Mastering
Active Directory for
Windows Server 2003

Mastering™
Active Directory for
Windows® Server 2003

Robert R. King

SYBEX®

San Francisco   London

Associate Publisher: Joel Fugazzatto

Acquisitions Editor: Ellen Dendy

Developmental Editor: Tom Cirtin

Production Editor: Lori Newman

Technical Editor: James Kelly

Copyeditor: Anamary Ehlen

Compositor: Scott Benoit

Graphic Illustrator: Scott Benoit

Proofreaders: Dennis Fitzgerald, Emily Hsuan, Laurie O'Connell, Yariv Rabinovitch, Nancy Riddiough, Sarah Tannehill

Indexer: Jack Lewis

Book Designer: Maureen Forys, Happenstance Type-o-Rama

Cover Designer: Design Site

Cover Illustrator: Tania Kac, Design Site

To my wife and best friend, Susan

Acknowledgments

I'M NOT SURE THAT I'd call myself an "old hand" in the publishing game, but I've got a few books out there. I'm still surprised by the number of people and the amount of work that go into producing any kind of high-quality material. There are numerous people who helped get this book into your hands—and each of them was critical to the process.

First of all, I'm deeply indebted to Bob Abuhoff for contributing to Part 3 of the book and to Marcin Policht for revising Chapters 11, 12, and 13. Without their expert help, I couldn't have completed this project on time.

My family deserves the most thanks. Every time I start a new Sybex project, I promise them that I'll "work a normal schedule," and every time I end up working into the wee hours more often than not. This book could not have been finished without their love and support.

I'd also like to thank James "Gibby" Gibson, who gave an inexperienced kid his first job in the industry. This doesn't sound like much until you realize that my previous job had been owner/operator of a small tavern in rural Wisconsin! Gibby: I was never sure if you saw some spark of intelligence or just wanted an experienced bartender for the company gatherings, but either way, thanks for taking a chance on me.

I also would like to thank the fine folks at Sybex. I have never worked with a more supportive and understanding group of people. Both Ellen Dendy, acquisitions editor, and Tom Cirtin, developmental editor, helped guide me in terms of changes to this revision, and editor Anamary Ehlen was insightful and really helped to ensure that I held to some sort of consistent style! Production editor Lori Newman and electronic publishing specialist Scott Benoit from Publication Services made the final product look sharp. Finally, my technical editor, James Kelly, ensured that I didn't embarrass myself—something I really appreciate! To these, and to all of those who helped put this book together, I'd like to say one big "Thank you."

Contents at a Glance

Contents

Introduction

EVEN THOUGH I HAVE written books revolving around Microsoft products, I have never tried to hide the fact that I started out as a Novell guru (heck—I was even a Novell employee for awhile). When Microsoft first released Windows NT, I was amazed at the number of people who bought into that "New Technology" (NT) marketing line. Their "new technology"—or at least the networking portion of it—had been developed a good 10 years earlier for an IBM product named LanManager. (A search through the Registry of any NT computer for the word "Lanman" will prove this.) So Microsoft was releasing a product based on a 10-year-old networking philosophy and which used a nonroutable communication protocol by default. It didn't seem all that "new" to me!

Windows 2000/Windows Server 2003 moved Microsoft networking away from the dated and limiting domain-based architecture of earlier releases and toward the true directory service–based architecture necessary in today's complex networks. Microsoft provides this service through the addition of Active Directory (AD), an open, standards-based, X.500-compliant, LDAP-accessible network directory. (Don't worry—we'll talk about X.500, LDAP, and what seems like an endless list of industry acronyms throughout this book.)

The first commercially viable, directory service–based operating system to hit the networking industry was Novell's NetWare 4 with NetWare Directory Services (NDS). At the time of its release, I was working as a senior technical instructor for a company in Minneapolis, Minnesota. In order to be one step ahead of the competition, my company sent me to the prep classes taught on the beta version of the software. After two weeks of intensive training on NDS, I returned home and started to reevaluate my career choices. It seemed as if everything I knew about networking was about to become out-of-date, and I would be forced to master this new paradigm known as a "directory service." I have to admit that when I first saw Novell's directory service, I didn't get it, didn't think I would ever get it, and wasn't sure I wanted to get it. I felt safe with earlier versions of NetWare, and I couldn't understand why *anyone* would want to add the complexity of a directory service to their network. In the long run, however, the benefits of a directory service far outweighed the painful learning curve. With the release of Active Directory as part of the Windows 2000 Server product, Microsoft finally provided these benefits to its customer base. (And, I hope, this manual will help reduce the pain involved in mastering the technology!)

AD provides the power and flexibility you need in today's changing computer world, but it provides these at a price. A large portion of that price is the steep learning curve that administrators need to climb in order to fully understand and utilize the potential of Microsoft Windows 2000/Windows Server 2003 and Active Directory Services. However, the benefits of using Active Directory speak for themselves:

A More Stable Operating System   You will see far fewer "blue screens" than ever before in a Microsoft environment. You can also say goodbye to the weekly (or more) reboots necessary to keep an NT server up and running.

Group Policies   Controlling the end user's environment—what they can see, what they can change, and what they can do—is critical as our operating systems become more and more sophisticated.

Software Distribution   Statistics show that we (network professionals) spend more time installing and maintaining end-user applications than any other aspect of our job. Automating these processes will allow us to (finally) use some of that vacation time we have accumulated over the years!

I wrote this book to help you avoid being caught by surprise by Microsoft Windows 2000/Windows Server 2003 and Active Directory. While a network directory might be a new paradigm in networking for you, try to remember that at its most basic, networking technology—whether Windows 2000/Windows Server 2003, AD, or anything else—is still just moving bits from one place to another. All of the knowledge you have gathered about networking is still valid; you'll just have a few more options available to you.

What's in This Book?

When I was planning the table of contents for this book, I struggled with how best to present a new paradigm for Microsoft networking—the concept of a network directory. It was suggested that I just write about Active Directory Services and leave it at that, but I wanted to give you a conceptual overview of the technology as well as a look at AD. I decided that a three-part book would suit my goals. Read on to learn what's in each part.

PART 1: NETWORK DIRECTORY ESSENTIALS

No matter what Microsoft would have you believe, network directories have been around for quite some time. Understanding earlier implementations (both their strengths and weaknesses) can help us understand why AD works the way it does—and perhaps help us realize some of its weaknesses. Part 1 is fairly short, but it is filled with conceptual information that can really help you tie AD to your environment. Part 1 contains four chapters.

Chapter 1: An Introduction to Network Directory Services and Their Benefits   This chapter gives a basic overview of what a directory is and what Active Directory is, and it compares directories to older technologies.

Chapter 2: Anatomy of a Directory   In this chapter, you will learn what a directory is by looking at examples of existing technologies, starting with basic paper-based directories and working up to the directories used in today's networks.

Chapter 3: Inside an X.500-Compliant Directory   Read this chapter for an overview of the X.500 recommendations, which are used to create the structure of the Active Directory database.

We also discuss the process of creating a directory service database from the ground up—a mental exercise that can really help you understand what makes Active Directory tick.

Chapter 4: Accessing the Directory   Chapter 4 explains DAP and LDAP, the two protocols used to access the information stored within the AD database.

PART 2: MICROSOFT ACTIVE DIRECTORY SERVICES

Once we have a firm grounding in directory technology, we can look at AD with a critical eye, trying to find its strengths and weaknesses. With this information, we can better apply the technology within our own environments. There are nine chapters in Part 2.

Chapter 5: Microsoft Networks without AD   To fully appreciate Windows 2000/Windows Server2003, and especially Active Directory, it is important to understand earlier versions of NT. If you are an NT expert, this chapter will be a review. If you are a newcomer to the NT world, this chapter should prepare you for some of the topics you will encounter later in the book.

Chapter 6: Active Directory Benefits   Just as NT was originally designed to overcome the weaknesses of server-centric environments, Windows 2000/Windows Server 2003 with AD was designed to overcome the weaknesses of domain-based environments. In this chapter, we will discuss how AD fits into the overall Windows 2000/Windows Server 2003 philosophy.

Chapter 7: Network Support Services   While Microsoft 2000/Windows Server 2003 can utilize many different protocols for communication, AD depends on TCP/IP. Before you can begin to install and configure an AD environment, you must have a strong foundation in TCP/IP tools and techniques.

Chapter 8: Designing the Active Directory Environment   In this chapter, you will read about the theories of designing a stable AD structure that does not place undue stress on any single component of your network.

Chapter 9: Implementing Your Design   Read Chapter 9 to find out about the mechanics of AD installation and building your AD structure.

Chapter 10: Creating a Secure Environment   If the AD database is going to be of any real use in a network, the information it contains must be secure. In this chapter, we will look at the various security options available with Windows 2000/Windows Server 2003.

Chapter 11: Implementing Group Policies   Group Policies are used to define user or computer settings for an entire group of users or computers at one time. As such, they will be a very important concept for administrators of networks based on Windows 2000/Windows Server 2003. In Chapter 11, we will discuss the concept of Group Policies and look at the procedures used to implement them.

Chapter 12: Modifying the Active Directory Schema   The AD database contains object classes, which define *types* of network resources, and attributes, which define *parameters* of those classes. The default list of classes and attributes might not be sufficient in some environments. Chapter 12 discusses the process of extending the design of the AD database to include custom object classes and attributes.

Chapter 13: Understanding and Controlling AD Sites and Replication   For any network operating system, no matter how logical we make the structure or how graphical we make the interface, when all is said and done, everything comes back to the plumbing—the "pipes" we use to move data. This chapter looks at design issues with an eye on available bandwidth and communication costs.

PART 3: ADVANCED ACTIVE DIRECTORY ADMINISTRATION

So far we have gotten a history of the technology upon which Active Directory was built—sort of a historical perspective, if you will—in Part 1. In Part 2, we looked at the basic structure of an Active Directory environment—design strategies, traffic considerations, and the peripheral components found in most Ad environments. In Part 3 we take an in-depth look at specific components of Active Directory implementations.

Chapter 14: Active Directory Network Traffic   A complete description of devices and services that generate traffic on your network. While no one could ever describe every bit that will pass through a network wire, we'll look at those services that revolve around Active Directory: DNS, WINS, DHCP, AD replication, and others.

Chapter 15: Backup and Recovery of Active Directory   Everyone knows that good backups are critical to job security—and just about everyone in the business can describe the basics of server backup. What many don't understand are the intricacies of backing up a complex database such as Active Directory. We'll look at the theories and the tools involved in backing up and restoring Active Directory.

Chapter 16: Active Directory Design   There are more ways to design a hierarchical system than there are people to describe them. We'll look at some of the network and business details that will impact your final AD design. We'll also provide a few "cookie cutter" designs that can act as the foundation of your own network.

Chapter 17: Migrating to Active Directory   Very few of us have the luxury of starting from scratch—we inherit a network and then want to upgrade it to match our perceived needs. In this chapter we'll discuss the options available when you want to upgrade your existing network to Windows 2000 and Active Directory.

Chapter 18: Integrating Active Directory with Novell Directory Services   Novell still holds a significant portion of the business networking market. Some recent surveys have even shown that NetWare's market share might be increasing. Even in those companies where all new servers are Microsoft-based, many still continue to support legacy NetWare servers. The odds are that you will face a mixed environment at some time in your career. In this chapter we'll discuss the tools and techniques available to help ease the pain of supporting two platforms: AD and NDS.

Who Should Read This Book?

This book was written for the experienced network administrator who wants to take a look at Microsoft's Active Directory Services. I'm going to assume a basic level of knowledge of networking in general, but no (or little) knowledge of directory-based technologies. It seems as though whatever Microsoft is doing is what the industry moves toward—and Microsoft is doing network directories in a big way! If you run a Microsoft house, you'll need to come up to speed on AD quickly. If you run a non-Microsoft house (or older versions of Microsoft NT), you can bet that sooner or later you'll need to understand how Microsoft views network directories.

In my 10 years as a technical instructor, I found that there were basically two types of students—those that just wanted to know the "how," and those who also wanted to know the "why." I feel that this book will satisfy both types of computer professionals. We certainly delve into the theoretical—discussing the history of network directories, the philosophy of management of directories, and the environment-specific aspects of AD that will effect your final design. We also discuss and describe many of the more common administrative tasks that you will be required to perform on a daily basis. That mix of both theory and concrete should prepare you for the task of implementing and maintaining an Active Directory structure in your work environment.

I guess the bottom line is this: if you are in networking today and you plan to be in networking tomorrow, you will have to master the concepts of a network directory at some point in your career. This book is designed to give you the information you need to understand and implement Microsoft's interpretation of that technology.

In Short

Microsoft Windows 2000/Windows Server 2003 is the hottest technology in networking today. To use it effectively, you might have to rethink how you characterize network resources and services. The days of putting in the network and *then* considering the environment are long gone! With today's technologies, each network will have to be designed around a "total business solution"—providing the resources and services necessary without unduly taxing the budget, staff, or infrastructure of the host company.

One last word of advice: enjoy what you do. New technology can be exciting, challenging, and downright fun. If you spend more time complaining about the technology than being amazed by it, perhaps a vacation is in order!

As with all my books, if you have questions or comments about the content, do not hesitate to drop me a note at bking@royal-tech.com. I always look forward to hearing from you.

Part 1

Network Directories Essentials

In this section you will learn how to:

- ◆ Evaluate network directory services and their benefits
- ◆ Understand the critical features of directory systems
- ◆ Design a generic directory
- ◆ Access the directory

Chapter 1

An Introduction to Network Directory Services and Their Benefits

THE COMPUTER INDUSTRY, ESPECIALLY in the networking arena, generates more acronyms, terms, phrases, and buzzwords than any other business in the world. The latest craze is the phrase *network directories*. Directories are nothing new—they have been around in one form or another since the late '60s. Now, however, they have entered the mainstream with the release of Microsoft's long-awaited Active Directory Services in Windows 2000 Server and the Windows Server 2003 product line. To get the most from this technology, you must have a firm understanding of what directories are, what they are not, and how they can be used to ease the management of your network. That is the goal of this book—to give you enough information to implement, manage, and utilize the services provided by Microsoft's Active Directory Services (ADS). (While this directory is just another feature of the Windows 2000/Windows Server 2003 environment, it has reached the status of some rock stars—a shortened name. Microsoft's directory service is usually referred to as just Active Directory or AD. This is the terminology that I'll use throughout the book.)

PC-based networks have become an integral part of the business world. They started out as simple solutions for the sharing of a few physical resources—hard disk space, printers, and so on. Over time, though, networks have become quite complex—often spanning multiple sites, connecting thousands of users to a multitude of resources. Today, networks control everything from payroll information to e-mail communication, from printers to fax services. As networks offer more services, they also demand more management. Easing the use and management of networks is the real goal of a directory service.

This first chapter is more about setting the appropriate mood for the first section of the book than it is about technology. Directories have the ability to ease (or sometimes even eliminate) some of the most common IT administrative tasks. In this chapter we'll look at a few of those tasks, think about how we would perform them in a "traditional" network, and then imagine the ways in which a directory could make them easier to deal with. The bottom line here is that directories are exciting technology—and I want you to start getting excited about them! To effect that excitement, though, you need to have a firm grasp on the "concept" of a directory. The first part of this chapter will define that term, explain the benefits of using a directory, and describe the basic structure used by most network directories on the market today.

I've been in this business for a long time, and I know the typical work environment in an IT department. First, IT workers are often assumed to be nocturnal—we do our most important tasks (server maintenance, data backups, upgrades, etc.) after everyone else has gone home for the day (or worse, for the weekend or holiday!). Second, IT staff members are assumed to be workaholics. Why else would they give us vacation time that we never seem to be able to use? I don't know how many times I've heard of IT staffers who lose their vacation time at the end of the year because they could never use it— there was always something going on that prevented them from leaving for a week or so. Lastly, we are assumed to know everything (and while we like this image, it sometimes causes problems). How many training classes have you attended in the last year? How many would you have liked to attend? If those two numbers are equal (or even close), you work for a great company! Too often, IT workers are given little training, and this results in more late hours, more headaches, and less opportunities to use vacation time.

Most administrators are overworked and underpaid. Most IT departments are understaffed and underbudgeted. This results in IT professionals who never see their families, never have time to attend classes (which just exacerbates the problem), and very seldom have time for relaxation—no wonder so many of us switch careers during our midlife crisis!

When properly installed and configured, Active Directory can often reduce the administrative overhead of maintaining your network. Certain tasks are completely eliminated, many redundant tasks are reduced to a single step, and most management processes are made easier to accomplish. The bottom line is that your workday is made more productive—allowing you to accept more responsibility, utilize your vacation time, and, just maybe, attend a few of the training events and industry seminars that you have on your wish list. (Okay, that's the optimistic view. More likely, your company will see that the number of IT staff members required is not as great, and you end up with a smaller IT staff. This isn't all that bad though, because a smaller staff often results in higher salaries… a win-win situation!)

Get excited about Active Directory! While it does require you to master a new paradigm (read that as a learning curve to climb), it also provides you with the opportunity to work more efficiently! This often results in the IT department adding new (and exciting) technologies to their systems. If you're like me, working with the latest and greatest technology is just another perk in the workplace!

In this chapter:

- What is a directory service?

- Why use a directory service?

- Before there were network directories…

- ◆ Traditional networks vs. network directories
- ◆ Benefits of Active Directory
- ◆ The Active Directory structure
- ◆ The Active Directory feature set

What Is a Directory Service?

In any business-level networked environment, there exists some sort of database of account information. In Windows NT, this database was known as the Security Accounts Manager (SAM) database, and in early versions of Novell NetWare, it was known as the bindery. No matter what network operating system you look at, there has to be a place in which information about valid users is stored—things like names, passwords, and maybe even a little security information.

In many operating systems, this accounts database is server- or resource-centric. By this I mean that the database only stores information about users who have access to the resources (files, printers, applications, etc.) located within the sphere of control of the device upon which the database is stored. Novell's bindery is a perfect example; it stored account information for users who could access a specific server (the server in which the bindery files were located). While this type of system is workable in smaller environments, it begins to fall apart as networks grow. Think about it: if every server has its own accounts database, and I have 100 servers, then I have 100 accounts databases to manage.

A *directory service* is a networkwide database that stores resource information, such as user accounts. In a directory-based environment, I create a single user account for each user, and that account is used to manage all aspects of the user's network (and sometimes desktop) environment. To put this another way, a directory service provides a place to store information about network-based entities, such as applications, files, printers, or people. Given the networkwide scope of such a database, it provides a consistent way to name, describe, locate, access, manage, and secure information about those individual resources.

The directory also acts as the central point of control and management for the network operating system. It acts as the central authority to properly identify and authenticate the identities of resources, and it brokers the relationships between distributed resources, thus allowing them to work together. The directory service must be tightly coupled with the underlying operating system to ensure the integrity and privacy of information on the network.

In a Microsoft-based network, the Active Directory Service plays a critical role in an organization's ability to manage the network infrastructure, perform system administration, and control the user environment.

Why Use a Directory Service?

When I first started in the networking industry, I worked on what, at the time, was a midsized environment—we had four servers and about 200 users. The Internet was still a thing of the future, e-mail wasn't mission critical (heck, most people didn't even know what e-mail was), there was no such thing as a "fax server" or any other kind of specialized server for that matter, and FedEx was used to transfer documents from one site to another (no one would have thought to invest in a wide area link for a medium-sized company—they were too expensive).

Today, a midsized environment can include 50 or more servers, support hundreds, if not thousands, of users, and include numerous special services that run on dedicated servers. Wide area links are common, and bandwidth demands are astronomic! Not to mention the dial-in, VPN, and other "new" services that end users are demanding. In these complex networks, the task of managing the multitude of network-based resources can be overwhelming.

Directories help administrators manage today's complex environments by:

◆ Simplifying management. By acting as a single point of management (and providing a consistent set of management tools), a directory can ease the administrative tasks associated with complex networks.

◆ Providing stronger security. Once again, the fact that access and authentication is controlled through a single service, administrators and users are only required to know a single set of tools, allowing them to develop a better understanding of them. Directories, since they offer a single logon facility, are usually able to provide a more secure authentication process (since all logons are managed through a central service, that service can be made extremely secure).

◆ Promoting interoperability. Most of today's commercially viable directory services (AD included) are based upon a series of industry standards—X.500 and LDAP to name a few (I'll describe these in detail later). Sticking with a standards-based solution makes it easier to share resources in a mixed environment or, better yet, to share resources with business partners without opening too many doors into your network.

Directories can be thought of as both a management and a user tool. From a management perspective, having a centrally controlled and consistent interface to resource information can drastically reduce administrative costs. From a user's perspective, a central service for authentication can make accessing resources throughout the network a lot easier. Gone are the days when users had to memorize (or worse, write on a Post-It note) multiple logon names and passwords!

Before There Were Network Directories...

To understand and appreciate the power and convenience of a directory-based solution, you must have an understanding of the technologies that it will replace. Before the advent of directories, most network operating systems (NOSs) were "server-based." In other words, most account management was done on a server-by-server basis. With older NOS software, each server maintained a list of users (the *accounts database*) who could access its resources and the users' permissions (the *Access Control List*, or ACL). If a system had two servers, then each server had a separate accounts database, as shown in Figure 1.1.

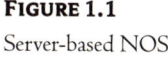

FIGURE 1.1

Server-based NOS

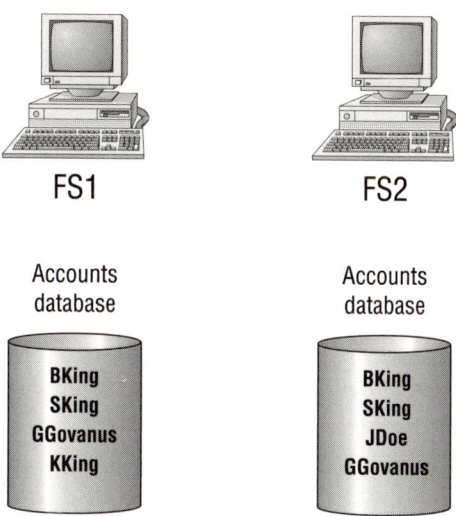

As you can see, each server in Figure 1.1 maintains its own list of authorized users and manages its own resources. While this system is simple and easy to understand, it becomes unwieldy once a system grows past a certain point. Imagine trying to manage 10,000 users on 250 servers—the user and resource lists would soon overwhelm you! To get around this limitation, some NOS software, such as Microsoft NT 4, was configured so that small groups of servers could share one list of users (called a *central accounts database*) for security and authentication purposes, as shown in Figure 1.2. This central accounts database gave administrators a single point of management for a section of their network, known as a *domain*. Once again, however, this system becomes cumbersome after it reaches a certain size.

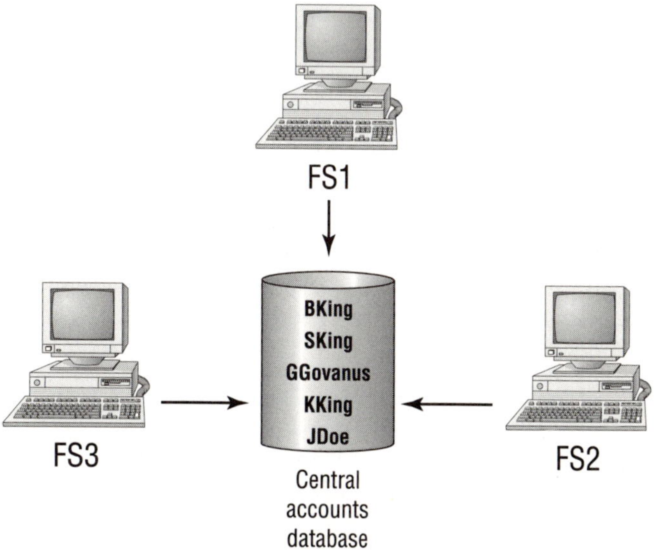

FIGURE 1.2

NT 4 security
accounts database

The shift from server-based to domain-based networks was the first step in creating an environment where all users and resources are managed through a single database. In a domain, all user information is stored in a single place and managed with a single set of tools, and users can access the network via a single account (no more having to remember multiple account names and passwords). Network directories take this approach to the next phase: a single database to hold *all* user and resource information across your entire network.

NOTE *I'm using the phrase "user and resource" to refer to the records within a directory database because that is how traditional administrators see their world: users accessing resources. In a directory-based environment, however, users become nothing more than another resource. This subtle shift in philosophy is critical in understanding the strengths of a directory-based network. This distinction should become clear as you become more familiar with directory concepts.*

Network directories are just databases that hold network information. They can contain many different types of information:

- User account information (logon name, password, restrictions)

- User personal information (phone number, address, employee ID number)

- Peripheral configuration information (printers, modem, fax)

- Application configuration (Desktop preferences, default directories)

- Security information

- Network infrastructure configuration (routers, proxies, Internet access settings)

If you can imagine it, a network directory can store it!

Once this information is stored in a centrally controlled, standards-based database, it can be used in many different ways. Most commonly, administrators will use such information to control access to the network and the network's resources. The directory will become the central control point for many different network processes. Here are examples of some of these processes:

- When a user attempts to log on to the network, the client software will request authentication from the directory. The directory service will ascertain whether the account name is valid, check for a password, validate the password submitted, and check any restrictions on the account to determine if the logon request should be granted.

- Individual users can use directories to store personal preferences. Each time a user logs on to the network, his Desktop settings, default printer, home directory location—even his application icons—can be downloaded to whatever computer he happens to be at. Users will no longer have to re-create their environment each time they use a new computer. All of their settings will be centrally located to ensure a "universal environment" and, if you desire, centrally controlled to lock them down.

- As directories mature, you will also be able to use them to monitor and control traffic across network devices. When a user attempts to access a remote network, for instance, the directory could be used to determine whether the request is valid for that user. Imagine controlling Internet access with the same tool you use to control other security settings. Or perhaps the directory could query various devices to determine the least congested network path to the destination. You might even be able to grant higher network priority to certain users, groups, applications, or services, allowing you to provide a guaranteed level of service.

Traditional Networks vs. Network Directories

Many network tasks can benefit from the capabilities of a network directory. Many of the hardest configuration issues of earlier networks will become a piece of cake when you use a network directory as the central controlling point for the network.

Traditional Network Solutions for Common Administrative Tasks

As food for thought, let's consider a few common networking tasks and the nondirectory solutions to them. Each of these scenarios is a "real-world" implementation that I have been asked to complete on production networks. As you will see, the nondirectory-based solutions often border on the ridiculous. In some cases, the service provided could not justify the time spent to provide the requested solution. In other words, the constraints placed upon networks by traditional management techniques often limit the services that a network can realistically provide.

SCENARIO 1: TO TRUST OR NOT TO TRUST

Your company's marketing department has a Color Wax Thermal Transfer Graphics printer, which is used to create camera-ready art for the company that prints your sales brochures. Because of the cost of consumables, which is somewhere in the neighborhood of $3.00 per page, you have been very careful about who is allowed to print to this device. Luckily, the marketing department is its own domain, so security has been fairly easy to maintain. Over in the engineering department, Susan has decided that she needs to print drawings of prototypes on this printer. Your job is to arrange the appropriate permissions.

In a multidomain environment, there are two basic ways to handle this situation:

- You *could* create a trust between the marketing domain and the engineering domain, create a global group in the engineering domain, place Susan's account in the group, and then place that global group in the appropriate local group in the marketing domain. While this solution is great for Susan, it does mean that you now have to keep track of another trust relationship, not to mention the associated local and global groups.

- You *could* create a local account for Susan in the marketing domain and teach Susan to "Connect As" to use the printer. Now, of course, you've lost one of the biggest benefits of the domain concept —one user, one login.

SCENARIO 2: WHERE'S JOE?

An executive calls to inform you that a user named Joe in the sales department has been overheard discussing confidential information, including future product designs and marketing strategies. This executive would like a detailed explanation about where Joe has permissions and how they are acquired. She would also like you to ensure that Joe only has rights to resources appropriate for salespeople.

In a multidomain environment, this problem can be overwhelming. Your first inclination is probably to delete Joe's account and start from scratch—but you want to ensure that no other salespeople have been granted inappropriate permissions. You'll have to track down every group that Joe is a member of and then check the permissions of each group. For each global group, you'll have to check to see which local groups it has been made a member of (including those local groups in other domains). You'll also have to search for any local accounts that might have been created for Joe in the marketing and R&D domains. Finally, you'll probably want to institute an auditing policy to track who is accessing the confidential data.

NOTE   *Of course, this scenario assumes that you have administrative rights in the other domains of your environment. If not, you will have to coordinate your actions with those of the other administrators.*

When you have completed your search, you will have to implement a corporatewide policy that defines how permissions should be granted, who should be able to grant rights to various types of resources, and the appropriate naming standards for things like global and local groups (this will make the next search a little easier). In a multidomain environment, enforcing these policies can be an administrative nightmare.

SCENARIO 3: THE SEARCH FOR INFORMATION

An expensive and mission-critical printer refuses to print. You know that the printer was purchased in the last few months, but you need specific information for dealing with the vendor. In a traditional office, you must contact purchasing. The purchasing agent will have to dig up the paper-based purchase order using the serial number or approximate date of purchase. If all goes well, the purchase order will contain the check number and date of purchase, as well as the name of the salesperson who sold you the device. Once that information is at hand, you can call the vendor and negotiate repairs or replacement.

SCENARIO 4: SETTING LIMITS

Your company has just adopted a policy to control Internet access: certain users have unlimited access, other users are allowed to surf the Web during nonbusiness hours, and some users are allowed to access only an approved list of websites. It's your job to make sure this policy is implemented. Luckily, all of this functionality is built into the new routers you have purchased. Unfortunately, those routers are not "NT aware," so you must enter all of the specifics (including usernames) in the vendor's proprietary format.

SCENARIO 5: COMPANY INFORMATION

You've been asked to design a database that can serve as a company phone book. The CEO would like to have the following information available for each employee:

◆ Company phone extension

◆ Home phone

- Company mail stop

- Home address

- Birthday

- Hire date

While all of this information is already in a series of databases controlled by the human resources department, the CEO would like this to be a companywide application. She also realizes that some of this data is confidential, so you must control access to certain fields based upon job function.

One solution might be to create a series of databases: one for nonsecure information and another for secure information. Each user would access the database that is appropriate for his or her needs. Not an elegant solution, but it is probably the quickest. The biggest problem will be keeping the information up-to-date.

Network Directory–Based Solutions

Most administrative tasks can be broken down into two basic functions:

- Providing resources

- Securing those resources

With that in mind, let's look at the five scenarios just described. You've been asked to:

1. Secure access to an expensive resource (a printer).

2. Provide security for confidential information.

3. Organize information (the purchase order for the printer).

4. Secure and control access to the Internet.

5. Provide (and secure) access to employee information.

Balancing the availability of resources with the need to secure those resources represents a large percentage of what LAN administrators do for a living. The implementation of a network directory service can help to make these tasks as straightforward as possible.

SCENARIO 1: TO TRUST OR NOT TO TRUST

Because a network directory provides a single logical database to manage all network resources, the directory-based solution to this problem is fairly straightforward. The users and the printer are no longer "separated" by any type of administrative grouping; in other words, both the user account and the printer now exist in the same logical database. When you use a directory, the solution can be as simple as giving Susan account permissions to use the printer.

SCENARIO 2: WHERE'S JOE?

Once again, the single point of management provided by a network directory offers a fairly simple solution to this problem. Since all groups exist in the same database, you can query that database for a list of all groups of which Joe is a member. Rather than checking each group by hand, you can use the database as a tool to limit your workload.

Once you've discovered the source of Joe's extra permissions (and fixed the immediate problem), you should be able to implement a directorywide policy to correct the errors that caused the problem in the first place. You might, for example, limit the administrator of the sales department so that he can only administer resources listed as belonging to the sales department. With this type of policy in place, the sales administrator could never grant permissions to nonsales resources.

SCENARIO 3: THE SEARCH FOR INFORMATION

Many people get so hung up on the fact that a directory "manages the network" that they forget that a directory is just a database. Why not store resource-related information as a part of that resource's record? A directory can easily store things like the serial number of a printer or any purchase information that you might need later.

If this information is in your directory, the directory-based solution would be to query the database for the printer's record. You can base your query on any known attribute—since the printer is not working, you probably have access to its serial number. Search the directory for a matching entry.

SCENARIO 4: SETTING LIMITS

Since there is an industry-standard protocol for accessing information in a directory (LDAP, which I will discuss in Chapter 4), it should not be difficult to manage a multivendor environment from a single point. You should be able to import the configuration information for things like a proxy server or router right into your network directory. (This capability is actually part of a Microsoft-suggested standard known as Directory Enabled Networks, or DEN.) Once such integration is possible, you might be able to drag and drop user accounts onto the router and configure limits for each user. Another option might be to create a series of groups in Active Directory Services and then assign permission to various router functions to those groups. The router can then query the AD database to determine what groups a particular user belongs to.

SCENARIO 5: COMPANY INFORMATION

The company phone book is probably one of the easiest tasks an administrator can accomplish in a directory environment. Most directories (AD included) will store most of the information that the CEO requests in this scenario. Directories also have built-in security so that users can be limited to viewing only certain data from the directory.

AD is accessible by most of the industry-standard directory tools. Once you have imported the information into the directory, you can use any of these tools to query for things like phone numbers and addresses. The internal security will determine whether or not the request is honored.

Now you've seen a few examples of how a directory can be used to solve some common issues administrators face every day. In the next section, I'll discuss the benefits of a specific directory server—Microsoft Active Directory.

Benefits of Active Directory

If you work in a Microsoft "house"—in other words, your company uses Microsoft networking products as their main network operating system—Active Directory either is, or will become, a critical piece of your environment. If you are not working in a Microsoft house, then the strong security, ease of implementation, and interoperability of Active Directory just might convince you to move to a Microsoft-based networking solution.

Basically, Active Directory improves upon the domain-based architecture of Windows NT to provide a directory service that is better suited to today's distributed networks. AD acts as the central authority for network security as well as the integration point for bringing diverse systems together. AD consolidates management tasks into a single set of Windows-based management tools, greatly reducing the management overhead inherent in many enterprise network operating systems. As shown in Figure 1.3, AD can act as the "center" for management of all of your network resources.

FIGURE 1.3

AD as the center of your enterprise network

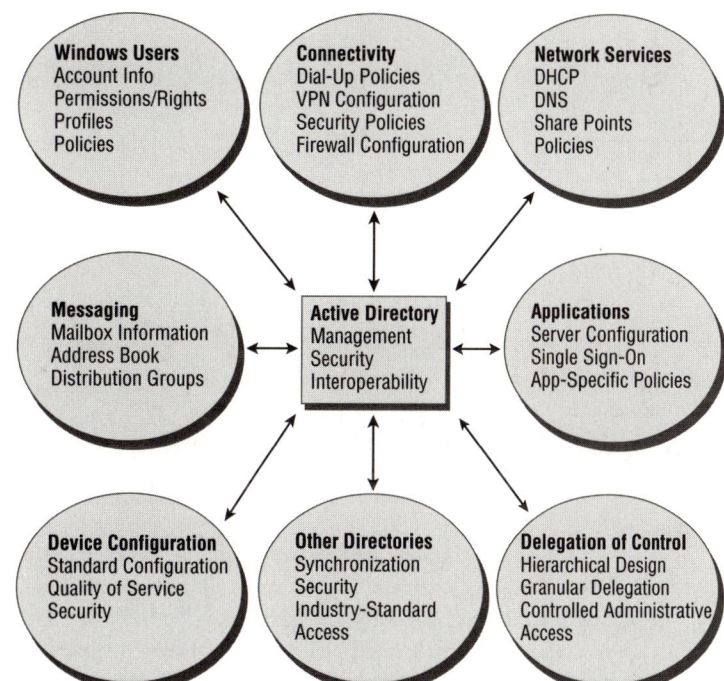

Active Directory provides a single point of management for Windows-based user accounts, clients, services, and applications. Its hierarchical nature allows network resources to be organized in a natural, intuitive nature. Because it is based upon industry-standard protocols, it can help integrate diverse (non-Microsoft) operating systems and applications into a cohesive whole, bringing management of those resources into a centrally controlled environment with a single set of management tools.

The Active Directory Structure

Active Directory allows you to organize your network resources in a hierarchical, object-oriented fashion, and in a manner that matches the way in which you manage those resources. While it is still "domain-based," replication between domain controllers has been redesigned, from the single master model used in Windows NT to a multimaster model in which all domain controllers are equal (or *peers*, to use the proper terminology). This means no more primary domain controller (PDC) and backup domain controller (BDC) issues, allowing for a much more efficient replication process and ensuring that no single point of failure exists within a domain.

The Hierarchical Design

Probably the most fascinating, and potentially powerful, feature of Active Directory is your ability to organize resources to match the IT management philosophy used in your company. This hierarchy, or tree, structure is the backbone of an Active Directory environment. As shown in Figure 1.4, a graphical representation of an AD tree looks much like a graphical representation of a DOS directory structure.

FIGURE 1.4

The AD tree allows you to organize your resources in a logical manner.

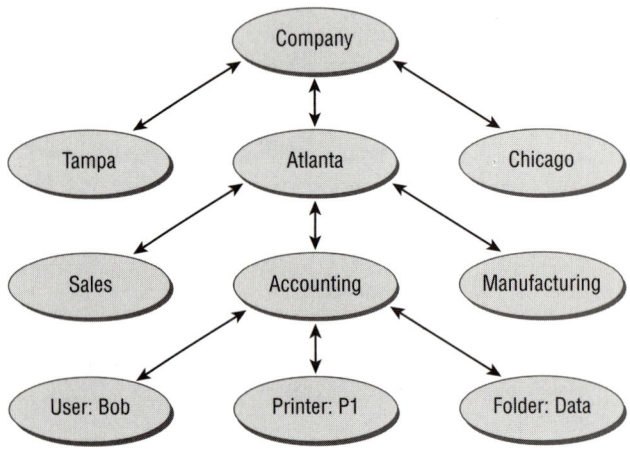

AD uses *objects* to represent network resources such as users, printers, or share points. It also uses specialized objects known as *containers* to organize your resources along the lines of your business needs. In Figure 1.4, for instance, the company has three offices: Tampa, Atlanta, and Chicago. Given that most users will utilize resources located physically near them, it makes sense (usually) to create containers that represent physical sites. Within the Atlanta office, the network resources (notice that users are nothing more than another resource on the network) are departmental, so the AD design reflects this through the creation of departmental containers.

The best analogy for the AD tree structure is to look at the DOS file system. In DOS, you would create directories and subdirectories to organize your files; directories were created for easier access (it's much easier to find your spreadsheets if they are all stored in a single directory) and to ease management (if all of your data is within a Data directory, you can easily configure your backup software to back up your critical data).

AD containers are used to group objects that have similar attributes. You might, for instance, want to apply a specific security policy to all salespeople. Grouping these user accounts together will facilitate this type of management in your environment. Active Directory manages the relationships between objects within the tree, by default creates the appropriate trust relationships between domains, and presents you with a consistent (and single) view of your network.

The Benefit of an Object-Oriented Structure

Take another look at Figure 1.4. You will notice that each object represents some "manageable" aspect of the network. Each container represents a grouping of resources, and each individual resource is represented by a unique AD object. Each of these object classes (container, user, printer, etc.) is assigned a set of attributes that describe the individual resource. User objects, for instance, have attributes that are pertinent to users: names, passwords, addresses, telephone numbers, and so on. There are two major benefits of this type of object-oriented design.

First, since each object within AD is really only a record in a database, it is possible to expand the list of attributes to match the specific needs of your company. You might, for instance, work in an environment in which almost all users travel for business. In this case, you might (or might not) want to store travel information (such as frequent flyer memberships, hotel preferences, and emergency contacts) within the security of the AD database. Since AD is "extensible" (open to modification), these types of changes are possible.

The second benefit of an object-oriented design is that each object represents an individual resource, and each attribute represents a unique aspect of that resource. This means the system can include an inherent security mechanism. In the case of AD, each object has an ACL that describes who has been given permissions to access the object. For example, you might want to allow your help desk personnel to change passwords, but not to perform any other administrative tasks.

Multimaster Domain Replication

As in earlier versions of Microsoft network operating systems (namely Windows NT), the domain represents a database of network resources. Each domain controller within a domain contains a complete copy of this database. If a new object is created, or an existing object is modified, this information must be replicated to all of the other domain controllers within the domain (in order to keep their copy of the database up-to-date). In Windows NT, this replication process was accomplished using what is known as a single-master model. There was one (and only one) PDC upon which all changes were created. The PDC would then replicate those changes to BDCs in order to keep their databases current.

The problem with the single-master model is that it produced a single point of failure. In the event the PDC was unavailable, administrators were not able to complete any domain administrative tasks. (They could promote a BDC to PDC status, but this was a manual process and required a full understanding of the ramifications to the environment.)

Active Directory uses a multimaster replication model in which all domain controllers are able to accept changes to the database and replicate those changes to all other domain controllers within the domain. Gone are the days of PDCs and BDCs, and gone are the days of a directory's single point of failure!

The Active Directory Feature Set

Over the last few years, I've helped a lot of companies make the critical decision to either upgrade or migrate to Windows 2000/Windows Server 2003 and Active Directory. I've also faced a lot of people who were resistant to this process—people who were comfortable with their existing network, confident in their ability to maintain their current environment, and intimidated by the new paradigm inherent in a directory-based network.

Many times administrators were just reluctant to change because they were not aware of the great benefits they would reap once the process was complete. I don't know how many times I've heard an administrator say, "AD doesn't offer anything that I need." My answer is always, "Hogwash!" (Of course, as a self-employed consultant I usually find a more politic method of expressing my opinion.) Most of the time, these IT professionals are just not aware of the many features inherent in an AD environment. If you are in the position of justifying a move to AD, perhaps Table 1.1 will help. Table 1.1 provides a fairly complete listing of the main features of Active Directory. I've broken the table into three main sections, representing the three areas in which a directory (especially Active Directory) can be of benefit.

TABLE 1.1: ACTIVE DIRECTORY FEATURES

FEATURE	DESCRIPTION
EASE OF MANAGEMENT	
Central database	Active Directory provides a consistent view of your network and a single set of management tools.
Group Policy	Group Policies allow administrators to take complete control of their users' environment—controlling access to the ability to make changes, distributing software, applying security settings, and redirecting system folders to a network location. Once set up and assigned, Group Policies are maintained and applied without administrative intervention.
Automated software distribution	While this feature is a function of Group Policies, it warrants its own discussion. Using GPOs (Group Policy Objects), you can automatically install and update software used by your users. This software can be available at any computer from which they work or only on specific computers.
Backwards compatibility	When older clients connect to a Windows 2000/Windows Server 2003, the server will respond as if it were a domain controller in an NT 4.0 domain.
Administrative delegation	Given the granular nature of Active Directory's security system, it is easy to delegate specific administrative tasks or specific levels of control over distinct areas of the AD tree.
Multimaster replication	Using a multimaster model for domain controller replication improves efficiency and eliminates the single point of failure inherent in NT domains.

Continued on next page

TABLE 1.1: ACTIVE DIRECTORY FEATURES *(continued)*

FEATURE	DESCRIPTION
SECURITY	
Kerberos v5 authentication	Kerberos v5 is considered to be the most secure method of authentication commercially available. Because Microsoft's implementation is compliant with the Kerberos standards, authentication with diverse environments is also possible.
Smart card support	Windows 2000/Windows Server 2003 networks fully support smart card authentication as well as other more sophisticated technologies (such as biometrics).
Transitive trust relationships	The user of transitive trusts greatly reduces the administrative overhead of managing a multidomain environment.
PKI/X.509 certificates	Windows 2000/Windows Server 2003 includes a fully functional PKI implementation package that is capable of issuing and managing X.509-compliant certificates.
LDAP (over SSL)	LDAP is an industry-standard protocol for accessing the information in network directories. Microsoft AD is fully LDAP accessible. LDAP requests can also be tied to an SSL security environment to provide security to network access.
Ability to mandate levels of authentication	Administrators can mandate the levels of authentication required to access a Windows 2000/Windows Server 2003/AD network. Kerberos v5, certificate-based, or even NTLM processes are supported.
Universal groups	Using groups across domains is easier than ever!
Group nesting	Groups can now be nested, allowing you to design a hierarchical group strategy.
DirSync	DirSync is a synchronization mechanism for exchanging information between multiple directories.
Active Directory Connectors	ADCs provide directory synchronization with foreign (non-AD) directories, allowing you to choose your method of managing a diverse network.
LDAP	LDAP is the accepted industry-standard protocol for accessing the information in a directory.
DNS	Windows 2000/Windows Server 2003 is TCP/IP-based, allowing the use of DNS for name resolution (and allowing the removal of WINS services).
Open API set	Having an open set of APIs allows developers the option of creating Directory Enabled Applications (DEAs), thus facilitating the use of AD programmatically.

Continued on next page

TABLE 1.1: ACTIVE DIRECTORY FEATURES *(continued)*

FEATURE	DESCRIPTION
SECURITY	
Extensible schema	The basic layout of the AD database (the definition of objects and attributes known as the *schema*) can be modified to meet specific business needs.

While the feature set can certainly be used to justify the move to AD, I find that the following aspects of Windows 2000/Windows Server 2003 and AD seem to be the deciding factors for my clients:

◆ A more stable operating system. (This one is especially useful when working with established NT environments. NT blue-screens and needs to be rebooted a lot more often than Windows 2000/Windows Server 2003.)

◆ Group Policies. Unlike the system policies found in NT, AD Group Policies actually work as advertised! The ability to take control of the users' environment can greatly reduce ongoing support costs.

◆ Software distribution. One of the major costs of supporting PCs in the workplace is keeping them up-to-date—both on the operating system (by applying patches and fixes) and on user applications (ever tried applying the latest MS Office service pack on 2500 computers?).

In Short

In this chapter we took a high-level view of directory services and the benefits that they provide to network administration. You'll find that many of your common tasks can be made easier in a directory-based environment.

As you can see from the scenarios presented in this chapter, moving to a directory-based environment should make administration of large networks a lot easier. The directory can act as:

◆ The central point of management for the network

◆ The central point of access for users

◆ A repository for administrative information that would otherwise be hard to manage

As we discuss the capabilities of AD, you will probably come up with some solutions for your own administrative nightmares.

In Chapter 2, we will dig a little deeper into the internal workings of network directories. There are many directories currently being used throughout the networking world, and we'll take a look at a few of them. As we examine these other directories, we'll build a "wish list" for AD. Later, we'll see how closely the reality of AD matches the potential of directory-based networks.

Chapter 2

Anatomy of a Directory

I DON'T KNOW ABOUT you, but over the years I've had to learn a whole bunch of new technologies—first CPM (remember that?), then DOS, then NetWare (all kinds of versions), then Windows, followed by Windows for Workgroups, NT, Windows 2000, XP, and now the Windows Server 2003 product family. (This list doesn't even touch upon the various user and server applications, network services, and Unix-type stuff!) I have to admit that there have been times when I wasn't sure I would learn the latest technology; sometimes the changes seemed too great.

Whenever I hit a mind-block, and it seems that perhaps I should consider a career in lawn maintenance, I try to find out what brought the technology to its current state. In other words, if I can understand the series of technologies that resulted in this new product, I can cut through the marketing propaganda and find the core value. That core value (what I call the "critical features list") often gives me an understanding of what the technology is supposed to do. Once I know what it's supposed to do, I can usually figure out how to make it work.

That's what this chapter is all about—taking a look at the technologies that preceded and helped form the features list of Active Directory. We'll start simple—looking at paper-based directories to get a feel for what a directory is. We'll then discuss a few of the limited directories that have been in use for quite some time in our industry. Last, we'll look at a competing network directory—both as an example of what a network directory can do and as a yardstick for comparison with Active Directory.

This chapter covers:

◆ Benefits and drawbacks of paper and computer-based directories

◆ Understanding DNS, WINS, and NDS network directories

Paper-Based Directories

We all use directories on a daily basis. Perhaps the most common directory is the plain old phone book. You might not see the telephone directory as a marvel of technology, but consider the services it provides.

The telephone directory acts as a repository of information, storing the names, addresses, and telephone numbers of the residents of your town (or state or nation, depending on the book you are using). This information is presented in an easy-to-use format—in most cases, as a paper-based book that can be used by anyone with a basic level of literacy. The book's information is organized in an easily understood manner: an alphabetical listing. All in all, as a directory, the telephone directory fulfills its purpose admirably, as evidenced by how long it's been around and how little its design has changed.

The telephone directory has become a standard piece of our culture: consider how many companies now offer such directories to the public. Many of these offerings are specialized—business-to-business listings, neighborhood directories, and even restaurant listings organized by type of food. Having such specific directories means that you don't have to search through page after page of information in order to find that great Mexican restaurant or a pizza parlor near your home.

An example of a common directory that is specific in scope would be the list of physicians in a particular health-care system. This is an example of a directory that is a little more "directed": a list of physicians, their specialties, their locations, and sometimes even their office hours. This information targets a specific audience. If you do not participate in the appropriate health-care plan, this information would be of no use to you. If, however, you belong to the plan, the information is critical to the health of your family. Once again, this information is presented in a manner that is appropriate for its use: usually a paper-based solution where the physicians are listed alphabetically by specialty.

The biggest problem with both of these examples—the telephone directory and the physician directory—is that a paper-based solution is usually out-of-date before you receive it. Think about the number of times you have dialed the listing for a local pizza parlor, only to find that it has gone out of business. While the list of physicians might be correct and current, wouldn't it be nice to have a list of physicians who are currently accepting new patients? Better yet, wouldn't you prefer to have a list that is so up-to-the-minute that you could check to see how far behind schedule the doctor is running today?

Computer-Based Directories

Paper-based directories illustrate the kinds of services that a network directory can provide, but they fall short of explaining the true benefits of a real-time, software-based solution.

A better example of a directory would be a personal information manager (PIM), such as Microsoft Outlook. PIMs store, organize, and display information that is specific to an individual. You can use a tool like Outlook to hold your addresses, keep track of appointments, and even warn you about important dates such as birthdays or anniversaries. PIMs are starting to take the place of paper-based address books because they store more information, they can display that information in more convenient ways, and they can be customized (and all without forcing you to write really small in the margin of the page).

It is not unusual for someone to use a PIM to organize a day's activities, add a list of friends' birthdays to her to-do list, send a copy of a good joke to all her friends, and automatically fax a sales announcement to her clients. A good PIM not only stores information but also makes information usable in real-world applications. With Outlook, for instance, you can use your contacts list (which contains names, addresses, telephone numbers, and other information about people) as the data list for a mail merge into a document created in a word processor.

While PIMs are convenient, they do have their drawbacks. To retrieve the information in your PIM, you must have access to both the software and a computer. Also, stand-alone PIMs, such as the software that runs on Palm Pilots, are not convenient for sharing information because their information is not stored on a central server. If your schedule is stored on your laptop or sitting in your pocket, your colleagues can't access it to find out whether you can attend an important staff meeting.

These limitations are being overcome by moving PIMs from the status of stand-alone applications to groupware products. *Groupware* can be defined as an application that is specifically designed to allow users to share and/or collaborate on projects or data. Most of today's groupware packages started out as e-mail applications and have grown from there. This makes sense; e-mail is a basic way to share information, and most collaboration is just that—shared information.

Microsoft has entered the groupware market in a big way with Microsoft Exchange Server. As an e-mail package, Exchange is about par for the course, although some might argue that Microsoft's traditional graphical interface makes it easier to configure and manage than many others on the market, such as Lotus Notes and Novell's GroupWise. Exchange really shines, though, in its collaborative tools. In an Exchange system, the administrator (or any user with the appropriate permissions) can create *public folders* that hold data. That data can be in just about any form you desire—from traditional e-mail messages to form-based, threaded conversations to executables. All of this data can be made available to users of the system based upon an internal security system.

Exchange was Microsoft's first attempt at a directory-based system. The Exchange system is managed through a series of containers and subcontainers—just like most network directories. Its access features include the following:

♦ It has an internal security system so that only specific individuals can access certain data.

♦ It can be accessed from various types of clients (from mail clients like Outlook, from Internet browser software, and even from LDAP-enabled applications).

NOTE *I'll talk about directory organization later in this chapter.*

COMPARING EXCHANGE SERVER TO ACTIVE DIRECTORY

If you've worked with earlier versions of Exchange Server (version 5.5 and earlier), you'll be comfortable with the Active Directory paradigm. If you can think of the mailboxes as "user accounts," then the philosophy of management is almost identical. "Accounts" represent real resources, and these accounts are grouped within containers. There are also other types of objects within the Exchange directory—objects that represent manageable aspects of the messaging system, things like connectors (the name implies its function) to foreign mail systems, or the web-access protocols. The bottom line here is that Microsoft produced an X.500-compatible directory (I'll talk about X.500 later, but for now, it's just an industry-standard method of organizing directories) to manage their messaging software. While this is just conjecture on my part, I believe they concentrated on Exchange in an effort to clarify their vision of how a directory should work (and used it as a test environment to work through any technical problems). They could then take the expertise they developed and use it to develop Active Directory. For administrators, this just means that Microsoft's development staff had years of experience in putting together a working directory *before* they released Active Directory.

While all of these examples—the telephone directory, a listing of physicians, a personal information manager, and even Microsoft Exchange Server—indicate the kinds of services that a network directory can provide, none exemplifies the true depth of the service that such a system can provide. A network directory encompasses all of these examples—and offers even more.

Understanding DNS, WINS, and NDS Network Directories

As you learned in Chapter 1, a network directory is a database that contains information used to access, manage, or configure a network. As thus defined, network directories have been in use for quite some time. Some examples of mature network directories include:

- Domain Name System (DNS)
- Windows Internet Name Service (WINS)
- Novell Directory Services (NDS)

Each of these directories holds information that is used to access or manage a network (or some aspect of a network), and each works in a slightly different manner. Let's look at each of them to determine what each does, how it is configured, and how it accomplishes its tasks. Each of these examples will include good traits and bad traits: things to be embraced or avoided by any new directories that enter the market, such as Active Directory. From each example, we will build a list of desired capabilities in a directory service which we can then use as a set of guidelines when considering Active Directory.

Domain Name Service (DNS)

The basic function of DNS is to resolve user-friendly domain names into IP addresses (called *name resolution*), but as such it barely qualifies as a true network directory. It does, however, include some features that can be useful in a true directory, or even useful *to* a true network directory. Active Directory utilizes DNS as its name resolution utility, so you must have a good understanding of how DNS works before you begin working with AD.

When a client enters a fully qualified domain name (FQDN), the DNS server is queried for the IP address of the corresponding server. DNS is the tool most commonly used to find resources on large IP networks such as the Internet. While DNS has been working as the main name-resolution service on the Internet for quite some time, it does have a few weaknesses. For our discussion, we'll look first at how DNS is structured, then at a few of its weak points.

WHY DNS?

Before the Internet was created, there existed a network known as the ARPAnet. This network tied together a few university and Department of Defense sites so that they could share research material.

NOTE   *This is a bit simplistic, but it will suffice for our discussion. For an overview of Internet history from the perspective of network security, see* Active Defense: A Comprehensive Guide to Network Security *by Chris Brenton (ISBN 0-7821-2916-1, Sybex, 2001).*

Since the network was small, each computer on the net had a small text file, known as a *hosts file*, that listed a user-friendly name for each host (computer) and its IP address. When another host was added to a site, the hosts file on each computer that might need to communicate with the new computer was updated with its address.

As an example, suppose that two networks were tied to this network—KingTech and PS Consulting. Each of these networks has five hosts that must be accessed across the network. The hosts file for each client device must include a "friendly name" and the IP address of all 10 hosts. A sample hosts file is shown in Table 2.1.

TABLE 2.1: SAMPLE HOSTS FILE

IP ADDRESS	HOST
131.107.2.100	Localhost1
131.107.2.101	Localhost2
131.107.2.102	Localhost3
131.107.2.103	Localhost4
131.107.3.100	Remotehost1
131.107.3.101	Remotehost2
131.107.3.102	Remotehost3
131.107.3.103	Remotehost4
131.107.3.104	Remotehost5

Each computer needing to access hosts on these two networks needs a hosts file with the IP address of all of the hosts it might access. In other words, keeping these "simple" text files up-to-date could require quite a bit of management.

WHAT ARE DNS DOMAINS?

DNS was created to alleviate some of this management overhead. Basically, DNS is this text file, broken into logical units known as *domains* and distributed across multiple computers known as DNS *servers*. The logical domains are organized in a hierarchical structure, much like the DOS file system. There is a very specific format for the names used in a DNS system, known as the *namespace* of the DNS system. The concept of a namespace will be very important in understanding how AD is accessed by clients, so let's define the term for future reference:

> *A namespace is a set of rules governing how objects (DNS records in this case) are referenced (named) within a directory.*

On the Internet, domain names are registered with a central consortium to ensure that they are unique and that their format follows the namespace rules set forth for the Internet. This consortium, known as InterNIC (short for Internet Network Information Center), controls the last section, or "upper level," of domain names and has created a specific set for use on the Internet. Domain names on the Internet will end with some standard name. Below you'll find the traditional first-level domain names, although the standard list has been expanded lately.

`.edu`	Educational institutions
`.com`	Commercial organizations
`.org`	Nonprofit organizations
`.net`	Networks
`.gov`	Nonmilitary government organizations
`.mil`	Military government organizations
`.num`	Telephone numbers
`.arpa`	Reverse DNS
`.XX`	Two-letter country codes (such as `.ca` for Canada)

TIP *Any directory service must include a set of clearly defined, standard rules for naming the objects that it contains—the namespace.*

NOTE *Actually, this list is not really complete. Most of us are used to typing in domain names like* `www.royal-tech.com`, *and we are taught that this is the resource's complete name. In this case,* `www` *represents the host (my web server), and* `royal-tech.com` *is the domain. In reality, the full name of any domain ends in a period. The period represents the root of the domain namespace, much like DOS paths should really start with* `C:\` *but are rarely typed that way.*

When a domain name is registered, InterNIC will determine if the requesting agency has chosen the appropriate upper-level domain. If so, and if the name is not already in use, InterNIC will reserve the name for the requesting party and add a record to DNS for the new domain.

NOTE *The InterNIC was established in 1993 by the National Science Foundation (NSF) and is operated by Network Solutions, Inc. and AT&T. For more information and a wonderful history of the Internet, try their "15 Minute Series" at* `http://www.medizin.fu-berlin.de/medbib/15min/index2.html`.

The following steps show how a DNS request is translated into an IP address during a typical query:

1. The client requests a resource; for our example, let's assume it's the web page `www.royal-tech.com`. One of the configuration parameters for IP clients is the IP address of a DNS server. The client software will query this server for the IP address of the corresponding resource.

2. The DNS server will process the query, first checking to see if information for the `royal-tech.com` domain is included. If not, it will check a local cache. The local cache contains the IP addresses of resources that have recently been resolved to IP addresses. If the IP address for `www.royal-tech.com` is in the cache, the server will return this information to the client.

NOTE   *The DNS cache is a physical file that holds the IP addresses that the DNS server has resolved; if someone accesses a site once, he might want to do so again. Caching the IP addresses speeds up response time, since the DNS server will not have to query any other servers for the information the second time. Because the Internet is a dynamic environment, these cached entries are given a time to live (TTL) so that they will be re-resolved every so often. In the Microsoft implementation of DNS, the default TTL for cached entries is 60 minutes.*

3. If the information is not available locally, the DNS server will forward the query to a root server. Each DNS server on the Internet contains a *public cache* file that holds the IP addresses of the root servers for each top-level domain tree (`.com`, `.edu`, `.org`, and so on).

4. The root DNS server will search its database for the record of a DNS server registered for the `.com` domain. If such a record exists, it will return the IP address to the local DNS server.

5. The local DNS server will then query the `.com` DNS server for the IP address of a resource named `royal-tech`. If such a record exists, the remote DNS server will return the IP address to the local DNS server.

6. The local DNS server will query the `royal-tech.com` DNS server for the IP address of a host named www. If such a record exists, the remote DNS server will return the IP address of the www server to the local DNS server.

7. The local DNS server will then return the IP address to the client. The client will then begin the process of connecting to the `royal-tech.com` web server. This process is depicted in Figure 2.1.

FIGURE 2.1

A typical Internet DNS query

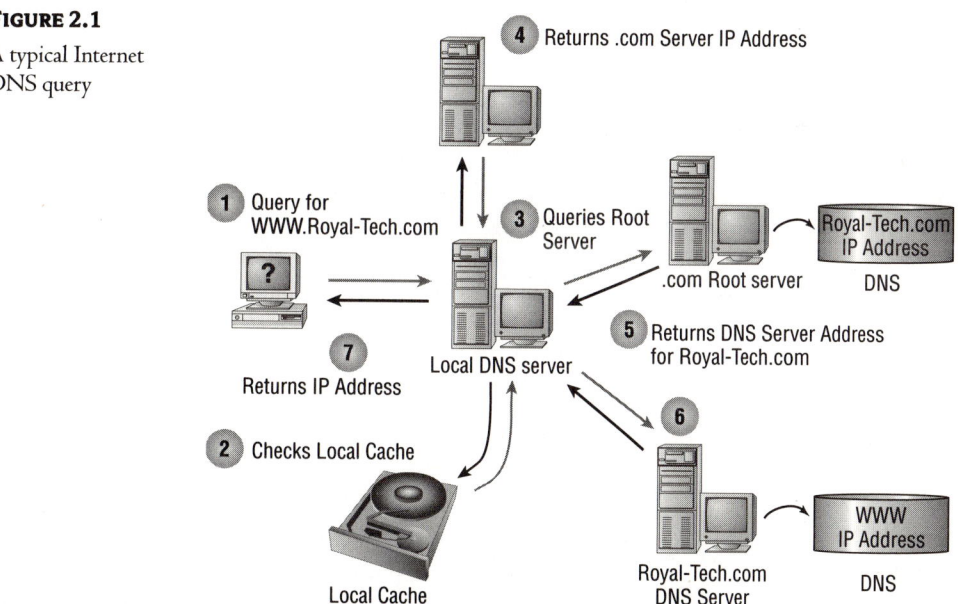

Steps 5 and 6 result in local DNS servers walking the DNS structure until the proper IP address is returned.

THE DNS STRUCTURE

The example in Figure 2.1 demonstrates both the distributed nature and the hierarchical design of DNS. Each DNS server contains only records for resources in the domains for which it is responsible. If the DNS server receives a request for information that it does not contain, it will pass that request up or down the structure until the appropriate DNS server is found.

You could see DNS as a DOS-like structure—a series of directories (or domains) organized in a tree-like format, as shown in Figure 2.2.

FIGURE 2.2

The DNS hierarchical structure

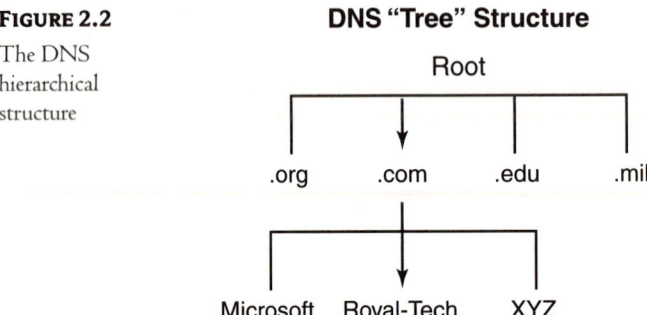

DNS "Tree" Structure

The hierarchy of domains within the DNS structure allows the database to be broken into smaller sections, which can, in turn, be distributed across multiple servers. This reduces the hardware required at any given server, as well as the network bandwidth required to support queries.

Imagine a system that was *not* broken into smaller pieces. First, the database would be huge (a record for *every* resource on the Internet). Few companies would be able to afford the kind of equipment that would be required: large hard drives, tons of memory, and multiprocessor servers would be mandatory. With fewer DNS servers available, each would have to handle more queries from clients. This would result in more network traffic, which would, in turn, require more bandwidth on the link to the Internet. Without the ability to distribute the workload across multiple servers, DNS would probably not work for name resolution on large IP networks.

This ability to break the database into logical pieces and distribute those pieces across servers is critical to any network directory that hopes to serve in medium or larger environments.

TIP   A network directory should include the ability to split the database (this is called partitioning) in order to distribute the maintenance and access overhead across multiple computers.

DNS RECORDS

Due to the various services that can be listed in the DNS database, the format of each record can get quite complex, but the bottom line is that DNS is a series of text files containing IP addresses for hosts in an IP-based network. This text file must be created and maintained manually—a task that can consume a lot of time in a large environment. If a company is forced to change its IP addressing scheme, the DNS records for each resource must be updated in DNS. If a resource is added (another mail or web server, for instance), a record must be added to the DNS database.

The manual nature of DNS management is both a blessing and a curse. On one hand, the simplicity of a text file offers advantages in a mixed environment. On the other hand, a database that does not offer any automation will require a lot of person-hours in a large environment.

TIP   A network directory should have the ability to dynamically confirm the validity of some of the information it contains.

To be quite honest, the drawback of manual maintenance has been overcome in the latest releases of DNS. DNS has also been expanded so that the database records are not limited to resolving IP addresses for hosts; recent versions support a new type of record known as an *SRV record* that resolves an IP address for a service (in other words, my DNS request can ask for a "domain controller" rather than a particular host). Both of these additions are critical to an Active Directory installation. If you are using a BIND-based (Berkeley Internet Name Domain) DNS solution (used by most Unix and Unix-like operating systems), then you will have to ensure that you are using DNS version 8.1.1 or later to support these newer functions.

DNS Fault Tolerance

In order to provide fault tolerance, DNS defines two types of DNS servers:

- ◆ Primary servers

- ◆ Secondary servers

Primary servers copy the domain information that they contain to secondary servers on a regular basis. Clients can be configured with the IP addresses of multiple DNS servers. If the client attempts to contact a DNS server and receives no response, it will proceed to the next DNS server in its list. This ensures that clients will continue to function normally even if the network loses a DNS server to some catastrophe, as shown in Figure 2.3.

FIGURE 2.3

Primary and secondary DNS servers

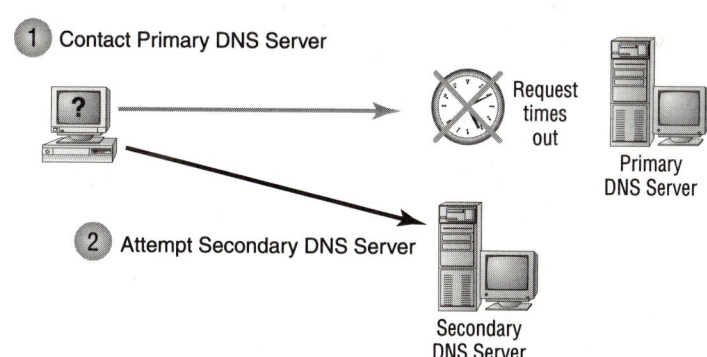

While the primary/secondary arrangement of servers provides a level of redundancy, it is configured in a limited manner known as a *single-master environment*. All changes to the DNS database *must* occur at the primary (or *master*) DNS server and be propagated to the secondary. If the master DNS server should fail, no changes can be made to the database until one of the secondary servers has been promoted to the status of master.

TIP   *A network directory in a large environment must be completely fault tolerant. The loss of a single server should in no way affect network functionality.*

There are certain shortcomings to the traditional DNS primary/secondary system. First, because all changes must occur on the primary server, the system has a single point of failure. In the event that the primary goes offline, no updates can be made to the domain information. The biggest problem with this system is that it really does not provide any fault tolerance. If the secondary servers do not receive an update (or at least some sort of "hello" message) from the primary server in a given time period, they assume that their data is out-of-date and begin refusing to service client requests. In other words, even though we have a complete copy of the domain information, it cannot be used unless the primary is online. (This simplifies the overall concept, but it works for our purposes.)

In order to eliminate these problems, Microsoft has configured their DNS software so that it can store the DNS database within Active Directory. Since AD utilizes a multimaster replication process, all AD-integrated DNS servers are consider to be primaries. (They can all accept changes and update all other DNS servers with the new information.) The loss of a single DNS server does not affect the overall system since all DNS servers consider themselves to be authoritative for the domain.

DNS IN SHORT

The Domain Name Service is a database used to resolve host names into IP addresses. The namespace it defines follows a set of rules, which is the industry standard. The database can be broken into smaller pieces (domains) and distributed across multiple servers. The service provides a mechanism for combining these separate files into a logical whole. Using a series of primary and secondary servers, the service adds a limited amount of fault tolerance to the database by replicating domain information to multiple servers.

All in all, DNS is a success. It has fulfilled its purpose in a large environment (the Internet) for quite some time. While there are a few things that might need improvement, for our purposes it acts as a very good example of a working directory.

You might be wondering, "If DNS is so great, why don't we use it as our network directory instead of implementing Active Directory Services?" The answer to this question revolves around functionality. DNS was designed for a specific purpose: resolving a host name into an IP address. DNS handles its intended function very well—so well, in fact, that AD incorporates DNS into its own design—but DNS could not handle the extra functions that would be placed upon it in an expanded role. DNS is based on a series of text files that are seen as a flat-file database. Adding additional functionality (holding the configuration information for a router, for instance) would stretch the limits of such technology.

Windows Internet Name Service (WINS)

WINS is another network directory currently used in Windows NT environments. Like DNS, WINS is used to resolve names into IP addresses. Unlike DNS, though, WINS is used to resolve NetBIOS names rather than host names. *NetBIOS names* are the unique identifiers, or computer names, given to resources on an NT (this includes NT, Windows 95/98, Windows Me, Windows 2000, XP, and even Windows Server 2003) network. Since these names identify computers on the network, each computer must have a unique NetBIOS name assigned to it.

NOTE *NetBEUI was "retired" with XP, but the DLLs are included with a README file for putting it on an XP machine. Microsoft has made an attempt to move away from NetBEUI and WINS altogether.*

REGISTERING A NAME

NetBIOS is a *broadcast-based protocol*. By default, as each client is initialized, NetBIOS sends out a broadcast announcing the name it intends to use. If another station is already using the intended name, that station will return a negative acknowledgment to the newcomer. Basically, this boils down to the first station yelling, "I intend to join the network as WS1—anyone mind?" If no response is returned, the station will assume that the name is unique on the network and will continue its initialization.

NOTE *While this sounds like a simple but effective technique, it is of limited use in a routed network. Most of today's routers are configured so that they do not pass broadcast packets. In effect, this means that the NetBIOS station is limited to confirming the uniqueness of its name to the local network. Conceivably, there could be another station with the same name on a different network.*

The first function of a WINS server is *name registration*. In a WINS environment, clients are configured with the IP address of a WINS server. Instead of using the broadcast method to announce itself (and determine if its name is unique), each client sends a registration request directly to the WINS server. The WINS server builds a database of the names of those workstations that have registered themselves. When the server receives a new request, it compares the requested name to those that have been registered. If the name is unique, it sends back a positive response; if not, it sends back a negative response. Since all of the traffic is made up of directed packets, routers will pass the request to a WINS server on another network.

Unlike DNS, the WINS server builds the database dynamically, adding records as workstations register with the service. The net effect is that the database is updated without intervention from a network administrator, greatly reducing the administrative overhead for networking staff.

Figure 2.4 depicts the four steps in the name registration process:

1. The client sends a message to the WINS server requesting registration.

2. The WINS server checks its database to ensure that the name is unique.

3. The WINS server sends a positive response to the client and adds the client's name and IP address to the database.

4. The WINS server adds the NetBIOS name and IP address to its database.

FIGURE 2.4

WINS name registration

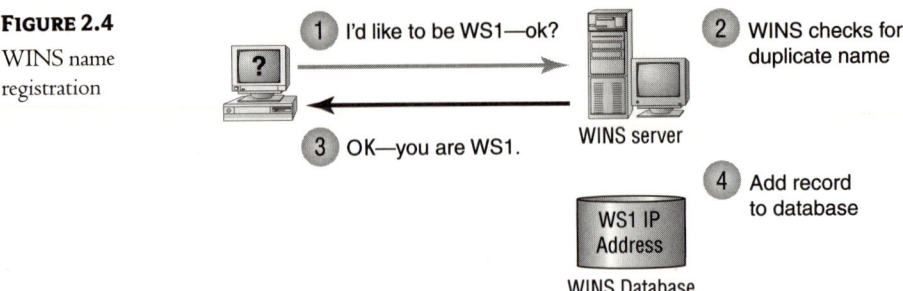

TIP   In a large environment, a directory service should have some mechanism for dynamically adding information to the database.

NAME RESOLUTION

Once a station has determined that its name is unique, it can begin to communicate on the network. In a traditional NetBIOS-based network, names are resolved to IP addresses using broadcast packets. Basically, a workstation yells on the wire, "Hey! I'm looking for a station named WS2—are you out there?" If WS2 is on the wire, it will respond with a packet that contains its IP address. Once again, though, because this process is broadcast-based, most routers will not forward the packets to other networks. In effect, this limits communication to the workstations within a single network segment.

The WINS server also provides a name-resolution service. Instead of using the broadcast method, clients send their request to the WINS server. The WINS server checks the requested name against its database of registered names. If the name is available, the WINS server will return the IP address to the requesting workstation. Once again, because this communication is performed using directed packets, rather than broadcast packets, routers do not interfere with the process. Figure 2.5 shows the name resolution process in a WINS environment, which occurs in the following steps:

1. The client queries the WINS server for the IP address assigned to a NetBIOS name.

2. The WINS server checks the database for a matching record.

3. The WINS server returns the requested information or an error indicating that the requested resource is unavailable.

FIGURE 2.5

WINS name resolution

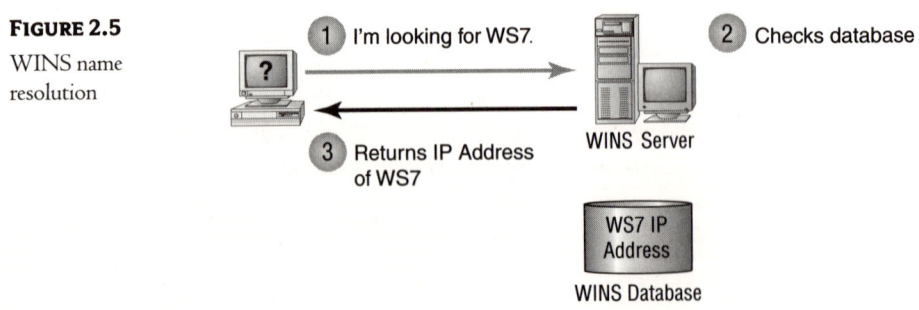

Lastly, WINS clients send a notification to the WINS server when they are about to go offline. This notification tells the WINS server to remove the record corresponding to the client from its database. (If a client shuts down without sending this notification, WINS has a mechanism that will delete the record automatically if it hasn't heard from the client in a specified period of time.) From an administrative perspective, this means that the WINS database is both built *and* maintained dynamically—without intervention from the network administrators.

TIP *Wherever possible, network directories should have mechanisms that automatically update and maintain the information that they contain.*

WINS ACROSS A WAN

WINS includes one last mechanism that warrants discussion here. Imagine a WINS network that includes wide area network (WAN) links, as shown in Figure 2.6. Because WINS uses directed, rather than broadcast-based, communication, the router can pass the requests across the WAN from City 2 to the WINS server in City 1.

FIGURE 2.6

WINS across a WAN link

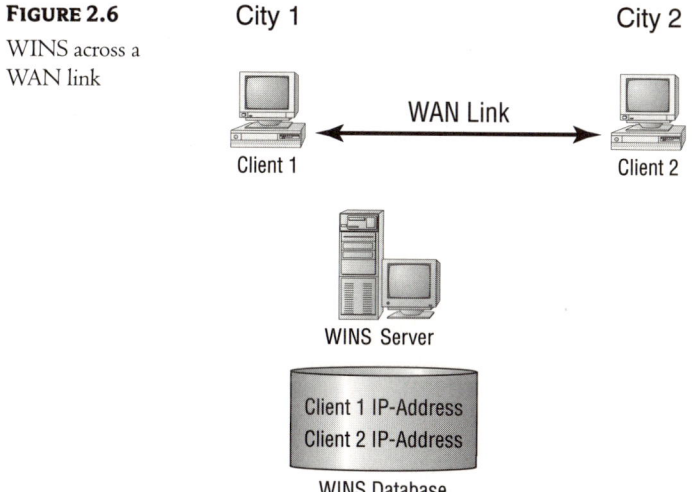

While this configuration is possible, it might not be appropriate to send all of the WINS registration and resolution traffic across the WAN link. Bandwidth is usually limited (and expensive) across this kind of line. WINS includes the ability to set up a partnership between WINS servers, overcoming this limitation. With a configuration like the one in Figure 2.7, there is a lot less traffic across the WAN link.

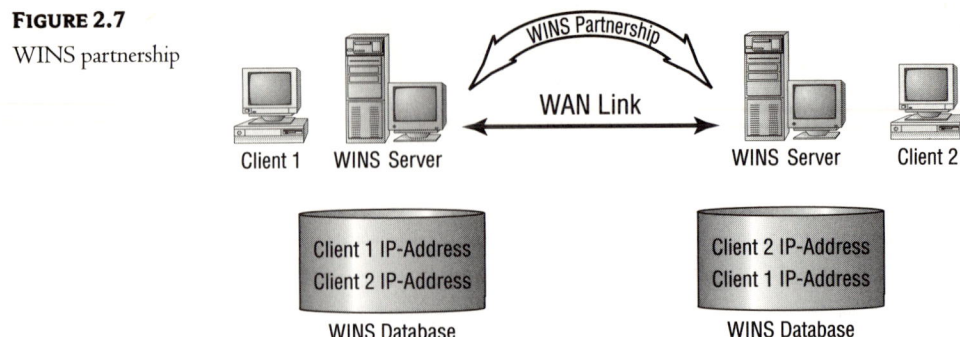

FIGURE 2.7

WINS partnership

When two WINS servers are configured as partners, they exchange their databases on a regular basis. They can be configured to exchange information based on the number of changes to the database or on a timed basis. In either case, there will be less traffic across the link, and the administrator has more control over when that traffic is generated.

TIP   *A network directory should include a mechanism that allows control over the update traffic generated to keep the information current.*

WINS IN SHORT

Unfortunately, WINS alone cannot provide the level of service demanded of a true network directory (although much of the WINS technology can be found in AD). Microsoft learned a few valuable lessons from the design and implementation of WINS—and these lessons have added to the functionality of AD.

Luckily, WINS is a technology on the decline. Microsoft has put forth a lot of effort to reduce dependence on WINS for name resolution and registration. The new solution is to rely upon DNS to provide these services.

Novell Directory Services (NDS)

With the release of NetWare version 4, Novell introduced what is arguably the most commercially successful network directory to date. NDS was intended to act as the central point of control for *all* network services in a NetWare environment. NDS is a fully functional, mature, and stable example of the kind of services that a network directory can provide. As such, it merits close examination here—if for no other reason than to serve as an example of a well-designed directory.

NOTE   *There have been numerous rumors concerning the demise of NetWare as a viable product. To paraphrase Mark Twain, the rumors of its death are greatly exaggerated! Case in point: Novell has recently released NetWare 6. NDS becomes more stable and provides more functionality with each release. Don't be surprised if the networks of the future are a mix of NDS and AD working together to provide network services!*

THE NDS STRUCTURE

The NDS database is critical to the proper functioning of a NetWare network. NDS is queried each time a network resource is accessed. When a user attempts to log on to the network, for instance, the client software submits the user's name to NDS for authentication. Later, this user might try to access some resource, such as a printer, and NDS would again be queried: first to determine whether the user had the necessary permissions and then to find the physical location of the resource. NDS is accessed during all network functions.

The best way to understand NDS (or any network directory) is to think of it as a database. Many administrators are intimidated by the "network" functions of a directory and forget that a network directory is nothing more than a database. The NDS database contains records, or *objects,* that represent network resources. There are many different types, or *classes,* of resources that can be managed through the NDS database. The record type for each class of object has a different set of fields, or *properties.* You wouldn't, for example, need a logon name property for a printer object, because printers do not log on to the network.

Table 2.2 lists a few of the more common classes of objects that exist in an NDS database.

TABLE 2.2: NDS OBJECT CLASSES

CLASS	DESCRIPTION OF OBJECT
User	Holds information specific to a user, such as logon name, password, account restrictions, telephone number, and address.
Printer	Holds information about a network printer. This object class contains properties such as network address, name, and amount of printer memory.
Group	Represents a set of users with similar resource needs. All members inherit permissions assigned to the group.
Volume	Acts as a pointer to a discrete portion of storage space (hard disk, optical, CD-ROM, and so on). This object has properties that pertain to storage devices: network address, the server upon which it resides, and certain permission information.
Print Queue	Represents a directory used to store print jobs until the system is ready to release them to a printer.
Alias	Acts as a pointer to an object that exists elsewhere in the NDS structure.

There are many other classes of objects that can exist in the NDS database. NDS is also *extensible:* custom object classes can be created to store information specific to a particular environment. The definition of the object classes contained within a directory is known as its *schema.* The ability to extend the schema to include new or custom object classes is critical for any directory to remain viable in the future.

TIP   A network directory contains information about network resources. The definition of a directory's resource records is known as the schema. For a directory to be a viable long-term solution, it must be able to adapt to new technologies. In other words, it must be easily extended to include new object types.

GLOBAL DISTRIBUTED REPLICATED DATABASE

NDS is marketed as a "global distributed replicated database" used for the management of network resources on a NetWare network. While most marketing phrases are more hype than substance, this phrase actually does a fairly good job of describing how NDS works on a network. By breaking the phrase down into its components, we can understand the basic functionality of the directory.

Global

In earlier versions of NetWare, each server held its own "accounts database" known as the *bindery*. When a user accessed a given server, this bindery (a flat database) would be queried to determine if the username and password submitted were valid. From an administrative perspective, this meant that a user account had to be created at each server that the user might need to access. Users were often required to submit to the logon process multiple times as they accessed different resources on different servers.

One of the many functions of any network directory is to centralize control of network functions. In an NDS-based system, there are no bindery files. Instead, the NDS database is used for all authentication processes. Notice that this implies that there is only one database for the network—no matter how large or geographically dispersed the network. This is what is meant by the term *global database*. When user Wu in Tokyo logs on to the network, he accesses the same database as user Bob in Chicago.

Distributed

Given that an object represents each network resource and each object is really only a record in a database, the NDS database in a global environment could grow into a large file. The next logical question is, "Where is NDS stored?"

Since NDS is critical to most network functions, it might be best to place it in a central location, as shown in Figure 2.8. Placing the database in the middle of your environment seems to put it in the "fairest" location. This placement actually mirrors other kinds of corporate access—it always seems that the offices farthest from the center are the last to know anything.

FIGURE 2.8

Centrally located NDS database

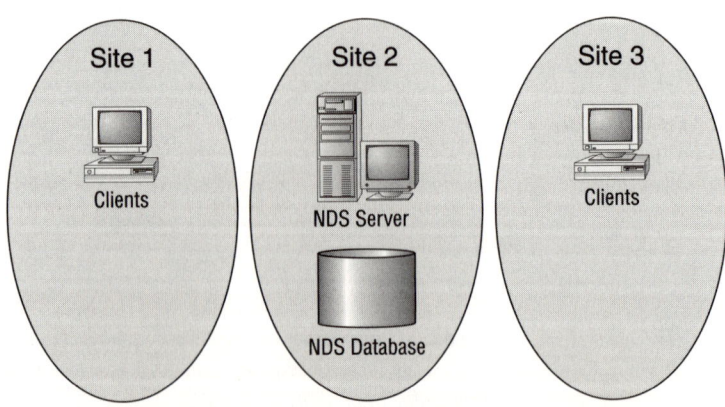

While this arrangement might look good on paper, what if Site 1 is in Tokyo, Site 2 is in Chicago, and Site 3 is in London? Do we really want users in Tokyo accessing a server in Chicago every time they need to utilize a network resource? Probably not! This configuration would not only be inconvenient for the user (imagine how long it would take to log in across the WAN link), it would also generate an unacceptable amount of traffic on what is probably an expensive link.

Since a centrally located database is not a good idea, another design would be to place the database on *all* servers in the network, as shown in Figure 2.9.

FIGURE 2.9

NDS on all servers in the network

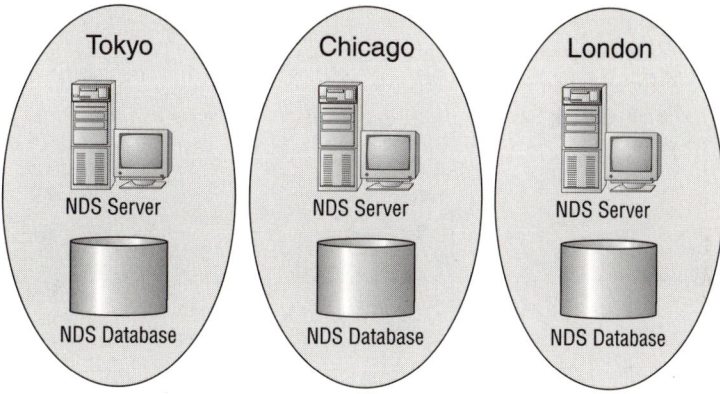

While this configuration would ensure local access to NDS for authentication, it is still not a viable solution. Imagine the traffic that would have to be generated to keep the multiple copies synchronized!

These two scenarios demonstrate the value of a distributed database. NDS can be divided into chunks—the technical term is actually *partitions*—that can be located on servers throughout the network, as shown in Figure 2.10. A good design would be to place the partition that contains records for Tokyo resources (including user accounts) on a server near those resources. This design has the added benefit of distributing the workload of maintaining the database across multiple servers so that no single server is overworked.

FIGURE 2.10

A distributed NDS database

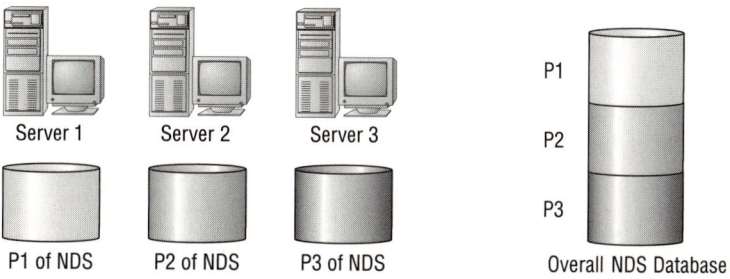

Replicated

While the design shown in Figure 2.10 does solve the problem of where NDS should be located, it does not provide any fault tolerance for the critical information stored in the database. Suppose that Server 1 were to go offline. Since the server that contains her authentication information is not available, user Susan in Chicago would be unable to access *any network resources*.

To solve this "single point of failure" problem, each partition of the database can be copied, or *replicated*, to multiple servers, as shown in Figure 2.11. In the event that Server 1 becomes unavailable, the system can still authenticate user Susan, because her account information is still available on Server 2.

FIGURE 2.11

Replication of partitions to multiple servers

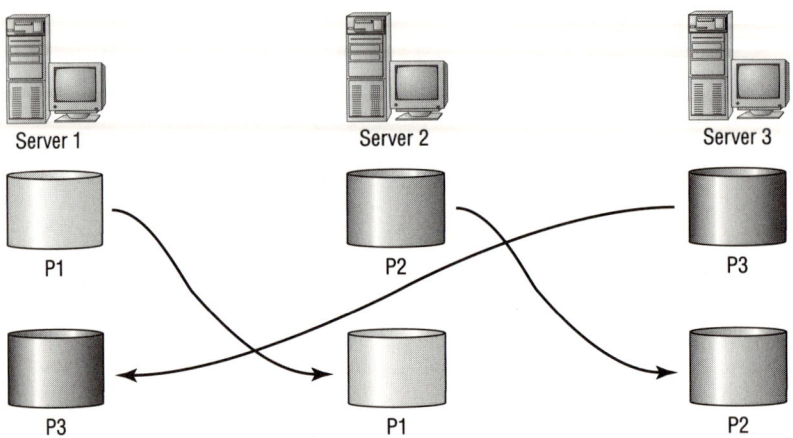

SCALABILITY

Figure 2.11 shows another important feature of NDS. Notice that we now have complete fault tolerance of the database: each partition exists on more than one server. To provide this fault tolerance, though, no server has to hold more than two-thirds of the database. As a network grows, each server will have to hold less and less of the database—and therefore spend less and less time managing NDS—but we will still have complete fault tolerance. This is known as *scalability*. As the number of servers increases, the amount of overhead placed on each server decreases. In other words, NDS becomes more efficient as the network becomes larger.

NDS IN SHORT

NDS is a mature, stable, and efficient network directory. It can be used as the measuring stick for all other directories. The only real weakness of NDS is its proprietary nature. When NDS was released, there were no other viable directories on the market, thus no industry standards were in place to guide Novell's development team. This resulted in a directory that is not as accessible to non-Novell environments as administrators might like. Given the track record of Windows 2000 and Microsoft, in the long run it is more likely that developers will be working on AD add-ons than NDS add-ons.

In Short

Each of the solutions that we have discussed—DNS, WINS, and NDS—offers lessons in how a directory should be implemented (and in a couple of cases, how one should *not* function). The "wish list" can act as our yardstick as we compare AD to these other directories:

◆ Any directory service *must* include a set of clearly defined, standard rules for naming the objects that it contains.

◆ A network directory should include the ability to split the database in order to distribute the maintenance and access overhead across multiple computers.

◆ A network directory should have the ability to dynamically confirm the validity of at least some of the information it contains.

◆ A network directory in a large environment must be completely fault tolerant. The loss of a single server should in no way affect network functionality.

◆ In a large environment, a directory service should have some mechanism for dynamically adding information to the database.

◆ Wherever possible, network directories should have mechanisms that automatically update and maintain the information the directories contain.

◆ A network directory should include a mechanism that allows control over the update traffic generated to keep the information current.

A network directory contains information about network resources. For a directory to be a viable long-term solution, it must be able to adapt to new technologies. In other words, it must be easily extended to include new object types.

In Chapter 3, we will discuss the ways that information can be organized within a database. Network directories serve a very specific function, so they use a very specific form of organization.

Chapter 3

Inside an X.500-Compliant Directory

IN THIS CHAPTER WE'RE going to look at the basic structure of a generic network directory. Why, you might ask? Well... I could say because I'm a geek and I think it's interesting. While that answer would indeed be truthful, it wouldn't justify your time in reading this chapter. The real reason to understand the basic building blocks of the directory database is that you are going to be working with it on a regular basis. Understanding how it is built (from the ground up) can help explain some of the issues you will face during your implementation. It can also help you design an AD structure that is stable and able to pass the test of time.

On a more practical note, the AD database is designed to be extensible. By that I mean you can add new types of objects and attributes. Okay, I know I haven't talked about these things yet; let's just say you might want to customize the information that is stored within the directory database. You might, for instance, want to differentiate between your full-time, permanent employees and your contractors or temporary staff. Perhaps you want to store different information about these users—the brokerage firm from which you hired them or their hourly rates. The bottom line here is that you might have management needs that are not met by the standard information stored within the AD database. You have the ability to change the basic data stored within AD (although the process is not as straightforward as you might like!).

A big part of understanding how a network directory works means understanding the X.500 recommendations for designing a directory. In the preceding chapters, we discussed network directories as repositories for network information. For this information to be of any use, it must be organized in a manner that makes it easy to access and secure. So, based on the specialized needs of a network directory, the industry developed the X.500 recommendations for organizing directories. Consider that a flat-file database would not work for a large directory. Imagine how large the file would be in a global network. The size limitations would confine its usefulness to networks so small that they don't really need a directory. Beyond even the physical limits, imagine trying to define a record type that could manage everything from user accounts to router configuration. A relational database also would not handle the needs of a full-fledged network directory. Given the diversity of the information that a network directory must store, the number of related files would grow so large that just the index of relationships would soon overwhelm even the fastest computers on the market. And so the X.500 recommendations were created.

Microsoft has adopted the X.500 recommendations in its design of the AD database. A firm understanding of these recommendations is necessary before any discussion of AD can continue. Since X.500 is a recommendation and not a standard, incompatibilities exist between the implementations of X.500. For example, Microsoft's implementation differs from Novell's, but since the namespace is consistent, the information stored in the directory can be accessed from either implementation.

If you are going to make changes to the structure of *any* database, you had better know how that database is put together! *That's* what this chapter is all about.

In this chapter:

◆ What is X.500?

◆ Designing a directory: the schema and hierarchical structures

What Is X.500?

Before I discuss what X.500 *is,* I should define what it is *not.* X.500 does *not* define the implementation of network directories. X.500 is instead a model upon which vendors can build their own products. In this, it resembles the seven-layer OSI (Open Systems Interconnection) networking model, which simply defines the functions that must be performed by networking software at each layer, without defining direct implementation techniques.

The X.500 Specifications

The X.500 specifications were originally developed in conjunction with the OSI networking model (the same seven-layer model that many of us learned, and then forgot, while studying for various networking certifications). The goal of the specification was to provide a mechanism that would allow products from different vendors the ability to access and share information. Exactly what type of information is not defined; that is left up to the implementation of the vendor. What *is* defined is a common method of organizing, naming, and accessing that information—in other words, a standard definition of the format that the directory will take to facilitate interoperability. Two international standards organizations—the ISO (International Standards Organization) and the IEC (International Electrotechnical Commission)—created a joint committee, the International Telecommunications Union (ITU), to oversee a set of technical documents with this goal in mind. The documents that make up the X.500 recommendations are listed below.

NOTE   *If you are overly curious or suffer from insomnia, the following nine documents make up the core of the X.500 technical suite. While most administrators will not need this level of expertise, these documents do give a wonderful feel for the goals of the international committee. It's interesting to note that if you read these documents and then work with any product on the market, you will have a firm understanding of the difference between compatible and compliant.*

◆ ITU-T Recommendation X.500 (1993) ISO/IEC 9594-1:1993, *Information Technology—Open Systems Interconnection—The Directory: Overview of Concepts, Models, and Services.* This is probably the best read of the bunch. It provides a great overview of what a directory is all about.

◆ ITU-T Recommendation X.500 (1993) ISO/IEC 9594-2:1993, *Information Technology—Open Systems Interconnection—The Directory: Models*. Provides a series of models to be used in the other documents.

◆ ITU-T Recommendation X.500 (1993) ISO/IEC 9594-3:1993, *Information Technology—Open Systems Interconnection—The Directory: Abstract Service Definition*. Defines, in an abstract way, the externally visible services provided by a directory (such as Read or Write services to the data).

◆ ITU-T Recommendation X.500 (1993) ISO/IEC 9594-4:1993, *Information Technology—Open Systems Interconnection—The Directory: Procedures for Distributed Operations*. Specifies ways in which the distributed components of a directory can interoperate.

◆ ITU-T Recommendation X.500 (1993) ISO/IEC 9594-5:1993, *Information Technology—Open Systems Interconnection—The Directory: Protocol Specifications*. Defines various protocols used by or to access the directory.

◆ ITU-T Recommendation X.500 (1993) ISO/IEC 9594-6:1993, *Information Technology—Open Systems Interconnection—The Directory: Selected Attribute Types*. Defines various attributes for the data stored in a directory, such as the naming of objects.

◆ ITU-T Recommendation X.500 (1993) ISO/IEC 9594-7:1993, *Information Technology—Open Systems Interconnection—The Directory: Selected Object Classes*. Defines a series of common types of data that might be stored. These classes can act as the starting point for vendors when creating their products.

◆ ITU-T Recommendation X.500 (1993) ISO/IEC 9594-8:1993, *Information Technology—Open Systems Interconnection—The Directory: Authentication Framework*. Defines two methods of authentication:

  ◆ Simple, in which passwords are exchanged

  ◆ Strong, which can take advantage of credentials formed using cryptographic techniques

◆ ITU-T Recommendation X.500 (1993) ISO/IEC 9594-9:1993, *Information Technology—Open Systems Interconnection—The Directory: Replication*. Defines methods for replication of the data within the directory to various directory servers and provides for automatic updates.

Guidelines to Using the X.500 Recommendations

As a guideline (rather than a detailed specification), the X.500 recommendations act as a frame upon which vendors can build their own implementation. The members of the ITU agency (hereafter referred to as the X.500 committee) had no idea what the scope of such products would be, but to help focus their efforts they did make a few assumptions about the environments in which directories would be used:

◆ The networks would be large and subject to constant change. Think of a large network: how many resources are completely static? Users move from place to place; devices are added, removed, or moved on a regular basis; and the attributes of objects (passwords, telephone numbers, or even network addresses) are extremely variable.

◆ While the overall rate of change will be high, the useful lifetime of the information will not be short. Stated another way, the information stored in the directory will be accessed by users more often than it changes.

◆ Most network resources are identified by some "address" that is chosen for efficiency rather than user convenience.

NOTE   *As you read over this list, you might assume that directories don't seem to offer much for small or midsized businesses. Remember that the X.500 committee was looking at the overall picture and had to create a set of recommendations that would scale up to the largest environments. Directories in smaller networks prove their worth through lower administrative costs and easier management.*

The overall goal was to provide users (*users* can be either people or other computer programs) with information about network resources, while insulating them from the mechanics of the network. At the same time, the directory should allow for the maintenance, distribution, and security of that information. Network resources can be just about anything that can attach to a network—from users to computers to printers.

Since a primary goal of the directory is to insulate users from the mechanics of the network, the information stored must be presented in a user-friendly manner. Each resource must be given a user-friendly name and the interface should be intuitive (or at least as intuitive as possible). This name can be thought of as a pointer to the resource. Since the name is just a pointer, it can remain the same even if something has changed on the networking side. A printer named ColorLaser, for instance, can still be named ColorLaser even if it is upgraded to the latest model or moved to another area of the office. From the users' perspective, these changes have no bearing on their access to the resource.

Developing Uses for a Directory

During the creation of the recommendations, the X.500 committee envisioned three generic, practical uses for a directory. These generic examples were intended to inspire developers to more complex uses.

Interpersonal Communication   The directory can play a role in many forms of interpersonal communication (such as e-mail) by providing the information necessary for users (or their software-based agents) to communicate with their counterparts in another system. Imagine a worldwide directory that includes things like telephone numbers and addresses. A user would have a single point of access to all of that data.

Intersystem Communication   The directory could also be used to provide the information necessary for one service to talk to another. A prime example would be one mail server trying to deliver mail to another mail server. Today, we use another database (DNS) for this type of mail delivery across the Internet. As you saw in Chapter 2, DNS is a great tool, but it does have its limitations.

Authentication Services   The directory could also act as a primary source for identification and authentication of users to resources. By using passwords or some other form of identifier, the directory could act as a single point of control over access to information and services.

Designing a Directory

Designing any database is really more a logical exercise than a technical one. First you must decide the purpose of the database, then you decide on an overall structure. For an X.500-compliant network directory, such as AD, these two steps are predetermined:

◆ Its purpose is to store information about network resources.

◆ Its structure is hierarchical.

With most databases, the next step would be to define records and fields. This is where the design of a network directory becomes a little more complicated than the Microsoft Access databases that most of us are comfortable with.

The Schema

One of the first tasks involved in designing any type of database is defining the types of records that exist within it and the information that each record will contain. Within an X.500 directory, there can be many different types of records. A record is called an *object,* and each type of record is known as a *class.* Each class of object is made up of different fields known as *attributes.* A record for a user would be of the class "user," have various attributes (like telephone numbers or passwords), and be known as a user object. The definition of the object classes and attributes available for any given directory is known as its *schema.*

Since the X.500 recommendations are just a model and not an implementation, there are very few object classes predefined. There is, however, a well-documented set of rules for how objects and attributes should be created to allow for interoperability between various vendors' directories. While an in-depth discussion of this process is beyond the scope of this book, an overview can be helpful when implementing a directory on a network.

The X.500 committee assumed that certain types of information might be made available through the directory. These include the following generic types:

◆ Information about people, such as e-mail addresses, telephone numbers, and public key certificates

◆ Information about servers and services, such as network port addresses

◆ Information about the directory itself, used to perform consistency checks and replication

You should note a couple of things about the list. First, it is extremely generic; there is very little detail provided about the class of objects that should exist. Second, the list is open to expansion should the need arise.

DETERMINING THE SCOPE

When designing a directory-based product, a vendor must first define the scope of the directory. That is, they must first decide the various classes of objects they wish to support. Basically, the vendor must decide which aspects of the physical world should exist in the directory database. The directory for a network operating system, for instance, would have to include things like user accounts, groups, servers, storage devices, printers—in other words, the various pieces of information that would be involved in a network. A manufacturer of network equipment, however, might have a completely different list. Here, it might be more appropriate to store things like routers, bridges, and gateways.

As you can see, deciding the scope determines what information will be available within the directory. The goal of the X.500 recommendations is that these different types of directories will be able to share information because they are based upon the same design framework.

WHICH ATTRIBUTES?

Once a vendor has determined the scope, the next step is to decide what attributes should be stored for each class of object. The attributes are a second step because the format of the directory allows multiple classes of objects to use the same attribute definitions. The name attribute, for instance, would be used for all records regardless of class. An IP address attribute, however, might only be used by physical devices or user accounts (documenting where the user is logged on to the system). It would probably not be a necessary attribute for a group object.

After these decisions have been made, a vendor can begin the process of building the schema of the database. The schema holds the definition for the object classes in the database and their attributes. The first step in building a schema is to define the attributes for objects. Then the developers combine attributes to build object classes.

Creating a Directory

Microsoft has claimed that the AD schema is easily extensible; in other words, you are able to define your own attributes and object classes. We're not going to get into the actual coding process, but it might be helpful to explore the thoughts behind building a schema.

DETERMINING THE DIRECTORY'S SCOPE

Begin by determining the scope of your directory. Microsoft has ambitious plans for Active Directory: at some point it will probably contain records for users, routers, applications, printers, and just about everything else you might associate with your networks.

DIRECTORY ENABLED NETWORKS

At one point Microsoft was touting a concept known as Directory Enabled Networks (DEN). This concept revolved around various vendors of network hardware (and some software) defining their own classes and attributes for the Active Directory database and creating an application that would add these new components to the schema. While the concept has not disappeared, Microsoft had a hard time convincing a few key (and major) players to actually join the "Microsoft Team." Many thought that by tying their products to Windows 2000/Windows Server 2003 (and Active Directory) they would lose market share in other arenas (most notably those networks that are Unix- or Linux-based). It will probably be a while before we see "router" objects in the AD schema, but once it happens, network administration will change drastically. Imagine installing a new router and configuring it by cutting and pasting the configuration from an existing device on your network!

For our purposes, let's keep your directory simple. You should design a few user-related object classes and leave the highly technical network components to the experts at Microsoft.

First, let's define the classes of objects to include the following:

User   Represents the network user to the system

Group   Represents a number of users for administrative purposes

Printer   Represents the physical device on the network

Storage Space   Represents some form of storage, such as hard drive, CD-ROM, or tape drive

Service   Represents some service provided to the network, such as e-mail, DHCP, or DNS

NOTE   *This list is not complete enough to act as an actual network directory, but it will suffice for our purposes.*

The next step is to define the information that you would like to store for each object class—in other words, the attributes that will be needed for each object.

For a user object, you might want to store some of the following attributes:

◆ Name: a unique identifier

◆ Password

◆ Security certificate: a place to store advanced security certificates

◆ Telephone number

◆ E-mail address: multiple forms for Exchange, SMTP, or other mail systems

◆ Mail stop

◆ Department

◆ Network address: multiple values to hold current IP, MAC, or other network addresses

◆ Description: a text field to be used for any nonstandard information

◆ Class: the type of object

◆ Location: physical location of the user

This list could go on and on. If your users do a lot of traveling, for instance, you might want to store things like frequent-flyer memberships, seating preferences, or rental car company preferences. Your human resources department might like your directory to store items such as benefits package options or dates of hire.

For the group object, your list might include these:

◆ Name: a unique identifier

◆ E-mail address: multiple forms for Exchange, SMTP, or other mail systems for all members to use as a built-in distribution group

◆ Telephone number: perhaps for the person responsible for the group's activities

◆ Description: a text field to be used for any nonstandard information

◆ Class: the type of object

◆ Member list: a list of all user accounts associated with this group

◆ Purpose: a text field used to describe the function of the group

Once again, this list could have numerous options. You might, for instance, want to store a pointer to a group web page on your intranet server.

Things should be a little simpler for your printer object:

◆ Name

◆ Network address: the IP or MAC address of the device

◆ Make/model: the manufacturer and model number for the device

◆ Serial number

◆ Date of purchase

◆ Warranty information: a text field describing any warranties in effect for the printer—perhaps you could even add a date option to alert you when the warranted time has expired

◆ Memory

◆ Fonts

◆ Client print drivers: multiple drivers for various clients that might use this printer

Your storage device object should also be fairly straightforward:

◆ Name

◆ Network address

◆ File system: FAT, NTFS, CDFS, etc.

◆ Configuration: RAID, mirrored, etc.

◆ Date of purchase

◆ Warranty information

◆ Size

◆ Writable media: Yes/No

◆ Removable media: Yes/No

Finally, we come to your service object. This object might be a little more complex. There are so many network services that coming up with a standard format might not be possible, but you can add attributes as needed later. Here are some attributes to get you started:

◆ Name

◆ Network address

◆ Description

◆ Location

As you can see, planning the information that should be held within the directory can be a complex job. You have to include any critical information (how would you find a print device without some sort of address?) as well as any information that might reduce either the management or user-access overhead.

DEFINING ATTRIBUTES

Once you have created your list of object classes and attributes, the X.500 recommendations determine how you should define these items. First, you should combine all of your attributes into one list and cross-reference those that can be used for more than one object class, as shown in Table 3.1.

TABLE 3.1: DIRECTORY ATTRIBUTE LIST

	USER	GROUP	PRINTER	STORAGE SPACE	SERVICE
Name	X	X	X	X	X
Password	X				
Security Certificate	X				
Telephone Number	X	X			
E-mail Address	X	X			
Mail Stop	X	X			
Department	X	X	X	X	X
Network Address	X		X	X	X
Description	X	X	X	X	X
Object Class	X	X	X	X	X
Location	X		X	X	X
Member List		X			X
Purpose		X			X

Continued on next page

TABLE 3.1: DIRECTORY ATTRIBUTE LIST *(continued)*

	USER	GROUP	PRINTER	STORAGE SPACE	SERVICE
Make/Model			X	X	
Serial Number			X	X	
Date of Purchase			X	X	
Warranty Information			X	X	
Memory			X		
Fonts			X		
Print Drivers			X		
File System				X	
Configuration			X	X	X
Size				X	

By creating the attribute definitions first, developers can save themselves a lot of redundant work. Objects are "built" by adding various attributes to a frame, rather than by building each object from the ground up. There are certain attributes that will be common to all object classes. Each object needs a unique name, for example, so that it can be referenced as a separate entity. Each object will also have to be classified as a member of a class, so that the system can properly identify the resource or service to users.

Hierarchical Structures: X.500 and DOS

X.500 presents a method of organizing the data stored within a directory that is easy to manage and that also makes it easy for users to access the information they need. The recommendations define the model as a hierarchical structure, often referred to as the *directory tree*. For some reason, many experienced network administrators have a hard time with the concept of a directory tree structure. For years, networks have had a server-centric design: each server was an island of services in a sea of connectivity.

The X.500 recommendations present a new paradigm for network management that can take some getting used to. While it *is* different, the concept is nothing new. Computer professionals have been working with a hierarchical system for quite some time—DOS! Since both DOS and an X.500 directory tree are based upon a hierarchical structure, the management of each is very similar. Let's review a few simple DOS basics before we look at the X.500 structure—basics that will help us understand a hierarchical network directory structure.

DEFAULT DIRECTORY

The first term to review is *default directory*. In DOS, the default directory is the directory in which you are currently working. Here's another way of looking at it: if you were to save a file (without specifying a path), it would be placed in your default directory. This is quite a bit different from Windows 98 and NT, which hold a default "save" location (usually a directory named My Documents) in the Registry. Because many DOS activities revolved around the default directory, we often configured our prompt to display the default directory. (Remember the `C:\` prompt?) Figure 3.1 shows a common DOS directory structure. Let's review a few more basic DOS recommendations before we go on.

FIGURE 3.1

DOS directory structure

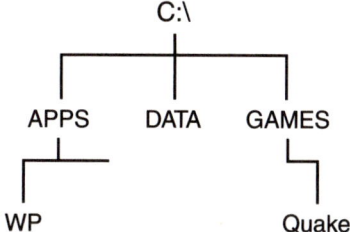

NAMING DOS FILES

First, let's review how DOS files are named. Most of us are probably used to simply typing in just the filename to start a program. In the example in Figure 3.1, for instance, we would probably start a game of Quake by typing **Quake**. In reality, though, that is not the full name of the file. The full name of the file includes the path back to the root of the drive: In this case, the full name of the file would be `C:\games\quake\quake.exe`. As a convenience, DOS includes the path function so that we don't have to type in the complete name to start a program.

NOTE *The concept of a "complete" name will be very important when we start looking at X.500 directories.*

MOVING AROUND IN DOS

In DOS, we use the CD (Change Directory) command to move around the structure. If your default directory were `C:\` and you wanted to move to the Quake directory, you would enter the following command:

```
CD games\quake
```

In the background, DOS would perform an append action, adding what you typed to your default directory to end up with your destination. If the named destination exists, you are moved there. If not, DOS will return an error.

If your default directory were `C:\apps\wp` and you wished to move to the `C:\data` directory, you would enter the following command:

```
CD \data
```

The backslash character (\) indicates the root in this command. DOS moves to the root and appends the path you have entered. Once again, if you have entered a correct path, you will be moved there.

For most of us, moving around a DOS file system is second nature. Luckily, this means that moving around an X.500 directory structure is also second nature!

The X.500 Hierarchical Structure

The structure of a directory specifies how the information within the directory will be organized. There are two main goals for the design of any network directory structure:

◆ Object identification

◆ Object organization

Both goals are critical to the proper functioning of any directory.

Object identification ensures that each object within the structure has some sort of unique identifier. Each unique identifier must map directly to some resource. Think of it this way: without some unique name, you would be unable to ask for information about a particular resource. At best, you could ask for information about all similar objects. Imagine that you needed to print a document. Instead of identifying the printer near your desk, you would have to present a request for all "HP printers in my building," or some other, less specific grouping. In this case, you wouldn't know whether your job would print at the nearest printer or at some HP printer on another floor. The unique identifier allows you to specify a particular object within the directory database.

Object organization allows the data within the directory to be broken into subsets for administrative purposes. Suppose you wanted a local administrator at the Tampa office to be able to create new user objects within a certain area of your structure. Without some sort of organizational plan, it would be difficult to limit the access of the administrator.

The X.500 recommendations not only fulfill these two requirements quite well (as you'll see in the next section) but actually exceed them. The X.500 structure defines a uniform way to uniquely name objects and provides a framework that can be used to organize those objects once they are created. It also provides for other necessary services: distribution of the database to multiple servers, replication of pieces of the database to more than one server, and various protocols to be used when accessing the directory.

THE X.500 TREE

As I stated earlier, there are many similarities between the DOS file structure and the X.500 directory structure. In DOS, you organize your files by creating directories and subdirectories. In an X.500 structure, we have the equivalent of directories, called *containers*. Instead of using containers to organize files, you use them to organize the objects within your database.

You may have heard the DOS structure referred to as a "tree" because of the way subdirectories branch off from the root of the drive. Since the X.500 structure acts in much the same way, we refer to it as the *tree*. You use the tree to organize your objects for ease of management or ease of access (just as you'd use directories to organize files for the same reasons in DOS). In an X.500 tree, we refer to the objects as *leaves*. A leaf object can be defined as any object that does not contain any other object. This can get complicated, so let's start with the container objects and ignore leaf objects for now.

In DOS there is no real difference between a directory and a subdirectory, except that subdirectories are beneath some directory in the structure. Unlike DOS, the X.500 structure does define different types of container objects. Each has a specific purpose and certain limits on placement within the tree. X.500 defines the following types of containers:

Country Represented as a C object. The highest container object in the schema as defined by the X.500 committee. It can only exist at the top, or root, of the tree.

Organization Represented as an O object. These containers can only exist off the root of the tree or below a country.

Location Represented as an L object. A grouping object that can exist at any level of the tree except directly below the root.

Organizational Unit Represented as an OU object. Another grouping object. Basically, this is the equivalent of a subdirectory in DOS. OUs can exist under Os or other OUs.

WARNING *Microsoft's X.500 directory (AD) does not necessarily implement all of these container classes.*

Figure 3.2 presents a graphical representation of an X.500 structure for the company King Technologies. King Technologies has offices in Tampa, Florida, and Berlin, Germany.

FIGURE 3.2

Directory tree
structure for
King Technologies

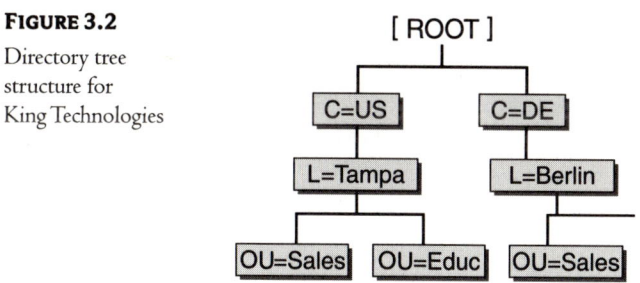

As with a DOS disk, there is no *right* way to organize a network directory. Many of the principles are the same, though. In DOS you create a directory for one of two reasons: to ease access or to ease management. The same holds true when creating containers in a network directory. Unnecessary levels only add to users' confusion and to management overhead.

Once you have planned the structure, the next step is to populate it with leaf objects. Within the directory, leaf objects are represented by CN, as shown in Figure 3.3.

FIGURE 3.3

A populated directory

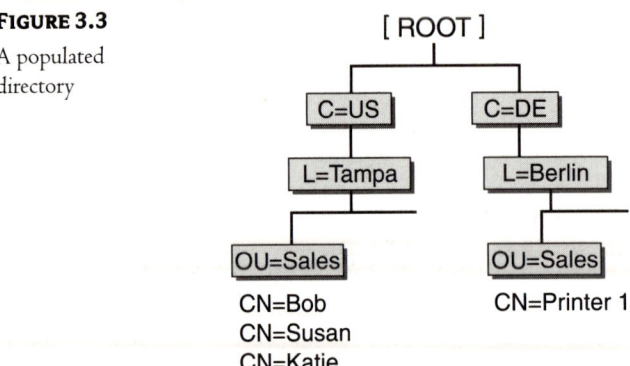

In Short

An X.500 network directory is nothing more than a complicated database. The database holds objects, which in turn have attributes (records and their fields). Because of the complicated nature of its job, the directory is organized in a hierarchical fashion. The structure is defined as a series of container objects connected in a tree-like manner.

There are numerous types of container objects and rules about their use, as you can see in Table 3.2.

TABLE 3.2: CONTAINERS IN AN X.500 DIRECTORY

NAME	REPRESENTATION	VALID PLACEMENT IN THE TREE
Country	C	Can exist only at the top, or root, of the tree
Organization	O	Can exist only directly below the root or a country container
Location	L	Can exist anywhere except directly off the root
Organizational Unit	OU	Can exist only under an organization object or another organizational unit

In this chapter, we discussed how a directory is designed, the types of information it can hold, and how that information is organized. Once any directory has been populated with data (user accounts, groups, peripherals, and so on), it must be made accessible if it is to have any value. In the next chapter, we will discuss an industry-standard set of protocols specifically designed to access information stored in a directory database.

Chapter 4

Accessing the Directory

SO FAR, WE HAVE concentrated on the structure of directory databases. Once you have defined the schema, the next step is to populate the database with objects. The mechanics of creating objects and filling the database with data will be discussed in detail in later chapters. For the moment, let's assume that you have created your environment. Now you can just sit back and relax, right? Hardly! You have entered a lot of useful information—the next step is making that information available to the right people. After all, why did you spend hours typing in addresses, phone numbers, and locations if that information was never going to be used?

If you were going to do all the administration of your AD environment and your users were going to access it *at the server*, then a discussion of accessing the directory would really just be an overview of the user interface. Of course, there are a couple of small problems with such an environment. First (and foremost), we do not want users sitting, logging in, or even touching our servers! Second, most companies place their servers in locked rooms, so even we (as administrators) rarely sit at the server to perform our administrative functions.

The reality is that users sit at their own computers, and those computers can be spread out from one end of the company to the other (and if you consider the mobile workforce, your users might be spread out across the entire globe). This means that users must access the information in the directory in a remote fashion. The same is true for administrators—who wants to go to the "server room" every time a change must be made to the directory? I guess that might not be a problem for much of the day-to-day management of a network directory; you could conceivably walk to the server once or twice a day to create new user accounts or add a new printer. But what about the ad hoc support that we all provide? You get a call from a user in accounting who has locked out their account because "the system screwed up." (This is usually a euphemism for "I fat-fingered my password six times and now the system says my account is locked out" or "Someone stole the Post-It note that had my password on it.") Do you want to leave whatever you are working on to go to the server room to fix each of the 100 small problems that crop up each day? We all know that the answer is "NO!"

That's what this chapter is all about. How, exactly, is the data in a directory database accessed? This question is especially important if you manage a heterogeneous environment. You might, for instance, have both Novell NDS and Microsoft AD running within your network. Since both are X.500 compliant, information placed in one directory can be made available to the other. There are a couple of industry-standard protocols used for accessing (and managing) the data stored within an X.500-compliant directory.

Understanding these protocols gives you an advantage when configuring various remote access tools *and* when trying to bridge the gap between dissimilar operating systems. Back to our example of NDS and AD: knowing the access protocols used to communicate between the two environments can make it much easier to install and configure the various product add-ons that facilitate this communication.

The first half of this chapter is more of a history lesson than anything else. Sometimes it helps to review what has been tried before to explain the current processes. In the case of directory access, the first protocol used (DAP) was proprietary in nature and placed a lot of overhead on the client computer (essentially limiting the types of hardware that could access the directory; full PCs could handle it, but other devices didn't have the necessary horsepower). While DAP is really a dead technology, knowing its background will help you understand the way that the current industry-standard access protocol (LDAP) works, and why.

In this chapter:

◆ Making information available to users

◆ Directory Access Protocol: modifying the directory, providing access, and analyzing the cost

◆ Lightweight Directory Access Protocol: comparing DAP and LDAP

Making Information Available to Users (or Not!)

At first, your users will not even be aware of the directory. Of course, if not for the splash screens of modern operating systems, many users wouldn't even know they were working on a network (until it goes down). They will log on to the network, access necessary resources, and fulfill their job functions without giving a second thought to the underlying mechanism of the network.

NOTE *In the early days of networks, administrators tried to hide the "plumbing" of networks so that users could do their jobs without having to be concerned with the mechanics of networking. The highest compliment an administrator could receive was a user's unwitting question, "Network, what network?" Of course, with today's operating systems this goal is impossible—it seems that users are constantly being presented with splash screens advertising the network software.*

As time passes, users will begin to see the directory as a source of useful information, asking, "What's Joe's phone number?" or "What's the mailing address of the marketing department?" or even "I need to e-mail the receptionist in the sales group—what is his name?" The answers to all of these questions can be stored within your directory and made available to users. Not only can you make the information available, you will be able to control access to specific attributes. Perhaps everyone should be able to access the e-mail addresses, but only managers should be able to access home telephone numbers.

The fact that this information *can* be made available implies that there must be some mechanism used for access. The design and capabilities of the directory itself will influence the methods used to access the data it contains. Certain aspects of a network directory must be taken into account when choosing an access method:

Hierarchical Database Structure An X.500 directory follows a hierarchical structure. Hierarchical databases organize data much differently than standard databases. In a flat-file or relational database, each record has some unique field (or combination of fields) that differentiates it from every other record in the database. In a hierarchical database, each object is identified by its place in the structure. The tools used to access information from an X.500-compliant database must understand the structure of the schema and must format requests appropriately.

Presentation Scheme A directory's *presentation scheme* defines the methods that can be used for accessing information stored in the directory. Without a well-defined presentation scheme, the data would be inaccessible. The X.500 specifications provide a standard set of access capabilities for presenting directory information to users. Access is accomplished through the use of a *Directory User Agent* (DUA) built into an application designed for directory access. The DUA interacts with a *Directory Service Agent* (DSA) at the directory server, as shown in Figure 4.1.

FIGURE 4.1

Client access to the directory

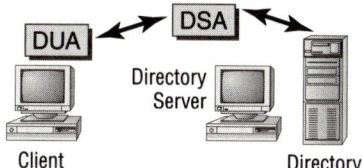

Two protocols are available for use in accessing an X.500 directory:

♦ Directory Access Protocol (DAP)

♦ Lightweight Directory Access Protocol (LDAP)

DAP was defined as a part of the X.500 specification. LDAP, on the other hand, was defined independently of X.500 as a method for accessing both X.500 and non-X.500 directories. Each has its strengths and weaknesses, but LDAP has become the preferred method of access because of its less proprietary nature and lower overhead on the client. LDAP clients with the proper permissions can search, add, delete, and modify objects and attributes within a directory. LDAP functionality consists of a series of calls, or functions, used for directory management.

Directory Access Protocol (DAP)

During the development of the X.500 recommendations, the X.500 committee spent time considering the ultimate use of the directory. There are certain functions that are standard with *any* database and other uses that would be specific to the function of the directory. Users of any database need to be able to perform the following tasks:

Lookup   This is the basic information retrieval used by users. Users request specific information about a known resource (such as "What is Bill's phone number?").

Searching and Filtering   A user can use information associated with resources to locate individual resources (such as "List all users in the Sales department").

Browsing   A DAP call can be used to present information in some sort of list from which users can choose specific resources. ("I don't remember the name of the object, but I will recognize it when I see it.")

Other tasks will be more directory oriented. These tasks are not *normal* database functions—they are applicable only to the purpose of a network directory:

Name Resolution   Resources can be located based upon easily remembered names. This can be thought of as a special case of lookup. (The corporate standard for user accounts is last name, first initial. Knowing this standard, and knowing the name of the person I'm looking for, allows me to easily find his object in the directory.)

Authentication   Authentication involves some type of security system used to positively identify a user in order to determine permissible access to resources. A user proves her identity by providing a password (or some other trusted identifier). Resource access can be based upon this "proven" identity.

The five tasks just listed—lookup, searching and filtering, browsing, name resolution, and authentication—are the end result of some action taken by the client software. They all revolve around the ability to interrogate the directory. DAP provides four functions that a client can initiate when accessing the database for information:

Read   A request aimed at a specific object. This action will return the values of some or all of the attributes of the object in question. If a limited set of attributes is to be returned, the client software (DUA) supplies the list of desired attributes to the server (DSA). A client might, for instance, request the phone number attribute of a particular user object.

Compare   This is a request aimed at a particular attribute of a particular object. In some implementations, a user might be able to compare an attribute without having the ability to actually read it. An example of this functionality might be security software that checks for the existence of a password without being able to read the passwords themselves.

List   This action will return a list of objects in the directory. A user might, for instance, request a list of all printers within (or below) the Tampa container in the directory tree.

Abandon   This action informs the directory to stop an action requested by a user. If a user is performing a search on a large directory, for instance, the desired information might be presented before the entire search has been completed, or the search is taking too long and has been terminated by the client, or the search has timed out. Issuing an Abandon request would cause the DSA to stop the search.

Client software will use these four basic functions to make the information stored within a directory available to users or network services. Users, for example, can search the database for the telephone numbers stored within it, basically eliminating the need for a special-purpose database for this task (or worse—a paper-based solution that is never up-to-date). Network services can query the database as part of their function. An e-mail package might query the database to determine whether a user is currently connected to the network, and if so, to find the address of the user's station. Once the database is made accessible, its uses are limitless!

Modifying the Directory

Reading the information is only half the story, though. While some of the information within the directory will be automatically maintained, much of the information must still be entered and maintained manually. This implies that there must be another set of functions that provide the ability to modify the directory. DAP defines four specific functions for modifying the directory:

Add Entry This request adds a new object to the directory.

Remove Entry This request deletes an object from the directory.

Modify Entry This request is used to change an existing object. This function is used to change attributes such as telephone numbers or addresses.

Modify Distinguished Name This request is used to rename objects within the directory (as well as any subordinate objects).

As you can see from the descriptions, these four functions allow complete management of the directory. Objects can be created, deleted, and manipulated using the DAP protocol and an appropriate tool.

Providing Access to the Directory

Once you have implemented a directory, it can become critical to the proper functioning of your network. Since it can be used to authenticate users during the logon process, for instance, there can be absolutely no question about the integrity of the information that the directory stores. Each DAP request can be configured so that security mechanisms can be included in the process.

To put it another way, consider that the directory can contain information that is either confidential (such as user passwords or other security certificates) or critical to network functionality (such as the address of a network printer). Clearly, you want to protect such information against inappropriate access or manipulation. Each of the requests defined in the DAP specifications can include security information that can be used to determine whether the requesting user is allowed to perform the function. Normal users, for instance, would not have the rights required to change the database—this ability would be reserved for administrative personnel.

NOTE Network directories must have some sort of internal security that can be used to limit access to the information they contain.

In a typical scenario, the directory will be used to authenticate the user during the logon process. The user will have supplied some unique fact, such as a password, that ensures his identity. Passwords are the most common method of authentication used today, but other methods are on the horizon. There are numerous hardware- or software-based tools that can use much more specific information to identify a user. Some of the options available either today or in the near future include:

◆ Hardware that accepts a magnetic ID card (much like a credit card) that contains a user's identification credentials

◆ Hardware that can scan a user's fingerprints or retinal patterns and match them against a stored value

◆ Software that uses a camera to "sense" a user's face and matches it against a stored picture

◆ Certificate software that uses a series of encrypted values to ensure identity (much like the software used to secure web-based transactions)

Whatever the method used for identification, an X.500 directory can be used to store the unique information necessary for authentication. During the logon process, the security subsystem can compare a value submitted by the user's client software against this particular attribute of the user account, as shown in Figure 4.2.

1. The user supplies identification information to the logon software (this can be a password, a certificate, or some other, more sophisticated identifier).

2. The client software then submits this information to a directory server.

3. The directory server finds the user's object and compares the information against the value of a security attribute.

FIGURE 4.2

User authentification

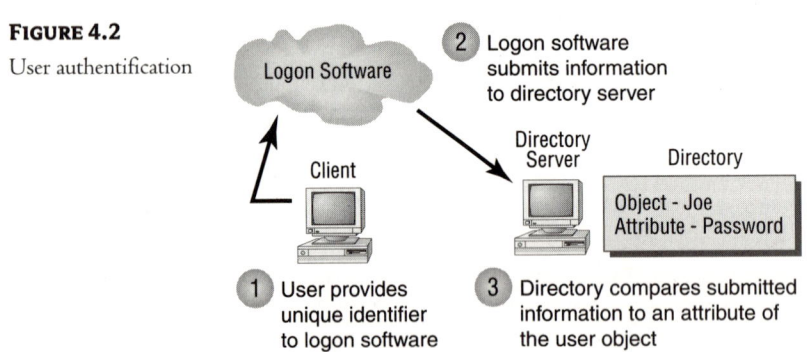

Once the user has been properly identified, this identification can control access to information within the directory. Each attribute of each object can contain a list of the users who are allowed to read or manipulate its value. DAP requests can pass the user's identity to the directory service with each request.

What's the Cost?

Any time you add another service to your network, it costs money. First there is the cost in person-hours. You will need to be trained in the capabilities and tools of any new technology. Users will also need training if they are going to see any benefit from the implementation. All of this training adds up to lost person-hours for your company. The hope is that the cost will be offset by higher productivity in the future. Such costs are hard to quantify and therefore hard to justify. They are also (thankfully) beyond the scope of this material. There are also, however, tangible costs associated with new services; these costs *are* within the scope of this book.

As anyone who has ever had to work with a large, complex database can confirm, performing complex searches can eat up server resources. The larger the database and the more complex the queries, the better your hardware will have to be to provide adequate performance. AD is no different from any other large database in this respect. DAP has defined a set of standard capabilities to help with this issue.

DAP is defined as a client-intensive protocol. Most of the "up-front" work is performed at the client computer. The client software is responsible for the proper formatting of any requests, which means that any client software must have a complete understanding of the directory it is designed to query. Moving these functions to the *client* reduces the overhead at the server, but it does have a few drawbacks.

CLIENT OVERHEAD

Because the client must fully understand the directory, the programs tend to be large and resource-intensive. The more complex the directory becomes, the more complex the client software must be to access it.

NOTE   *Client overhead might seem like an unimportant issue given the power of today's computers. Actually, it is critical to industry acceptance of X.500 directories. DAP was developed to allow remote access to the information stored within a directory. DAP works fine if a user is sitting at his high-powered work station, but it might not work so well for a user who is away from her desk. Consider the type of information stored in the directory: user names and addresses, phone numbers, e-mail addresses—exactly the kinds of things stored in most electronic Rolodexes or palmtop computers. It would be great if a user could access the directory from his Palm Pilot! Unfortunately, most of these types of components have limited resources—usually not enough to handle the overhead of DAP client software.*

PROPRIETARY SOFTWARE

Since any client software must understand the directory that it will query and since the X.500 standards are a model, not an implementation, vendors will need to produce proprietary client software to access their directory. In effect, this will either limit networks to a single-vendor solution or force users to master multiple programs to access the information in different brands of directories.

LIMITING USE OF RESOURCES

As well as moving much of the work to the client, DAP also includes the ability to limit the server resources used by any request. Users can set limits for the actions they take, as in the following examples:

Time Limits DAP client software can set a limit on the length of time to be spent on a given request. In a large database, this can prevent a client from performing a search that "spans the globe." If a request exceeds its time limit, the server will abandon the action.

Limits on the Size of the Results DAP client software can also limit the size of the returned information set. If a user inadvertently asks for all "User" accounts, for instance, this could restrict the amount of information returned.

Limits on the Scope of the Request These limits allow a user to configure the query so that only a portion of the directory is searched. When asking for a "Printer" object, for example, the user could limit the search to the local portion of the directory tree.

Setting Priority DAP client software can be configured so that certain requests have a lower priority than others. For example, looking up a telephone number should not have the same priority as finding the address of the nearest WINS server.

These limits can be implemented in various ways. During the installation of the client software, default maximum values for each limit could be set—thereby limiting any user who performs a query from that computer. The directory itself could easily hold limits on an individual or group level. Using the directory to hold limits would mean that users would have their default maximums set *any* time they perform a query (the directory would check the "query limits" attributes of a user when she accessed the database). Another option would be to limit queries on a server-by-server basis. This option would allow administrators the option of reducing the workload on servers that are already overworked.

DAP in Short

In an effort to standardize the methods used to access an X.500 directory, the X.500 committee created a protocol specifically designed for this purpose: the Directory Access Protocol. DAP defines the methods used to both read and modify the directory database.

DAP has a few built-in design features that merit discussion. Knowing that a directory must contain internal security, each DAP function is capable of including security information in its requests. This security can be as simple as using the logon credentials of the user's account (in other words, trusting the directory to have properly identified the user at first access using some sort of password-security scheme) or as complex as including various industry-standard security certificates.

Since the X.500 directory recommendations allow for many types of security (simple password authentication, X.509 certificates, or even more complex identification like fingerprint or retinal matches), DAP is extensible so that it can take advantage of any of these security procedures.

DAP was specifically designed to reduce the workload at directory servers by moving much of the functionality to the client computer. While this design benefits the directory, it does mean that client computers must have the necessary horsepower to perform these functions. Another feature is the ability to limit resource usage at the server. User queries can be limited in the time, size, scope, or priority of the searches they perform.

All in all, the DAP specifications achieve their goal—defining a standard method of accessing an X.500 directory. As you will see in the next section, however, the weaknesses of DAP have forced the development of another protocol—one that is better designed for real-world applications.

Lightweight Directory Access Protocol (LDAP)

While DAP is the access protocol defined within the X.500 specifications, it is not the access method that is getting the most press. That honor goes to the Lightweight Directory Access Protocol, a protocol that is *not* defined within the X.500 recommendations. LDAP was developed in direct response to the major weaknesses of DAP:

◆ Using DAP-based software places a tremendous amount of overhead on the client computer. Many client machines, especially PCs or Macintosh-based computers, lack the resources necessary to support any DAP services.

◆ DAP was designed specifically to communicate with X.500 directories. This means that many vendor-specific products will not be accessible using DAP-enabled software.

These two limitations of the DAP protocol have hindered the implementation of X.500 directories on production systems. While the X.500 specifications are a great model, they are limited by the fact that they *are* only a model. Most commercial products will be X.500 compatible but will not conform 100 percent to the model set forth by the standard. In effect, this lack of a multivendor access protocol has made X.500 directories an interesting theory but not a real-world solution. Combine this with the fact that even if you take a chance and implement an X.500 directory, many of your client computers will lack the necessary horsepower to access the database—and you end up with a great idea whose time has not yet arrived!

LDAP was developed to overcome these limitations. Rather than becoming part of the X.500 recommendations, LDAP has been developed through a series of RFCs (Requests for Comment). This ensures that the protocol is developed as an open standard, available to anyone wishing to develop a directory-based product.

How LDAP Differs from DAP

The major difference between DAP and LDAP is that LDAP is not a client-based service. Yes, clients will use LDAP-enabled client software to communicate with a directory server, but they will communicate with an LDAP service on a server instead of directly with the DSA (Directory Service Agent) of the network directory. The LDAP service will interpret a client request and pass it along to the DSA.

In effect, this means that a vendor can build into their directory software an LDAP service that can accept standard LDAP requests and convert them into whatever format is necessary for the vendor's product. It also means that one client software package will be able to access information from the directories of multiple vendors. In addition, each software developer can develop their own LDAP server-side service, and these services can run side-by-side with those of other developers. This is a major selling point for LDAP-compliant directories. We'll talk about the specific services in a little bit, but you can see the basic process in Figure 4.3.

1. The client sends a Read request to the LDAP service on a network server. This service can be running on a directory server or on any server that can connect to a directory server.

2. If necessary, the LDAP server can authenticate the user to whatever operating system is in use. This allows the user access to cross-vendor directories. (LDAP can even query the directory for authentication.)

3. The LDAP service then converts the request into a format appropriate to the directory being accessed. If the directory were X.500 compliant, for example, the LDAP service would convert the request into a DAP request.

4. The LDAP service submits the request to the DUA at the directory server.

5. The directory server returns the requested information to the LDAP service.

6. The LDAP service returns the requested information to the client.

FIGURE 4.3

The LDAP communication process

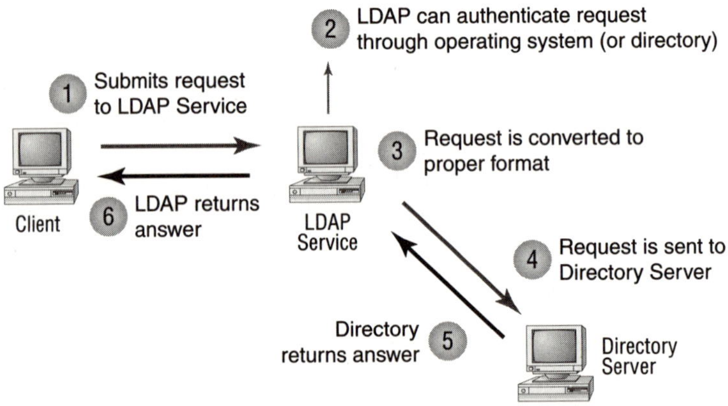

Cross-vendor support is not the only benefit of an LDAP implementation. Take another look at Figure 4.3 and notice that the overhead has been moved from the client to whatever server is supporting the LDAP service. This allows users with limited resources access to the information within the directory. Don't be surprised to see some geek at the ballpark using a palmtop computer with the capability to access a directory remotely through use of an LDAP solution.

DIRECTORY-ENABLED APPLICATIONS

Actually, the reduction in client-side resource use opens up a slew of possibilities for directory-based applications. One of the more basic uses might be the set-top box for a cable company. The cable company could easily configure a directory-based application that would provide current schedules or authenticate users to view special programming, as shown in Figure 4.4. For example, this would allow the cable company to demand authentication for a viewer to watch shows intended for mature audiences. The user account could store the birthdates of everyone in your household. When you chose a program to watch, the cable's directory server could compare your age against the age requirements of the program.

FIGURE 4.4

LDAP set-top cable implementation

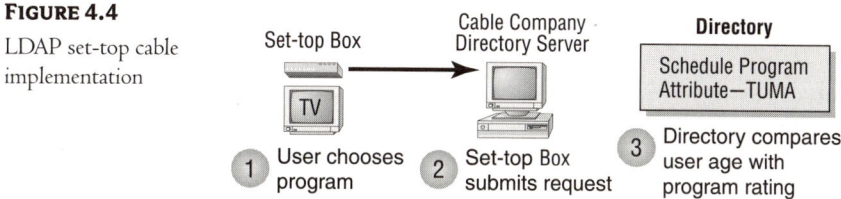

NOTE   *Why stop at the obvious—how about a directory-enabled refrigerator? Imagine a refrigerator that could scan the bar codes on the products it held and build a shopping list for you. Using LDAP, that list could then be sent to a directory at your market, and your weekly groceries could be waiting for you when you arrived at the store. I'm not sure I'd want a refrigerator that is quite so intrusive, but the possibility is interesting!*

These types of directory-enabled applications are available only because of the low demands that LDAP places on the client device. LDAP can be used by just about any device that can hold a microprocessor.

LDAP and DAP: The Similarities

While the methods of their implementations differ, LDAP is really nothing more than a subset of the functions available in DAP. The development of LDAP centered around five design considerations to reduce the load on the client device:

- ◆ Implementing only a subset of the functions provided by DAP

- ◆ Offloading the complex operations necessary to locate resources in a distributed environment

- ◆ Simplifying the encoding of attribute types and values

- ◆ Using ordinary strings to represent data

- ◆ Using standard communication protocols (such as TCP), instead of complex, function-specific protocols

Whereas DAP has five "Read" functions defined, LDAP only defines three actions:

Compare   Works just like the DAP Compare function. The client can compare object attributes for a match to given criteria.

Search   Works just like the DAP Search capability. The client can search all or some of the directory for objects that have attributes matching a given set of values. LDAP also uses the Search function to emulate the DAP Read and List functions. (Basically, the "search" is conducted using predefined search conditions.)

Abandon   Works just like the DAP Abandon function. The client can use this request to inform the LDAP service that it no longer needs to continue the query.

LDAP also defines functions that can be used to modify the database:

Modify   This is the equivalent of the DAP Modify request. LDAP simplifies the language involved by supporting three operations:

◆ Add values

◆ Delete values

◆ Replace values

Add   This request is used to add a new entry to the database.

Delete   This function allows the deletion of an entry from the database.

Modify RDN   This function requests that the name of an object be changed.

While LDAP defines a more modest list of functions than DAP, it has sufficient functionality to satisfy most user or administrative needs. LDAP has become the access protocol of choice for most directories on the market. Having an industry de facto standard provides a lot of benefits to network administrators. Software vendors can develop a single LDAP application that can access multiple types of directories, giving them the time (since they only have to write one version) to add functionality that they might otherwise not add. LDAP also makes administration a whole lot easier when supporting a mixed network. Since LDAP can act as a common communication method across different vendors' directories, we can build tools to either search across or manage data across multiple directories.

In Short

LDAP provides most of the functionality of DAP while avoiding its weaknesses. First, LDAP puts a lot less overhead on the client device. This allows almost anything with a microprocessor the opportunity to access and use the information in a directory. Second, by making LDAP a more server-centric service, you can use this standard to communicate with vendor-specific directories.

These two facets of LDAP (less client overhead and multivendor support) have made it the de facto standard of the directory industry. Most, if not all, directories on the market include an LDAP service as part of the basic package. Using LDAP-enabled software, a client could easily pull information from an AD server, as well as from most other directory services available.

Part 1 of this book has given you a non-vendor-specific overview of network directories—in other words, a view of the technology without reference to specific Microsoft solutions or products. The Microsoft marketing department has already flooded the market with AD product propaganda. As you weed through the press releases on Windows 2000/Windows Server 2003 and AD, this background should help you separate the sales pitch from the technical information. (Not always an easy task!)

Part 2 will discuss the Microsoft-specific directory service—AD. We'll look at how Active Directory has changed the way NT networks are accessed, managed, and designed. We'll also take a peek at the tools and techniques used in a Windows 2000/Windows Server 2003 environment based upon Active Directory Services.

Part 2

Microsoft Active Directory Services

In this section you will learn how to:

- ◆ **Understand Microsoft networks before Active Directory**
- ◆ **Understand the benefits of Active Directory**
- ◆ **Understand the Services Windows 2000** can provide to the network
- ◆ **Design the Active Directory environment**
- ◆ **Implement your own design**
- ◆ **Create a secure environment**
- ◆ **Implement Group Policies**
- ◆ **Modify the Active Directory schema**
- ◆ **Understand and control Active Directory sites and replication**

Chapter 5

Microsoft Networks without AD

NOW THAT WE HAVE discussed the theories behind directories, we can begin our discussion of Microsoft's Active Directory Service. Microsoft has utilized many of the time-tested methods used in current directory technologies. You will find pieces of DNS, WINS, and even NDS in AD. You will also find that Microsoft has taken great pains to remain open to industry standards. AD is modeled after the X.500 directory recommendations, is accessible using industry-standard protocols, and has the ability to incorporate complex authentication technologies.

Given Microsoft's position in the computer industry, AD will probably become a de facto standard within a short period of time. The extensible nature of the schema, combined with a large base of NT-based application developers, should produce new tools and techniques that will benefit the entire networking industry.

Microsoft Windows NT has been a major network operating system for quite some time. Before the release of AD, NT used a domain-based solution for network management. While domains were nothing new, they did provide solutions to many of the problems inherent in server-based operating systems. Three major benefits that NT's domain structure provided were as follows:

◆ Single login capability for users

◆ Central management of users, groups, and network resources

◆ Universal access to resources

NT's domain structure was often difficult to manage, especially on larger networks, but it did (and does) support some very large networks. The success of earlier versions of NT has had an influence on the design of Windows 2000/Windows Server 2003. First, Microsoft needed to provide a level of backward compatibility so that existing clients could leverage their current investment in Microsoft technologies. Second, those components that *did* work well have not been discarded—they have carried over into the latest version. Some of these components are now "new and improved," but others have come across unchanged.

When my friends read the first (and second) editions of this book, a few asked, "Why should I care about how NT worked? I'm studying Windows 2000/Windows Server 2003; just show me Windows 2000/Windows Server 2003 stuff!" Well, that's a great theory, but unfortunately it's not very realistic. First, Microsoft's operating systems are an ongoing development project at Microsoft. In other words, each revision (starting way back in Windows for Workgroups, or WFWG) has contributed a little to the operating systems that followed. Windows 2000/Windows Server 2003 is no different; you will find aspects of all of Microsoft's preceding products within its environment, although there's very little WFWG left! From an administrator's view, this is both good and bad. It's good because much of what you already know (assuming that you've worked with earlier Microsoft operating systems) is still valid. It's bad because many of your preconceived notions about Microsoft products will have changed, and that can cause some confusion.

In answer to my friends' confusion, there are two very important reasons to understand how Windows NT worked. First, most companies are not going to jump headfirst into a fully Windows 2000/Windows Server 2003 world. We, as IT professionals, will probably be supporting Windows NT (and Windows 95/98, Me, and XP) for quite some time. Few consultants get the chance to build a new network from the ground up—we usually inherit an existing infrastructure—and we add to or modify that existing system as appropriate.

The second reason to understand Windows NT is because Microsoft included a certain level of backward compatibility in Windows 2000/Windows Server 2003. Many of the underlying technologies of AD are based upon technologies developed in Windows NT. In fact, much of what you may have learned when working with NT will be directly applicable to your work with Windows 2000/Windows Server 2003. That's the good news! Of course, any good news is usually balanced by some not-so-good news. There are certain aspects of AD that are close enough to what you may have seen in NT in appearance, but different enough in actual deployment, that you might face some confusion.

In short, to fully appreciate Windows 2000/Windows Server 2003—and especially Active Directory Services—it is important to understand the strengths and weaknesses of earlier versions of NT. If you are an NT expert, this chapter will be a review. If you are a newcomer to the NT world, this chapter should prepare you for some of the topics we will discuss later.

In this chapter:

◆ What is a domain?

◆ Primary and backup domain controllers

◆ Trusts between domains

◆ The four domain models

What Is a Domain?

Microsoft has defined a *domain* as a logical grouping of users and computers. Unfortunately, this definition can also be applied to workgroup (or peer-to-peer) networks. A better definition would be:

> A domain is a logical grouping of users and computers *managed through a central shared accounts database.*

The idea of a centrally located management database is the key to understanding domains and their functions. In older technologies, each computer that provided a service to the network had its own database of accounts. As you can see in Figures 5.1 and 5.2, this could result in a single user having accounts located on several computers.

FIGURE 5.1

Typical user needs

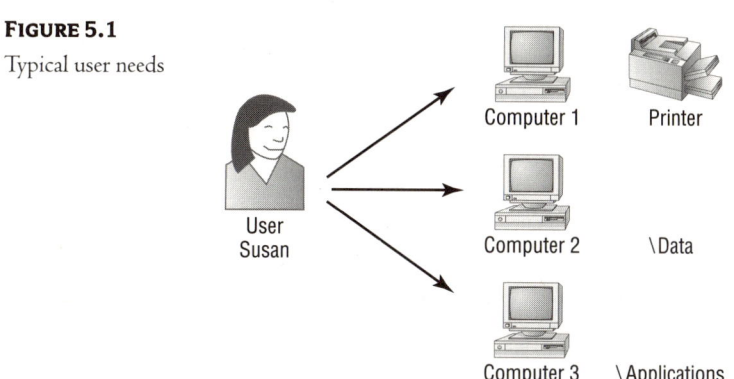

Susan needs access to the printer attached to Computer 1, the data located on Computer 2, and the shared applications located on Computer 3.

FIGURE 5.2

Accounts databases

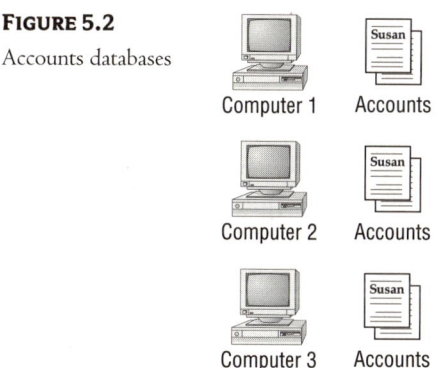

Susan needs to have an account created on each computer that contains resources she must access. For Susan, this might mean remembering multiple passwords and logging on numerous times. For the system administrator, this means that "Susan" must be managed in multiple locations. The bottom line is that this arrangement mandates redundant work for both the user and the administrator.

In a domain, the accounts database is located on a central server. This server, known as a *domain controller*, handles all logon attempts, authentication to resources, and management tasks. Remember the three big benefits of a domain?

◆ Single login capability for users

◆ Universal access to resources

◆ Central management of users, groups, and network resources

The central location of the accounts database is the key to these functions, as shown in Figures 5.3, 5.4, and 5.5.

FIGURE 5.3

Single logon for users

When Susan wants to log on to the network, her workstation (or whatever computer she is sitting at) sends the authentication request to a domain controller. The domain controller checks its accounts database to determine whether Susan has a valid account and, if she does, whether there are any restrictions placed on her account that would prevent her from logging in at this time or from this location. The domain controller then returns a yes/no answer to her workstation. If the answer is yes, Susan is allowed access to the network using this single logon procedure.

FIGURE 5.4

Universal access to resources

When Susan attempts to print to the shared printer attached to Computer 1, as shown in Figure 5.4, her request is authenticated using information from the accounts database located on a domain controller. Computer 1 permits or denies access based on this authentication process.

NOTE *Actually, this description simplifies the authentication process. We'll expand upon the process a little later in this chapter.*

FIGURE 5.5

Central management

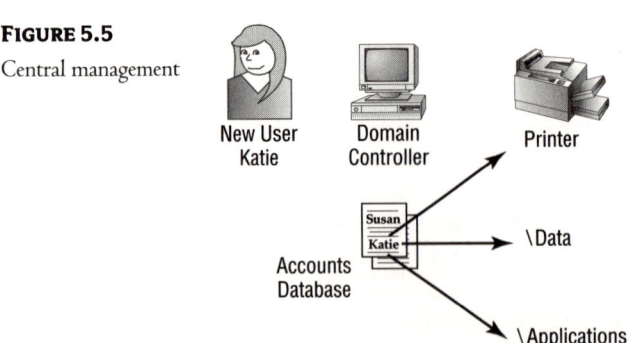

Account administration is managed through the central accounts database stored on a domain controller. When a new employee is hired, such as Katie in Figure 5.5, her account is created at a domain controller. This account is then granted permissions to use resources throughout the network.

To summarize, when I think "domain," I think "database." Perhaps it's because I started as a database administrator. For me, it is easier to picture a database handling the authentication requests than it is for me to picture some nebulous idea like a domain. In reality, my perspective is closer to the actual technology than not. Seeing the domain as representing a database also helps in understanding various functions that are inherent in domain functionality. The bottom line here is what I always tell my students in the classroom: when you think of domains, think of a database that defines an area of responsibility (or management or security, depending upon what aspect of NT you are currently considering).

Authenticating in NT 4 and Earlier

As a user logs on to the network, the authentication request is forwarded to a domain controller. The domain controller determines whether the logon request is valid (checking passwords, time restrictions, station restrictions, and other items that might limit a user's access to the network). If the request is valid, the domain controller gathers that user's system identifier (SID) and the SIDs of any groups that the user belongs to, and passes them back to the client computer as a *security token*. This token is used during authentication to network resources.

During the authentication process, the user's security token is compared to the Access Control List (ACL) of the resource. The ACL contains the SIDs of all users and groups that have been assigned permissions to the resource. If this comparison of the SIDs in the user's security token with the SIDs in the object's ACL produces a match, the user is granted the appropriate level of access. Hence the name Access Control List.

As you can see, our earlier description of the domain's ability to provide universal access was an oversimplification. The domain controller is not consulted each time a user attempts to use a network resource. Instead, the domain controller is consulted only during the initial logon process. It provides the user with a "set of keys" that can open the door to a distinct group of resources.

It is important to understand this distinction because it highlights a weakness of a domain-based environment. Users are only authenticated to a resource during logon. If a user's permissions are changed while that user is logged on, the change will not take effect until the next time he logs on to the network. The following dialog represents a common exchange between users and administrators:

User: I need to change the data in the XYZ data area.

Administrator: Okay, I'll make sure you've got the rights to do that.

User (*five minutes later*):   I still can't get at that data I called about.

Administrator: Oh, did you try restarting your computer?

NOTE   *The user could have just logged on again, but most administrators simply give the first rule of troubleshooting NT—restart the computer—rather than explaining the process of logging back in.*

One of the nice things about a directory service is that it is used for multiple purposes. Not only does it contain the user's SID, but it also is used by the user's computer to locate the resource. Since AD is being accessed to find the physical location, why not do an authentication process as well? This means that changes to security are indeed effective immediately.

Authentication Protocol

As in any transaction between computers on a network, certain protocols are utilized. Remember that a protocol is just a set of rules that govern how the transaction will occur—the order in which processes will happen, the levels of encryption, what forms of identification will be utilized, etc. You are probably already aware, for instance, that the typical communication protocol used on most networks today is TCP/IP. You should already know the process used by TCP when opening a connection, a process commonly referred to as the Three-Way Handshake.

The process of authentication also uses a specific *functional* (or service-level) protocol. In earlier versions of Microsoft network operating systems, this protocol was NTLM (NT Lan Manager). In Windows 2000/Windows Server 2003, a new protocol is used by default: Kerberos v5 (Kv5). Windows 2000/Windows Server 2003 still uses NTLM for logging on to legacy systems (providing backward compatibility), but Windows 2000/Windows Server 2003 domain controllers prefer using Kerberos.

A complete description of the differences between the two authentication protocols is not really necessary (and I'll be discussing Kv5 in more detail in Chapter 10), so I won't get into the gory details here. There are, however, a few things of which you should be aware.

The NTLM protocol has been around for a very long time. It relies upon the Netlogon service for authentication. While this, in itself, doesn't sound so bad, a good number of the security breaches that occurred in NT involved holes in the Netlogon service. In other words, NTLM is not necessarily the most secure authentication method.

In a Windows 2000/Windows Server 2003 domain environment, domain controllers will attempt to use Kv5 authentication first. They will only fall back to NTLM if Kv5 is not an option; in other words, Kv5 will be used in any Windows 2000/Windows Server 2003 to Windows 2000/Windows Server 2003 authentication. In the event that one side of the process or the other is not running Windows 2000/Windows Server 2003, the system will downgrade to NTLM.

When you log on to a computer running Windows 2000/Windows Server 2003 Professional or Server, the following process occurs. (I know that this chapter is supposed to be about NT, but since NTLM is an NT protocol, we'll discuss it here.)

1. You type your name and password.

2. The Graphical Identification and Authentication (GINA) process collects this information and passes your name and password (in a secure manner) to the Local Security Authority (LSA).

3. The LSA passes the information to the Security Support Provider Interface (SSPI). This interface communicates with both the Kerberos and NTLM services. (This component is very important to developers; it allows them to develop security-aware applications without having to master either Kerberos or NTLM.)

4. SSPI passes the information to the Kerberos Security Support Provider (SSP).

5. The Kerberos SSP checks to see if the target computer name is the local computer or the domain name. If the name is local—in other words, the user is attempting to log on to the local computer rather than the domain—the Kerberos SSP generates an error, and the process is handed back to the GINA. If this is a domain logon attempt, the Kerberos SSP will continue to process it (I'll discuss this process in Chapter 10).

6. If the logon attempt is local, then GINA will resubmit the request, and the system will fall back to the NTLM authentication process. (The NTLM SSP will pass the request to the Netlogon service for authentication against the local Security Accounts Manager database.)

Notice that the system will always attempt to use Kerberos v5 authentication first, only falling back to NTLM if Kv5 fails.

What does this mean to us? Well, only Windows 2000/Windows Server 2003 and XP clients support Kv5 authentication. This means that all of your Windows NT, 95/98, and Me clients will still be using NTLM. You can increase the security of the process by installing the Directory Services client software (found on the Windows 2000/Windows Server 2003 CD-ROM) or installing the latest service packs on your client computers. This will upgrade them to NTLM version 2, a more secure version of NTLM.

NOTE *For information about enabling NTLM version 2 on your Windows and NT clients, see the Microsoft article Q239869 on the* `support.Microsoft.com` *website.*

Primary and Backup Domain Controllers

There are three types of servers in an NT network:

- Primary domain controllers (PDCs)
- Backup domain controllers (BDCs)
- Member servers

Each type of server has a function in the overall design of the network. Administrators must decide what type of server a particular computer will be during the installation of the NT Server operating system. After installation, domain controllers can switch roles (a BDC becoming a PDC, for example). Member servers cannot become domain controllers without reinstalling the operating system. Member servers can, however, move from one domain to another, while domain controllers cannot.

Member Servers

Member servers are computers using NT Server as their operating system that do not contain a copy of the domain accounts database. There are many reasons why a server might be configured in this manner. Perhaps the server will be dedicated to a task that places a heavy load on the device (such as an e-mail application). In this case, you would not want to burden the server with the additional overhead of user authentication.

Also, you might already have enough domain controllers for your environment. Each copy of the domain accounts database that exists adds overhead to your network. Keeping a backup domain controller synchronized with the primary domain controller produces network traffic and, once again, adds overhead to your system. In any event, member servers are really irrelevant to our purpose. Since they do not hold account information, they do not need to be discussed in this context.

How PDCs and BDCs Work

The copies of the domain accounts database for an NT domain are organized in a *single-master environment*. By this, I mean that changes to the database can occur at only one of the copies: the copy held by the PDC. All other domain controllers are BDCs. BDCs receive updated information from the PDC for their domain. In other words, there is one, and only one, *master* copy of the database, as you can see in Figure 5.6.

FIGURE 5.6

Single-master environment

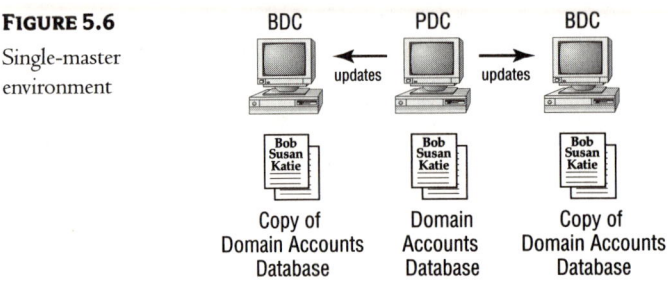

NOTE *I'll discuss the single-master domain model in detail later in this chapter.*

One drawback to the single-master environment is that it creates a single point of failure. Since there can be only one master copy, and it resides on the PDC, this implies that there can be only one PDC for each domain. In the event of the PDC going offline, no changes can be made to the domain accounts database, as shown in Figure 5.7. While it is easy to promote a BDC to the status of PDC, it is not an automatic process. In other words, the promotion requires administrative intervention.

FIGURE 5.7

Results of a PDC going offline

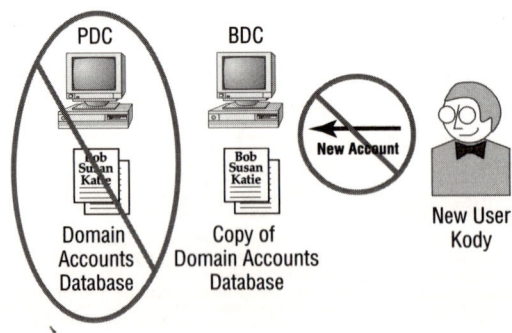

On the plus side, though, a single-master environment does make synchronization of the backup copies fairly straightforward. Since only one copy of the database can be changed, all updates originate from this copy.

The Synchronization Process

Keeping the domain accounts database synchronized across multiple locations can consume a lot of processing power and produce a lot of network traffic. While limiting changes to the copy stored on the PDC does simplify the process, any procedure that is both automatic and occurring across a network is going to be complex.

To understand the process used to synchronize the BDCs, we must delve a little deeper into the structure of the domain accounts database and its supporting files. One attribute of each object in the database is known as the *version ID*. Think of this value as an overall "change counter" for the database. Each time a change is made, the version ID is incremented.

The PDC also creates a log file that documents the version ID for each change made to the database. This process is shown in Figure 5.8.

FIGURE 5.8

Version ID

If a new user is added to the domain, the information is placed in the database. The system's version ID is incremented, and this value is placed in the version ID attribute of the new user. The change log is also updated with a record of the change.

The PDC keeps a record of the value of the system version ID at the time of last update for each BDC. Every five minutes, the PDC checks the database to see if any changes have been made. If any have, it then checks the value of the version ID for each BDC against its last update, as shown in Table 5.1.

TABLE 5.1: VERSION IDs FOR EACH BDC

SERVER	VERSION ID AT LAST SYNCHRONIZATION
BDC1	2
BDC2	3
BDC3	1

In our example, the current version ID is 3. Any BDC with a value of less than 3 would not have received this change to the database. These servers will be notified that changes exist. The PDC only notifies 10 BDCs at a time to avoid saturating the network with synchronization traffic.

NOTE *Changes are documented only at the record level—not at the field level. This means that if user Bob changes only his password, then Bob's entire record will be sent to each BDC.*

The change log is of a fixed size. By default, it can hold about 2,000 changes. When the change log fills, the system will begin writing over the oldest records in the log file. This can lead to a situation where the PDC is not sure which changes have occurred since the last update of a BDC. As an example, look at Figure 5.9.

FIGURE 5.9

Full change log

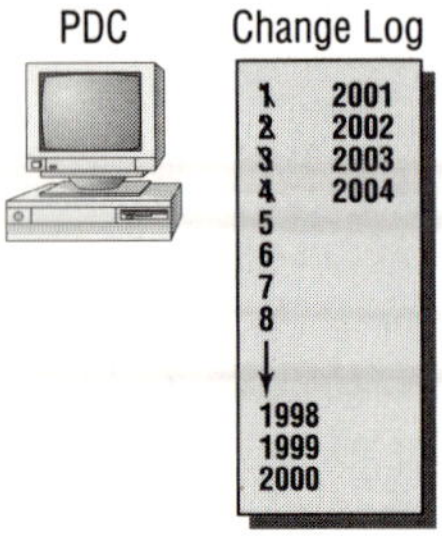

As changes occur, the system increments the value of the version ID. If a BDC was last updated when the system version ID was 27, the PDC could not be sure how many changes had been overwritten in the change log. When this occurs, the BDC will be sent the entire database. This is known as a *full synchronization*.

The bottom line is that the synchronization process generates overhead on many components of a network. The PDC must check for changes, notify the BDCs of any changes, and then update the BDCs. The BDCs must process the incoming changes on a regular basis. This can affect network bandwidth, especially in an environment with frequent changes.

Trusts between Domains

Microsoft has defined a *domain* as a "logical grouping of users and computers organized for administrative purposes." Unfortunately, this is also the phrase Microsoft uses to define the term *workgroup*.

Let's take the definition to the next level. The major difference between a workgroup and a domain is where users are authenticated to the resources they wish to access. In a workgroup, user accounts are defined on the machine that holds the resource. In a domain, user accounts are defined and managed in a central database. This database, called the *Security Accounts Manager (SAM)*, is managed by NT's Directory Services. So a more accurate definition of an NT domain would be *an administrative grouping of users and computers, defined and managed through a single database*.

The SAM is a secure database that contains information about the users, computers, global groups, and local groups defined in a domain. Each of these is called an object in the database. The maximum number of objects that can be organized in a single SAM is 40,000. The SAM is stored on an NT server, which plays the role of domain controller for your network. A domain controller is an NT server that contains the domain accounts database. Domain controllers are responsible for the authentication of users—in other words, for the logon process.

Although the accounts database can support up to 40,000 objects, a network might be designed with multiple domains (accounts databases) for various reasons. These reasons include the following:

- Having more than 40,000 objects consisting of users, computers, and groups

- Wanting to group users or resources for management purposes

- Wanting to reduce the number of objects viewed in management tools (Yes, it's great to have all users in one place, but do you *really* want to scroll through a list of 40,000 objects every time you need to manage an account?)

Partitioning the Database

The act of splitting the users and resources into multiple domains is called *partitioning the database*. There are two main benefits to this type of design:

- You can delegate administration for each domain. This gives each department or location the ability to manage its own resources.

- It reduces the length of the list you have to scroll through to find a given object.

THE TERM *PARTITIONING*

When I wrote the previous editions of this book, my technical editor objected to my use of the term partition when referring to the NT database. His view was that I was too closely tied to my Novell background, because partitioning is an important aspect of the NDS database. In a Novell environment, partitioning carries with it a lot more meaning than it does in an NT-based environment. In both, however, the term refers to the difference between the physical location of the database (on domain controllers in NT and Windows 2000/Windows Server 2003) and the logical view of the overall environment. The bottom line here is that the term partitioning is used in many Microsoft white pages and other forms of documentation. If you have a Novell background, you'll just have to differentiate the term; it will have one meaning here and another in your Novell system.

Establishing Trust

By default, each domain is a separate entity. By this I mean that domains do not share information, nor are resources from one domain made available to users defined in another domain. To allow users to access resources in another domain, a *trust* must be established between the domains. A trust can be defined as a communications link between two domains. There are two domains involved in a trust:

- One that contains the user accounts that should have access to resources

- Another that contains those resources

The domain with the user accounts is called the *trusted* domain; the domain with the resources is called the *trusting* domain.

TIP   *Deciding which domain should be the trusted domain and which should be the trusting domain can sometimes be confusing. Think of it this way: You never hear the phrase "trusted computer," but most companies do have "trusted employees." The domain where the employees are defined is always the "trusted" domain.*

TRUST ISN'T ALWAYS A TWO-WAY STREET

When you are documenting your system, you should represent trusts with arrows. The arrows should point to the trusted domain. When one domain trusts another, this is known as a *one-way trust*, and you can see this in Figure 5.10.

FIGURE 5.10

One-way trust

When each domain has users who need to access resources in the other domain, you will create a *two-way trust*. As you can see in Figure 5.11, a two-way trust is really just two one-way trusts.

FIGURE 5.11

Two-way trust

NT 4.*x* trusts are *nontransitive*. This means that trusts are never *inherited* from one domain to another. If Domain A trusts Domain B, and Domain B trusts Domain C, this does not imply that Domain A trusts Domain C. This trust would have to be created manually.

NOTE   *Let's say you are going on vacation. You give your house keys to Harry, a friend from work. In this scenario, you have made Harry a trusted friend (and, as you'll find out, you are maybe just a bit too "trusting"). When you get back from vacation, you find that Harry let his friends Tom and Dick use your keys. You'd probably be angry, right? You didn't expect that Tom, Dick, and Harry would have access to your house! Giving your keys to Harry was a nontransitive trust. You trusted Harry—not all his wild friends!*

AGLP is an acronym that describes the fundamental process for granting permissions to resources across trusts: Accounts go into Global groups, which go into Local groups, which are then granted Permissions.

The steps for granting these permissions are shown in Figure 5.12.

FIGURE 5.12

AGLP

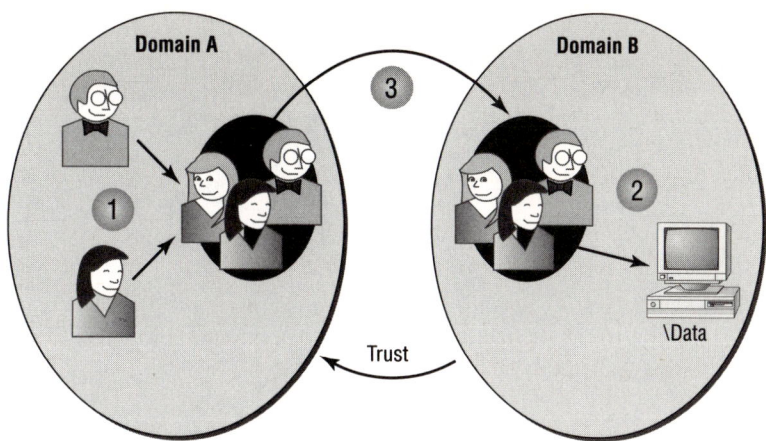

Here's what the figure illustrates:

1. In the domain where the users are defined (Domain A), either use an existing or create a new global group and make the appropriate users members of this group.

2. In the domain that contains the resource (Domain B), create a local group with the necessary permissions.

3. Make the global group from Domain A a member of the local group in Domain B.

The Four Domain Models

How you design your NT environment can have a big impact on its performance. A *domain model* defines how you will use directory services in your environment. There are four basic domain models; each has some definite advantages and disadvantages. The four models are as follows:

◆ Single domain

◆ Single master

◆ Multiple master

◆ Complete trust

Single Domain Model

The *single domain model* is the easiest of the four models to implement. In it, all users and computers are defined in a single domain, as shown in Figure 5.13. The single domain model is most appropriate when there are fewer than 40,000 objects and you require central administration of the domain environment.

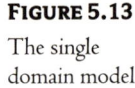

FIGURE 5.13

The single domain model

Since all resources are defined in a single accounts database, no trusts need to be established. Users have access to all resources to which they have been granted permissions.

ADVANTAGES AND DISADVANTAGES

The advantages and disadvantages associated with the single domain model are listed in Table 5.2.

TABLE 5.2: ADVANTAGES AND DISADVANTAGES OF THE SINGLE DOMAIN MODEL

ADVANTAGES	DISADVANTAGES
Simple to implement and manage.	Performance can degrade as the number of resources increases.
Central control of user accounts.	All users are defined in the same database: no grouping by location or function.
Central control of all resources.	All resources are defined in the same database: no grouping by location or function.
No trusts are necessary.	Browser performance will slow with large numbers of servers.

Single-Master Domain Model

A *single-master domain model* consists of at least two domains. In it, all user accounts are defined in a master domain. The other domains are used to manage physical resources, as you can see in Figure 5.14. This design is most appropriate when you want central control of user accounts, but local administrators are responsible for departmental or geographic control of physical resources.

The single-master domain model is also appropriate when the number of objects defined in the database exceeds the maximum of 40,000. In this case, moving the computer accounts to another domain spreads the object records over multiple domains. (Although in a company of this size, you would probably start with the next model: multiple-master domains.)

NOTE   *If you think your company might grow into multiple locations or might grow past the 40,000-object limit, it is best to start with the single-master domain design. This offers more growth options than the single domain model.*

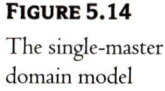

FIGURE 5.14

The single-master domain model

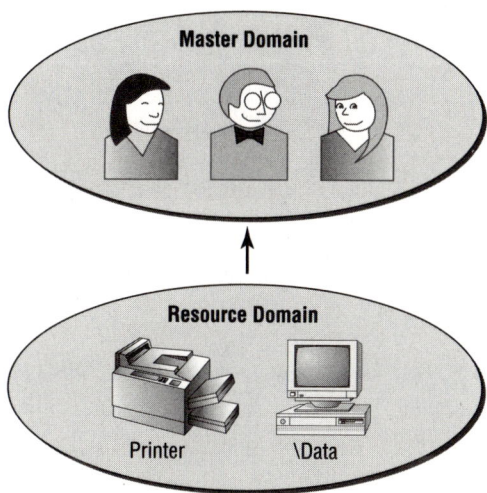

NOTE   *In this model, each resource domain establishes a one-way trust with the master domain.*

ASSIGNING RIGHTS

Use the AGLP process to assign users in the master domain permissions to the resources defined in the resource domains, as demonstrated in Figure 5.15.

1. Create a global group in the master domain with the appropriate members.

2. In the resource domain, create a local group and assign it the necessary permissions.

3. Next, make the global group from the master domain a member of the local group from the resource domain.

FIGURE 5.15

Groups in a
single-master
domain model

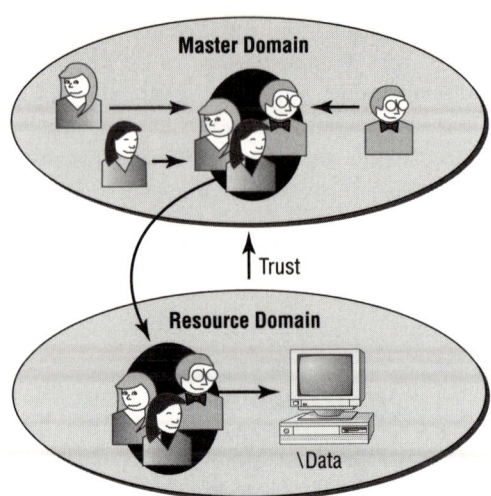

ADVANTAGES AND DISADVANTAGES

You can see the advantages and disadvantages associated with the single-master domain model in Table 5.3.

TABLE 5.3: ADVANTAGES AND DISADVANTAGES OF THE SINGLE-MASTER DOMAIN MODEL

ADVANTAGES	DISADVANTAGES
Best choice if resources need to be managed by different groups.	Performance can degrade as the number of users defined in the master domain increases.
User accounts are centrally located.	Local groups must be defined in each resource domain.
Resources are grouped logically (either by department or by geographic location).	Administrators of resource domains must "trust" the administrator of the master domain to set up global groups correctly.
Global groups must be created only once.	

Multiple-Master Domain Model

The *multiple-master domain model* is shown in Figure 5.16. It is the most scalable of the four models. It looks quite a bit like the single-master model, except that there is more than one domain where user accounts are defined. There are various reasons why you might choose this model:

♦   The accounts database is limited to a maximum of 40,000 objects (users, groups, and computer accounts). If your environment were large enough, you might be forced to partition the database just to stay within the defined limits.

♦ Your company's management strategy might also lead to this model. If each location or department wants to manage its own user accounts, you might want to create separate domains for management purposes.

♦ You might also create multiple master domains for ease of administration. Let's face it—just because the accounts database *will* hold 40,000 accounts doesn't mean that you are going to like paging through such a large list to find stuff.

♦ In a WAN (wide area network) environment, you might make multiple domains in an effort to reduce the amount of network traffic that crosses the wide area links.

FIGURE 5.16

The multiple-master domain model

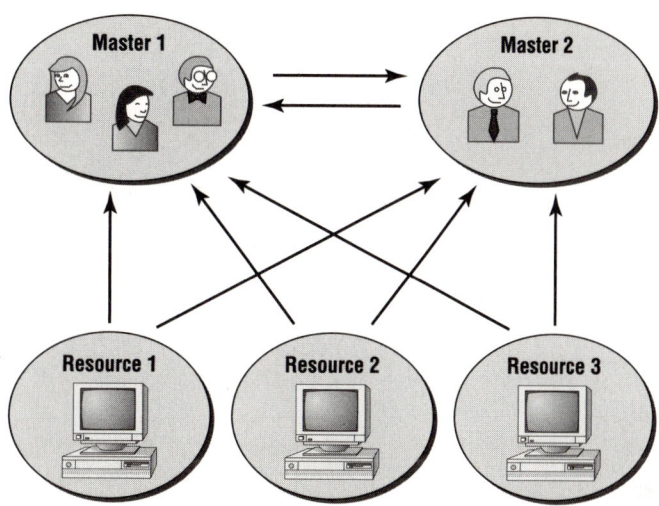

> **NOTE** *Master domains have two-way trusts between themselves, and each resource domain has a one-way trust to each master containing users who might have to access its resources. You can determine the number of trusts in a multiple-master structure by using this formula: $M \times (M - 1) + (R \times M)$, where M is the number of master domains and R is the number of resource domains. (This assumes that each resource domain trusts each master domain.)*

ASSIGNING RIGHTS

Assigning rights in a multiple-master domain environment is a bit more confusing than in the preceding models. You still use the AGLP method, but you might have to create the global groups in each of the master domains, as shown in Figure 5.17.

FIGURE 5.17

The use of groups in a multiple-master domain model

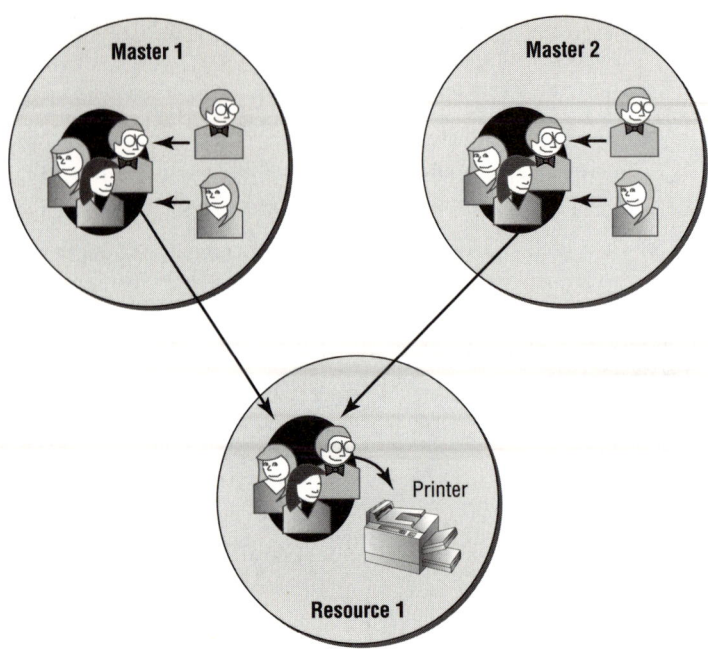

ADVANTAGES AND DISADVANTAGES

The advantages and disadvantages of the multiple-master domain model are listed in Table 5.4.

TABLE 5.4: ADVANTAGES AND DISADVANTAGES OF THE MULTIPLE-MASTER DOMAIN MODEL

ADVANTAGES	DISADVANTAGES
Best model for large environment with central MIS department.	Both local and global groups might have to be defined in multiple domains.
Scales to any size network.	Large number of trusts to manage.
Each domain can have a separate administrator.	Not all user accounts are in one domain database.

Complete Trust Model

The *complete trust model* takes full advantage of directory services. In the complete trust model, each domain has both user accounts and resources. Each domain must trust all other domains. This model, as shown in Figure 5.18, is perfect for a company where each department or location wants control over both its physical resources and user accounts.

NOTE   *The reality is that most complete trust environments happen by accident. First, each department or location installs NT for its own use. Somewhere down the line, they realize that it would be nice if they could share resources. At that point there are only two options: back up all data on all domain controllers and start from scratch with one of the other domain models, or implement a complete trust model and deal with the large number of trusts to manage.*

FIGURE 5.18

The complete trust model

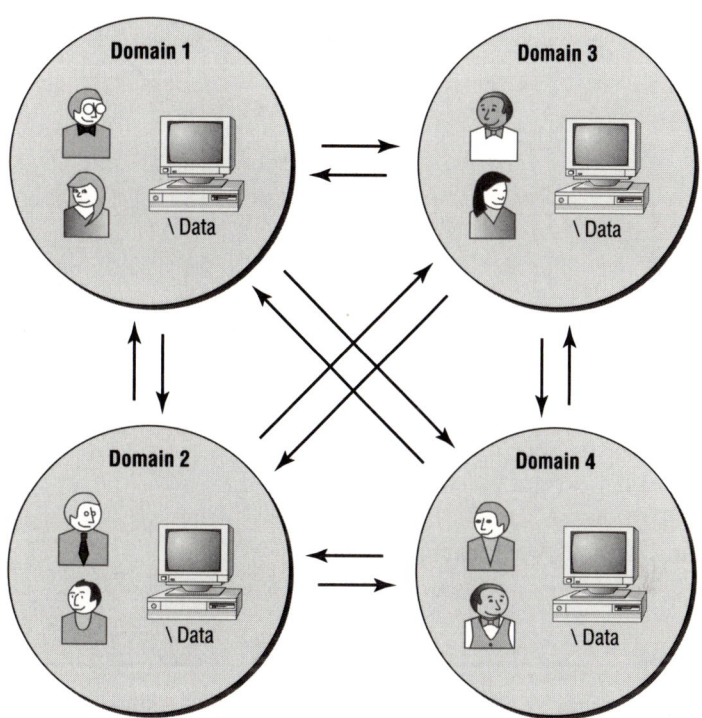

NOTE   *In a complete trust model, all domains trust all other domains. Determine the number of trusts with the following formula:* $D \times (D - 1)$, *where* D *is the number of domains in the network.*

ASSIGNING RIGHTS

Assigning rights in a complete trust environment can be extremely confusing. In this model, you must create both local and global groups in every domain, as shown in Figure 5.19.

Figure 5.19

Groups in a
complete trust
domain environment

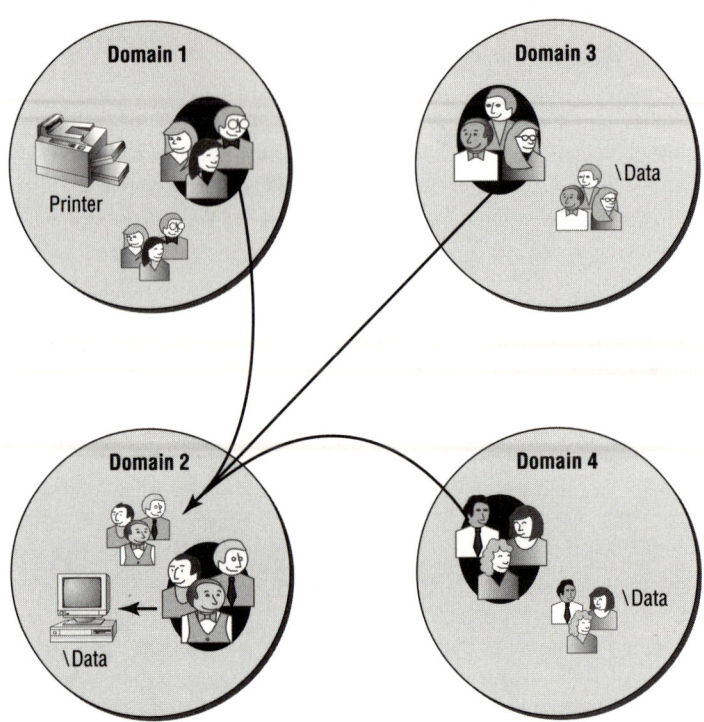

Advantages and Disadvantages

The advantages and disadvantages of the complete trust domain model are listed in Table 5.5.

Table 5.5: Advantages and Disadvantages of the Complete Trust Domain Model

Advantages	Disadvantages
Works for companies with no central number of trusts to manage.	Large MIS department.
Scales to any number of users.	More domains mean more points of management.
Each domain can have its own administrator.	Each administrator must trust that all other administrators know what they are doing.
Resources and user accounts are grouped into management units.	

Supporting a Single Logon Account

In a traditional server-based network, each server maintained its own list of users who could access its resources. Since there were multiple lists of users (one for each server), users often had to remember several user account names and passwords. This could be confusing for the users. From an administrative perspective, having users defined in multiple places added complexity and redundant management.

As an example, let's imagine a small manufacturing firm in St. Paul, Minnesota. This firm has two servers—one for engineering tasks and the other for accounting—each using a traditional server-based operating system. If I were hired as the Head of Engineering, with both design and financial responsibilities, the LAN administrator would have to create a user account for me on each server, and I would have to remember both user account names and passwords.

This is clearly unacceptable in anything other than a small network. Microsoft Windows NT lets you use a single user account to access resources on the entire network.

PASS-THROUGH AUTHENTICATION

A process called *pass-through authentication* makes it possible for users to log on from computers or domains on which they have no account. When a user sits down at a computer defined in a domain that trusts her "home" domain, she will have the option of choosing her domain from a drop-down list.

The NT server in the computer's domain will then use the trust relationship to pass the authentication request to the user's home domain. For example, if user Bob from Domain 1 attempts to log on at a machine in Domain 2, the logon process will use the procedure depicted in Figure 5.20.

FIGURE 5.20

Pass-through authentication

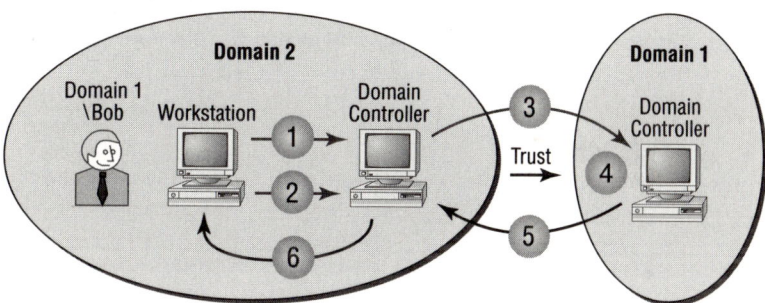

Here's what happens:

1. When the Windows NT machine boots, its Netlogon service locates a domain controller in Domain 2. As part of this process, the computer receives a list of all trusted domains to present in the logon screen.

2. When the user identifies himself as Bob from Domain 1, the Netlogon process passes the request to a domain controller in Domain 2.

3. The domain controller in Domain 2 recognizes that the request is for a user defined in a trusted domain, so it passes the request to a domain controller in Domain 1.

4. The domain controller in Domain 1 checks its accounts database to ensure that the username is valid and the right password has been entered.

5. If the request to log on is valid, the domain controller in Domain 1 passes the user's SID and group information to the domain controller in Domain 2.

6. The domain controller in Domain 2 trusts that the authentication was done properly, so it passes the information about user Bob back to the NT machine where Bob is trying to log on, completing the logon process.

Allowing Users to Access Resources in Different Domains

To grant a user rights to a resource in a trusting domain, follow these steps:

1. Create a global group in the user's home domain.

2. Create a local group in the trusting domain. Grant the local group permission to the appropriate resource.

3. Make the global group a member of the local group.

NOTE *I always picture the trust as a highway between the two accounts. You can't use a highway to travel unless you have a vehicle. When using a trust, the global group is the vehicle; user accounts are the passengers.*

In Short

Earlier versions of NT, based upon a domain environment, provided three main benefits over earlier network operating systems:

◆ Single logon for users

◆ Central management for administrators

◆ Universal resource access through pass-through authentication

Before NT and the domain environment, most network operating systems were server-based, meaning that each server was managed as a separate entity. This type of management scheme resulted in redundant management and increased workload for both users and administrators.

The NT domain environment was Microsoft's first foray into enterprise networking. While it does alleviate many of the headaches of earlier network operating systems, it also introduces its own problems to the network:

◆ The overhead of synchronizing multiple copies of an accounts database can overwhelm servers and saturate network segments.

◆ The single-master synchronization scheme creates a single point of failure in the PDC.

- Managing multidomain environments was basically the same as managing server-based networks—each domain was seen as a separate entity.

- Trusts added administrative overhead and security risks to the network.

When all is said and done, Microsoft Windows NT versions 4 and earlier represented an attempt to overcome the limitations of a flat-file accounts database. While they accomplished much of this goal, the performance, security, and management capabilities left much to be desired.

Unfortunately, much of AD has been designed to be backward compatible with domain-based networks. While most of these capabilities can be turned off or ignored, mixed environments will be very common for quite some time. A mixed environment will not show AD in its best light—a fact that might slow down its acceptance.

Now that we've taken a look at NT *without* AD (most of this chapter was probably a review for you), we can begin to look at NT *with* AD. In Chapter 6, we'll discuss how AD overcomes the limitations inherent in a domain-based environment. We'll also look at how AD fits into the overall Microsoft product line and how AD has been added to the architecture of NT. Once we've discussed how AD is supposed to work, in later chapters we can look at how it actually does work.

Chapter 6

Active Directory Benefits

JUST AS NT WAS originally designed to overcome the weaknesses of server-based network operating systems, Windows 2000/Windows Server 2003 with AD was designed to overcome the weaknesses of an NT domain-based environment. While Microsoft is loath to admit it, NT domains created as many problems as they fixed, especially in larger networks. Most of NT's weaknesses revolved around scalability. To put this another way, the NT domain structure was designed to overcome the limitations of server-based operating systems, which it did in an admirable fashion. The problem was that this domain model was designed with a "workgroup" philosophy. NT's domains were designed to represent the resources of small groups within a company, not the overall network resources. This is where Windows 2000/Windows Server 2003 and Active Directory enter the picture.

Active Directory was designed, from the ground up, to support what Microsoft has labeled "enterprise environments." These enterprise environments can span huge physical areas, support thousands (if not millions) of users, and can provide services that are critical to the overall success of the company. For us, as network administrators, this scalability does come with a cost; we must master a new technology. The benefits, though, are astounding!

While Active Directory was built for huge environments, most, if not all, of its features are also applicable to small and medium networks. In fact, many of the new features built into Windows 2000/Windows Server 2003 and Active Directory can ease the management of those smaller environments that perhaps do not have a large IT staff or a staff with extensive networking expertise!

The bottom line here is that Active Directory is a great addition to any network—large or small. IT professionals working on any size network will benefit from the new utilities, technologies, and features available once their network has become AD-based.

In this chapter we will discuss a few of the features of Active Directory as well as a few of the fundamental technologies that you must master in order to take advantage of those new capabilities.

In this chapter:

- ◆ How networks develop

- ◆ The general goals of AD

- ◆ Enterprise management: vendor and user acceptance

- ◆ Uniform Naming Convention

- ◆ Active Directory in the Windows 2000/Windows Server 2003 architecture

How Networks Develop

Very few networks are installed all at once, especially in medium to small companies. Most networks grow over time—almost like a fungus! First the accounting department installs a server. They get it configured properly (this *can* take some time) and start bragging it up around the company. The folks in the production department see what the accountants are doing and decide to install their own server, creating their own domain in the process. The sales department staff suddenly wants Internet mail, so they bring in a consultant and have their own server installed, creating yet another domain. Before you know it the company is NT-based, but there are no connections between the various departments.

The next step in the development of the network is sharing resources between departments. First someone in sales needs access to the quarterly accounting reports. Then someone in production decides she wants to look over the marketing materials in order to stock inventory based upon what the company is advertising. Departmental administrators start creating local accounts and trusts between domains to allow for this unplanned resource-sharing. Before you know it, a complete trust domain structure is born!

Remember the three big benefits of domains over older, server-based networks?

◆ Single logon

◆ Universal resource access

◆ Central administration

The "network on the fly" scenario described above has the potential to provide all three. The question is, do the benefits outweigh the costs? Management of a larger domain-based network with lots of trusts can be overwhelming! In a complete trust design, the number of trusts is $D \times (D - 1)$, where D is the number of domains involved. This doesn't seem like a lot—until you do the math for a few networks, as shown in Table 6.1.

TABLE 6.1: TRUSTS IN A COMPLETE TRUST NETWORK

NUMBER OF DOMAINS	NUMBER OF TRUSTS
2	2
3	6
4	12
5	20
6	30
7	42
8	56
9	72
10	90

As you can see, even a small company with five or six departments (or sites) will generate a relatively large number of trusts. This is compounded by the fact that most small companies either have no staff administrators or have an administrator without a lot of experience.

Of course, there's really not a lot of management involved with trust relationships once they are created—it is the global groups, local groups, global accounts, and local accounts that will turn you in circles. As an example, look at the environment shown in Figure 6.1. Jim works in the Seattle office, but he needs access to resources in Tampa.

FIGURE 6.1

Jim's dilemma

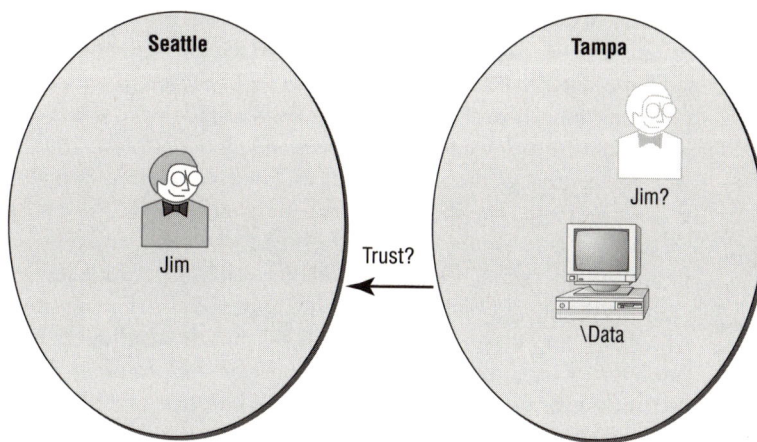

In a domain-based system, there are two possible solutions:

◆ Connect the two domains by a trust relationship.

◆ Create a local account for Jim in the Tampa domain.

In either event, the administrators have to decide which is the appropriate method. If they choose to create the trust, they will have to remember that the Tampa domain now trusts the entire Seattle domain. While NT's inherent security should protect against the abuse of this trust, that risk is still a consideration. If the administrators decide to create an account for Jim in the Tampa domain, they will have to train Jim in the skills necessary to connect to resources in Tampa. Either way, they will have increased the potential amount of management required on their system.

The General Goals of AD

The overall goal of Microsoft Windows 2000/Windows Server 2003 and Active Directory Services can be stated simply:

Reduce both the user and administrative overhead associated with computer networks.

As a proposal, it's fairly simple. As an implementation, it becomes much more difficult. This has been the goal of most network operating systems since networking began. The biggest problem is that this "goal" is really made up of two areas:

◆ User access

◆ Network administration

Often these two goals are at odds: Making a network easier for the user ends up creating more administrative overhead. Conversely, giving more responsibility to users usually means less work for the administrators. Placing higher demands upon system users is not a realistic expectation. Given the complex nature of today's networks, users cannot be expected to understand many of the necessary technologies.

The result is that the complexity of networks has forced both end users and administrative personnel to become more network literate. Users are becoming more and more aware of the network, and administrators are being forced to master more and more complex technologies. At some juncture, this spiral will reach a point of diminishing returns. Users will be forced to master technology at the expense of their ability to perform their job functions (in other words, users will spend more time worrying about the network and less time being productive). Network administrators will spend such a large amount of time managing existing systems that no time will be left for improvement or optimization.

Since technological advances do not appear to be slowing (much to the relief of those of us who make our living writing about them) and these advances have the potential to increase the productivity of end users, something must be done to avoid that point of "diminishing returns." Network directories in general, and Active Directory specifically, attempt to accomplish this by providing a simpler, more intuitive interface to the increasing complexities of a network. AD attempts to provide two things:

◆ A common interface to network resources

◆ An intuitive interface to network resources

At first glance, these two goals might appear to be identical. The truth is, however, that we have intuitive interfaces in many of today's technologies. Almost every vendor realizes that easing access and management—through GUI interfaces, online help systems, and the like—is critical to success. The problem is that there is not a "standard" method of presenting information to end users, administrators, or even other vendors.

Enterprise Management

AD aims to allow you to manage your entire network (and all of its associated resources) in a consistent manner: more specifically, through a series of tools used to access configuration information stored within the AD database. At first glance, this might not seem like such a revolutionary change to network management. If you stop and think about it, though, a *single* set of tools to manage *all* network resources—users, printers, servers, routers, switches—is indeed a lofty goal. If successful, accomplishing this goal could change the way that network administrators approach their current responsibilities.

Three prerequisites must be met before this goal can be reached:

◆ Design of an industry-standard method for storing and accessing configuration information

◆ Acceptance of this standard by third-party vendors of hardware and software

◆ Customer buy-in to the products created (and brought to market) by these vendors

An Industry Standard

AD is the embodiment of the first of these three prerequisites. In AD, Microsoft provides the framework for an industry-standard method of storing, accessing, and using configuration information for network resources. Through AD, Microsoft defines how information should be formatted. By embracing industry recommendations and standards, such as X.500 and LDAP, Microsoft makes AD accessible to any vendor who wishes to take advantage of it. More important, by creating a system for easily extending the schema of the AD database, Microsoft creates an environment that all vendors can take advantage of.

I cannot overstress the importance of an open environment. By creating a directory service that is easy to access and utilize, Microsoft brings the first truly "open" directory service to the networking industry. While there have been other commercially successful directories (Novell's NDS, for example), none has been as easily accessible or extensible as AD. Developers can use simple tools to extend the capabilities of AD to meet their needs. This openness is the first step in fulfilling the second of our three prerequisites.

Vendor Acceptance

With an open environment, backed by Microsoft, the stage is set for the completion of the second prerequisite: acceptance of a standard by product vendors. Given the clout that Microsoft wields in the industry, it would seem that this is a foregone conclusion. In reality, however, AD must provide some added value (over older, proven technologies) before products will be written to take advantage of AD.

NOTE   *At a trade show soon after the release of Windows 2000, it was rumored that Microsoft offered incentives to any vendor that would fly an "AD-ready" flag on its booth. While many booths had this logo, most were demonstrating products that did nothing more than trust AD to perform user authentication. In other words, most of the products were not, in fact, AD-based; rather, they were AD-friendly. A large difference!*

This added value currently consists of products that utilize AD services to authenticate users to control access, use information stored in AD, or automatically add data to standard attributes of an object class. For instance, consider the following:

◆ Most so-called AD products accept the identity of a user once authenticated through the AD database. This information is then used to control access to specific features of the product.

◆ Other products access the information stored within the directory. A simple example is a company directory (phone book) that gathers its information dynamically from user attributes and provides a user-friendly interface to LDAP queries of that data.

◆ Some products have actually made the jump to placing data in the AD database. The installation software for a printer, for instance, can automatically fill in the make, model, and serial number attributes of a printer object in the directory.

While each of these applications is an improvement over non-AD-enabled products, none of them is really revolutionary in design. Before AD can become the industry standard, Microsoft must entice developers to create products in which AD is an integral component. Such products would depend upon AD for a portion of their functionality. A few examples might include these:

◆ Devices that store their configuration in the directory database rather than in a local file. These devices will have to include firmware that can find an AD server so that this information can be gathered as they initialize.

◆ Software that stores a user's preferences (things like default fonts, colors, or even the location of stored data) in AD. By moving this information to a central database, a user's preferences will be available to her no matter where she is on the network.

NOTE   *Actually much of this functionality is built into AD already—since a user's profile can be stored on a network and since most applications now store user preferences in the user profile.*

◆ Software that knows where other copies of itself are located. If a server becomes unavailable, a user can be routed to another copy of the software—without any interruption of normal network services.

Given the strength of a directory service, these few suggestions are just the tip of the iceberg. The big question is, "What will Microsoft do to justify the costs involved in reengineering products to be AD-aware?" Without this justification, third-party providers will not take a chance on this new technology. Three aspects of AD provide this justification:

◆ Microsoft's large market share in both the desktop and networking arenas. Developers are confident that any Microsoft product will be successful—and a large installed base increases their own odds of success.

◆ Microsoft has made programming AD applications as easy as possible. AD applications can be created using most of today's prevalent tools, including Microsoft Visual Basic and C++.

◆ Microsoft has made AD easy to access through the use of industry-standard protocols such as LDAP.

User Acceptance

The last of the prerequisites to the success of AD is user acceptance. There are two types of users that must be considered:

◆ End users

◆ Administrators

Each type will have its own criteria for accepting any product.

END USERS

A common maxim of older networks has always been: "The best networks are those of which the user is unaware." In a nutshell, this credo of network administration refers to the fact that end users should not have to be concerned with the mechanics of networking. Users should see their computer as just another tool—no different from a screwdriver—for doing their jobs.

With Windows 2000/Windows Server 2003 and Active Directory Services, this credo might be changed to: "The best networks are those that intuitively guide users to the resources they need." As I mentioned earlier, networks (and the resources they provide) have become much more sophisticated over the last few years. Networks provide many more services than they used to, and this increase in service has pushed users into becoming more computer (and network) savvy. Typical office workers are now required to understand both the specific applications they use to manipulate information *and* the networks that connect them. The argument over whether or not this is a good trend will probably continue for years. The simple truth is that users must have a basic understanding of networks to survive in today's business world.

From an end-user perspective, some of the most basic aspects of AD might be the best selling points. AD promises the following benefits to users:

◆ A single logon for *all* network resources. Many users are faced with multiple logons to access the varied resources on their networks—one for the LAN, another for the mainframe, and yet another for some legacy system down the hall. With AD, the user will be authenticated to the Windows 2000/Windows Server 2003 network, and this authentication should be valid across multiple environments.

◆ Dynamic mapping to network resources. Users are often overwhelmed by the task of remembering the locations and names of resources throughout a large network. Using AD to represent resources, such as applications, printers, and shared data, makes the process of accessing resources as easy as clicking an icon.

◆ A consistent set of services on the network. Users are often confused by changes to their environment. By providing a central database to store all of a user's preferences, policies, and other unique configuration information, AD can re-create a user's environment—no matter where he logs on to the network.

For AD to become successful, Microsoft must make the information that the directory database holds easily (and readily) available to end users. Moving to a graphical interface is a first step. The simple fact that Microsoft owns the most popular end-user operating systems (the entire Windows OS family–9x, NT, 2000, XP, and Windows Server 2003) gives AD a leg up on the competition. Almost every end user will understand the process of using a Windows-based application.

NOTE *The next step is to design the killer application—in other words, some application that becomes indispensable to the average end user. We've discussed quite a few applications for directory services, everything from an employee telephone directory to automatic configuration of network devices. None of these examples, however, is really indispensable to the average end user. What is needed is a new application that insinuates itself so thoroughly into business that it becomes as commonplace as the calculator and as indispensable as the fax machine. While I'm sure that this application will be developed, there is no telling at this point what its purpose will be.*

ADMINISTRATIVE USERS

While AD can provide numerous services to end users, its primary function is that of network resource management. As such, AD will first and foremost have to be sold to network administrators—administrators who have little time or patience for new technologies that promise the world but do not deliver! As a group, network administrators are mostly overworked and underappreciated (until an information emergency, that is) but are fascinated by the possibilities of technology. Given the promises of AD, it should be an easy sell to these individuals. For administrative personnel, AD can provide the following:

◆ A single point of management for each user. Administrators will no longer have to create multiple accounts for a user who needs to access multiple environments. The same account information (or at least the same account object within the database) can be used to access many different types of systems: NT servers, Novell NetWare servers, mainframe systems, and even Unix boxes.

◆ A single interface for managing products from multiple vendors. Since AD can be extended to hold the configuration information for any type of object, a single set of tools should be able to manage any resource that can be represented by an object within the database.

◆ The ability to provide a uniform configuration for a like set of resources. AD provides the ability to *copy* objects. From an administrative perspective, this means that like objects (for instance, two routers) should have to be configured only once; the second can be configured by copying the configuration of the first.

◆ The ability to provide a standard set of policies across an entire network. For resources that are so enabled, administrators can use AD tools to create policies of use. Such resources will accept the identity of the user (as confirmed by the NT network) to enable or disable services. A router, for example, might limit access to a particular route (the Internet, perhaps) based on membership in an AD-defined group.

◆ The ability to selectively delegate administrative responsibility based on an object's location in the tree structure. Earlier we discussed the concept of containers within an X.500-compliant directory structure. In AD, each container can act as a security boundary. In other words, if you have created a "users" container, you can delegate the administrative tasks for the objects it contains. This allows you to limit the areas in which a particular user might have administrative powers.

◆ The ability to selectively delegate administrative responsibility based on an object's attributes. You can, for instance, allow all members of the Help desk group to change passwords for all user objects, without allowing them any other administrative privileges.

◆ The ability to distribute printer drivers from a central location. AD will store the drivers necessary for a client to use a particular printer. When a user attempts to print, the driver can be automatically installed (or upgraded) on her computer.

NOTE *This ability is not new—both NT 4 and Novell NetWare also have this capability.*

All in all, what administrators need is an environment where new technologies mesh easily with old technologies, where management tasks do not consume every waking hour, and that can be customized to fit the specific needs of the business. In other words, what administrators need is AD! Active Directory includes many tools that bring it close to achieving these lofty goals, the most important of which are discussed in the following sections.

Extensibility

One of the major features of the Active Directory database is that it can be extended to include *any* information that might be necessary in a particular environment. Suppose, for instance, that Company XYZ is in a business that requires employees to travel on a regular basis. In this type of company, each office probably has one person who is responsible for arranging travel—flights, hotels, auto rentals, perhaps even tickets to activities like plays or ballgames.

If user Carrie is based in Grand Rapids, Michigan, the local travel personnel probably know all about Carrie and her travel preferences. They know whether she likes window or aisle seats, nonsmoking or smoking rooms. They are aware of the appropriate type of automobile for her— e.g., whether she needs a van to carry equipment or whether a compact car can cover her needs. When Carrie needs to travel, she just calls the local person and gives her destination and travel dates, and everything is arranged for her.

If Carrie is away from home, though, this scenario changes a bit. Either Carrie calls her office to arrange travel (which means faxing itineraries, and lots of phone time) or she talks to the travel person at the branch nearest her. The problem is that this travel person doesn't know all of Carrie's preferences. He either has to ask Carrie—who is busy working on her project—or call her office and have the material faxed to him (okay—he would probably be able to do this through e-mail). Either way, information that should be readily available, based upon the type of company we have described, is not!

In an AD-based environment, this scenario changes quite a bit. After analyzing the business needs of the company, the administrators decide that the AD database should store travel preferences as properties of the user account. Using fairly straightforward tools, they extend that property list of user accounts to include things like airline of choice, frequent flyer identification, smoking/nonsmoking, special diet needs, and perhaps even hobbies (so that entertainment arrangements can be made or suggested). Now, wherever Carrie travels, her preferences are available to the local staff. If her plans change, they can make arrangements easily. If she's doing a really great job, they can check her entertainment preferences and arrange tickets to a ballgame. In other words, the data that is needed is readily available.

The process of changing or adding to the properties of objects is known as *extending* the schema of the database. Extensibility ensures that AD can be customized to fit the needs of any size or type of business.

NOTE *This scenario might not be a "real-world" solution. It might actually be easier to build a "travel" database using your database application of choice (SQL Server, Access, etc.) and then share it across the network. The big news here is that with Active Directory, you have another choice! For information that* must *be available, AD might be the better option, since that information will be replicated to all domain controllers within the domain automatically, ensuring availability even if the WAN links are down.*

Integration with DHCP (Dynamic Host Configuration Protocol)

Since TCP/IP is the protocol of choice for Windows 2000/Windows Server 2003 networks, and is mandatory for Active Directory Services, many of the traditional TCP/IP tools have been improved upon in Windows 2000/Windows Server 2003. One of the most basic, yet critical, tools is that of DHCP. DHCP is used to dynamically configure the TCP/IP protocol stack on clients—automatically as they boot rather than manually at each computer.

Traditionally, as DHCP clients initialize, they broadcast a packet on the network requesting the services of a DHCP server. This DHCP server responds with an offer that includes all of the pertinent TCP/IP configuration parameters. The DHCP server keeps a database of available IP addresses and is responsible for ensuring that no duplicate addresses are given out.

In Windows 2000/Windows Server 2003, DHCP services have been integrated with AD. First, the DHCP database of IP addresses has been moved into the Active Directory database. This allows central control of all DHCP services; more important, it also negates the necessity to implement DHCP relay agents or configure routers to pass BootP broadcast packets.

Another benefit of integrating DHCP into the Active Directory database is that the IP addressing information is moved to a more accessible forum. We'll see the benefit of this in the next section.

Integration with DNS (Domain Name System)

As we discussed in Chapter 2, DNS is used to resolve user-friendly names, such as www.royal-tech.com, into the IP address of a resource. The biggest drawback to DNS was its static nature—each entry had to be created manually for each resource or service. This limitation meant that while DNS was great for some resources (e-mail servers, web servers, and the like), it wasn't all that great as an all-around resource locator. (This was why WINS was created.) For Windows 2000/Windows Server 2003, Microsoft has integrated a new version of DNS—Dynamic Domain Name System (DDNS)—into Active Directory. With DDNS, a resource can dynamically register itself in the DNS database. The bottom line here is that the resource records can be created on the fly as each resource initializes. This turns DNS into a dynamically maintained database of active resources—in other words, it replaces the DNS/WINS combination that was used in earlier versions of Microsoft networking.

Global Catalog Server

We've discussed the various protocols used to access the data in the Active Directory database—DAP and LDAP. We've also discussed the various uses that this information can be put to—the company phone book, holding parts of the Registry so that user preferences are available from multiple locations, even checking the settings on various types of hardware. What we haven't talked about is the network traffic generated by these types of queries. Think about it: if I use the Active Directory database to find phone numbers for users around the globe, the traffic generated could outweigh the benefit of the central database.

In order to reduce this network overhead, Windows 2000/Windows Server 2003 includes a component known as the Global Catalog. This service is installed by default on the first domain controller in your environment.

The Global Catalog contains a partial replica of every object defined in every domain in your forest—in other words, here is a list of everything in your environment, but with only part of the actual data. Only selected properties of each object are stored in the Global Catalog, specifically those properties that are most likely to be searched upon.

Let's take my company phone book as an example. If my company's network spanned the globe, I would probably have created multiple domains. Remember that each domain represents a partition of the overall Active Directory database. As such, if I were to search my local partition (domain database) for the phone number of a fellow employee whose account resides in another domain, the information would not be available (at least not from my local server). Without any additional components, my local server would have to access a domain controller at the remote domain and perform the query on my behalf, ultimately returning the information that I requested. The problem here is that my request has now traveled across the WAN links that connect my network. The amount of traffic generated for a single query would probably not affect the performance of my network, but if we extrapolate that traffic for 1,000 users—well, suddenly we have a problem.

The Global Catalog acts as a reference point for these types of queries. In the scenario above, my local server would forward my query to the Global Catalog server. There, we would hope, the requested information would be found. The best part of this entire process is that I have complete control over which properties are stored in the Global Catalog and who can access the information.

I can also designate multiple servers to hold the Global Catalog, thus ensuring that a catalog is available locally to all of my users. (Of course, the more Global Catalog servers I have, the more traffic is generated to keep the replicas up-to-date.)

Policy-Based Administration

Earlier versions of Windows NT had the ability to create policy files to control certain aspects of a user's environment. While this capability was useful, it was limited in scope—you could create policies only for users, groups, or computers. The level of control was also limited to a very select set of parameters, things like access to the display options on a computer or ability to disable the Run option on the Startup menu. All in all, administrators had more control than was available with earlier operating systems, but the capabilities were too limited.

In Windows 2000/Windows Server 2003, policies have been expanded so that they can apply across a site, domain, or organizational unit (OU) as defined in the Active Directory database. The controls available have also been expanded so that administrators can now control just about every aspect of a user's environment.

Policies now include options that allow central administration of items like operating system updates, installation of applications (either mandatory or user-controlled), user profiles, and the traditional Desktop.

Uniform Naming Convention

Within the realm of networks and network applications, there are numerous ways to identify resources. Within a single environment, administrators and users are often forced to understand (and use) multiple methods for naming and finding the resources they need.

One common method of naming servers and share points is to use *UNC (Uniform Naming Convention)* names. UNC names adhere to the following format:

```
\\<server name>\<share point>\<path to resource>
```

where:

◆ `<server name>` refers to the name of the device that holds the resource.

◆ `<share point>` refers to the name given to the shared data area.

◆ `<path to resource>` refers to the logical directory structure used to find the requested information.

NOTE *The acronym UNC is also interpreted as Universal Naming Convention in many current texts. Since UNC is a Microsoft term and this book is about Microsoft technology, I've decided to go with the original.*

While users have grown accustomed to this format, it is not necessarily either intuitive or convenient. Users must know the entire UNC name to use an object on their network. This is one of the reasons why graphical interfaces are so popular: users can click to an object rather than have to remember its name.

Another confusing environment can be that of messaging systems. Exchange Server, for instance, generates multiple names for each recipient created. These names follow the format of various standards and foreign mail systems (thus allowing mail to be routed to and from other environments). A typical recipient will have names matching the following standards:

◆ Distinguished names (or X.500 names)

◆ X.400 names

◆ Lotus cc:Mail names

◆ Microsoft Mail names

For our purposes, we do not need to examine each of the naming standards in detail. Besides, most of this is done behind the scenes, meaning that the mail administrator doesn't necessarily have to understand each naming standard. There are, however, times when such knowledge is critical to troubleshooting a message delivery problem. The problem with this type of system is that no one can be expected to have detailed knowledge of all of these standards (especially not for systems one has never worked with).

With Windows 2000/Windows Server 2003 and AD, each object in the directory has one unique name that can be used to reference it. AD uses X.500 names to represent each of the objects that it contains. In an X.500 environment, the complete, or *distinguished*, name of any object is a complete path to the top of the tree structure, as shown in Figure 6.2. From an administrative perspective, this means that there is only one naming format in use on a network.

FIGURE 6.2

Distinguished object names

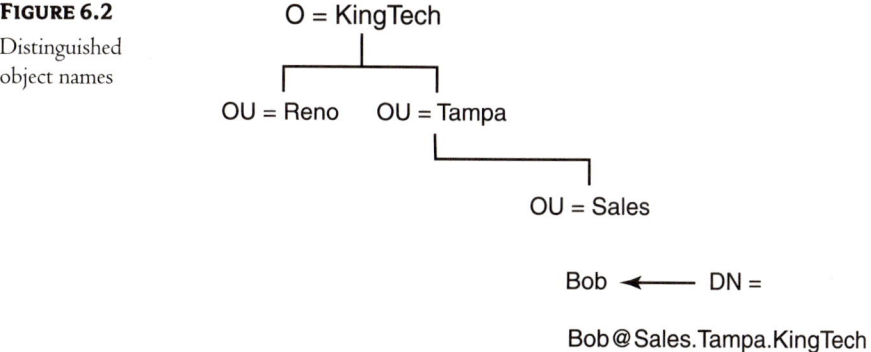

As you can see in Figure 6.2, there are certain similarities to all objects named within a particular AD tree. At the very least, every object share's name includes the name of the root object, much as all members of a family share a common last name. Just as you can refer to my family as "the King family," you can refer to an AD tree by its topmost object (the root).

Namespace and Name Resolution

The root object of a tree defines the beginning of a namespace. The concept of a namespace is critical to understanding AD. A *namespace* is a structure in which a name (in this case, the name of the root object of the AD database) is applied to all of the objects it contains. In other words, a namespace is any specific context in which a name can be resolved to a resource.

Name resolution is the process that uses the name of an object to find some information about that object. Probably the most common name resolution process is using the telephone book. With a telephone book, you use a name to find a telephone number or address.

In AD you can use the name, or even just a portion of the name, of an object to find the value of its attributes, as shown in Figure 6.3. Susan is looking for the mail-stop of a user named Bob in the sales department. She uses a tool to submit a query, and AD returns the resources that match her criteria. This is the process of name resolution.

FIGURE 6.3

Name resolution

Susan

Query: Show me all Bobs in
the Sales Department

Result: Bob.Sales.Tampa.KingTech
Bob.Sales.Reno.KingTech
BobP.Sales.Tampa.KingTech

When you create the tree structure for an AD tree, its contents are organized in a hierarchical (and, ideally, logical) manner. Each department, workgroup, or object class can be given its own container. These containers relate back to the original Active Directory namespace, as shown in Figure 6.4.

FIGURE 6.4

The AD hierarchical structure

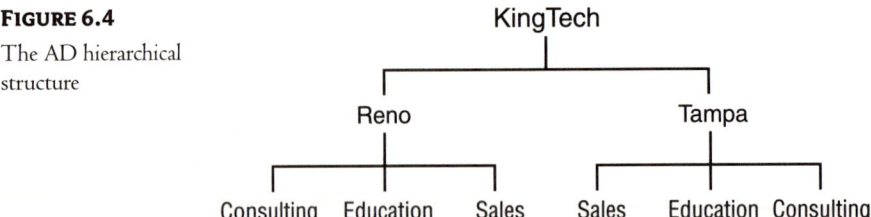

The King Technologies tree has two regional containers, or organizational units:

◆ `Tampa.KingTech`

◆ `Reno.KingTech`

Each region is divided into three departmental OUs. For the Reno office, these are `Sales.Reno.KingTech`, `Education.Reno.KingTech`, and `Consulting.Reno.KingTech`. In our previous example, if Susan had known which office Bob worked in, she could have limited her search to the appropriate area of the AD structure by specifying the `Sales.Reno.KingTech` container. This shows the hierarchical nature of the AD tree structure. It also demonstrates the concept of namespace: each object in the context `KingTech` can be resolved to a unique name.

Active Directory Names

In an AD directory, each object has a unique name within the structure. There are three different types of names used depending upon the function being performed:

◆ Distinguished names

◆ Relative names

◆ User principal names

I know that I said there was a single naming standard; as we discuss each of the three name types in the following sections, you will find that they are all derived from the same single namespace.

DISTINGUISHED NAMES

The *distinguished name (DN)* of any object identifies the entire path through the AD structure to find that object. Every object within an AD tree has a DN. For example, Katie King, who works in the Reno sales department of King Technologies, would have the following DN:

`Katie King@Sales.Reno.KingTech.com`

◆ `Katie King` is the actual name given to the object in the AD database.

◆ `Sales` is an OU within the `Reno` container.

◆ Reno is an OU within the KingTech container.

◆ KingTech is the organization at the top of the structure.

◆ com represents the container in which the KingTech namespace is defined on the Internet.

A distinguished name is the most complete and accurate way to represent any object within the AD tree. DNs can, however, be cumbersome to use in a productive manner—can you imagine typing Katie's entire DN each time you wanted to send her an e-mail or manage her object? Luckily, there are a few shortcut naming standards that can reduce the length of names used to access resources.

RELATIVE NAMES

A *relative name (RN)* is made up of the parts of an object's DN that are attributes of the object itself. For Katie, her RN would be Katie King because this is the only part of her DN that is specific to her object. The rest of her name is made up of RNs of the containers used to make up her DN. Sales, for instance, is the RN of her parent container.

NOTE   *The term* parent *is used to describe any object above another in an AD tree.*

USER PRINCIPAL NAMES

The *user principal name (UPN)* is the name a user uses to log on to the network. Katie *could* use her DN—Katie King@Sales.Reno.KingTech.com—but this could be confusing for her. The UPN is a shortcut made up of her RN and the DNS name of the domain in which she resides: Katie King@KingTech.com.

NOTE   *I'll discuss DNS naming in more detail in Chapter 9.*

A major goal of AD is to simplify the process of finding information about resources on a network. By using a standard set of rules to create DNs, RNs, and UPNs for objects, Microsoft begins the process of removing multiple naming formats from large environments. This can help to reduce both user and administrative confusion, easing the process of resolving names to resources.

Active Directory in the Windows 2000/Windows Server 2003 Architecture

When reading (or writing) a book about Active Directory, one tends to forget that AD is just one small piece of the overall Windows 2000/Windows Server 2003 environment—although a critical small piece! Before we begin our discussion on the specifics of AD, we need to see how AD fits into the overall architecture of Windows 2000/Windows Server 2003.

As you can see in Figure 6.5, the Active Directory subsystem is contained within the security subsystem of NT—more specifically, within the *Local Security Authority (LSA)* subsystem of the security environment. The specific module that contains Active Directory within the LSA is the *Directory Service module*. Understanding how these modules are organized can help when designing your AD network for optimal efficiency and performance.

FIGURE 6.5

AD in the Windows
2000/Windows
Server 2003
architecture

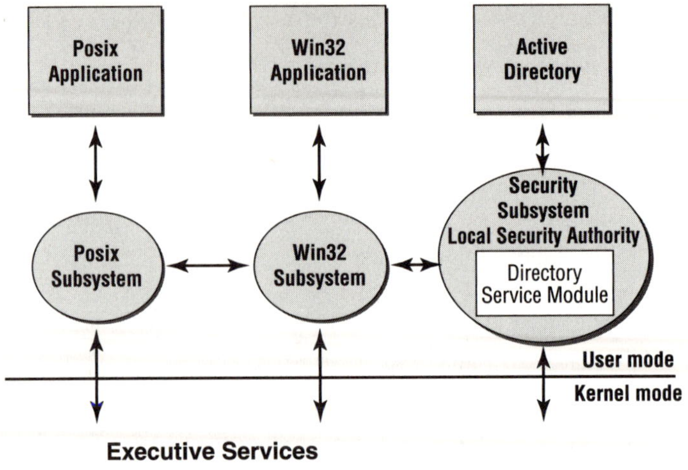

The modular design of Windows 2000/Windows Server 2003 means that each component is a separate and distinct piece that is responsible for a particular function. These components work together to perform operating system tasks. Active Directory is a part of the component called the security subsystem, which runs in user mode. *User mode* is a separate section of memory in which applications are executed. Applications running in user mode do not have direct access to the operating system or hardware; each request for resources must be passed through various components to determine whether the request is valid. One such component is the security subsystem. *Access Control Lists (ACLs)* protect objects in the Active Directory structure. ACLs list who or what has been given permission to access the resource. Any attempt to gain access to an AD object or attribute is validated against the ACL by Windows 2000/Windows Server 2003 access validation functions.

The Windows 2000/Windows Server 2003 security infrastructure has four primary functions:

◆ It stores security policies and account information.

◆ It implements and enforces security models for all objects.

◆ It authenticates access requests to AD objects.

◆ It stores trust information.

The security subsystem for Windows NT is a mature, stable component. Using this subsystem to manage AD ensures that the information stored within the AD database will be secure against unauthorized access.

NOTE *There have been a few changes to the overall NT architecture with Windows 2000/Windows Server 2003: the addition of Plug and Play and power management modules; the addition of Quality of Service (QOS), asynchronous transfer mode (ATM), and other drivers to the I/O manager; and some low-level changes to the operating system kernel.*

The Security Subsystem

Active Directory is a subcomponent of the LSA, which is in turn a subcomponent of the security subsystem. The LSA is a protected module that maintains the security of the local computer. It ensures that users have system access permissions. The LSA has four primary functions:

◆ It generates tokens that contain user and group information, as well as the security privileges for that particular user.

◆ It manages the local security policy.

◆ It provides the interactive processes for user logon.

◆ It manages auditing.

The LSA itself is made up of various components, each of which is responsible for a specific function. These components are shown in Figure 6.6.

FIGURE 6.6

LSA components

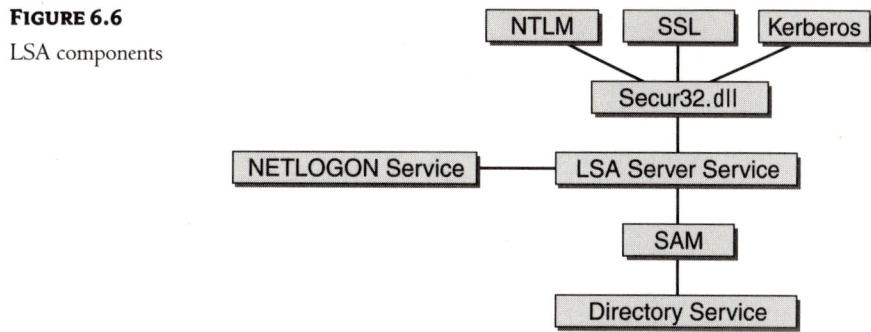

Netlogon.dll   Maintains the secure connection to a domain controller. It passes the user's credentials to a domain controller and returns the domain security identifiers and user rights for that user. (In Windows 2000/Windows Server 2003, the Netlogon service uses DNS to locate the domain controller.) In the event that the environment is a mix of NT 4 and Windows 2000/Windows Server 2003, the Netlogon service also controls the replication process between the PDC and BDCs.

Msv1_0.dll   The Windows NT LAN Manager (NTLM) authentication protocol.

Schannel.dll   The Secure Sockets Layer (SSL) authentication protocol.

Kerberos.dll   The Kerberos v5 authentication protocol.

Lsasrv.dll   The LSA server service, which enforces security policies.

Samsrv.dll   The Security Accounts Manager (SAM), which enforces stored policies.

Ntdsa.dll   The Directory Service module, which supports LDAP queries and manages partitions of data.

Secur32.dll   The multiple authentication provider, which manages the rest of the components.

The Directory Service Module

The Directory Service module is itself made up of multiple components that work together to provide directory services. These modules are arranged in the following three layers, which you can see in Figure 6.7:

◆ Agents layer

◆ Directory System Agent layer

◆ Database layer

These three layers control access to the actual database itself, which is known as the *Extensible Storage Engine (ESE)*.

FIGURE 6.7

Directory Service module components

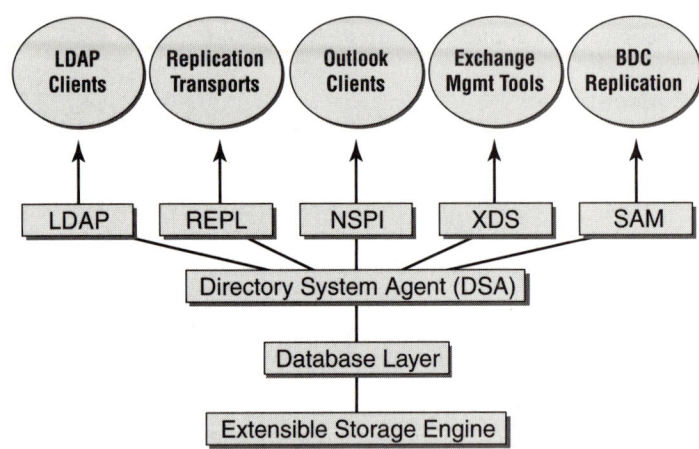

AGENTS LAYER

There are five interface agents that gain access to the directory through internal functions:

Lightweight Directory Access Protocol (LDAP) The industry-standard protocol for directory access. This interface makes it easy for third-party developers to utilize the AD database.

Intersite and Intrasite Replication (REPL) Changes to the AD database must be replicated throughout the environment. The REPL interface is used to facilitate this function.

Name Service Provider Interface (NSPI) This interface provides a uniform method of naming objects.

Exchange Directory Service (XDS)   This interface directly connects to an Exchange e-mail system (if one exists).

Security Accounts Manager (SAM)   This interface accesses the AD database as if it were the accounts database in an NT environment.

Each of these interfaces uses a different method to access the information stored within the database.

DIRECTORY SYSTEM AGENT (DSA) LAYER

The DSA is responsible for creating a hierarchical tree-like namespace from an existing flat namespace. This allows you to view objects in a more logical manner, rather than as a flat list. The database itself is not really a "tree"—the DSA uses the information found for containers to create the logical structure that we see in the various management tools. The DSA has the following responsibilities:

◆ Enforce all Directory Service semantics

◆ Process transactions

◆ Enforce the common schema

◆ Support replication between AD servers

◆ Provide Global Catalog services

◆ Propagate security descriptors

DATABASE LAYER

The database layer provides the functionality needed to access and search the directory database. All database access is routed through the database layer. It controls the ways in which the data is viewed.

EXTENSIBLE STORAGE ENGINE

The ESE is the actual database used to store the Active Directory database. It is a modified version of the Jet database used in Microsoft Exchange versions 4 and 5. The ESE enables you to create a 17-terabyte database that (theoretically) can hold up to 10 million objects.

The Jet database engine has been used for Microsoft Exchange Server for quite some time. The version used by AD comes with a predefined schema (the definition of object classes and their attributes). ESE reserves storage only for the space actually used. If you create a user object, for example, which *could* have 50 predefined attributes, but you only give values to four of them, then ESE will only use as much storage space as needed for the four attributes. As you add values to other attributes for that user, ESE will dynamically allocate space for the growth in record size. ESE can also store multiple values for a single attribute (such as telephone numbers). It will allocate space as needed for each telephone number added to a user object.

The Internal Architecture of the Active Directory Module

The rootDSA object is inside the DSA in the Directory Service module. It is the top of the logical namespace defined by the AD database and therefore at the top of the LDAP search tree, as shown in Figure 6.8.

FIGURE 6.8

AD internal architecture

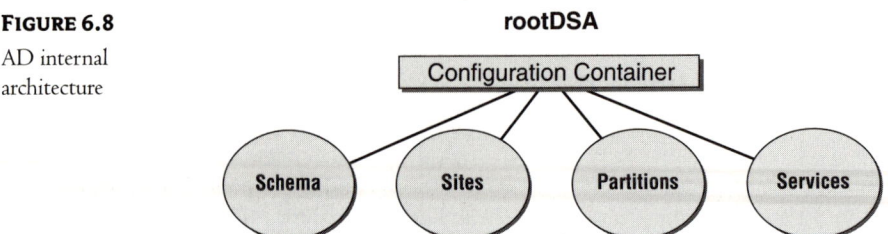

The rootDSA object contains a configuration container, which in turn holds data about the entire AD network. The information stored in the configuration container provides the data necessary to replicate the directory database, how this server relates to the overall namespace, and how the database is partitioned. This information is known as the *name context* for the various types of information. The following four name contexts are described under the configuration container:

Schema   Contains the definitions of all object classes and their attributes.

Sites   Contains information on all of the sites in the enterprise network, the domain controllers in those sites, and the replication topology.

Partitions   Holds pointers to all of the partitions of the directory database.

Services   Holds the configuration information for networkwide services such as Remote Access Service, system volumes, and DNS.

In Short

Microsoft Active Directory Services is intended to tie together all of the diverse aspects of network management within a single database, which can be accessed using a single set of tools. Once implemented, AD should ease the administrative burdens placed upon network administrators.

Now that we've looked at the goals and the architecture of AD, we can turn our attention to specific pieces of AD. In the next chapter, we'll take a closer look at how domains exist in a Windows 2000/Windows Server 2003 environment and how AD implements backward compatibility with older NT systems.

Chapter 7

Network Support Services

ACTIVE DIRECTORY DOESN'T HAVE a lengthy history, but it has been around long enough to require a third update of *Mastering Active Directory*. The first edition of the book was based upon the functionality of a few beta versions of Windows 2000 (and Active Directory). The goal was to provide a good look at Active Directory as soon as possible after its release. The purpose of the second edition was to correct any discrepancies between the beta releases of Windows 2000 and the final product. In both cases, neither I nor anyone else had any real-world experience upon which to base our comments because the product was so new. In other words, I (along with a host of other authors) wrote material based upon experience with other directory services and the documentation provided by Microsoft.

Needless to say, basing technical information upon Microsoft material often results in a book with a pro-Microsoft slant. In this version of the book, I can begin to offer real-world, experience-based assessments of the technologies and skills used in designing, installing, configuring, and maintaining an Active Directory environment. When producing a new edition of a manual, an author is torn between simply updating the salient information and rewriting large portions of the material, depending upon the topic at hand. This chapter is the first in which I felt that significant changes needed to be made.

As much as I hate to use marketing terms, the release of Windows 2000 began a whole new paradigm in Windows networking. While earlier versions of the NT product family included support for TCP/IP and its associated services, they were in no way mandatory to a successful implementation. With Windows 2000/Windows Server 2003 and Active Directory, TCP/IP and some of the TCP/IP-based technologies are critical to success. Earlier versions of NT also revolved around domain-based technology. While domains still exist in Windows 2000/Windows Server 2003, there have been significant changes to the way they fit into an overall design.

One of the biggest, and possibly best, changes that we see in Windows 2000 revolves around the demise of NetBIOS-based technology. Don't get too excited yet; NetBIOS is still integral to most installations, but the new focus on TCP/IP (especially DNS) shows us a light at the end of the tunnel. The foundation has been laid for a complete removal of NetBIOS traffic from our future networks!

In this chapter we'll review a few TCP/IP basics—foundation material that you must understand with implementing Active Directory. We'll also take a look at WINS (see, I told you NetBIOS was still hanging around) and how it fits into the AD picture. Lastly, we'll look at DHCP and DNS and see how these two technologies will soon replace NetBIOS and WINS in our networks.

In this chapter:

◆ Windows Server 2003 vs. Windows 2000

◆ TCP/IP basics

◆ The Windows Internet Name Service (WINS) processes

◆ Dynamic Host Configuration Protocol: installing DHCP and examining how it works

◆ Domain Name System (DNS): planning DNS naming and integrating DNS and Active Directory

Regarding Windows Server 2003 vs. Windows 2000

I had a difficult decision to make when writing this edition: how much effort should I put into covering the Windows Server 2003 release? From a strictly Active Directory perspective, the basic functionality really hasn't changed much (although there are a few changes that I'll cover when appropriate). This reference is dedicated to an understanding of AD, and that reduces the importance of the operating system version considerably! For those of you coming from a Novell NDS background, discussing this is like the difference between NDS 4.1 and 5; sure, there are some changes, but the underlying concepts are pretty much the same.

I also had to consider the real-life situations of most companies out there. Microsoft has released new versions of its operating systems on such a regular basis lately that many companies are getting a little fed up! Many of my own clients are currently running mixed systems—a few Windows 2000/Windows Server 2003 servers, a few NT 4.0 servers, and just about every client operating system since Windows 95. Most of these companies have expressed the same thing about upgrades:

1. Upgrades will only occur when the benefit is clearly defined and documented.

2. New servers and workstations will be installed with a standard operating system (usually Windows 2000/Windows Server 2003), but existing servers and clients will remain until number 1 (above) is met.

3. Given Microsoft's track record, new operating systems (first releases) will be thoroughly tested before being utilized in a production environment. (Many clients say they'll let "someone else beta-test Microsoft's product in the field;" they'll wait until the smoke clears before adopting any new technology.)

As you can see, this leaves me in kind of a bind. As an author, I have two directives: stay on topic (Active Directory) and provide useful information. Personally though, it's a lot more fun to write about the "latest and greatest" than it is to discuss an operating system that is being replaced. To this end, I have decided to include both operating systems—Windows 2000 and Windows Server 2003—wherever appropriate. You'll find screen shots from both, whenever they differ enough to make a difference.

The bottom line is that our discussions will pertain to Active Directory—in both Windows Server 2003 and Windows 2000—unless specifically noted.

TCP/IP Basics

The Transmission Control Protocol/Internet Protocol (TCP/IP) is a suite of protocols specifically designed to fulfill two goals:

◆ Allow communication across WAN (wide area network) links

◆ Allow communication between diverse environments

Understanding the roots of these protocols leads to an understanding of their importance in today's networks.

The Development of TCP/IP

In the late 1960s and early 1970s, the U.S. Department of Defense Advanced Research Projects Agency (DARPA) conducted a series of tests with packet-switching networks. These tests had two goals:

◆ The development of a network that would allow research facilities to share information (at the time, DARPA discovered that numerous universities were conducting the exact same research but did not have the ability to share their results)

◆ The development of a network that would act as a link between defense sites in the event of a nuclear attack

NOTE *The second of these goals might sound kind of silly in light of today's global political situation, but at the time, the threat of "nuclear holocaust" was a fact of life. Many of today's most important technologies were developed with the Cold War in mind.*

These experiments developed through numerous stages until they finally came together in what we now call the Internet. The TCP/IP suite was developed as part of these experiments. The TCP/IP suite itself is still developing to meet the needs of changing technology.

The development of TCP/IP is overseen by the Internet Society. The Internet Society is responsible for the internetworking technologies and applications used on the Internet. The Internet Architecture Board (IAB) is an advisory group of the Internet Society that is responsible for setting Internet standards. Internet technologies are defined through a series of articles known as RFCs: Requests for Comments.

If a member of the IAB believes that she has a new technology for the Internet or an improvement to an existing technology, she would write a Request for Comments that outlines her idea. This RFC is submitted to the IAB and posted for discussion. (Hence the name Request for *Comments*.) If the idea has merit, it might eventually become part of the standard definition of the TCP/IP suite. Having each proposed change posted on a public forum for discussion fosters an environment of cooperative development. This process also helps to ensure that any change is well thought out and tested before implementation.

Common TCP/IP Protocols and Tools

Over the years, many RFCs have been added to the standard definition of the TCP/IP suite. TCP/IP has developed into a rich, if somewhat complex, set of protocols perfectly suited to the task of managing a complex network. The mature status of most of the technologies is one reason that Microsoft has selected TCP/IP as its protocol of choice for Windows NT networks. Table 7.1 lists some of the more common TCP/IP protocols and the purpose of each.

TABLE 7.1: TCP/IP PROTOCOLS

PROTOCOL	PURPOSE
Simple Network Management Protocol (SNMP)	A protocol designed to be used by network management software. Specifically designed to allow remote management of network devices. This definition has been expanded to include the management of just about any network resource.
Transmission Control Protocol (TCP)	A communication protocol that is connection-oriented and provides guaranteed delivery services.
User Datagram Protocol (UDP)	A communication protocol that uses a connectionless delivery scheme to deliver packets. This is a nonguaranteed delivery protocol.
Internet Control Message Protocol (ICMP)	A protocol used for special communication between hosts, usually protocol management messages (errors and reports).
Internet Protocol (IP)	A protocol that performs addressing and routing functions.
Address Resolution Protocol (ARP)	A protocol used to resolve IP addresses into hardware addresses.
Simple Mail Transfer Protocol (SMTP)	A protocol specifically designed to handle the delivery of electronic mail.
File Transfer Protocol (FTP)	A protocol used to transfer files from one host to another.

NOTE *While this is not a complete list of the various protocols that make up the TCP/IP suite, it shows some of the more important protocols in use. As we add complexity to our networks, so must we add complexity to the protocols that provide network functionality.*

There is also a standard set of TCP/IP-based tools that every network administrator should be aware of. Table 7.2 lists a few of the more common utilities and their functions.

TABLE 7.2: COMMON TCP/IP UTILITIES

UTILITY	FUNCTION
File Transfer Protocol	This was listed as a protocol in Table 7.1, but it is also considered a critical TCP/IP utility. FTP can be used to test the transfer of files to and from hosts.
Telnet	Provides terminal emulation to a host running Telnet server software.
Packet Internet Groper (Ping)	Used to test TCP/IP configurations and connections.
IPCONFIG	Verifies the TCP/IP configuration on the local host.
NSLOOKUP	A command-line tool used to read records in the DNS database.
TRACERT	Used to display the route taken between two hosts.

You will need to be proficient with each of these tools in order to set up and troubleshoot an AD environment.

TCP/IP Addressing

In a TCP/IP environment, each network host (any device that uses TCP/IP to communicate) needs a unique identifier. This identifier is known as its *IP address*. IP addressing is well beyond the scope of this book, but I will cover the basics just to ensure that we are speaking the same language.

Without getting into too much detail (I'll suggest some additional reading at the end of this chapter), here's an overview. Each IP address is made up of 32 bits. Since computers use a binary system to represent information, each of those bits has one of two values: 0 or 1. The arrangement of those bits must be unique against all computers on any network that a host can communicate with. A typical IP address would look something like this:

10000011.01101011.00000010.11001000

Notice that the 32 bits are divided into four *octets* (an octet is a grouping of 8 bits). Each octet is 1 byte of data. While this is actually what the computer "sees," it is not how humans think (or at least most of us don't think in binary). Rather than using the binary value, IP addresses are converted into their decimal equivalent. We see IP addresses in a format known as *dotted decimal*. The dotted decimal representation of the address shown above is

131.107.2.200

An IP address has two parts:

◆ The network address

◆ The host address

The *network address* is used to route information to the correct network segment, and the *host address* identifies a particular device within that segment. This is really no different from the street addresses used by the U.S. Postal Service, as you can see in Figure 7.1.

FIGURE 7.1

IP addresses

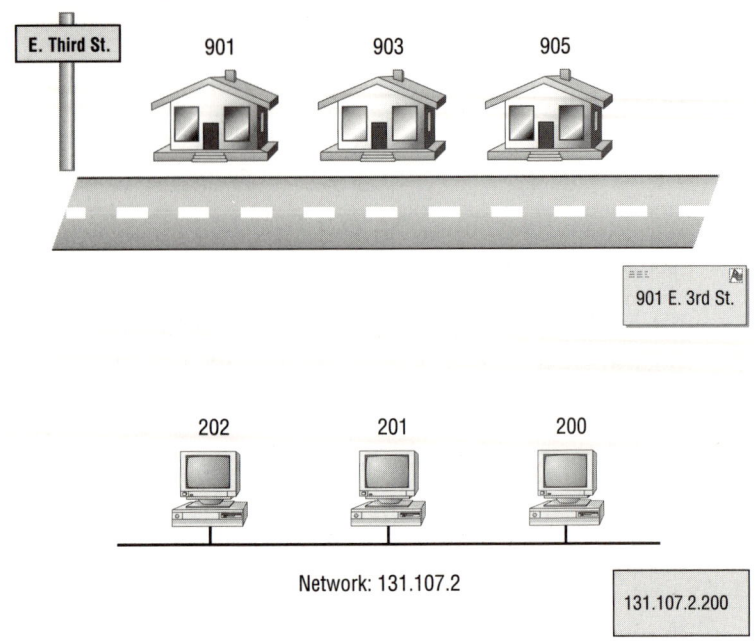

The address line on a letter contains both the house number and the street name. This allows the post office to sort the mail (using the street name) so that the appropriate carrier receives it and can identify which house it should be delivered to. The same process is used with IP addresses: the network portion allows routers to deliver packets to the correct network (city and street), and the host portion identifies which host should receive them (building or apartment number).

IP Subnetting

IP addressing is a little more complex than I just described. When a company receives a network address (either from the Internet authorities or from an Internet Service Provider), the company is given a range of possible addresses. There are three main classes of addresses available: A, B, and C.

NOTE   *There are actually more than three classes of IP network addresses, but we will stick with the more common classes here.*

THE ABCS OF IP ADDRESSES

Class A addresses begin with a first octet value between 1 and 126. In other words, there are only 126 class A networks available on the entire Internet. (Needless to say, there are no more class A addresses available.) The first octet is the network portion of the IP address, and the last three octets represent the host portion. Each class A network can support over 16 million hosts. Now you can see why only a few of these addresses are needed—not many companies have that number of hosts on their networks.

NOTE   *How do you calculate the number of hosts a network can support? On a class A network, only the first octet represents the network. This means that three octets—or 24 bits—are used to provide the host portion. In a binary system, you can determine the number of unique combinations by raising 2 to the number of bits available. In this case, 2 raised to the 24th power equals 16,777,214—more than 16 million available combinations. Without going into the binary math involved, two of the possible combinations are illegal, so really there are 16,777,212 hosts available on a class A network.*

Class B networks begin with a first octet value between 128 and 191. In a class B network, the first two octets represent the network and the last two represent the node portion of an IP address. This means that there are only 65,534 class B networks available, each of which can support 65,534 nodes (2^{16}–2).

Finally, class C networks begin with a first octet value between 192 and 223. On a class C network, the first three octets represent the network and the last octet represents the host portion. This means that there are a little over 16 million class C network addresses available, but each can only support a maximum of 254 hosts.

SUBNETTING IP ADDRESSES

The problem with the standard address classes is that they assume no routers between the various hosts on the network. In other words, if you were given a class B network address, it is assumed that you have somewhere in the neighborhood of 65,000 hosts on a single network. In reality, this situation would be intolerable. Even if you could find a topology that would support it, the amount of traffic on such a network would slow performance to a crawl.

To overcome this limitation, IP network addresses can be *subnetted*. The process of subnetting can be extremely confusing (especially since this is not something you consider every day), but the theory is fairly straightforward.

When a company is given a network address, it is given the *network portion* of each valid IP address for the network. In other words, if a company is given a class B address of 131.107.0.0, each IP address on its network *must* begin with 131.107. This is the portion of the address used by network devices to route packets to the network.

Another way to look at this is to see the network portion as mandated by some external entity (the Internet, for instance). The local administrator owns the host portion, such as the last two octets in our example. He can do what he likes with them. This means that with a class B license, the local administrator has 16 bits to use as he sees fit. In order to control traffic, the local administrator might choose to use some of these bits to represent local network addresses. While this *does* make the process of assigning IP addresses much more complex, it offers a few advantages that cannot be ignored:

♦   Since internal routers will direct traffic to the appropriate local network, congestion is reduced. Each network segment will carry only traffic intended for local hosts.

♦   Each topology has limitations on the number of hosts that can be physically attached to a single network wire. Subnetting allows the administrator to control how many hosts are on each internal network.

♦   Later we will see that we can define AD *sites* that are used to control directory database replication. These sites are based upon IP subnet addresses.

NOTE   As you can see, TCP/IP addressing can be a complex subject, well beyond the scope of this material. For more information, I would suggest you read one of the books recommended at the end of this chapter.

That last bullet item—the ability to define AD sites—is a critical piece of the Active Directory puzzle. Microsoft has claimed that the AD database is capable of handling millions of objects—well beyond the capabilities of the NT domain database. While this allows a wider latitude when it comes to designing your environment, it could result in an overabundance of replication traffic. AD site objects are used to define areas of replication, and they are based upon grouping IP subnets.

Now that we've taken a look at some of the basic principles of TCP/IP, we can examine a few of the utilities designed to make managing a network easier.

Windows Internet Name Service (WINS)

Let's start our discussion of management tools with the one we'd really like to get rid of: WINS. WINS is used to resolve user-friendly NetBIOS names to their associated IP addresses. While this sounds like a fairly simple process—and a lot like DNS—you'll see that WINS is really yesterday's news.

First, let's talk about NetBEUI. NetBEUI is an old, nonroutable communication protocol that was actually designed quite some time ago to support an Application Programming Interface (API) set named NetBIOS. When Microsoft first entered the network operating system business, they decided to use NetBEUI as their default communication protocol. After all, their first networking product was Windows for Workgroups (WFW)—not a really robust or scalable product. WFW was designed for small, departmental-sized environments—in other words, environments without multiple IP networks (and their associated routers). Most of Microsoft's first networking endeavors revolved around the use of NetBEUI to support NetBIOS.

NetBIOS was first designed to act as an API so that applications running on different computers could share information or work together. It includes various processes to facilitate this communication. Rather than rewrite a networking process from scratch, Microsoft incorporated NetBIOS into their own networking scheme.

For our discussion, there are a few important NetBIOS functions you should know about:

NetBIOS Names   NetBIOS names are the unique, user-friendly names associated with devices in a NetBIOS-based environment. They are 16 bytes in length; the first 15 bytes are assigned during the installation/setup of the hardware, and the last byte represents services on the device.

NetBIOS Name Registration   NetBIOS devices use (by default) a broadcast technique to ensure that the name being used by the device is unique on the network. Basically, the device sends out a broadcast packet declaring its name. If no negative response is heard (in other words, some other device is using the name and protests), then the device assumes its name is unique and begins using it.

NetBIOS Name Resolution   While NetBIOS uses the user-friendly computer name, the lower layer communication protocols use other identifiers. When one device wants to communicate with another, it will broadcast the destination's NetBIOS name. The destination device will respond with its IP address. At that time, communication can commence.

NetBIOS Name Release   When a device is properly shut down, it will broadcast a packet notifying other devices on the network that it is going offline. This allows them to update any NetBIOS name tables that they might have built.

Have you noticed the problem with this yet? Everything is broadcast-based. This works great in a single-segment environment, but as soon as you add a router to the mix, it starts to fall apart.

WINS Processes

There are actually a few different ways to deal with the issues surrounding NetBIOS in a routed network, but we'll concentrate on the Microsoft solution: WINS. In a WINS-based environment, NetBIOS clients use directed traffic rather than broadcasts to register, resolve, and release NetBIOS names. The processes involved are fairly straightforward. They include:

- Client setup

- Name registration

- Name resolution

- Name release

- Server partnerships

CLIENT SETUP

Each client in a WINS environment must be configured with the IP address of a WINS server. Once this configuration has been made, NetBIOS functions will use a directed (or unicast) IP process rather than broadcasting over the local segment. You can configure your clients manually if desired, or you can include the WINS options as part of your DHCP configuration.

NAME REGISTRATION

Once configured with the IP address of a WINS server, the client will send its proposed name to that WINS server during operating system initialization. The WINS server builds a database of all names that have been registered. When it receives a new request, it checks this database to ensure that the name is not already in use. If it is not, an acknowledgement is sent to the client, and initialization can continue. If the name is already in use, the WINS server will attempt to contact the original client, to ensure that it is still online and using the name (this protects against a machine being accidentally rebooted and then being denied its name because it is still in the WINS database). If the original client is still online, the new client will receive a negative acknowledgement informing it that its proposed name is already in use. (The user will see the dreaded message, "Computer name already in use. Please contact your network administrator.")

NAME RESOLUTION

In a traditional broadcast-based NetBIOS network, computers "find each other" by broadcasting a request for a response. Basically, if computer A needs to talk to computer B, A will send out a broadcast packet with B's NetBIOS name. In B's response will be his IP address. Once A has obtained the IP address of the destination, communication can begin.

When WINS is added to the network, the process changes a little. First, A no longer broadcasts to find B's IP address. Instead, computer A will send a directed packet to the WINS server requesting the IP address of a computer named "B". The WINS server will search its database (see "Name Registration" above) to see if computer B has been registered. If so, the WINS server will send computer A the IP address of computer B.

NAME RELEASE

When a WINS client is properly shut down, one of the last things it will do is send a message to the WINS server letting it know that it is going offline. This alerts the WINS server to remove all of the records for the device from its database. Basically, this ensures that the WINS database only contains records for active devices—a dynamically created, self-maintaining, database of network devices.

In the event that a computer is taken offline in an inappropriate manner (such as an unplanned reboot or a user hitting the off button instead of properly shutting down the machine), each record is given a time limit. In effect, each device "leases" its name and must "re-lease" on a regular basis. If a record reaches the end of its lease period without reestablishing contact with the WINS server, the record will be flushed from the database.

SERVER PARTNERSHIPS

While WINS can definitely cut down on the amount of broadcast traffic on your network, and it does alleviate the problems associated with a routed environment, there can be a few problems. Say, for instance, that you have offices in London and Tokyo. If your WINS server is located in London, the Tokyo computers would have to register themselves to a database located in London—not necessarily the best use of expensive WAN bandwidth. They would also have to utilize the London service to resolve the IP address of local devices, again placing unwanted traffic on the WAN link.

The solution is to put two WINS servers in place—one in London and one in Tokyo. Each WINS server would service the needs of local clients. Of course, without some additional configuration, neither would have records for the computers in the other location. This would mean that Tokyo clients would not be able to resolve the IP address of (or, in effect, communicate with) clients in London (or vice versa).

WINS includes the ability to create partnerships between servers. In effect, the WINS servers exchange databases on a regular basis. This allows each WINS server to hold records for all WINS clients on the network. In our example, we would create a partnership between the two WINS servers. After database synchronization occurred, clients in London could resolve the IP addresses of Tokyo resources through their local WINS server.

Why WINS?

Okay, by now you are probably wondering why you should worry about WINS at all. All of the Microsoft marketing material states that Windows 2000/Windows Server 2003 uses DNS (which we'll discuss later in this chapter) for name resolution. NetBIOS (and the NetBEUI protocol) was probably one of the least-efficient components of Windows NT. Since Windows 2000/Windows Server 2003 uses DNS *and* defaults to TCP/IP, you should be able to shelve the whole WINS experience, right? Wrong!

While Windows 2000/Windows Server 2003 can live without NetBIOS, none of the older legacy operating systems (and their associated server-based applications) can. Until you eliminate all legacy workstations and servers, as well as any older server-based applications, you will have to deal with the limitations of the NetBIOS environment. In other words, WINS will probably exist on your network for the foreseeable future.

Now, you might ask, why mention it in a book devoted to Active Directory? Surely AD doesn't use such an antiquated technology, right? This time you are correct! Active Directory utilizes DNS for all name resolution. So from a strictly AD perspective, NetBIOS and WINS are no longer necessary. I mention them here, in passing, because they will probably be critical to your environment.

Dynamic Host Configuration Protocol (DHCP)

Each host on a typical routed IP network must have certain parameters set correctly in order to communicate. These are the three most common parameters:

IP Address   Used to uniquely identify the host

Subnet Mask   Used to determine which portion of the IP address represents the network address

Default Gateway   Used to represent the IP address of the router to which all nonlocal traffic will be directed

Traditionally, these parameters were configured manually on each device on the network. From a management perspective, this meant that an administrator had to visit each device to configure its IP parameters. Entering this information manually took a lot of time and was prone to error. While there is a better way to accomplish this task, you can still opt for manual configuration of a Windows 2000/Windows Server 2003 computer if you desire.

TCP/IP addresses are configured in much the same way as they were in NT 4. There are, however, a few changes to the interface. To access the configuration window, right-click the My Network Places icon on the Desktop and choose Properties. You will be presented with the window shown in Figure 7.2.

FIGURE 7.2

NetworkConnections

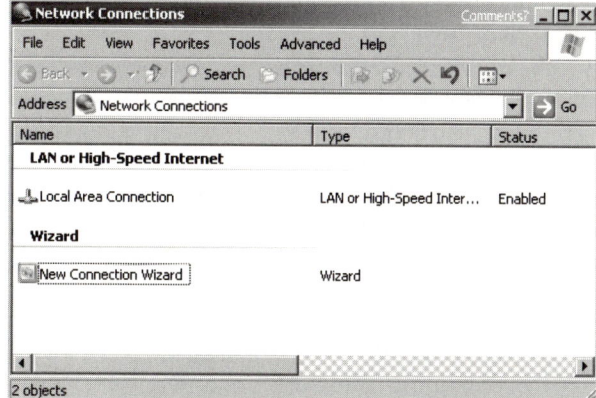

From this window, right-click the Local Area Connection icon and choose Properties. Highlight the Internet Protocol (TCP/IP) option and again choose Properties. At this point, you will be presented with the window shown in Figure 7.3. Check the box labeled Use the Following IP Address and enter your parameters.

FIGURE 7.3

Internet Protocol
Properties window

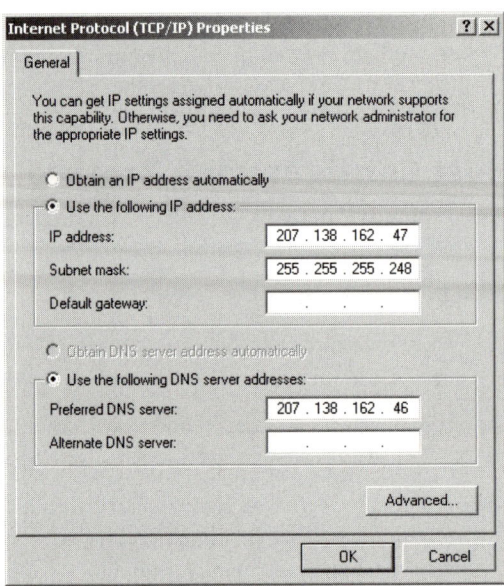

Our discussion of how to manually configure the IP parameters on a Windows 2000/Windows Server 2003 computer is mostly academic. You will use this method mostly to configure static IP addresses for special-case devices. Microsoft's preferred method for configuring IP hosts is to use Dynamic Host Configuration Protocol (DHCP), which we'll turn to next.

Installing DHCP Service

DHCP uses the BootP protocol to automatically configure TCP/IP clients as they join the network. DHCP services must be installed on a server. The basic premise of DHCP services is that clients can be configured automatically as they join the network, rather than manually as the computer is installed. Since configuration occurs each time the client computer attaches to the network, changes to the configuration are dynamically updated on the client.

The DHCP installation process has been modified from the NT 4 process, so let's take a good look at it.

To install DHCP services on your Windows 2000/Windows Server 2003, open your Control Panel (by choosing Start ➢ Settings ➢ Control Panel) and click Add/Remove Programs. You will be presented with a new interface, as shown in Figure 7.4.

FIGURE 7.4

Add/Remove
Programs in
Windows 2000/
Windows
Server 2003

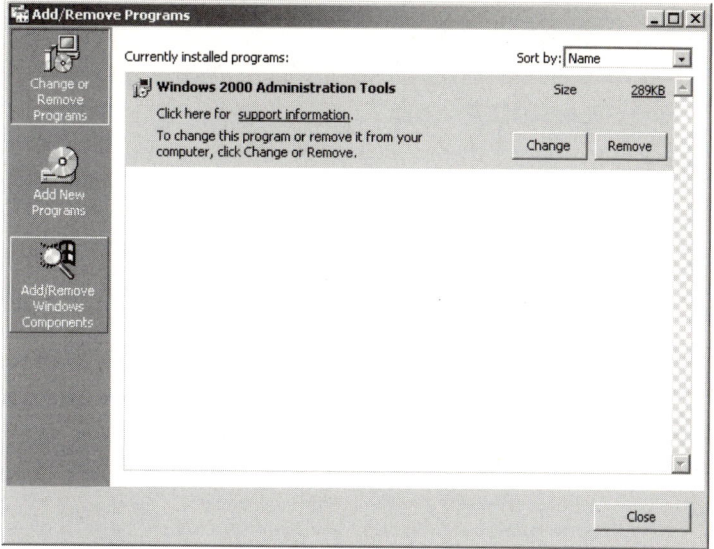

Click the Add/Remove Windows Components button. The Windows Components Wizard (A wizard is just a graphical interface designed to accomplish a specific task.) will appear, as shown in Figure 7.5. This window displays the various NT components that you can install on your server. The DHCP service is part of the Networking Services selection. Make sure that Networking Services is chosen and click Details. You will notice that there are numerous components to this option; make sure that only the items you want installed at this time are chosen. Then click OK and press the Next button and then the Finished button to complete the installation.

FIGURE 7.5

The Windows
Components Wizard

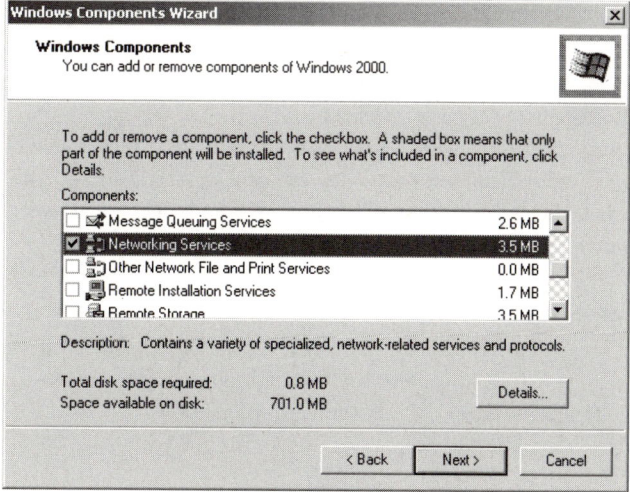

Once DHCP services have been installed, you will find a new tool in your Administrative Tools group: DHCP Server Management.

How Does DHCP Work?

There are two processes to consider when looking at DHCP services:

◆ Configuring the DHCP server

◆ Configuring clients as they attach to the network

The next couple of sections discuss these processes.

CONFIGURING THE DHCP SERVER

When configured properly, DHCP servers provide an important service to the network. As with most important functions, though, an incorrectly configured (or worse, unplanned) DHCP server can wreak havoc on your orderly world. Remember the major task of DHCP servers: to give IP addresses and other configuration parameters to clients as they join the network. If a DHCP server is incorrectly configured, it could conceivably hand out IP addresses that are either invalid or—worse—already in use on your network. For this reason, each DHCP server must be authorized before it can function in an Active Directory environment.

Each server in an Active Directory environment will function in one of the following three roles:

Domain Controllers   Contain a copy of the Active Directory database and perform account management for domain members.

Member Servers   Do not maintain a replica of the Active Directory database, but they have joined a domain and have an associated record in the AD database.

Stand-alone Servers   Do not hold a replica of the AD database and are not members of any domain. Basically, stand-alone servers announce their presence as members of a workgroup.

Only domain controllers and member servers can act as DHCP servers in an AD environment. By mandating that all DHCP servers be verified as legal, Windows 2000/Windows Server 2003 provides a level of security that was unavailable in earlier operating systems. Not only does this protect against "industrial espionage" (I've always wanted to use that phrase in a book—of course, I had a spy novel in mind), but it also epitomizes one of the biggest advantages of a directory service: central control. The central information services department no longer has to worry about some hotshot in Cleveland installing a DHCP server without understanding IP addressing or subnetting.

AUTHORIZING A DHCP SERVER

To authorize a server to act as a DHCP server, first install DHCP services as described earlier. Then open the DHCP management tool located in the Administrative Tools group. You will be presented with a screen similar to the one shown in Figure 7.6.

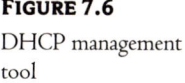

FIGURE 7.6

DHCP management tool

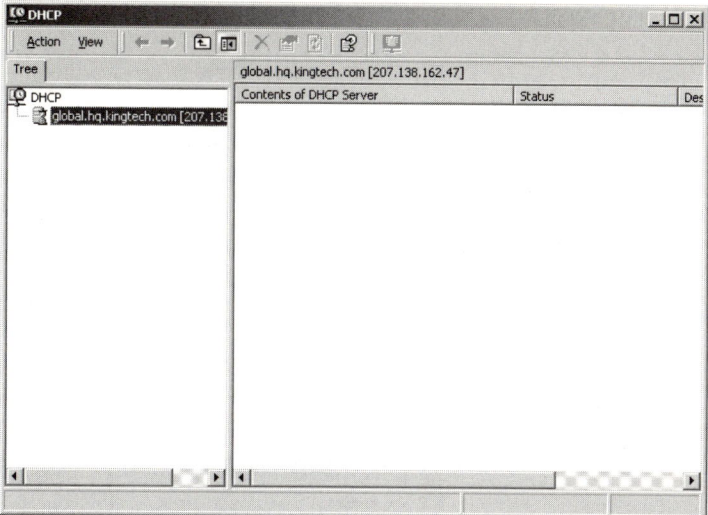

From the opening screen, choose Manage Authorized Servers from the Action menu. You will be presented with the screen shown in Figure 7.7.

FIGURE 7.7

Authorizing DHCP servers

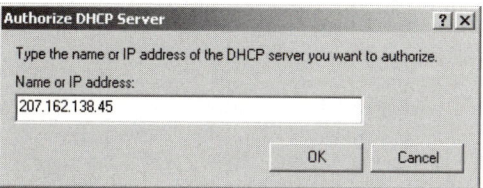

Type in the name or IP address of the server that you wish to add to the authorized DHCP servers list.

Note   Okay, let's be realistic. While the authorization process does indeed prevent unauthorized Windows 2000/Windows Server 2003 DHCP servers from functioning on your network, it does not have any effect on DHCP servers running some other operating system. Basically, the Windows 2000/Windows Server 2003 DHCP server sends out a request to proceed to Active Directory. Upon receiving the go-ahead, the server will then initiate the DHCP service. Other operating systems (such as Windows NT), on the other hand, do not send the request; they just start doing their job. Don't count on this as the ultimate in security; it's just a nice feature!

CREATING A SCOPE

At the server a *scope* must be created. A scope is a database of the parameters that the DHCP server will pass to clients as they initialize. The DHCP server can provide more than just an IP address, subnet mask, and default gateway—there are numerous TCP/IP parameters that might need to be configured on any given client, and DHCP can designate all of them!

To create a scope, open the DHCP management tool located in the Administrative Tools group. There are two ways to complete most tasks: manually or with the aid of a wizard. Personally, I like the wizards—even though I'm fairly comfortable with most items, Wizards ensure that I don't inadvertently forget something. To start the New Scope Wizard, first highlight the server you wish to add the scope to, then from the Action menu choose New, then Scope. The opening screen is the standard "Welcome to our wizard" message. Click Next and you will be presented with the window shown in Figure 7.8. Here you will give your scope a name and perhaps add a few comments to document your system.

FIGURE 7.8

New scope name
and comments

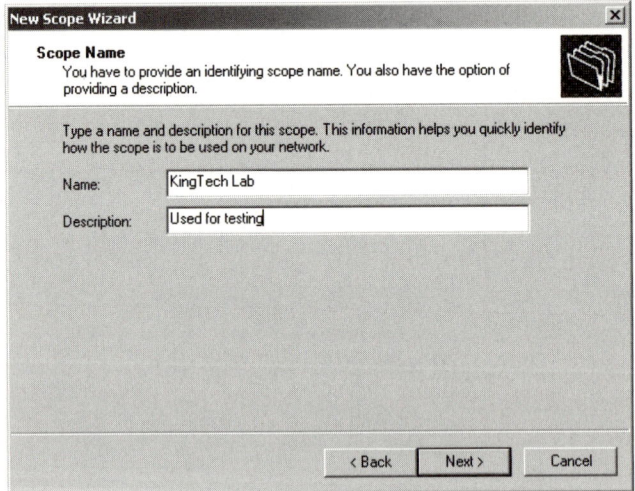

TIP *The scope name should be something that will remind you of the purpose of the scope, such as "KingTech Test Lab." You can also add an administrative comment, such as "IP addresses not valid on the Internet."*

The first technical configuration option is on the next page of the wizard, shown in Figure 7.9. Here you will be asked to give a range of addresses that should be given out by the DHCP server when using this scope. (This is where knowledge of the IP addressing scheme discussed earlier will come in handy!) You should also configure the subnet mask for this network.

FIGURE 7.9

Defining the range
of addresses

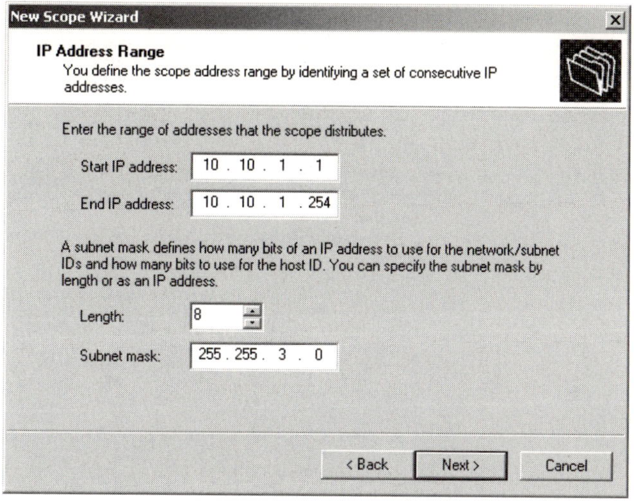

FIGURE 7.9 — New Scope Wizard: IP Address Range. You define the scope address range by identifying a set of consecutive IP addresses. Enter the range of addresses that the scope distributes. Start IP address: 10 . 10 . 1 . 1 End IP address: 10 . 10 . 1 . 254. A subnet mask defines how many bits of an IP address to use for the network/subnet IDs and how many bits to use for the host ID. You can specify the subnet mask by length or as an IP address. Length: 8 Subnet mask: 255 . 255 . 3 . 0

You will then be asked for a list of any IP addresses that should be excluded from the range, as shown in Figure 7.10. You might need to exclude addresses if you have devices that are manually configured with an address from your range.

NOTE *Manually configured addresses are also known as static addresses because they should never change.*

FIGURE 7.10

Excluding IP
addresses

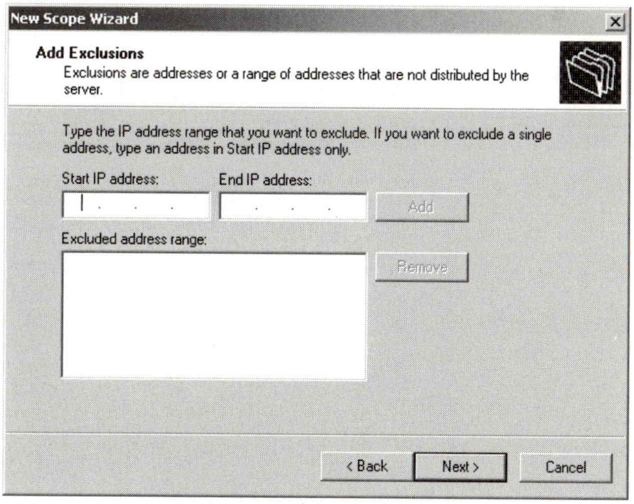

FIGURE 7.10 — New Scope Wizard: Add Exclusions. Exclusions are addresses or a range of addresses that are not distributed by the server. Type the IP address range that you want to exclude. If you want to exclude a single address, type an address in Start IP address only. Start IP address: End IP address: Add. Excluded address range: Remove.

The next screen, shown in Figure 7.11, will ask you for the duration of IP address leases. When a client receives an IP address from the DHCP server, the client "leases" it for this amount of time (the default is eight days). This allows the DHCP server to free up the address if the computer goes offline for an extended period of time.

FIGURE 7.11

Setting lease duration

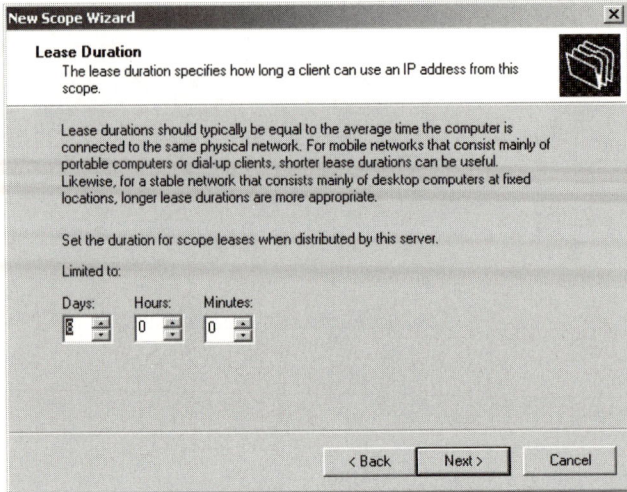

The last screen of the wizard reminds you that you will still have to configure any additional parameters that should be passed to clients by the DHCP server and that you will have to activate, or turn on, the scope before it will function. By selecting the appropriate button, as shown in Figure 7.12, you can choose either to configure these options now or to do so later.

FIGURE 7.12

Additional options

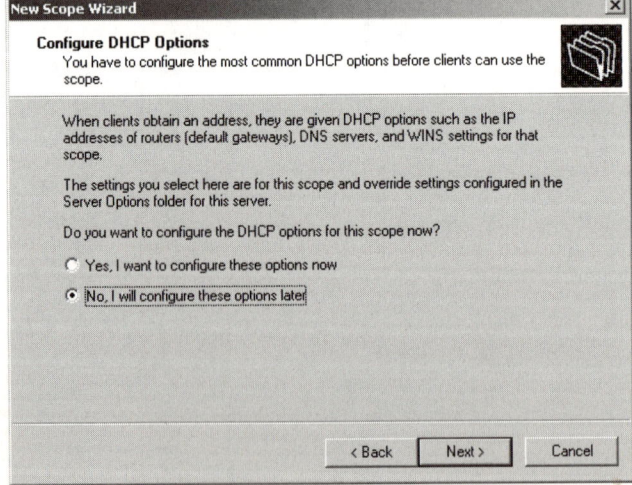

There are numerous options that can be added to a DHCP scope for inclusion in the configuration of clients. Once you have finished creating the scope, it will be added to your view in the DHCP management tool, as shown in Figure 7.13.

FIGURE 7.13

KingTech Lab scope

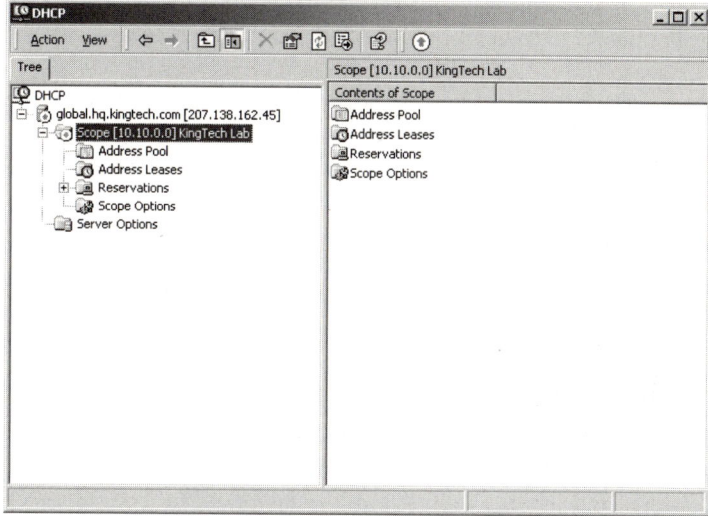

To configure additional parameters, right-click Scope Options and choose Configure Options. The window shown in Figure 7.14 will appear. A complete discussion of the options available is beyond our purposes, but you should be aware that no scope is complete without a few additional options. As an example, you will probably want to configure the default gateway option for most clients.

FIGURE 7.14

DHCP options

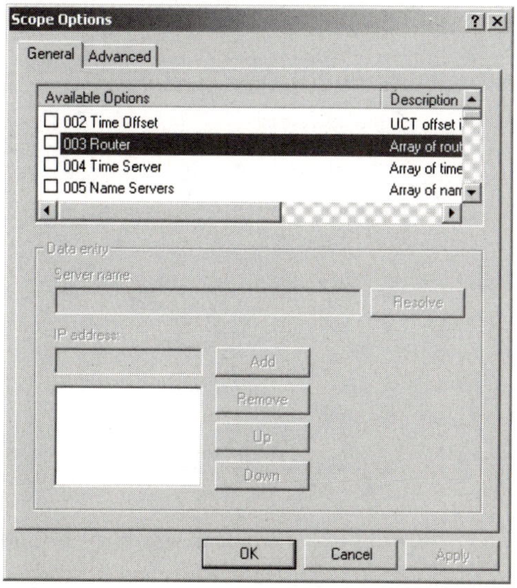

DHCP AUDITING

While DHCP is an established and reliable process, there might be circumstances where you need to track the DHCP actions taken on a server. Perhaps you suspect that unauthorized computers are being placed on your network, or you want to track who is utilizing your services. (Tracking who uses your services can be used to "charge back" to other departments or to justify an increase in the IS budget.) For these and other reasons, the version of DHCP services included with Windows 2000/Windows Server 2003 includes the ability to audit its services.

Once enabled, DHCP logging will create comma-delineated text files that document the actions taken by the DHCP service. Administrators have quite a bit of control over the placement, size, and use of DHCP auditing. You can set the following parameters for DHCP auditing:

◆ Placement of the log files.

◆ Maximum size limit (in megabytes) for all DHCP log files.

◆ How often the DHCP service checks for available disk space before writing new records to a log file. (This one is useful for limiting the overhead on your server.)

◆ Minimum available space restriction that will be used to determine if there is enough disk space available to continue logging. This prevents the DHCP auditing service from filling your hard disks.

To enable DHCP auditing, open the DHCP management tool, click the appropriate DHCP server, and choose Properties on the Action menu. You will be presented with the window shown in Figure 7.15. Make sure that the Enable DHCP Audit Logging option is selected.

FIGURE 7.15

Enabling DHCP audit logging

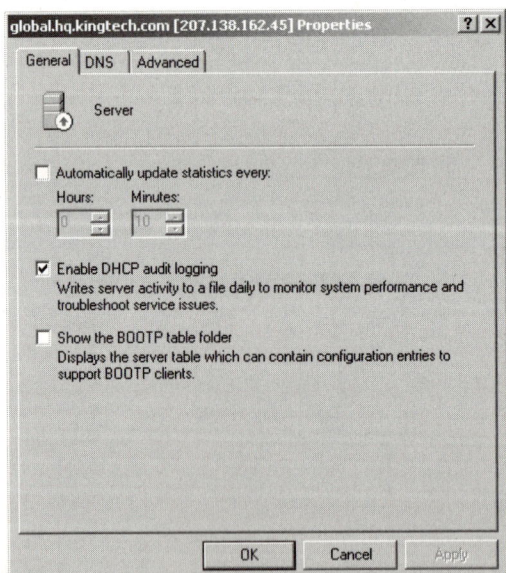

On the Advanced tab, you will be able to set the path to the audit files. This allows you to place them on a partition that has enough available disk space.

Once logging has been available, you will want to check the audit files on a regular basis (and possibly save and print them for record-keeping purposes). Below is the output from a sample log file:

```
Microsoft DHCP Service Activity Log

ID Date,Time,Description,IP Address,Host Name,MAC Address
00,11/26/99,13:34:12,Started,,
55,11/26/99,13:34:43,Authorized(servicing),,WORKGROUP,
01,11/26/99,13:51:10,Stopped,,
```

As you can see, each entry provides an event code that identifies the action taken, the date, the time, and a short description. Notice the trailing commas in our sample—these represent other fields that will be available when appropriate: IP address, host name, and MAC address. Our sample is a very simple example of a DHCP log file. There are numerous event codes that you will want to be familiar with. I've listed a few of the more important ones in Table 7.3.

TABLE 7.3: DHCP Log File Event Codes

EVENT ID	NAME	DESCRIPTION
00	Start	The log was started.
01	Stop	The log was stopped.
02	Pause	The log was paused due to insufficient disk space.
10	Lease	A new IP address was leased to a client.
11	Renew	A lease was renewed for a client.
12	Release	A client has released its IP address.
13	Duplicate	An IP address was found in use on the network.
14	Out of addresses	A lease request was denied because the DHCP server had no available addresses.
15	Denied	A lease request was denied.
50	Unreachable domain	The server was unable to find the domain in which it is configured (probably followed by more events).
51	Authorization succeeded	The service was authenticated and started.
52	Upgraded to Windows 2000/Windows Server 2003	The service was recently upgraded to Windows 2000/Windows Server 2003 so unauthorized DHCP server detection was disabled.
53	Cached authorization	The server was unable to contact AD but used cached information to start.

Continued on next page

TABLE 7.3: DHCP LOG FILE EVENT CODES *(continued)*

54	Authorization failed	(Usually followed by more event records to explain the problem.)
55	Authorization (servicing)	Successful authorization occurred.
56	Authorization failure, stopped servicing	The attempt to authenticate failed so DHCP services were stopped.
59	Network failure	The system was unable to communicate on the network so services were stopped.

While this is not a complete list of the available event codes (more can be found in both the DHCP help file and the Windows 2000/Windows Server 2003 resource kits), it includes the more commonly seen events.

DHCP AND CLUSTERING

In this book, we are concentrating on "Mastering" one very specific topic—Active Directory. Windows 2000/Windows Server 2003 includes many other new technologies, tools, and advances to make your computing environment more efficient, easier to manage, and more reliable. We can only touch on a few of those in this book. One noteworthy new technology is *clustering*. Clustering, available only with Windows 2000/Windows Server 2003 Advanced Server, allows a group of independent computers, known as *nodes*, to work together as a single unit. There are many advantages to a clustering environment: the ability to manage a group of servers as a single entity, improvement in workload distribution, and fail-over in the event of hardware failure.

A basic cluster is made up of two or more computers attached to one or more storage systems. Each of the nodes runs software that allows it to monitor the status of the other nodes in the cluster. In the event of a failure, the cluster can be configured to restart the affected computer's critical services or applications on other computers in the cluster. The system can also be configured to spread the workload of an application or service across multiple machines.

The DHCP service can be configured to take advantage of a clustered environment. This configuration allows you to ensure that DHCP services will be constantly available through cluster fail-over. This type of fault tolerance is critical in today's high-volume, constant-use, mission-critical networks.

To configure DHCP to take advantage of clustering, certain prerequisites must be met. The cluster itself must have a shared disk resource configured and working. You must then create an IP address resource (to act as the IP address of the DHCP service) and a name resource (to represent the DHCP service).

The IP address cluster resource represents the IP address that will be assigned to the DHCP service (as opposed to a specific host). This "virtual IP address" must be statically configured and must be valid on your network. The DHCP service will bind to the virtual IP address instead of the address of a physical device.

Each node in the cluster must also be configured with its own IP address. The DHCP named cluster resource is then configured with the IP address of the preferred node and the IP addresses of any node that should take over in the event of failure. Since the cluster shares a disk subsystem, the DHCP database is available even though the original DHCP server might be unavailable. In the event of a failure, the clustering software will start the DHCP service on another node, and service will continue normally.

THE DHCP CLIENT CONFIGURATION PROCESS

There are four packets involved in the configuration of a DHCP client:

◆ Discover

◆ Offer

◆ Request

◆ Acknowledgment

The process is as follows:

1. As a DHCP client initializes, one of the first things it does is send a *discover packet* out on the wire. This packet is a broadcast, so all computers on the local network will pick it up to determine whether they need to respond.

2. Any DHCP server that receives the broadcast discover packet will respond. Each such server first checks its scope to determine whether it has an IP address available. If so, it marks an address as temporarily in use and sends an *offer packet* to the client. The offer also uses a broadcast packet because the client is not yet configured with an address.

3. The client accepts the first offer that it receives (there might be more than one DHCP server that responds). It broadcasts a *request packet* on the wire. The client uses a broadcast for two reasons:

    ◆ The client still has no IP address, so broadcasts are mandated.

    ◆ This informs all other DHCP servers that the client has made a selection.

4. Finally, the DHCP server broadcasts an *acknowledgment packet* and marks the client's IP address as being in use. Any other DHCP server that responded also receives the broadcast and can free up the address that it had temporarily marked as unavailable.

There are many different types of clients that can take advantage of the DHCP service—all of the modern Microsoft operating systems (Windows 9*x*, Windows NT 4, Windows 2000/Windows Server 2003), of course, plus various other local operating systems currently on the market (e.g., various flavors of Unix, LAN Manager). Each local operating system will be configured to act as a DHCP client in a slightly different manner. Most, however, will have certain things in common. For instance, most will be configured in the same way as other network-related options (text files, some applications, or perhaps as part of the operating system installation). Microsoft products, for example, are configured in the same place as the TCP/IP protocol is configured.

While DHCP does reduce administrative overhead by centralizing control over IP configurations, there are a few problems with the traditional implementation. First and foremost, DHCP is a broadcast-based technology. Most administrators tend to avoid broadcast-based technologies for two reasons:

◆ Broadcast packets place unwanted overhead on the network. Every computer that receives a broadcast packet must open it up to look inside and determine whether it needs to respond. In effect, broadcast packets use processing power on every computer that receives these packets.

◆ More important, most modern routers are configured to prevent broadcast packets from being forwarded to other networks. This means that broadcast packets are limited to the home network of the originating computer. With DHCP, this means you must have a DHCP server on each segment or you must manage some other solution (either configuring your routers to forward broadcasts or installing a DHCP proxy).

Microsoft has integrated AD, DHCP, and DNS to solve these problems, as you'll see later in this chapter.

Domain Name System (DNS)

As we discussed earlier, DNS is the directory used by traditional TCP/IP environments (like the Internet) to resolve user-friendly names into IP addresses. DNS is a group of name servers linked together to create a single namespace.

NOTE   *Remember that a namespace is just a system in which all resources share a common trait. In the case of the Internet DNS, the common trait is the root object.*

The namespace defined by the DNS system is logical in nature—in other words, it presents a group of text files as a single entity. The servers that hold these data files are known as *name servers*. Clients that query the name servers for name resolution are known as *resolvers*.

The DNS namespace itself is presented graphically as a hierarchical system, much like the system of folders and subfolders that makes up a file system. In DNS, each folder would be considered a DNS *domain* (not to be confused with an NT domain). Any domain that contains subdomains would be considered the *parent* of those domains, and the subdomains would be considered *child domains*. (A domain can be both a child of one domain and the parent of another.) Each domain has one, and only one, parent domain. At the top of the structure is the *root domain*; this is the only domain that has no parent. Planning the structure of domains and subdomains is a large part of planning any DNS installation.

Domains are named by the complete path to the root domain. In Figure 7.16, the complete name of the Royal-Tech domain would be `royal-tech.com`.

NOTE   *Notice that the root domain is not included as part of the complete name. It is assumed that every DNS name ends with the root domain.*

FIGURE 7.16

Royal-tech.com

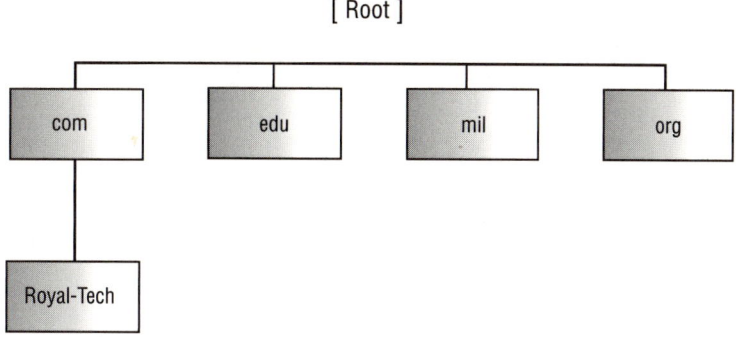

DNS is critical to an Active Directory environment because AD uses DNS to resolve host names into IP addresses for internal functions, such as the replication of the directory database. Without a properly functioning DNS system, AD will not function correctly. In other words, DNS is something that you will have to be very familiar with in order to properly plan your AD-based network.

So What Exactly Is a DNS Domain?

There are two ways to look at DNS domains:

◆ Physically

◆ Logically

You will need to understand both views in order to properly install and configure the DNS service on your Windows 2000/Windows Server 2003.

Physically, a DNS domain is really a piece, or partition, of a large distributed database. It exists as a text file stored on a server that is running DNS services. The file that holds the records for a domain is often called the *zone file*. The syntax used in the zone file is arcane—remember, the same people who designed the original Unix interface created this technology. Luckily, Microsoft's implementation of DNS uses a graphical interface to create the records in the zone file.

NOTE *We'll look at the DNS Manager tool a little later in this chapter.*

Logically, a DNS domain represents a boundary of responsibility. Whoever controls the server on which the zone file is located is responsible for the maintenance of the records within the file. Think of this in terms of the Internet. If there were one big DNS file located on a server somewhere, whoever was responsible for that server would also have to maintain the DNS records for all of the resources on the Internet—a big job, to say the least!

Breaking the DNS namespace into domains allows for a *distributed database*. A distributed database allows for delegation of responsibility. Even if your company is not connected to the Internet, you can still use these principles to distribute both the overhead on your DNS servers and the administrative tasks.

Planning DNS Naming

When planning your DNS naming structure, you must answer a series of questions:

◆ Will this system be attached to the Internet?

◆ How heavily will DNS be used?

◆ How can the system best be organized to provide an intuitive environment for end users?

◆ Which DNS design strategy will you use? (We'll look at a few of the more common designs as we discuss this question.)

We'll look at each question in turn.

WILL THIS SYSTEM BE ATTACHED TO THE INTERNET?

If your system will be attached to the Internet, certain aspects of the DNS namespace will be mandated for you. You will need to register a domain with the Internet Society and follow certain rules governing your configuration. More information about this process can be found at `http://rs.internic.net`.

NOTE   If you are not connecting to the Internet, the same rules will apply, but you will have a little more freedom in naming your domain. Just remember that the name must be unique if you are ever going to connect.

HOW HEAVILY WILL DNS BE USED?

If you expect your DNS system to be heavily utilized, you might want to consider setting up multiple DNS servers. DNS has the ability to replicate zone files from a master DNS server to secondary servers. While changes can be made only to the primary copy, the secondary servers can act both as a fault-tolerant copy of the zone file and as another name server to split the workload of resolving names. This consideration is not applicable if you decide to implement DNS as a portion of AD, a choice we'll discuss in a bit.

HOW CAN THE SYSTEM BEST BE ORGANIZED TO PROVIDE AN INTUITIVE ENVIRONMENT FOR END USERS?

This is probably the hardest part of designing a DNS system. Creating multiple subdomains can ease the overhead on each DNS server (since each server holds less of the database), but this can be confusing for your users. Microsoft recommends that the DNS structure not be more than three to five layers deep and that you keep names as short as possible. This reduces the users' learning curve considerably. Table 7.4 lists the common steps involved in designing a DNS domain structure.

TABLE 7.4: PLANNING YOUR DNS DOMAIN STRUCTURE

LEVEL	EXAMPLE	CONSIDERATIONS
Top	`.com`	This level will usually be mandated by the Internet Society. There are certain top-level names associated with different types of businesses: `.com` for commercial, `.org` for nonprofit organizations, `.edu` for educational facilities, and so on.
Top of local domain	`royal-tech`	This should be descriptive of your company, such as its name, product, or function. This is the domain name you register on the Internet, and it is often not exactly what you want. (My company's name is King Technologies, but the closest I could get was `royal-tech`.)
Child domains	`Sales.royal-tech.com`	The entire purpose of creating child domains is to be able to delegate responsibility for administration of the zone file. Usually these names will indicate the department or organization that is responsible for each.

WHICH DNS DESIGN STRATEGY SHOULD YOU USE?

IF DNS has a fault, it's that it is too "public" in nature. Since DNS is used to located resources (or find the IP addresses of those resources, to be more specific), the DNS database must be available to users *before* they authenticate to that resource. To drive this point home, let's look at an example of how DNS is used.

Imagine you are managing a large corporate network for some company—let's call it RT. RT has registered a domain name on the Internet, RT.com. Your company has a public web server, an FTP site for customers to download patches for your product, and a company e-mail server. We'll concentrate on the e-mail service for this example. When mail needs to be delivered to your e-mail server, the originator of the message submits it to their e-mail server. That e-mail server does a DNS lookup to find a special kind of DNS record: an MX (Mail Exchange) record. The MX record tells the server where to send any messages destined for your domain. Once the other e-mail server has obtained the IP address of your e-mail server, the message(s) can be sent.

So far this seems like a fairly good process, doesn't it? Here's the problem: if the other e-mail server can read the DNS database (and it must to deliver mail to you), then the database must be open, or readable, to unidentified requests (unless you want to make a security entry for everyone who might want to send you mail!). Many DNS implementations include another type of mail-related record known as a *Mail Information* record. This entry contains the e-mail address of the person responsible for maintaining the mail system. Hackers have been known to "read" this record and then impersonate that person by sending e-mail messages with his or her return address, requesting information.

In a Windows 2000/Windows Server 2003/Active Directory environment, DNS can potentially contain quite a bit of information that you might not want available to the public. Windows 2000/ Windows Server 2003 computers, for instance, use DNS to resolve names for other hosts on the network. As each client initializes on the network, it creates its own DNS record so that other devices can locate it. (We'll discuss this DNS feature in a little bit.) In effect, this creates a complete map to your environment—host names, IP addresses, services offered, etc.—that is available to anyone who can access the DNS server.

The bottom line here is that DNS is a necessary part of any Active Directory environment, but its implementation must be given careful consideration. While a few variations exist, there are four basic design strategies for the implementation of DNS in an AD environment that is attached to the Internet:

- Single DNS structure

- Subdomains

- Separate, same-name DNS structures

- Separate DNS structures

Each design has its strengths and weaknesses (although some are weaker than others). We'll discuss each of these choices in the following sections.

Single DNS Structure

In a single DNS structure model, you create and maintain a single DNS domain, named to match the name your company registered for use on the Internet. In this implementation, your DNS server (or servers) are directly accessible from the Internet. Foreign systems access, read, and utilize the information stored with the DNS database to locate resources within your network.

While this is the easiest method to implement, there are some definite security issues inherent in this design. First and foremost, in a Windows 2000/Windows Server 2003 environment, each client registers itself with DNS as it initializes. This means that the DNS database has the IP address of not only your "service" providers (your web server, FTP server, mail server, etc.), but also the IP address of each of your Windows 2000/Windows Server 2003 clients.

Since DNS is by design an open database—accessible by anyone—this means that your internal IP address scheme becomes public knowledge. The first thing that any hacker wants to gather is a list of valid hosts and their associated IP addresses. You should also be aware that DNS is no longer limited to providing IP address resolution for hosts; the relatively new SRV records now allow the resolution of a service, such as domain controller, to an IP address.

In a single DNS structure environment, your entire environment becomes an open book; anyone can obtain a list of valid IP addresses, host names, and even the location of certain key services. Given this, the single DNS structure model is definitely not the suggested strategy for implementing DNS!

Subdomains

Another option is to use DNS subdomains to limit the DNS information that is available to the public. In this scenario, you could either manage the public DNS server yourself or have a service provider maintain it for you.

If you had registered `royal-tech.com` for use on the Internet, you might have one server that held the public records for that domain. You might then create a subdomain, such as HQ, to handle the DNS records for local hosts (such as your client computers).

This design is usually implemented in an environment that contains a DMZ, or screened subnet, that contains their public servers, as shown in Figure 7.17.

FIGURE 7.17

DMZ configuration

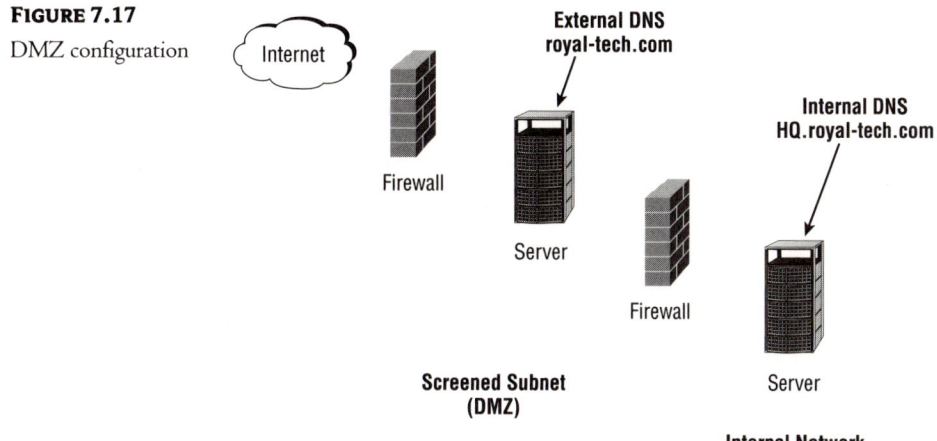

In this type of strategy, the external DNS server resides in the DMZ. This server holds only those records that are appropriate for resources accessible to the Internet: the web server, the mail server, or other public resources. The internal DNS server supports a child domain, for our example, `HQ.royal-tech.com`. It contains DNS records that refer to resources on the internal network.

Clients on the internal network are configured to use the internal DNS server for address resolution. For any external resources, this internal DNS server would query the external DNS server, which would, in turn, query other DNS servers on the Internet.

While this DNS design strategy does work, you should be aware of a couple of drawbacks. First, there is a certain amount of inconvenience for your users. They are probably used to accessing your company's website by using your publicly register domain name, `www.royal-tech.com` in our example. In this scenario, the host names of internal resources would end in `HQ.royal-tech.com`. While this might not be a big problem, it is something you should keep in mind.

Another, and potentially more serious, problem with this design revolves (once again) around the public nature of DNS. The external DNS server, which is accessible to the general public, has a record describing its child domain (`HQ.royal-tech.com`). A good hacker could use that information to query the internal DNS server—potentially gathering information that you might rather remain private.

Separate, Same-Name Domain Structures

I have to admit that this model is my personal favorite. It combines the necessary security with a consistent naming standard. In this scenario, you create two DNS servers, both servicing the same DNS domain (usually the domain you registered for use on the Internet). You do not, however, configure them as primary/secondary. In other words, there will be no replication between the two servers. The DNS server that is accessible to the Internet contains only public DNS records—records that you create and maintain manually. The internal DNS server contains all of your internal resource records (many of which are created dynamically; we'll discuss that later in this chapter).

This design usually works best in an environment using a DMZ. It is set up as shown in Figure 7.18.

FIGURE 7.18

Same-name DNS configuration

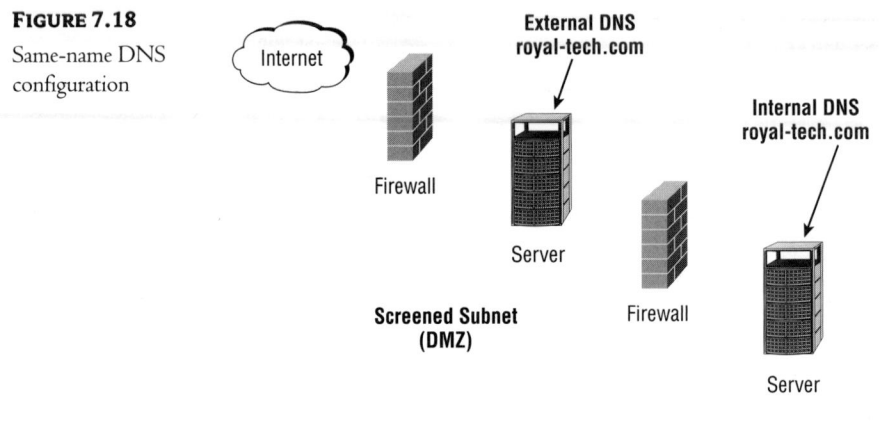

Clients register themselves with the internal DNS server and use it for all DNS queries. For local resources, it provides the IP address to clients. For external (unknown) requests, it is configured to forward to the external DNS server.

While this configuration requires some manual maintenance—you must manually create the DNS records on the external server—the administrative overhead should be fairly low. After all, how many public resources do most environments have? A web server, a mail server, maybe a VPN server—that's really about it.

The nice thing about this design is that it provides a consistent naming standard to your users. All resources fall within the same DNS domain. This design is also great if you currently have an ISP supporting the DNS entries for your registered domain. If that's the case, you really don't have to make any changes to the public side of your DNS strategy. Continue to let the ISP service your DNS records for your public resources, and let them worry about security, hack attempts, Internet-spread viruses, and all of the other issues involved in opening up a server to access from the Internet! You just put up your internal DNS server and use theirs as a forwarder!

Separate DNS Structures

Another philosophy toward a DNS design is to avoid giving anything away: have an external DNS server that supports your registered DNS domain and another internal DNS server that supports a completely different naming strategy, as shown in Figure 7.19.

FIGURE 7.19

Separate DNS structures

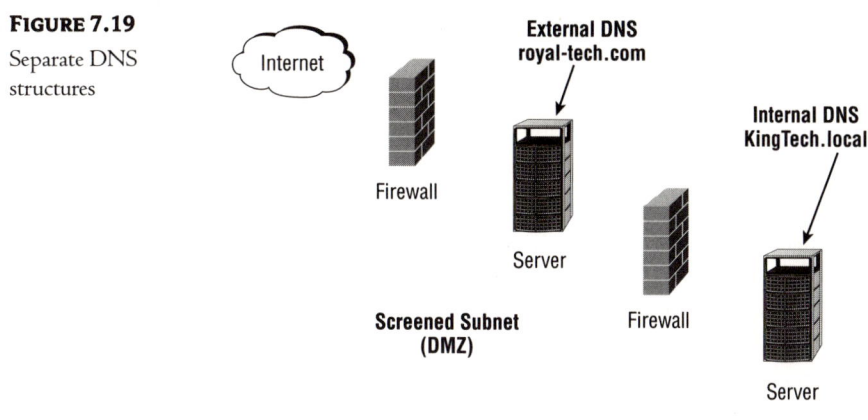

As you can see in Figure 7.19, two different DNS domains are supported: an external domain to handle public resources and an internal domain to handle internal resources.

This design is considered to be the most secure DNS design available. Your internal DNS server is not available to, nor does it communicate with, your external DNS server (except to forward DNS queries from your internal clients out to the Internet).

This model also fits well into another Microsoft suggested security configuration—using a completely separate Active Directory forest (not connected to or involved in any kind of trust with your internal AD forest) in the DMZ. We'll discuss overall design issues later, but for now, this might be the overall best DNS model in the long run.

For those of you who are currently using an ISP's DNS services, this design can be utilized without changing your current DNS solution. Your ISP continues to support your registered domain, and your internal DNS server supports your in-house needs.

Integrating DNS with Active Directory

When you deploy Microsoft DNS services in an AD environment, you have two choices:

- ◆ Use traditional, text-based zone files.

- ◆ Integrate the zone information with Active Directory.

Microsoft suggests the latter option! When you integrate DNS with AD, all zone information is stored in the AD database: a distributed, replicated, fault-tolerant database, which is then stored on all of the AD servers within your organization.

AD can store one or more DNS zones. All domain controllers can then receive dynamic DNS information sent from other Windows 2000/Windows Server 2003 computers. Each Active Directory server can also act as a fully functional DNS authority, updating the DNS information stored on all of your AD servers.

NOTE   *In other words, once DNS has been integrated with AD, every AD server acts as a primary DNS server for all zones. In fact, all zones stored by AD must be primary—if you need to implement old-fashioned secondary zones (perhaps in a mixed DNS environment), you will have to stick with the old-fashioned text-file-based DNS.*

In addition to integration with Active Directory, the Microsoft implementation of DNS provides the following functionality:

SRV Resource Records   These are a new type of record (defined in RFC 2052) that identifies the location of a service rather than a device.

Dynamic Update   Microsoft DNS is more properly called DDNS: *Dynamic* Domain Name System. It is capable of allowing hosts to dynamically register their names with the zone, thereby reducing administrative overhead. (More about this important feature in a little bit.)

Secure Dynamic Update   Windows 2000/Windows Server 2003 Server security is used to authenticate hosts that attempt to dynamically register themselves within the zone.

Incremental Zone Transfer   Only changed data is replicated to other AD servers, rather than a complete replication of the zone as was the case in older versions of DNS.

Interoperability with DHCP   A server running DHCP services can register host names on behalf of its clients. This allows non-DDNS clients to dynamically register with the zone. (More on this topic later, too.)

Active Directory uses DNS to locate domains and domain controllers during the logon process. This is made possible by the inclusion of SRV-type records in the DNS database. Each Windows 2000/Windows Server 2003 domain controller dynamically registers an SRV record in the zone. This record represents the domain Netlogon service on that server. When a client attempts to log on, it will query its DNS server for the address of a domain controller. The bottom line here is that even if you are not going to use DNS for anything else, you will have to install and configure it for the logon process to work properly. Let me stress this one more time—DNS is critical to an AD environment! The worst offender appears to be Microsoft's XP operating system. In some tests, the logon process took as long as eight minutes to complete—try explaining that to your users!

Installing and Configuring DNS on an AD Domain Controller

If you are upgrading an existing NT 4 server that has DNS installed and configured, the installation of AD will automatically upgrade DNS for you. If not, you will have to install DNS as a separate step (part of the Networking Services you installed with DHCP services).

If you have to configure a new DNS server, you will use the DNS Manager tool located in the Administrative Tools group. Here you will see your server listed, as shown in Figure 7.20.

FIGURE 7.20

DNS Manager

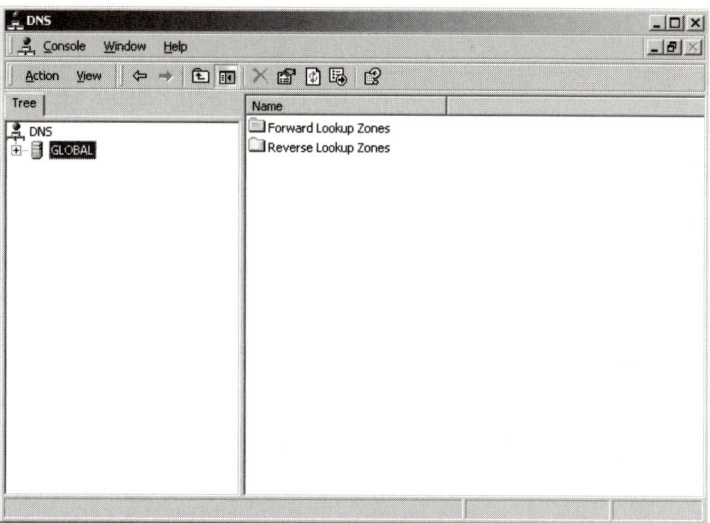

To create a new zone, right-click your server and choose Create a New Zone. A wizard will walk you through the steps involved. While the basic concepts of this process have remained the same, Windows Server 2003 has brought a few changes. You will first be asked whether you would like to have a traditional DNS system (stored in text files) or have DNS integrated into AD, as shown in Figure 7.21. You can also create a *stub zone*, which is used to hold records (but cannot accept changes). This type of server is useful for load-balancing your DNS query traffic. Also note the new option at the bottom of the window: the DNS database can be integrated with Active Directory, but only if the server is also a domain controller.

FIGURE 7.21

New Zone Wizard

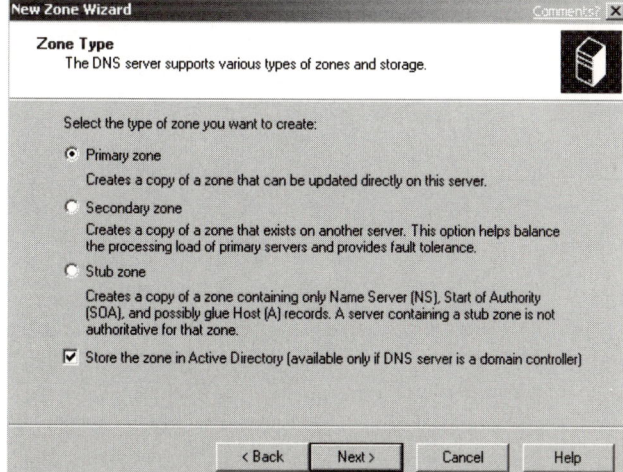

The next screen allows you some very granular control over the replication of the DNS database—whether it should be stored on all domain controllers or on only DNS servers, and in which AD domain they should exist, as shown in Figure 7.22.

FIGURE 7.22

Active Directory Zone Replication Scope

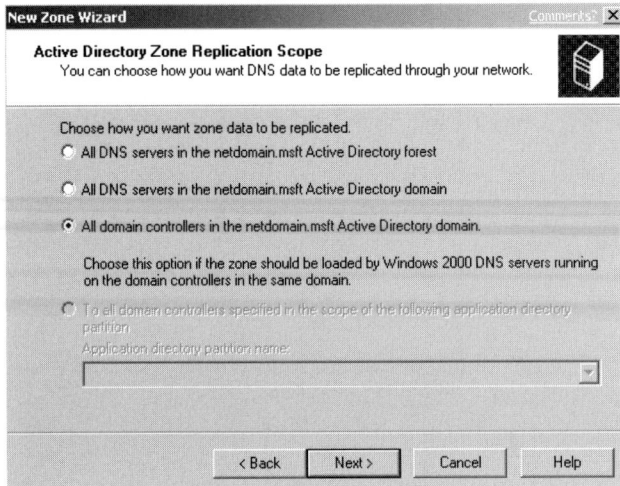

If you are going to create a reverse lookup zone, you are asked for its network address, as shown in Figure 7.23; otherwise you only provide the name for the new domain.

FIGURE 7.23

Configuring a reverse lookup zone

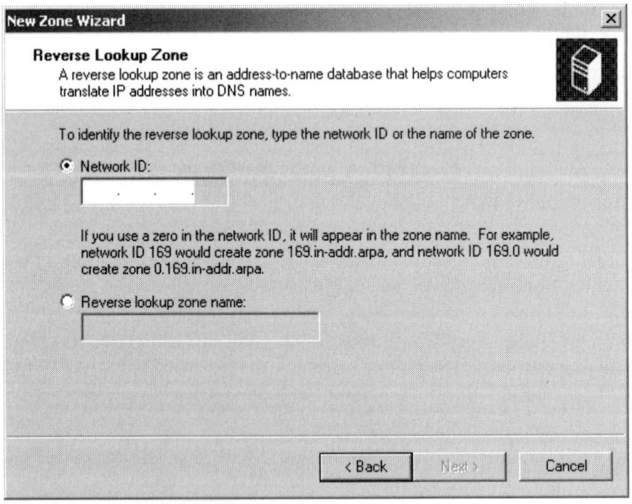

A new addition to the process in the Windows Server 2003 product is the final screen, in which you decide how the system should handle dynamic updates. Your choices are to allow only secure (authenticated) updates, allow any updates, or allow no updates, as shown in Figure 7.24.

FIGURE 7.24

Dynamic updates

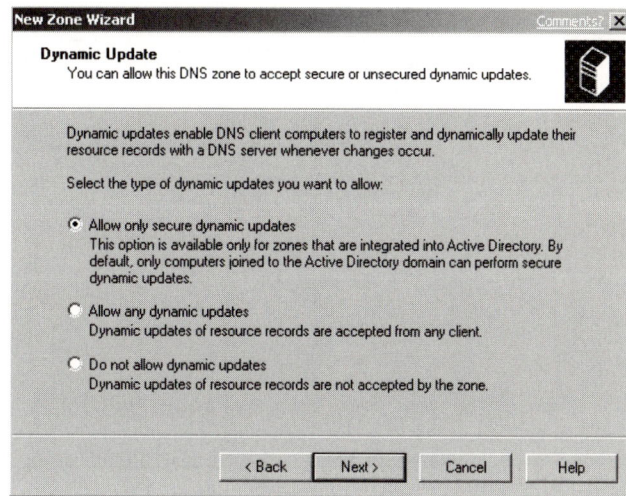

NOTE   *For more information about the specifics of DNS (such as reverse lookup zones), I suggest reading* MCSE: TCP/IP for NT Server 4 Study Guide, *4th ed., by Todd Lammle with Monica Lammle and James Chellis (ISBN 0-7821-2725-8, Sybex, 2000).*

DNS AND DYNAMIC UPDATES

One of the most exciting new features of Windows 2000/Windows Server 2003 DNS is the ability to configure the system to accept dynamic updates from clients. This allows clients to register and dynamically update their DNS records as they boot or as their configuration changes. In older systems, especially those where computers were frequently moved or reconfigured, keeping the DNS files up-to-date was a full-time job. Windows 2000/Windows Server 2003 clients and servers support dynamic updates as defined in RFC 2136—in other words, through an industry standard method.

In Windows 2000/Windows Server 2003 DNS servers, dynamic updates can be enabled or disabled on a zone-by-zone basis. By default, all Windows 2000/Windows Server 2003 clients will attempt to dynamically register themselves with DNS as they boot or as changes occur. Enabling or disabling dynamic updates is a fairly simple process. In the DNS Manager, right-click the zone, choose Properties, and on the General tab configure the Allow Dynamic Updates? option as shown in Figure 7.25.

FIGURE 7.25

Allowing dynamic updates

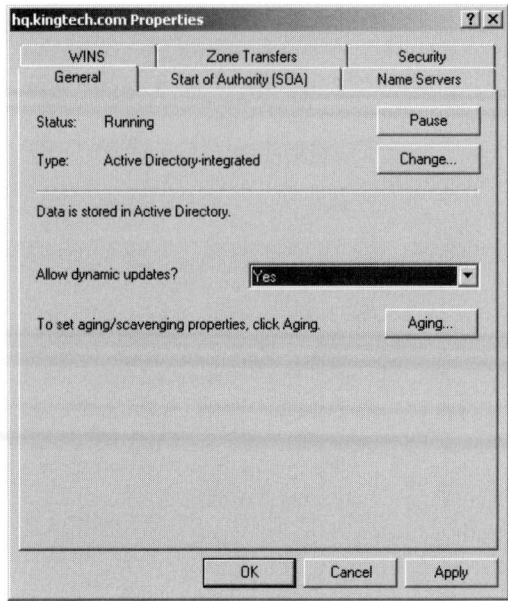

Clients will register themselves using their fully qualified domain name (FQDN). The FQDN is the NetBIOS computer name followed by the text placed in the Primary DNS Suffix of this Computer configuration parameter. This parameter can be found in the Network Identification tab of the System applet in Control Panel as shown in Figure 7.26. (Notice that the computer in the graphic is a domain controller, so this parameter cannot be changed.)

FIGURE 7.26

Fully qualified domain name

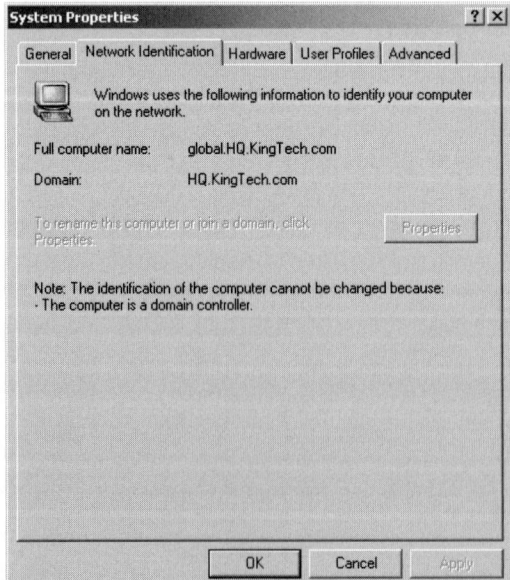

The goal here is to replace the NetBIOS name resolution process that was inherent in earlier versions of Microsoft networking products with DNS name resolution. This brings us to a potential problem: how do we ensure that all machines get registered in the DNS database, and how do we ensure that the proper information is registered?

Combining DNS and DHCP

While the dynamic registration of host records in the DNS database sounds like a great idea, a few potential problems come to mind. First, how do I, as an administrator, ensure that all of my machines (including my non-Windows 2000/Windows Server 2003 clients) get registered? And second, how do I ensure that the proper information is included (such as the correct domain name)?

The secret is to use DHCP. The version of DHCP included in Windows 2000/Windows Server 2003 has the ability to register DNS records on behalf of its clients as they are given their TCP/IP configuration. The process happens as shown in Figure 7.27.

FIGURE 7.27

Dynamic DNS registration by DHCP

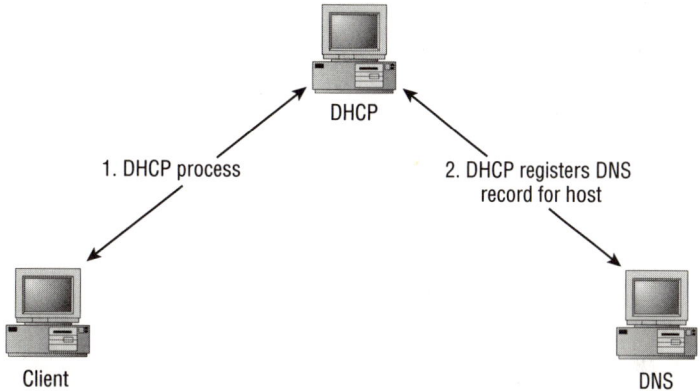

DHCP

1. DHCP process

2. DHCP registers DNS record for host

Client

DNS

First, the client computer and the DHCP negotiate an IP configuration as normal—the four-step process we talked about earlier in this chapter—step number one in Figure 7.27. Once the client has accepted an IP address from the DHCP server, it (the DHCP server) then registers a DNS record on behalf of the client (step number 2 in Figure 7.27).

This system allows for the creation of host records for those clients that are unable to register themselves, such as Windows 95, 98, etc. In other words, your legacy clients can be included in the dynamic registration process.

Why is this important, you might ask? Well, remember our goal here. The goal is to remove dependence upon NetBIOS functions. As long as the only method of resolving those older clients is NetBIOS-based (either through broadcasts or a WINS server), we are stuck with the NetBIOS traffic on our networks. For now though, you'll probably end up with both as you begin the switch to an Active Directory environment.

CONFIGURING THE DHCP SERVER

There are only a couple of configuration issues to be concerned with when using the DHCP server to register DNS records for its clients. The first involves the options you send down to the clients. In a strictly NetBIOS-based environment, the host name and domain set at a client often didn't matter. If you are using DNS to resolve names, though, you have to ensure that the appropriate host name is configured.

One of the options you should set (either at the server or scope level) is that of DNS Domain Name (option number 015). With this option, you can correctly set the DNS domain name that the computer will register, ensuring that the correct name can be resolved to an IP address.

To set the DNS domain name, from within the DNS management tool, choose Scope (or Server) Options. Scroll down the list until you find the DNS Domain Name option, and fill in the correct domain information, as shown in Figure 7.28.

FIGURE 7.28

Configuring the DNS Domain Name option

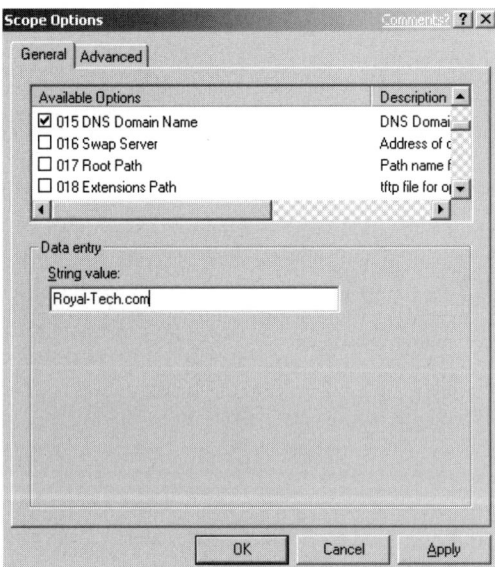

To configure the DHCP server to create or update DNS records for clients, from within the DHCP management tool, right-click the server and choose Properties. On the DNS tab, shown in Figure 7.29, enable the appropriate options for your environment.

FIGURE 7.29

Enabling DHCP to manage DNS host records

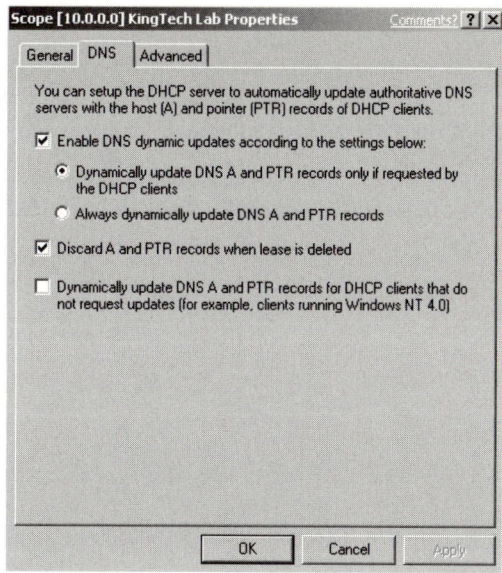

The options available are fairly self-explanatory—the only thing to remember is that you must configure a DNS server for the DHCP server; the system uses that configuration to determine which DNS servers to update.

One Word of Warning

Microsoft has made a very strong case against installing DHCP on a domain controller if you plan on having the DHCP register client host records. Doing so creates a potential security hole that can allow an unscrupulous individual to modify records within your DNS database. *DO NOT DO THIS!*

The problem occurs because the DHCP server service runs under the computer services account of the computer upon which it is installed. In such a scenario, this results in the DHCP server service running under the computer account of a domain controller. This account has access to all records within the DNS zone that it supports... resulting in the security problem.

There are three ways to avoid this issue—two easy and one hard. The easy way is to do two things:

◆ First, do not install the DHCP service on a domain controller!

◆ Second, configure your DNS zones to require Secure Dynamic Updates (this only works if you are using AD-integrated DNS).

The third, hard way:

◆ You can configure your DHCP service to impersonate another account. This can cause problems, so rather than describing the process, here's the article number from the Microsoft Knowledge Base: Q255134. Read the article, and the associated articles, before you decide to use this method!

In Short

A basic level of TCP/IP knowledge is mandatory when configuring AD. Since none of this is really specific Active Directory information, our discussion has been limited to an overview. For a more detailed explanation of the technologies presented, I suggest you read the following title, available from Sybex:

◆ *TCP/IP JumpStart: Internet Protocol Basics* by Andrew Blank (Sybex, 2002)

In the next chapter, we will take a look at NT domains in an AD environment: why they exist, their function in today's networks, and how to manage them.

Chapter 8

Designing the Active Directory Environment

So FAR IN THIS book, I've concentrated on "directory services" without an emphasis on Microsoft's Active Directory. In other words, I've tried to build a basic understanding of directory services in general. I've also discussed a few of the additional network services that are required in a Microsoft-based network, things like DHCP, DNS, and WINS. Now, finally, I think it's time to turn our eyes to Active Directory!

In my opinion, this chapter starts the "cool" stuff. Here we take our foundation (our basic understanding of directory services) and put it all together to build a working environment—an environment in which our IT resources can provide their services in a secure and efficient manner. As far as I'm concerned, designing a great network—whether I'm talking about the infrastructure, the security policy, or the directory service—is where the fun starts!

In this chapter we will take a look at the basic building blocks of AD: domains, trees, and forests. We'll look into a few specific components of every AD environment—specifically servers that perform AD functions. We'll also discuss how you can use AD to organize your network resources for easier management.

By the time we're done with this chapter, you will be able to look over an environment and design a great AD structure—one that works well, doesn't place too much of a burden on any of your network segments, and will be easy to manage in the long run.

A few months ago, I was mentoring a medium-sized company through an upgrade to Windows 2000/Windows Server 2003 and Active Directory. My job was to provide "expert" opinions during the design phase, steer the design team in the right direction, and then leave. If everything went well, I'd never have to touch a keyboard or argue a point to upper management. That would be left to the company's internal IT staff; I was just a resource.

During the project I got to know the IT staff fairly well; there's something about designing a system that forces you to get to know the people you work with—their strengths, their weaknesses, and their prejudices. (We had, for instance, one gentleman in our midst who wanted to skip the whole process and go back to NetWare. While this was a valid opinion, it was not a serious option in this case.) We discussed (or argued, depending upon the topic and the day) every aspect of the AD design—structure, server placement, hardware requirements, client-side upgrades, everything! I made the mistake of allowing a few decisions to be made on the basis of "what Bob said" rather than on a foundation of technical merit—a mistake that, as you'll see, I paid for later!

When we were done, I was invited to sit in on the presentation to upper management. The purpose of the presentation was to describe the reasons for the upgrade, explain the benefits of the move, request a budget for the project, present a tentative schedule, and present the AD design—nothing too technical (this was upper management after all), but enough to make the accountants feel comfortable with the expenses and time involved. I wasn't involved in the presentation; my presence was more of a courtesy than anything else.

The presentation went well, until someone asked a "why" question: why did they need additional servers at a remote site (we had decided on a separate domain for a particular location, mandating two domain controllers to provide redundant authentication services). The IT person who was making the presentation understood why we wanted two servers, but not why we wanted a second domain. The end result was that the project was delayed. The upper management team gathered for a second meeting, and by then they were ready to tear everything apart, looking for ways to cut costs. The moral of this story is, "Don't just talk; understand!"

That's my goal: by the time you are done reading this chapter, you will not only be able to choose the correct (or most correct) design for your AD structure, you'll be able to explain why yours is the best choice!

In this chapter:

◆   Active Directory building blocks: domains, trees, and forests

◆   Active Directory server functions

◆   Active Directory organizational units: planning and designing an OU model

AD Building Blocks

Any discussion of Active Directory design must begin with a discussion of a few key components and concepts. AD structures, or trees, start with the most basic of components: the AD domain. AD domains can then be combined to create a more complex environment, known as an AD tree. AD trees can be connected to create AD forests. Understanding each of these fundamental entities is critical to making the correct design choices for any given environment.

Active Directory Domains

You might recall the definition of a *domain* from earlier versions of NT: a logical grouping of computers and users managed through a central security accounts database. According to this definition, a domain was:

◆ Logically, an organizational grouping of resources allowing central management of those resources

◆ Physically, a database containing information about those resources

Combining the logical with the physical gave you a management or security boundary; administrators for a domain could manage all resources in that domain (database) by default.

The definition of a domain has not changed in Windows 2000 or the Windows Server 2003 products. A domain still represents a group of resources and is still really just a logical description of a database (the Active Directory database). But as we've already discussed, what have changed—and changed considerably—are the types of information that the domain database can contain.

Domains now act as the basic building blocks of an AD environment. As such, AD design starts here, at the domain level. It's imperative that you have a solid, secure, and efficient domain plan in place before you move to any other aspect of creating your Active Directory tree.

THE ROOT DOMAIN

It all starts at the top of the structure with the creation of the first domain in your environment. This domain, the first created, is known as the *root domain*. It acts as the beginning of your AD namespace. All subsequent domains will be influenced by your choices here in the beginning!

The name given to the root domain will act as the base for the name of all domains created later. As each subsequent domain is added to the structure, it will be added somewhere below the root domain. Additional domains are always children of some other domain in the tree. The only domain that is not a child is the root (topmost) domain. This concept is illustrated in Figure 8.1.

FIGURE 8.1

The root domain

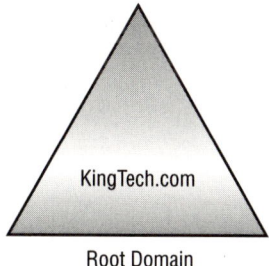

KingTech.com

Root Domain

In Figure 8.1, the first domain for the company King Technologies has been named `KingTech.com`. As the first domain added to the tree, it becomes the root domain. All subsequent domains will follow the naming pattern of `<something>.KingTech.com`, as shown in Figure 8.2.

FIGURE 8.2

Subsequent domains

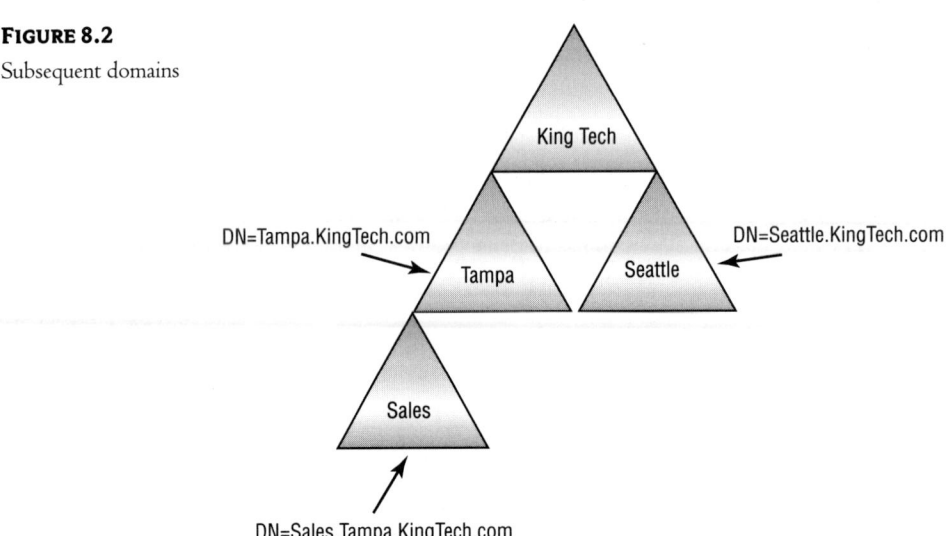

DN=Tampa.KingTech.com

DN=Seattle.KingTech.com

DN=Sales.Tampa.KingTech.com

Figure 8.2 demonstrates the principle of *hierarchical naming*. Each subsequent domain adds the names of all domains above it together to create a distinguished name.

THE DIFFERENCE BETWEEN DNS AND AD DOMAINS

For some reason, our industry often uses the same term to represent completely different things. In Chapter 7 we discussed DNS (Domain Name System) domains. A DNS server is used to resolve TCP/IP host names into IP addresses. A DNS domain represents a piece of the overall DNS namespace. DNS is a service used to find resources: A process submits a host name, and DNS attempts to find a record that matches. If a match is found, DNS returns the appropriate IP address to the requestor. As such, we could define a DNS domain as *a bounded portion of a DNS namespace used to find IP host information.*

In this chapter, we will discuss NT domains, concentrating on how they relate to Active Directory. For our purposes, we can define an NT domain as *a bounded area of an AD namespace used to organize network resources.*

Comparing the two definitions, we can make two generalizations:

◆ DNS domains are for finding resources.

◆ AD domains are for organizing resources.

I know that we have said that the Active Directory database is used to "find" resources, so let me clarify. While AD holds information about resources on the network, it (or the client, depending upon the process involved) uses DNS to find and resolve distinguished names into IP addresses. In other words, AD and DNS work together to return connection information to users or to other processes that request such information, as you can see in Figure 8.3.

FIGURE 8.3

AD and DNS work together to provide services.

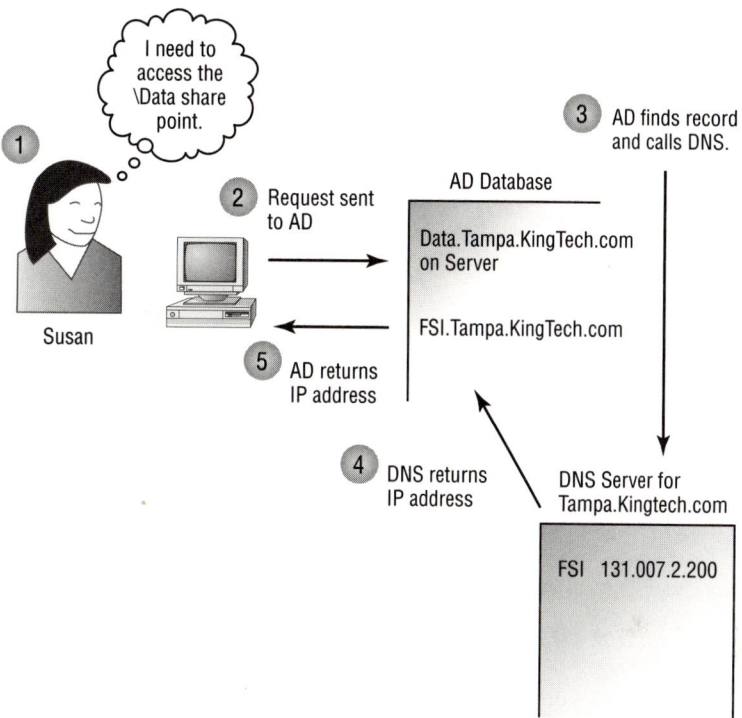

In Figure 8.3, Susan uses the AD database to find a share point. Here is what happens:

1. Susan browses the directory and clicks the \Data resource.

2. The client software sends a request to an AD server.

3. The AD server searches the directory database for the resource record. In the record, it finds the DNS name of the server on which the share point is located. AD queries DNS for the IP address of the appropriate server.

4. DNS searches its database for the record for server FS1.Tampa.KingTech.com. Once it finds this record, DNS returns the IP address to AD.

5. AD returns the IP address of server FS1.Tampa.KingTech.com to the client.

At this point, the client software can establish a connection with the server using the appropriate TCP/IP technologies.

NOTE *DNS is a critical piece of the AD puzzle. Without DNS, AD cannot resolve user requests into IP addresses of resources. To put this into perspective, AD will not allow itself to be installed without DNS: either by access to an existing DNS server or through the installation of DNS on the first AD server. For this reason, you must have a good grounding in DNS before installing and configuring Active Directory.*

USING DNS TO FIND A DOMAIN CONTROLLER

One of the most important uses of DNS in an Active Directory environment is that of locating domain controllers. Remember that one of the goals of moving to a DNS-based name resolution process was to reduce or eliminate our dependence on NetBIOS broadcast technology. On a network that consists of only Windows 2000/Windows Server 2003 (or newer) computers, NetBIOS and WINS traffic can be completely eliminated.

Since finding a domain controller is critical to the process of logging in, let's take a closer look at the process.

1. First, the client runs a process called the Locator, which initiates a DsGetDcName query at the local Netlogon service. This is done through a Remote Procedure Call (RPC) that passes information about the client's configuration (domain membership and IP configuration) to the Netlogon service.

2. The Netlogon service uses this information to look up a domain controller for the specified domain. This can be done in a couple of different ways, depending upon the type of name submitted—DNS or NetBIOS.

    ◆ If the name presented to the Netlogon process is a NetBIOS name, the older name resolution process is used. This allows backwards compatibility in environments that have not yet upgraded to Active Directory. In this case, either a broadcast is performed or, if configured, a WINS server is queried. In either event, this is not the process we prefer—remember, we're trying to get rid of NetBIOS-based procedures!

    ◆ If the name presented to the Netlogon process is a DNS host name, then the Netlogon service queries the DNS server for SRV and A records for the appropriate domain. The query takes the following format:

    `_service._protocol.DnsDomainName`

    ◆ Since Active Directory services utilize the Lightweight Directory Access Protocol (LDAP) services over TCP, the query identifies that service and protocol:

    `_ldap._tcp.DnsDomainName`

3. After receiving a list of domain controllers from the DNS server, the Netlogon service sends a datagram to each domain controller.

4. The domain controllers respond by sending their operational status to the Netlogon service on the client computer. This information is cached by the Netlogon service so that the process will not be required on subsequent requests. (This helps to ensure the consistent use of the same domain controller.)

5. The client establishes an LDAP session with a domain controller. As part of that process, the domain controller identifies which AD site the computer belongs to (based upon the IP subnet of the client). If the domain controller is in the same site as the client, authentication begins. If not, the client again queries DNS, looking for a domain controller in its site. That query follows the format:

```
_LDAP._TCP.dc.msdcs.DomainName
```

The bottom line here is that the client uses DNS to find a list of domain controllers for its domain. Part of the process attempts to locate a domain controller "near" the client, using AD site information (which is based upon IP subnetting). Once an appropriate domain controller has been located, communication has been established, and any secure channels have been created, the logon and authentication processes can begin.

So, What Exactly *Is* a Domain?

It seems that every book I read about NT and Windows 2000/Windows Server 2003 wants to sidestep this question: what is a domain? The answers are often mystical—a "grouping of computers and resources" begin the most common—and they really don't give you any concrete information. Different authors also have different definitions and uses for domains. Well, here's mine:

> *A domain represents a database. That database holds records about network resources—things like computers, users, groups, and other things that use, support, or exist on a network. In Windows 2000/Windows Server 2003 and later releases, the domain database is, in effect, Active Directory.*

Simple? I hope so. Taking this view of Active Directory makes it easier (and less intimidating) to work with. I've never liked those references that try to make AD into some magical management environment. The bottom line is that AD is a database—a complex, secure, and replicated database—but just a database.

Things to Consider about Domains

As with any component of a complex system, you have to consider certain key concepts when dealing with domains. These include:

- Number of objects
- Replication traffic
- Domains as security boundaries
- Language
- Security policies

While some of these might not make sense right now, they will when put in context with our upcoming discussions.

Number of Objects Domains really have no limit to the number of objects they can support. To put this another way, the domain database in NT 4.0 had a physical limit to the number of records that it could hold—approximately 40,000. While the limit could be expanded under the right circumstances, the 40,000-object limit was the Microsoft-approved maximum number of objects that the database could efficiently contain. In reality, in most circumstances, 40,000 users, computers, and groups in a single NT domain would not have been realistic; the "workable" limit was much lower!

The Active Directory database, on the other hand, has no real limitations to the number of objects (records) it can contain and efficiently support. Tests have been conducted in which the Active Directory domain contained millions of user objects and the associated support objects, such as computers and groups. In all of these tests, the database performed efficiently. Of course, the hardware required to manage such a large database is extreme, but if you've got millions of users, you probably have a fairly large budget anyway!

Replication Traffic All domain controllers within a domain must contain the same database. In other words, a replication process is used to synchronize any changes made to the database to all domain controllers for the domain. The net effect is more network traffic.

The larger the database (meaning more user, computer, group, and other types of records), the more potential replication traffic will be generated. A corollary to this is that the more domain controllers you have, the more replication traffic will travel through your network.

Domains As Security Boundaries Since a domain represents a separate database, the domain boundary is often seen as a built-in security boundary. Administrators of a domain are limited (by default) to the management of resources within their own domain.

While administrative accounts can be given privileges in more than one domain, this is a manual configuration—in other words, a conscious decision, rather than a default.

Language Considerations Within a domain, servers can be configured for a single language: French, German, etc., although English is supported by all installations. This means that if your company crosses international boundaries, you might need additional domains so that local administrators can manage their resources in their native tongue.

Security Policies While we haven't discussed security policies yet (that's coming up in Chapter 11), we need to touch upon them in our discussion of domains. Certain policy elements are "domainwide." In other words, certain security decisions must be made with an eye toward the entire domain, rather than a subset of the domain. These include some very common settings, things like password policies (complexity, length, and lifetime), account lockout policies (when and for how long an account will be locked due to unsuccessful logon attempts), and Kerberos v5 policies (ticket lifetimes, renewal, and logon restrictions).

The bottom line here is that if you have different areas of your environment in which these policy elements need to differ, you might be forced to create multiple domains.

Active Directory Trees

The general philosophy of directory service–based environments is to see the directory as a network-wide component. Our discussion so far of directory services has always implied a single database holding information about resources throughout the network. In some cases, maybe even most, this "single database" approach will make sense. Let's face it, the AD database can easily hold hundreds of thousands of records. Most of us will never work in an environment in which the physical capabilities of the database itself are pushed even close to its limits. What I'm trying to say here is that in a majority of environments, a single AD domain will be sufficient. This is a big difference from the days of Windows NT!

There are, however, certain conditions in which multiple domains will be mandated. As we saw earlier, the X.500 recommendations (upon which Active Directory is based) specify a method of breaking the database into smaller pieces, known as *partitions*, and distributing them across multiple servers. The X.500 recommendations also include a methodology for replicating changes to copies stored on multiple servers. Logically, we can still see the database as a cohesive whole, containing information about resources throughout our entire network. Physically, though, each domain acts as a partition of the overall "logical" database, as shown in Figure 8.4.

FIGURE 8.4

Each domain is
a partition of the
logical AD database.

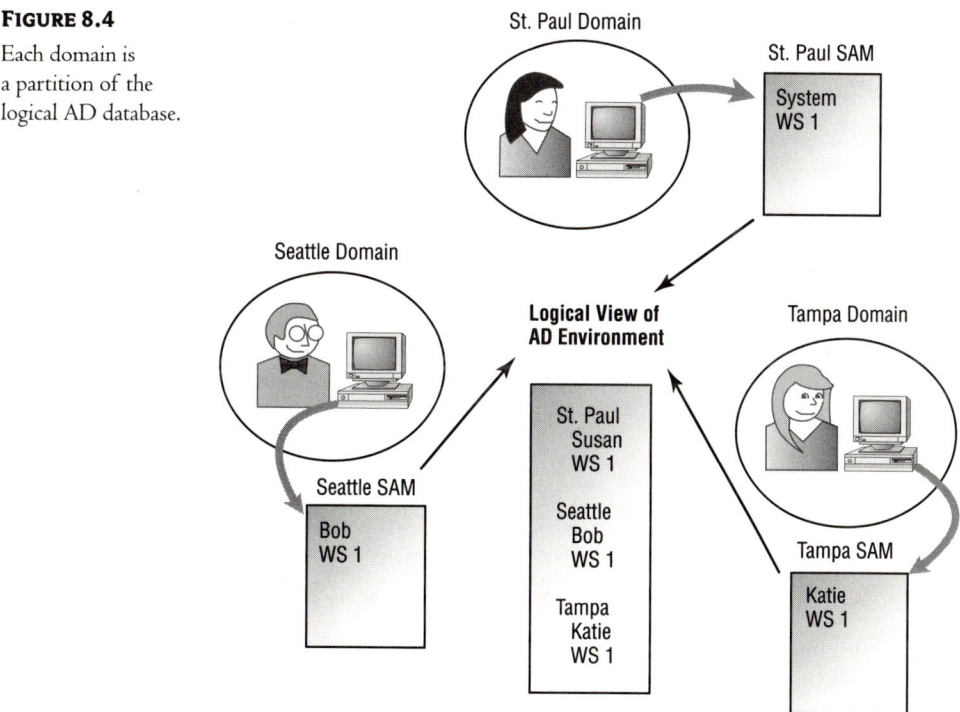

Breaking the database into smaller pieces places less overhead on each Active Directory server. It also grants the administrator more control over the amount and route of traffic generated by the database replication process. Consider the environment depicted in Figure 8.5. Since there is only one domain defined, each AD server holds records for every resource in the enterprise. If a new printer is installed in Seattle, information about that printer will have to be updated on every AD server in the entire company. The same holds true for *every* change made to the database. If user Katie in Tampa changes her password, that change will have to be replicated to every AD server across the entire network. While this design is functional, it is probably not the best design possible for the network.

FIGURE 8.5

Company XYZ domain structure

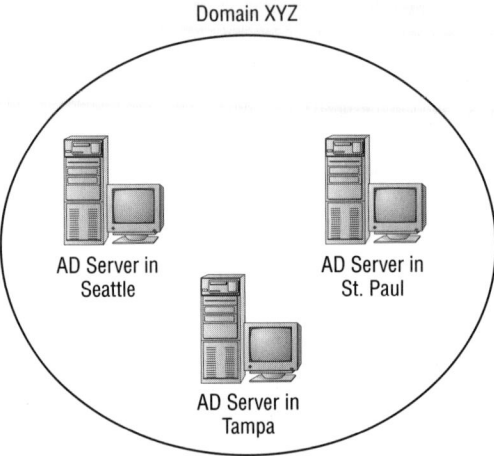

The thing to remember here is that within a domain, all changes to the database must be replicated to all domain controllers. Conversely, there is no replication between domain controllers in different domains. Limiting the scope of the domain would limit the impact of any changes made.

The KingTech Company has come up with a much better design, as you can see in Figure 8.6. In this design, each server contains records only for objects that are in its own geographic area. Notice that this design has two benefits:

♦ It limits the amount of traffic generated between the two locations.

♦ It ensures that no server is overburdened by holding records that are of no real value to its purpose.

We'll look at various design strategies in more detail later in this chapter.

FIGURE 8.6

KingTech domain structure

Reno Domain

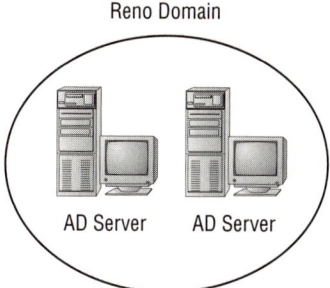

AD Server   AD Server

Fresno Domain

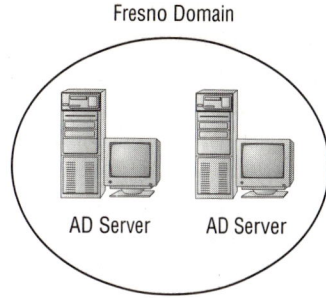

AD Server   AD Server

   This concept of creating multiple domains brings us to the topic of this section: creating Active Directory trees. We've already discussed the importance of the first, or root, domain. It sets the beginning of the namespace for the AD tree—in other words, the name given to the topmost, or first, domain in the structure will impact the name of all subsequent domains. As you create additional domains, they will join the AD tree somewhere below the root domain, forming a treelike structure (with the root at the top).

   Remember that each domain represents a separate directory database. Each database also acts as a security boundary and is individually protected against unwanted access (we'll discuss AD security in Chapter 10). As I mentioned earlier, for instance, administrators of one domain are not necessarily administrators of any other. But you can set up your system so that a small group of administrators have security privileges over the entire structure, or you can give a group administrative abilities in a select few domains. You can also give users permission to access resources throughout the tree. This implies that there is some mechanism that allows security to be managed and maintained between domains. This mechanism is known as a *trust*.

TRUSTS BETWEEN DOMAINS

Domains not only act as partition boundaries for the database; they also act as boundaries for various administrative functions. In our review of NT 4 domains, we discussed the concept of *trusts* between domains. Put simply, a trust is a secure connection between two domains. Without some sort of trust, domains will not communicate and cannot share resources. This is also true in Windows 2000/Windows Server 2003—except that trusts are created automatically and they work a little differently.

   The creation of a trust does not imply any specific permissions—only the ability to grant permissions. This is an important concept. Many NT administrators were overly concerned about the security ramifications of creating trusts; they assumed that once the secure path had been created, some "rights" would inherently exist. This is not true. The trust itself grants nothing. All it does is allow the trusting domain's administrator access to the domain accounts database of the trusted domain (so that accounts from the trusted domain can be granted permissions to resources in the trusted domain).

Trusts in NT 4 and Earlier

As a quick review, let's take a look at how trusts worked in NT 4. In version 4 there were two types of trusts: one-way and two-way. In Figure 8.7, the Tampa domain trusts the Reno domain. In effect, this means that accounts that exist in the Reno domain can be granted permissions to access resources in the Tampa domain. *But not vice versa!* A one-way trust implies that only one of the domains is trusted and only the trusted domain can access resources in the other.

FIGURE 8.7

One-way trust

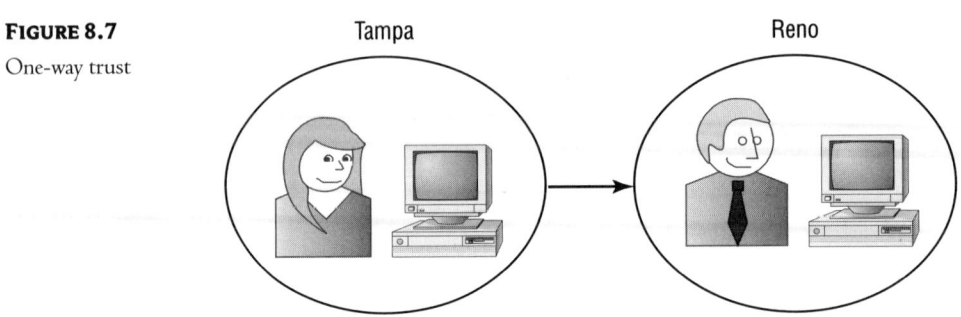

In Figure 8.8, a two-way trust has been established between the Tampa and Reno domains. In this configuration, accounts from both domains can be granted permissions in either domain.

FIGURE 8.8

Two-way trust

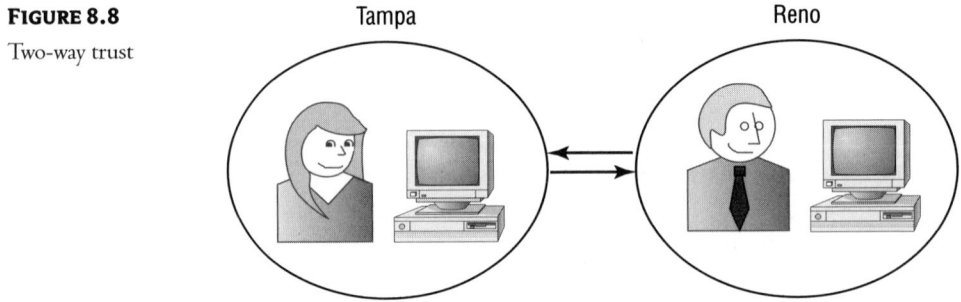

In NT 4 and earlier, trusts were nontransitive. This meant that trusts had to be explicitly defined between any two domains. As an example, look at Figure 8.9. In this figure:

- The Tampa domain trusts the Reno domain.

- The Reno domain trusts the St. Paul domain.

- The Tampa domain does not trust the St. Paul domain.

NOTE   *To put it simply, if A trusts B, and B trusts C, this does not imply that A trusts C.*

FIGURE 8.9

Nontransitive trusts in NT 4

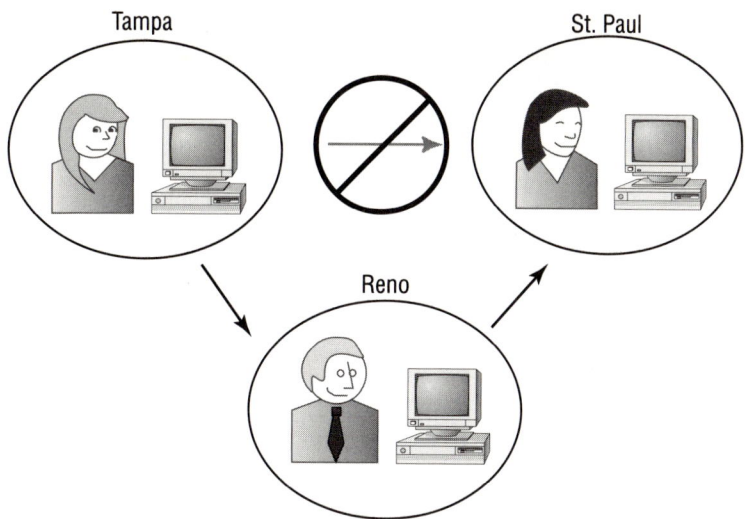

Trusts in Windows 2000/Windows Server 2003

In Windows 2000/Windows Server 2003, trusts have changed quite a bit from what we've just seen. First, in earlier versions of NT, no trusts were defined automatically. All trusts had to be set up manually. In Windows 2000/Windows Server 2003, a two-way trust is established between every domain and its parent domain in the tree, as shown in Figure 8.10.

FIGURE 8.10

Windows 2000/ Windows Server 2003 default trust configuration

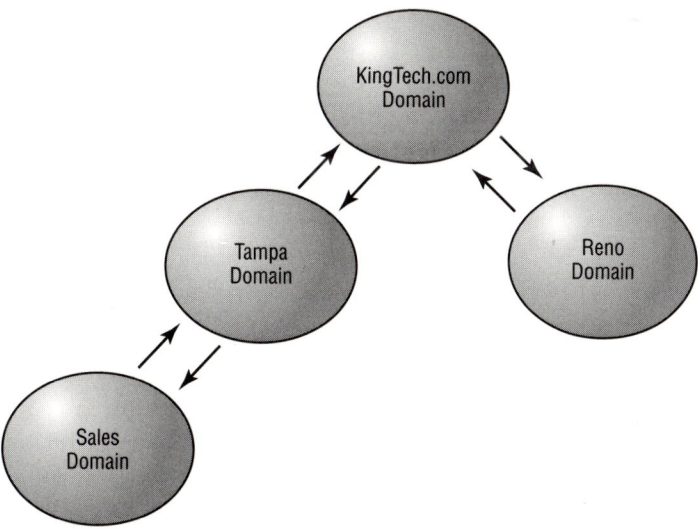

The second (and probably more significant) change in trust relationships in Windows 2000/Windows Server 2003 is that trusts are now transitive. To put it another way, if A trusts B, and B trusts C, then A trusts C. Take another look at Figure 8.10.

NOTE *With transitive trusts, every domain in the tree trusts every other domain by default.*

The result of these changes is that every domain within the tree trusts every other domain. This rids administrators of the headache of designing and manually configuring an environment in which users can be given permissions to all resources within the enterprise.

SPECIAL TRUSTS

While the default trusts will suffice in most Active Directory environments, a few conditions might mandate the manual creation of what I call "special trusts." These manually created trusts act just like the trusts in Windows NT 4; they are nontransitive in nature, must be manually created and maintained, and imply a one-way agreement (although you can create two one-way trusts between domains to allow for a two-way trust relationship).

Explicit Trusts

Explicit, or short-cut, trusts help to alleviate one of the drawbacks to a hierarchical database structure. Take another look at Figure 8.10. Notice that for a user in the sales domain to access resources in the Reno domain, the request must pass through a series of trusted relationships: the trust between sales and Tampa, the trust between Tampa and `KingTech.com`, and, finally, the trust between `KingTech.com` and Reno.

This path of trusts actually defines the path that a request must take between the two domains. Let's say that a user in sales wants to print to a printer in Reno. The user is authenticated to a local (sales) domain controller. To "find" the printer, the user opens their network neighborhood and begins searching through the AD structure. Ultimately, they submit a request for the printer in Reno—let's call it `P1.Reno.KingTech.com`.

The user's request is submitted to their local domain controller (a domain controller for the `sales.Tampa.KingTech.com` domain). This domain controller has no information about the resource (remember, domain controllers only have records for resources defined within their own domain). The sales domain controller recognizes, however, that the distinguished name includes the name of its parent domain (`Tampa.KingTech.com`). It submits the request to a domain controller in the Tampa domain. The same process occurs there; the Tampa server does not recognize the resource, but it realizes that the name includes the name of its parent domain and submits the request to a server in the `KingTech.com` domain. This server, in turn, submits the request to a domain controller in the Reno domain.

As you can see, the process of authenticating a sales user to a printer in Reno involves communication with at least four domain controllers—one for each domain between the user and the resource. (This process is often called "walking the tree.")

If users in sales use resources in Reno on a regular basis, you might want to eliminate this network overhead by creating an explicit trust between sales and Reno. Now, when the request is submitted to the sales domain controller, it knows about the Reno domain, through the establishment of the explicit trust. It can submit the request for authentication directly to the Reno domain controller.

The creation of explicit trusts is not a common design feature. Let's face it, one of the precepts of "good" design is to place users and their resources in the same domain whenever possible. In reality, the creation of a short-cut trust does not reduce network or server overhead by much, but in a busy environment (where the domain controllers are overworked or network bandwidth is limited), they can help to create a more efficient environment.

Explicit trusts should only be created when resources from one domain will be accessed on a regular basis by users from another domain. An explicit trust is not necessary between two domains that share a parent-child relationship, since the default trust is already in place between them.

External Trusts

External trusts allow access from domains that are not part of your AD environment. They function exactly as Windows NT domains: they are manually configured, nontransitive, and one-way in nature (although, once again, two one-way trusts—one in each direction—form a two-way trust).

There are two major uses for an external trust. The most common is to create a trust between your "new" AD domain and your legacy NT domains. The trust can go in either direction, or both. Most of the time, this is a temporary situation that is implemented during the upgrade to Windows 2000/Windows Server 2003 and Active Directory. You upgrade a central domain (or create a new Windows 2000/Windows Server 2003 domain) and then create two-way trusts between your new environment and your old NT domains. This allows you to slowly upgrade your domains without losing access to resources. Most commonly, you upgrade your account domains first, so the trusts are one-way, with the old NT resource domains trusting the accounts in the new AD domain.

Another use for an external trust is to grant external environments access to your AD resources. Say, for instance, a certain vendor makes parts for your widget. Traditionally, you would have to let them know how many parts you need each time you place an order. If they have an AD tree (or a legacy NT domain environment), you can create a one-way trust in which your domain trusts their domain. After the trust is established, you can give their users permissions to your resources—perhaps to your production schedule so that they can proactively monitor your stock, sending you a new shipment when appropriate.

This concept of "extranets" has become quite popular lately. Personally, I'm not sure I like giving some external entity permissions to my resources. I have no idea about their environment's security policies, the trustworthiness of their employees, or even what types of connections they allow. Personally, I prefer a nice authenticated-access website, with pages that are dynamically created through calls to my (secured) SQL server.

I had a client who created a trust between their AD domain and a vendor's AD NT domain. It took about a month before they realized that the vendor's IT staff (or whoever was managing their network) had no idea how security should be implemented. It wasn't long before everyone—not just employees of the other company—was accessing my client's production databases. Needless to say, one of my first actions was to kill the trusted relationship and come up with another way for them to access the information they needed. We ended up using an authenticated website, with SSL connections—just as easy to accomplish, and less susceptible to unauthorized use.

WHEN TO USE A NEW DOMAIN

A Windows 2000/Windows Server 2003 domain can grow to one million objects, or until the database takes more than 17 terabytes of storage space. This means that most companies will not be forced into a multiple-domain configuration by the limitations of the directory. Multiple domains will be used to facilitate solutions to common network problems. Here are the primary reasons for creating an additional domain:

- When you need decentralized management of users or resources where administrators do not want to share control of a domain. In other words, in an environment in which the administrative tasks are distinctly split between areas. You might, for instance, have a corporate IT staff that handles most administrative tasks, but the research and development department wants complete and autonomous control over their own resources (and has their own IT staff).

- When you want to make delegation easier in cases of diverse environments, such as a network in which different languages are spoken. Remember that Windows 2000/Windows Server 2003 is available in many languages. Servers within a single domain must be of the same language version (other than the English version that can be mixed with any other language).

- If unique, domain-level security policies are mandated. Certain security policies are applied to a domain as a whole—password, account lockout, and Kerberos policies must apply to an entire domain as opposed to a subset of a domain.

- When you want to control directory replication traffic (for instance, across a WAN link with limited bandwidth). Replication traffic only occurs between domain controllers within the same domain. If you want to limit replication traffic across a link, have the servers on each side be members of different domains.

- If you will have over one million objects in the database. Even this limit has been stretched in the lab; in reality, this is not a common reason to create additional domains. (How many businesses have more than a million objects?)

- When you are upgrading from an earlier version of NT that was configured as a multidomain environment. Even this is usually a temporary fix; in most cases, the additional domains will be merged into larger AD domains at a later time.

- When you are preparing for future changes to the company.

- If the default trust relationships do not meet your needs.

To be truthful, new domains will usually be created to control network traffic. A prime concern in most wide area networks is bandwidth limitations on the wide area links. Controlling the traffic placed on these links is the driving force behind most directory designs. Once this consideration is taken into account, the administrator is left with the task of designing the OU model for each domain. We'll discuss OU models a little later in this chapter.

Active Directory Forests

In our discussions so far, we have limited ourselves to environments with only one AD tree. In a single-tree environment, each domain is added to the structure as a new partition of a single database to create the tree, as shown in Figure 8.11.

FIGURE 8.11

Single-tree environment

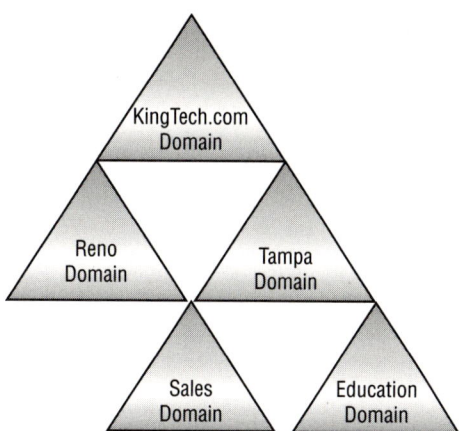

This configuration works well in most environments, but it has one big limitation: all objects within the structure *must* be a part of the same namespace.

NOTE   *Remember that within a namespace, all objects have some common component to their name.*

In the case of KingTech, the name of every object will end in `.KingTech.com`. Therein lies the problem: what if a company has a reason for some objects to belong to one namespace and other objects to a different namespace? Such a situation might occur when an environment requires a substantial amount of separation between domains that must still share resources. For instance, partnerships or joint ventures might require that two distinct businesses share resources. These two companies would each have a unique namespace, so both could not fall under a single root domain.

Two separate AD trees can establish a relationship, thereby forming an AD *forest*. A forest is just a collection of trees that share a common schema and Global Catalog server (I'll discuss the Global Catalog in a few pages). The trees establish a two-way transitive trust relationship between their root domains, as shown in Figure 8.12.

FIGURE 8.12

An AD forest

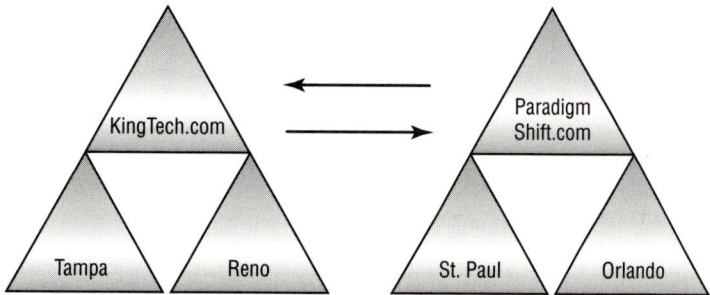

Once you've established this relationship, you have formed a forest. A forest allows you to do the following:

◆ Search across all domains through a common Global Catalog server.

◆ Maintain existing DNS names (during an acquisition, for instance).

WHEN TO CREATE A FOREST INSTEAD OF A SINGLE TREE

This is actually a fairly simple decision. If your company requires multiple namespaces, then separate trees are mandated. Once this decision has been made, you must then decide if the trees should create a formal relationship (create a forest) or if a single external trust will suffice. Remember, an external trust is nontransitive.

Ask yourself how much interaction occurs between the two environments. If the two namespaces represent two divisions or separate companies that fall under the umbrella of a single controlling company, then a forest is the best way to go. If the entities represented by the two namespaces are in fact completely separate companies—for example, business partners—then an external trust might suffice.

Here's the crux of the problem: the trees within a forest must share a couple of things—a common Global Catalog and a common schema. We've discussed the function of the AD schema; it defines the structure of the AD database. Since trees within a forest must share a common schema, then any changes to the schema must be replicated to all domains within the forest. This doesn't sound like too big an issue until you realize that someone must have Schema Admin rights to the schema of the overall structure. If all the domains fall within a single parent company, this is usually not too big an issue. If, however, the domains truly represent separate business entities, then this often becomes a bone of contention. Not many IT departments want some "outside group" of administrators to have that level of access to their environment. We'll discuss the function of the Global Catalog in a little bit, but the same issue exists there—within a forest, the common Global Catalog must be accessible to someone.

Microsoft's marketing literature suggests creating a forest of the AD trees of your company and one or more trees of your business partners or vendors. I've tried this a couple of times in the field, and it usually becomes a political minefield. Neither company wants to give the other company's IT department the ability to change their schema. If one company, for instance, decides to install Microsoft Exchange 2000 Server (a program that requires changes to the standard AD schema), then those changes must be replicated to the schema of all other trees in the forest. If those changes are done incorrectly, then the schema of all trees within the forest can be adversely affected.

NOTE *Exchange 2000 Server was probably a bad example here since its schema change routine is extremely stable. Instead, imagine some hotshot administrator who decides to create their own object class—without having the expertise to do so correctly. If that administrator is a member of the Schema Admins group, then their mistake could bring down every AD tree in the forest!*

Don't let me scare you away from creating forests when appropriate! If your company needs to support multiple namespaces and wants to delegate administration between the various trees (or wants to be able to search for objects across the entire environment), then separate trees in a forest configuration is your only option.

AD Server Functions

In general, from an administrative perspective, servers fall into three broad categories: stand-alone, member, and domain controller. Stand-alone servers are not a member of any domain, so they are not really pertinent to a discussion of Active Directory. Member servers do not hold a copy of the AD database, so they too are not all that pertinent to our discussion. Domain controllers are where the AD action happens. They hold a copy of the AD database, can accept changes to the information within that database, and can replicate those changes to all of the other domain controllers within the domain.

So far, so good, right? We've discussed the concept of a replicated, distributed database. We've also discussed the concept of a multimaster environment—an environment in which each of the replicated copies can accept changes and pass those changes to all other copies (domain controllers) through the process of replication. The AD replication process does indeed utilize a multimaster strategy, but there are certain functions that are server-specific.

If you think about it, it makes sense that certain functions in such a complex operating system must be managed through a single point. Maintaining unique SIDs for objects, for instance, has to be centrally controlled. If every server "randomly" created a SID for each object they created, duplicate SIDs could be "randomly" issued. Numerous functions within the AD environment are managed through a single server; some of these functions are forestwide and others are domain-specific. There are also servers that hold the Global Catalog; we'll discuss these first since they have a fairly large impact on AD design.

Global Catalog Servers

A *Global Catalog server* is an AD server that holds a partial replica of the entire tree. This replica holds a limited amount of information about every object within the forest, usually those properties that are necessary for network functionality or those properties that are frequently asked for or searched against. The Global Catalog is referenced when a user "looks" for an object outside of their domain, thus eliminating the call to a domain controller at the destination domain.

The list of properties is different for each class of object. User objects, for instance, need to store certain information for network functions—a great example is their "Group Membership" list. During the logon process, the user's object is checked to retrieve this list. AD then confirms the user's membership with each group using information stored in the Global Catalog. Once membership is confirmed, the Security IDs for each group can be added to the user's security token. The Global Catalog might also contain various properties that are frequently searched upon—telephone numbers, for example. On the other hand, the Global Catalog will probably store less information about Printer objects because fewer of their properties are needed on a regular basis.

For those of you with a curious nature, Table 8.1 lists the properties stored (by default) in the Global Catalog. You can change this list, but remember that any additions to the Global Catalog properties list can have a great impact on your network.

NOTE *To be honest, my search for this list was quite confusing. A search of Microsoft's support website returned multiple hits; unfortunately, each page offered a different list of attributes as the default list in the Global Catalog. The list I've included in Table 8.1 seems to be fairly complete, although if you want the nitty gritty, you'll have to search the Microsoft website.*

TABLE 8.1: DEFAULT GLOBAL CATALOG CONTENT

NAME	DESCRIPTION
alt-Security-Identities	Alt-Security-Identities
common-Name	Common-Name
display-Name	Display-Name
given-Name	Given-Name
group-Type	Group-Type
keywords	Keywords
l	Locality-Name
lDAP-Display-Name	LDAP-Display-Name
legacy-Exchange-DN	Legacy-Exchange-DN
location	Location
mail	E-mail-Addresses
mSMQ-Digests	MSMQ-Digests
mSMQ-Label	MSMQ-Label
mSMQ-Owner-ID	MSMQ-Owner-ID
mSMQ-Queue-Type	MSMQ-Queue-Type
mS-SQL-Alias	MS-SQL-Alias
mS-SQL-Database	MS-SQL-Database
mS-SQL-Name	MS-SQL-Name
mS-SQL-Version	MS-SQL-Version
name	RDN
netboot-GUID	Netboot-GUID
object-Category	Object-Category
object-Guid	Object-Guid
object-Sid	Object-Sid
organizational-Unit-Name	Organizational-Unit-Name
primary-Group-ID	Primary-Group-ID

Continued on next page

TABLE 8.1: DEFAULT GLOBAL CATALOG CONTENT *(continued)*

NAME	DESCRIPTION
sAM-Account-Name	SAM-Account-Name
sAM-Account-Type	SAM-Account-Type
service-Principal-Name	Service-Principal-Name
sID-History	SID-History
surname	Surname
uNC-Name	UNC-Name
user-Account-Control	User-Account-Control
user-Principal-Name	User-Principal-Name
uSN-Changed	USN-Changed
uSN-Created	USN-Created

The reality is that this list is not that important. I cannot think of a single reason to remove one of the default attributes from the list. If you decide to do so, however, test the change in a lab environment first. Many of these attributes are included to provide specific functionality to the Windows 2000/Windows Server 2003 environment. You might, however, want to add an attribute to the Global Catalog. Remember, the Global Catalog is used to perform searches of the Active Directory database. If a user tries to search on an attribute that is not included in the Global Catalog, then the search must access domain controllers in each domain—adding network traffic, processing overhead to the servers involved, and increasing the time necessary to perform the search. We'll discuss this process a little later in this section.

By default, the first domain controller created in the AD forest is made a Global Catalog server. This is the only Global Catalog server that is created automatically. If you desire more than one Global Catalog (and you probably will), you have to manually configure them. The process is fairly straightforward.

CHANGING THE ATTRIBUTES STORED IN THE GLOBAL CATALOG

As I mentioned earlier, you can control which attributes of object types are stored in the Global Catalog. The partial list of attributes stored by default includes those attributes that are most frequently used in search operations—things like common name, location, or e-mail address. By adding attributes, you can speed up search queries. If your company uses a lot of interdepartmental faxes, for instance, your users will probably spend a lot of time searching for the fax number of other departments. Adding the fax number attribute to the Global Catalog will speed those searches up.

It is important for you to note, however, that in Windows 2000 adding a new attribute to the Global Catalog causes a full synchronization of all object attributes—not just the information that changed. Since the Global Catalog holds information about every object in the forest (not just a single domain), this one-time synchronization process can generate a significant amount of network traffic! This has been changed in the Windows Server 2003 operating system: Windows Server 2003 replicates only the new information. Of course, for backward compatibility, if the Windows Server 2003 communicates with a Windows 2000 Global Catalog, a full replication will occur.

If you are going to customize the content of the Global Catalog, remember that static data causes less synchronization traffic in the long run than data that changes on a regular basis. The fax number attribute is a perfect example; fax numbers for departments usually do not change very often. Once the data has been synchronized to all of the Global Catalog servers, very little additional replication traffic relating to this attribute will be generated. The only time synchronization traffic will be generated is when a fax number changes.

The content of the Global Catalog is managed through the Active Directory Schema snap-in to the MMC. If this snap-in is not available, you must install the Windows 2000/Windows Server 2003 Administration Tools from the Windows 2000/Windows Server 2003 CD-ROM. Since it is copied during a default installation, you can just run `Adminpak.msi` from the %systemroot%\System32 folder.

To modify the AD schema, you need to be a member of the Schema Admins group. First open the MMC and add the Active Directory Schema snap-in, as shown in Figure 8.13.

FIGURE 8.13

Adding the Active Directory Schema snap-in to the MMC

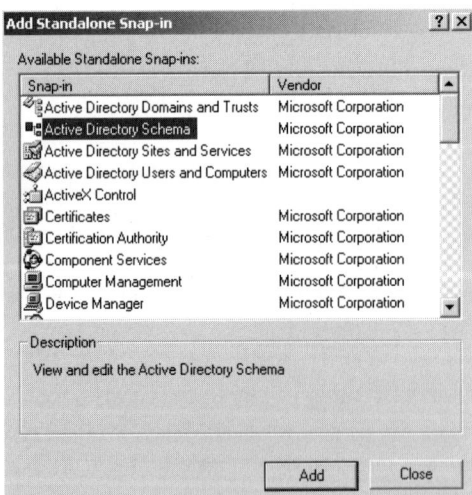

Expand the Active Directory Schema folder and click on the Attributes folder. You will see a list of all the attributes available within the AD schema, as shown in Figure 8.14.

FIGURE 8.14

Attributes within
the AD schema

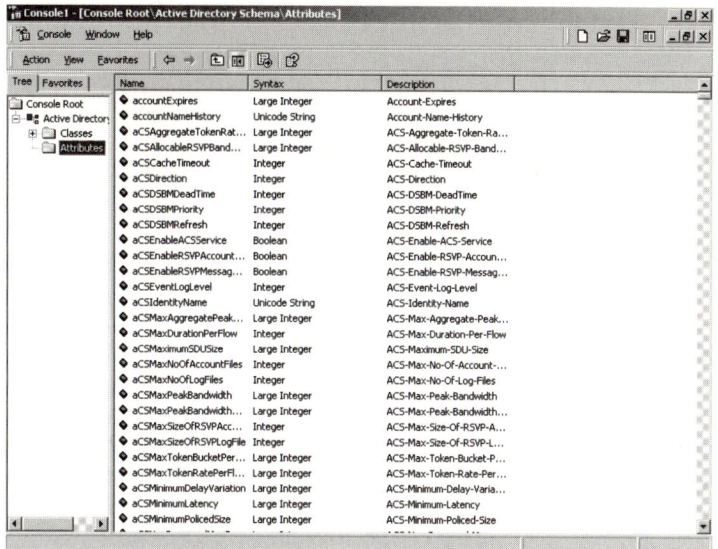

Right-click the attribute you want to add to the Global Catalog and click Properties. On the resulting window, ensure that the Replicate This Attribute to the Global Catalog option is selected, as shown in Figure 8.15.

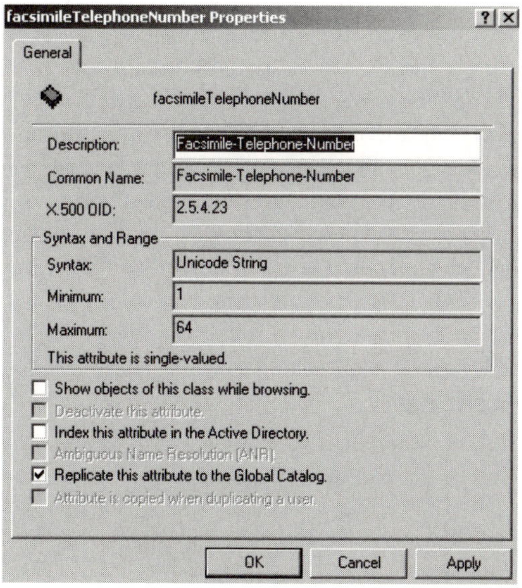

FIGURE 8.15

Adding an attribute
to the Global
Catalog

That's all there is to it! You'll also want to take note of another option in Figure 8.15: Index This Attribute in Active Directory. As with most databases, AD has the ability to index certain "fields," which increases the efficiency of queries. If you are adding an attribute to the Global Catalog, the odds are that the attribute you are selecting will be searched upon quite often. You can increase the efficiency of the process by selecting this option. AD will, however, create an index file for the attribute—increasing the size of the AD database files marginally. (This is usually not a problem, and since you are going to search on the attribute, you accept the slightly larger file size in exchange for lower processing requirements on the server.)

THE BIG DIFFERENCE BETWEEN WINDOWS 2000 AND WINDOWS SERVER 2003 GLOBAL CATALOG

While there really aren't a lot of AD-related differences between Windows 2000 Server and the Windows Server 2003 product line, one of the most important differences impacts the use of Global Catalog servers during the logon process.

In a Windows 2000 environment, a Global Catalog is critical to the logon process. When a user logs on to the network, a security token is created for them. This token includes information about the groups of which they are a member. If a Global Catalog server is not available during the logon process, the user will not be able to log on to the network—instead they will be limited to logging on to the local computer.

NOTE *Members of the Domain Admins group can log on to the network without accessing the Global Catalog. If this wasn't the case, a malfunctioning Global Catalog server could conceivably prevent an administrator from logging on to fix the problem.*

In Windows Server 2003 the requirement of contacting a Global Catalog has been eliminated. The domain controller closest to the user caches the user's complete group memberships. The cache populates at the first logon, and subsequent logons use this cached information. The cached information is refreshed periodically from a Global Catalog.

This is a major change to the way logons are processed! It might actually justify the cost of moving to Windows Server 2003. Many Windows 2000 environments experience extreme performance issues during periods of heavy logon (like Monday morning when everyone logs on at the same time). Most of this slowdown is caused by the dual access involved—first a domain controller is accessed, and then the domain controller accesses a Global Catalog.

In a Windows 2000 environment, it is recommended that each physical location have at least one Global Catalog server, otherwise the logon process will include accessing the Global Catalog over whatever WAN links are in place—not a pretty picture!

Forestwide Functions

As I mentioned in the beginning of this section, certain functions within a multimaster database just do not lend themselves to the multimaster model. Some things need to be controlled through a single point to provide a level of consistency that is just not available if "any old domain controller" was allowed to do them. Let's call these functions *single master functions*. Some of these functions are specific to a domain, while others affect the entire forest. Let's start our discussion with those that have the widest possible impact: the forestwide functions.

NOTE *I've had a couple of Novell guys laugh when we talk about the single-server functions. They seem to believe that NDS is multimaster in all functions. Nothing could be further from the truth! Any complex, replicated, and multimaster database has certain things that need to be tightly controlled—even NDS. I started off with Novell products, and I still like them. Heck, I'm even a former Novell employee. Read the documentation: Novell will tell you, in no uncertain terms, that certain management tasks (usually those that involve changes to the structure of the directory tree) need to be performed by specific servers.*

For these operations, one server is designated as the *operation master*. All updates or changes occur at the operation master, and this server is responsible for synchronizing the changes to all other servers. Because these responsibilities can be moved from server to server (as best fits your network), Microsoft refers to them as *flexible single-master operations (FSMOs)*.

NOTE *Do not let the word "flexible" confuse you—this is mostly a marketing phrase. These operations are truly "single-master." They are "flexible" only in the fact that you can determine which server will perform them.*

There are two forestwide operation master roles:

♦ Schema master

♦ Domain naming master

These two roles are fairly straightforward, but once again, let me stress that only one server in the entire forest performs these tasks. You must ensure that this server is reliable and has enough horse-power to perform them. You should also place it in a physical location where any outside links are fairly reliable. If these servers or the links to them are unavailable, certain administrative functions will not be accessible.

The *schema master* controls the structure of the AD database. Any updates or modifications made to the database structure must be made on this server first. It will then replicate these changes to the rest of the AD servers in your forest. This ensures that all AD servers are "speaking the same language." There should never be a case where one server knows about a new object class or property but another server does not.

By default, the first server installed in the Active Directory forest (your first domain controller) assumes the role of schema master. To change the server that is performing this role, or to confirm which server is performing this function, use the Active Directory Schema snap-in to the MMC. Right-click Active Directory Schema in the left pane of the window and choose Operations Masters. You will be presented with the dialog box shown in Figure 8.16.

FIGURE 8.16

Locating or changing the schema master server

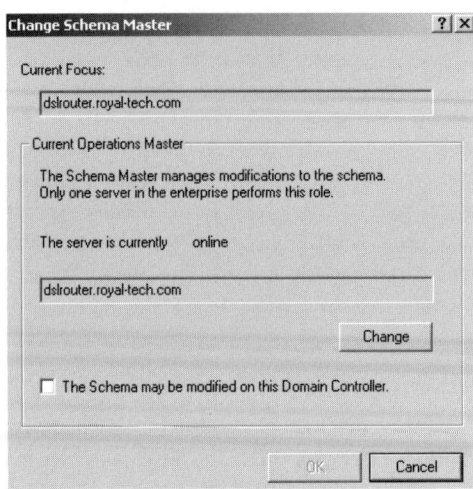

You should note something else in Figure 8.16. You must manually configure a server to allow schema changes by selecting the modification option near the bottom of the figure. Until this option is selected, you will be allowed to look at the schema, but changes will not be accepted. It is suggested that only one server in the forest have this option selected!

The *domain naming master* is responsible for adding or removing domains from the forest. It ensures that each domain is given a unique name when added to the forest and that any reference to a removed domain is cleaned up.

Once again, only one server in the AD forest performs this function. To locate or change which server is acting as the domain naming master, run the Active Directory Domains and Trusts application located in the Administrative Tools group. Right-click Active Directory Domains and Trusts in the left pane of the window and choose Operation Masters. You will be presented with the dialog box shown in Figure 8.17.

FIGURE 8.17

Locating or changing the domain naming master server

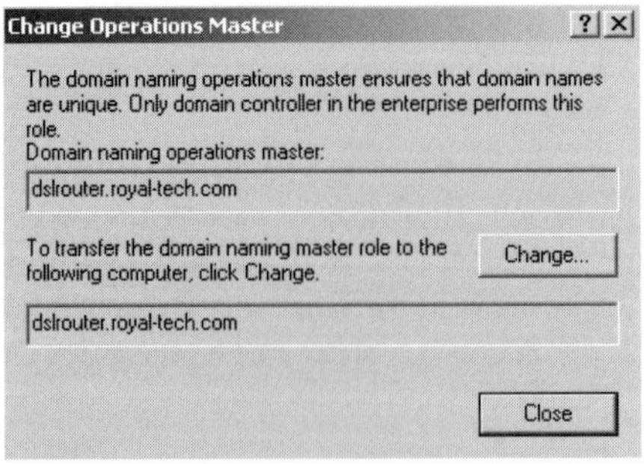

Domain-Specific Functions

There are three domainwide operation master roles:

◆ Relative ID master

◆ Primary domain controller (PDC) emulator

◆ Infrastructure master

Once again, only one server in each domain performs each of these tasks. These servers will need to be both powerful enough to handle the extra workload and reliable enough to be available when necessary.

The *relative ID master* controls the creation of security IDs for new objects created in the domain. Each object has a security ID that is made up of a domain identifier (the same for every object in the domain) and a unique relative ID that differentiates the object from any other in the domain. To ensure that these IDs are indeed unique, only one server in each domain generates them. To ensure that new objects can be created even if the relative ID master is offline, each domain controller is given 10,000 unique identifiers when they join the domain. If all 10,000 unique identifiers are used, the domain controller requests another 10,000 from the relative ID master.

The *PDC emulator master* has the ability to act as a PDC for non–Windows 2000/Windows Server 2003 clients and NT 4.0 (and earlier) BDCs. This allows for a mixed environment of Windows 2000/Windows Server 2003 and earlier NT version servers on the same network. Even in a completely Windows 2000/Windows Server 2003 AD environment, though, the PDC emulator performs an important function. When a user changes their password, whichever domain controller accepts the change will first pass the change to the PDC emulator operation master. This server then uses a high-priority function to replicate this change to all of the other domain controllers in the domain.

Each domain controller in a domain knows which server is acting as the PDC emulator. If a user tries to log on to the network but provides an incorrect password, the domain controller will first query the PDC emulator to ensure that it has the latest password for the user before denying the request to log on. This prevents a denial of service in the event that a user attempts to use their new password before it has had a chance to be replicated to all of the domain controllers in the domain.

The *infrastructure master* is responsible for updating group-to-user references when group members are renamed or relocated. It updates the group object so that it knows the new name or location of its members.

All of the domain-specific operation master servers can be confirmed and changed from the Active Directory Users and Computers application located in the Administrative Tools group. Right-click the domain in the left pane of the window and choose Operations Masters. You will be presented with the dialog box shown in Figure 8.18.

NOTE *There was confusion in our "beta-readers" of this chapter: they felt I gave the same instructions for checking the domain naming master and the infrastructure master. Here's the difference: when looking for forestwide information, you right-click Active Directory Domains and Trusts. When working on domain-specific items (such as the infrastructure master), you right-click the domain in question.*

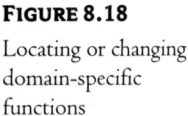

FIGURE 8.18

Locating or changing domain-specific functions

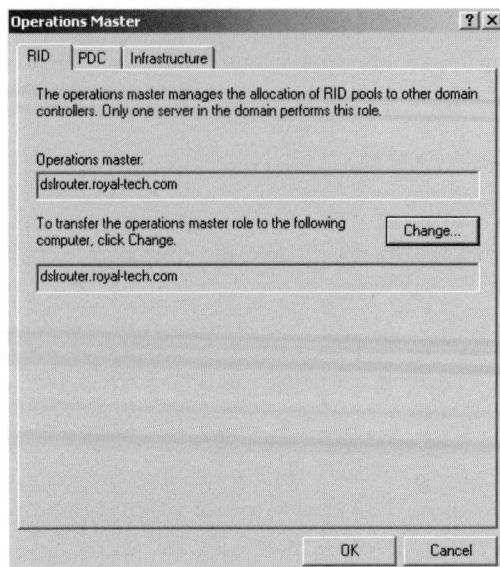

Notice that the system automatically selects another domain controller (if you have more than one, which I don't in the figure) that acts as the "standby" server. Do not get your hopes up here. In the event that the original master server becomes unavailable, the role does not automatically switch to the backup; you still have to click the Change button. This makes sense: you wouldn't want it to change automatically every time a server was temporarily unavailable! That would also require some sort of timed communication to manage, which would just add more traffic to your network.

General Guidelines for Operation Masters

You should be aware of certain facts and suggestions when planning for the location of your operation master servers. While I've never had a problem related to a malfunction of or even the inability to connect to an operation master server, I'm always careful to follow the guidelines for placement within the environment.

First let's review what happens by default: The first domain controller in the AD forest is assigned all five roles: schema master, domain-naming master, relative ID master, PDC emulator, and infrastructure master. This makes sense; because there is only one domain controller, it must assume all five roles. Each time a new domain is created, the first domain controller in the new domain is assigned the three domain-specific roles: relative ID master, PDC emulator, and infrastructure master.

Microsoft also makes the following recommendations:

♦ Place the relative ID and the PDC emulator roles on the same domain controller. Since legacy clients target the PDC emulator for services, it is usually a large consumer of relative IDs, so the two services communicate quite a bit.

- If the workload justifies placing the relative ID and PDC emulator roles on different domain controllers, make sure that the two computers are in the same AD site, and that the connection between them is reliable.

- In general, the infrastructure master role should not be assigned to a server that is acting as a Global Catalog server. The reason for this limitation is a little confusing. Remember that the Global Catalog contains a record for every object in the forest. Also remember that the infrastructure master is responsible for updating things like group membership changes to other domain controllers. The infrastructure master will only replicate changes for objects that it does not hold. Since the Global Catalog holds "all objects," the infrastructure master will not update any records on other domain controllers. (Weird little gotcha, huh?) There are two exceptions to this rule:

  - In a single-domain forest, all domain controllers will be updated through the AD replication process anyway (the infrastructure master really has no work in a single-domain environment), so it does not matter where you place this role.

  - In a multidomain forest in which all domain controllers are Global Catalog servers, this role can be placed anywhere. Once again, since all domain controllers know about all objects, the infrastructure master has no real work to do.

- The schema master and domain-naming master roles should be placed on the same server (remember these are the two forestwide functions). They actually do little work and so add very little overhead to the server, but they are critical services that should be tightly controlled. In addition, the server acting as the domain-naming master should also be a Global Catalog server.

AD Organizational Units

So far in this chapter, we've discussed Active Directory domains, trees, and forests. We've also discussed a few of the AD roles that servers can be assigned to provide directory functionality. Let's think for a minute of what some of our discussions so far imply in a real-world environment.

First, I've said that an AD domain can support more than a million objects—users, computers, groups, etc. I've also suggested that you limit the scope of a domain, either to reduce the overall number of objects within the database or to control replication traffic between physical locations. After our discussion of AD trees—multiple domains tied together with transitive trusts—the next logical step was to tie these trees together to form forests, usually to support multiple namespaces while still retaining the ability to centrally manage the environment. So far, so good, right?

In your mind's eye, you should be visualizing a series of domains tied together to represent your company's network resources. If you are, then you are on the right track, and you have the proper mindset for AD—it's all just a graphical representation of the things you need to manage on your network. See any problems yet?

Think about managing the AD tree of a large company. You've got multiple locations, so you create multiple domains. Maybe you've got a few independent business units that demand you support their established naming standards, so you create multiple trees and bring them together into a single forest.

Okay, great, but now what? In a large company, a single site can easily have thousands of users. In AD terms, this would result in thousands of user objects, their associated computer objects, a large number of group objects, and tons of other objects created in a single domain.

Now imagine trying to manage that number of objects. In your mind, see yourself opening the Active Directory Users and Computers tool. What do you see? An endless list of thousands of objects—hopefully at least sorted alphabetically—from which you need to pick and choose when managing? In reality, this type of representation of your resources would be unmanageable, and it's one of the reasons that an NT environment needed so many domains.

When we talked about the X.500 recommendations, we discussed the use of container objects to organize the resources represented in the directory. These container objects did not represent physical resources; instead they acted as tools to organize the resources into logical groupings. Since they are used to organize your resources, it makes sense that they are called *organizational units (OUs)*.

In many ways, planning the structure of the OUs in your environment is more complex than designing the domain, tree, and forest structure. Since domains usually represent physical locations or separate business units, finding the scope of any given domain is usually fairly straightforward. Likewise, AD trees are just groupings of domains—again, fairly easy to visualize. The same holds true for forests: each represents a unique namespace; finding its limits is easy!

OUs, on the other hand, are used to organize actual resources—user accounts, printers, servers, etc. While the scope of a domain is usually easy to find, creating OUs can be confusing. OUs tie resources into logical groupings; as we'll see later, these groupings can represent departments, locations, or even projects. Placing your resources into the appropriate OUs can greatly ease long-term administration—it's planning the groupings that cause the headaches. Take printers, for instance. In most companies printers are used by whichever users are located near them. If your OU structure mirrors the departmental structure of your company (sales, marketing, production, administration, etc.), which OU should contain the object of a printer? The printer might be used by people from many of these departments, but the printer can have only one record in the tree.

Okay, you say, then I'll create OUs to represent locations. That will fix the problem; now the printer object goes in the OU that represents its location. But what if you need to manage user accounts by department?

See what I mean? Planning an OU structure that helps you manage your resources can be kind of tricky.

What Are OUs Used For?

OUs form logical administrative units that can be used to delegate administrative privileges within a domain. Rather than add another domain to an existing structure, it is often more advantageous to just create another OU to organize objects.

Organizational units can contain the following types of objects:

- Users
- Computers
- Groups
- Printers

- Applications
- Security policies
- File shares
- Other OUs

NOTE   *Remember that the AD schema is extensible, so the preceding list might change if you change the schema of your tree.*

NOTE   *There is only one type of object that an OU cannot contain, and that is any object from another domain.*

EASIER ACCESS, EASIER MANAGEMENT

You could define an OU as a container object designed to allow organization of a domain's resources. An OU is used in much the same way as a subdirectory in a file system. There is an old adage about creating subdirectories in DOS:

> *There are only two reasons to create a subdirectory: to ease access or to ease management.*

You might, for instance, create the DOS structure shown in Figure 8.19. Most of us would find this type of layout comfortable (and familiar). If you take the time to analyze why this structure works so well, you'll find that all subdirectories were created for one of two reasons: management or access.

FIGURE 8.19

Typical file structure

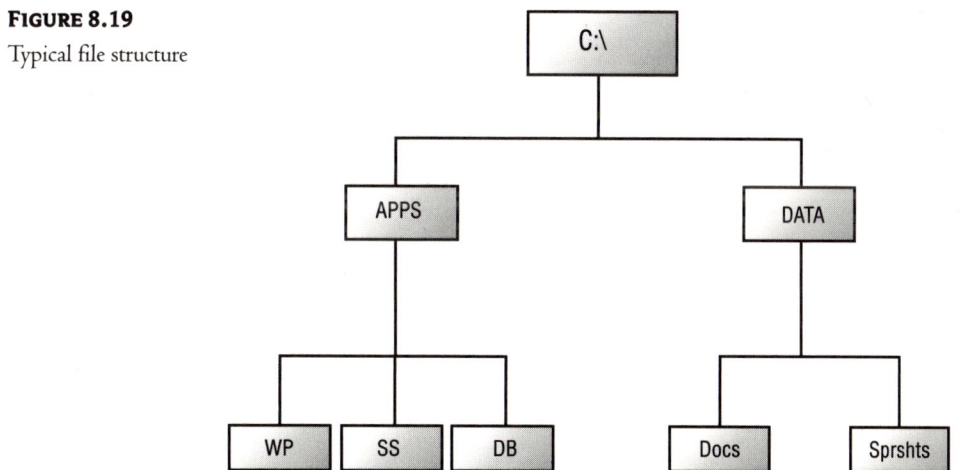

APPS   Naming a directory APPS lets a user know exactly where to find applications, making access easier. It also lets an administrator know where to place any applications stored in the file system, making management easier.

DATA Again, the name helps both access and management. Placing both the APPS and DATA directories directly off the root of the drive makes navigation easier for users. Separating the data from the applications also simplifies setting up backup programs (you can back up everything under DATA rather than all .doc files in \apps\wp and all .xls files in \apps\ss, and so on).

OUs in Active Directory have even fewer "rules" than in DOS. In DOS, your structure had to make sense to end users. They had to be able to use the directory names to "walk" through the structure to find the files they were looking for. In AD, organizational units are created strictly to ease the administration of the environment. In a properly designed and implemented Active Directory environment, users should not even be aware of the existence of the AD hierarchical OU structure!

OUs are created for one of two reasons (in most cases): either to facilitate the *delegation* of administrative privileges or to facilitate the assignment of *Group Policies*. Let me expand upon these two choices.

Delegation

While certain administrative tasks must be centrally managed (mostly concerning the management of the AD domain structure), most administrative tasks can easily be delegated to specific individuals or groups. In other words, you have the ability to choose specific sets of administrative privileges and assign them to specific people or groups of people.

As an example, you might have a help desk group that supports most calls for support. While this group of people needs to have access to the information in AD, and maybe even make changes, they should not have full control over the entire tree or domain. One common task that most help desks perform is changing passwords. You've probably had this type of call at your workplace:

User: "The network won't let me log on."

Support: "Can you explain what is happening?"

User: "I type in my name and my password, and it says something about incorrect username or password. Why won't it let me in?"

Support: "Are you sure you're typing in the right password?"

User: "Of course!"

Support: "Is the light on above the words Caps Lock?"

This conversation usually ends up with the support person changing the user's password to something simple (like "password"), forcing them to change it the next time they log on.

In Microsoft NT, it was actually quite difficult to give your help desk personnel the ability to change passwords without also giving them way too many other permissions in your system. In Windows 2000/Windows Server 2003, it's quite easy! (We'll discuss security in Chapter 10.) Even better, with a proper OU structure, you can limit the scope of the assignment to a select set of resources within your domain.

When planning for delegation, you create OUs that represent administrative areas of responsibility. If you have an administrator for a remote office who is supposed to handle all management tasks for the resources in that office, create an OU that represents the location, place the appropriate resource records (objects) within the OU, and delegate the necessary privileges to that administrator.

Group Policies

I haven't discussed Group Policies yet; I'm saving that for Chapter 11. Yet Group Policies can influence your OU structure, so I'll have to introduce them here and finish the discussion later. Group Policies are basically a set of rules that can be applied to a client workstation; these rules influence, or control, the environment presented to users. While that is a fairly good definition, it sounds a little vague. Perhaps an example would start things off on the right foot.

Have you ever had a user who just couldn't seem to stop tinkering with their computer? They read an article in some magazine, believe everything they read, and try whatever the author suggests. While the authors of these articles might know what they are talking about, they do not know your particular environment. Often the suggestions they make cause problems or are at odds with your preferred configuration. A Group Policy can let you take control of that user's environment, limiting their options to what you decide they should be able to access. One of the most common settings, for instance, allows you to determine which of the configuration tabs should appear on the Display applet. You can allow users to set their backgrounds or screen savers, but you can completely remove the Display Settings tab.

Group Policies are so powerful that you can literally control every aspect of the user environment, even locking their machine down so that they cannot do anything you have not specifically allowed them to do! Conversely, a Group Policy can be created to limit their access to just those functions that have been causing the most help desk calls. Either way, you, as the administrator, decide how much control users should have over their Desktops.

As I said, we'll continue this discussion in Chapter 11. We'll look at the options available and how to implement them. For now, though, you need to know how Group Policies are assigned.

First, policies can be assigned to either users or computers. Think of it this way: you might have a user, Bob, who is constantly calling the help desk to correct problems of his own making. You could create a Group Policy Object (GPO, the actual AD object that holds your configuration decisions) and assign it in such a way that it implements every time Bob logs on to the network—no matter which computer he sits at! Conversely, you might have a computer that is located in a public place. This computer needs to run one, and only one, application. You could create a GPO that accomplishes this level of control and then apply it to that particular computer (or group of computers).

I've used both techniques, and both are effective, depending upon your needs. Just recently I designed an attendance sign-in system for a vocational school. They had an Access database located on a server and a series of computers in their classrooms and computer labs. They wanted to track their students—take attendance and track lab use—without placing an additional burden on their instructors. We placed "kiosk" computers in each classroom and lab. These computers were assigned to a Group Policy that limited them to running the front-end for the database. In effect, we created a machine dedicated to a particular task. Now students "sign in" when they enter a room. The application tracks the time of sign-in and attendance records for every class—without any additional burden placed on the teachers. (If you've been watching the news lately, you know how underfunded our schools are. Automating basic administrative tasks can free up teachers so that they can spend more time with their students.)

Group Policies can be assigned at the OU level (as well as at a few other places that we'll talk about later). In other words, you can create an OU and assign (or *link*, to use the proper term) the GPO to the container, and it will be applied (by default) to all users and computers within that OU. Since GPOs are a very big part of the management capabilities of AD, planning your OU structure to efficiently use them is a big part of a good AD design!

THINK AHEAD

When designing the OU structure for your domains, you must plan ahead. If you are going to use them as administrative boundaries (to facilitate delegation of administrative privileges), then you must know who will be responsible for what resources before you create the structure.

If you are going to design your OU structure to facilitate GPO assignments, once again, you must know what GPOs you plan to use, and who (or which computer) they should affect, before creating the OUs and populating them with objects.

While OUs are a great way to logically organize your resources for easier management, you can have too many! Remember our DOS analogy? In DOS we use directories to organize files. Have you ever sat down at a computer where the user had created way too many subdirectories? If the structure is too complex, it can be impossible to find specific resources. Utilize OUs, but do not create a structure that is so complex you can't find things later!

TIP *The bottom line is: if a container does not help you manage a set of resources, then you probably don't need that OU!*

CREATING CONTAINERS

With that said, there are a few good business reasons why you *should* create containers:

◆ To delegate administrative control, allowing an individual the ability to add, delete, or modify objects in a limited portion of the tree.

◆ To ease management by grouping like objects. You might, for instance, create a container to hold users with similar security requirements.

◆ To control the visibility of objects.

◆ To make administration more straightforward, assigning permissions once to the OU rather than multiple times for each object.

◆ To make administration easier by limiting the number of objects in a single container. Even though the limit on the number of objects within a single container is large (well over a million), no one wants to page through a huge list every time they need to manage one object.

◆ To control policy application. We'll discuss changes to the system policy process later, but for now just be aware that policies can be set at the OU level.

◆ To be used as a holding container for other OUs. This would be the same as the APPS directory in our DOS example. The APPS directory does not really hold any files; it just acts as an organizer for other directories.

◆ To replace NT 4 domains. In earlier versions of NT, delegation of administration was achieved by creating multiple domains.

Designing the OU Model

Organizational units provide structure within a domain. This structure is hierarchical in nature, just like the structure built by adding domains together. Each OU acts as a subdirectory to help administrators organize the various resources described within the directory. This structure must be meaningful to your administrators for it to be of any value to the network. A structure designed without people in mind can be of more harm than good, as demonstrated in Figure 8.20.

FIGURE 8.20

Bad OU structure

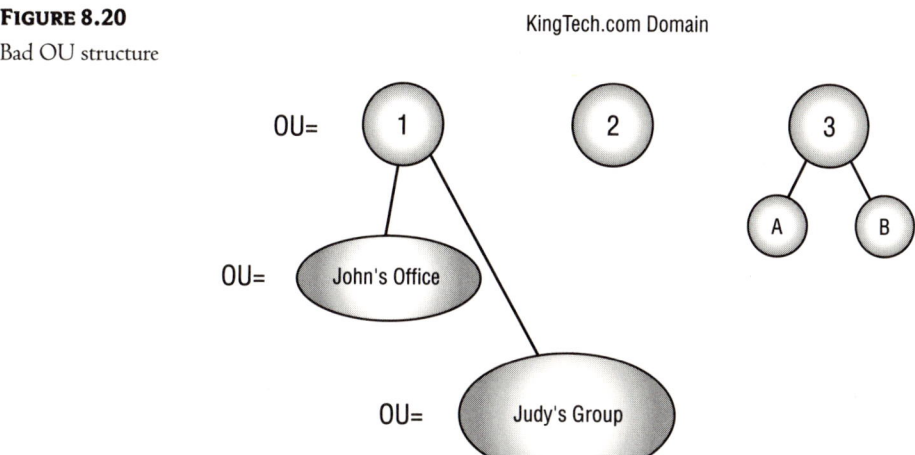

There are a couple of problems inherent in this design:

◆ Many of the OU names are not user friendly. A name of 1 might mean something to the administrator who created it, but it will probably mean nothing to anyone else.

◆ Naming containers after people *might* make things easier for a while, but as soon as there is a change in personnel or business structure, all such containers will need to be renamed.

WHAT MAKES A GOOD OU MODEL?

There are various *models* of good OU structures. A model defines categories of OUs and the relationships between them. The model you create for your tree should follow the business practices of your company. More than in any other form of network, a directory-based network demands that administrators understand the business practices and workflow of their company before designing the system.

Creating an OU model can be a difficult task—especially on your first attempt. Since a good design makes your life (and the lives of your fellow administrators) easier in the long run, you would like to come up with a good, stable design the first time! With this in mind, some "cookie-cutter" models have been designed to act as guides during the planning stage of your own design.

Microsoft suggests seven different basic models for OU structures:

◆ Geographic

◆ Object-based

◆ Cost center

◆ Project-based

◆ Division or business unit

◆ Administration

◆ Hybrid or mixed

In the sections that follow, we will take a look at the advantages and disadvantages of each design model.

Geographic Model

A geographic model structures its OUs by geographic location, as shown in Figure 8.21. The KingTech Corporation has created a first level of OUs to represent continents and a second level to represent countries. This type of configuration is helpful if each country has its own administrator; you can easily grant administrative privileges to a local user account.

FIGURE 8.21

Geographic model

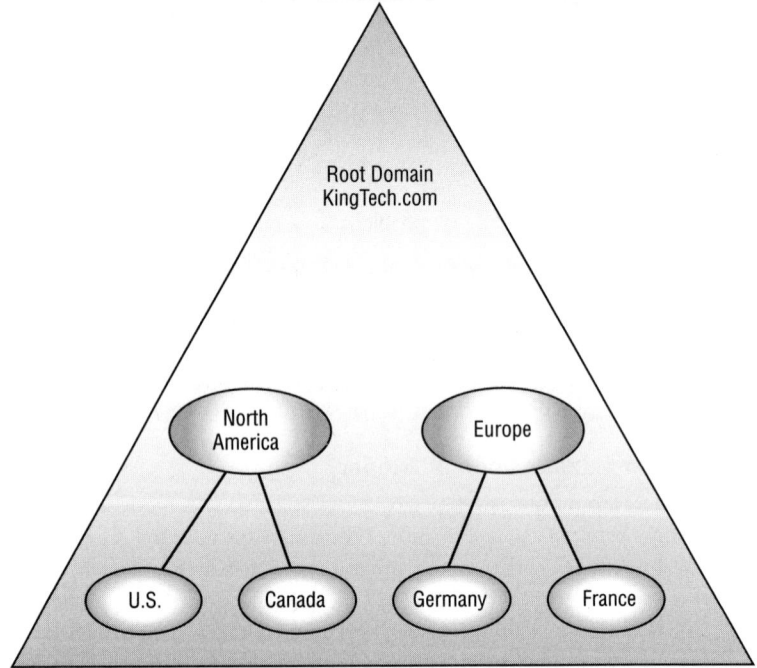

A geographic model offers a number of advantages:

◆ OUs will be fairly stable: most companies sometimes reorganize internal resources, but the locations of their offices are usually stable.

◆ Corporate headquarters can easily dictate domainwide policies.

◆ It is easy to determine where resources are physically located.

◆ A geographic naming standard is easy for both users and administrators to understand.

A geographic model also has some disadvantages:

◆ This design does not mirror the business practices of KingTech in any way.

◆ The entire structure is one large partition (single domain). This means that *all* changes to all objects must be replicated to all AD servers worldwide.

NOTE *In most cases, the replication traffic on the wide area links will outweigh any of the benefits of using this model.*

Object-Based Model

The design of an OU structure can also be based on object types, as illustrated in Figure 8.22. A first-level container would be created for each class of object that exists in the tree. Below this first level, a geographic layout might make administration easier.

FIGURE 8.22

Object-based model

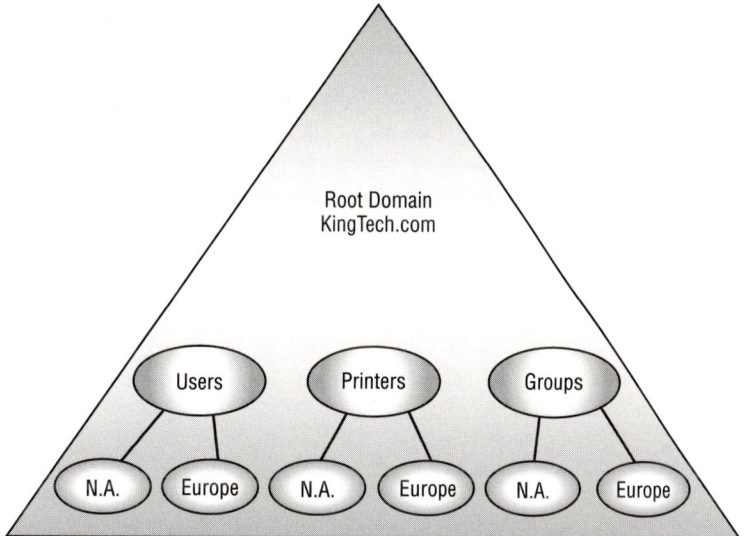

Here are some advantages of the object-based model:

◆ Resource administration is easier because each OU represents a specific class of object.

◆ Permissions are based upon OUs. It's easy to create OU-wide permissions, such as "All users should be able to use all printers."

◆ Administration can easily be delegated by resource type. For example, you can create a Printer Administrator who has permissions to add, delete, and modify all printers in the enterprise.

◆ A company reorganization should have little effect on the design. The same resources (with the possible exception of users) should exist no matter how the company is organized.

◆ Distinguished names are consistent for all objects in a class.

◆ It resembles the DNS structure, so it may lessen the learning curve for some administrators.

Disadvantages of the object-based model include the following:

◆ It is harder to define OU-based policies because all users are in the same containers.

◆ This flat structure will have to be created in each domain.

◆ There are too many top-level OUs. This can make navigating the administrative tools more difficult.

◆ If the schema is extended to accept new object types, new OUs will have to be created.

I've been working with directory-based networking for quite some time, and I've never liked the object-based design. It offers the administrator little opportunity for customizing the environment to meet a particular business need. I might, for instance, have a printer that should be visible only to a particular group of users. While this goal is possible with the object-based model, accomplishing it is more work than it might be in other models.

Cost Center Model

A company may decide that the OUs within its AD tree should reflect its cost centers, as shown in Figure 8.23. This model might be used in a company where budgetary concerns outweigh other considerations. A nonprofit organization, for example, might have separately defined divisions, each of which is responsible for its own management and cost controls.

FIGURE 8.23

Cost center model

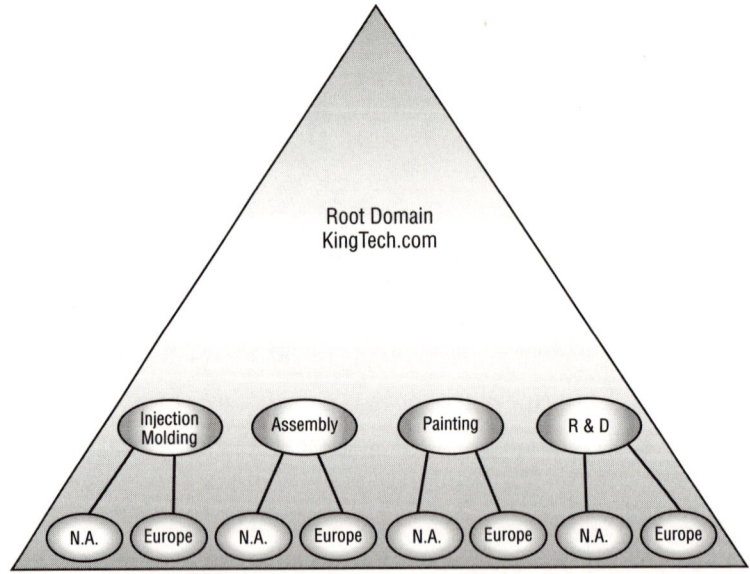

The cost center model has one main advantage: Each division or business group manages its own resources.

This model also has some disadvantages:

◆ Users might not be grouped together in a way that reflects their resource usage. A color printer, for instance, might belong to one department but might also be used by other departments as needed.

◆ Delegation of administrative privileges can be confusing.

The cost center design does not really take full advantage of the power of Active Directory. Most companies have departments, and each department might have its own budget—but there is usually some overlap of resources.

Project-Based Model

Some companies might prefer an OU structure that is based on current project teams. A manufacturing firm, for instance, might want to create an OU for each resource group in a shop floor manufacturing process. The project-based model is shown in Figure 8.24.

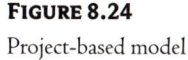

FIGURE 8.24

Project-based model

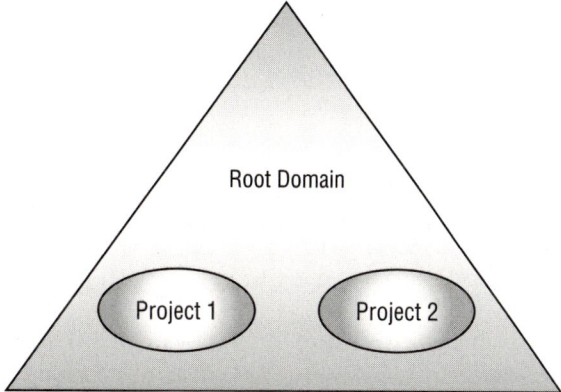

For certain environments, the project-based model offers some definite advantages:

◆ This model works well in an environment where resources and costs must be tracked.

◆ Because each project group is a separate OU, security between groups is easy to maintain.

Project-based design also has a couple of disadvantages:

◆ Projects often have a finite lifetime, so many OUs will have to be deleted and the resources redistributed on a regular basis. (Of course, consultants love this design since it requires that they come back to shuffle resources.)

◆ If projects change frequently, this type of structure will require a lot of maintenance.

I've found that a project-based structure will work for smaller companies with a limited product line. As a company grows (along with the number of active projects), the workload of maintaining a project-based design gets out of hand.

Division or Business Unit Model

The OU structure can also reflect a "well known" business structure if such a structure exists. A typical well-known structure would be the various departments within a law enforcement agency. You can see an example in Figure 8.25.

FIGURE 8.25

Division or business unit model

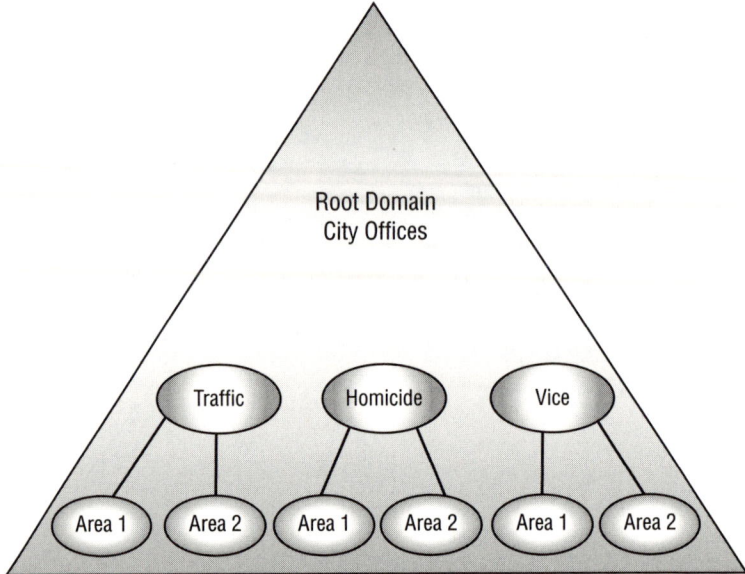

Here are some advantages of the division or business unit model:

◆ This structure is very user friendly, because it is based upon a structure with which users are already familiar.

◆ For the same reason, it is easy to locate resources.

And here is a disadvantage: although the structure is based on a "well-known" environment, there is always the chance that the business divisions will change. Any such change would force a redesign of the OU structure.

TIP   This model works very well in environments that are defined in a very rigid fashion, such as police departments and government offices.

Administration Model

One of the more frequently used models is a structure based upon common administrative groupings within a company, as shown in Figure 8.26. This model works well because it is based upon the actual business structure of the particular company.

FIGURE 8.26

Administration
model

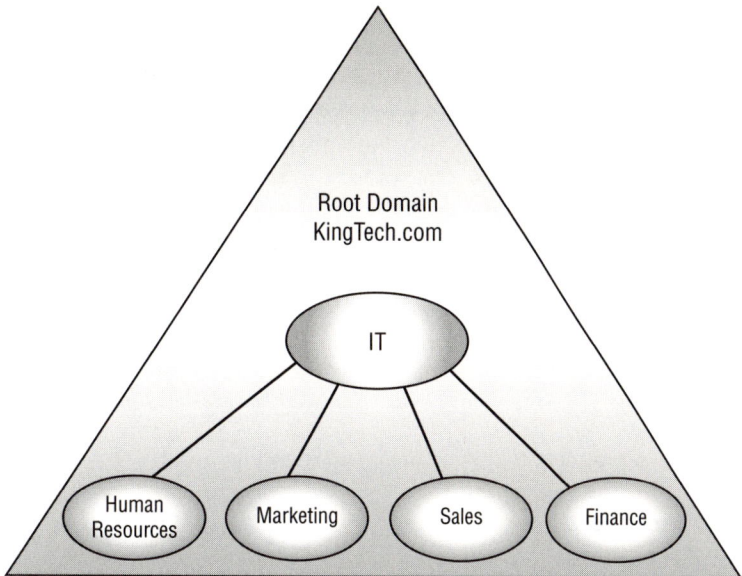

The administration model offers these advantages:

◆ This model is designed from the perspective of the network administrator and makes the administrator's job easier.

◆ Since most companies are departmental—from both a physical and a logical perspective—this model fits most enterprises.

It also has these disadvantages:

◆ Since this model is division oriented, all resources from a single division or department will be grouped under a single OU. This might be confusing for users.

◆ In companies where many resources are shared between departments, this model might not reflect the business model of the company.

This is one of the more commonly implemented OU models. It works reasonably well for most companies.

NOTE *Probably the biggest advantage of the administration model is that in most companies this design matches the organizational chart. In other words, the design has already been created—all the network administrator has to do is implement it!*

The administration model also matches the way many NT 4 networks were created. First one department would install an NT server, creating its own domain and user accounts. Later, another department would see the benefits enjoyed by the first department and would in turn install its own NT server. In the process, this department would create its own domain and SAM (Security Accounts Manager) database. Next, the two departments would see the potential benefits of sharing resources and would create trusts. The end result is a network already modeled on the administrative groupings within the company.

During the upgrade to Windows 2000/Windows Server 2003, the administrator has the option of redesigning the structure, but since the users are already familiar with the "departmental" concept of multiple domains, it makes sense to keep the structure as it is. This results in less confusion for end users, less retraining, and less productivity lost due to confusion.

Hybrid or Mixed Model

Most companies will settle on a hybrid structure that combines two or more of the "standard" models.

TIP   Remember that a structure will be more stable and need fewer adjustments if it accurately reflects the business structure of your company. The standard models are often too rigid to do this.

A typical hybrid structure is shown in Figure 8.27.

FIGURE 8.27

Hybrid model

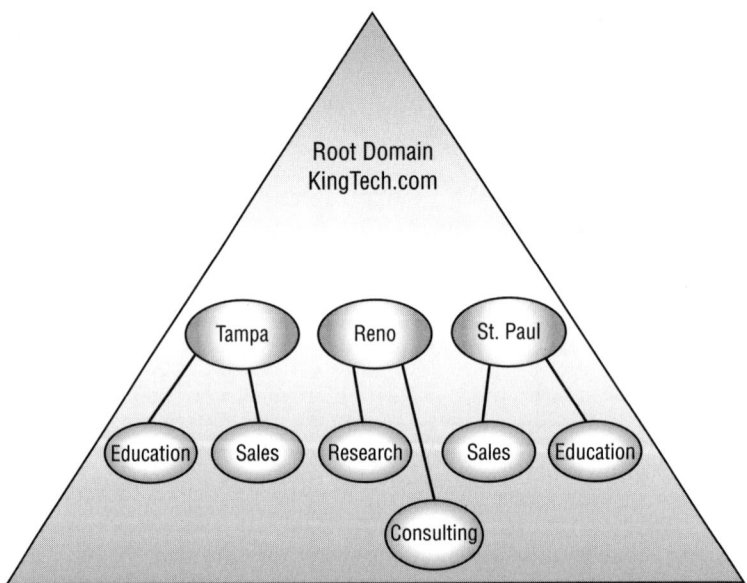

Advantages of a hybrid model follow:

◆ The structure can be customized to closely match the way in which business is conducted by the company.

◆ Employees are usually comfortable with the design, since it reflects the way they actually work.

This model does have one disadvantage: it requires a greater understanding than the other models do of the company for which it is intended. For this reason, many outside consultants will avoid hybrid models.

Because of its flexibility, the hybrid model is probably the best overall design. It does, however, require more planning before implementation than the other models. Administrators of a hybrid model AD will have to create a set of rules governing when, why, and where new containers will be created. Here are some questions to ask yourself during this process:

◆ Which resources are departmental?

◆ Which resources are regional?

◆ Which resources are dedicated to a specific project?

Once you have answered these questions, you can start designing a structure that closely mirrors the way in which your business is structured.

NOTE   The biggest problem with the hybrid model is that most businesses are dynamic. In other words, the way that they do business changes as the market changes. Such changes could result in a design that no longer meets the needs of the organization.

OTHER ASPECTS OF PLANNING AN OU MODEL

After you have chosen the overall structure that you will use for your OU model, there are a few other things to consider before you start implementation. Most of the following topics are administrative concerns. Proper planning of these details will make administering your network easier down the line.

Name Standards

The names you give to OUs are used internally within the domain and can be seen when searching for particular objects. It is important, therefore, that the names you choose are meaningful *both* to your users and to your administrators.

NOTE   OU names are not part of the DNS namespace. Users do not use DNS services to "find" an OU. This makes sense, since OUs are not physical resources—they are logical structures used to organize the objects in your database.

OUs are identified by a distinguished name—also known as a *canonical name*—that describes their location in the hierarchical structure. Basically, this is the X.500 name for the object in the tree. An OU named `Tampa` that is located in the `KingTech` container would be known as `Tampa.KingTech`. These names are used most often for administrative tasks.

OU Ownership

Each OU in the structure has an object that acts as its owner. The owner of an OU can:

◆ Add, delete, and update objects within the container

◆ Decide whether permissions should be inherited from the parent container

◆ Control permissions to the container

◆ Decide whether permissions should be propagated to child containers

NOTE   *By default, the user who creates an OU is its owner.*

Delegating Administration of OUs

For every OU in a domain, there is a set of permissions that grant or deny Read and Write access to the OU. This allows for a delegation of administrative privileges down to the lowest level of your structure. Any permissions assigned at the OU level pertain to all objects within that OU. There are various levels of authority that you might want to delegate to other administrators:

Changing Container Properties   Administrators can change OU-wide properties, such as OU policies and other attributes.

Creating, Deleting, and Changing Child Objects   These objects can be users, groups, printers, and so on.

Updating Attributes for a Specific Class of Object   Perhaps your help desk personnel should *only* be allowed to change users' passwords (but not any other attributes of a user account).

Creating New Users or Groups   You can limit the class of objects that an administrator has the permission to create.

Managing a Small Subgroup of Objects within the Tree   You might want an administrator to manage only objects in a particular office.

In Short

Designing the structure of your Active Directory is an important task that should be completed *before* implementation. As you have seen, proper planning of domains and organizational units can make life easier for both users and administrators. Here are some suggestions for your design:

- ◆ Use as few domains as possible. Windows 2000/Windows Server 2003 greatly increases the capacity of a single domain. You should use multiple domains only when there is a specific need for such a configuration.

- ◆ Limit the number of OU levels. As with the file system, the deeper things are hidden, the harder they are to find! Because of the way AD searches for objects, deep structures are less efficient than shallower ones.

- ◆ Limit the number of child objects for any given OU. While a Windows 2000/Windows Server 2003 domain can now support up to a million objects, no one wants to page through that many objects to find a specific user or printer.

- ◆ Remember that administrative privileges can be delegated at the OU level. You no longer have to create a new domain in order to limit administrative power.

In Chapter 9, we'll look at the actual implementation of AD: creating domains, OUs, and other objects.

Chapter 9

Implementing Your Design

MANY PEOPLE WHO READ reference manuals such as this one often want to start "doing" right away, rather than read through the explanations until a complete understanding is in place before taking any action. To placate those of you who are getting impatient, this chapter describes the mechanics of creating various objects within the AD forest. We'll look at the tools and techniques used to install Active Directory, create organizational units, delegate administrative privileges, create users, create groups, create printer objects, and describe the process for creating a few other types of objects.

A few people have asked me (people who have read the first and second editions) why I put this chapter in the middle of the book. Some of those people wanted the "how to" stuff in the beginning, and others thought it should wait until the end. Those who wanted it in the beginning complained that there was too much theory without any real "hands-on" descriptions. Those who wanted it at the end said that I talked about the creation of a few objects before talking about the implications of their use.

I have no defense against either complaint. Both groups are correct: this is not necessarily the ideal location for the "hands-on" chapter. Nevertheless, I placed it here for two main reasons:

♦ I don't want you to concentrate on the mechanics of management before you have a firm grasp of the theory of directory services. Installing and populating Active Directory takes a little thought, and I want you to have the basics before you start clicking through the tools.

♦ I also realize that many of you have a home lab in which you practice. Many of you said that you wanted to create objects while you were reading to get a visual reference for the topic being discussed. This makes perfect sense to me! Hear, see, do is the basic learning process. In a book this translates to read, see (the figures), do (in a home lab environment).

The bottom line here is that this chapter will present the mechanics of creating objects within the AD environment—where to click and a few short discussions of the consequences. Most of the complete discussions, though, take place in later chapters. As we move into the later chapters, I want you to have enough information to practice the techniques so that I can concentrate on the discussion at hand.

NOTE *This chapter also makes a pretty good reference point for later. If you forget how to do something (like creating a printer), you know this chapter is most likely to have a step-by-step guide.*

With that said, we can now move into the meat of the chapter. We've discussed most of the variables involved in designing an AD structure; now we can look at the mechanics.

In this chapter:

◆   Installing Active Directory

◆   Creating organizational units

◆   Creating users

◆   Crating groups

◆   Creating printers

◆   Creating other objects

Installing ADS

In earlier, domain-based versions of Windows NT, the accounts database (the Security Accounts Manager) was stored on special servers known as *domain controllers*. There were two types of domain controllers:

◆   One primary domain controller (PDC) for each domain

◆   An unlimited number of backup domain controllers (BDCs)

NOTE   *As you will recall, the PDC was responsible for synchronizing changes to the database to all of the BDCs.*

One of the biggest problems with this older system was the inability to reconfigure servers "on the fly." While you could promote a BDC to the position of PDC, it was impossible to demote a domain controller or promote a member server (any NT server that was not acting as a domain controller) without reinstalling Windows NT. In other words, once you chose a role for an NT server—domain controller or member server—you were stuck with that role. The only way to change a server's role was to pull out the NT CD-ROM and reinstall the operating system.

One of the biggest "incidental" advances that Microsoft has made to Windows 2000/Windows Server 2003 is that AD can be installed or removed without affecting the underlying operating system. If you decide that a certain server should act as an AD server, only to learn later that the server just doesn't have the necessary horsepower to perform the task, you can remove AD. If you install a Windows 2000/.NET server without AD and later decide you need to add the service, all you have to do is run an Administrative Wizard.

AD has become "just another network component" of the Windows 2000/Windows Server 2003 operating system. This flexibility allows network administrators the opportunity to make mistakes without fear of losing network functionality while yet *another* reinstallation takes place.

Before You Begin

Before you can begin the actual installation of the Active Directory service, you must complete certain preliminary tasks. Specifically, DNS *must* be configured and working properly before you begin the installation process. You should verify the following:

- You have decided on and configured DNS names for each of your Active Directory servers.

- DNS is installed and working.

- You have configured DNS for your environment. Specifically, ensure that:

    - Lookups work properly.

    - All DNS servers are configured for forward lookups as needed.

    - Your reverse lookup zones are working properly.

- You have configured DNS to allow dynamic updates.

TESTING DNS

Testing DNS is beyond the scope of this book, but here are a couple of suggestions:

- Use Ping to confirm communication between *all* Active Directory servers. If you ping each server by its host name, you will also test DNS at the same time.

- Use NSLOOKUP to test functionality for forward lookup, reverse lookup, and root zones.

NOTE *For more information on these tools, I suggest* Mastering Windows 2000 Server, *4th ed., by Mark Minasi, Christa Anderson, Brian M. Smith, and Doug Toombs (ISBN 0-7821-4043-2, Sybex, 2002) or* MCSE: TCP/IP for NT Server 4 Study Guide, *4th ed., by Todd Lammle, Monica Lammle, and James Chellis (ISBN 0-7821-2725-8, Sybex, 2000).*

MIXED MODE OR NATIVE MODE?

You must also decide on one other facet of your AD environment: whether your AD server should be configured to run in *mixed* or *native* mode.

A mixed-mode AD server can interact with domain controllers running earlier versions of NT. Basically, the AD server becomes the PDC for the existing NT domain, and it will update the older servers in a manner similar to that of an NT 4 server. This allows you to update your servers one at a time without having to be concerned about backward compatibility issues. While this process is certainly not as efficient as moving everything to AD, it does allow you a gradual upgrade of your environment.

NOTE *Unfortunately, terminology in the Microsoft world is often a little confusing. A Windows 2000/Windows Server 2003 acting as an AD server has the ability to emulate the functions of a domain controller from earlier versions of Windows NT. Since it is performing the same functions as an NT domain controller, many documents will refer to it as just another domain controller. You should be aware that there is a subtle difference between old and new—and an AD server, performing the role of PDC emulator, just acts like a PDC.*

A native-mode AD server does not have the ability to act as part of an older environment. As soon as all of your older servers have been upgraded to Windows 2000/Windows Server 2003 and AD, you should switch your servers to native mode. Mixed mode basically refers to a process running on your Windows 2000 server, using processor power and memory.

NOTE *It is not necessary to use mixed mode if all of your domain controllers are running Windows 2000/Windows Server 2003. It is perfectly acceptable, however, to have older member servers still running Microsoft NT. The only servers that force you to run mixed mode are domain controllers (PDC, BDC).*

While mixed mode is certainly convenient during the implementation of Windows 2000/Windows Server 2003, there are certain limitations to the environment. Depending upon the size of your environment and the functionality that you need, mixed mode can end up being a mixed blessing! While a Windows 2000/Windows Server 2003 environment is running in mixed mode, certain administrative capabilities are disabled. Probably the one with the most far-reaching effects is the disabling of universal groups. You are also unable to nest group membership (placing global groups within other global groups or domain local groups within other domain local groups). We'll discuss the various types of groups and their functions a little later in this chapter.

Of course, running in native mode also has its limitations. Once a domain has been configured to run in native mode, no Windows NT 4.0 BDCs can exist in the environment. If you plan on running a mixed environment (with NT and Windows 2000/Windows Server 2003), you either have to separate the domain controllers into distinct domains (NT and Windows 2000/Windows Server 2003 domains) or run in mixed mode.

The AD Installation Wizard

AD is installed by using the Active Directory Installation Wizard (the actual file is named `DCPromo.exe` and is located in the `<windows_root>\System32` directory). The wizard leads you through the entire installation process, asking you for information on the first domain controller, domain, site, and other configuration information. AD must be installed on a volume that has been formatted with NTFS 5 or higher.

The wizard itself is fairly straightforward. It starts with the obligatory Microsoft Welcome screen to identify what you are about to do (just in case you ran the wrong program). On the second screen, you are asked to select your server type, as shown in Figure 9.1.

There are two choices on this screen:

Domain Controller for a New Domain This server will be the first domain controller. Make this choice if this is the first AD server for a domain.

Additional Domain Controller for an Existing Domain Use this option if there is already an AD server within this NT domain. This server will receive a replica of the local domain's partition.

In Windows 2000, the next screen also has two choices, as shown in Figure 9.2. You must decide whether to create a new domain tree or add this domain to an existing tree.

FIGURE 9.1

Domain controller type

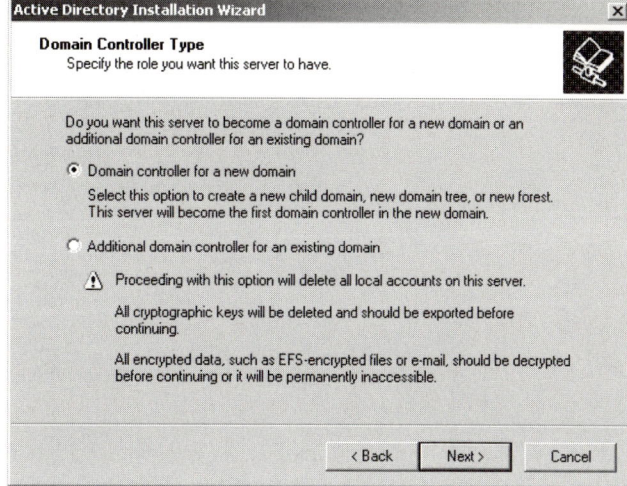

FIGURE 9.2

Create a tree or child domain in Windows 2000

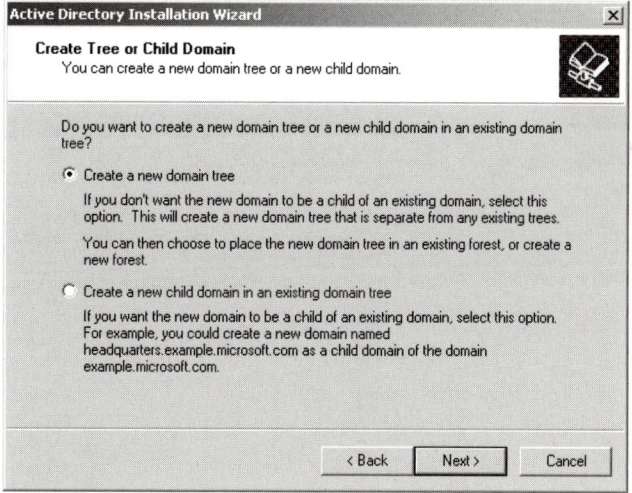

On Windows Server 2003, this dialog box offers more options, as shown in Figure 9.3. The first option, Domain in a New Forest, creates a new AD forest, with this server acting as the first domain controller (and thus accepting all of the operation master roles). The second option, Child Domain in an Existing Domain Tree, adds a new domain to your existing domain. The last option, Domain Tree in an Existing Forest, creates a new AD tree and adds it to your existing forest (remember this is usually used to support an additional namespace). If you choose either of the last two options, this server will assume all of the domain-specific operation master roles.

FIGURE 9.3

Create a tree or child domain in Windows Server 2003

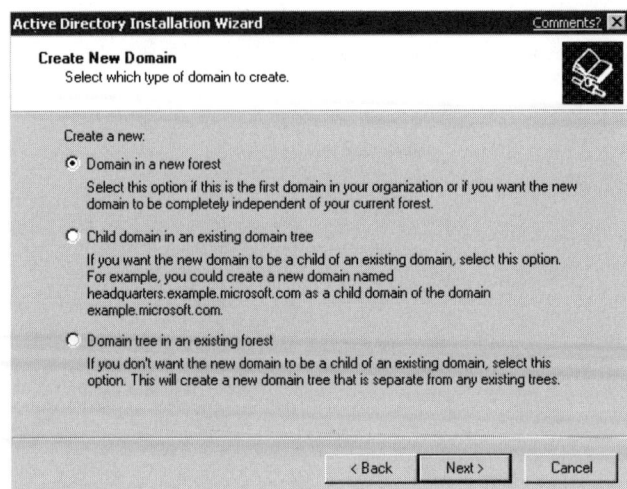

We discussed the tree and forest issue in the last chapter. Here you make decisions that will affect the number of domains in your environment and how their namespaces will interact.

FINISHING YOUR INSTALLATION

If you choose to create a new child domain, you are asked for an administrative account and password for an existing domain in the tree, as shown in Figure 9.4.

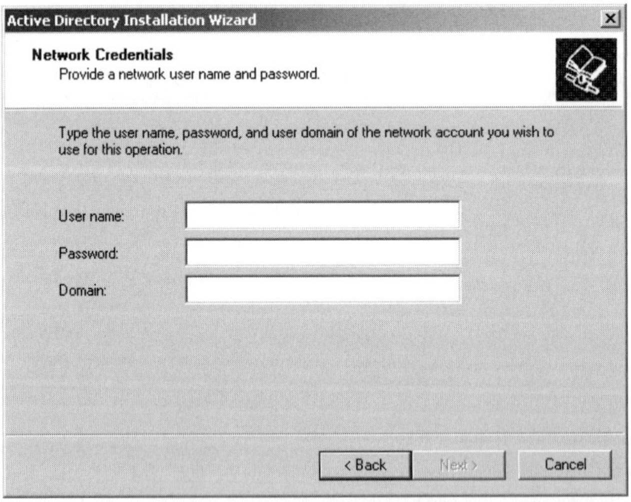

FIGURE 9.4

Establishing network credentials

If you choose to create a new tree, the next screen asks you for the full DNS name for the new domain, as shown in Figure 9.5. Remember that this name *must* be resolvable through DNS.

FIGURE 9.5

Naming the
new domain

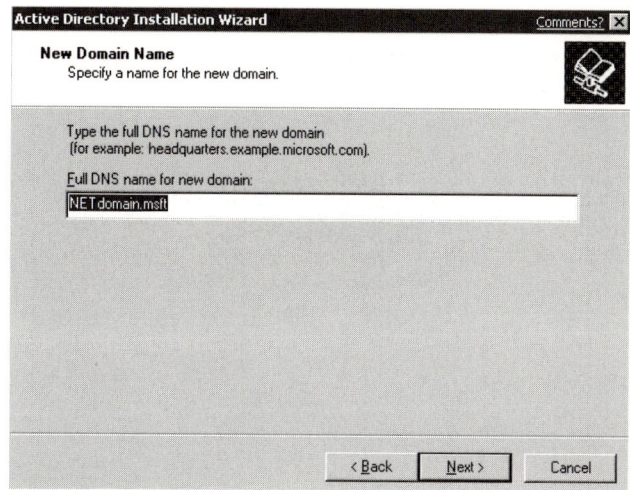

You are also asked for a NetBIOS-compatible domain name, as shown in Figure 9.6, that legacy operating systems (such as Windows 95/98, Me, and NT) can use to refer to the domain. This provides backward compatibility for those computers that have not been, or will not be, upgraded.

FIGURE 9.6

Setting a
NetBIOS-compatible
domain name

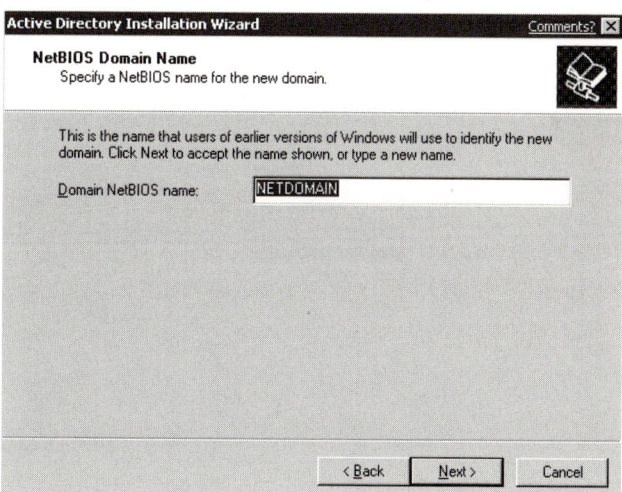

The next dialog box asks you where to store the NDS database and log files. As we'll see in Chapter 15, placing the database and log files on separate physical hard disks is recommended. Notice, in Figure 9.7, that the default places both on the local system partition.

FIGURE 9.7

Storing the database
and log files

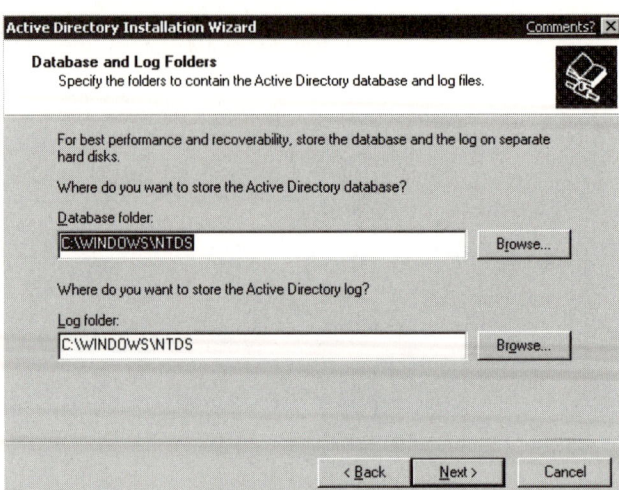

The next dialog box asks you to decide where the SYSVOL folder should be located, as shown in Figure 9.8. The SYSVOL folder contains all of the domain's publicly accessible files. Its contents are replicated to all domain controllers in the domain.

FIGURE 9.8

Locating the
SYSVOL folder

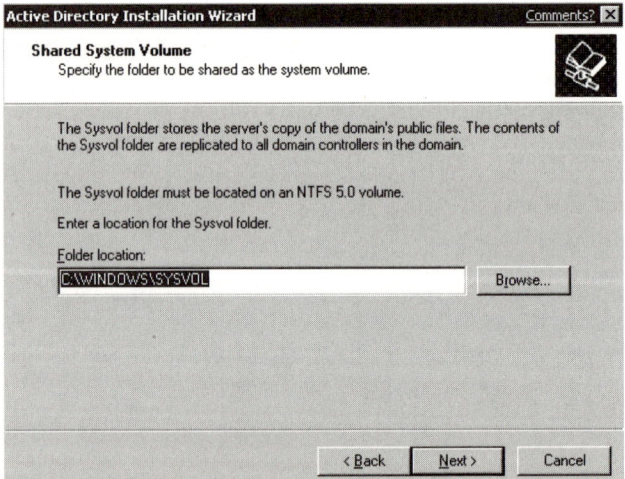

In the event the DCPROMO application cannot resolve the domain name through an existing DNS server, the dialog box shown in Figure 9.9 will appear. As you can see, the error message clearly describes the problem. You are presented with a few choices: fix the problem now, have the system automatically install and configure DNS on this computer, or fix the problem later. Notice that not addressing the problem at some point is not an option! Without DNS, AD cannot function.

FIGURE 9.9

The DNS
Registration
Diagnostics
window

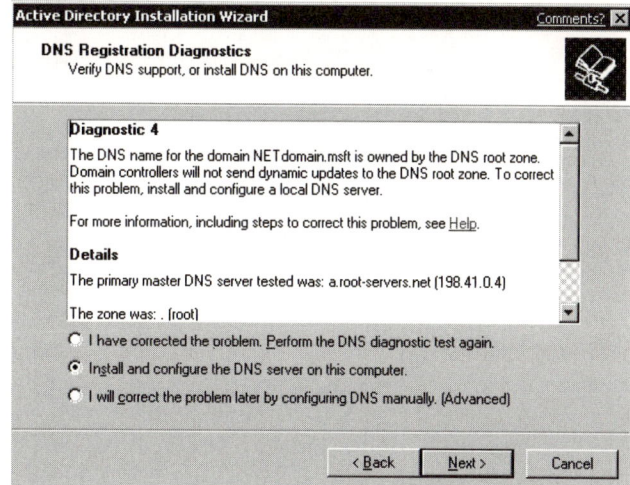

If you decide to have DNS automatically installed and configured at this time, you should confirm a couple of configuration options *before* continuing! Failure to do so can result in an incorrectly configured DNS environment, and that can be a real headache to correct. First, ensure that the primary DNS suffix for this computer is correctly configured. You can confirm this by right-clicking the My Computer icon on the Desktop. On the Computer Name tab, click the Change button. On the Computer Name Changes dialog box, shown in Figure 9.10, click the More button.

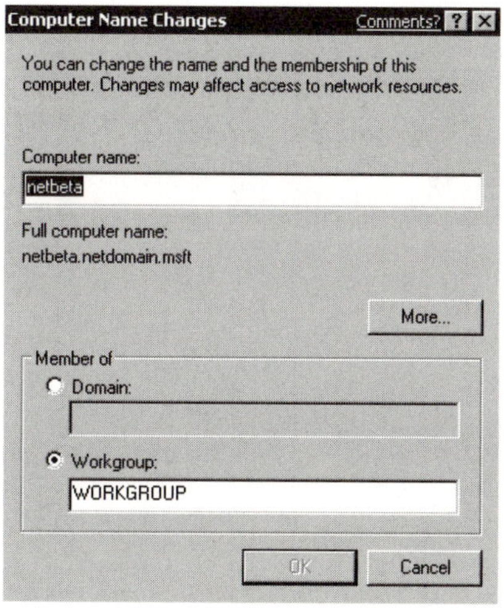

FIGURE 9.10

Confirming the
configuration of the
primary DNS suffix

The next dialog box, the DNS Suffix of and NetBIOS Computer Name, is where this option is confirmed. Ensure that the Primary DNS Suffix of This Computer option lists the DNS domain for which this computer will be a domain controller, as shown in Figure 9.11.

FIGURE 9.11

Confirming the
DNS domain

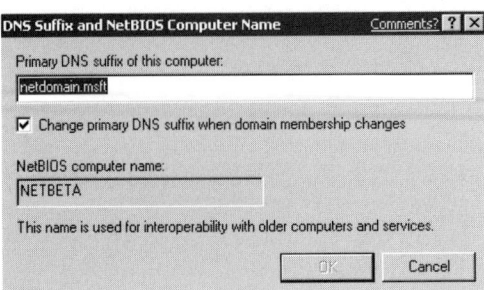

The second configuration you should confirm can be found in the properties of the TCP/IP configuration. Right-click the My Network Places icon on the Desktop and choose Properties. Highlight and right-click the LAN connection, then choose Properties. Highlight Internet Protocol (TCP/IP) and click the Properties button. Click the Advanced button and access the DNS tab on the Advanced TCP/IP Settings dialog box, as shown in Figure 9.12. Ensure that the appropriate DNS domain is listed in the DNS Suffix for This Connection option.

FIGURE 9.12

Setting DNS
options in the
Advanced TCP/IP
Settings dialog box

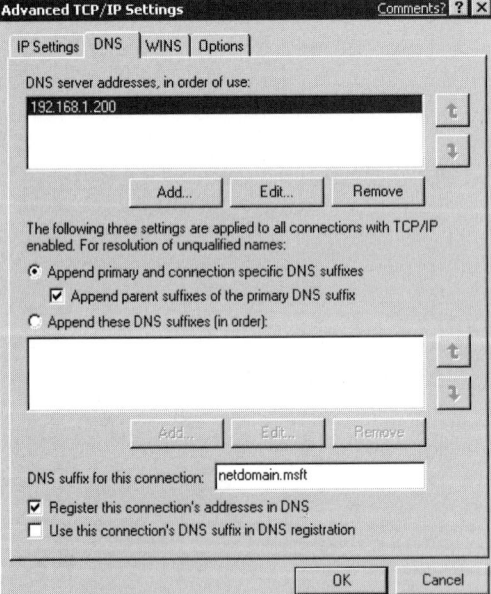

NOTE *I learned the hard way not to skip these steps. It is much harder to fix an incorrectly configured DNS domain than it is to avoid the problem in the first place!*

The next decision to be made concerns security, as shown in Figure 9.13. If you run server-based applications (such as a database or messaging program) on pre–Windows 2000/Windows Server 2003 *or* if you run server-based applications on Windows 2000/Windows Server 2003 that are members of pre–Windows 2000/Windows Server 2003 domains, then you need to configure your environment to be compatible with the needs of those older environments. This description can be confusing, so I'll explain the reasoning. Older server-based applications often used an unauthenticated (or Null) session for server-to-server or server-to-client connections. These types of connections present a security hole that has been removed from Windows 2000/Windows Server 2003. To provide backward compatibility, though, you can configure your server to support them. If at all possible, I recommend utilizing the newer, tighter security configuration available in Windows 2000/Windows Server 2003. If you must provide backward compatibility, I recommend doing so as a temporary solution—until you can upgrade any applications that require them.

FIGURE 9.13

Allowing backward compatibility

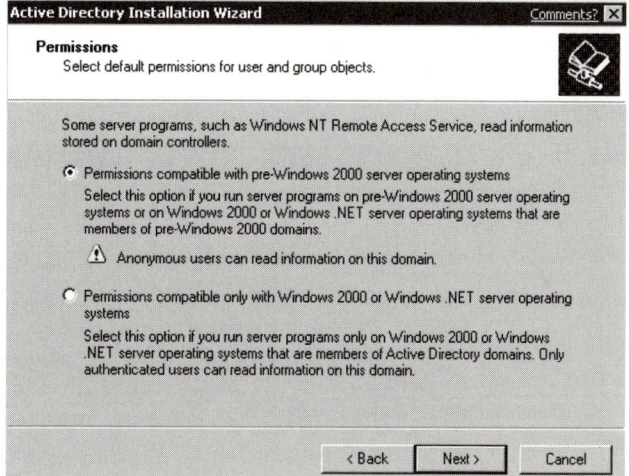

The next dialog box, as shown in Figure 9.14, asks you to provide a password that is used when starting the computer in Directory Services Restore Mode. This password allows the recovery of AD from a backup. Knowing this password grants you the ability to overwrite AD with an older version (from a backup set). Use a complex password, store it in a secure location, and limit the number of individuals who know it!

FIGURE 9.14

Setting the Restore Mode administrator password

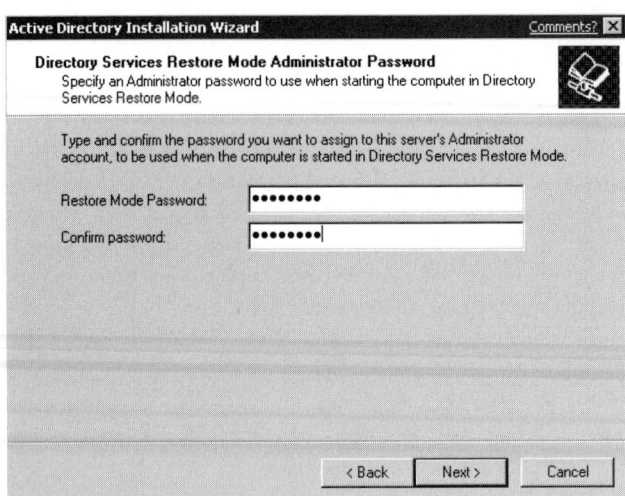

The last window, shown in Figure 9.15, provides a summary of the choices you have made in the DCPROMO process. Now is a great time to review your actions—avoiding mistakes, rather than correcting them, is always an easier route!

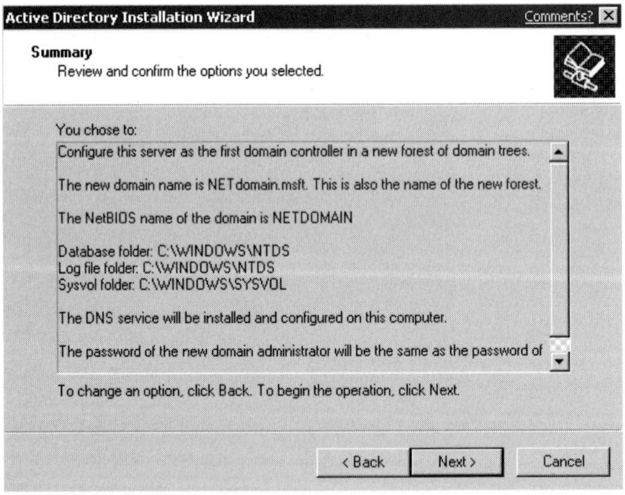

FIGURE 9.15

Reviewing your choices

That's all there is to the installation of AD. So far, so good! Actually, creating a good design is the hardest part of moving to a directory-based environment—the mechanics are just knowing where to click.

WHAT DOES THE WIZARD CREATE?

The following items are created during the AD installation process:

Database   This is the directory database for the new domain. The default location for the database and its associated log files is <*systemroot*>\Winnt\Ntds.

Shared System Volume   All Windows 2000 domain controllers have a share point used to store scripts that are part of the Group Policy objects for both the local domain and the enterprise. The default location for these files is <*systemroot*>\Sysvol\sysvol.

Domain Controller   The first domain controller for the domain is created during the first installation of AD.

First Site Name   A *site* is a logical grouping of servers. By default, the first site contains the first domain controller.

Global Catalog Server   The first domain controller in a site becomes the Global Catalog server. The Global Catalog server holds a partial replica of every domain in the forest. This replica holds a subset of the attributes for each object—those attributes most commonly used for searches. The Global Catalog server facilitates forestwide searches for objects.

Root Domain   If you create a new tree (rather than join an existing one), this domain will become the root domain for the new tree.

The installation also creates a series of organizational units:

Built-in Container   This contains default security groups, such as Account Operators, Administrators, and so on.

Foreign Security Principals Container   When a trust is made with a domain outside of the tree, this container is used to hold references to objects from the outside environment that have been granted local permissions.

Users Container   This is the default location for user accounts.

Computers Container   Likewise, this is the default location for computer accounts.

Domain Controllers Container   I bet I don't even have to tell you. (Just in case, though, this container is the default location for domain controller accounts.)

After your installation is complete, all components are ready to go. The process even creates an OU structure for you, as shown in Figure 9.16. The original containers created are not really intended to be the final location for your resource objects. For instance, from a security perspective, it does not make sense to leave user objects in a container named Users. Not only does the name give away too much information to anyone who manages to hack their way in, it is also a known default. Staying with known defaults makes a hacker's job easier—they already know the name of the object.

FIGURE 9.16

The default OU
structure

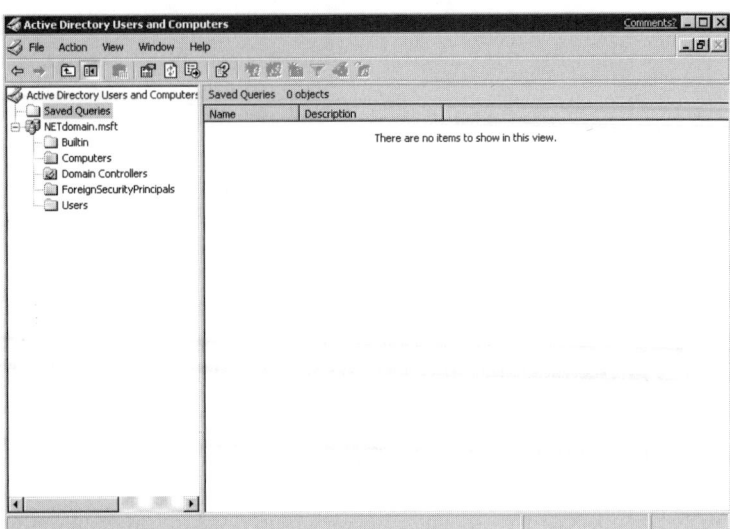

You'll notice a difference between Windows 2000 and Windows Server 2003 in Figure 9.16. In a Windows Server 2003 installation, a folder named Saved Queries is created. Right-clicking this folder and choosing New Query, opens the dialog box shown in Figure 9.17. Here you can define a set of search parameters for querying the AD database. Figure 9.18 shows the interface for defining the parameters. These predefined queries can be a great aid when managing AD.

FIGURE 9.17

Defining a new
query in Windows
Server 2003

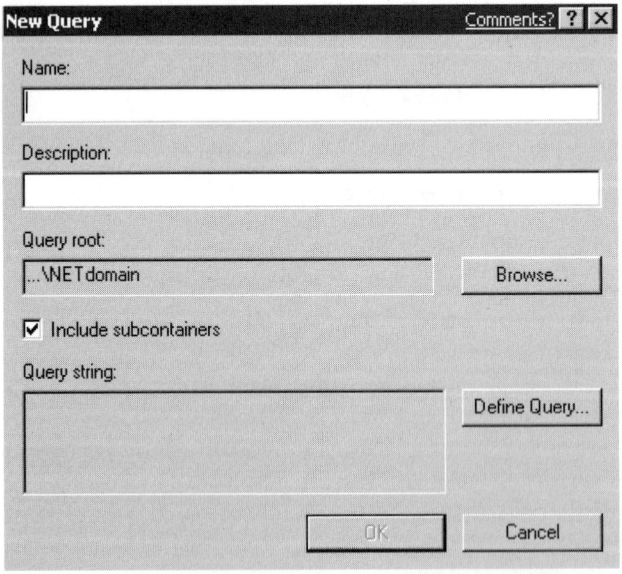

FIGURE 9.18

Finding common queries

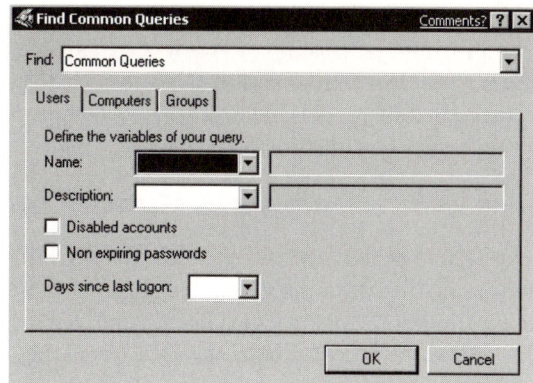

Notice the two available check boxes: Disabled Accounts and Non Expiring Passwords. Both of these are commonly searched (for AD cleanup and security). You can search for the name of objects or the value of attributes. You have options to search for partial names (for instance, all users whose names begin with *BK* or end with *KING*), for exact matches or nonmatches (all user accounts whose company does not equal *Royal Technologies*), or even for the existence or nonexistence of an entry (all users who do not have a telephone number entered). All in all, learning to use the query tool can make managing your AD environment quite a bit easier!

The installation process also creates a log file that lists the results of each step in the process. This log file is located in the `\winnt\debug` folder. Figure 9.19 displays the beginning of one such file. This file is a great beginning for your documentation of the server!

FIGURE 9.19

The DCPROMO log file

```
DCPROMO - Notepad
File Edit Format View Help
02/15 11:26:18 [INFO] Promotion request for domain controller of new domain
02/15 11:26:18 [INFO] DnsDomainName  netdomain.msft
02/15 11:26:18 [INFO]   FlatDomainName  NETDOMAIN
02/15 11:26:18 [INFO]   SiteName  Default-First-Site-Name
02/15 11:26:18 [INFO]   SystemVolumeRootPath  C:\WINDOWS\SYSVOL
02/15 11:26:18 [INFO]   DsDatabasePath  C:\WINDOWS\NTDS, DsLogPath  C:\WINDOWS\NTDS
02/15 11:26:18 [INFO]   ParentDnsDomainName  (NULL)
02/15 11:26:18 [INFO]   ParentServer  (NULL)
02/15 11:26:18 [INFO]   Account (NULL)
02/15 11:26:18 [INFO]   Options  6336
02/15 11:26:18 [INFO] Validate supplied paths
02/15 11:26:18 [INFO] Validating path C:\WINDOWS\NTDS.
02/15 11:26:18 [INFO]   Path is a directory
02/15 11:26:18 [INFO]   Path is on a fixed disk drive.
02/15 11:26:18 [INFO] Validating path C:\WINDOWS\NTDS.
02/15 11:26:18 [INFO]   Path is a directory
02/15 11:26:18 [INFO]   Path is on a fixed disk drive.
02/15 11:26:18 [INFO] Validating path C:\WINDOWS\SYSVOL.
02/15 11:26:18 [INFO]   Path is on a fixed disk drive.
02/15 11:26:18 [INFO]   Path is on an NTFS volume
02/15 11:26:18 [INFO] Domain Creation -- check that the flat name is unique.
02/15 11:26:23 [INFO] Start the worker task
02/15 11:26:24 [INFO] Request for promotion returning 0
02/15 11:26:24 [INFO] Using supplied domain controller:
02/15 11:26:24 [INFO] Using supplied site: Default-First-Site-Name
02/15 11:26:24 [INFO] Stopping service NETLOGON
02/15 11:26:24 [INFO] Stopping service NETLOGON
02/15 11:26:24 [INFO] Configuring service NETLOGON to 1 returned 0
02/15 11:26:24 [INFO] Stopped NETLOGON
02/15 11:26:24 [INFO] Creating the System Volume C:\WINDOWS\SYSVOL
02/15 11:26:24 [INFO] Deleting current sysvol path C:\WINDOWS\SYSVOL
02/15 11:26:29 [INFO] Preparing for system volume replication using root C:\WINDOWS\SYSVOL
02/15 11:26:29 [INFO] Created the system volume
02/15 11:26:29 [INFO] Copying initial Directory Service database file C:\WINDOWS\system32\ntds.dit to C:\WINDOWS\NTDS\ntds.di
02/15 11:26:32 [INFO] Installing the Directory Service
02/15 11:26:32 [INFO] Calling NtdsInstall for netdomain.msft
02/15 11:26:32 [INFO] Starting Active Directory installation
02/15 11:26:32 [INFO] Validating user supplied options
02/15 11:26:32 [INFO] Determining a site in which to install
02/15 11:26:32 [INFO] Examining an existing Active Directory forest
02/15 11:26:32 [INFO] Configuring the local domain controller to host Active Directory
02/15 11:27:14 [INFO] Creating directory partition: CN=Schema,CN=Configuration,DC=netdomain,DC=msft; 1585 objects remaining
02/15 11:27:32 [INFO] Creating directory partition: CN=Configuration,DC=netdomain,DC=msft; 139 objects remaining
02/15 11:27:32 [INFO] Creating directory partition: CN=Configuration,DC=netdomain,DC=msft; 138 objects remaining
02/15 11:27:32 [INFO] Creating directory partition: CN=Configuration,DC=netdomain,DC=msft; 137 objects remaining
02/15 11:27:32 [INFO] Creating directory partition: CN=Configuration,DC=netdomain,DC=msft; 136 objects remaining
02/15 11:27:32 [INFO] Creating directory partition: CN=Configuration,DC=netdomain,DC=msft; 135 objects remaining
02/15 11:27:33 [INFO] Creating directory partition: CN=Configuration,DC=netdomain,DC=msft; 134 objects remaining
02/15 11:27:33 [INFO] Creating directory partition: CN=Configuration,DC=netdomain,DC=msft; 133 objects remaining
02/15 11:27:33 [INFO] Creating directory partition: CN=Configuration,DC=netdomain,DC=msft; 132 objects remaining
02/15 11:27:33 [INFO] Creating directory partition: CN=Configuration,DC=netdomain,DC=msft; 131 objects remaining
02/15 11:27:33 [INFO] Creating directory partition: CN=Configuration,DC=netdomain,DC=msft; 130 objects remaining
02/15 11:27:33 [INFO] Creating directory partition: CN=Configuration,DC=netdomain,DC=msft; 129 objects remaining
```

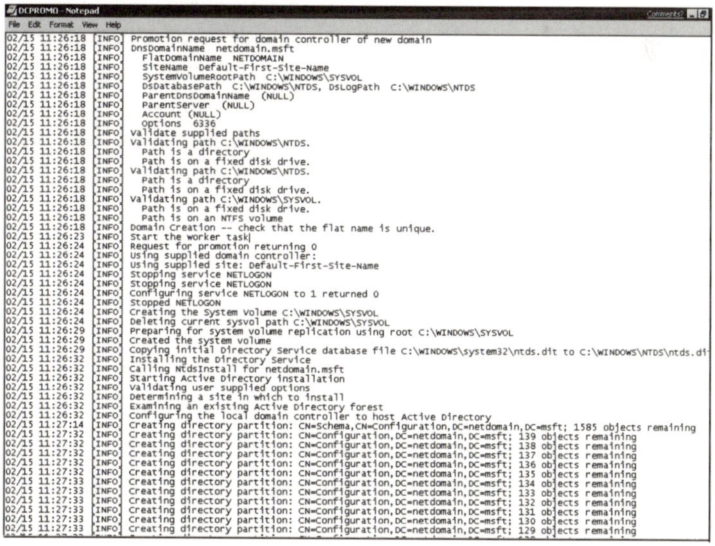

VERIFYING YOUR INSTALLATION

Once you have completed the installation of AD, it is a good idea to confirm that everything went as planned. The only real problem with wizards is that you click, they do, and you are never sure if they have done what you wanted them to do! The most important process that must be completed during the installation is the addition of the service records, or *SRV records*, to the DNS database.

NOTE *Since AD uses DNS to find domain controllers, it is imperative that each server has a record in the database.*

To confirm that DNS has been updated correctly, you need to do two things.

First, check the local DNS file to ensure that the proper entries have been made. This file is located in the *<systemroot>*\System32\Config folder and is named `Netlogon.dns`. The first record you should see is the server's LDAP service record. The LDAP SRV record should look something like this:

`_Ldap._tcp.<Active_directory_domain_name> IN SRV 0 0 389 <domain_controller_name>`

Here's an example:

`_Ldap._tcp.KingTech.com IN SRV 0 0 389 ADS1.KingTech.com`

You can also use the DNS Management tool, located in the Administrative Tools group. Within this tool, expand your DNS domain and highlight the _tcp folder. In the right pane you will see the record, as shown in Figure 9.20 (I've highlighted the appropriate record in the figure).

FIGURE 9.20

Confirming the LDAP record in DNS

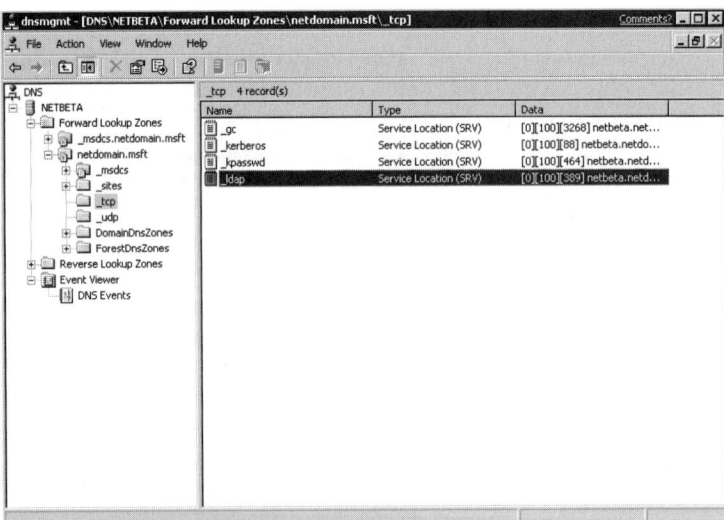

Second, to ensure that the SRV records in the DNS database are working correctly, use the NSLOOKUP tool. The following steps will confirm their functionality:

1. At the command prompt, type **NSLOOKUP** and hit the Enter key.

2. Type **SET TYPE = SRV** and press Enter.

3. Type `ldap.tcp.<Active_directory_domain_name>`, where *<Active_directory_domain_name>* is the name of your company's Active Directory domain. Press Enter.

If this process returns the server name and IP address, the SRV records are performing correctly.

Creating Organizational Units

To review: organizational units are used to organize the objects within your tree and to act as administrative boundaries. Many different types of structures can be created using OUs as the building blocks.

NOTE *The only real limitation is that no OUs can be created within the default OUs created during the installation of ADS.*

A user must have the appropriate permissions to create OUs within the tree. By default, members of the Administrators group have the permissions necessary to create OUs anywhere within a domain.

To create an OU, use the Active Directory Users and Computers tool, located in the Administrative Tools group. Expand your domain, and you will see the default containers shown in Figure 9.21.

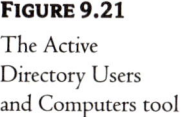

FIGURE 9.21

The Active Directory Users and Computers tool

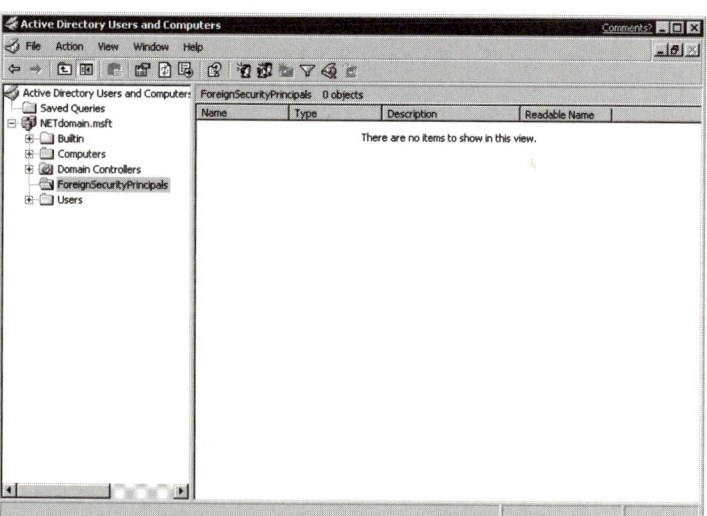

NOTE *We'll discuss the uses of the default containers in Chapter 10.*

Right-click the level where you want to create a new OU and choose New, then Organizational Unit, as demonstrated in Figure 9.22.

FIGURE 9.22

New organizational unit

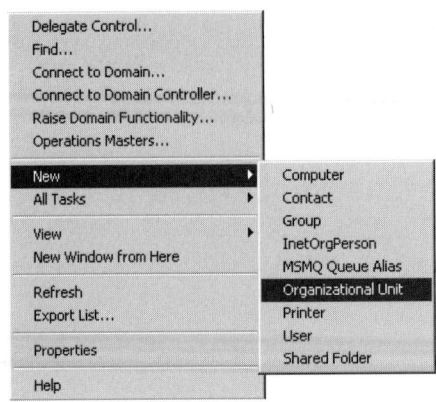

You will see the window shown in Figure 9.23.

FIGURE 9.23

Creating a new organizational unit

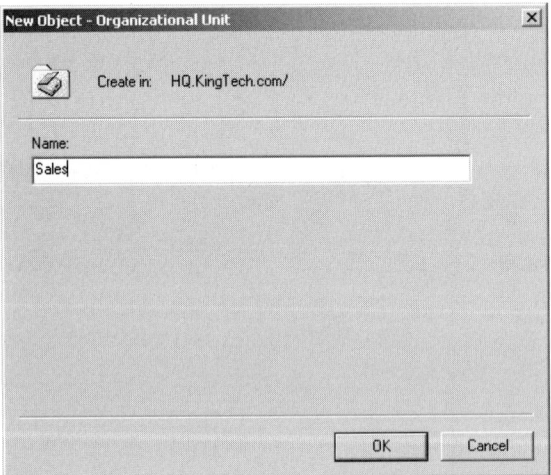

Provide a name for your new organizational unit and click the OK button. As you can see, creating new organizational units is about as easy as creating new directories in a DOS file system. Just as in DOS, there will be those people who create too many and those who create too few. In either case, we have a name for them: future consulting customers. Take the time to plan your structure (and play with a few test systems) before implementation!

Delegating Administration

One reason to create multiple OUs is to delegate administrative tasks. While the mechanics of delegation are straightforward, you will need to be aware of how permissions work in the AD structure.

Permissions granted to an AD container flow down the structure in the same way they do in the NTFS file system, as you can see in Figure 9.24.

FIGURE 9.24

Permissions
inheritance

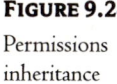
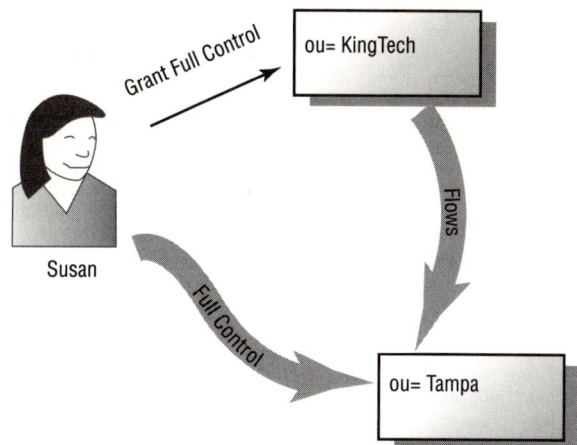

If Susan is granted Full Control to the KingTech container, by default that set of permissions will flow down the AD structure so that she has Full Control in every container below KingTech. As you will see when we walk through the process, you can limit the flow if you desire.

DELEGATING CONTROL OF A CONTAINER

To delegate control of a container, right-click the container in the Active Directory Users and Computers tool and choose the Delegate Control option. This starts the Delegation of Control Administrative Wizard. As with all wizards, the first screen is a Welcome screen. Clicking Next brings you to the window shown in Figure 9.25. Here, you are asked to choose which users or groups should be given permissions.

FIGURE 9.25

Users or groups

In Windows 2000, clicking Add brings you to a list of available users and groups, as shown in Figure 9.26.

FIGURE 9.26

User or group selection in Windows 2000

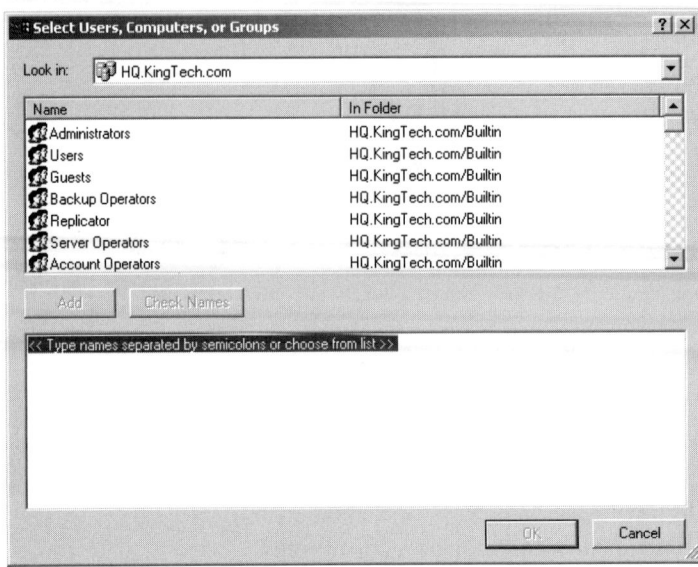

The Windows Server 2003 interface, however, has changed quite a bit, as shown in Figure 9.27. The new look is more than just a pretty face; you have quite a few more options than were available in Windows 2000—options that can make your life easier!

FIGURE 9.27

Selecting users or groups in Windows Server 2003

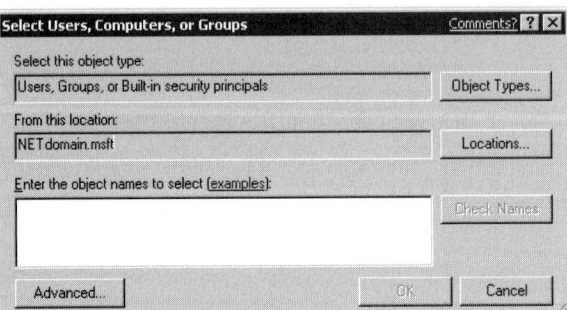

Let's work through the options one at a time. First, the Object Types button allows you to control which types of objects should be shown, as you can see in Figure 9.28. This allows you to filter the list to match your needs.

FIGURE 9.28

Controlling object types

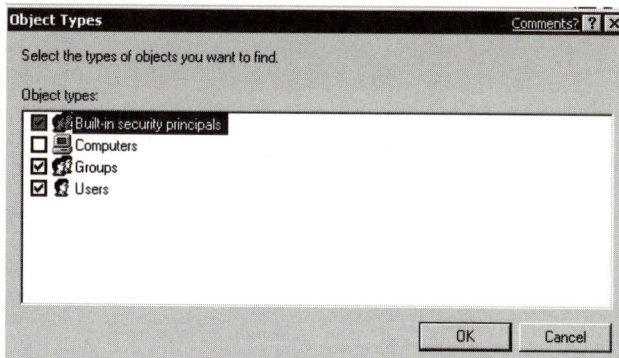

The Locations button allows you to control the list of objects by their placement in the AD structure, as shown in Figure 9.29.

FIGURE 9.29

Finding locations

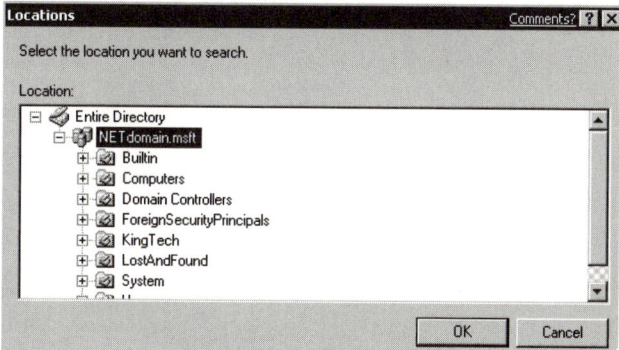

To actually choose the person or group to whom you want to delegate permissions, you have the option of either typing them in or using the Advanced button. Notice the "examples" link; it brings up a list of the types of names that are acceptable and their formats, as shown in Figure 9.30.

FIGURE 9.30

The Examples window

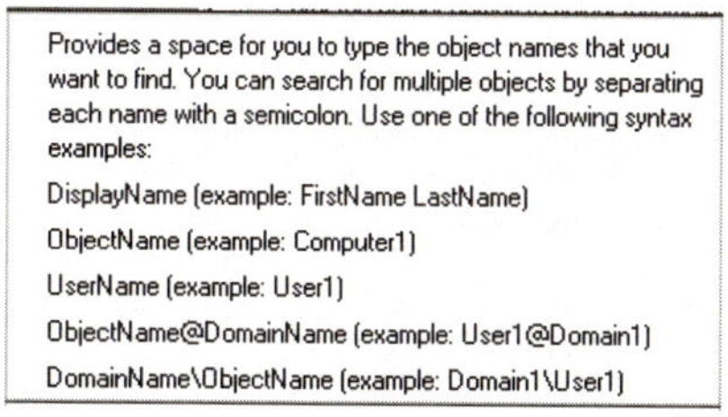

> Provides a space for you to type the object names that you want to find. You can search for multiple objects by separating each name with a semicolon. Use one of the following syntax examples:
>
> DisplayName (example: FirstName LastName)
>
> ObjectName (example: Computer1)
>
> UserName (example: User1)
>
> ObjectName@DomainName (example: User1@Domain1)
>
> DomainName\ObjectName (example: Domain1\User1)

The Advanced button is where this utility really shines. You can run some very sophisticated searches to find the accounts or groups you need. First, you can type in the first few letters and be shown all matching records, or you can specify that only exact matches be displayed. The Columns button allows you to customize the information about each object shown in the display box. In Figure 9.31, I have entered nothing in the Name box, so the entire content of my AD domain is displayed. I've also added the Employee ID column to the output.

FIGURE 9.31

Searching with the Advanced options

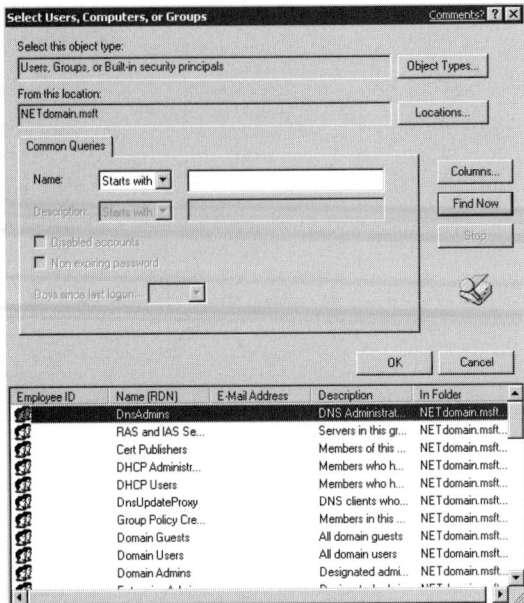

The next screen in Windows 2000, shown in Figure 9.32, lets you either choose from a list of commonly delegated tasks or create a custom delegation. The list of available common tasks has been expanded for the Windows Server 2003 environment, as shown in Figure 9.33.

FIGURE 9.32

Tasks to delegate in Windows 2000

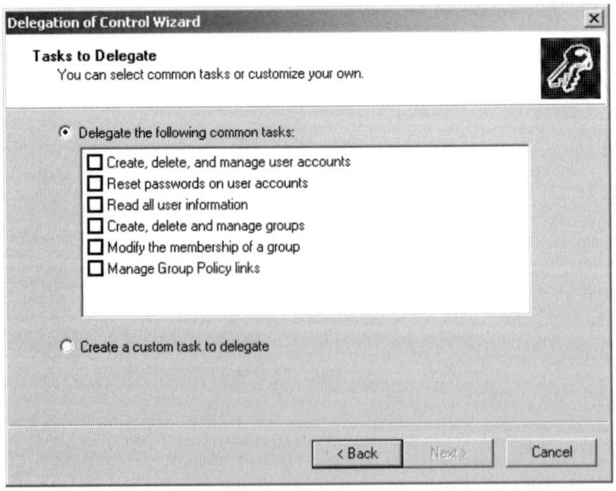

FIGURE 9.33

Tasks to delegate in Windows Server 2003

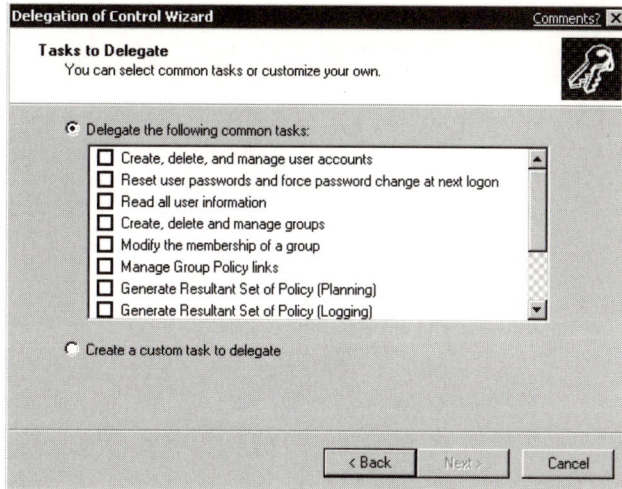

If you choose to create a custom delegation task, in Windows 2000, you will be presented with the window shown in Figure 9.34. Here you can either allow management of all objects in the container or limit the delegation to certain object classes.

FIGURE 9.34

Managing object types in Windows 2000

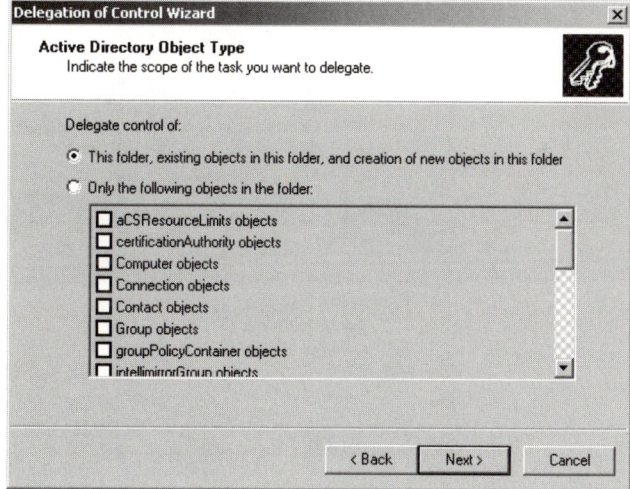

A couple of convenient check boxes have been added to the Windows Server 2003 interface, as shown in Figure 9.35. While you could manually choose the appropriate permissions to accomplish these two tasks in Windows 2000, it is very convenient to just select a check box to allow the user or group to create or delete the selected object types.

FIGURE 9.35

Managing object types in Windows Server 2003

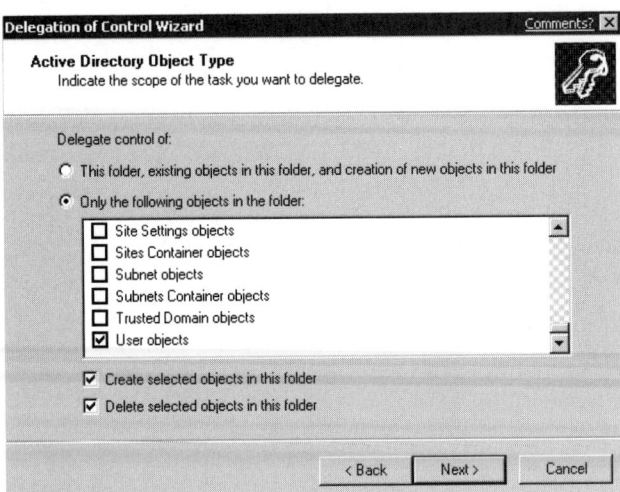

In the next window, shown in Figure 9.36, you determine exactly what administrative powers you wish to grant. Notice that there are three check boxes.

FIGURE 9.36

Permissions

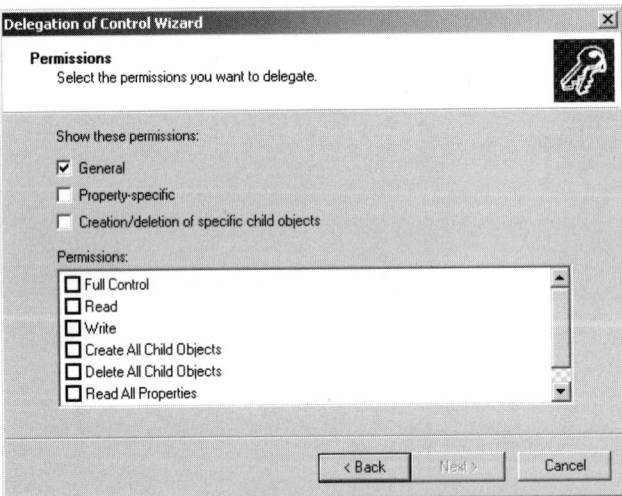

The General check box gives a basic set of permissions as options. These permission are:

Full Control Grants all other permissions (and the ability to take ownership) to all objects in the container

Read Allows the recipient to read the Access Control List (ACL) of all objects

Write Allows the recipient to write to the ACL of all objects within the container

Create All Child Objects   Allows the creation of any class of object within the container

Delete All Child Objects   Allows the deletion of any class of object within the container

Read All Properties   Allows the recipient to read the properties of objects within the container

Write All Properties   Grants the ability to change all properties for objects within the container

In reality, the list of permissions above should be sufficient in most cases. Actually, most companies will not even be as specific as this first list allows—most companies will give administrators Full Control and leave it at that. You have, however, the ability to micromanage the delegation of administrative permissions. If you check the "Property-specific" option (shown back in Figure 9.36), the list will expand to include a list of all of the various properties available. As an example, the list will include Read Street and Write Street, allowing you to determine if the recipient can see or change the Street property of objects within the container. This level of granularity allows you to easily grant a person in human resources the ability to change user information such as addresses and phone numbers *without* having to give that person rights to any other properties.

Lastly, if you check Creation/Deletion of Specific Child Objects, the list will expand to include the various classes of objects that can be created. Now you can control exactly what types of objects an assistant administrator can create. Perhaps you've got a person who is in charge of all printers in the company. You can easily give this person the ability to create printing-related objects *without* giving them the permission to create anything else.

The last screen of the Administrative Wizard confirms the changes that you are about to make. Clicking Finish will implement these changes.

Creating Users

Once you have created your AD structure, the next step is to populate it with objects representing the resources on your network. While many different classes of objects are available, there are a few that *every* network requires. To tell the truth, most objects within the directory are created in a similar manner. In the Active Directory Users and Computers tool, right-click the container in which you wish to create the object and choose New; you will be presented with a list of valid object classes, as shown in Figure 9.37. Choose the object class that you wish to create and enter the required information.

FIGURE 9.37

Creating new objects

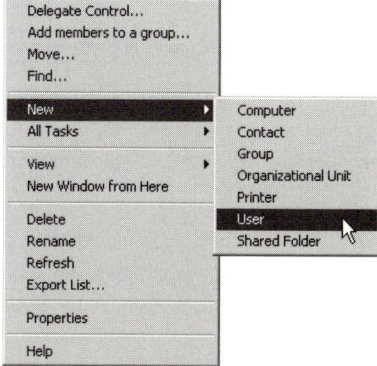

Without a doubt, the most important class of object is that of *user*. User accounts are the backbone upon which all network functionality is built—without them, no one accesses resources.

You are probably pretty comfortable with the concept of a user account. User accounts of one sort or another have been used since the dawn of networks to allow users to identify themselves to the network. Networks also use user accounts to authenticate access to resources. When a user—let's call him Tom—attempts to access the network, he will be asked for his logon name (Tom's user account). The network operating system will then check to see whether the account he provides exists and, if so, whether there are any restrictions that would mandate denying his request (such as time or station restrictions). If Tom successfully logs on to the network, his account information will be used to authenticate his requests for resource access. Every action that Tom takes on the network will be allowed or denied based on information in a user account (although not necessarily his own—many processes are accessed through system accounts, such as many web-based resources).

Creating a New User Account

To create a user account, access the Active Directory Users and Computers program located in the Administrative Tools group. Right-click the container in which you wish to place the user account, then choose New ➤ User. You will be presented with the screen shown in Figure 9.38. Here you will enter the user's first, last, and logon names.

FIGURE 9.38

Creating a user account

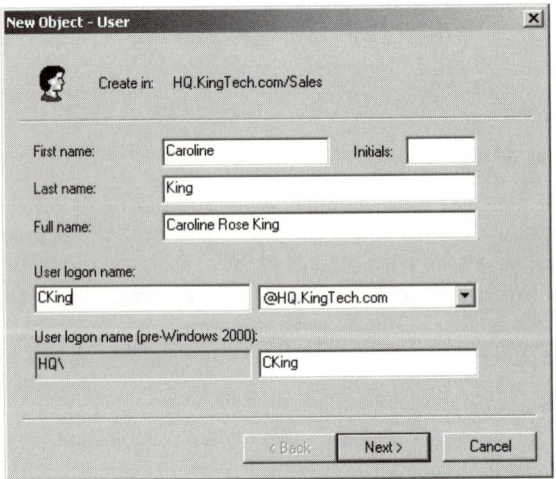

Click Next to move to the next window in the process, shown in Figure 9.39. Here you can assign the user's first password and make a couple of choices regarding this account. Your choices are explained in the following list:

User Must Change Password at Next Logon   The next time the user logs in to the network, she will be forced to change her password. This forces the user to change her password from the one provided by the administrator, so that the user is the only person who knows her password.

User Cannot Change Password   Some companies use a centrally controlled list of passwords, set by the administrator. If this is the case, this option will prevent a user from changing her password.

Password Never Expires   Most companies force users to change their passwords periodically. This option overrules that policy.

Account Is Disabled   This option can be used to disable an account.

TIP   *Usually, the Account Is Disabled option is used when an employee has been terminated or goes on an extended leave. In a seasonal business, however, you might want to create user accounts for seasonal employees before your busy season, disable them, and then just reenable them as the employees come online.*

FIGURE 9.39

User account setup

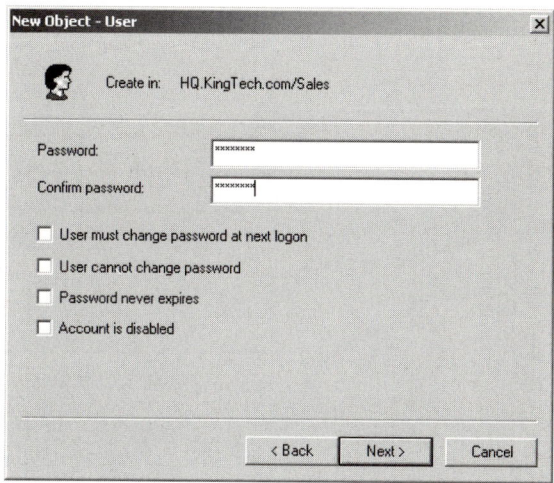

The process ends with a screen that confirms the choices you have made, as shown in Figure 9.40. Clicking Finish will create the account.

FIGURE 9.40

Finishing the creation

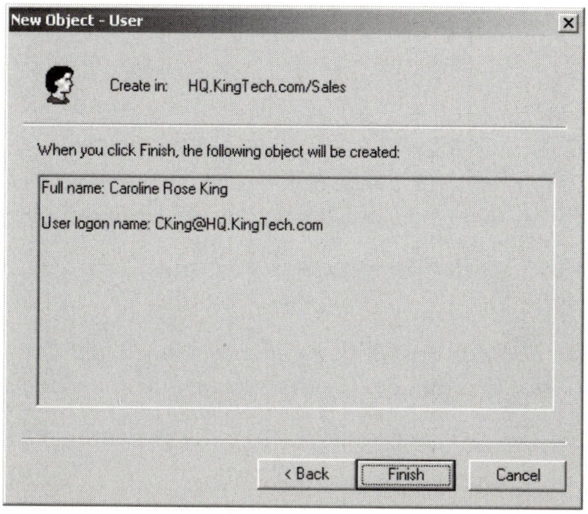

Adding Information about Users

Once you have created a user account, there is still a lot of information that you can add. To perform searches based on such criteria as location, department, or manager, you will have to enter that information into the user's attributes. To do so, double-click the user account in the Active Directory Users and Computers tool. You will be presented with the User Properties window shown in Figure 9.41.

FIGURE 9.41

General tab of the User Properties window

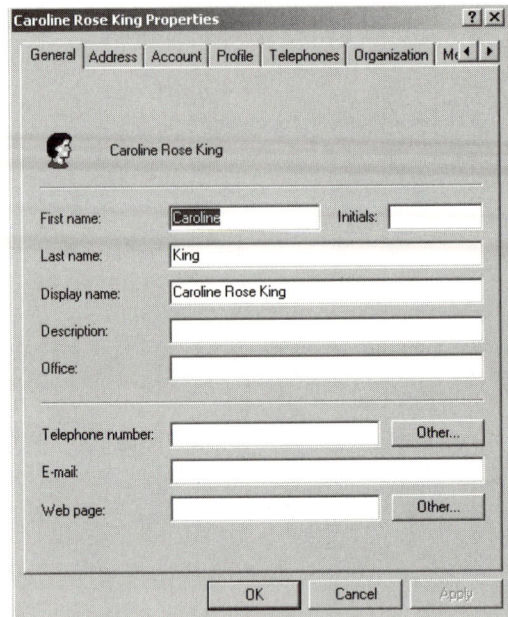

Most of the attributes are self-explanatory; the e-mail attribute, for instance, is the user's e-mail address. Other attributes will need some explanation; for example, phone number and home page are both multivalue attributes. Clicking the Other button allows you to add multiple values for these attributes.

Figure 9.42 shows the Address tab of the User Properties dialog box. This tab contains parameters that pertain to the user's mailing address.

Figure 9.43 shows the Account tab. Notice that you can use this tab to set an expiration date for a user account. This option is handy if you hire a lot of temporary or seasonal personnel and do not want their accounts to be valid indefinitely. You can also provide values for the following:

Logon Hours   One of the initial access securities is the ability to limit when users can log on to the network.

Log On To   Controlling which computers a user logs on to can help to control those "social butterflies" who flit from desk to desk, logging on but never logging off!

Account Options   This area allows you to set parameters for controlling password security.

FIGURE 9.42

The Address tab of the User Properties window

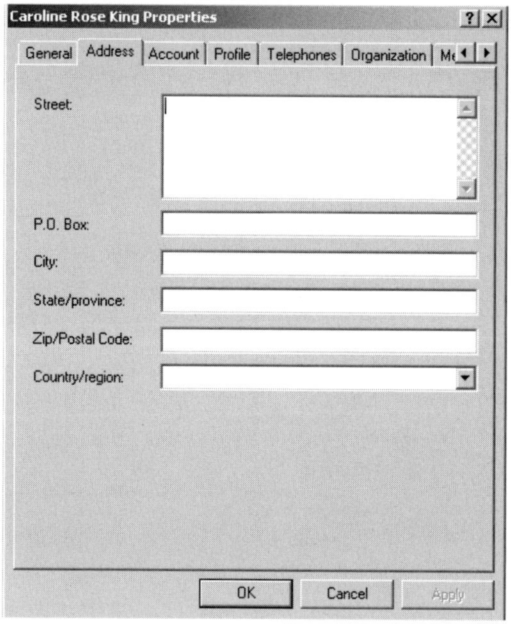

FIGURE 9.43

The Account tab of the User Properties window

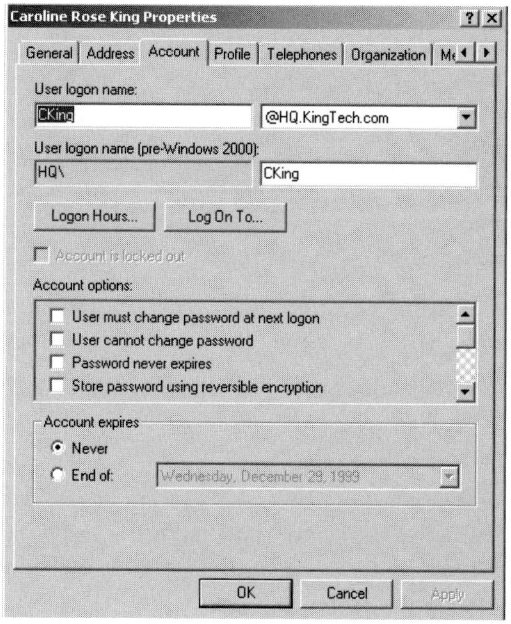

Figure 9.44 shows the Profile tab. This tab contains attributes pertaining to the placement of network files. There are two distinct areas of configuration:

User Profile   Here you can set the location of a user's profile and login script.

Home Folder   This lets you control the placement (local or network) of a user's home directory.

FIGURE 9.44

The Profile tab of the User Properties window

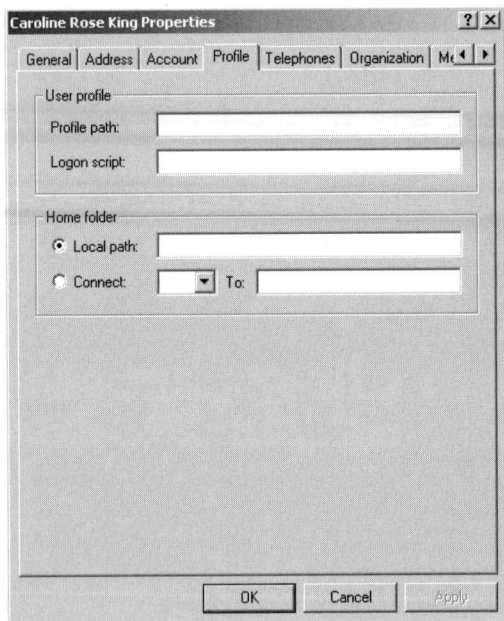

Figure 9.45 shows the Telephones tab, which contains contact information for the user.

NOTE   *The attributes on the Telephones tab are all multivalue fields—clicking the Other button allows you to enter multiple values.*

Figure 9.46 shows the Organization tab. This tab contains attributes that allow you to document the organizational hierarchy of your company. You can set the following values:

Title

Department

Company

Manager   This refers to the employee's manager (as opposed to the next attribute, Direct Reports).

Direct Reports   This refers to the people who are managed by this user.

FIGURE 9.45

The Telephones
tab of the User
Properties window

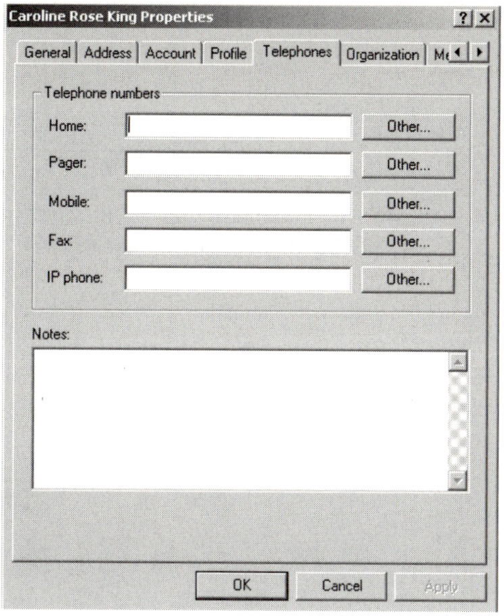

NOTE *At this time, AD does not use the information stored on the Organization tab except for LDAP searches. Later, we can expect other applications to take advantage of this information. For example, imagine an e-mail system—Exchange Server, perhaps—that lets you send messages to "All users whose department attribute is Sales."*

FIGURE 9.46

The Organization
tab of the User
Properties window

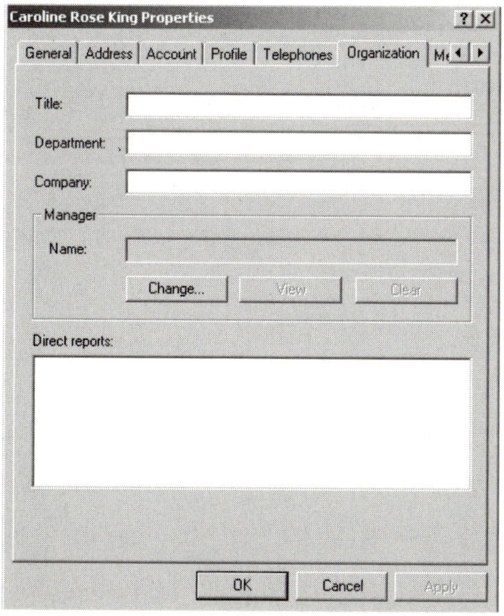

The Member Of tab is shown in Figure 9.47. On this page you can add or remove users from Windows NT security groups.

FIGURE 9.47

The Member Of tab of the User Properties window

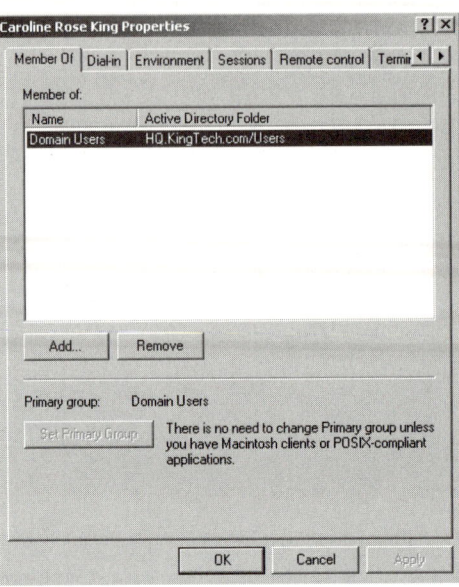

The Dial-in tab, shown in Figure 9.48, is used to configure a user's dial-in privileges. This tab is only valid if RAS has been configured.

FIGURE 9.48

The Dial-in tab of the User Properties window

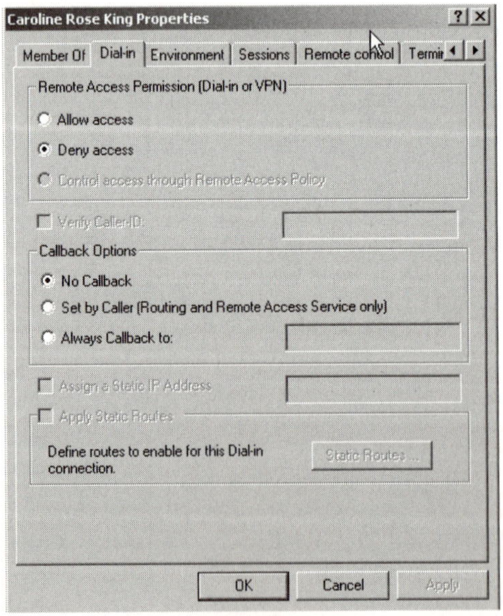

The Environment tab (Figure 9.49) allows you to configure the user's initial network environment as they log in. This is useful for users who move from computer to computer. Settings here will take effect no matter where the user is sitting.

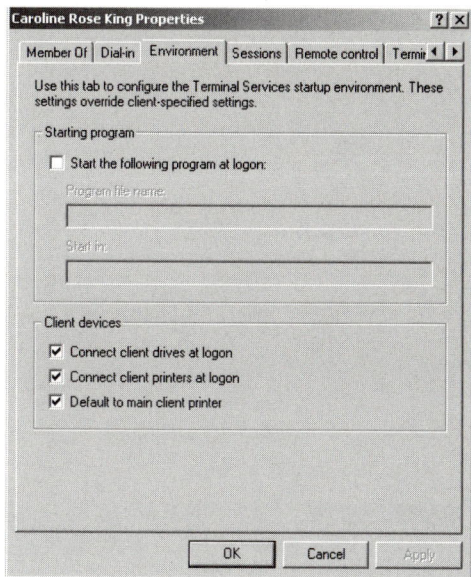

The Sessions tab, shown in Figure 9.50, allows you to configure connections for clients utilizing the Terminal Services capabilities of Windows 2000.

NOTE   *Terminal Services is really beyond the scope of an AD book. In short, it allows you to use less powerful PCs or dumb terminals to connect to Windows 2000/Windows Server 2003. All applications actually run on the server, with only screen updates being sent to the client machine. We use this quite effectively in the training industry—it allows us to move out-of-date equipment from technical classrooms into application training rooms. Here, they can run Windows 9x or NT applications without having to have the horsepower necessary to run those operating systems.*

The Remote Control tab also pertains to Terminal Services. As shown in Figure 9.51, you can configure aspects of observing or controlling a user's session from a remote location.

NOTE   *This can really save time for help desk personnel. They can call a user on the phone and walk him through the process he is having trouble with—without ever leaving their own desks!*

FIGURE 9.50

The Sessions tab of the User Properties window

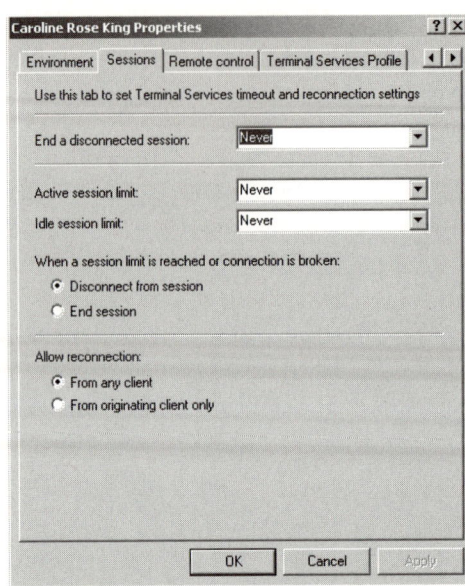

FIGURE 9.51

The Remote Control tab of the User Properties window

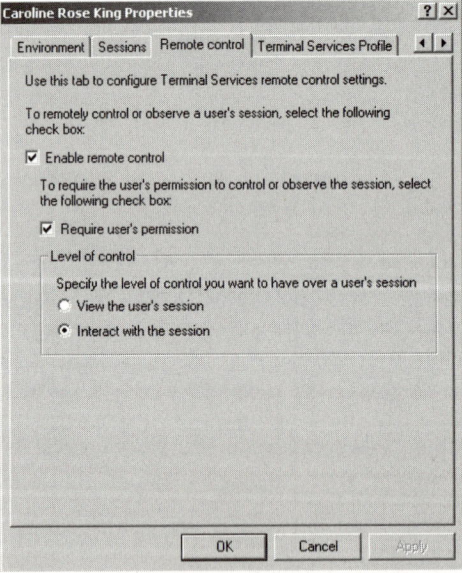

Lastly, the Terminal Services Profile tab, shown in Figure 9.52, allows you to configure the location where Terminal Services clients should find their session profile and to assign the folder they should use as their home directory.

FIGURE 9.52

The Terminal Services Profile tab of the User Properties window

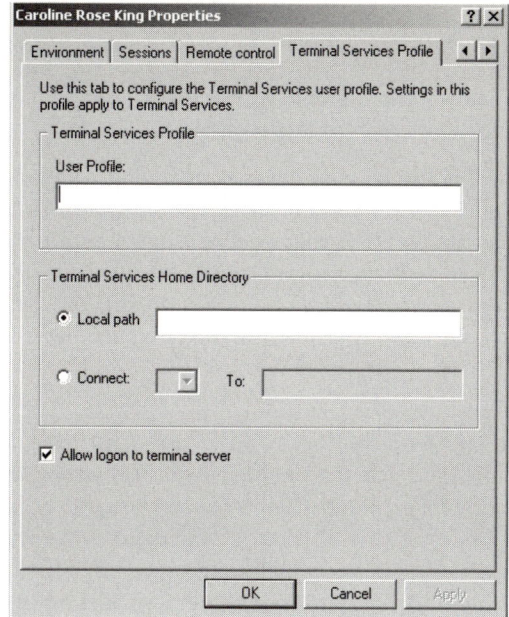

I know that this seems like a lot of information about a user—especially when compared to earlier network operating systems. Remember the big difference here is that in AD we are not just creating a user account for network access, we are trying to create a database of user information. This information, once entered, can be utilized in many ways.

Creating Groups

Groups are a means to organize individual user or computer accounts. They are used for security and distribution purposes. Most of your management should be done through groups, rather than to individual users or computers. The *scope*, or area of influence, for a group can be limited to a single domain, to multiple domains (through trusts), or to the entire network. Group objects are named in the same way as any other object in the directory.

TIP   Take special care to give each group a name that describes its purpose. If a group is used to grant access to accounting information, for instance, its name should imply that, such as AcctInfo.

Types of Groups

New to Windows 2000/Windows Server 2003 are two types of group objects, each used for a specific function:

Security Groups   These are used to grant permissions to resources. Computers, users, and other groups can be members of a security group. If you wanted to grant users permissions on a share point, for instance, you could create a group, grant that group the appropriate permissions, and then add users (or other groups) as members of that group.

Distribution Groups   These groups are used for nonsecurity functions, such as e-mail. Distribution groups cannot be assigned permissions or rights.

In reality, you will probably create only security groups unless a compelling reason to use distribution groups arises. Here's the bottom line: distribution groups can act as "mail recipients" but cannot be assigned permissions. Security groups can be assigned permissions *and* act as mail recipients. Since the security groups can perform both functions, it is usually better to use them, even if all you want is for the group to act as a mail distribution point. If, at a later date, you decide that the members of a group should be assigned permissions, you can do so without having to create a second group.

Access Tokens

When an object is created in the directory database, it is given a unique identifier known as a SID (system identifier). Rather than the user-friendly X.500 names, the operating system uses SIDs to identify objects. SIDs are used to control access to all resources on the network.

When a user logs in to the network, the system requires that she provide a valid login name (and password if one exists for her account). NT then puts the SID for the user, and the SIDs of any groups that she is a member of, into an object known as the *access token* and sends the access token back to the user.

As the user attempts to access resources, she will send her access token to the resources for authentication. The SIDs in the token are compared against a list of SIDs for objects that have permissions to the resource. This list, known as the Access Control List (ACL), controls who may access the resource. If the user's access token contains the SID of an object that has been granted the necessary permissions to use the resource, the user's request is granted.

Scopes of Groups

Windows 2000/Windows Server 2003 provides the ability to limit the area of influence for a group. A group can be one of the following three types:

Domain Local Groups   Limited to a single domain. They can be used to grant permissions to resources only within that domain, but can have members from any domain. These groups should be used when the permissions are to be granted specifically within a domain: domain local groups are not visible outside of their own domain.

Global Groups   Used to grant permissions to objects in multiple domains and are visible to all trusted domains. Global groups, though, can have as members only users and groups from within their own domain. If your AD database is configured for native-mode operation, global groups can be *nested*; in other words, a global group can contain other global groups.

Universal Groups   Similar to global groups in that they can be used to grant permissions across multiple domains. The big difference is that universal groups can contain any combination of user and global group accounts from *any* trusted domain in the forest. Microsoft suggests the following procedure for granting permissions across multiple domains:

1. Create a global group in each domain and add the appropriate users as members.

2. Create a universal group and grant it the appropriate permissions.

3. Add the global groups as members of the universal group.

Adding groups to other groups is known as *nesting*. Each group "deep" into a nest is called a *layer*, as shown in Figure 9.53. Group 1 is a member of Group 2; this is one layer. Group 2 is a member of Group 3; this is another layer.

NOTE *While there is no limit to the number of layers that can be applied, tracing permissions becomes much more complex as the depth increases.*

FIGURE 9.53

Nesting groups

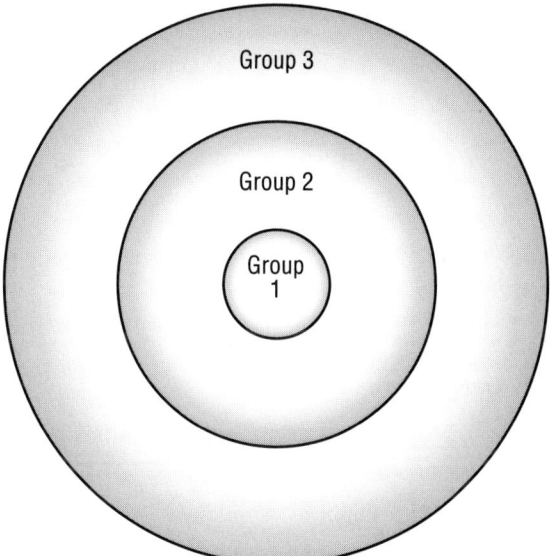

The Mechanics of Creating Groups

Groups are created using the Active Directory Users and Computers tool located in the Administrative Tools group. Right-click the container in which you wish to create a group, choose New, and then choose Group. This will bring up the Create New Object - Group screen depicted in Figure 9.54. Here you will name your group, choose a type (Security or Distribution), and choose a scope (Domain Local, Global, or Universal). The Universal option will be available only in a multidomain environment (in other words, in AD structures where trusts exist).

FIGURE 9.54

Creating a group

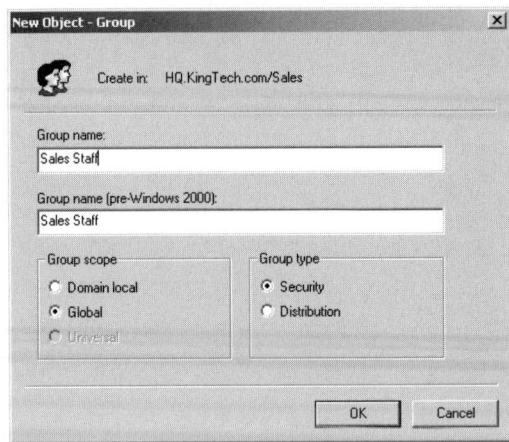

Once you have created the group, you can manage the object's properties by double-clicking the group object in the AD Management tool. You will be presented with the Properties page for the group. As you can see in Figure 9.55, the Properties page for a group object has four tabs:

◆ General

◆ Members

◆ Member Of

◆ Managed By

On the General tab, you can change a group's type, scope, and name, and even provide an e-mail address for addressing mail to the group.

FIGURE 9.55

The General tab of the Group Properties window

The properties on the other three tabs are fairly straightforward.

The Members tab, shown in Figure 9.56, lists those users and groups that are members of this group.

FIGURE 9.56

The Members tab of the Group Properties window

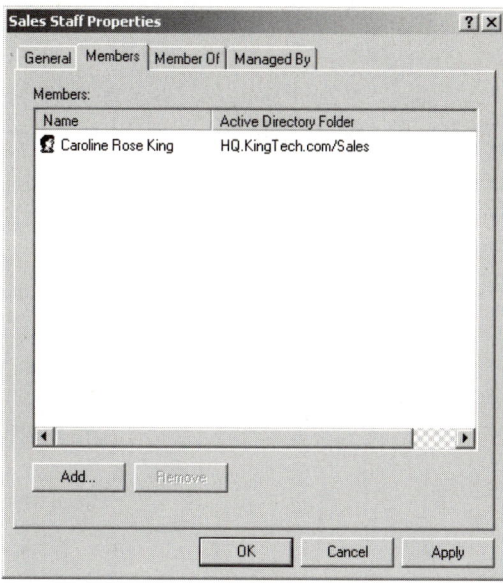

The Member Of tab, which you can see in Figure 9.57, lists the groups that this group is a member of. (I've added the guest group as an example.)

FIGURE 9.57

The Member of tab of the Group Properties window

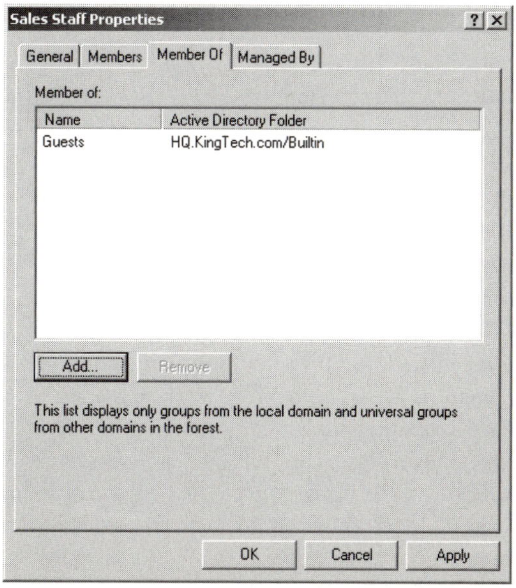

Figure 9.58 shows the Managed By tab, which allows you to document who is responsible for management of this group.

FIGURE 9.58

The Managed By tab of the Group Properties window

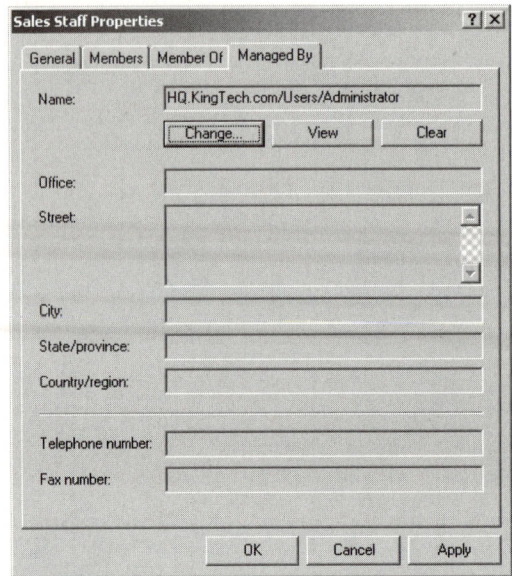

Creating Printers

There are two types of printers that you might create in your Windows 2000/Windows Server 2003 environment:

◆ Those that are attached to Windows 2000/XP/Windows Server 2003 computers

◆ Those that are not

Since Windows 2000/Windows Server 2003 is fully AD enabled, publishing a printer in the AD database is as simple as creating a new printer. For printers attached to non–Windows 2000/Windows Server 2003 computers, use the Active Directory management tool to create a printer object.

Printers in Windows 2000/Windows Server 2003

Printers are created on a Windows 2000 computer in the same manner that they are created in earlier versions of NT. There have, however, been a few interface changes in the Windows Server 2003 products. Let's start with a look at creating printers in Windows 2000. Access the Printers folder and double-click the Add Printer icon. This will run the Add Printer Administrative Wizard. The wizard opens with a Welcome screen. Clicking Next brings you to the first configuration window, in which you determine whether you are adding a local printer or attaching to a printer across the network. If you are adding a local printer, the next window, shown in Figure 9.59, asks you which port the printer is attached to.

FIGURE 9.59

Port selection

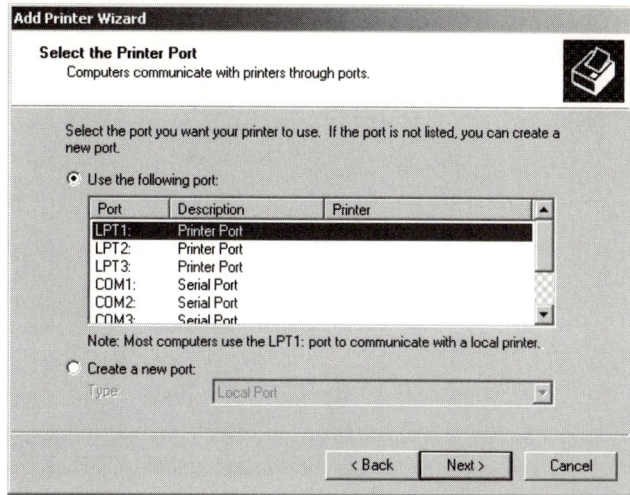

The next screen, which you can see in Figure 9.60, asks you to identify the make and model of your printer. This ensures that the appropriate printer drivers are installed.

FIGURE 9.60

Choosing a printer model

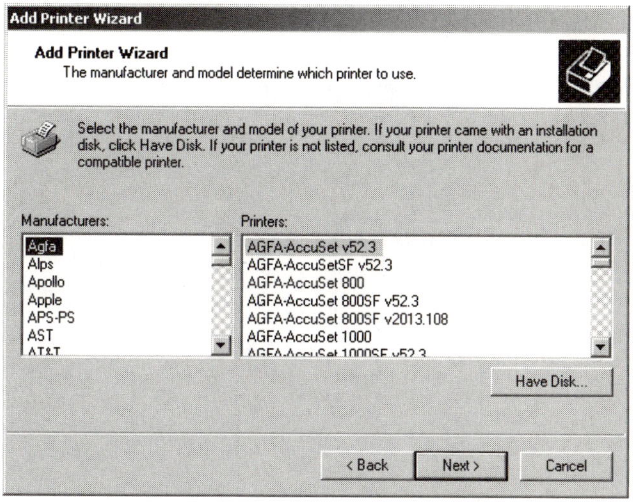

The next screen asks you to name the printer. After you have done that, you are asked if you want to share the printer, and if so, what the shared printer should be named.

A new option for Windows 2000 Server (when compared to NT) appears in the next screen, shown in Figure 9.61. Here you can add a few comments about the printer. These comments will be available to users through an AD query.

FIGURE 9.61

Supplying a location
and comments

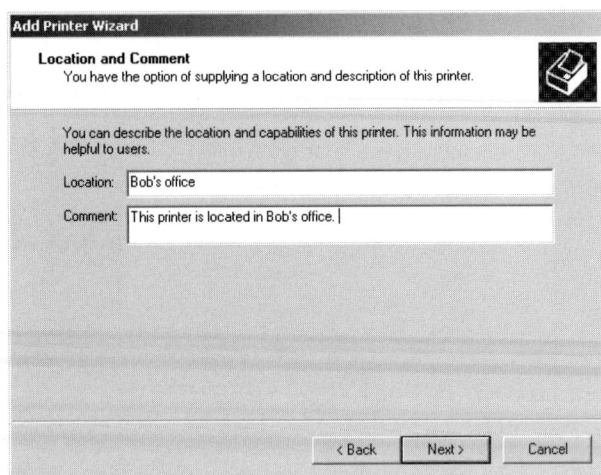

The rest of the Wizard is standard. It asks whether you want to print a test page and shows you a review of the choices you have made. Clicking Finish on the last page completes the process.

Once the printer has been created, you can right-click it and access its properties. On the Sharing tab, shown in Figure 9.62, you will see that the List in the Directory option is selected by default. In other words, this printer will automatically be listed in the AD database.

FIGURE 9.62

Printer properties

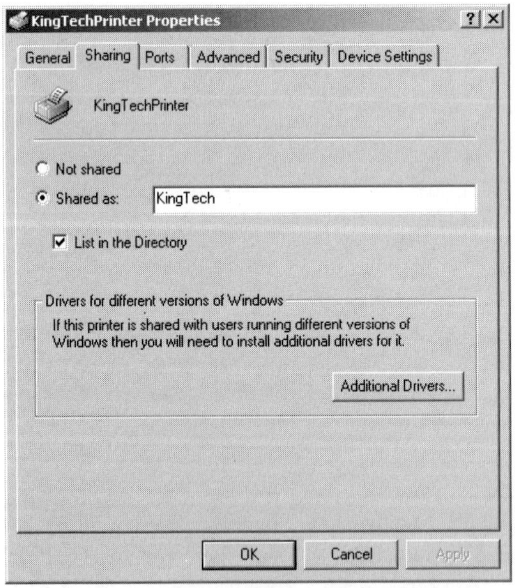

Now let's take a look at the process on Windows Server 2003. The first difference is that the title of the group on the Start menu has changed from Printers to Printers and Faxes. (The inclusion of a fax server service is a great addition to the core components of the operating system, but it doesn't impact our topic, Active Directory. We'll concentrate on objects that are more central to AD.) Take a look at Figure 9.63. Notice that the interface is much more useful—with a series of collapsible menus in the right pane on the window. At the top of the list is a menu offering the various options available in the printer and fax group: adding a printer, accessing print server properties, and setting up faxing. Below that is a direct link to the printer section of the help and support system (this is very handy when you are having trouble with your print environment), and below that is a list of other system-related groups that you might need to access. At the very bottom is a general description of the folder in which you are working. This new interface is common to most of the system folders on your Start menu, and makes working with the operating system more convenient than ever!

FIGURE 9.63

The Printers and Faxes group

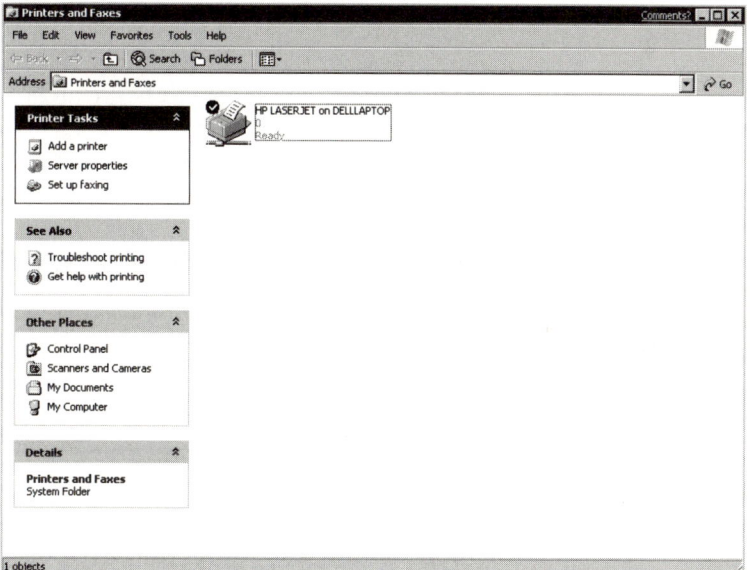

Clicking the Add a Printer option brings up the obligatory Welcome screen for Microsoft wizards (what I call the "Aren't you glad you bought Microsoft?" dialog box). Clicking Next brings you to your first choice, as shown in Figure 9.64. This is the same choice that is available in Windows 2000: installing either a local printer or a printer attached to another computer.

FIGURE 9.64

Installing a local or network printer

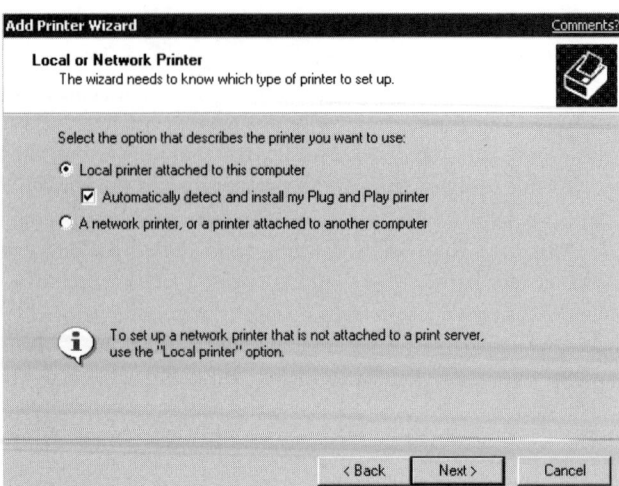

If you choose to install a network printer, the next screen determines which printer is chosen, either by searching Active Directory, connecting to a printer by NetBIOS name, or connecting to a printer by URL, as shown in Figure 9.65. In any event, once your choice is made, the wizard attempts to communicate with the print server supporting the printer. If this communication is successful, you will have added the printer.

FIGURE 9.65

Specifying a printer

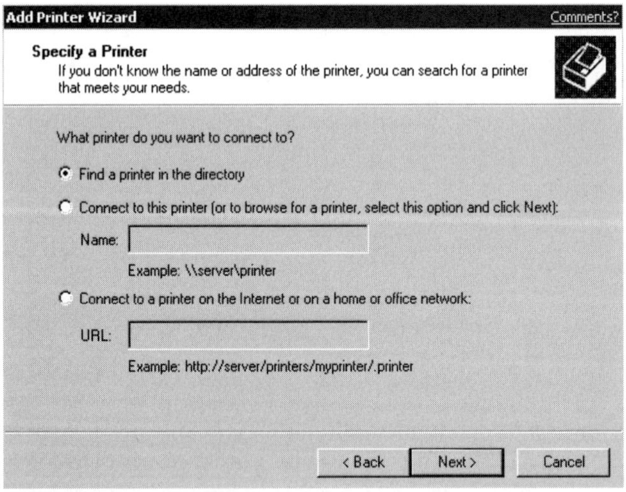

If you are adding a local printer, the next screen, shown in Figure 9.66, asks you where the printer is attached. Notice that it defaults to LPT1. The drop-down list, however, lists all of the available ports on the local machine (as well as an option to print directly to a file).

FIGURE 9.66

Selecting a
printer port

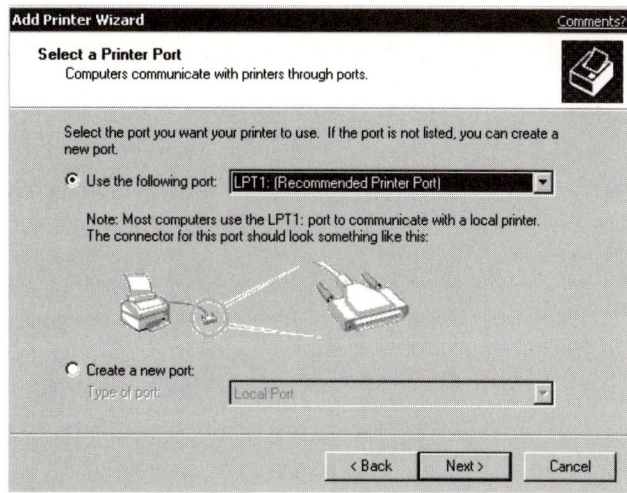

If necessary, you can choose to create a new port for this printer. The drop-down list will vary, depending upon which components you installed with the operating system, but by default it contains the options to create a local port or a standard TCP/IP port. Since TCP/IP printing is very common in today's networks, let's look at that option. This process is very simple; the only dialog box, shown in Figure 9.67, asks you to provide the printer name or IP address of the print device.

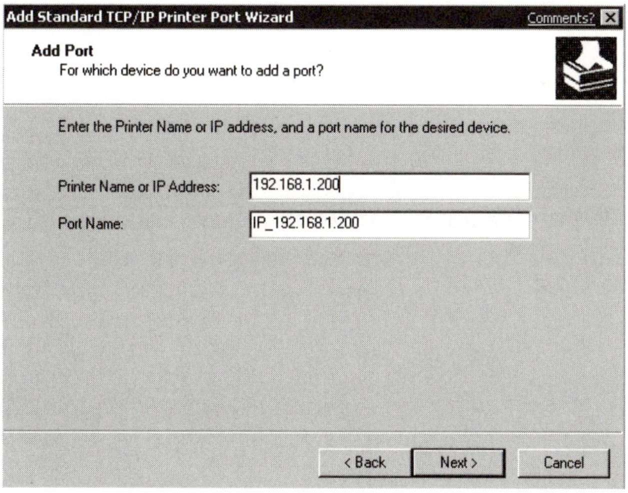

FIGURE 9.67

Adding a
standard TCP/IP
printer port

From this point forward, the process is much like adding a printer in Windows 2000 (or 95/98, Me, or XP for that matter). You choose a driver, give the printer a name, decide if you want to share it, add your comments, print a test page, and click Finish. The same properties exist for Windows 2000 as shown in Figure 9.62.

One great new feature in the Windows Server 2003 operating system is the change to the options available in the Printers and Faxes window, once you highlight a printer. Look at Figure 9.68. Notice that I've highlighted the printer that I just added. Look at the left pane of the window. The list of options in the Printer Tasks menu has expanded to include common printer management tasks. Also notice that the See Also menu now contains a link to the manufacturer's website! This doesn't seem like a big deal, but is sure makes managing printers a lot more convenient.

FIGURE 9.68

Managing printers and faxes

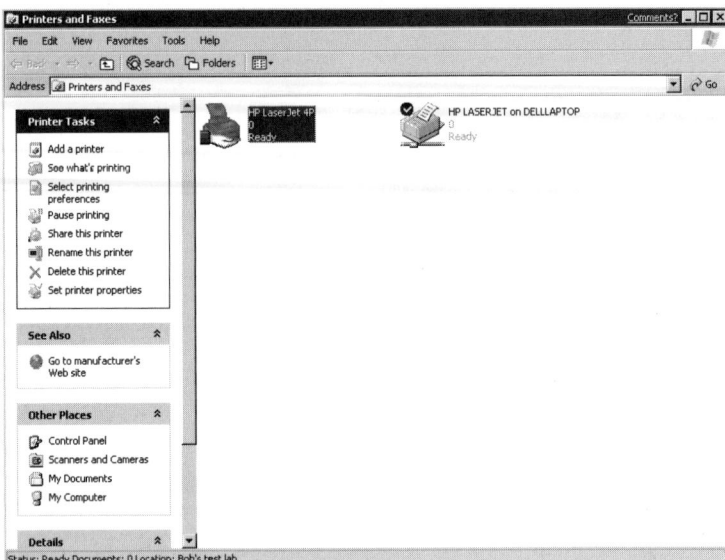

Non–Windows 2000 Printers

To add to your directory any printers that are attached to computers not running Windows 2000, you must use the Active Directory Users and Computers management tool. Before you begin, ensure that the printer is properly configured on the host computer. Document the make, model, and name of the printer for use in this process.

In the Active Directory Users and Computers tool, right-click the container in which you want the printer created. Choose New and then Printer. You will be presented with the Create New Object–Printer dialog box, as shown in Figure 9.69. Provide the UNC path to the printer, and you are done!

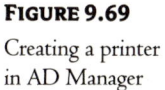

FIGURE 9.69

Creating a printer
in AD Manager

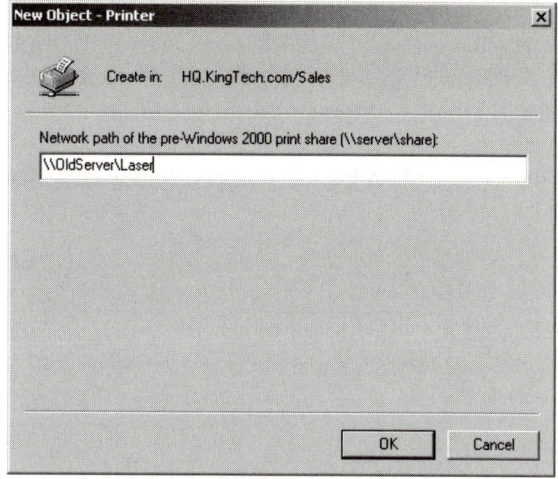

Creating Other Objects

While OUs, users, groups, and printers will be the mainstay of most directories, AD defines numerous other types of objects: computers, contacts, shares, and more. Some of these object types are for special use and beyond the scope of this book, but others will become an integral part of your environment as you get more and more comfortable with Windows 2000 Server. As an introduction to some of the other types of objects available, we'll take a look at the following classes:

- Computer
- Contact
- Shared folder

Creating each of these objects starts in the same way: in the Active Directory Users and Computers tool, right-click the appropriate container, choose Properties ➢ New, and then choose the class of object you wish to create.

Computer Objects

A *computer object* is used to represent computers that have joined the domain. Creating a computer object requires one screen, shown in Figure 9.70. Here you provide the computer name and the DNS name of the host, and you identify the type of computer (Windows 2000 workstation, member server, or domain controller). Notice the two check boxes at the bottom of the dialog box. The first option, Allow Pre–Windows 2000 Computers to Use This Account, allows computers that are running legacy operating systems to register themselves as the computer for which this account has been created. The second option (which is available only in Windows Server 2003 operating systems) lets you control whether the account can be utilized by an NT BDC. This option is a great way to ensure that no new NT servers are added to your environment. (Notice the default is that the check box is cleared.)

FIGURE 9.70

Creating a
computer object

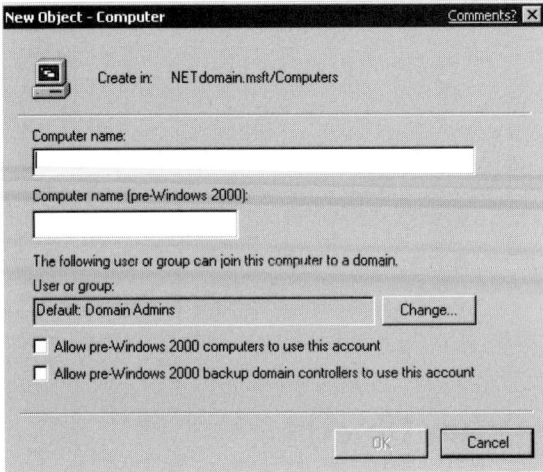

Once you have created a computer object, you can configure the properties of the object by double-clicking it. Figure 9.71 shows the tabs that are available for configuration in Windows 2000/Windows Server 2003.

FIGURE 9.71

Configuring a
computer object

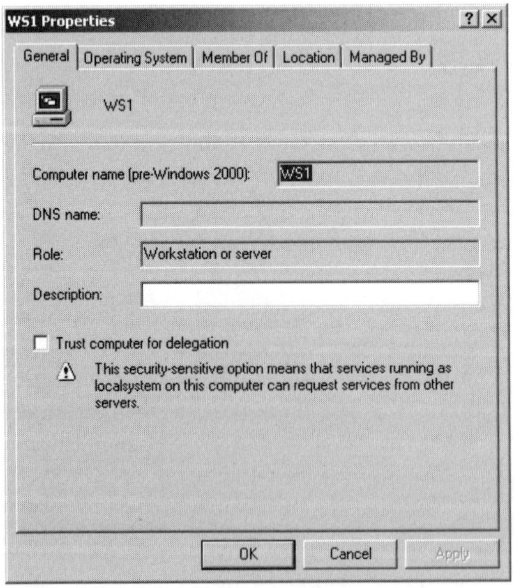

Each tab represents a different type of information:

General   This tab shows the information given during the creation of the device, names, and roles.

Operating System   This tab documents the name and version of the operating system running on the machine, as well as any service packs that have been applied to the operating system.

Member Of   This tab shows the ADS security groups of which this computer is a member.

Location   This tab allows you to document the physical location of the computer—Tampa Building 1, for instance.

Managed By   This tab shows properties that describe who is responsible for this computer.

The Windows Server 2003 operating systems offer an additional tab, as shown in Figure 9.72. The Dial-in tab is used to control whether this computer is allowed to utilize dial-in services.

FIGURE 9.72

Controlling dial-in services in Windows Server 2003

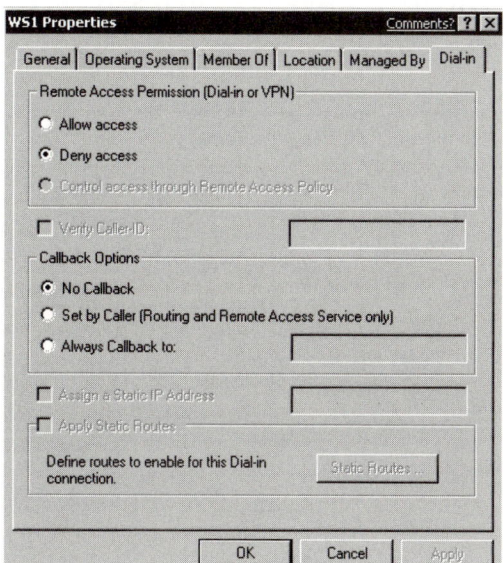

Contact Objects

A *contact* is an object designed to hold information about a person who is not a part of the local forest. Users can then access this information using an LDAP-enabled tool. The creation process involves providing first, last, and full names for the contact, as shown in Figure 9.73.

FIGURE 9.73

Establishing a new contact object

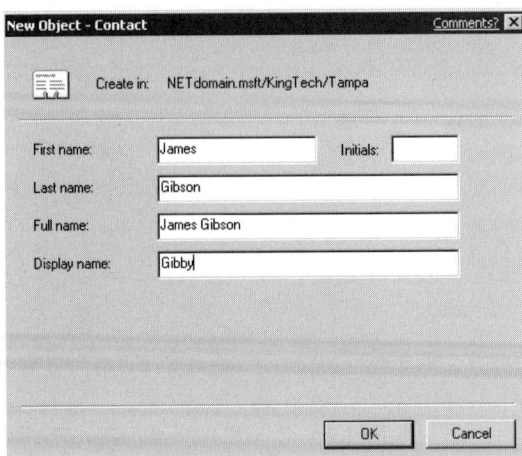

Once created, the contact has numerous properties. The Properties page of a contact object is shown in Figure 9.74.

FIGURE 9.74

Configuring a contact object

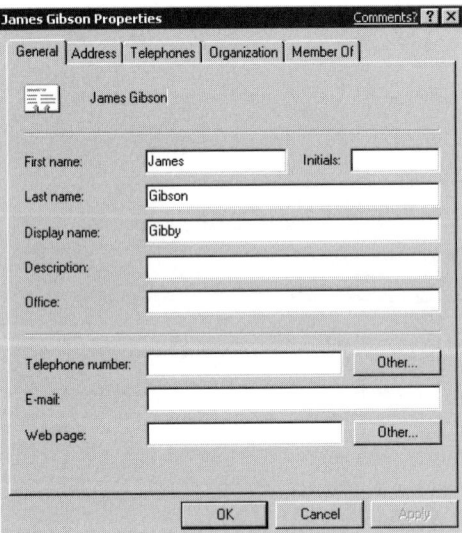

Each tab represents a different type of information:

General   This tab contains generic contact information such as names, phone numbers, and e-mail addresses.

Address   This tab shows the mailing address of the contact.

Telephones/Notes   This tab lets you record more contact information.

Organization This tab shows title, department, and company information.

Member Of This tab shows the AD security group of which this contact is a member.

Share Objects

Share points can also be published through the AD database. Once the share has been created at the host computer, you create a share object in AD. Configuring a share is just a matter of providing the UNC path to the actual share point, as shown in Figure 9.75.

FIGURE 9.75

Creating a
share object

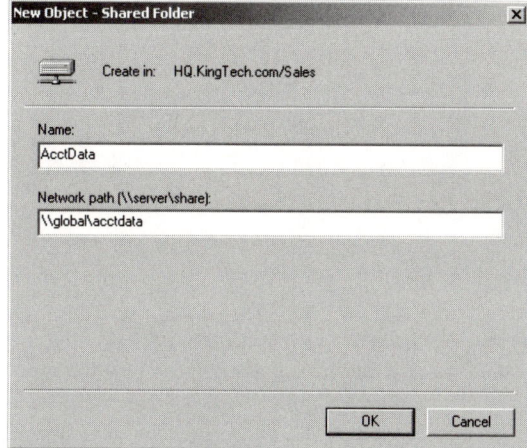

Share objects do not have a lot of properties, as you can see in Figure 9.76.

FIGURE 9.76

Configuring a
share object

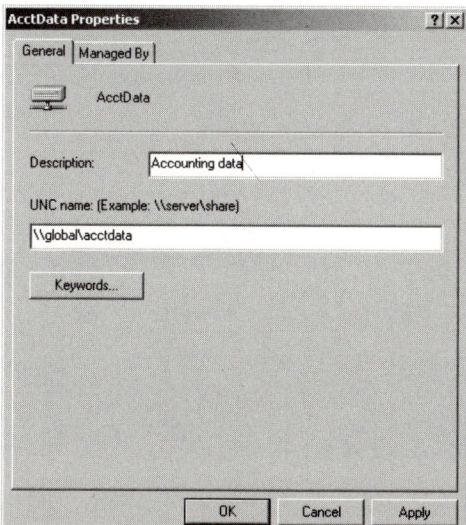

The most interesting property of a share object is the ability to create a list of keywords that can later be used to find this share with an LDAP query, as shown in Figure 9.77.

FIGURE 9.77

Creating a keyword list for a shared folder

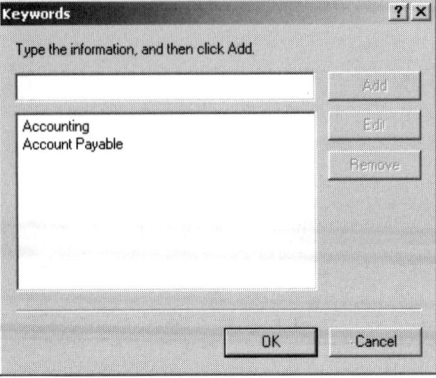

In Short

Installing and populating an Active Directory database is really just a matter of knowing where to click. More important than the mechanics is a firm understanding of the design principles discussed in Chapter 8 and the function of each object class, as discussed in this chapter.

Now that you have created your AD structure, the next step is to ensure that it is secure. In Chapter 10, we will discuss the theory and techniques of securing an AD directory database.

Chapter 10

Creating a Secure Environment

SECURITY IS PROBABLY THE hottest topic in our industry today. Everywhere you turn, there are stories about this leak or that hole; it seems that every operating system and every application is being compromised on a regular basis. It's impossible to keep up with the service packs, hot fixes, and suggested practices for all of the diverse environments in which we work; and when you finally think you are ahead of the game, some 13-year-old kid finds another area of vulnerability or writes a newer version of some destructive code. There are actually "virus" kits available on the Internet that make creating a sophisticated virus as easy as dragging and dropping!

Luckily, Windows 2000/Windows Server 2003 was created, from the ground up, using the latest in security enhancements. That is not to say, however, that it is inherently a secure operating system. It certainly has the potential to be secure, but not without some careful consideration by the person or group configuring the system.

Let me put this rumor to rest: Windows products have fared no better or worse than most of the products released to the market in the recent past. Yet we seem to see an inordinately large number of "Microsoft" security holes in every trade magazine. I was around when Novell was just taking off, and I've worked with various flavors of Unix—heck, I even work with Linux. None of these products was "perfect" upon release. Most provide security by either being so proprietary that it's hard to develop malicious code for them (which means it's also hard to write productive code for them) or by using the same methods used by Microsoft: release, listen, patch.

The reason that more security issues are found in Microsoft products (when compared to other vendor's offerings) is quite simple: Microsoft owns a larger share of the overall market. Think about it—if you were going to write a virus that would propagate through a network, which network operating system or product would you choose to attack? Linux with five percent of the market or NT with 50 (or better) percent?

That's not to say that Microsoft products are perfect, or that they are the "best" available. First, nothing's perfect. I had a college professor who said, "There's no such thing as perfect code, only code that hasn't experienced the unique set of circumstances necessary to break it." Second, the term "best" is open to interpretation; too much depends upon the use to which a product will be put to be able to define "best" in any simple manner.

No matter what the "experts" say, there is no way (short of taking a bunker approach and cutting yourself off from the world) to stop a determined and professional attack on your system. You can, however, slow it down. That's the secret to most successful security implementations; they place enough roadblocks in the way of an attack that they can discourage the amateurs and slow down the professionals.

The focus of this book is Active Directory, with the specific goals of helping you understand how AD works, how to install and configure it, and how to use it to your advantage. Given the tight integration of AD into all aspects of the Windows 2000/Windows Server 2003 networking environment, however, our discussion of security will need to include some non-AD topics. We'll touch upon the fundamental security components of all Microsoft networking operating systems since the first versions of NT; we'll discuss the difference between rights and permissions; we'll talk about permissions within the AD structure; we'll look at the proper uses of group, user, and computer objects; we'll analyze the default objects in AD; and we'll talk about delegating administrative privileges. Lastly, we'll discuss the various ways to authenticate to an AD environment.

The first question you might ask is, why bother with securing the AD database? After all, most of the information stored within the AD directory database is specifically designed to be for public consumption: things like telephone numbers, departments, and company names. There are, however, certain attributes of objects that you might *not* want to be published to the world at large. A user object, for instance, has certain properties that could be considered confidential (depending upon the types of data you store). For example, in some companies the human resources department uses "job titles" to describe employees' salary ranges. In such a case, federal, state, or local legislation might mandate that salary information (and thus the data in AD) be kept confidential.

One way to avoid this problem is to ignore the title attribute of all user accounts—after all, if the information is not there, it most certainly is not at risk of disclosure. Another way to approach this issue is to secure the title attribute so that only members of the appropriate groups can see this information.

Another issue, one that we touched upon earlier, is that of delegating administrative privileges. The ability to limit administrative capabilities is one of the most important security features of Active Directory. We'll revisit this topic in this chapter, not so much for new information as to drive home the concepts presented earlier.

NOTE *Although this is not one of those "test preparation" manuals, if you are considering chasing your Microsoft Certified System Engineer (MCSE) certificate, you should understand the concept of administrative delegation inside and out! Microsoft is pushing this feature very hard—and they are known for testing on the features that they are most proud of.*

We'll begin this chapter, though, with a discussion of the basics of security. While most of the Windows 2000 Server security features work the same as they did in NT 4, there are a few subtle differences, as well as a few new features pertaining to Active Directory.

When you are done with this chapter, I hope to have given you enough of a grounding in security so that you can design and implement a secure Active Directory–based network. Be aware, though, that security does not end with AD, nor does it end at your server. Security is one of those topics that must (if it is to be effective) include every aspect of your business, from the servers to the routers, from controlling hard copy output to training your users in dealing with questions on the phone. This chapter should only be a small part of your research into securing your network!

In this chapter:

◆ Security components: SIDs, ACLs, ownership, and trust relationships

◆ Permissions

◆ Authentication security: Kerberos, public-key, and certificates

Security Components

The security systems in use in the Windows 2000/Windows Server 2003 products are, in most respects, the same as those that were used in Windows NT. NT, in turn, followed a security model that was created in the '60s for mainframe environments. Because this model is a mature technology, we can rest assured that Windows 2000/Windows Server 2003 security is stable and well supported in the industry. This does not mean, however, that it is intuitive or simplistic. Security can be extremely complex, but that is the price we usually pay for sophisticated and powerful systems.

You must understand two main concepts to fully appreciate the strengths (and weaknesses) of Microsoft security:

◆ System identifiers (SIDs)

◆ Access Control Lists (ACLs)

SIDs and ACLs work together to provide security for the resources on your network. We'll look at each in turn.

System Identifiers (SIDs)

As each object is created in the directory database, it is assigned a unique value known as its *SID*. The SID is used by internal operations to identify that object when it attempts to access some resource.

NOTE   *For our purposes, we will limit our discussion to the use of SIDs for user and group objects, but you should be aware that every object in the tree has a unique identifier assigned to it.*

Any discussion of how SIDs are used starts with the logon process. As a Windows 2000/Windows Server 2003 computer boots, a series of processes starts. One of these processes is the *NETLOGON* process. Among its tasks, the NETLOGON process is responsible for the act of "logging on" (hence the name) to the network.

The NETLOGON process, working in conjunction with a few other components, opens a secure communication channel to a domain controller. The user provides a username and password, and is either granted or denied access to the network. If the user is granted access, the domain controller will gather together the user's SID and the SIDs of all groups that the user is a member of. These SIDs are placed in an *access token* and sent back to the user, as shown in Figure 10.1.

FIGURE 10.1

Acquiring the access token

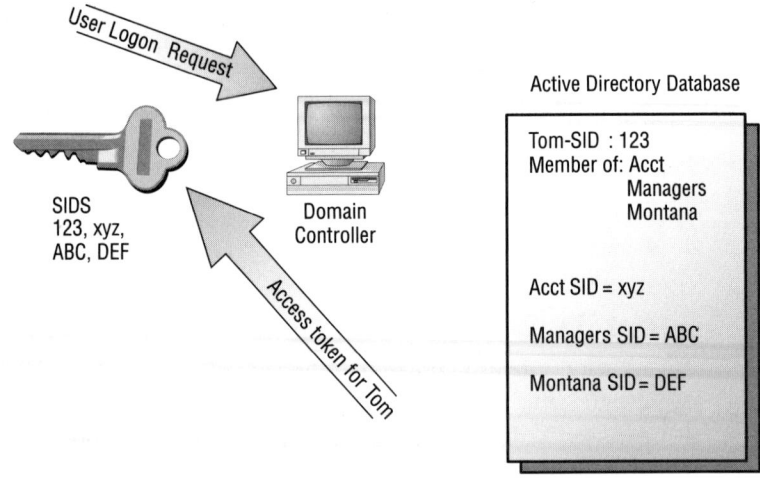

NOTE *Many people picture the access token as a set of keys. Each key opens a different aspect of some network resource. If you attempt to read a file and you have the "read key" for that file, for example, you will be granted access.*

The system identifier is only half the story. For it to have any value, there must be a mechanism for connecting SIDs to resources. That mechanism is the *Access Control List*.

Access Control List (ACL)

The record for each object in the directory database (as well as the file system) has a header known as the *security descriptor*. The security descriptor defines the access permissions that have been granted to the object. To be more specific, the security descriptor contains:

- The SID of the owner of the object

- A group SID (used only by the POSIX subsystem and Services for Macintosh)

- Two Access Control Lists

You can see the contents of a security descriptor in Figure 10.2. The object being granted rights is known as the *security principal*. Security principals receive rights or permissions.

FIGURE 10.2

Security descriptors

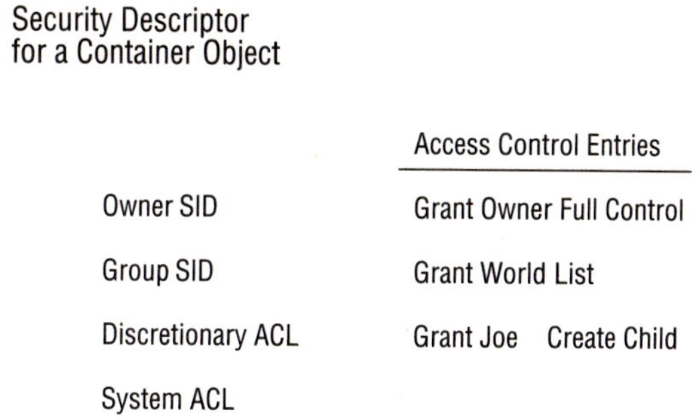

Security Descriptor
for a Container Object

	Access Control Entries
Owner SID	Grant Owner Full Control
Group SID	Grant World List
Discretionary ACL	Grant Joe Create Child
System ACL	

The *Discretionary Access Control List* (DACL) contains the SIDs of objects that have been granted permissions to the object and the specific permissions granted. The objects within the DACL are referred to as *access control entries* (ACEs). All permissions and rights are assigned through ACEs. The *System Access Control List* (SACL) contains systemwide policies, such as the settings for auditing. As such, it is not really relevant to our discussion.

ACCESS CONTROL ENTRIES

Access control entries are part of the DACL and are designed to protect the object. There are many levels of ACEs available:

Object Class   You might set an ACE for every instance of a class of object in the tree. You might, for example, want to create an ACE that allows your help desk personnel to change user passwords.

Object   You can create ACEs that apply only to a specific object in the tree. You might, for instance, want to protect a particular application object from being tampered with.

Object Properties   You can also protect specific attributes of an object. For example, you might want to limit the anonymous user account's ability to view the configuration parameters of your e-mail server.

This combination of abilities lets administrators get as granular as they want in their management practices. You can make assignments that are sweeping in nature (affecting large numbers of objects, such as all user objects), more controlled (such as the ability to read and write to all properties for a specific printer), or very specific (such as the ability to read all properties of user Joe *except* his title property).

APPLYING ACES TO A REQUEST FOR ACCESS

ACEs are applied to requests in the same manner in which ACEs are applied to requests in the NTFS file system (both the newest version that ships with Windows 2000/Windows Server 2003 and earlier versions). We'll look at a standard request first and then at the exception that makes the rule.

In a standard request, a user—Tom, for instance—wants to change the value of the telephone number property of user Susan. Tom's computer will send his request, along with his access token, to the Active Directory server, as shown in Figure 10.3.

FIGURE 10.3

Request for information

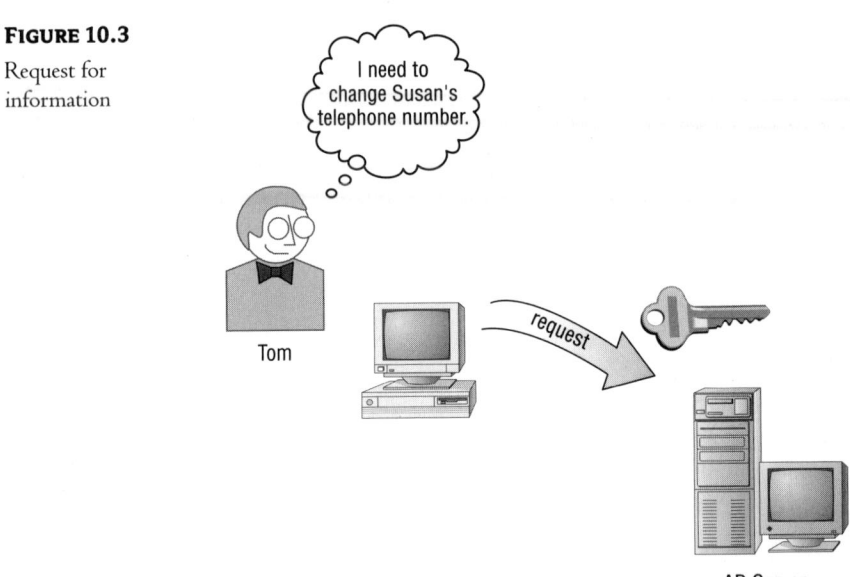

The AD server finds Susan's object and compares the SIDs in Tom's access token with the SIDs in Susan's DACL. You can see this in Figure 10.4.

FIGURE 10.4

Authenticating a request

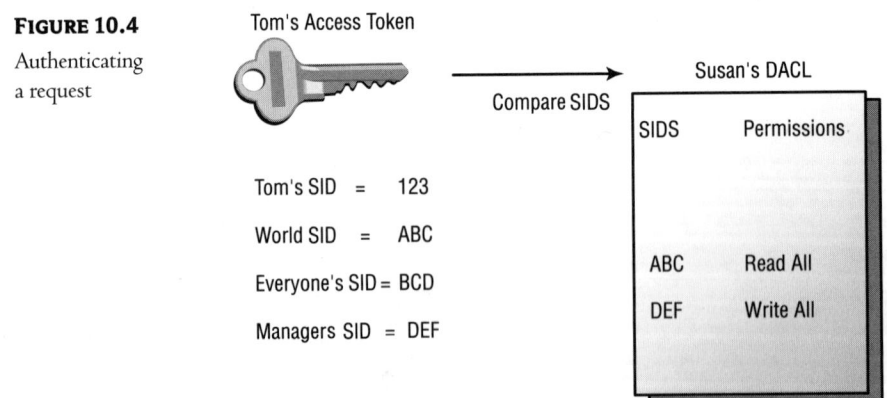

AD will search for a matching SID that allows Tom to change the attribute in question. If a match is found, Tom can make the change. If not, Tom's request will be denied. Note, though, that the system will stop searching once a relevant match is found. It doesn't look for all of the records that might affect Tom, only the first ACE that will have an effect on this request. This point becomes important a little later in our discussion.

There is one exception to the statement "AD will search for a matching SID." If the access token contains a SID for an object that has been granted the Deny Access permission, the object will be denied access. Notice the blank space at the beginning of Susan's DACL in Figure 10.4. All Deny Access permissions are placed at the beginning of the DACL. Let's change the scenario a bit and see what happens. Tom will still be a member of the Managers group, but we'll also make him a member of the Security Problems group. (Either Tom is a manager who knows just enough to be dangerous or his position is such that he shouldn't be granted excessive permissions.) In Figure 10.5, the graphic has been updated to reflect this small change.

FIGURE 10.5

Deny Access permission

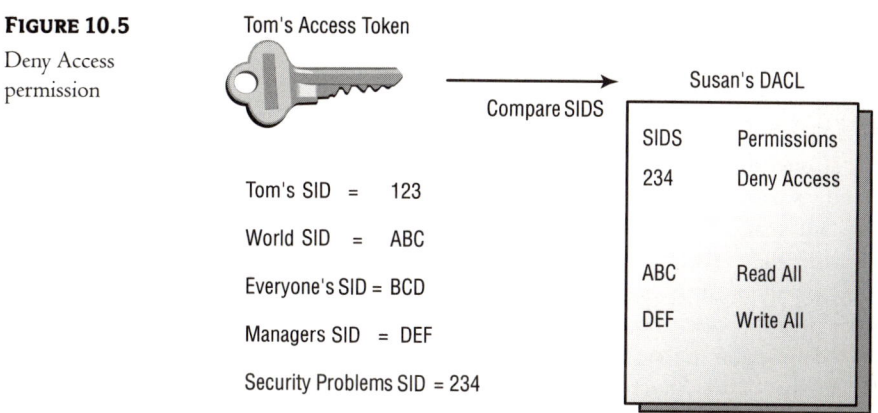

Figure 10.5 shows the Deny Access permission at the top of the DACL. When the comparison is made, ADS will see that Tom is a member of a group that has been denied access. Even though Tom is a member of another group with the appropriate permissions, his request will be denied. ADS will search no further once it finds a Deny Access permission.

The bottom line here is that the system will work its way through the SIDs in the ACL, looking for an entry that should be applied to Tom's request—either an explicit "deny" or a record allowing him to perform the requested action. As soon as it finds a match, it stops looking. Since all denies are at the beginning of the list, any deny associated with Tom will be found first, effectively ending the process.

Ownership

Every object in the AD database has an *owner*. The person who creates an object becomes the owner of that object. The owner has complete control over an object. The owner has the ability to control how permissions are set for an object and to whom permissions are granted. In short, ownership of an object delegates administrative responsibility of that object to the listed owner.

If a member of the Domain Administrators group creates an object, the group (rather than the individual) is listed as its owner. Members of the Domain Administrators group also have the ability to take ownership of any object within their domain.

Taking ownership of an object is as simple as right-clicking the object in Active Directory Users and Computers, choosing Properties, choosing the Security tab, and then clicking Take Ownership.

From a security perspective, it is important to note that anyone with the Take Ownership permission can assume ownership (and thus all permissions) to an object. Controlling who has the Take Ownership permission is critical to an effective security strategy. Also note that members of the Domain Administrators group can always take ownership of any object within their domain.

Also important is that fact that ownership can be taken, but not given. Say, for instance, that a malicious administrator wants to look at the contents of a file to which they have been denied access. That administrator can easily take ownership of the file and then peruse its contents. They cannot, however, change the ownership back to the original owner—you can take, but you cannot give! In the event that the administrator's actions are noted, it will be easy to see that ownership has been changed. (Of course, you still won't know which administrator was to blame since the Administrators group will be listed as the owner; that's where auditing comes in handy.)

Trust Relationships

As we discussed in Chapter 8, two-way transitive trusts are created between each domain in an AD tree and its parent domain. When we extend our view to a forest environment, the same type of trust is automatically established between the root domains of all the trees within the forest. This mechanism allows users to be granted permissions and rights throughout the entire structure, without forcing administrators to be concerned with the various trust relationships necessary. All in all, this is a great process. Trusts, in and of themselves, do not grant permissions or rights; they only create a connection so that these assignments can be made. We also discussed the creation of special trusts in Chapter 8—shortcut trusts to reduce the number of domain controllers involved in connecting to a resource in another domain within the forest, and external trusts to establish a relationship with a foreign environment (another forest or a legacy NT 4 domain). Once again, these types of trusts are convenient mechanisms used to facilitate the sharing of resources, but they do not grant permissions or rights.

What we didn't cover in Chapter 8 are the mechanics of managing trusts: how do we modify the defaults, how do we create shortcut or external trusts, and what are some of the security issues that must be considered? We'll discuss those mechanics now.

SECURITY ISSUES

As I've said before, and I want to stress again, trusts, in and of themselves, do not constitute much of a security threat. They do not inherently give users permissions nor do they grant any types of rights. They do, however, create a path, or connection, over which those actions can be taken. From a security perspective, controlling who has the ability to grant those privileges becomes the critical key to creating a secure environment

It goes without saying that controlling membership in those groups that have administrative privileges is important. I've actually seen environments in which every user was made a member of the Domain

Admins group, because it was "easier." If that sounds like an acceptable strategy for your network, then you might as well skip this chapter (and any other reference manual that uses the word *security* within its pages!). In particular, watch membership in both the Domain Admins and Enterprise Admins groups, although only membership in the Domain Admins group is necessary to begin the process of creating a trust relationship. I said "begin the process" because it takes membership in the Domain Admins group of both domains to complete the process.

MANAGING TRUSTS

Let's start with the basics—where do we go to confirm the current trust relationships in our environment? In the Administrative Tools group, open the Active Directory Domains and Trusts tool. Right-click the domain you are interested in and choose Properties. On the Trusts tab is a list of all trusts in which the domain is included, as shown in Figure 10.6.

FIGURE 10.6

Domain trusts

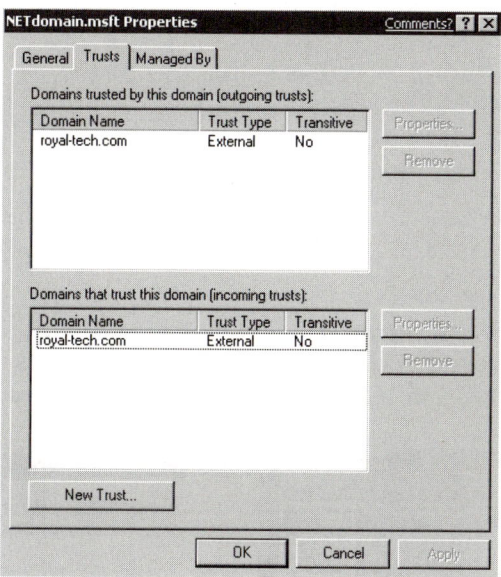

Any changes to the trust environment for the domain are accomplished from this dialog box. The figures in this section were created using a Windows Server 2003, but the principle is the same in Windows 2000.

To delete a trust, highlight the trust you wish to delete and click the Remove button. You will see the dialog box shown in Figure 10.7. Here you decide whether to remove only the local side of the trust or to remove both sides. As the dialog box states, you must have administrative privileges in both domains to perform the latter choice. (Notice that you can identify an administrative account on the other domain during the process.) You will be presented with one more dialog box—the obligatory "Are you sure you want to remove the . . . ?" one—click Yes to continue.

FIGURE 10.7

Removing a trust

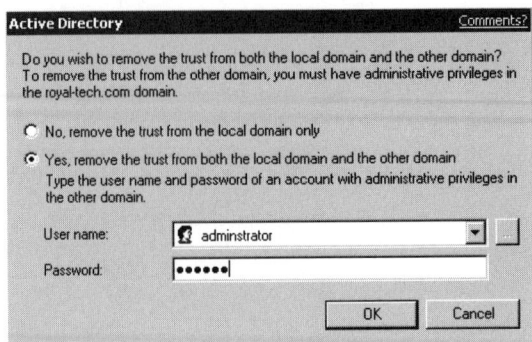

To create a trust, use the Active Directory and Trusts utility. You'll have the following four options:

◆ Create a trust with another domain in the same forest or in another forest.

◆ Create a trust with an NT 4.0 domain.

◆ Create a trust with another Kerberos v5 environment (known as a *realm*).

◆ Create a trust with another AD forest.

The process is identical for each of the options; the design implications, however, are quite different. First let's look at the mechanics, and then we'll discuss the reasoning behind each of the four choices. Follow these steps:

1. Right-click the appropriate domain, choose Properties, and select the Trusts tab. Click the New Trust button to start the New Trust Wizard. The first window is the mandatory "Welcome" screen, shown in Figure 10.8, which reviews your four options.

FIGURE 10.8

The New Trust Wizard

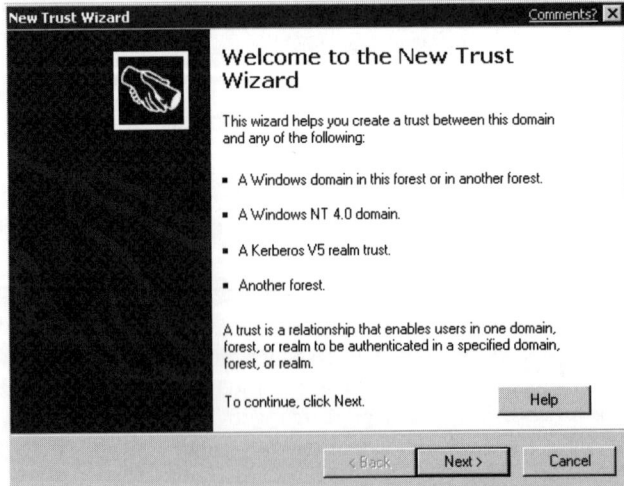

2. After the Welcome screen, you are asked to identify the domain, realm, or forest to which you wish to create a trust relationship. As shown in Figure 10.9, you can enter the NetBIOS name or DNS name of the target. To create a trust to a forest, you must use the DNS name.

FIGURE 10.9

Entering a trust name

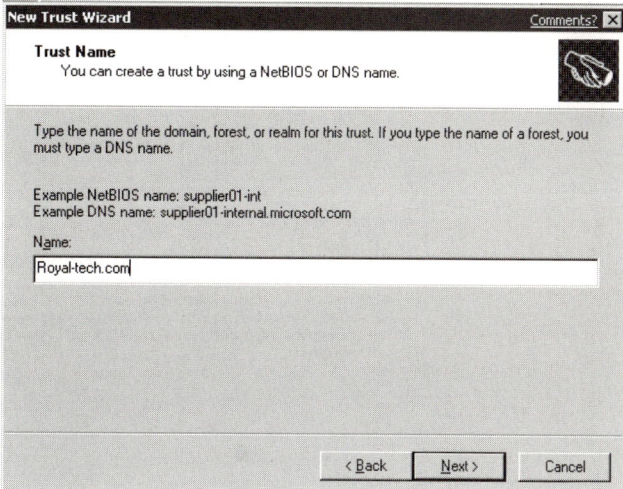

3. Once you have identified the target, you must determine the scope of the relationship. Should it be a two-way trust, one-way in which the target domain trusts your domain (your users can be granted permissions to resources in the target domain), or one-way in which your domain trusts the target domain (their users can be granted permissions to resources in your domain)? You can see these choices in Figure 10.10.

FIGURE 10.10

Choosing the direction of the trust

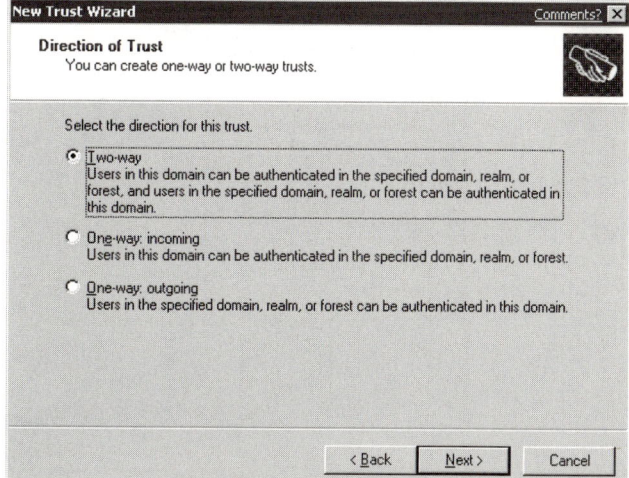

4. In the next dialog box, shown in Figure 10.11, you can create both sides of a two-way trust, if you have the appropriate permissions. If not, the administrator of the target domain will have to configure that end of the relationship.

FIGURE 10.11

Creating both sides of the trust

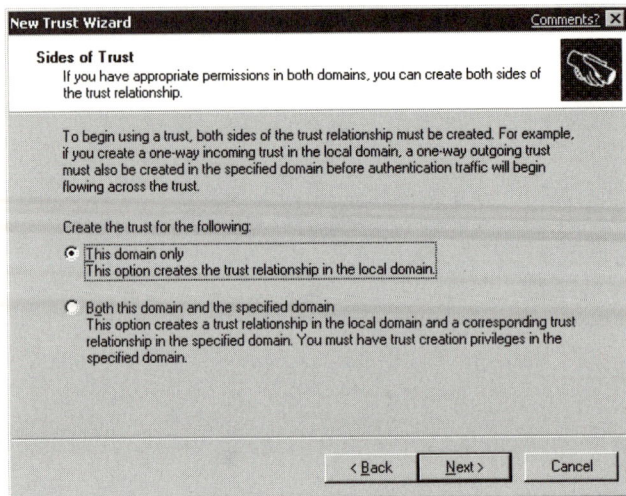

5. Next you must choose a password for this trust, as shown in Figure 10.12. If the administrator of the target domain is going to configure the other side of the relationship, they will have to enter the same password. Even if you are configuring both sides, you must still choose a password for the trust. Active Directory modifies this password automatically on a regular basis. This password is then used as part of the authentication process between the domains.

FIGURE 10.12

Setting the trust password

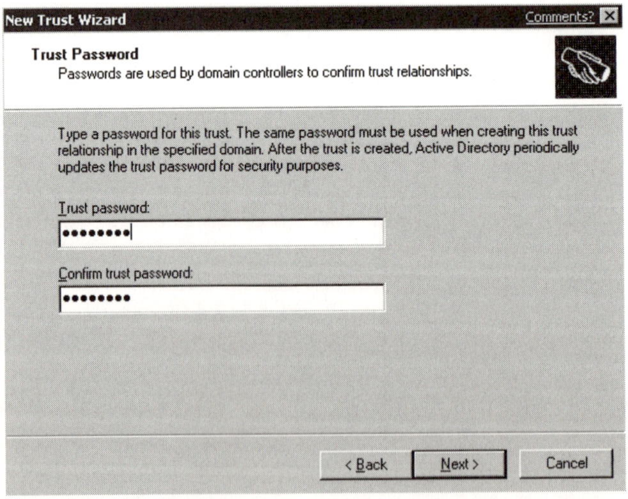

![New Trust Wizard dialog box - Trust Password. Passwords are used by domain controllers to confirm trust relationships. Type a password for this trust. The same password must be used when creating this trust relationship in the specified domain. After the trust is created, Active Directory periodically updates the trust password for security purposes. Trust password: •••••••• Confirm trust password: ••••••••   Back Next> Cancel]

6. Finally, you review a summary of the choices you have made (shown in Figure 10.13). Read this carefully as it describes the results of the selections. This is a great way to ensure that you didn't inadvertently create a trust in the wrong direction!

FIGURE 10.13

Reviewing your trust selections

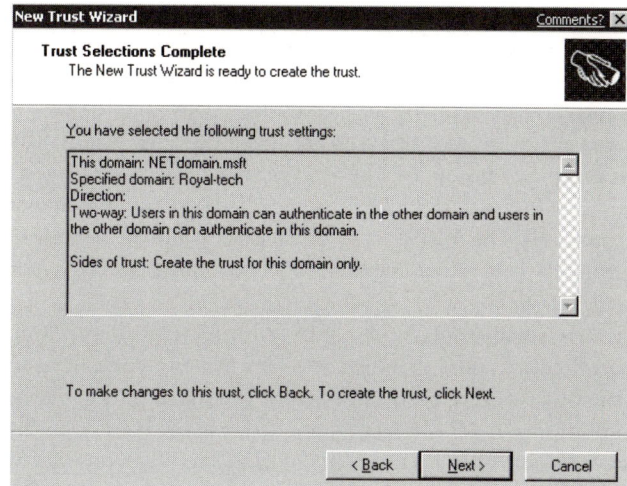

Now that you know where to click, let's take a look at the issues you must consider when creating the four different kinds of relationships.

Creating a Trust with Another Domain in the Same Forest or in Another Forest

From both an administrative and an AD perspective, these two options are functionally identical. In the overall design process, however, they are used for quite different purposes.

You create an explicit trust between two domains within the same AD forest as a tool to reduce the number of servers that will be impacted by users in one domain accessing resources in another. As you may recall, when a user attempts to access a resource in another domain, multiple domain controllers can be involved in the pass-through authentication process. To sum it up, the user submits their request to a domain controller within their own domain. This domain controller looks at the distinguished name of the resource and determines if it exists in a domain that is below it in the AD structure, above it in the structure, or on a completely different branch of the AD tree. As an example, let's look at user Bob, whose distinguished name is CN=Bob,OU=Sales,DC=Farmington,DC=RoyalTech,DC=com as he tries to access a shared resource named CN=Resource,OU=Education,DC=Tampa,DC=Royal-Tech,DC=com.

Looking at the two names, you can see that both objects exist in the same AD tree (whose root domain is named `royal-tech.com`). They are located, however, in different domains—Bob exists in the Farmington domain, and the resource exists in the Tampa domain. Whatever domain controller Bob submits his request to will look at the names and realize that both objects are under the `royal-tech.com` domain. The request will be passed from Bob's domain controller to a domain controller in the `royal-tech.com` domain. From there it will be passed to a domain controller in the Tampa domain. This final domain controller will trust that the preceding domain controllers have authenticated Bob, and it will check Bob's access permissions (and those of groups to which Bob belongs) to determine if he has the appropriate permissions necessary to access the resource. In this small example, the request is processed by at least three domain controllers. In a larger AD structure (one with more domains), the request might be processed by numerous domain controllers.

To avoid the overhead of the pass-through process, an explicit trust can be created between the Tampa and the Farmington domains. Bob's domain controller will then have a direct path to a domain controller in the Tampa domain, avoiding the pass-through path completely.

Creating a trust between two domains that are located within different AD forests has a completely different function. This can be seen as an "extranet" connection, and it is usually implemented to grant permissions to external entities (perhaps a vendor or another independent business unit within your parent company). The trust created works exactly like the nontransitive trusts in Microsoft NT 4.0. The bottom line here is that one domain will trust accounts from another, even though they are located in different forests.

I've always found this second option (creating trusts between domains from different forests) to have more security issues than business benefits. In most cases I will look for another technology before creating this type of trust. The bottom line is that some external users need access to your internal resources. I will often suggest a dedicated web server, utilizing server and client certificates to control access. Using a web-based solution allows me to grant access without having to trust the IT staff in control of the other forest.

Creating a Trust with an NT 4.0 Domain

Many companies move to Windows 2000 and Active Directory from an existing Windows NT environment. In most cases the upgrade is planned as a gradual process, both to spread out the costs involved and to limit the impact of any unforeseen problems. There have also been reports of server-based applications that do not migrate well to the Windows 2000 operating systems (in my experience, these applications have almost always been custom programs written by the in-house development staff). In any event, if you have a mixed environment of Windows 2000 and Windows NT domains, you will probably want to create a trust between those two environments. As we've seen, the process is straightforward. There are no real issues involved—except, perhaps, that you will become disenchanted with the management capabilities of NT once you start working with Windows 2000.

Creating a Trust to Another Kerberos v5 Realm

While Microsoft's implementation of the Kerberos authentication process is compliant with the industry standards—specifically, Microsoft wrote their implementation to RFC 1510—it is not exactly easy to implement. If you are looking for some in-depth information about Kerberos, RFC 1510 has a lot of interesting information; unfortunately, it is also a great cure for insomnia. Luckily, most administrators will never need to create a trust between Windows 2000 and a foreign Kerberos implementation. Even in the unlikely event that you are forced to create such a trust, you can accomplish this task without having a deep understanding of the underlying protocols. Let's go over the basics—enough to understand the process, but not enough to put you to sleep!

A Kerberos environment is often referred to as a *realm*. The Kerberos realm acts, in many ways, much like a Windows domain. Users belong to a realm, applications and services use the Kerberos services of a realm for authentication, and users are "known" (or have a unique identity) within a realm.

A trust can be created between a Windows 2000 domain and any standards-based Kerberos realm. The mechanics of the process differ depending upon the needs of the foreign operating system. The bottom line is that either or both environments can be configured to trust the session tickets generated by the other.

Creating a Trust with Another AD Forest

There is a new option available in the Windows Server 2003 product line: the creation of a transitive trust between domains within two different AD forests. In earlier releases of Active Directory, trusts between domains in different forests were, by definition, nontransitive trusts to a foreign environment. These trusts worked exactly the same as Windows NT 4.0 trusts. With the release of the Windows Server 2003 environment, two AD forests can be tied together with a transitive trust between any two domains. In effect, this creates a large structure in which users can be granted permissions to resources in any domain in either forest. Because of the potential scope of this type of trust relationship, you must be very sure of the nature of the relationship before creating this type of trust! Since the trust will impact all domains in both forests, convention is to create the trust between the root domains, tying the two (or more) forests together at their roots.

Why, you might ask, would I want to tie two forests together in this manner? Isn't the whole point of creating separate forests to limit the administrative or user crossover between the environments? Remember: we create trees to support multiple namespaces, and forests to create separate entities.

Microsoft's marketing department sells this idea on, what I consider to be, a silly premise. They suggest that you might want to tie together your AD forest with the AD forests of your business partners, such as vendors or customers. This would allow you to share resources with these foreign environments. Personally, I believe this to be rather risky. I don't trust the IT department of my customers (or vendors) enough to want to do this! There is, however, a plausible reason for this capability.

Remember that all of the trees (and hence the domains) within a forest share two things: a common schema and a common Global Catalog. You might create multiple forests within your company to limit the size of the Global Catalog or to reduce the impact of schema modifications. Doing this, however, has always limited the ability to share resources—you were forced to manage trusts between the forests as if you were still running Windows NT. Now you can create the single trust between the forests, share your resources across the environments, and even delegate administrative privileges but still control the Global Catalog and the scope of schema changes.

Permissions

If you think about it, the list of actions you might want to take regarding any given type of network resource is pretty limited. Let's say, for instance, that you have a file (your resume, perhaps) located on a network server. You, of course, want to be able to do anything to your file; after all, it's yours, isn't it? (Let's ignore the legal side of this question: if you place it on a company server, is it really still yours?) There are other people, though, who might need to take certain actions with regard to your resume.

You might ask your buddy in human resources to look your resume over and, based upon her expertise, make a few adjustments to increase its effectiveness. You might also want your good friend in sales to look it over—he meets with a lot of clients, maybe someone will mention an opening that matches your qualifications. There's your friend in marketing who volunteered to redo your resume in PageMaker, punching up its appearance. Lastly, your current boss might be a little perturbed to find your (freshly updated) resume being circulated; you want to make sure that she can't even see the file in the folder.

Each of these actions—to see that your resume exists, to look at its contents, to correct or add to it, and even to copy it into another format—can be controlled through NTFS file permissions. Permissions control the actions you can take upon a resource. Active Directory includes its own set of permissions that control the actions you can take upon objects and their attributes within the AD database.

Microsoft uses two terms in its security descriptions that can be unclear, especially to anyone coming from a Novell background. Novell calls the controls listed above *rights*, as in you have certain rights to perform actions on a resource. Microsoft, as I've already indicated, calls these *permissions*. Unfortunately, Microsoft uses the word *rights* to describe another set of security functions, and this is where the confusion begins. To set matters straight: In a Microsoft world, the term *rights* refers to the ability to perform system-related actions (things like login, changing the time or date, or even downing the server). The word *permissions* refers to the ability to access and/or change static network resources (AD objects or files).

For our discussion, we'll concentrate on the permissions available within the AD database. This becomes a tricky subject because Microsoft has gone to great pains to make this function as straightforward as possible—and when Microsoft tries to make something "simple," the results are often confusing. Securing the contents of a complex directory services database can be a daunting project; there are numerous types of records (objects), each record has various types of fields (attributes), and we really want the ability to control each aspect in a granular manner if necessary. (You might, for instance, want to allow your help desk personnel the ability to change passwords but not any other aspect of user objects.) Since each object class differs in its attributes, the security options available must also be different—in other words, the list of available "permissions" will vary from object class to object class. Talk about your convoluted environment! The more object classes that are added to the AD schema (remember, the schema can be extended to include new classes and attributes), the more security options you will have available.

You must also understand the difference between assigning permissions to manage the object as opposed to managing specific attributes of the object. Some permissions affect the overall object. You might, for instance, want your help desk to be able to look at or change all of the attributes of a user. In this case, you could assign the help desk users the Read permission to the object, thus allowing them to read all information (including attributes) about the user. On the other hand, you might want to limit your help desk personnel to certain attributes—the address, phone numbers, and group membership attributes, for instance—but not allow them access to any other information. In this case, you would assign them permissions to the specific attributes you want them to either see or change.

At this point, you are probably wondering if a career in IT is really the best choice you can make. Rest easy; it is actually easier to do than to describe! The best way to get a handle on this is to see it in action, so I'll be making liberal use of screen captures from this point on!

In an effort to reduce the confusion (an effort that is partially successful), Microsoft gives us two views of security: a view based upon overall functionality and a granular view. The easiest way to discuss the difference between the two is to take a look at a couple of screen captures—one of each view. Our example will use a user object—the list of security options (permissions) will be different for other classes of objects.

First we'll look at the functionality view. Figure 10.14 shows the contents of the Security tab of a user's Properties pages. As you can see, the list of permissions scrolls out of the dialog box.

FIGURE 10.14

Security page for
user objects

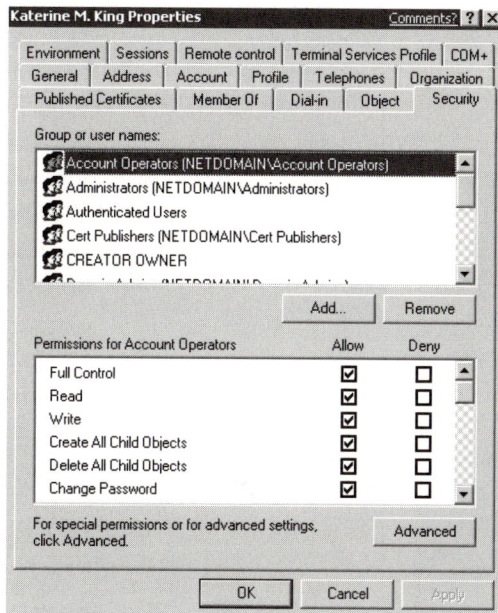

Tables 10.1 and 10.2 list the permissions available for a user object (with a default installation of the schema—remember, this list might change if you have extended the schema manually or through the installation of an application). They also provide a short description of what each permission allows (where the name does not adequately describe its purpose).

TABLE 10.1: GENERAL PERMISSIONS AVAILABLE FOR A USER OBJECT

PERMISSION	DESCRIPTION
Full Control	Just what the name implies: a combination of all the other permissions.
Read	Allows the viewing of all attributes of the user object (see the address or phone number).
Write	Allows the ability to write to the attributes of an object (change the address or phone number).

Continued on next page

TABLE 10.1: GENERAL PERMISSIONS AVAILABLE FOR A USER OBJECT *(continued)*

PERMISSION	DESCRIPTION
Create All Child Objects	Allows the ability to create AD objects below this object in the AD tree.
Delete All Child Objects	Allows the ability to delete AD objects below this object in the AD tree.
Change Password	In most environments, users have this permission to their own user object. It allows them to change their own password, but does request that they enter the old password before allowing the change.
Receive As	Applies to Microsoft Exchange environments. It allows the user to receive mail as a given mailbox. In other words, the user assigned this permission can receive mail addressed to the user account.
Reset Password	Grants the ability to change a user's password without knowing the original password. (This is often assigned to help desk personnel so that they can change passwords for those users who forget theirs.)
Send As	An Exchange mail attribute; allows the recipient to send mail as if they were this user. (An administrative assistant, for instance, could send mail with the name of their boss in the From field.)

TABLE 10.2: PERMISSIONS THAT ALLOW FOR THE VIEWING OR CHANGING OF SPECIFIC TYPES OF INFORMATION ON A USER ACCOUNT

PERMISSION	DESCRIPTION
Read Account Restrictions	Self explanatory.
Write Account Restrictions	Self explanatory.
Read General Information	Self explanatory.
Write General Information	Self explanatory.
Read Group Membership	Self explanatory.
Write Group Membership	Self explanatory.
Read Logon Information	Self explanatory.
Write Logon Information	Self explanatory.
Read Personal Information	Self explanatory.
Write Personal Information	Self explanatory.
Read Phone and Mail Options	Self explanatory.
Write Phone and Mail Options	Self explanatory.
Read Public Information	Self explanatory.

Continued on next page

TABLE 10.2: PERMISSIONS THAT ALLOW FOR THE VIEWING OR CHANGING OF SPECIFIC TYPES OF INFORMATION ON A USER ACCOUNT *(continued)*

PERMISSION	DESCRIPTION
Write Public Information	Self explanatory.
Read Remote Access Information	Self explanatory.
Write Remote Access Information	Self explanatory.
Read Web Information	Self explanatory.
Write Web Information	Self explanatory.
Special Permissions	This option is used if none of the above choices provides the degree of control you desire. (This is our next topic.)

The lists of permissions in Tables 10.1 and 10.2 are really just the tip of the iceberg! In reality, these are not the "permissions" at all; these "tasks" are really combinations of the real permissions that are necessary to perform common administrative functions. As an example, think about the Read Phone and Mail Options permission. This option gives you a single place to click to grant someone (perhaps someone in human resources) the ability to look at (but not change—that's the Write permission) the information entered in all of the phone and mail attributes. You could, however, be more specific. Perhaps your human resources personnel are not supposed to look at mail-related information. In this case, you would have to utilize the Special Information option to grant more granular permissions.

The special permissions option is accessed by clicking on the Advanced button. This opens the Advanced Security Settings dialog box shown in Figure 10.15.

FIGURE 10.15

Advanced security options

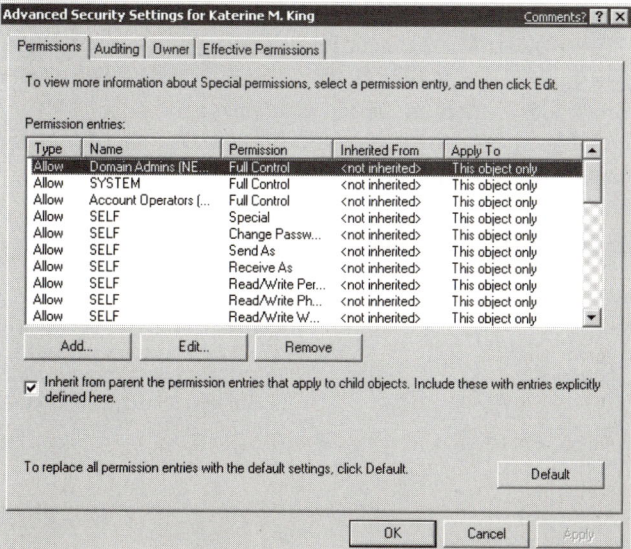

Click the Add button and choose the appropriate user to grant the permissions to. This opens the Permission Entry for <*User*> dialog box, as shown in Figure 10.16.

FIGURE 10.16

Granting object permissions

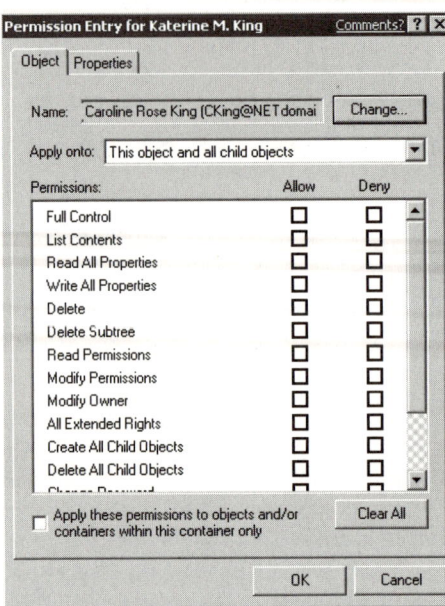

Here is where things can get a little confusing. For some reason, most documentation for directory services (whether it be Active Directory, Novell Directory Services, or whatever) use similar terms at this point in the process. Look at Figure 10.16 again. Take note of the two tabs available in this dialog box: Object and Properties. As we'll see, these two tabs refer to: (1) management of *objects* as they exist in the AD tree, what I call "Tree Management," and (2) management of the *properties* of the object, what I call "Object Management." For me, the two terms "Tree Management" and "Object Management" make more sense—although be aware that they are my own terms and are not found in any Microsoft documentation. Let's look at what I mean.

The Object tab of the Permission Entry dialog box (for a user object) includes the following permissions, as shown in Table 10.3.

TABLE 10.3: OBJECT PERMISSIONS

PERMISSION	DESCRIPTION
Full Control	Just what the name implies—a combination of all the other permissions.
List Contents	This allows you to view any objects that are subordinate to the object within the hierarchical structure of the database.

Continued on next page

TABLE 10.3: OBJECT PERMISSIONS *(continued)*

PERMISSION	DESCRIPTION
Read All Properties	Read (and Write below) allows you to quickly give sweeping administrative powers, without having to check every single property. Both properties are available for every class of object within AD.
Write All Properties	See above.
Delete	Self explanatory.
Delete Subtree	Allows you to delete this object and everything below it in the AD tree.
Read Permissions	Allows you to see the contents of the ACL for this object (basically the information shown in Figures 10.14, 10.15, and 10.16).
Modify Permissions	You can only grant permissions equal to what you have been granted. In other words, if I am given the Read All Properties and Modify Permissions properties, I cannot grant another user the Write All Properties permission.
Modify Owner	This permission allows you to take ownership of the object.
All Extended Rights	Self explanatory.
Create All Child Objects	Create any class of object that can exist under this object within the AD tree structure.
Delete All Child Objects	Self explanatory.
Change Password	Self explanatory.
Receive As	Self explanatory.
Reset Password	Self explanatory.
Send As	Self explanatory.

As you can see, most of the permissions on the Object tab refer to managing the object within the AD structure—create, delete, permissions, ownership. A few permissions refer to properties (read all, write all, reset password, etc.), but they are mostly just common administrative tasks placed here for convenience.

The Properties tab, shown in Figure 10.17, lists each and every property of the object, and it allows you to set permissions on each. That list includes over 225 properties for the user class of object on a default installation of Active Directory (remember: certain applications will extend the schema to include new object classes and properties). In other words, if you want you can spend your entire life taking extremely granular control over your AD environment!

FIGURE 10.17

The extensive Properties tab for the user object

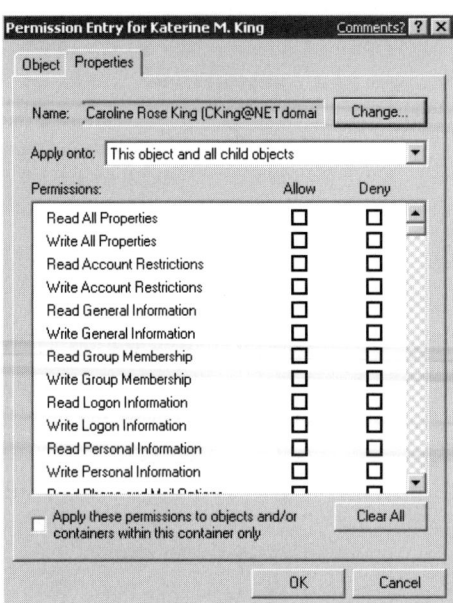

Unlike the permissions listed on the Object tab, I'm not going to build a table with all of the properties of the user class of object. First, the list is way too long, and second, the list is only pertinent to user objects. You'd have to memorize a different list for every class of object. There are, however, a few things you should note about this list:

◆ Every manageable property of the object class is listed. If you want to control access to a specific property, you can do so.

◆ Permissions are matched: read and write. You can grant someone the ability to read the value of any property without giving them the ability to change it.

◆ You can control the scope of the assignment with the Apply Onto drop-down list. (We'll discuss this list next!)

The Apply Onto drop-down list lets you control how much of your AD tree is included when you grant administrative permissions. Look at Figure 10.18; it lists the objects that will be affected by your action. Notice that it defaults to applying this permission to the object and everything below it in the AD tree. Microsoft does not expect you to control every property of every object individually. You can apply your assignment to this object and everything below it, to this object only, or to every instance of a particular object class. This last option comes in real handy. You might, for instance, want to grant your human resources department the permissions necessary to update the phone and address information of all users. We'll look at some specific uses of these tools a little later in this section.

FIGURE 10.18

The Apply Onto list lets you control the scope of the permissions assignment.

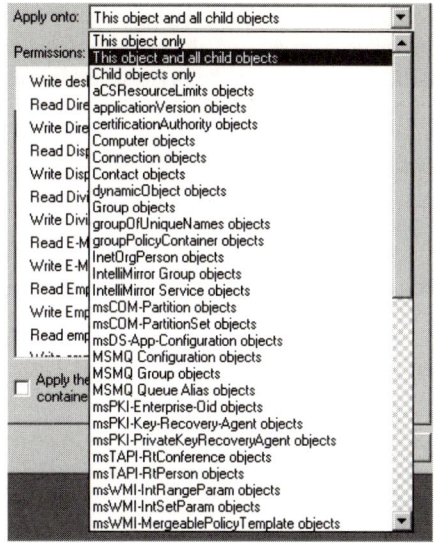

Real-World Implementations

So now that we've looked at the security system on a theoretical level, let's switch gears and apply what we've seen to a few real-world scenarios. I've always believed that a security system is only as good as you make it—the most sophisticated system on the market isn't worth anything unless you can use it to your advantage.

Before we start, though, let's talk about a real-world approach to security. I follow a few rules and guidelines when working with my clients:

> *Ensure that you have indeed secured that which you want to protect.* Don't rely upon your "theory;" audit resources to ensure compliance. Implementation doesn't mean much if you don't test your process beforehand and monitor its success in the long run.

> *Security has a cost; spend your resources wisely.* I've had many an argument with technologists who always want the "best" or "most secure" solutions. In reality, you should implement a level of security that meets both the needs and budget of your environment.

> *If curiosity kills the cat, complexity kills the administrator.* If your security plan is so complex that you can't keep track of it, it will fall apart sooner or later. I firmly believe in the KISS system: Keep It Simple and Secure. (You might have your own definition for KISS, but I didn't want to offend anyone.)

> *Less is better.* This guideline has a lot of meanings:

♦ Users should be granted the minimum set of permissions necessary to perform their job—nothing more!

- Security should be implemented with the least number of actions (in other words, the fewer times you have to grant permissions, the better—use group objects so that a permission is granted once, rather than granting the permission to each individual user object).

- The lower the number of administrators over any given set of resources, the better (too many cooks spoil the broth, and make it harder to keep track of who can do what, and where).

- Fewer domains (usually) means fewer headaches.

- Fewer Group Policies (usually) means easier management.

- And the more controversial meaning: fewer freedoms mean fewer help desk calls (lock 'em down as much as possible).

NOTE *My "Less Is Better" philosophy has been developed over years in the field. I find that the more administrative actions I have to take, the harder it is to manage the system. In systems where every little aspect of the environment is managed separately, the level of complexity soon rises to the point where troubleshooting a security-based issue becomes a nightmare.*

Using the Defaults

Traditionally I've been a firm believer in living with the defaults—making changes after circumstances warrant. Unfortunately, Microsoft makes this theory kind of hard to live with. Whoever heard of giving the Everyone group Full Control by default? Up until the latest releases of their operating systems, I've been inclined to say scrap the defaults and start from scratch. Until now, that is!

The default security implementations in the Windows Server 2003 operating system—at least those that pertain to Active Directory—actually make sense for most environments. For those of you who were wondering, this is good news! This means that in many cases, you can set up an AD structure and not have to spend a lot of time configuring security—notice that I didn't say you could ignore it!

My basic philosophy when it comes to AD security has been to live with the defaults and then plan for any exceptions given the needs of my client's specific environment. With that said, it becomes necessary to understand the default assignments so you'll know when you can live with them and when you'll need to make some changes.

This is another of those areas where the default permissions will depend upon the class of object in question—in other words, the default permission assignments differ when looking at a group object or a user object or an OU object. It's not important that you memorize the default assignments for each type of object; there are too many classes and too many default assignments (that's why GUIs were invented!). If you did take the time to memorize them, the list would likely change the first time you installed a high-end server-based application—something like Exchange Server 2000—since many high-end applications are now extending the schema to fit their needs. What you want to do, however, is get a feel for the thought process that went into choosing the defaults, and then look at each object class as you use it on your network.

Without getting into specifics (remember, the specifics will change, and there are too many to remember), the bottom-line default is that the Domain Admins group can pretty much do what it wants within a given domain, the Enterprise Admins group can do pretty much what it wants throughout the entire forest, and the Schema Admins group can modify the Active Directory schema—a dangerous ability, to say the least!

Normal users, on the other hand, have a much more limited range of permissions in a default installation. Every user can read the properties of all objects within the tree. This facilitates their use of the AD database, but it does mean you have to either be careful about what information you store in AD or change the defaults to protect any information that should have controlled access. In the phone number property for a user object, for instance, if you enter a user's business phone number, you probably do not have to worry too much about security. In most companies (and for most users), a business telephone number should be public knowledge. In this case, the default permissions work just fine! If, on the other hand, you decide to store the user's home phone number in Active Directory, you will have to take steps to safeguard that information against unwanted access.

I follow two basic rules when deciding which information should be stored in AD:

1. The information should not be confidential. Not because of a lack of security, but because the AD database is the perfect vehicle for accessing basic, public information. Any LDAP tool can be used to access the Active Directory database—in other words, you have a ready-made company "phone book" without designing a database on your own.

2. The information should be fairly static in nature. While Active Directory's replication process is fairly efficient, I don't want to store data that changes on a regular basis. Constant changes will result in constant replication.

A great example of the importance of static information occurred on a recent consulting job. My client has one of those dynamic environment in which the emphasis is on projects rather than traditional departments. A user, for instance, might have multiple managers in any given year, depending on the number of projects upon which they worked. The client developed their own LDAP utility to query the AD database to determine the project to which a user was assigned, their manager, and anyone who reported to them. The client thought AD was the perfect vehicle since each user object has properties to store all of this information. The company has around a thousand employees, and we took the time to enter in all of the information for each of them—and updated it every time someone moved from one project to another. Since moving between projects was a common occurrence, we ended up flooding their frame network with AD replication traffic on a regular basis. It wasn't long before I was called back to the client site and asked to implement my original suggestion: using AD as a repository for static information (phone numbers, mailing addresses, etc.) and using a web-based solution for the more dynamic information (pulling information out of a series of databases managed by the human resources department).

A Few Examples

Let's take a look at a couple of real-world examples of how Active Directory security can be used to facilitate real-life management of network resources. When I talk to my clients, a few requests seem to be common across just about every type of business environment:

◆ The help desk needs to change passwords, but not be given excessive administrative permissions.

◆ The human resources department wants to manage all employee record keeping, including any "HR" information stored within the AD database.

Let's use these examples for learning the flexibility built into the AD security system.

PASSWORD CONTROL

One of the most common issues that I faced with NT revolved around giving help desk personnel enough power to do their job, but not enough power to mess things up. The biggest issue was granting them the ability to change or reset user passwords, without having to give them full administrative privileges. In an AD environment, this is actually a simple delegation; as a matter of fact, you can choose exactly what properties the help desk group should be able to access!

Let's take a look at the process. I ask myself three simple questions to help me focus my security assignments: Who? What? Where? Let's apply my three questions to our current issue:

Who?

To whom will I grant more power or permissions? In this case, the answer depends upon the company involved. In some companies, the help desk is a separate group of IT professionals—people who spend their days answering end-user questions and solving end-user problems. In this type of environment, I create a group with an imaginative name—something like "Help Desk"—and add the appropriate users to the group.

In other companies, the help desk is the entire IT staff—in which case, I have to determine if there are certain individuals who should or should not have this level of administrative power. Once again, I create a group (or use an existing group) and assign the permissions.

In a more distributed management type of environment, the help desk might be made up of an individual in each location. This makes the decision a little more tricky, and I might have to answer the "Where?" question before I can decide on my implementation. In any event, I create a security group that represents each location (or area of responsibility) and add the appropriate user(s) as members.

The bottom line to answering the "Who?" question is to create a security group or set of security groups that represent the individuals who should be granted the privilege.

What?

Now I consider exactly what the group(s) should be able to do. In this case, the privilege to be granted is very specific: these groups should have the ability to reset user passwords.

Where?

The answer to this question revolves around the management philosophy of the company. Does it have a centrally controlled management system? If yes, I'm going to assign this privilege so that the users have the power throughout the entire AD structure. If, on the other hand, I am working with a distributed management environment, each group might need to be assigned the ability to change passwords in a specific area of the AD structure (either within a specific tree, domain, or even OU).

Once I've answered my three questions, I'm ready to begin implementation. First I create any security groups and add the members. I then assign the permissions to the group or groups. For our example, let's assume that the company has a distributed management philosophy with a small number of IT support personnel for each physical region. Since the regional IT staff members are responsible for the management of resources within their area, they must have the appropriate permissions. The basic AD structure looks like that shown in Figure 10.19.

FIGURE 10.19

The AD structure of a company with distributed management

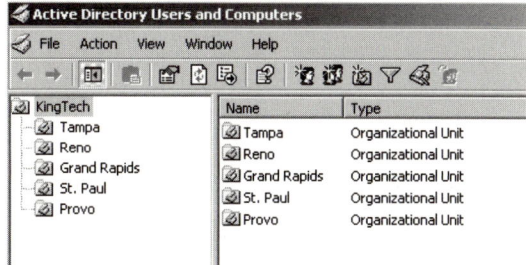

Each of the regional organizational units contains the account of the local IT administrator. This account should be given the permissions necessary to manage user passwords. The St. Paul container is shown in Figure 10.20. Notice that I have created a security group named "St. Paul Admins"—not very imaginative, but functional. The local IT person's account has been made a member of this group.

FIGURE 10.20

The St. Paul OU

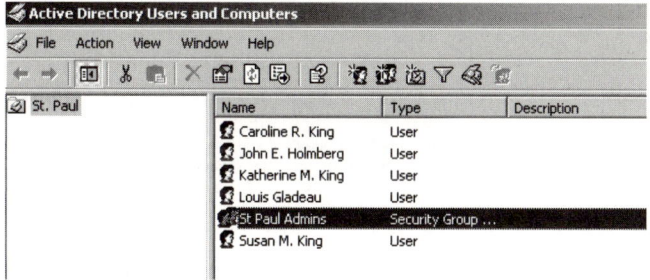

My next task is to assign the St. Paul Admins security group the appropriate privileges. Within Active Directory Users and Computers, I right-click the St. Paul OU and choose Delegate Control—notice that by choosing the correct OU, I've basically used the answer to my third question, Where? This starts the Delegation of Control Wizard. The first screen is the usual "Welcome to the wizard" and "Aren't you glad you bought Microsoft" message. Clicking Next opens the window shown in Figure 10.21.

FIGURE 10.21

Choose users
or groups.

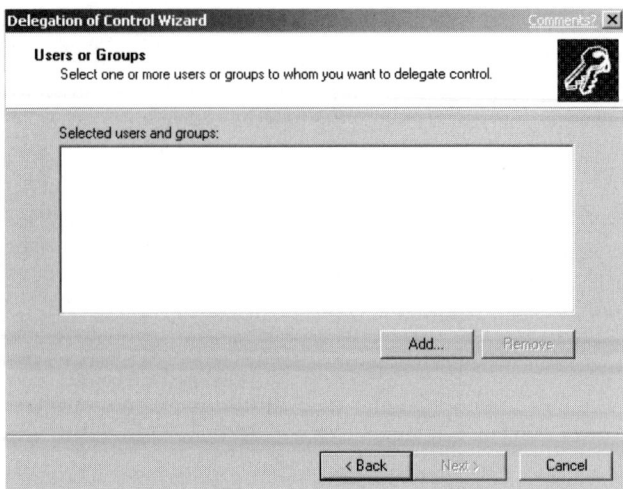

As you can see in Figure 10.21, the first step is the answer to my first question, Who? I've added the St. Paul Admins group to the list. Clicking Next opens the window shown in Figure 10.22. As you can see, the wizard actually makes our task very easy. Microsoft has included some common administrative tasks in a built-in list that we can choose from. I've checked the appropriate option: Reset User Passwords and Force Password Change at Next Logon. In other words, the answer to my second question, What? We'll see a more complex choice later.

FIGURE 10.22

Assigning the
appropriate
privileges

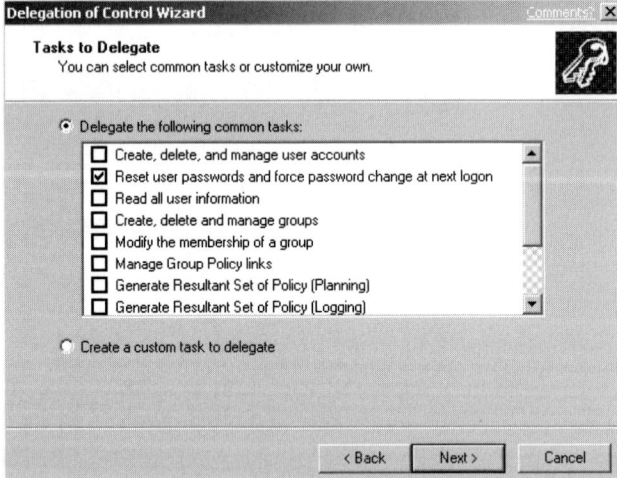

That's all there is to it! Now any member of the St. Paul Admins group has the power to reset user passwords.

MANAGING HUMAN RESOURCE INFORMATION

To be truthful, I'm not all that thrilled with the following example. It is based upon the assumption that I trust someone in the human resources department enough to allow them administrative (no matter how limited) access to Active Directory. I'll present my personal preference to this issue at the end of our example. I include this case because I have actually been asked to provide this type of scenario for numerous clients. Not surprisingly, I also talked all but one of those clients into using my workaround (described later).

So the scenario is this: the HR department wants to (or has been assigned to) manage any personal data stored within AD—things like phone numbers, titles, departments, etc. While this frees you from the task of entering this information, it means that someone in HR must be given the appropriate permissions (and no more!).

The mechanics of this process start the same as they did for the preceding example. Within Active Directory Users and Computers, right-click the appropriate container (in this case, the top of the structure) and choose Delegate Control. The first few screens will be familiar—the Welcome screen and the Choose the User or Groups screen. The first change will be apparent on the third window. Instead of picking one of the prebuilt tasks, you will create a custom task to delegate. Notice in Figure 10.23 that I have checked the appropriate option.

FIGURE 10.23

Create a custom task.

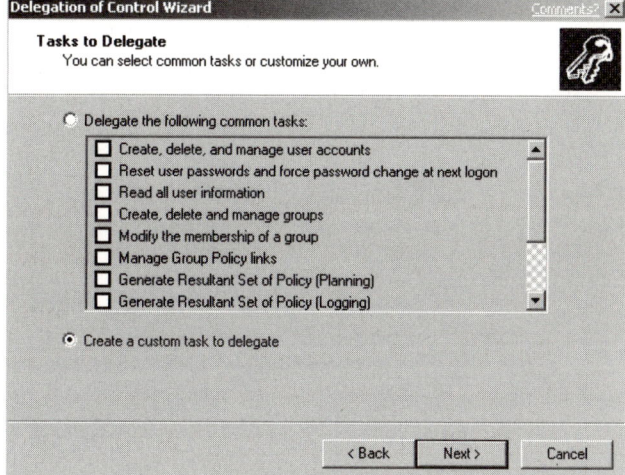

The next dialog box, shown in Figure 10.24, allows you to choose which types of objects the user or group should be given control of—users, printers, groups, etc. In our case, HR should only have access to user objects, so I have selected the option that limits their access to chosen object types. Notice that I have also *not* checked the options to allow the creation of new or the deletion of existing user objects. Some would argue that the HR department should have the ability to create user objects. Me, I'd rather have them call me or my staff so that I can enforce corporate standards for setting up users (like "last name, first" in the display field.)

FIGURE 10.24

Choose the
object types.

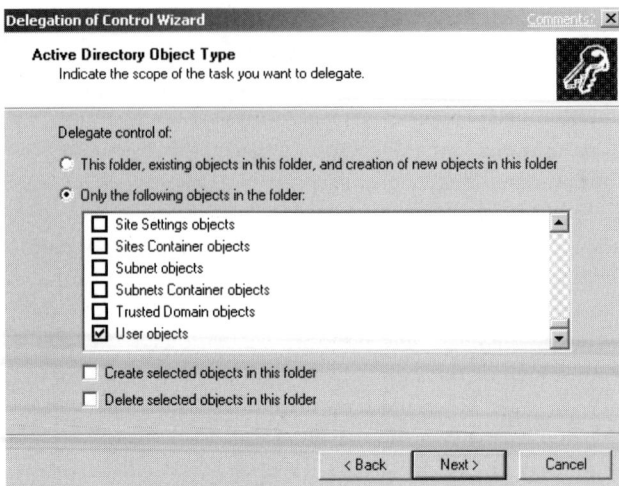

FIGURE 10.24

Choose the
object types.

Next I choose which properties the HR group should have permission to, as shown in Figure 10.25. Here is where I must carefully consider which properties should be considered "HR" and which should not. This usually entails creating a list of available properties and then presenting it to HR—and letting them choose what they feel they should manage.

FIGURE 10.25

Choose the
properties.

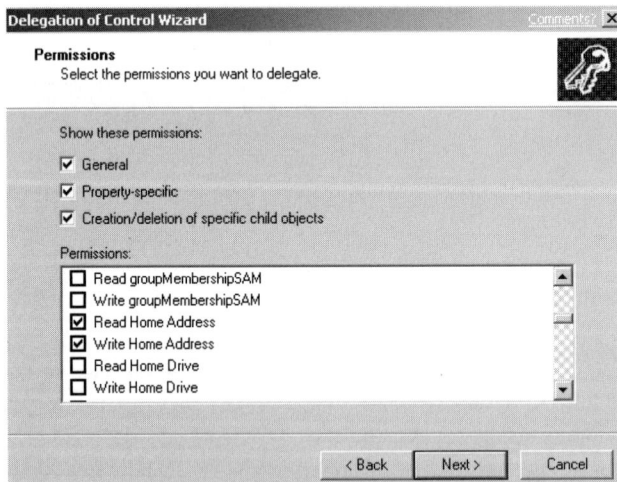

That's all there is to it! Once again, delegating control of specific aspects of AD is fairly easy.

I promised you a more real-world solution to this issue. Let's face it: First, we probably don't want HR personnel making changes to our AD database, nor do we really want the responsibility of training them to do so correctly. To be honest, the HR department is probably overworked as it is, so they probably aren't all that thrilled with the prospect either.

Luckily, there is a tool called `Addusers.Exe` that allows you to import information from a text file into AD. While the specifics are beyond the scope of this book, the basic concept is fairly simple. First, most HR departments have some sort of existing database of employee information—a database that they keep up-to-date as part of their job. Second, every database I've ever seen has the ability to export data in some sort of text file (usually comma-delimited at the very least). `Addusers.exe` has the ability to create new objects, add new values to existing properties, and overwrite the values in existing properties. Using a text file generated from the existing HR database, you can update the information in AD on a regular basis. This is also a great way to create user accounts in a new system; rather than typing them in by hand, you can contact HR and get a list of employees in a text file!

Authentication Security

The initial security that any user encounters is the security involved in the logon, or authentication, process. Windows 2000/Windows Server 2003 supports multiple protocols for network security and authentication. In a perfect world, one—and only one—security protocol would be used to access the network. Unfortunately, in the heterogeneous networks of today's business market, most networks must use multiple security protocols. Rather than force administrators to make a choice, and in an effort to provide an open architecture, Microsoft has designed a security architecture that is both modular and extensible. Windows 2000/Windows Server 2003 will support the following network security protocols:

Windows NT LAN Manager (NTLM) NTLM is the security protocol used by earlier versions of Windows NT. NTLM will continue to be supported to provide backward compatibility with these operating systems.

Kerberos Version 5 The Kerberos protocol replaces NTLM as the primary security protocol for access to resources within or across NT domains. Kerberos provides:

♦ Mutual authentication of both client and server (in other words, authentication becomes a two-way street)

♦ Less overhead on the server during authentication

♦ Support of delegation of authority from clients to servers through the use of proxy mechanisms

NOTE *We'll take a closer look at Kerberos in the next section of this chapter.*

Distributed Password Authentication (DPA)   DPA is the shared secret authentication protocol used by some of the largest Internet membership organizations, such as CompuServe and MSN. It was specifically designed to allow members to use the same username and password to access multiple Internet resources that are part of the membership organization. In other words, a user can access different resources without having to enter (and remember) multiple usernames and passwords.

Public-Key-Based Protocols   Secure Sockets Layer (SSL) is the *de facto* standard for secure connections between Internet browsers and Internet servers. These protocols use public-key certificates to authenticate clients.

NOTE   *We'll discuss certificates in more detail later in this chapter.*

The ability to mix and match security mechanisms as needed is critical in any large organization. Microsoft has implemented a modular security architecture known as the *Security Support Provider Interface* (SSPI) to provide this functionality. This SSPI architecture is shown in Figure 10.26.

FIGURE 10.26

The Security Support Provider Interface architecture

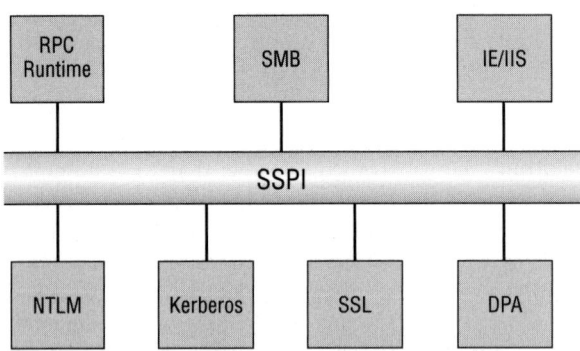

SSPI is a Win32 system API that acts as an interpreter between application protocols (such as those used by Internet Explorer) and security protocols (such as Kerberos).

Kerberos Basics

Kerberos version 5 has been implemented in numerous systems and can be used to provide a single point of authentication to mixed resources. Kerberos provides a common protocol that allows a single account database to authenticate users across a heterogeneous environment. As such, utilizing Kerberos security can greatly reduce the administrative overhead involved in supporting a mixed network.

Kerberos security uses a computer designated as the Key Distribution Center (KDC). Kerberos is known as a *shared secret authentication protocol* because both the client and the KDC know the user's password. The KDC acts as the middleman between clients and resources during the authentication process. You can see this process in Figure 10.27.

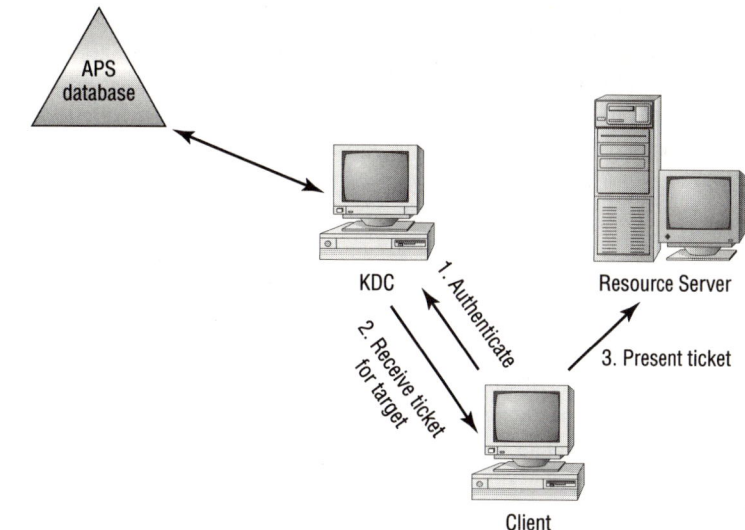

FIGURE 10.27

The Kerberos authentication process

Here's what happens:

1. The client authenticates to the Key Distribution Center computer, using a valid username and password. In Windows 2000/Windows Server 2003, this account information is held in the Active Directory database. In other words, Kerberos is fully integrated into the AD environment.

2. The client requests a *session ticket* for the target server. The Kerberos session ticket identifies the user. In a Windows 2000/Windows Server 2003 environment, the session ticket contains the user's SID as well as the SIDs of any groups the user is a member of. The session ticket also contains an encrypted key that the target server can use to ensure that the ticket was generated by the KDC.

3. The client then presents the session ticket to the target server. The target server checks whether the ticket is valid and grants or denies access as appropriate.

The session ticket is stored on the client computer for a random amount of time (between five minutes and eight hours) so that it can be used to request access to that resource in the future. If the ticket expires, it is flushed from memory and the process is repeated at the next access attempt.

Kerberos is a great technology—secure, dependable, and mature. It is not something that most administrators will, under normal circumstances, have to concern themselves with. The Kerberos authentication process happens in the background as users attach to network resources, much as the NTLM authentication process did in earlier releases of NT.

Public-Key Security

Windows 2000/Windows Server 2003 also supports the use of public-key schemes, the most common being X.509, for granting resource access to users who do not have Kerberos credentials.

Most commonly, this scenario will involve granting access to someone outside of the organization. You might, for instance, wish to allow clients the ability to access an inventory database, rather than forcing them to call a salesperson for information. Another potential X.509 certificate user would be a company that uses contractors to perform internal functions. Rather than create an internal account for the contractors, an administrator could use certificates to authenticate contractors to the resources they need. Whatever the purpose, using public-key security, or certificates, for authentication is common practice in today's world.

PUBLIC KEY BASICS

Public-key security is based on the science of *cryptography*. Cryptography uses mathematical algorithms that combine input (plain text) and an encryption key to generate encrypted data, known as *ciphertext*. With a good algorithm, it is mathematically infeasible (notice I did not say "impossible") to reverse the encryption process with only the ciphertext; some additional data is needed to perform this task, namely an *encryption key*.

In traditional cryptography, the same key is used to encrypt and decrypt messages. You have probably seen such encryption in some spy novel you have read. The spy steals the master code for all communication from the enemy, and the hero is one step ahead of the enemy from that point on. Usually, the master key is stolen during its transfer from one party to another. This is the biggest weakness of traditional cryptography: both parties must have the key, so some secure method of transferring that key is crucial.

In public-key cryptography, the encryption and decryption keys are related, but different. An encryption key is used to encrypt data, but it has no place in the decryption process. A different key (mathematically related but not identical), known as the *decryption key*, is used for decryption. In a public-key environment, every user has a pair of keys: a public key (to encrypt) and a private key (to decrypt). By making the public key available, you can enable others to send you data that is encrypted in such a way that only your private key can decrypt it. Public-key encryption schemes avoid the biggest weakness of older systems: the key used to decrypt data does *not* have to be transferred and thus can be kept in a secure location.

This separation of public and private keys has allowed the creation of a number of new technologies that are becoming a part of today's networks:

- ◆ Digital signatures

- ◆ Distributed authentication

- ◆ Bulk data encryption without prior shared secrets

The following sections give an overview of these technologies.

DIGITAL SIGNATURES

A *digital signature* is used to validate the authenticity of a message by the receiver. Using the private key, the client creates a small piece of data that can be decrypted only with the use of the corresponding public key. This electronic signature provides the following benefits:

- ◆ It ensures that the data is from someone who possesses the matching private key (either the originator of the message or a trusted certificate server).

♦ Anyone with access to the public key can verify the signature.

♦ Any change to the data (as small as modifying a single bit) invalidates the signature—letting the recipient know that the message has been tampered with or corrupted in transit.

Using digital signatures can provide a high level of confidence in the integrity of transferred data. Not only is this a good security mechanism, it can also be used to ensure that network problems have not corrupted data in transit.

DISTRIBUTED AUTHENTICATION

Public-key security can also be used as a form of authentication security. The public/private key combination can be used to guarantee the identity of the sender of data, much like using the digital signatures described in the previous section. This allows an NT/2000/2003 system to grant access to users outside of its environment. As long as both parties (the operating system and the user) trust a third-party key provider or certificate server, users can use their public/private key mechanism to identify themselves to an NT/2000/2003 server.

BULK DATA ENCRYPTION WITHOUT PRIOR SHARED SECRETS

Current public-key technologies are processor intensive compared to more traditional cryptographic methods. They are secure, though, because the decryption key does not need to be passed from sender to recipient. Bulk encryption takes advantage of the security of public-key mechanisms without incurring the greater processor overhead. If two computers need to transfer data, the sender will use the recipient's public key to encrypt a *master key* and send it to the recipient. Since only the recipient has the private key to decrypt this message, we can trust that the master key has arrived securely. Now that both parties have the master key, traditional encryption can be used during the actual transfer of data.

Certificates

A service known as the Certificate Authority (CA) issues *certificates* that guarantee the binding between a public key and the originator of data. In other words, both the sender and the recipient trust that the CA will correctly authenticate the certificate that the sender transfers to the recipient. If it does so, the recipient can trust that the certificate is from whom it is supposed to be from, and the rest of the public/private key security mechanism can proceed.

Another way to look at this is to think about the process of sending a signed message. The sender creates a message and attaches the digital signature. The recipient performs the algorithm against the signature to determine whether the message has been tampered with. What the recipient cannot guarantee is that the message came from the appropriate sender. In other words, the recipient can use the public key to verify the message, but what do they use to verify that the public key belongs to the appropriate sender? In other words, *anyone* can request a public/private key pair from a KDC using any name at all. How does the recipient know that some other user hasn't generated a key pair under a false name?

This is where CA services enter the picture. CA services guarantee the binding between the originator and the public key. As long as the recipient trusts the CA to do its job correctly, the recipient can rest assured that the sender is indeed who they claim to be.

In a large environment, the recipient might need to verify the CA server by using another CA server. This second CA server might also need to be verified using a third server. Ultimately, the recipient will build a chain of "trusts" back to a CA server that the user implicitly trusts, known as a *trusted root certificate server*.

Microsoft Windows 2000/Windows Server 2003 ships with the software to build a Microsoft Certificate Server. This software is compliant with the industry's leading certificate standard—X.509. Once in place, an Active Directory server can trust X.509 certificates and thus allow outside accounts access to internal resources.

In Short

The ability to selectively delegate administrative privileges is a *very* big selling point of Windows 2000 Server! Also important is the ability to incorporate external security methods into your NT network. Understanding the implications of these new features can be the turning point in the learning curve for AD.

In the next chapter, we will expand upon our discussion of security with the addition of Group Policies. This tool gives you the power to completely control who accesses your network and what their environment will look like.

Chapter 11

Implementing Group Policies

In NT 4, you could create System Policies (using the System Policy Editor) to configure user and computer settings stored in the Windows NT Registry. System Policies could be used to control the user environment and user actions, as well as to enforce system configuration settings for computers running Windows NT Workstation, Windows NT Server, and Windows 95. Basically, though, System Policies are just Registry settings that define the behavior of operating system components.

Windows 2000 Server introduced a whole new level of central control over user environments. The Group Policy Editor, a utility included in Windows 2000, extended functionality of the System Policy Editor and enhanced administrators' abilities to configure user and computer settings on the domain, site, or organizational unit level by leveraging the Active Directory database.

Windows Server 2003 not only enhances the power of Group Policies by significantly increasing the number of configurable settings, but it also makes their scope much more granular (through the introduction of Windows Instrumentation Management, or WMI, filters) and simplifies their management (with tools such as Resultant Set of Policies and Group Policy Management Console).

In this chapter:

- ◆ Defining Group Policies
- ◆ The Microsoft Management Console
- ◆ Configuring policy objects in AD
- ◆ Settings in the Computer Configuration node
- ◆ Administrative Templates in the Computer Configuration node
- ◆ The User Configuration node
- ◆ Configuring Group Policy settings
- ◆ Determining which policy will be applied
- ◆ Group Policy management tools

What Are Group Policies?

Total cost of ownership (or simply TCO) has become one of the most popular buzzwords among technology managers in recent years. TCO represents not only the original cost of the hardware and software used on the desktop, but also the ongoing support costs associated with personal computers. Lost productivity due to errors and inconsistencies in computer configuration is cited as one of the largest costs involved in long-term support. Continuous effort to lower this cost is the primary reason for the attention that Microsoft dedicated to the development and refinement of *Group Policies*.

Group Policies are used to define user or computer settings for an entire group of users or computers at one time. The settings that you configure are stored in a *Group Policy Object* (*GPO*), which is then associated with Active Directory containers such as sites, domains, or organizational units. Many different aspects of the network, desktop, and software configuration environments can be managed through Group Policies. The following list describes, in general terms, the different types of policies that can be created (and enforced) using Windows Server 2003's Group Policy Editor:

Application Deployment Policies   These policies affect the applications that users can install from the network. In general, installation can be performed in one of two ways:

Application Assignment   The Group Policy installs or upgrades applications automatically. Installation is triggered at computer startup, user logon, or the first time the application is used.

Application Publication   The Group Policy causes the list of published applications to be displayed in the Add/Remove Programs applet in Control Panel. This gives users the ability to install and remove programs manually, using the process with which they are already familiar.

Script Policies   These policies allow an administrator to specify scripts that should run during user logon/logoff or system startup/shutdown.

Security Policies   These policies provide many different ways of securing the computing environment, ranging from restricting access to files, folders, and Registry keys to controlling system services and applications running on computers, limiting certain privileges to selected users or groups, and determining domainwide password settings.

Folder Redirection Policies   These policies are intended to alter the default location of special user folders, such as Desktop or My Documents.

Software Components Policies   The majority of these policies are Registry-based, so they work similarly to System Policies. Administrators can use them to configure various Windows software components. This includes applications such as Internet Explorer, NetMeeting, or Windows Messenger, as well as features closely integrated with the operating system such as Offline Files, user profiles, or even Group Policies themselves.

As you can see from this list, you can make policies do more than in earlier versions of Windows. Most of this additional functionality comes from the integration of policies with Active Directory Services.

Microsoft Management Console

Before we begin our discussion of policy-based administration, this is as good a time as any to introduce a new tool: the Microsoft Management Console (MMC). In earlier chapters, we discussed specific tools to do specific jobs—for instance, using Active Directory Users and Computers to create organizational units and the objects that populate them. While this is a valid method (using a separate tool for each management function), Microsoft has provided us with a single tool that is capable of performing almost every administrative task required in a Windows Server 2003 and Windows 2000 environment: the MMC.

I think of the MMC as a big software pincushion. On its own it does very little, but if you plug in additional software, known as *snap-ins*, its functionality knows no bounds.

To run the MMC, type **MMC** in the Run window. Before any snap-ins have been added, the interface will look like the window shown in Figure 11.1.

FIGURE 11.1

The Microsoft Management Console

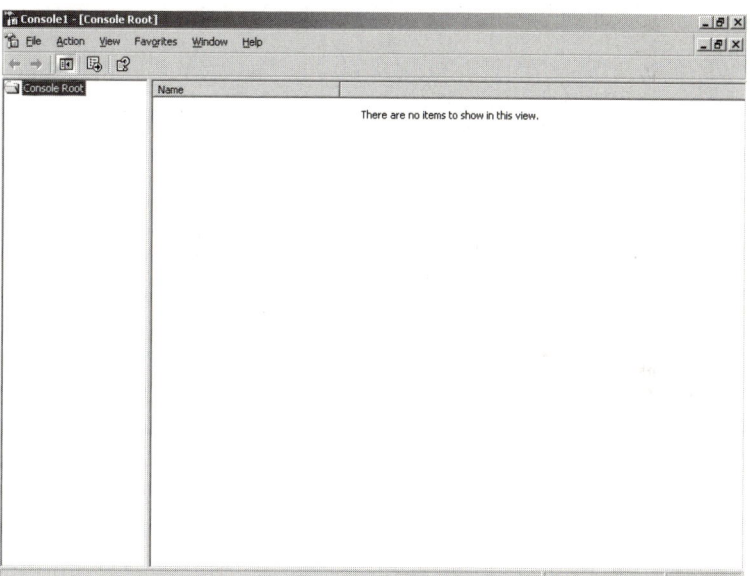

From here you'll need to install a few snap-ins. On the Console menu, choose Add/Remove Snap-in. You'll be presented with the list shown in Figure 11.2. As you can see, I've already added the Active Directory Users and Computers snap-in.

FIGURE 11.2

The Add/Remove
Snap-in dialog box

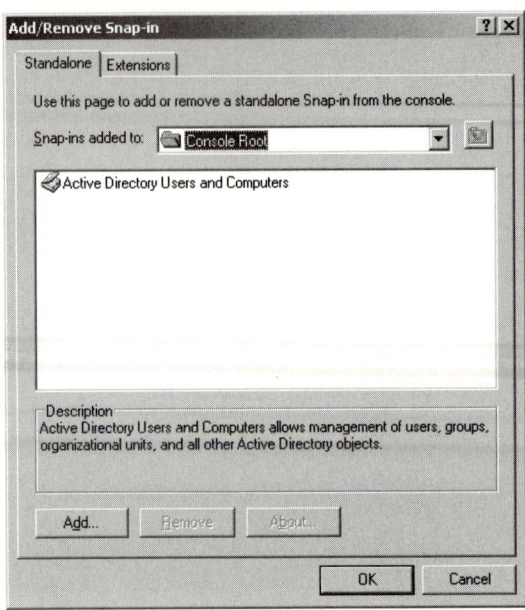

Click the Add button to be presented with a list of available snap-ins. For our purposes here,
I'll add the Group Policy Object Editor snap-in by highlighting it and choosing Add, as shown in
Figure 11.3.

FIGURE 11.3

Adding the Group
Policy snap-in

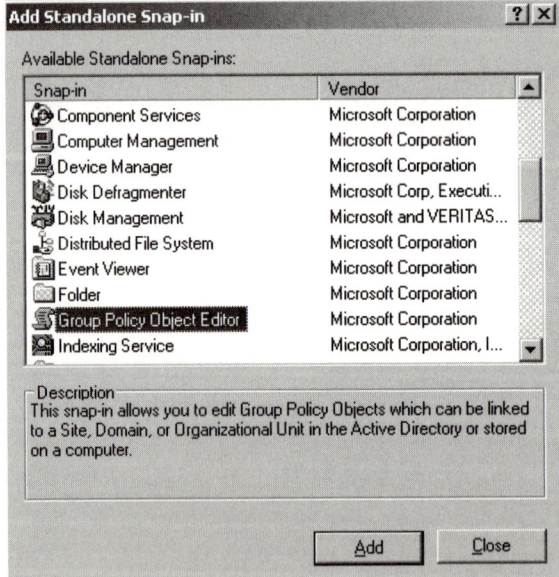

The next screen allows you to choose where the Group Policies will be stored, whether on the local machine or in Active Directory . I've decided to create a Group Policy Object named "KingTech Education Policy" and associate it with the Education OU, as shown in Figure 11.4. We'll discuss the significance of this association a little later in this chapter. For now, be aware that policies can be associated with sites, domains, or organizational units.

FIGURE 11.4

Creating the
policy object

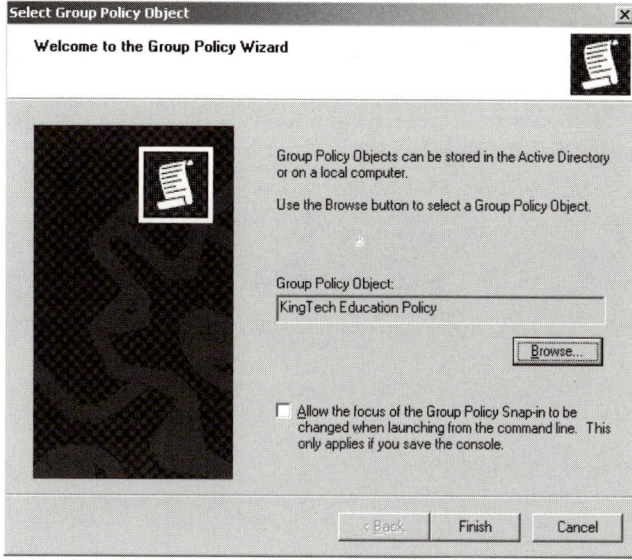

Now that I have created the Group Policy, the MMC reflects its existence, as shown in Figure 11.5. From now on, I can manage the policy using my customized MMC, rather than some other tool.

FIGURE 11.5

KingTech
Education
Policy

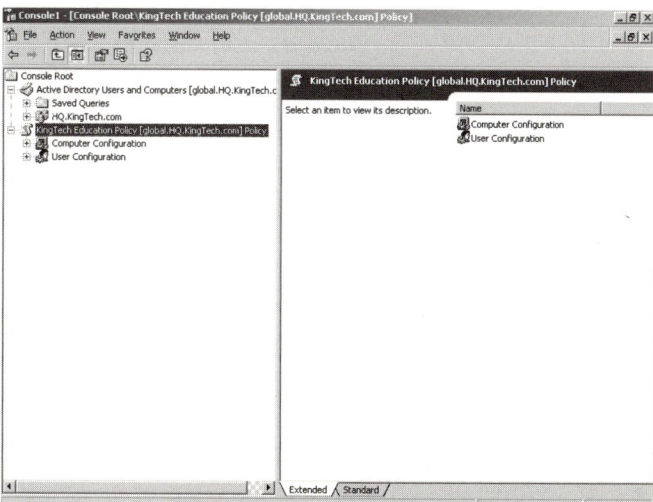

Policy Objects in AD

As you've seen, Group Policies are stored in Group Policy Objects, which are associated with sites, domains, or organizational unit objects within the directory. We'll discuss the procedures for creating and modifying Group Policies later in this chapter. We will begin, though, by looking at the structure of Group Policies and their relationship to Active Directory.

Group Policy Objects are tied to one of the three places in the Active Directory tree: site, domain, or organizational unit. The placement determines which users or computers will be affected by the settings in the GPO. The first rule to remember with Windows Group Policies is that they can be applied only to users or computers—they will have no effect upon other classes of objects in the AD tree.

At the root of the GPO structure are two subfolders, Computer Configuration and User Configuration, as shown in Figure 11.6.

FIGURE 11.6

The root of the GPO structure

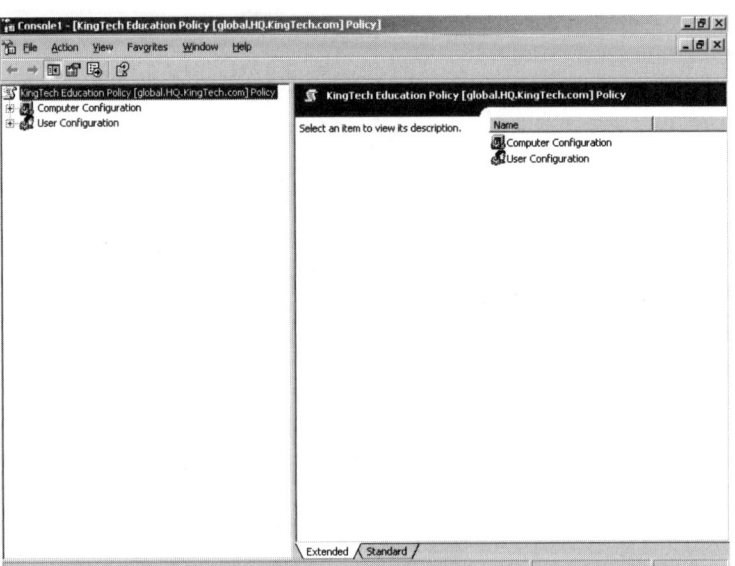

As the names imply, each of these subfolders contains parameters that can be configured for either the computer (Computer Configuration) or the user (User Configuration), whose accounts reside in the site, domain, or organizational unit associated with the GPO.

Computer Configuration

The options available within the Computer Configuration area can be used to:

◆ Launch automatic installation of applications at computer startup.

◆ Increase system security.

◆ Specify computer startup and shutdown scripts.

◆ Configure settings of software components for all users on a computer.

NOTE   Computer-related policies are applied whenever the operating system initializes. Most of them are also reapplied periodically, within configurable time intervals (set by default to 5 minutes for domain controllers and 90 minutes—with up to a 30-minute offset—for all other computers).

User Configuration

The options available within the User Configuration area can be used to:

◆ Launch automatic installation of applications at user logon or allow a user to perform installation manually afterward.

◆ Assign user logon and logoff scripts.

◆ "Lock down" a user's settings by hiding Desktop icons and removing Control Panel configuration options.

◆ Configure user-specific settings of various software components.

NOTE   User Configuration policy options are applied whenever a user logs on to the computer. As with computer-related policies, many of them are also reapplied periodically using a separately configured interval (defaulting to 90 minutes, with up to a 30-minute offset).

Using Computer and User Configuration

There are two essential differences between the Computer Configuration and User Configuration settings. The first one is rather obvious and concerns the type of object that Group Policy affects (computer and user, respectively). What might be less obvious is the fact that some of the settings exist only within a computer or user context. For example, it would not make sense to configure permissions on a Registry key that would change depending on which user logs on to a computer. Similarly, Desktop configuration is irrelevant from the computer configuration point of view, since a computer object does not run any interactive sessions and does not use the Desktop.

NOTE   There might be scenarios (such as shared, open-access kiosks) in which you want to ensure that every user logging on to the computer has the same Desktop configuration. This is possible by using loopback processing of Group Policies (a setting located in Computer Configuration folder).

The second difference deals with the time when each type of policy is initially applied. For Computer Configuration options, this happens as the operating system boots. User Configuration policies, on the other hand, are applied as the user logs on (*after* the operating system has initialized). As I mentioned before, some user and computer settings are also reapplied at configurable intervals.

Each of these folders—Computer Configuration and User Configuration—acts as the root of a GPO structure. Within each you will find a series of folders and subfolders. Each of these folders, also known as *GPO nodes*, contains configurable options for a specific area of your environment.

While NT 4–based System Policies are stored entirely in files with the extension `.pol` located in the NETLOGON share (on all domain controllers), the contents of Group Policies are split between Active Directory and files. The Active Directory part is called the *Group Policy Container* (*GPC*). The remaining part, known as the *Group Policy Template* (*GPT*) resides in the System Volume (SYSVOL) folder on all Windows 2000 and Windows Server 2003 domain controllers. Both locations (Active Directory and file system) contain a uniquely named subfolder structure within the Policies folder, as shown in Figures 11.7 and 11.8. Each subfolder is named with the Globally Unique Identifier (GUID) of the GPO that it contains. The GUID uniquely identifies Active Directory objects. As you can see on the right side of both figures, within each GPO folder are two subfolders, MACHINE and USER. The Group Policy Template also contains a file, `GPT.INI`. One of its purposes is maintaining a version number that is used to determine if the policy has been changed. The Group Policy Container stores similar information in the Version Number Active Directory attribute. Both version numbers are used to prevent unnecessary processing of the GPO (when no changes have occurred since the GPO was last applied) and keep the GPC and GPT synchronized.

FIGURE 11.7

Structure of the Group Policy Template

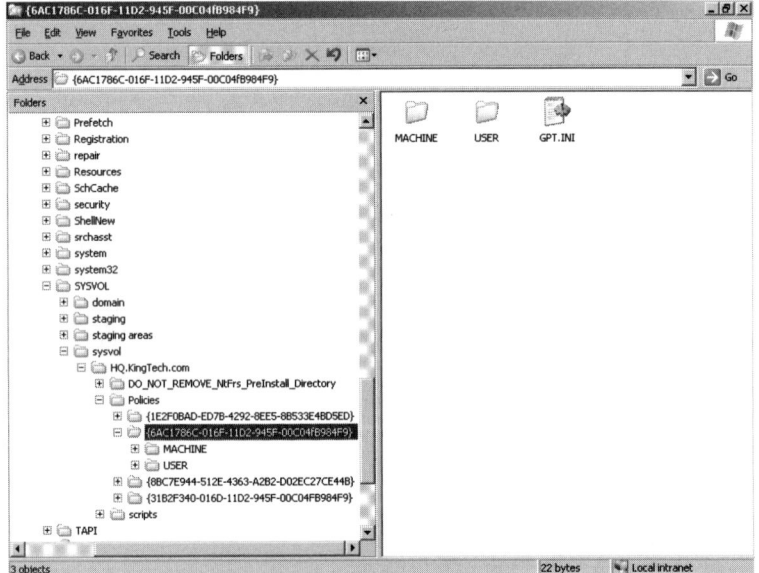

The following sections highlight the various nodes of the Group Policy Object and some of the specific configuration parameters that can be controlled. The reality is that there are so many options available in Group Policies that there is no way anyone could adequately describe them unless they were writing a book about Group Policies. We'll limit our discussion to an overview of the types of parameters that can be controlled—and concentrate on the impact of Group Policies on managing Active Directory.

FIGURE 11.8

Structure of the
Group Policy
Container

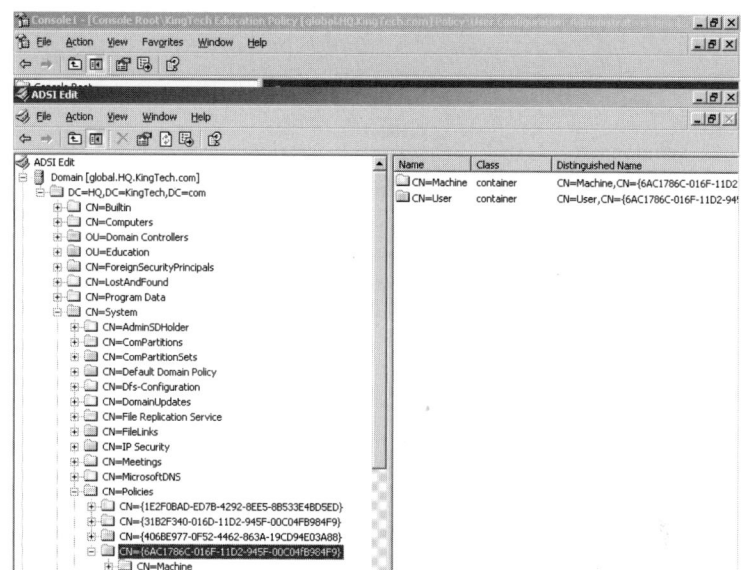

Software Settings Node

The Software Settings node of the GPO has the same structure for both user and computer policies. This node allows you to manage the installation and maintenance of software for a user or computer. Applications can be managed in one of two different modes: assigned or published.

ASSIGNED MODE

Assigned mode is used when you want everyone using the policy to have an application on his or her computer. Suppose, for instance, that you want everyone in the education department at KingTech to have Microsoft PowerPoint on their computers. Your first step would be to create a *package*. A software package contains all of the files necessary to install an application along with a description of all system changes needed (Registry changes, file locations, etc.) and the installation steps. The package has to be based on Windows Installer technology (such packages have .msi extensions). Many applications now include pre-made .msi packages when you purchase them (or have a package available for download on their website). If the application does not have a package, one must be created. There are several third-party products on the market that can accomplish this task. Place the application package in some shared folder available to the network.

Once you have your package, adding it to a policy is a straightforward procedure. First, decide if you wish to assign the application to a user (which will trigger installation on every computer this user logs on to) or a computer (which will make the application available to every user who logs on to this computer). The answer to this question will determine whether you should work in the Computer Configuration node or the User Configuration node of the policy. In either event, open the appropriate node (Computer or User), expand the Software Settings subnode in the MMC as shown in Figure 11.9, right-click Software Installation, and choose Package on the New menu.

FIGURE 11.9

Software installation

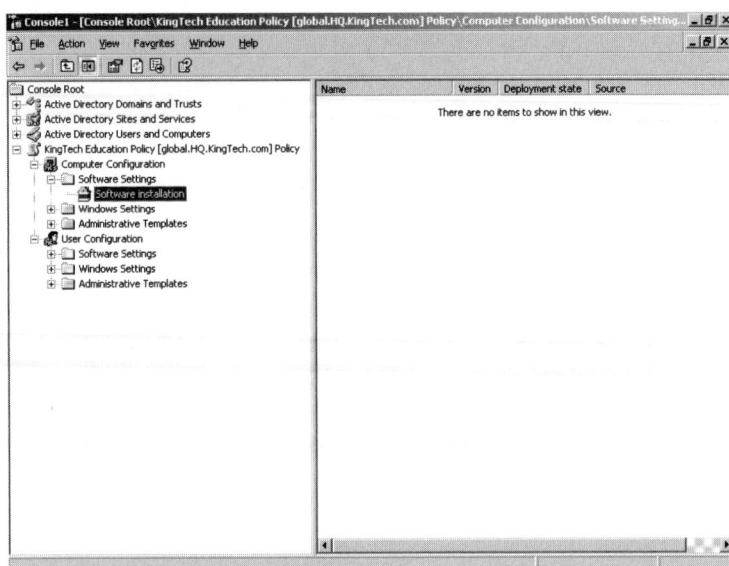

You will be presented with the dialog box shown in Figure 11.10. Browse to the location of the package file and select it for the application that you wish to associate with this policy.

FIGURE 11.10

Choosing the package

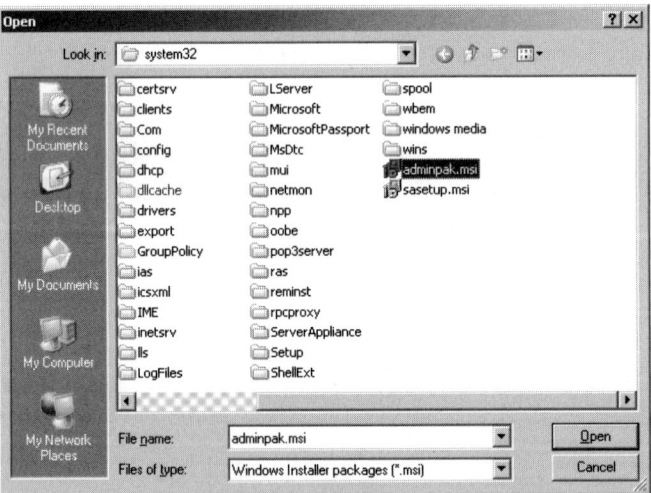

If you create the package as part of Computer Configuration, your only choice for deployment mode will be the Assigned option. If you are deploying a package to a user, you can choose between Assigned and Published, as shown in Figure 11.11. The Advanced option allows you to customize assigned or published applications, for example, by applying transforms (in the form of .mst files) during the installation.

FIGURE 11.11

Software deployment

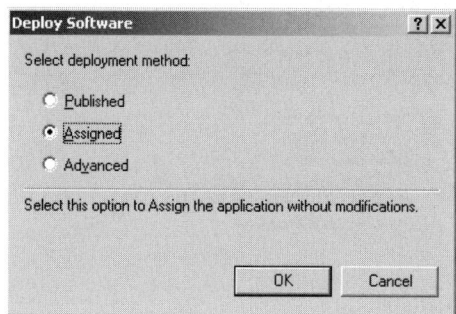

When an application is assigned to computers, the policy will advertise and install it at startup. If an application is assigned to users, it will be either installed or advertised (depending on the configuration option selected) at their next logon. The advertisement is different from installation and involves only the creation of so-called application entry points. These are, basically, different ways in which the application can be launched (e.g., menu and Desktop shortcuts or file extension associations). For example, the advertisement of Microsoft PowerPoint would create an appropriate icon in the Start menu and file associations for extensions such as .ppt and .pps.

The first time a user runs an advertised application (by either using the icon on their Start menu or attempting to open an associated file type), the application will be automatically installed on the computer. The user can uninstall an assigned application, but since it is advertised, the icon and associations will be re-created the next time they log on, which, in turn, will trigger automatic reinstallation.

Using the software installation mechanism of Group Policies can greatly ease administration of the applications in use by your users. You can use the same clean image on all of the computers; who logs in at a computer will determine which applications are made available.

If your users move from computer to computer, you can reap the same benefits. Administrators no longer have to worry about installing applications on computers—that task will happen automatically when a user tries to use the tools they need.

PUBLISHED MODE

Another option available only when deploying applications to users is to *publish* the application package. When an application is published, nothing is advertised or installed automatically on the client computer. Instead, the application is added to the list of available programs in the Add/Remove Programs applet in Control Panel. This allows users to install the application on their own if they so desire. They do so by using a familiar interface—the Add/Remove Programs applet. They also do not need the disks (floppies or CD-ROM) at their computer—all of the files needed to install the application are part of the package.

Computer Configuration Node

The settings in the Computer Configuration node are applied to the local machine as the computer initializes. As soon as the network components of the operating system load and connection to the domain is established, the computer will obtain a list of Group Policies that should be applied.

As you can see in Figure 11.12, the Computer Configuration node has quite a few subnodes. All of them are covered in the following sections.

FIGURE 11.12

Subnodes in Computer Configuration

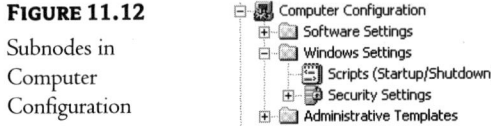

Computer Configuration\Windows Settings

In Figure 11.13 you can see the subnodes in the expanded Computer Configuration\Windows Settings area of the Group Policy structure.

FIGURE 11.13

Computer Configuration\Windows Settings

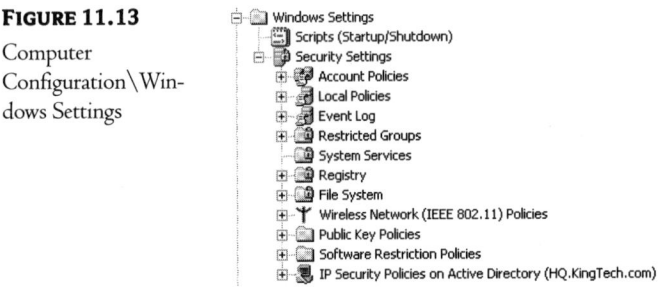

WINDOWS SETTINGS\SCRIPTS

In this subnode you can designate scripts or batch files that will run at either system startup or shutdown. Some of the actions you might include in these scripts are:

◆ Deleting temporary files

◆ Running antivirus software

◆ Performing system diagnostics

The list is limited only by your imagination!

WINDOWS SETTINGS\SECURITY SETTINGS

This section of the Computer Configuration node covers various settings dealing with system security.

WINDOWS SETTINGS\SECURITY SETTINGS\ACCOUNT POLICIES

As you can see in Figure 11.14, this section has three subnodes.

FIGURE 11.14

Account Policies

◆ Password Policy includes options to control the use of passwords such as minimum length, maximum age, and whether a password history should be maintained. You can also increase security by applying password complexity requirements, which force users to choose passwords at least six character long and containing three out of four possible types of characters (uppercase characters, lowercase characters, decimal digits, and nonalphanumeric characters).

◆ Account Lockout Policy includes options determining how long an account is locked out and how many bad login attempts will trigger lockout.

◆ Kerberos Policy includes the ability to configure various attributes of the Kerberos security environment.

WINDOWS SETTINGS\SECURITY SETTINGS\LOCAL POLICIES

As shown in Figure 11.15, the Local Policies node also contains three subnodes.

FIGURE 11.15

Local Policies

◆ Audit Policy allows you to control which events should be audited on this computer.

◆ User Rights Assignment includes the ability to control who can use specific system rights (such as the right to change the system time or shut down the system) on this computer.

◆ Security Options include parameters to control numerous aspects of the computer's environment—everything from who can eject removable media to what the name of the administrator account should be.

The next few nodes are shown in Figure 11.16.

FIGURE 11.16

Additional Security
Settings nodes

⊞ 🗿 Event Log
⊞ 📖 Restricted Groups
⊞ 📖 System Services
⊞ 📖 Registry
⊞ 📖 File System
⊞ 📶 Wireless Network (IEEE 802.11) Policies
⊞ 📁 Public Key Policies
⊞ 📁 Software Restriction Policies
⊞ 🖳 IP Security Policies on Active Directory (HQ.KingTech.com)

WINDOWS SETTINGS\SECURITY SETTINGS\EVENT LOG

Using settings in this node, you can configure options such as the maximum size of the log files and what should happen when the log files are full.

WINDOWS SETTINGS\SECURITY SETTINGS\RESTRICTED GROUPS

You can define which user accounts can be a member of any group by making it a *restricted group*. In the policy, the computer will honor only those users who are listed in the allowed member list. This prevents someone from managing to add him- or herself to an administrative group and then using those privileges. In addition, you can restrict which groups the restricted group is a member of.

WINDOWS SETTINGS\SECURITY SETTINGS\SYSTEM SERVICES

In this node, you will find settings that allow you to control the various services that load on the computer. The options for each service are the following:

◆ Load automatically at system startup

◆ Set for manual load

◆ Disable

NOTE *You might want to consider disabling such nonessential services as Computer Browser, which generates additional network traffic, or Distributed Link Tracking, which has a negative impact on the size of the Active Directory database.*

WINDOWS SETTINGS\SECURITY SETTINGS\REGISTRY

In this node, you can set permissions on Registry keys.

WINDOWS SETTINGS\SECURITY SETTINGS\FILE SYSTEM

In this node, you can set permissions to files or folders.

WINDOWS SETTINGS\SECURITY SETTINGS\WIRELESS NETWORK (IEEE 802.11) POLICIES

Introduced in Windows Server 2003, this collection of policy settings allows you to configure wireless network properties, such as authentication and encryption methods (WEP), and types of networks to connect to.

WINDOWS SETTINGS\SECURITY SETTINGS\PUBLIC KEY POLICIES

Here you can manage various aspects of certificate-based security.

WINDOWS SETTINGS\SECURITY SETTINGS\SOFTWARE RESTRICTION POLICIES

This is a powerful set of Group Policies, not available in Windows 2000, that can be used to prevent certain programs from executing on computers, based on such criteria as executable file paths, hashes, certificates, the Internet zone they originated from, or Registry entries they use. This provides an efficient way of preventing the spread of viruses or restricting use of unlicensed software.

WINDOWS SETTINGS\SECURITY SETTINGS\IP SECURITY POLICIES ON ACTIVE DIRECTORY

Here you can create and modify IPSec policies.

Computer Configuration\Administrative Templates

This node has four subnodes, as shown in Figure 11.17.

FIGURE 11.17

Administrative
Templates

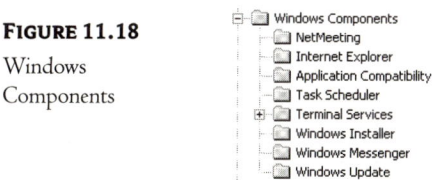

- ◆ Windows Components
- ◆ System
- ◆ Network
- ◆ Printers

ADMINISTRATIVE TEMPLATES\WINDOWS COMPONENTS

This node has the subnodes, shown in Figure 11.18. The basic functionality of this area is to configure aspects of some of the fundamental pieces of the Windows 2000/Windows Server 2003 environment.

FIGURE 11.18

Windows
Components

- ◆ NetMeeting
- ◆ Internet Explorer
- ◆ Application Compatibility
- ◆ Task Scheduler
- ◆ Terminal Services
- ◆ Windows Installer
- ◆ Windows Messenger
- ◆ Windows Update

ADMINISTRATIVE TEMPLATES\SYSTEM

This node contains the 12 subnodes shown in Figure 11.19. This is one of the more useful areas of the Group Policy Object—there are many options here that will be useful in even the smallest of environments.

FIGURE 11.19

System

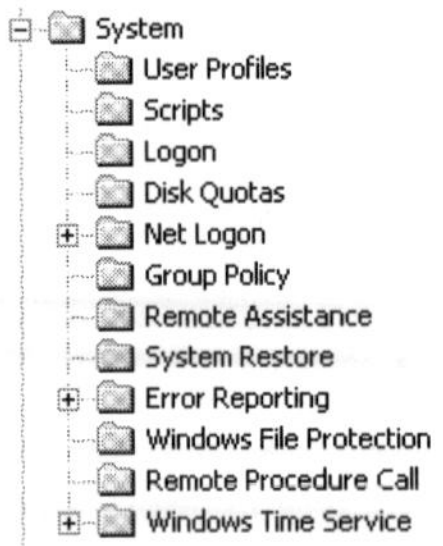

- ◆ User Profiles
- ◆ Scripts
- ◆ Logon
- ◆ Disk Quotas
- ◆ Net Logon
- ◆ Group Policy
- ◆ Remote Assistance
- ◆ System Restore
- ◆ Error Reporting
- ◆ Windows File Protection
- ◆ Remote Procedure Call
- ◆ Windows Time Service

SYSTEM\USER PROFILES

These settings deal mostly with different features of roaming profiles, such as slow link behavior and permissions and their interaction with local profiles.

SYSTEM\SCRIPTS

These settings control execution of logon/logoff and startup/shutdown scripts.

SYSTEM\LOGON

Here you can configure various aspects of the logon process, such as the selection of programs to be run automatically or delaying startup and logon until network connectivity is established.

SYSTEM\DISK QUOTAS

The Disk Quota functionality, included first in Windows 2000, provides the ability to set usage limits on disk space. This section allows you to turn this feature on and then configure various options, such as the space limit and what should happen when the limit is reached.

SYSTEM\NET LOGON

New in Windows Server 2003, this collection of policies is intended primarily to optimize the domain logon process. For example, it permits administrators to explicitly specify the site name or set parameters for caching domain controller information on the client workstation. The Net Logon folder also contains a number of settings grouped together in DC Locator DNS Records folder. These settings deal with DC Locator records registered in DNS and are relevant only when applied to domain controllers.

SYSTEM\GROUP POLICY

In this node, you can configure how group policies are processed on the computer. You can determine which nodes should be processed, whether they should refresh in the background, and how slow links should be dealt with.

SYSTEM\REMOTE ASSISTANCE

The settings in this node can be used to enable or disable offered and solicited remote assistance and to determine security features for both (such as level of control, helper list, or maximum ticket time).

SYSTEM\SYSTEM RESTORE

With entries in this node, you can allow or disallow users to configure parameters of System Restore or disable its functionality altogether.

SYSTEM\ERROR REPORTING

Error reporting has been significantly enhanced since Windows 2000. Using settings in this node, you can select the level of reporting your users will be comfortable with and customize it to match your environment (for example, you can upload all error reports to one of your servers). The Advanced Reporting subnode gives you even more granular control, allowing the admin to decide, for example, which applications will trigger generation of a report.

SYSTEM\WINDOWS FILE PROTECTION

Windows Server 2003 (like Windows 2000) scans system files on a regular basis to determine if changes have occurred. This protects against corrupted or missing system files causing problems in the operating system itself. Here you can configure various options of this process.

SYSTEM\REMOTE PROCEDURE CALL

Remote Procedure Call is one the protocols used for Windows interprocess communication. The Windows Server 2003 implementation of RPC includes additional features, such as the ability to use RPC over HTTP connections, which can be managed using settings from this node.

SYSTEM\WINDOWS TIME SERVICE

Time Service is essential to keeping all machines synchronized. With settings from this node, you can control a number of global configuration parameters for this service, enable your servers as NTP sources, as well as enable and configure NTP clients.

The next two subnodes of Administrative Templates are shown in Figure 11.20.

FIGURE 11.20

Network and Printers nodes

```
⊟ 📁 Network
     📁 DNS Client
     📁 Offline Files
     📁 Network Connections
  ⊞ 📁 QoS Packet Scheduler
     📁 SNMP
  📁 Printers
```

- ◆ Network node

- ◆ Printers node

In the Network node, you will find options to control the DNS Client and Offline Files settings, as well as the Network and Dial-up Connections, QoS Packet Scheduler, and SNMP parameters. The Printers node controls behavior related to printing and Active Directory Printer objects, such as publishing, pruning, browsing, and web-based printing.

User Configuration Node

In the User Configuration node, shown in Figure 11.21, you will find three subnodes:

- ◆ Software Settings, which we discussed earlier

- ◆ Windows Settings, which include options to control aspects of the Windows 2000/Windows Server 2003 environment

- ◆ Administrative Templates, which expand upon the capabilities available in the Computer Configuration node

FIGURE 11.21

User Configuration

```
⊟ 🖳 Computer Configuration
  ⊞ 📁 Software Settings
  ⊟ 📁 Windows Settings
       📄 Scripts (Startup/Shutdown)
    ⊞ 📁 Security Settings
  ⊞ 📁 Administrative Templates
```

The Windows Settings and Administrative Templates subnodes are covered in the following sections.

User Configuration\Windows Settings

The Windows Settings node contains the following subnodes (as shown in Figure 11.22):

FIGURE 11.22

Windows Settings

- ◆ Remote Installation Services allows you to configure options appearing on the Choice screen, which is part of RIS Client Installation Wizard. This method of installation is available for all versions of Windows 2000 and Windows Server 2003 servers (except for the DataCenter edition) and Windows XP Professional.

- ◆ Scripts allows you to specify scripts to run as the user logs on or off the domain.

- ◆ Security Settings contains entries relating to Public Key and Software Restriction Policies.

- ◆ Folder Redirection allows you to redirect a user's Application Data, Desktop, My Documents, and Start Menu folders. Enabling this option means that a user can log on at *any* computer and always have the same environment (assuming you have redirected it to a place accessible from the network).

- ◆ Internet Explorer Maintenance allows you to configure various options for a user's use of Internet Explorer. Some of the more interesting options include the ability to define entries for the user's Favorites List or setting the Home Page parameter.

User Configuration\Administrative Templates

For users, this area contains options most like those found in System Policies, used primarily in Windows NT. As shown in Figure 11.23, there are seven subnodes to the Administrative Templates node:

- ◆ Windows Components is similar to the one under the Computer Configuration node although it contains several additional folders (Help and Support Center, Windows Explorer, Microsoft Management Console, and Windows Media Player).

- ◆ Start Menu and Taskbar allows you to configure the various options that will affect the appearance of the Start menu and the Taskbar. You can, for instance, remove the links to the Windows Update, common program groups, Help, or Logoff menu options.

- Desktop allows you to configure the appearance of the user's Desktop. Options include the ability to hide specific icons (My Network Places or Internet Explorer), prohibit the user from changing the My Documents path, or prevent saving settings at exit.

- Control Panel allows you to configure the appearance and availability of most common Control Panel applets.

- Shared Folders provides control over publishing shared folders and DFS roots in Active Directory.

- Network contains options dealing with Offline Files and Network Connection.

- System allows you to configure various options of the operating system, such as disabling AutoPlay and Registry-editing tools, or preventing access to the command prompt.

FIGURE 11.23

Administrative Templates

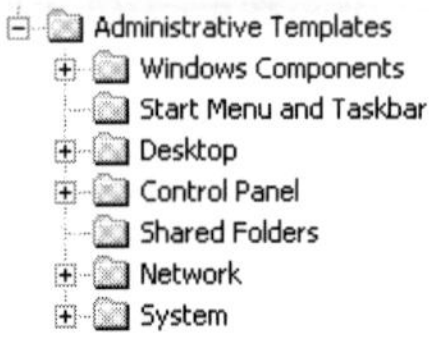

Whew—quite a list, isn't it? The amount of control available through the use of Group Policies in Windows 2000/Windows Server 2003 is staggering (and maybe even overwhelming). Now that we've looked at the types of things you can control, let's look at the procedures involved in using Group Policies.

Configuring Group Policy Settings

Since the options available within the Group Policy realm are so diverse, there are differences in the ways that many of them are configured. Fortunately, there will be certain similarities among "types" of parameters. In this section, we will look at a few of the different configuration procedures that you will use to set policy parameters.

The Three-Way Toggle

Many of the policy settings will be a basic on/off switch with a twist. *Enabling* the policy turns the setting on; *disabling* the policy turns the same setting off. The twist takes the form of the *Not Configured* option. When selected, this option no longer matters and has no effect on effective settings. This way the effective setting either will be the one currently set for the computer or user, or will be the result of the remaining policies interacting with each other. We will talk about this interaction more in the next section. You can see these three options in the sample shown in Figure 11.24.

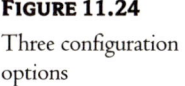

FIGURE 11.24

Three configuration options

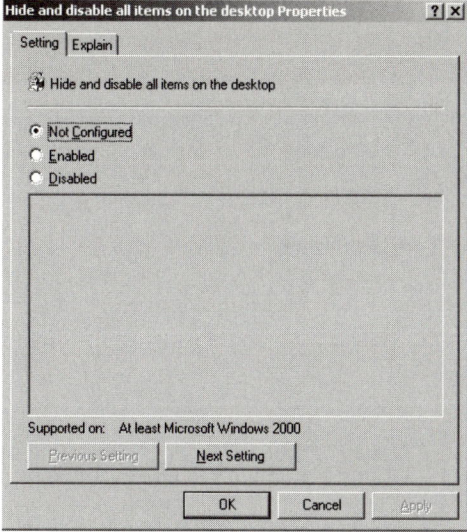

Make sure that you read the description of each policy option carefully. Often descriptions are written in the negative, such as, "Don't turn on XYZ." If you enable this type of policy option, XYZ will be turned *off* instead of *on*. Watch for double negatives!

Setting Amounts

Some options allow you to configure a limit of some sort. You might, for instance, want to place a default limit on the amount of disk space that users can use. This option is shown in Figure 11.25.

FIGURE 11.25

Setting volume quotas

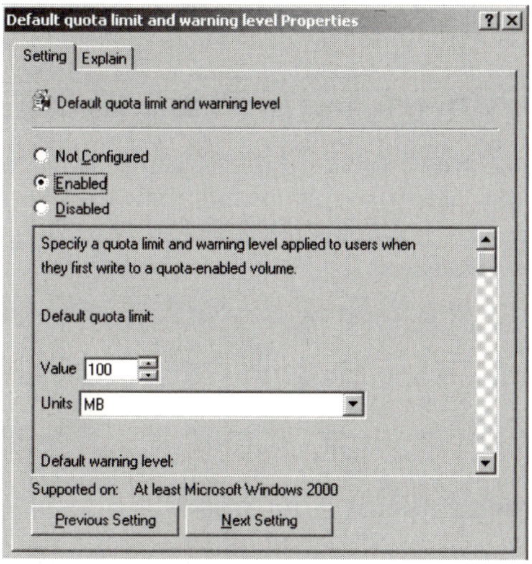

Here you type your value in the dialog boxes provided.

Creating Lists

Some options might be made up of a list, such as the option to limit the applets available in Control Panel. Here you would add the name of the applet to the list by clicking the Show button, as shown in Figure 11.26.

FIGURE 11.26

Creating a list

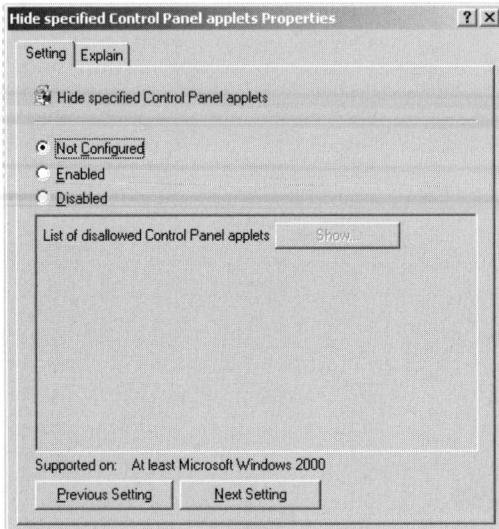

As you can see, configuring most of the options will be a matter of common sense (and figuring out where they are in the list of available options).

Determining Which Policy Will Be Applied

Having looked at the options available and how to configure them, the next step is to determine how and why policies are applied to users, groups, and computers. We'll look at how policies are applied by default, and then we'll look at how those defaults can be changed.

First, let me stress one last time:

◆ User policies are first obtained when a *user* logs on to the network.

◆ Computer policies are first obtained when a computer boots.

No other classes of objects receive policies—just users and computers.

The Order in Which Policies Are Applied

As we discussed earlier, policies can be associated with various objects in the Active Directory structure: domains, sites, and organizational units. There is also a local policy that is stored on and managed at the local client computer. Since we have the option to place policies at various points in our hierarchy, the first question that should come to mind is, "Which policy or policies will apply to which users and computers?" In a perfect world, the answer to this question would be short and sweet. Unfortunately, a simple answer would probably also imply a simple solution, and a simple solution would not meet the needs of today's complex networks. The truth of the matter is that most of the rest of this chapter will revolve around answering that "simple" question.

DEFAULT ORDER OF APPLICATION

The default order in which Group Policies are applied is:

1. The local policy, if one exists.

2. Policies assigned to the AD site object, in an order specified by the administrator.

3. Policies assigned to the domain, in an order specified by the administrator.

4. Policies assigned to organizational units, starting at the top of the AD tree and working from parent to child OU until the context of the object (user or computer) has been reached. Once again, if an OU has more than one policy, they will be applied in an order set by the administrator.

This order can be influenced in numerous ways, but the default behavior is that the policies are applied in the order listed above. Each policy that is processed will override those settings made in policies applied earlier in the process. In other words, if a parameter is set to "true" in the local policy, the site policy could change it to "false," the domain policy could change it back to "true," and then various OU policies could change it back and forth so many times that it could be hard to determine what the settings will be once the process is done! The point here is that the implementation of Group Policies takes some prior planning to avoid these kinds of issues.

UNDERSTANDING POLICY ORDERING

The general philosophy is that the policies should be designed so that the most general settings are applied first and the most specific are applied last. This means that:

◆ Use of local policies should be very limited. In most companies, local policies won't be used at all so that all policy management can occur within the Active Directory database.

◆ Site policies should also be used sporadically. Since sites typically correspond to geographical locations, separated by slower network links, you should limit use of site policies only to settings that are somehow related to the site structure. For example, when deploying applications using the Software Installation Group Policy, for each application you want to install, you need to specify the source path of the installation files. If the source files reside in a different site than the computer on which the installation is performed, the files need to be copied over slower, inter-site network links. You can prevent it by creating a separate GPO for every site, each containing a different path (local to the site) pointing to the application installation files.

NOTE *We'll talk about sites in Chapter 13, "Understanding and Controlling AD Sites and Replications."*

◆ Domain policies should contain configurations that are specific to the needs of the users and computers defined within the domain. This sounds obvious, but as you'll see in Chapter 13, it is possible for a single site to contain resources from multiple domains. This option allows you to be a little more specific as to who or what will be affected by a policy. Since Account Policies (part of Computer Configuration Security Settings) for domain accounts can only be configured as part of domain policies (settings on the site and organizational unit level are ignored), they will be the most commonly used components of domain-level policies. Other security settings are also established typically as part of the company standards, and as such should be part of domainwide policy settings.

◆ Organizational unit policies are by far most commonly used for more granular Group Policy management. They contain configuration parameters that apply to branches of your AD tree. Perhaps no users in the Sales OU (and those OUs under it in the tree) should be allowed to run programs other than those that are company-approved. Here you could configure the policy with the list of approved programs.

You can use this cascading effect to reduce the number of places in which you have to manage certain parameters—sweeping parameters only have to be configured once (in the site, domain, or higher-level OU policy), rather than for each OU.

Creating Policy Objects

Look at the AD organizational unit structure shown in Figure 11.27. In our example, we have an education OU that contains a Michigan OU and also contains OUs for each of the levels of schools that we support. This seems like a workable design—resources from each type of school can be placed within a container that represents their type (K–6, Middle, or High Schools). (Under these three containers, we could also have containers for each individual school—but we'll leave out that level of container to avoid confusing the issue.)

FIGURE 11.27

The education department

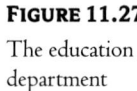 

Within this type of structure, certain aspects of our users' environment will be similar. All of our students, for instance, should be able to use Internet Explorer. Other items of control, though, will differ based upon age group—first-graders should probably have a different Home Page setting than high-school students. This is where the cascading nature of Group Policies comes in handy.

Our first step will be to determine which type of policy files we wish to use—local, site, domain, or organizational. Because we won't discuss AD sites until Chapter 13, we'll avoid them here. The process of assigning a policy to a site is the same as for assigning one to a domain or OU. In real life we would sit down with the teachers and administrators and ask for input: what types of controls do they desire, and how sweeping should those decisions be? After our research we might come up with a list that looks something like this:

All students:

♦ Advertise basic programs to all computers—word processing, spreadsheet, and database.

♦ Run a script that checks for viruses each time a user logs on.

♦ Do not allow printers to be published to AD.

♦ Limit access to the Display Options in Control Panel.

Based upon grade:

♦ Add appropriate URLs to the Favorites List in Internet Explorer.

♦ Assign specific applications.

♦ Redirect all data, Desktop settings, and other personal information to network locations.

In a real-world scenario, the list would probably cover pages, but for our purposes this should be sufficient. As you can see, there are certain policies that should apply to all students, and others that should only be applied to specific groups of students.

The second step in our process will be to determine which policies should be applied to computers and which to users. Some of the parameters will only be available to one or the other, but some can be configured in either manner.

The next step is to determine the type of policy to use—local, site, domain, or organizational unit. Since our environment is a single domain and a single site, we could use either a site or a domain policy as our most generic. Given our single-branch scenario, we could even use a higher-level OU as our least restrictive policy—but since this would be rare in a true business, we'll follow a more conventional strategy.

CREATING A POLICY FOR A SITE, DOMAIN, OR ORGANIZATIONAL UNIT

To create a policy, start the MMC. Follow these steps:

1. On the Console's File menu, choose Add/Remove Snap-in, as shown in Figure 11.28. The Add/Remove Snap-in dialog box, shown in Figure 11.29, will appear. This dialog box shows the snap-in modules that you have already added to your console. (Remember that the point of the MMC tool is to allow you to manage almost everything using a single application. Notice that I've added quite a few snap-ins to my interface.)

FIGURE 11.28

Selecting Add/Remove Snap-in

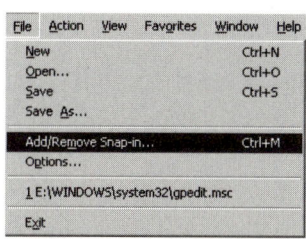

FIGURE 11.29

The Add/Remove
Snap-in dialog box

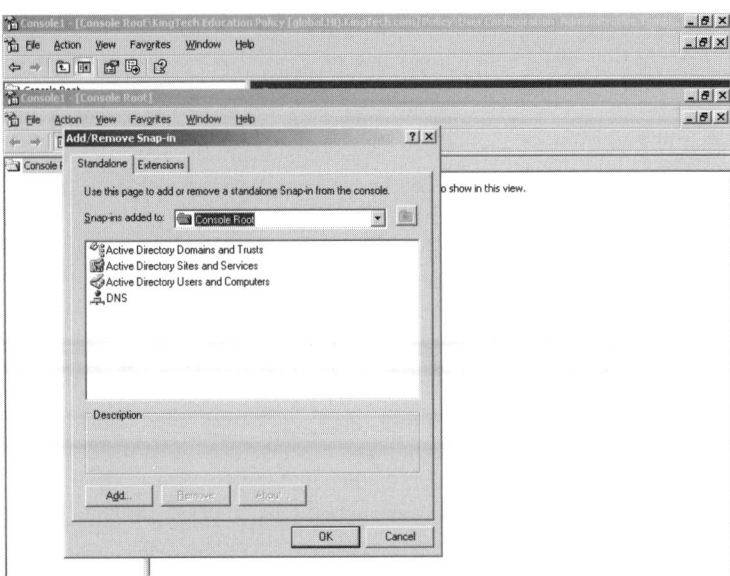

2. Click the Add button, and you will be presented with a list of the available snap-ins. Double-click the Group Policy Object Editor option, and the Group Policy Object Wizard will begin, as shown in Figure 11.30.

FIGURE 11.30

The Group Policy
Object Wizard

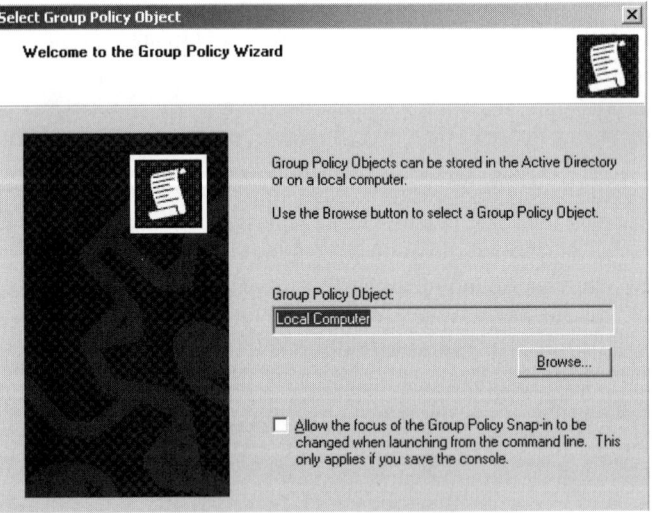

3. Your first decision is whether to work with the Group Policy of the local machine or to work with/create an AD Group Policy Object. To accomplish the latter option, click the Browse button. As you can see in Figure 11.31, you will then be able to determine what type (site, domain, or organizational unit) of policy you wish to work with.

FIGURE 11.31

Browse for a Group Policy Object

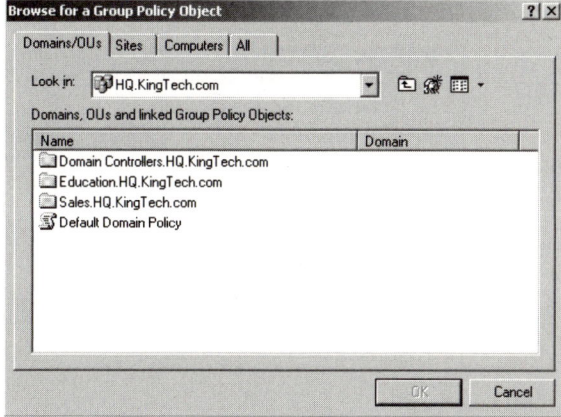

4. If you wish to add an existing policy to your MMC console, browse this screen and select it.

5. To create a new GPO, browse to the domain, site, or container you wish to associate your new GPO with, right-click empty space in the list, and choose New, as shown in Figure 11.32.

FIGURE 11.32

Creating a new GPO

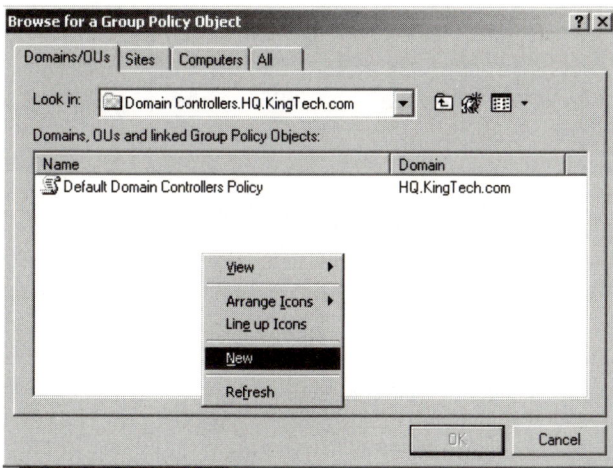

6. Click OK and Finish, and your new GPO will appear in the MMC console.

We follow the same steps to assign policies to each of the organizational units. For our example, I'm also going to create another GPO and link it to the K–6 container. Our final MMC console will contain both GPOs, as shown in Figure 11.33.

FIGURE 11.33

KingTech domain policies

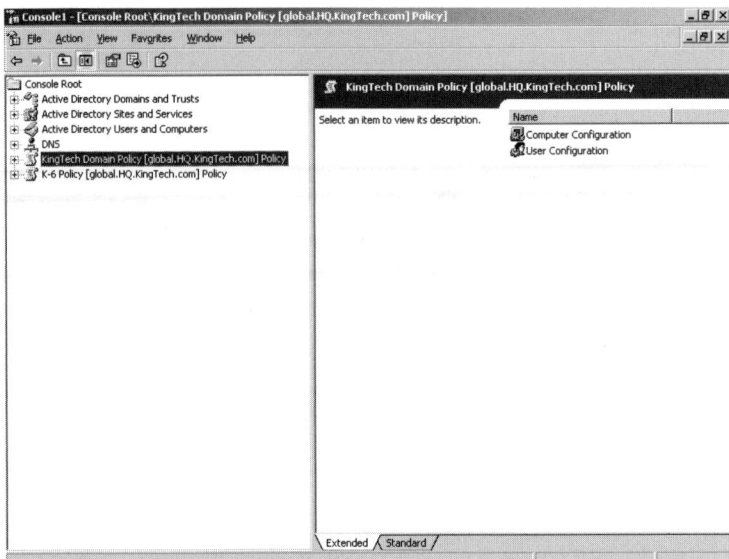

NOTE   *Notice that the names I've given my Group Policy Objects readily identify the container in my AD structure to which they are linked. Look at Figure 11.33 again—without proper naming standards, it wouldn't be clear where they would be applied.*

Linking Policies to Containers

While basic inheritance will see to it that a policy applied to one organizational unit will flow down the AD structure to lower OUs, there might be instances where you would like to apply the same policy to containers that are not related in a parent/child relationship—in other words, one policy that applied to two different branches of your structure. To do this, link the GPO containing the policy to whichever container you want it to apply to. Linking is accomplished by accessing the properties of the container itself. In MMC, highlight the container, right-click, and choose Properties. On the Group Policy tab, shown in Figure 11.34, you will find a list of GPOs that have been linked to this container.

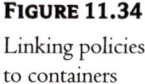

FIGURE 11.34

Linking policies
to containers

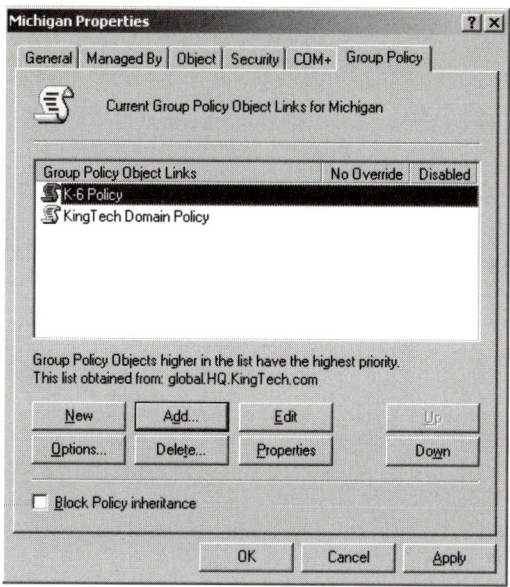

If more than one GPO is linked to a container, this same list will determine the order in which they are processed. Those higher in the list have higher priority, which means they are processed last. (That can take a little thought—just remember that since policies can overwrite each others' settings, the last one to process will make the final changes.)

Taking Control

If planned carefully, the default order of cascading Group Policies can work fairly well. The problem is that it is often necessary to have a policy apply to one group of users but not another, even if those users exist in the same organizational unit. At other times, you might want to allow one container within your AD structure to set its own policy without having to worry about it being overwritten by a policy in a lower container. The opposite is also true—there might be a time where you want a lower-level policy to be the *only* policy applied to the users in an organizational unit.

Based upon what we've discussed so far, these cases would require very careful planning of both the placement of policies *and* the very AD organizational units themselves. Luckily, Microsoft has provided us with four methods for taking control of which policies will be applied in any given situation. Those four methods are:

♦ Filtering policies by security group membership

♦ Blocking policy inheritance

♦ Preventing a policy from being overwritten by policies above it in the AD tree

♦ Filtering policies using WMI filters

By understanding the mechanisms involved in policy inheritance and filtering, an administrator can use Group Policies to take complete control over their network.

FILTERING POLICIES THROUGH GROUP MEMBERSHIP

Each GPO created has its own set of properties as an object in the AD structure. These properties refer to the *object*—not to the parameters that the GPO passes to the user or computer applying the policy itself. To see these properties, right-click the GPO in the MMC and choose Properties, as shown in Figure 11.35.

FIGURE 11.35

Accessing the properties of a GPO

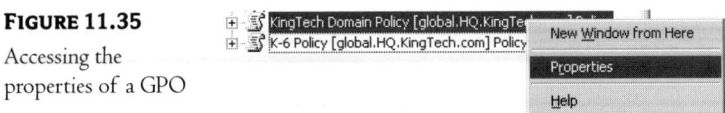

You will be presented with the Properties dialog box of the Group Policy Object, an example of which is shown in Figure 11.36.

FIGURE 11.36

Properties of a GPO

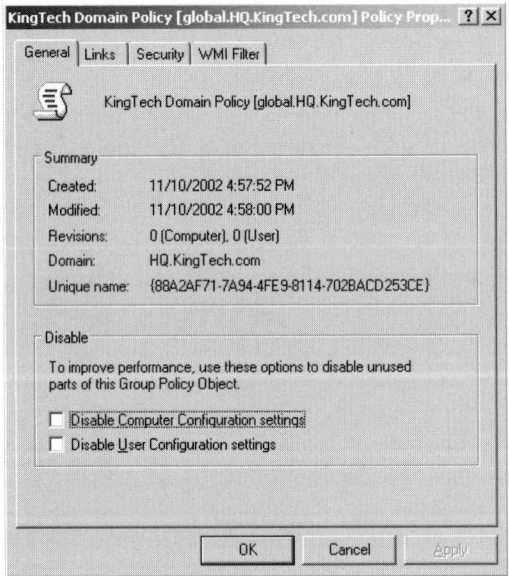

The Properties dialog box of a GPO can be used to gather information about the policy, manage the policy, determine where the policy will be applied, and manage who will use the policy.

Figure 11.36 shows the General tab of the GPO Properties dialog box. As you can see, this opening screen provides some useful information, such as when the GPO was created, the last time it was modified, and its GUID. You can also disable the computer or user portion of the policy to improve performance: if you create a policy but only use one portion or the other (user or computer), you can disable the other, thus preventing the unused portion from being downloaded to the client computer for processing.

The Links tab of the GPO Properties dialog box is shown in Figure 11.37. Here you can have the system perform a search to determine which sites, domains, and organizational units will use this policy. Because of the complex set of inheritance rules for GPO application, it used to be fairly difficult to determine which policies are in effect in each container. This has, however, been greatly simplified with the introduction of a new tool called Resultant Set of Policies in Windows Server 2003 and Windows XP Professional. I will describe Resultant Set of Policies later in this chapter.

FIGURE 11.37

The Links tab of the GPO Properties dialog box

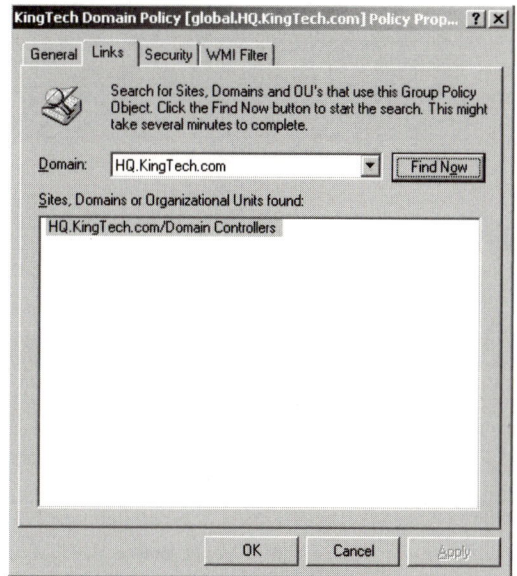

The Security tab of the GPO Properties dialog box is shown in Figure 11.38. Like any other object in the AD database, GPOs have Access Control Lists (ACLs). The ACL lists those objects that have been granted permissions to the object itself. GPOs have a unique permission—look at the bottom of the permissions list in Figure 11.38 and you will see the Apply Group Policy permission.

The permissions shown in Figure 11.38 are the default permissions granted when a Group Policy Object is created. Table 11.1 lists these default permissions.

FIGURE 11.38

Security tab of the
GPO Properties
dialog box

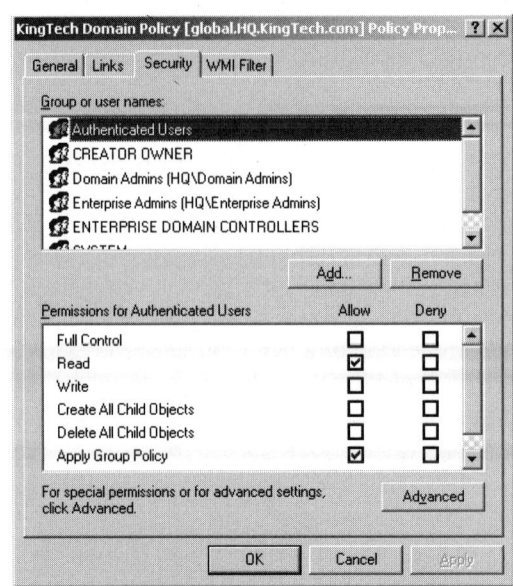

TABLE 11.1: DEFAULT PERMISSIONS TO A GPO

USER OR GROUP	PERMISSIONS
Authenticated Users	Read, Apply Group Policy
Creator Owner	Special
Domain Admins	Read, Write, Create All Child Objects, Delete All Child Objects
Enterprise Admins	Read, Write, Create All Child Objects, Delete All Child Objects
Enterprise Domain Controllers	Read
System	Read, Write, Create All Child Objects, Delete All Child Objects

NOTE   Even though it appears that Creator Owner does not have any permissions to the GPO, obviously this is not the case. If you click the Advanced button, you will be able to see all of them (the simplified interface of the Security tab cannot appropriately display them).

The important assignment for our discussion here is the assignment made to all authenticated users. Basically, this assignment is what makes the policies work. As long as Read and Apply Group Policy permissions to the GPO are granted to the user (or the group the user is a member of), policies defined within that GPO will apply to that user at logon. On the other hand, if these permissions are not granted, the GPO will not be processed.

As an example, let's return to the KingTech education department. The policies we've discussed so far have all revolved around the needs of the students—limiting their ability to change configurations, or adding tools that they will need to their Desktops and applications. The problem with the default GPO assignments is that this policy will also be applied to the teachers and administrative staff at KingTech (since they too will be authenticated users in this domain). To correct this, we could create a security group—perhaps named "Students"—and change the default permissions to this GPO. Remove the Authenticated Users from the list and add the Students security group, as shown in Figure 11.39.

FIGURE 11.39

Using security
groups to
limit GPOs

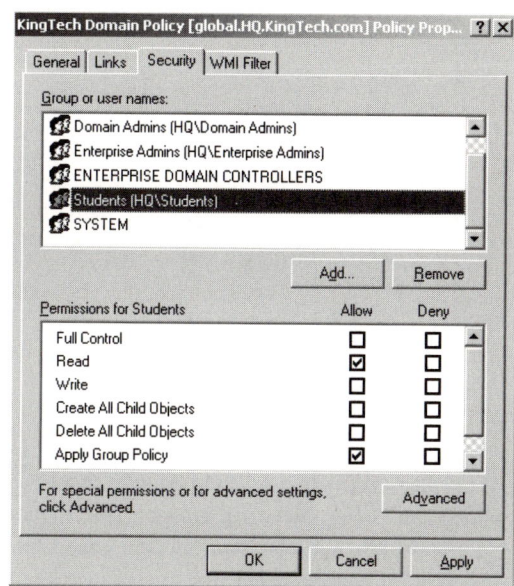

Make sure to give the Students group both the Read permission and the Apply Group Policy permission. Without the Read permission, they would be unable to read the policy itself.

BLOCKING POLICY INHERITANCE

Group Policy inheritance can be blocked at the domain and organizational unit level (blocking cannot be set on the site level). Because this setting is made directly at the domain or OU level, instead of to a particular GPO, it will block *all* policies from reaching the designated container. In effect, you are creating an autonomous branch of your structure that will not inherit policies from above itself in the tree.

To block the inheritance of Group Policies, access the properties of the domain or OU where you wish the block to begin. To do this, highlight it in the MMC, right-click, and choose Properties. You will be presented with the Properties dialog box of the object. On the Group Policy tab, shown in Figure 11.40, you will find an option to Block Policy Inheritance. Select this option, and inheritance will be blocked.

FIGURE 11.40

Blocking inheritance

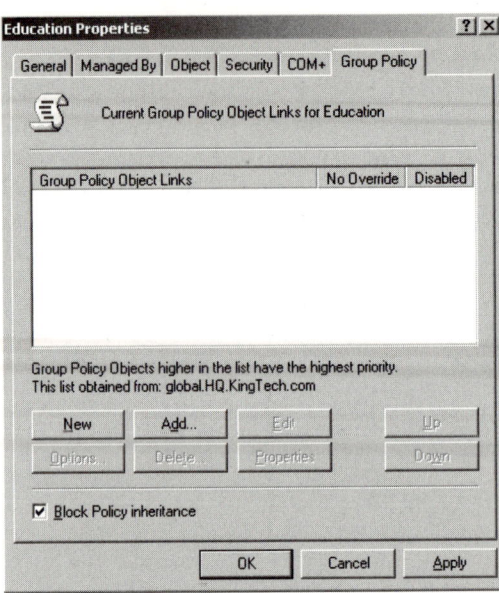

MANDATING A POLICY

While there will be times when you want to block inheritance as we just discussed, there will be other times when you want to ensure that a higher-level policy setting is not overwritten by a policy processed later. To prevent a policy from being overwritten, access the properties of the container in which you wish to protect the policy. On the Group Policy tab, click the Options button. You will be presented with the dialog box shown in Figure 11.41.

FIGURE 11.41

The Policy Options dialog box

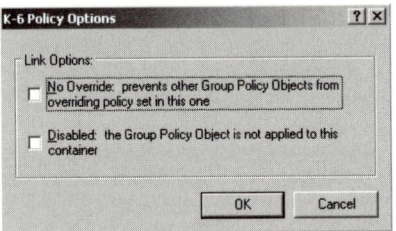

Here you can either select the No Override option or disable the policy in this container.

FILTERING POLICIES USING WMI FILTERS

Windows Server 2003 introduces a very flexible method of filtering the way GPOs are applied. This method is based on Windows Management Instrumentation (WMI). WMI provides access to properties of practically every hardware and software object in the computing environment (for example, the list of Windows Installer applications installed on a computer, free disk space on all its drives, amount of physical memory it has, maximum speed of its modem, profile settings of the currently logged-on user, just to list a few). Each object type is represented in WMI by a class (for example, the `Win32_LogicalDisk` class represents logical disks, and the `Win32_PhysicalMemory` class represents the computer's memory). As you can imagine, the number of objects (and corresponding classes) is enormous. In order to provide some kind of ordering, speed up searches, and prevent accidental name conflicts between classes, objects are organized in a hierarchy of namespaces starting at the one called `root`. The majority of the objects that Windows administrators deal with on a regular basis reside in the namespace called `root/Cimv2`.

Windows Server 2003 allows you to use user or computer properties, extracted with WMI, to decide whether policy settings should be applied or not.

WMI filters consist of two parts, separated by a semicolon. The first one is the namespace where the class representing the object you check for resides. The second part is a query where the results determine whether a particular GPO will be applied or not. The query is written in WMI Query Language (WQL), similar to (although much more limited than) Structured Query Language, which is used to work with relational databases.

You can use WMI in any type of scenario where standard group-based filtering does not satisfy your requirements. For instance, let's imagine that you want to deploy software only to Windows XP Professional systems that belong to one of your organizational units. Some of your machines, however, still have Windows 2000 installed. You can quickly solve this problem by setting a WMI filter for the GPO that contains the Software Installation settings. The filter would have the following format:

```
Root\CimV2; SELECT * FROM Win32_OperatingSystem
➥ where Caption = "Microsoft Windows XP Professional"
```

As you can see, this allows you to apply the GPO only to the computers that are running Windows XP Professional.

Only a single WMI filter can be applied to an individual GPO. To set it up, open the GPO Properties dialog box (using the same sequence of steps as described in previous sections) and select the WMI Filter tab. Select the This filter option and click on Browse/Manage. This will display the Manage WMI Filters dialog box, which you can expand with the Advanced button. You can either select an existing filter from the list or create a new one by clicking New (shown in Figure 11.42). For new filters, type in their name, description, and the text of the filter.

Following the same approach, you can create other queries and link them to other GPOs. This way, you will be able to apply Group Policies based on any characteristic that is accessible via WMI.

FIGURE 11.42

The Manage WMI
Filters dialog box

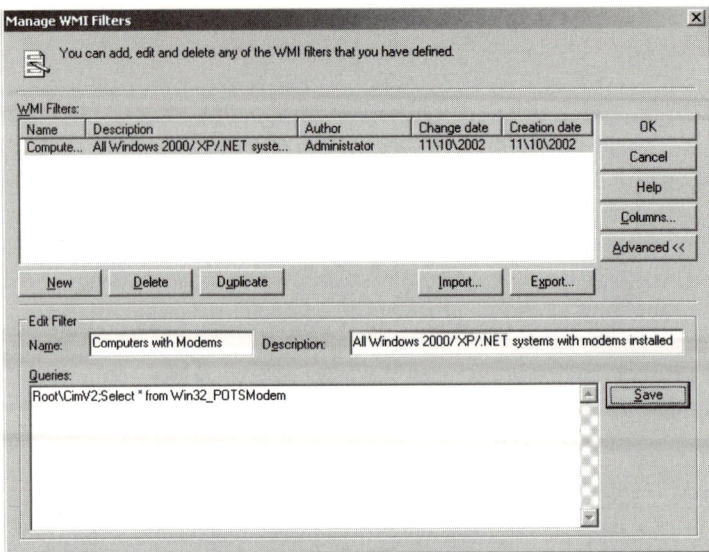

WMI filters are just one of many new Group Policy features in Windows Server 2003. Significant improvements have been made in the area of Group Policies management. In addition to the tools also available in Windows 2000 (the Security Configuration and Analysis Console and its command-line equivalent `secedit.exe`), Windows Server 2003 includes the Resultant Set of Policies Console and the Group Policy Management Console. However, before I discuss Security Configuration and Analysis and `secedit.exe`, we first need to take a closer look at security templates.

Security Templates

A *security template* is a plain-text .inf file containing entries corresponding to security-related Group Policy settings—the same ones that you can find in the Security Settings folder of the Computer Configuration node of the Group Policy Object Editor. This includes entries contained in the Account Policies, Local Policies, Event Log, Restricted Groups, System Services, Registry, and File System folders. The remaining ones (Wireless Network Policies, Public Key Policies, Software Restriction Policies, and IP Security Policies) are not available with security templates.

Security templates can be used to configure the security settings of a Group Policy Object. This, in effect, allows modifying in the same, uniform way the security configuration for all computers that are part of the domain, site, or organizational unit that the GPO is linked to. To apply a security template to a GPO, from the Group Policy Object Editor, right-click the Security Setting folder of the Computer Configuration node, select Import Template, and point to the .inf file that contains the desired settings.

Microsoft provides eight (two default and six incremental) predefined security templates, which contain recommended security settings for various types of environments. To view them, launch an empty Microsoft Management Console. Add to it the Security Templates snap-in. The end result should resemble the window shown in Figure 11.43 (possibly with the exception of the DC Security template, which appears only on domain controllers).

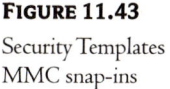

FIGURE 11.43

Security Templates
MMC snap-ins

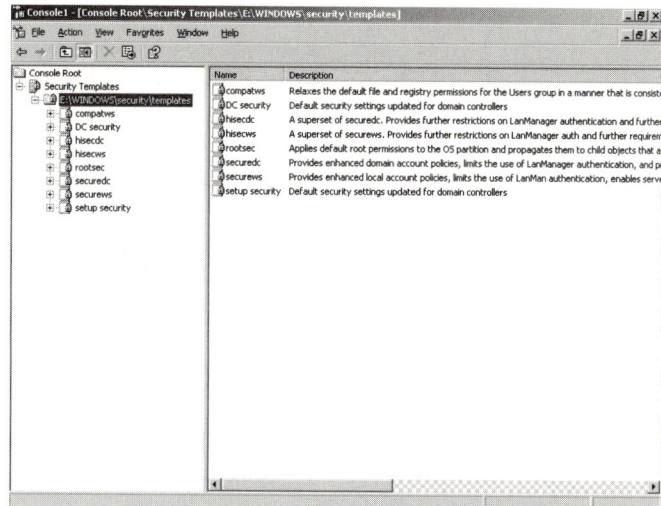

The predefined templates include the following:

setup security Default security settings for workstations or member servers, used typically to restore original settings and in combination with incremental templates. This template should never be applied to a GPO. This is due to the fact that the Setup Security template contains a large number of settings, which could seriously impact network bandwidth. I will discuss alternative ways of applying security templates later.

DC security Default security settings for domain controllers, applied as part of the Active Directory Installation Wizard (DCPROMO), typically used to restore original settings and in combination with incremental templates.

compatws Incremental template, which relaxes permissions on the file system and Registry, in order to allow nonprivileged users to run legacy applications. It is used typically in cases where applications do not run with the existing workstation configuration.

rootsec Incremental template, which applies default permissions to the root of the partition containing operating system files (the Windows folder) and propagates them to subfolders. It is used typically in cases where the default permissions need to be restored.

securews Incremental template, which increases security on a workstation or member server with default security settings.

securedc Incremental template, which increases security on a domain controller with default security settings.

hisecws Incremental template, which provides a higher degree of security than the one set by the securews template.

hisecdc Incremental template, which provides a higher degree of security than the one set by the securedc template.

Incremental templates are not intended to be used alone, but always in combination with their respective defaults. For example, in order to configure your domain controller with high security settings, you should apply the DC security template, followed by hisecdc.

You can create your own custom security templates. Although you can edit the template files using Notepad or any other text editor, it is much easier to use the Security Templates MMC snap-in. This way, you will be working with the same, already-familiar interface that you have seen in the Group Policy Editor. The snap-in allows you to copy one of the existing templates, modify individual settings, and save the results as a new file. However, you should never modify predefined templates. Keep in mind that you might need them some day to restore your original security settings.

SECURITY CONFIGURATION AND ANALYSIS AND SecEdit TOOLS

As we explained before, applying security templates via Group Policy Objects might not be feasible if the number of settings is large. In such situations, you can use the Security Configuration and Analysis MMC snap-in or the SecEdit command-line utility. In addition, both of these utilities allow the use of security templates as baselines for analyzing computer security. To understand the way they operate, we need to take a look at the technology behind them.

SECURITY DATABASE

As the entries in a security template are applied to a target computer, they are also stored in a special database called secedit.sdb. Such a database is maintained on each computer in the %System-Root%\Security\Database folder. Its content reflects current local security configuration. You can create similar databases (identical in format but not necessarily the same in content) for the purpose of security configuration or analysis with the Security Configuration and Analysis snap-in.

By importing one or more templates into your own copy of the security database, you can test different combinations of security settings before you decide which one should actually be used. At any point, you can overwrite the configuration stored in the database or merge its settings with another security template.

ANALYZING AND CONFIGURING SECURITY

Analyzing security is the process that compares security settings stored in your private copy of the security database with the existing computer security settings. Note that the existing computer settings might be the result of a combination of factors (such as local security settings and those applied from site, domain, or organizational unit policies). You can use this process to quickly evaluate whether settings on a particular computer conform to whatever your security standards are.

To analyze security, first add the Security Configuration and Analysis snap-in to an empty MMC. Right-click the node, select Open Database, and type in any name (as long as it is unique). This will create your own copy of the security database, located, by default, within your profile folder. Next, you will be prompted to select a security template to import into the database you just created. From this point on, you can use the Import Database menu option to import another template and further change the security settings stored in your private copy of the security database. During import, you can decide whether you want to merge or replace existing settings.

Once the database contains all the settings you need, select the Analyze Computer Now menu option. After you specify the location of the Error Log file path, the analysis will start. Its progress will be displayed on the screen.

The results are presented in a similar format to the one used by the Group Policies Editor, as you can see in the Figure 11.44.

FIGURE 11.44

Analyzing security settings

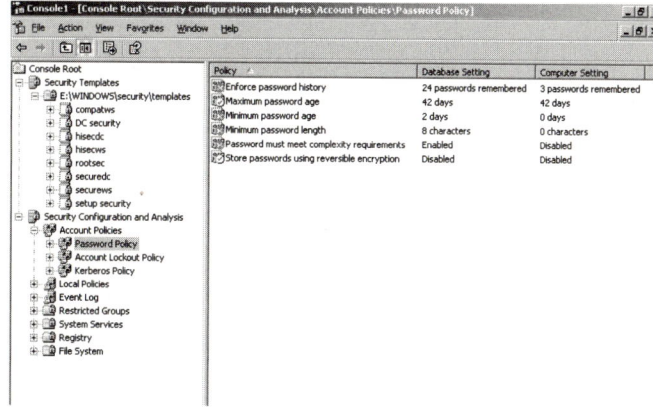

The details pane contains three columns: the name of the policy setting, its value in your private copy of the database, and the current value in the computer security database. A green check mark next to a setting indicates that corresponding entries in both databases are identical. A mismatch between two entries is designated by a red X.

In case of a mismatch, you have two options. If your existing computer settings are correct, you can manually adjust the settings in your database (to be the same as the computer settings) and export them into a security template. This way, you can reapply them to the same computer or another computer at any time. If the settings contained in your copy of the database are correct, you can apply them to your computer. To do this, right-click the Computer Configuration and Analysis node and select Configure Computer Now.

SecEdit

Once you get familiar with the way the Security Configuration and Analysis console works, you will find out that checking or applying security settings for individual computers is extremely easy. However, using this approach to modify the local security database on a larger number of computers would be very time-consuming. Fortunately, you can automate analyzing and configuring computer security, as well as importing or exporting security templates, with the SecEdit command-line utility. In addition, SecEdit offers a /GenerateRollback option for creating a rollback template, if security settings need to be restored. To view the syntax of all of its available options, type:

    SECEDIT /HELP

at the command prompt, or refer to the online help files.

Group Policy Management Tools

Even though Group Policies have been available since the release of Windows 2000, Microsoft failed at that time to provide management and troubleshooting tools that would meet the needs of an enterprise customer. While configuring Group Policies was certainly possible and relatively convenient in smaller domains, managing them in larger, multidomain environments required significant skills and effort. Troubleshooting was difficult and time-consuming. Common administrative tasks—such as backup, restore, or copy—required cumbersome workarounds or third-party tools. Fortunately, with the release of Windows Server 2003, this has changed. Two utilities, implemented as MMC snap-ins, offer previously missing functionality:

◆ The Resultant Set of Policies snap-in lets you evaluate and troubleshoot the impact of Group Policies.

◆ The Group Policy Management Console allows practically any other operation, including the backup and restore of individual GPOs.

Let's look at both utilities in detail in the next two sections.

Resultant Set of Policies

The Resultant Set of Policies snap-in works in two modes:

Logging   Allows reviewing of cumulative policy settings applied to an existing computer or user. It is used primarily for troubleshooting.

Planning   Allows evaluation of a resulting Group Policy based on information contained in Active Directory. It is typically used to find out the impact of the Group Policy on computers or users before they are placed in containers to which GPOs are linked.

I explained earlier about the rules that are followed when multiple GPOs are applied on different levels of an Active Directory hierarchy. The interaction among them, in addition to group or WMI filtering, as well as blocking or forcing inheritance, can make analysis of a resulting policy very complex. This was the challenge that Windows 2000 administrators had to face. The Resultant Set of Policies tool makes this task trivial.

Start by adding Resultant Set of Policies to the MMC console and selecting Generate RSoP Data from the right-click menu. This launches the wizard, which first prompts you for the mode you want to use (logging or planning).

If you select the logging mode, you will need to specify an existing (and reachable) computer (either local or remote) and a user whose profile exists on that computer (either currently logged on or who has logged on to that computer in the past, providing that profiles are cached locally).

If you select the planning mode, either you can select a user and computer object from Active Directory, or you can specify containers in which users and computers would be located. This way, you can test the impact of Group Policies on objects residing anywhere in the Active Directory hierarchy prior to placing them there. In addition, you can also specify other information that might affect the way Group Policies are applied, such as:

◆ Site name

◆ Slow network connection

- ◆ Loopback processing (in replace or merge mode)
- ◆ User and computer group membership (for group filtering)
- ◆ User and computer WMI filters

The results in both planning and logging mode are displayed in a format similar to the one used by the Group Policy Editor, shown in the Figure 11.45.

FIGURE 11.45

Analyzing security settings

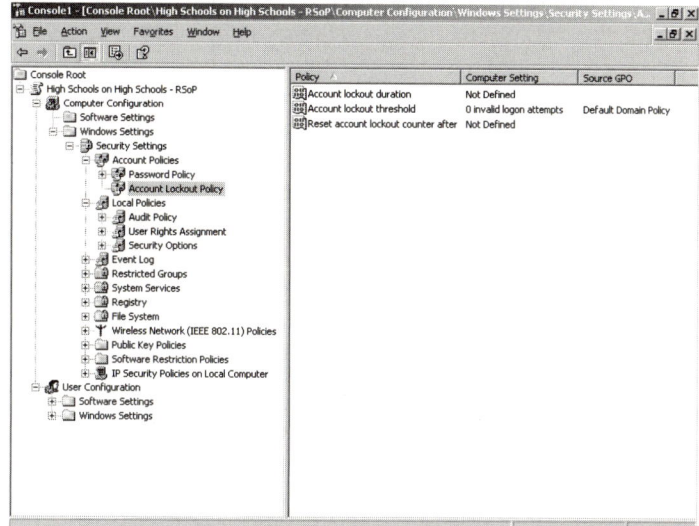

For each Group Policy entry, you will see the resulting setting and the source GPO where its value came from. You can find out other GPOs that were configured to modify the same setting by double-clicking the entry and checking the content of the Precedence tab in the Properties dialog box.

Group Policy Management Console

The Group Policy Management Console offers a number of Group Policy management features. It allows you to:

- ◆ Run forest- or domainwide searches for GPOs based on different types of criteria
- ◆ Back up individual GPOs
- ◆ Copy settings from one GPO to another
- ◆ Restore individual GPOs (along with their original GUID and all characteristics, such as WMI and group filters and permissions)
- ◆ Assign permissions to all GPOs from a single interface
- ◆ Create WMI filters and link them to one or more GPOs
- ◆ Configure group filtering for one or more GPOs

All these actions can be performed conveniently from the single interface. Within the same interface, you can search for the GPO you want to edit, and once you find it, open it in the Group Policy Object Editor. The Group Policy Management Console is extensible (new functionality can easily be added to it) and scriptable (its actions can be automated through scripts).

In Short

Group Policies give a network administrator complete control over the user's environment. Given that many help desk calls revolve around user configuration errors—"I was just trying to change my color scheme" or "I didn't know I couldn't pick my own IP address"—properly configured Group Policies should reduce the administration necessary to support end users. With the improvements introduced in Windows Server 2003, this task is not only easier to accomplish, but also easier to plan and troubleshoot.

In the next chapter, we will look at the process for extending the AD schema to include objects that are specific to your environment—perhaps some software package needs a new object class defined or perhaps you would like to store additional employee identification as an attribute of each user's network account. Whatever the reason, you may need to extend the AD schema at some point.

Chapter 12

Modifying the Active Directory Schema

WHILE THE STANDARD AD schema that ships with Windows 2000/Windows Server 2003 will probably be sufficient for most installations, there might come a time when you need to modify it. Microsoft allows you to add new classes and attributes and disable them if they are no longer needed. New in Windows Server 2003 is the ability to redefine disabled attributes. Your goal is to create an AD database that is customized for the way in which your company does business and flexible enough to accommodate changes and accidental mistakes.

Before you can effectively modify the AD schema, however, you must understand what it is and how it works. This chapter lays the foundation, and then teaches you to make changes to the AD schema to meet the needs of your enterprise.

Featured in this chapter:

◆ Schema basics

◆ Modifying the schema

Schema Basics

To review, the *schema* of the Active Directory database defines the objects that can be stored there. It is the formal definition of the object classes and attributes that exist in the database. The AD database is no different from any other database that you have worked with in the past. Before you can place information within it, you must lay out a structure to define how to store that data.

What's in a Schema?

A *schema* is total description of a database, including the description of each field, the relationships between files, any premade drop-down lists, and any other information about how the database is structured. Every database has a schema, some more complex than others. For example, imagine you were going to build a database to hold the telephone numbers and addresses of your business contacts. You wouldn't just start entering names and addresses, would you? The first step would be to decide exactly what information you would like to store. Your list might include:

- Company
- First name
- Last name
- Nickname
- Address
- City
- State
- Zip code
- Country
- Telephone number
- Pager/cellular phone number
- Fax number
- E-mail address

The next step would be to lay out the fields for each record, as shown in Table 12.1. You will need to decide the type of data each field will hold and the maximum size of each field, as well as add any special formatting requirements that are necessary for consistency.

TABLE 12.1: CONTACT DATABASE STRUCTURE

FIELD	TYPE	SIZE (CHARACTERS)	FORMATTING
Company	Text	50	
First name	Text	20	
Last name	Text	20	
Nickname	Text	20	
Address	Text	50	
City	Text	25	
State	Text	2	Should provide a pick list for consistent abbreviations.
Zip code	Text	9	#####-####

Continued on next page

TABLE 12.1: CONTACT DATABASE STRUCTURE *(continued)*

FIELD	TYPE	SIZE (CHARACTERS)	FORMATTING
Country	Text	2	Should provide a pick list for consistent abbreviations; use the two-letter abbreviations provided by the X.500 committee.
Telephone number	Text	11	#-###-###-####
Fax number	Text	11	#-###-###-####
Pager/cellular phone number	Text	11	#-###-###-####
E-mail address	Text	25	

Once you have decided the structure of each record, you are ready to build your database—unless you decide to add a bit more functionality. (To programmers this is known as *feature creep.*) You might also want to store records of each time you have been in touch with each of your contacts. You could do this by expanding the list in Table 12.1 to include a unique identifier, then using that unique field to relate to another database file. In the second file, you would then repeat the process of defining the fields that it would contain, as shown in Table 12.2.

TABLE 12.2: RELATED FILES

FIELD	TYPE	SIZE	FORMATTING	RELATED TO
Unique ID	Numeric	3		Unique ID in contact list
Date	Date		US standard	
Length of contact	Numeric	10	Number of minutes	
Notes	Text	Variable length		

The Active Directory Schema

The schema of the Active Directory database is much more complex than that of our contact list database. Within the AD database, each different type of record defined is known as an *object class*. The fields, known as *attributes*, for each class might be different from those for other defined classes. The AD schema attributes are designed so they can sufficiently represent the following types of information stored in Active Directory:

Multivalued properties Certain characteristics of an object class need to store more than one value. A user's home telephone number attribute, for instance, might need to store multiple telephone numbers for a single user.

How the various pieces of the database fit together   This is necessary due to the distributed nature of the AD database. Remember that this database is divided into partitions (domains), which are spread across multiple servers. Something in the schema must define how these partitions find each other, communicate, and share information as needed.

Attributes holding pointers to all other replicas of the same partition   There might be multiple copies of a single partition; without these attributes, the replication of database changes could not take place.

A mechanism to track changes   The replication process requires this of each object and each attribute of each object. This mechanism includes both the up-to-date vector and a time stamp.

Variable, rather than static, attribute lengths   Some of the data that the database will hold might be textual and the database might grow quite large—over a million objects in a single partition. In other words, each record in the database should take up only as much disk space as necessary but should have the ability to grow as more information is added.

A hierarchy of object classes   To reduce redundant design, the schema is built upon this hierarchy, with subordinate classes inheriting attributes from higher-level object classes.

To make matters even more complex, the Active Directory database schema must be fully—and easily—extensible so that it can grow to meet the changing needs of a dynamic business environment. In other words, the schema must be readily accessible so that changes to the database structure can be made. Make changes to the Active Directory schema by using the Active Directory Schema Manager included with Windows Server 2003.

NOTE   *You can also write scripts that make Active Directory interface calls to accomplish this task. We'll discuss the Active Directory Schema Manager later in this chapter.*

At the top of any LDAP-compliant directory service (such as Microsoft Active Directory), there is a special container known as rootDSE. When referring to this container, the appropriate syntax is to refer to `LDAP://rootDSE`. The rootDSE container contains a number of entries, including the definition of the namespace of the LDAP structure and the schema of the database. The schema itself is stored in the subcontainer that follows the naming context:

```
CN=schema,CN=configuration,<DC=forestroot>
```

where `<DC=forestroot>` is the distinguished name of the forest root domain, e.g., `DC=KingTech` or `DC=com`.

NOTE   *For our purposes, we really don't even have to know where the actual schema is stored—the tools provided by Microsoft will find it. But it is interesting to note that Microsoft has used the industry-standard location so that other LDAP-compliant directory services can communicate (and perhaps synchronize) with AD.*

Who Can Modify the Schema?

To make changes to the schema, a user must be a member of the Schema Admins group. By default, only a single user account—the Administrator from the root domain of the forest—is a member of this group. While you can add other user accounts to the Schema Admins group, due to the nature of the task—which is complex and has far-reaching consequences—most companies will probably stick with the default.

What Can Be Modified?

When modifying the directory schema, you may perform the following tasks:

- Create new classes.
- Modify existing classes.
- Create new attributes.
- Modify existing attributes.
- Deactivate classes.
- Activate deactivated classes.
- Deactivate attributes.
- Redefine deactivated attributes (Windows Server 2003 only).
- Activate deactivated attributes.

WARNING   *When you modify the schema, you are making a change that impacts the structure of the Active Directory database. This is not something that should be done lightly! Before you modify the schema, Microsoft suggests that you review the existing schema to determine if an existing object class or attribute can fulfill your needs.*

MODIFYING EXISTING CLASSES OR ATTRIBUTES

Once you have determined that no existing class or attribute will fit your needs, consider modifying the schema. If at all possible, try to modify an existing object or attribute rather than creating a new one.

A user object, for example, has many attributes that might not be applicable to your environment. There are numerous tabs filled with attributes for a user object. You will probably not use all of these attributes in your environment.

TIP   *Changing a display name for an existing attribute is one of the least intrusive ways to modify the schema to meet your needs.*

Modify an existing object class if all you need are new attributes. User objects are probably the best example of this situation. Many companies will want to store specific information about users in the directory. Often the generic definition of a user will not contain the additional attributes necessary. If your users do a lot of traveling, for instance, you might want to add attributes that store travel preferences, such as airline frequent-flyer information or smoking/nonsmoking preferences.

CREATING AN AUXILIARY CLASS

An *auxiliary class* is used to extend another object class. For example, suppose you have two types of users: permanent and temporary. While the normal user object is perfect for your permanent employees, it does not contain attributes sufficient for your temporary workers. To resolve this, you first create an auxiliary class (called, for example, tempWorker) that contains a number of additional attributes, and then you declare it as an auxiliary class for the user class. This makes these additional attributes available within the user class.

ADDING NEW CLASSES AND ATTRIBUTES

Add new attributes when no existing attribute meets your needs or can be modified to meet your needs. This can be an extensive change to the directory database, and you should think carefully before you do it.

WARNING   One of the most intrusive and potentially dangerous changes is to add a new object class. You should take this action only when no other option will fit the needs of your environment.

CAN CLASSES AND ATTRIBUTES BE DELETED?

There is no way to delete an object class or attribute that is in the schema. You can, however, *deactivate* either a class or an attribute. We'll discuss deactivation in the next section.

WARNING   As you can see, there are numerous types of modifications that can be made to the Active Directory database. While the process is straightforward (albeit not exactly easy), modifying the schema is not something that you should do without prior planning. Any time you change the structure of a database you risk damaging it—not something you want to happen to your network's directory!

DEACTIVATING CLASSES AND ATTRIBUTES

Classes and attributes are never removed from the schema. Instead, they are deactivated and marked as unused. This prevents irreversible mistakes and improves performance by not forcing a time-consuming cleanup of removed items.

NOTE   Deactivating an item is functionally the same as deleting it, but deactivation leaves you the option of reversing your action at a later date.

Here is what happens when you deactivate an object class or attribute:

◆ That object class or attribute is no longer replicated throughout the network or to the Global Catalog server.

◆ You may no longer create objects that are part of the deactivated class or enter data into the attribute. Attempts to do so will return the same error as if the class or attribute had never existed.

◆ When an attribute is deactivated, you may no longer use it in definitions of new object classes or add it to an existing class.

◆ Objects created prior to the deactivation remain in the AD database and will appear in the various tools. You may not, however, change attributes of them; your only real management option is to delete them.

♦ Deactivated object classes and attributes still appear in searches, for two reasons:

  ♦ You can search for the deactivated information in order to clean up your directory.

  ♦ You might not have deleted those objects that were created before the deactivation (which means you might need to search for them at some point).

♦ New in Windows Server 2003, you can redefine deactivated classes or attributes reusing the same LDAP display name or object identifier. (We'll discuss object identifiers later in this chapter.)

What Cannot Be Modified?

The bulleted list at the end of the previous section seems to imply that you can make just about any type of change to the directory that you desire. However, this is not really the case, since there are a number of rules you need to follow when modifying Active Directory.

For example, you cannot disable a class that is a parent or auxiliary class of another active class. You also cannot modify default system classes. Similarly, any attribute that is part of an active class cannot be disabled. Some of the attributes (starting with the word **system**) cannot even change after the class is created. The reason for these restrictions is to prevent changes that would be destructive to Active Directory's stability.

Modifying the Schema

Earlier, you read about the concepts of multiple-master and single-master environments. Both *multiple master* and *single master* refer to the process used to replicate changes throughout a distributed replicated database. In a multiple-master environment, all copies of the database can accept changes and can replicate those changes to all other copies. In a single-master environment, such as the PDC/BDC relationship used in Windows NT domains, only one copy of the database can accept changes, and the server that holds the copy (the primary domain controller) is responsible for replicating them to all other domain controllers.

While Active Directory functions as a multiple-master environment when replicating changes to the information stored within the directory database, it is a single-master environment when replicating changes to the schema. In other words, there is only one domain controller, known as the *schema master*, on which schema modifications can be made at any given time. In Active Directory, these single-master operations are known as *operations masters* or *flexible single-master operations* (FSMOs). The domain controller that is acting as the schema master is also known as the *schema operations master*.

What Happens When the Schema Is Modified?

When the schema is modified, there is a delay before the changes take effect. This delay is incurred because there are actually two copies of the schema:

♦ One in memory

♦ One in the Active Directory

When a modification is made, the change is written to the Active Directory database. Active Directory waits for five minutes (for performance reasons) after the schema update before it commits the changes to the copy in memory. The copy in memory, known as the *cache schema,* is the schema that is current. In other words, the copy of the schema used by various system processes and threads is the one stored in memory. This means that approximately five minutes will pass between the time you stop making changes to the schema and the time those changes become apparent.

During this five-minute interval, you cannot add objects that use a new or modified class or attribute. In other words, you must wait until the update has completed before making use of your changes. You can, however, force the schema to reload using the Schema Manager MMC snap-in or through manual programming.

Preparing for Schema Modifications

There are three preliminary steps you must complete before you can proceed with the task of modifying the Active Directory schema:

1. Obtain an OID (object identifier) for each new class or attribute you intend to create.

2. Verify your membership in the Schema Admins group.

3. Install Active Directory Schema Manager.

So far, we've discussed the process of making modifications to the directory as if it were a common administrative practice. As you'll see, this is far from the case!

OBTAINING OIDS

OIDs are globally unique object identifiers. By global, I mean that these identifiers are used to define objects and attributes as they are applied to *any* directory service, from Microsoft Active Directory to Novell Directory Services. OIDs are issued by the International Standards Organization (ISO) issuing agency. By having a central group control how object classes and attributes are implemented, the industry can avoid incompatible network directories.

OIDs uniquely define data elements, syntaxes, and various other parts of distributed applications. ISO-issued OIDs are used in many standard technologies, including Open System Interconnection (OSI) applications, X.500 directories, Simple Network Management Protocol (SNMP), and many other applications where a unique identifier is important. Each object class and attribute must have a unique OID if it is to exist in the AD schema. OIDs are organized in a hierarchical structure managed by the ISO.

NOTE *While you probably won't need to understand the entire OID naming process, it is important to know that the OID represents a tree-like structure much like the container/subcontainer structure of AD.*

LDAP is an important protocol used for accessing information in network directories, such as Microsoft Active Directory. LDAP applications use the ISO-issued OIDs to identify the objects and attributes that are available in *any* directory to which they connect. In other words, to be LDAP-accessible, every object and attribute within a directory must have an OID. (The OID itself becomes an attribute of each object defined.)

As stated earlier, the International Standards Organization acts as the issuing agent for new OIDs. To create a new object class or attribute within the AD schema, the first step is to apply to the ISO for an OID. The OID will be expressed as a string of numbers delimited by decimals, such as `1.2.840.xxxxxx.w.y.z`. Table 12.3 describes the purpose of each piece of our sample OID.

TABLE 12.3: DECODING OID 1.2.840.xxxxxx.w.y.z

NUMBER	REPRESENTS
1	This value acts as the root of the ISO hierarchy.
2	American National Standards Institute (ANSI).
840	United States.
xxxxxx	The organization applying for the OID is given a unique identifier.
w	A location within the organization.
y	A division within the location.
z	A group within the division.

VERIFYING MEMBERSHIP IN THE SCHEMA ADMINS GROUP

Before anyone attempts to make any schema modifications, verify that the person who will perform the procedure is a member of the Schema Admins group. By default, the only member of this group is the Administrator account of the root domain in the forest. (This Administrator account is automatically made a member of the Administrators, Domain Admins, Domain Users, Enterprise Admins, and Schema Admins groups.) Verify membership using the Active Directory Users and Computers tool found in the Administrative Tools group or in the MMC (after adding the appropriate snap-in). The process requires the following steps:

1. Start the Active Directory Users and Computers utility.

2. Click the domain, then double-click the Users OU. Groups and users will appear in the details pane, as shown in Figure 12.1.

FIGURE 12.1

Active Directory
Users and Groups

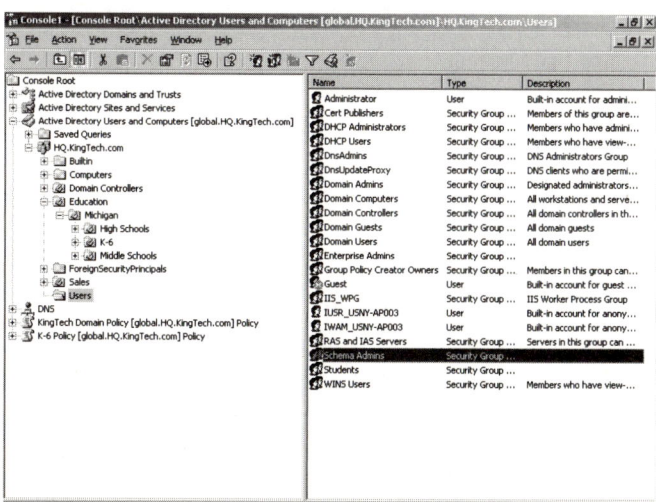

3. Find the Schema Admins group and double-click it. You will see the Schema Admins Properties dialog box, which is shown in Figure 12.2.

FIGURE 12.2

The Schema Admins Properties dialog box

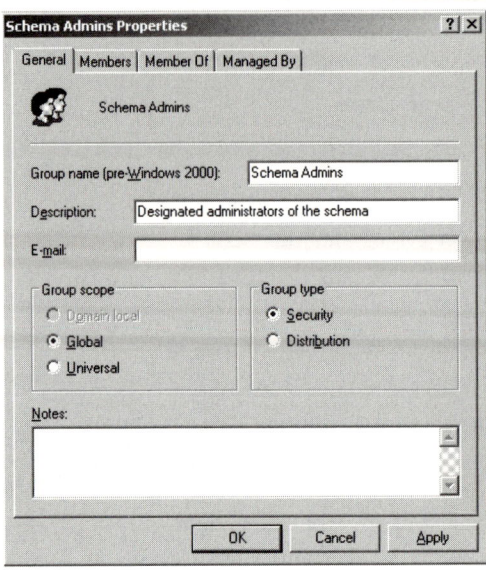

4. Click the Members tab and ensure that the appropriate user is listed as a member. You can see this tab in Figure 12.3.

FIGURE 12.3

The Members tab of the Schema Admins Properties dialog box

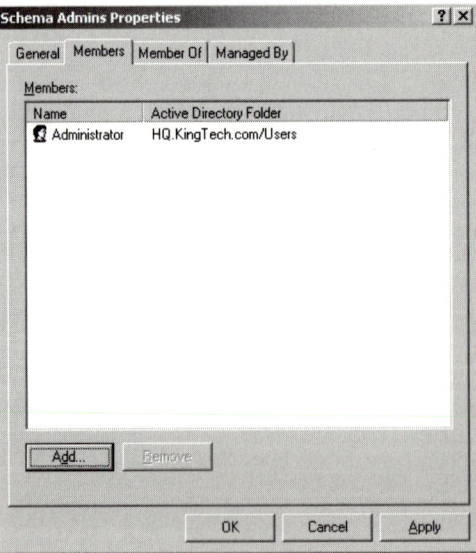

The default membership list, consisting only of the Administrator account, will be sufficient for most organizations.

WARNING   *Modifying the directory schema is not something that many people should be doing, and there should never be multiple people performing modifications simultaneously!*

INSTALLING ACTIVE DIRECTORY SCHEMA MANAGER

Administrators do not modify the schema as a matter of course, so Microsoft has not installed the Active Directory Schema Manager utility as part of the standard Windows 2000/Windows Server 2003 installation. Follow these steps to add this tool:

1. On the Run command, type MMC (for Microsoft Management Console). The MMC will appear, as shown in Figure 12.4.

FIGURE 12.4

The Microsoft Management Console

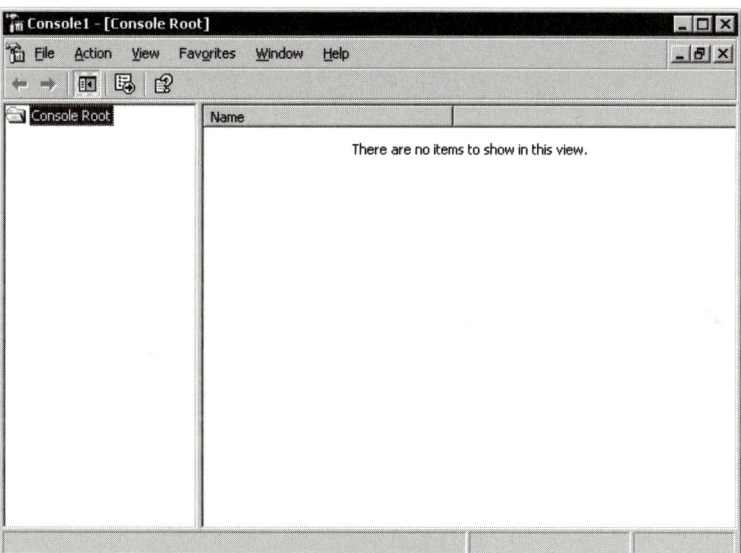

2. From the Console menu, choose Add/Remove Snap-in. The Add/Remove Snap-in dialog box will appear, which you can see in Figure 12.5.

FIGURE 12.5

The Add/Remove Snap-in dialog box

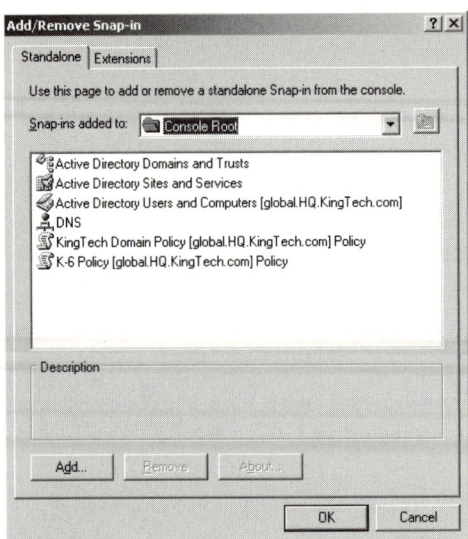

3. Click the Add button to access the Add Standalone Snap-in dialog box, as shown in Figure 12.6.

FIGURE 12.6

The Add Standalone Snap-in dialog box

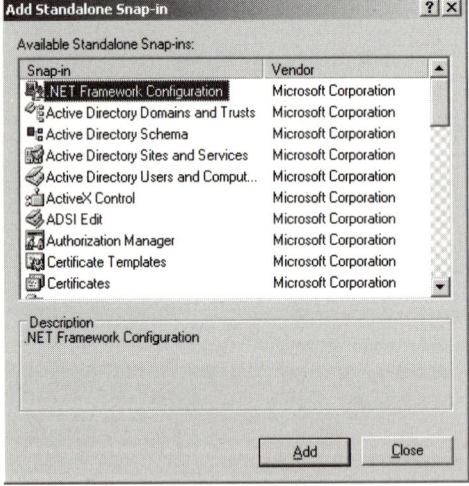

4. Highlight the Active Directory Schema option and click Add. If you do not see an entry for Active Directory Schema in the Add/Remove Snap-in dialog box, you will first need to register the Schema Manager extension. Do this by typing the following at the command prompt:

```
regsvr32 schmmgmt.dll
```

and press the Enter key. You should get the confirmation that the .dll has been properly registered.

5. Click Close, and the Active Directory Schema option will be added to your MMC.

The Active Directory Schema Manager utility must be connected to the current FSMO before modifications can take place. To ensure that the utility is pointing to the correct server, highlight the Active Directory Schema entry in the MMC, right-click, and choose Change Domain Controller. The Change Domain Controller dialog box will appear. You can see this dialog box in Figure 12.7.

FIGURE 12.7

The Change Domain Controller dialog box

From here you can change the server that the Active Directory Schema Manager utility points to when making schema modifications.

By right-clicking on Active Directory Schema node and selecting the Permissions option, you can grant permissions for users and groups to perform certain functions in the ADS database, as shown in Figure 12.8.

FIGURE 12.8

The Permissions for Schema dialog box

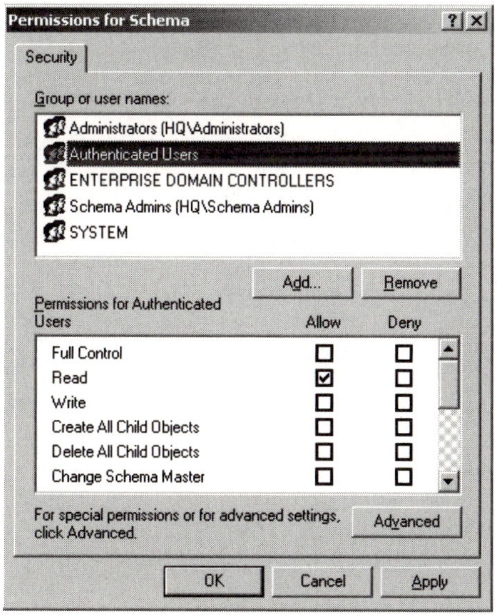

Here are the permissions available for the schema:

- Full Control
- Read
- Write
- Create All Child Objects
- Delete All Child Objects
- Change Schema Master
- Manage Replication Topology
- Monitor Active Directory Replication (Windows Server 2003 only)
- Reanimate Tombstones (Windows Server 2003 only)
- Replicate Directory Changes
- Replicating Directory Changes All (Windows Server 2003 only)
- Replication Synchronization
- Update Schema Cache
- Special Permissions

Click the Advanced button to set Special Permissions. The default permissions assignments are described in Table 12.4.

TABLE 12.4: DEFAULT SCHEMA PERMISSIONS

USER OR GROUP	PERMISSIONS
Authenticated User	Read, Special
Local System	All permissions
Schema Admins	All permissions except Full Control and Delete All Child Objects
Administrators	Manage Replication Topology, Replicate Directory Changes, Replicate Directory Changes All, Replication Synchronization
Enterprise Domain Controllers	Manage Replication Topology, Replicate Directory Changes, Replicate Directory Changes All, Replication Synchronization

The Seven Types of Schema Modifications

As you read earlier, there are seven types of modifications that you can make to the schema:

- Creating a new class
- Modifying an existing class

◆ Creating a new attribute

◆ Modifying an existing attribute

◆ Deactivating a class or an attribute

◆ Activating a deactivated class or attribute

◆ Redefining a deactivated class or attribute

The next few sections discuss the procedures for accomplishing each of these tasks. All of them can be accomplished through the Active Directory Schema Manager (ADSM) snap-in to the MMC that you read about earlier.

CREATING A NEW CLASS

To create a new class, you create a *class-definition object*. In effect, this class-definition object becomes a container for the attributes that describe the object class. Within the ADSM utility, right-click the Class container and choose New Class (or Create Class). First you will be presented with a dialog box reminding you that schema object creation is a nonreversible operation. Next, you will see the Create New Schema Class dialog box, shown in Figure 12.9.

FIGURE 12.9

The Create New Schema Class dialog box

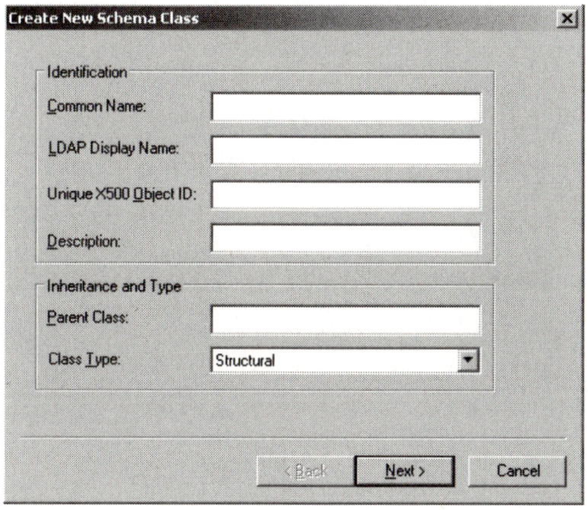

You will have to provide the following information:

Common Name   This is mandatory and is used as the Common Name attribute for the object class. This is an indexed field and is used for searches of the database.

LDAP Display Name   This is another mandatory field. This is what LDAP tools will display to users when they access the directory.

Unique X.500 Object ID   This is the OID you received from the ISO.

Description   This optional field provides a short description of the class.

You will also have to determine whether this class should be a child to another class and what type of class this should be.

Children inherit the attributes of their parents. This section can be used to create a subtype of object or set up redundant attributes. An example would be my company's AD tree. While we have "normal employees," we also have a subset known as "instructors." The instructors subclass inherits all of the properties of the user object class, but it also has attributes that are specific to that type of user (vendor certifications, a list of courses taught, and so on).

There are three types of classes:

Structural   Structural object classes are those from which AD objects can be created.

Abstract   Abstract object classes are templates used to build structural objects. An example of an abstract object class is the Top class. It contains all of the attributes that are mandatory for *every* other object class.

Auxiliary   Auxiliary objects are just a list of attributes that can be added to other object classes.

MODIFYING AN EXISTING CLASS

To modify a class, expand the Class container within the ADSM. Right-click the appropriate class and choose Properties. You will see the class Properties dialog box illustrated in Figure 12.10.

FIGURE 12.10

The class Properties dialog box

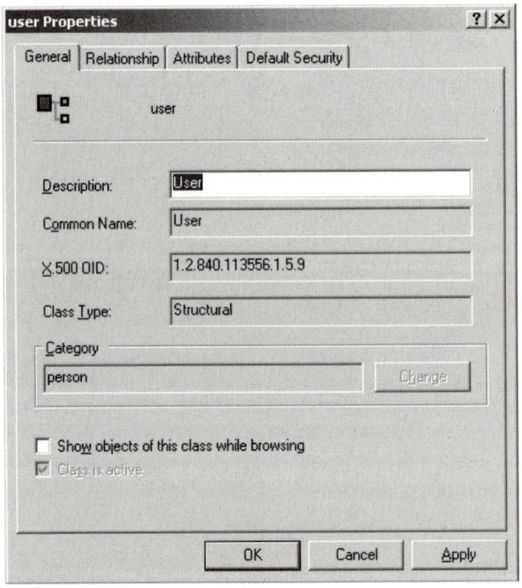

There are four tabs available:

◆ General

◆ Relationship

◆ Attributes

◆ Default Security

Each of these tabs controls a different aspect of the object class.

Figure 12.10 shows the General tab. Here you can change items pertaining to how the class fits into the schema.

Figure 12.11 shows the Relationship tab. Here you can assign auxiliary object classes to this structural class.

FIGURE 12.11

The Relationship tab of class Properties

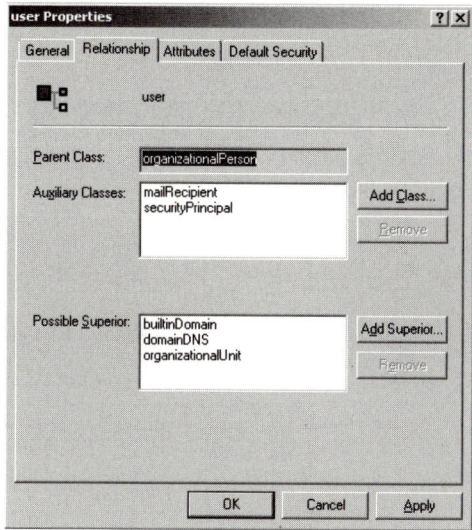

The Attributes tab is shown in Figure 12.12. Here you can view mandatory attributes as well as add optional attributes to the object class.

FIGURE 12.12

The Attributes tab of class Properties

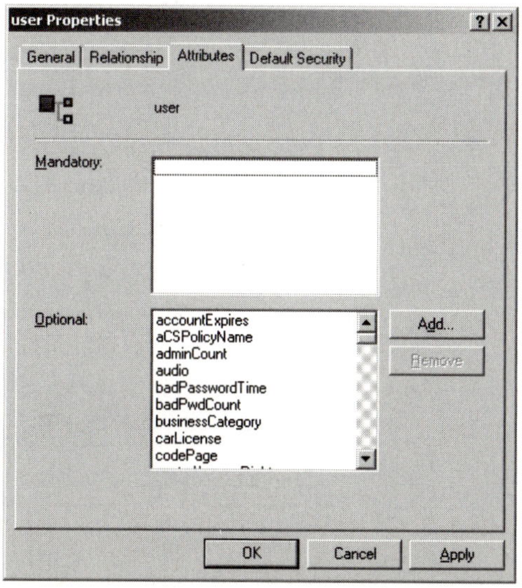

Finally, Figure 12.13 shows the Default Security tab. Here you can assign default permissions to this class of object.

FIGURE 12.13

The Default
Security tab of
class Properties

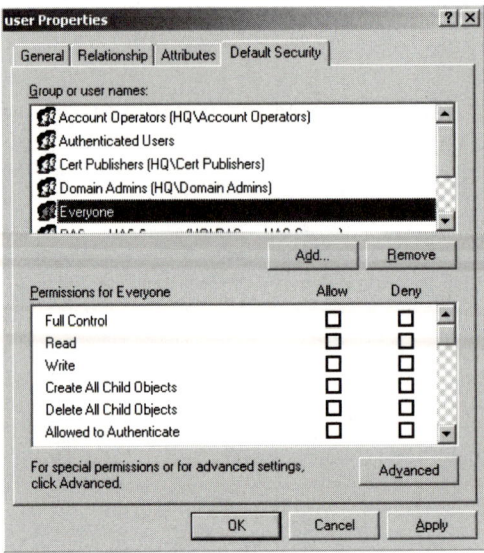

CREATING A NEW ATTRIBUTE

To create a new attribute, you create an *attribute-definition object.* The process is much like that of creating a new object class. Within the ADSM, right-click the Attributes container, then choose New Attribute (or Create Attribute). As with the creation of classes, you will first be reminded that creating a schema object is a nonreversible process. Next, you will see the Create New Attribute dialog box, shown in Figure 12.14.

FIGURE 12.14

The Create New
Attribute dialog box

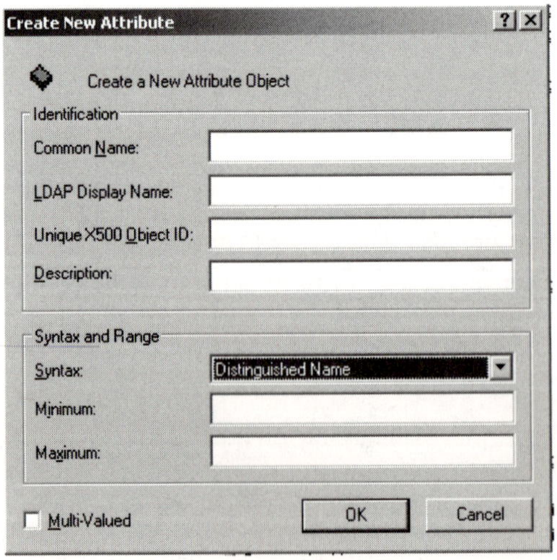

Here you enter the following information:

Common Name   This field becomes the Common Name attribute of the attribute.

NOTE   *Yes, attributes themselves have attributes—it can become confusing.*

LDAP Display Name   This is the string that the LDAP utility will display to users when they access the directory.

Unique X.500 Object ID   This is the OID you received from the ISO.

Description   This optional field provides a short description of the attribute.

You must also configure the type of data that the attribute will hold. In the Syntax box, you choose one of the predefined data types that the attribute will hold, such as a string of characters (Unicode, case-insensitive), numbers, SID, OID, and so on. You may also set valid ranges for the data entered to avoid incorrect information. Finally, check the Multi-Valued box if the attribute will contain more than one value (such as the telephone number attribute).

MODIFYING AN EXISTING ATTRIBUTE

To modify an existing attribute, right-click the attribute and choose Properties. This will display the single General tab, with the following fields:

Description   Modifiable description of the attribute.

Common Name   Used in the Relative Distinguished Name.

X 500 OID   OID assigned by ISO.

Syntax   Data type of the attribute.

Minimum   Lower boundary of the data type.

Maximum   Upper boundary of the data type.
It also includes the following check boxes:

Allow this attribute to be shown in advanced view   Restricts the view of the AD Administrative Tools to the Advanced view only.

Attribute is active   Used for disabling the attribute.

Index this attribute in the Active Directory   Speeds up searches.

Ambiguous Name Resolution (ANR)   Allows searches when an exact value of the attribute is not known.

Replicate this attribute to the Global Catalog   Includes the attribute in the Global Catalog.

Attribute is copied when duplicating a user   The value of the attribute remains the same when copying one user account to create another. Obviously, it applies only to attributes, which are part of the user class.

Index this attribute for containerized searches in the Active Directory Speeds up searches within AD containers.

DEACTIVATING A CLASS OR AN ATTRIBUTE

In the ADSM, expand either the Class or the Attribute container, depending on what you want to deactivate. Within the container, find the item you wish to deactivate, right-click it, and choose Properties. On the General tab, deselect the check box titled Attribute Is Active.

NOTE *If you choose to deactivate an item that another object is dependent upon, ADS will return an error describing the problem. This prevents you from making a deactivation that would interfere with the functionality of another class or attribute.*

ACTIVATING A DEACTIVATED CLASS OR ATTRIBUTE

Activating a deactivated class or attribute is accomplished simply by selecting the check box titled Attribute Is Active. You might not be able to activate a deactivated class or attribute if you have redefined them with the same LDAP display name or OID value. When activating a class, you also need to make sure that all of its attributes and classes referred to by its attributes are active as well.

REDEFINING A DEACTIVATED CLASS OR ATTRIBUTE

This new feature in Windows Server 2003 allows you to redefine a class or attribute. This offers new possibilities not available in Windows 2000. Imagine, for instance, that you created an attribute and mistakenly assigned an incorrect value to one of its attributes. A number of attributes cannot be changed after a class or attribute is created (such as common name or syntax). In a Windows 2000 environment, if this happened to be one of these attributes, your only option was to deactivate the newly created class or attribute and create a new one with a new LDAP display name and OID value. This could create problems if some of your applications were designed to rely on these values to work with Active Directory objects. However, in a Windows Server 2003 forest, you can deactivate the incorrectly created class or attribute and create a new one, reusing the same LDAP display name and OID values used previously. To create such a class or attribute, follow the sequence of steps described in the previous sections.

In Short

While you can make changes to the structure of the Active Directory database, this is not something you would do as part of the day-to-day administration of an AD environment. The modification process involves acquiring a valid OID for any new classes or attributes and, since it changes the schema, could have a negative effect on your network due to increased replication traffic.

Microsoft offers the following suggestions for schema modifications:

◆ Modify the schema only when absolutely necessary.

◆ Use existing attributes when creating new object classes. This allows you to avoid the process of applying for numerous attribute OIDs.

◆ Avoid multivalued attributes as much as possible. Large attributes are costly to store (in terms of disk space) and to retrieve (in terms of network bandwidth), and therefore should be avoided.

◆ Use meaningful names for any new classes or attributes to avoid ambiguity.

In the next chapter we will change gears, moving from the logical structure of the database to its impact on the physical aspects of the network. Through proper design and implementation of AD sites, an administrator can avoid much of the overhead involved in maintaining a large, distributed, replicated database like the Active Directory database.

Chapter 13

Understanding and Controlling AD Sites and Replication

SO FAR IN OUR discussion of Active Directory, we have concentrated on AD as a logical representation of your computing environment. Our entire focus has been on creating an environment that matches the logical manner in which a company does business. In other words, we have looked at AD with no regard for physical factors, such as networking infrastructure and its two most relevant characteristics:

◆ Bandwidth

◆ Cost

Every network consists of some medium, be it copper, fiber, or air (when dealing with wireless technology). On that medium we move packets of information from one point to another. This means that no matter how logical we make the structure or how graphical we make the interface, when all is said and done, everything comes back to the plumbing—the "pipes" we use to move data. It's just not feasible to design any portion of your network without taking into consideration available bandwidth and communication costs. This includes the design of your Active Directory environment.

Previously, we looked at the logical organization of AD to meet business needs. In this chapter, we will change our perspective, focusing on the organization of the AD environment to meet the realities of your physical network.

In this chapter:

◆ Understanding Active Directory sites

◆ Implementing Active Directory sites

◆ Understanding replication

◆ Behind the scenes of replication

Understanding Active Directory Sites

Within the Active Directory hierarchy, the directory tree structure does not need to match the physical organization of resources on the network. By "physical organization" I mean the physical location of computers and the connections between them. Take, for example, the AD tree presented in Figure 13.1.

FIGURE 13.1

Typical AD
structure

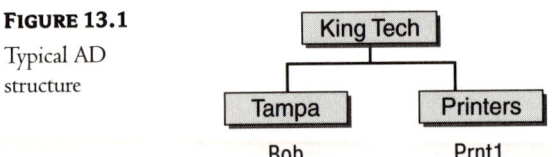

If user Bob needs to print to the printer named Prnt1, it would appear as a "local" resource. In other words, as Bob uses his graphical interface to the network, Prnt1 appears in a container named Printers. Based on the structure of the AD tree and the naming conventions used, we have no idea where printer Prnt1 is physically located. In Figure 13.2, we see that Bob works in the Tampa office, but the printer named Prnt1 is located in the Reno office.

FIGURE 13.2

The physical layout
for KingTech

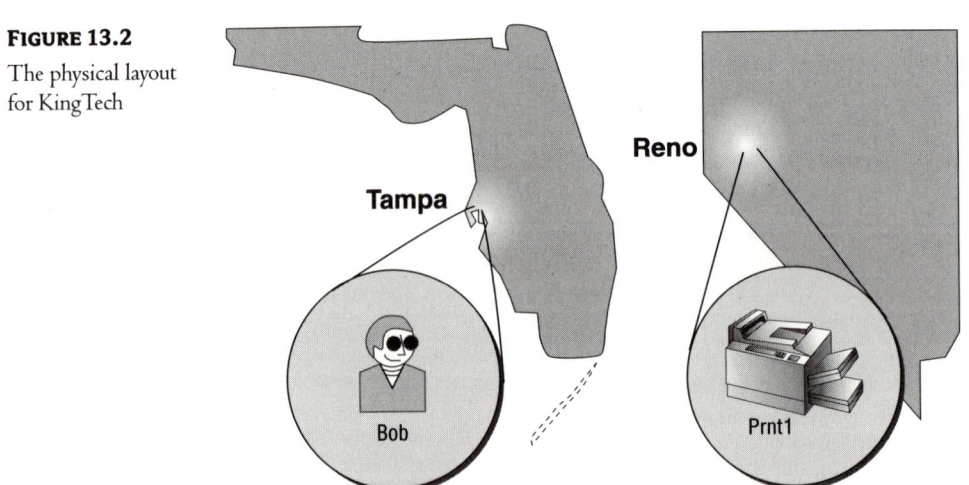

NOTE *Figures 13.1 and 13.2 drive home the fact that AD is logical in nature. Bob doesn't have to know anything about the physical layout of the network; he just accesses a printer and uses it. From the user's perspective, this simplicity is exactly what AD is all about.*

Network administrators, on the other hand, need to consider the physical path between resources when designing their networks. Within Active Directory, the physical nature of the LAN is registered by defining *sites*. A site is a grouping of one or more Transmission Control Protocol/Internet Protocol (TCP/IP) subnets. Sites are defined to control two types of traffic generated on the network:

Logon Traffic   Every time a user logs on to the network, Windows 2000/Windows Server 2003 attempts to find a domain controller in the same site as the workstation.

Replication Traffic   The act of updating domain controllers with changes to the database is known as *replication*. Sites can be used to control how and when this traffic will be generated on the network. (We'll discuss replication in detail later in this chapter.)

TIP   The subnets defined within a single site should be connected by high-speed, reliable links. The bottom line is that LAN lines (as opposed to WAN links) should connect all resources within a site. Any resources that connect through a slow or unreliable link should be defined as separate sites.

Sites are not associated with the Active Directory namespace in any way, so a site can contain servers from multiple domains, and the servers from a single domain can be spread out among multiple sites.

Determining Site Boundaries

As we've already discussed, sites should reflect the structure of your network. Each site should correspond to an area sharing fast network links. Note, however, that there is also another factor to consider— the mutual dependency between the site design and the number and placement of domain controllers.

NOTE   To review, sites are used to control two types of traffic: logon traffic and directory replication traffic. All of this traffic is specific to domain controllers. Users generate logon traffic as they attach and authenticate to the network through a domain controller. Replication is the process of updating changes to the directory database between the copies stored on multiple domain controllers. In other words, sites exist to control the traffic to and from domain controllers. Therefore, you should decide on the placement of your domain controllers as you design your site boundaries.

For each of your business locations, you will need to determine whether a domain controller is necessary. Numerous factors will determine your final decision. Table 13.1 lists the tradeoffs involved in having no domain controller at a location.

TABLE 13.1: No Domain Controller at a Location

ADVANTAGES	DISADVANTAGES
No AD database replication traffic to and from the location.	Since there is no local domain controller, all logon traffic has to cross whatever links exist to a location with a domain controller.
No need to define a site for the location.	Slower logons and authentication to network resources.
No remote domain controllers to manage.	If all domain controllers are in a single location, you have a single point of physical failure (a natural disaster or even a telephone outage could cut all users off from network resources).

Table 13.2 outlines some of the tradeoffs of having a domain controller at a location.

TABLE 13.2: PLACING A DOMAIN CONTROLLER AT A LOCATION

ADVANTAGES	DISADVANTAGES
Logon traffic does not cross the WAN link.	Replication traffic crosses the WAN link.
User logons are faster.	Multiple locations are needed, which might require on-site management.

When you are deciding on domain controller placement, the two most important factors to consider are the following:

◆ User convenience

◆ Available bandwidth

In most cases, users will see the best performance if they are authenticating through a local domain controller. A lack of available bandwidth, however, could result in periods where replication traffic floods the WAN link, slowing down access to resources on the other side of that link.

TIP *When it's all said and done, domain controller placement starts out as a judgment call. I usually err on the side of user convenience.*

Placing a server at a site provides two big benefits:

◆ The logon process is much faster, since users are not crossing the WAN link for authentication.

◆ Placing a domain controller at a site gives me another server to play with. If the link has limited bandwidth, this might provide an opportunity to move resources or services to the new server (and thus local to the users), reducing the WAN traffic.

BANDWIDTH CONSIDERATIONS

Available bandwidth will often be the determining factor in domain controller placement, so we should take the time to properly define the phrase. *Available bandwidth* refers to the amount of throughput that is left after normal traffic has been taken into account. Many administrators assume that the fastest line will always have the most available bandwidth. This is not always the case. The "fastest" line is often also the most used line.

Think of it this way: Most companies will not purchase more bandwidth than necessary. If a company leases a fast T1 line, it is usually because they plan on using the link for large amounts of traffic. While the line might have a faster overall rating, it is also more likely to be near saturation (without the addition of logon or replication traffic). A smaller pipe, such as a 256Kbps leased line, might actually have more bandwidth available.

The only way, therefore, to accurately determine the amount of available bandwidth on a link is to analyze traffic with a protocol analyzer, such as Microsoft Network Monitor. You will need to analyze the traffic on each segment over a period of time. This period should include peak-usage and nonbusiness hours so that you have a fairly good idea of how the link is utilized at different times of the day. Later in this chapter, we will discuss the ability to schedule replication traffic. If you know when a line usually has available bandwidth, you can easily determine the replication schedule that will be most efficient for your environment.

Along with the amount of available bandwidth, you will have to consider the cost of transmission on each link. Some telecommunications companies charge for the amount of data transmitted. If this is the case, even though a link might have plenty of bandwidth available, you might not want to add traffic to the line.

Analyzing traffic patterns and balancing use versus cost is one of the most challenging tasks facing network administrators. The cost structure for many WAN lines is confusing at best (and downright misleading at worst). Spending some time considering these factors can prevent unnecessary costs in the future—or worse, a complete redesign of your structure to control those costs.

Domain Controller Placement Strategies

There are three main strategies you can use when planning for the placement of domain controllers:

◆ Placement to control logon traffic

◆ Placement to control replication traffic

◆ Placement to provide a balance between replication and logon traffic

Each type of design has its advantages and disadvantages. You should analyze each network in order to choose the correct placement strategies for its unique properties.

PLACEMENT TO CONTROL LOGON TRAFFIC

One reason to create sites is to control logon traffic on the network. When a user logs on to the network, a workstation will attempt to find a domain controller in its local site. To determine this, the workstation compares its own TCP/IP address and subnet mask against those that define sites within the Active Directory database. If a primary focus of an organization is ensuring fast and reliable user logon, then the site boundaries should match the physical boundaries of each location, as shown in Figure 13.3.

NOTE   *We'll discuss the mechanics and objects pertaining to sites a little later in this chapter.*

FIGURE 13.3

Location-based boundaries

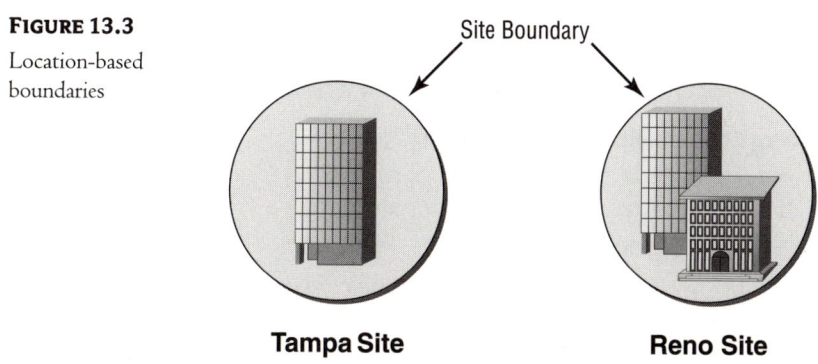

Tampa Site   Reno Site

If, however, a company would like more control over which domain controllers are used by each user to log on, multiple sites can be created in a single physical location, as you can see in Figure 13.4. You should place each workstation in a site that contains the domain controllers the workstation should use during the logon process.

FIGURE 13.4

Controlling domain controller overhead

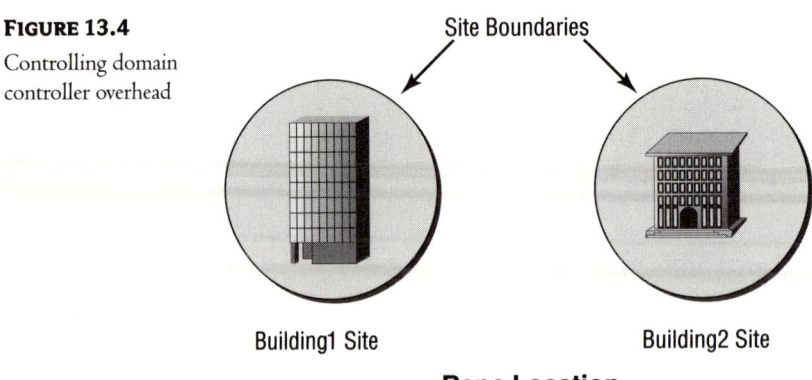

Site Boundaries

Building1 Site

Building2 Site

Reno Location

Keep in mind, however, that there is one potential problem with having multiple sites defined for a single location. In the event that a domain controller from the same site is not available, the workstation will be forced to search for a domain controller from another site. This search, however, does not take into consideration physical proximity, so it is conceivable that a user would be sent to a domain controller that is across a WAN link (even though there might be a local server available).

NOTE This is not as big a deal as it sounds. While the login and authentication process will be slower than normal, the user will still be able to access the network resources that they need. Since most users will access resources that are local to them, most functions will not be affected. In other words, it'll take a little longer to be authenticated, but everything else should function normally.

While this could degrade performance during the logon process, the workstation will correct the problem as soon as possible. Every so often, the workstation will check to see if a domain controller from its own site has become available. If so, all future authentication requests will be routed to that local server.

PLACEMENT TO CONTROL REPLICATION TRAFFIC

The other reason to create an AD site is to control replication traffic. You do not have as much control over replication within a site, also known as *intra-site replication*, as you have over the replication traffic between two sites, also known as *inter-site replication*. Inter-site replication offers the following advantages:

◆ Control over when replication occurs. Replication occurs on a schedule, as long as the physical link is available.

♦ Control over the network transport that is used.

♦ Compression of replication traffic (down to 10 to 12 percent of the original volume).

Windows Server 2003 does its best to reduce the amount of traffic generated by the replication process. Changes are replicated at the attribute level; in other words, if a user's telephone number is changed, only the *new* information is replicated to other domain controllers (as opposed to the entire record for that user object). In case of a group membership attribute, the replication mechanism is even more granular.

Windows 2000 treats this attribute as a single replication unit. This unnecessarily causes a large amount of traffic when adding a user or removing one from a large group (since the full list of its members have to be replicated). In addition, this could lead to replication conflicts, if two administrators independently update membership of the same group before the replication completes. Both problems are resolved in Windows Server 2003, since changes are now replicated on the group member level.

Data transferred is compressed (as long as the compression offers noticeable gains, which applies to data larger than 32KB, decreasing traffic to approximately 10 to 12 percent of the original volume.

NOTE *The main disadvantage of compression is its negative impact on the domain controller's performance. If the bandwidth between two sites is sufficient and a high CPU-utilization level becomes a problem, you can disable compression for the domain controllers involved in replication.*

Ultimately, though, the amount of traffic that is generated by the replication process depends on the number of changes made to the database. Companies that experience constant growth, numerous reorganizations, or just plain old changes will generate more traffic than companies that experience little change.

PLACEMENT TO PROVIDE A BALANCE BETWEEN REPLICATION AND LOGON TRAFFIC

Neither a design based upon optimization for replication traffic nor a design that solely reflects controlling logon traffic will be the perfect solution for most environments. In most cases, you will need to design the site boundaries with both considerations in mind. For each location in your intranet, you will need to analyze the links to other locations and decide (on an individual basis) whether each link should support logon or replication traffic.

The Default Placement

When you install Active Directory for the first time within a Windows 2000/Windows Server 2003 environment, a default site is created. This first site is named `Default-First-Site-Name`. You can rename this site later using the Active Directory Sites and Services tool. Until additional sites are created, all domain controllers are placed in the default site.

All new domain controllers are placed in the site that applies to them at the time of installation. In other words, during the installation process, the AD Installation Wizard searches the AD database for a site that includes the subnet upon which the server is placed. The new domain controller is placed within this site. Figure 13.5 demonstrates this principle. The new domain controller, FS1, is created in the Reno office. AD contains a site definition that describes the Reno site as all TCP/IP subnets that exist in the Reno network. Since the server is installed with an IP address that is defined as part of the Reno site, the server is placed within the Reno site.

FIGURE 13.5

Placing a domain controller

Later, if you were to move the FS1 server shown in Figure 13.5 to somewhere in the Tampa location, you would need to redefine the site property of the server. If you don't, the server will still think it is a part of the site defined in Reno and will replicate with the Reno servers (across that expensive and slow WAN link).

WARNING   *Moving a server from one site to another is easy, but be careful when you do it. Placing a server from one site within the defined boundaries of another site could result in unnecessary logon or replication traffic.*

Implementing Active Directory Sites

All information contained in the Active Directory database is divided into separate areas called *naming contexts*. The *schema naming context* contains the definition of all Active Directory objects—this is what makes the Active Directory a self-describing database. The *domain naming context* contains the objects that form the logical structure of an Active Directory domain—such as users, computers, and organizational units—which are part of the AD namespace. Sites are separate from this namespace and form their own structure stored in the *configuration naming context*. This context (just like the schema naming context) contains objects that are not specific to any particular domain, but shared by all domains in the forest.

If you look at the data stored in Active Directory for each site, you will probably find its format rather cryptic. Fortunately, you can access it using the friendly interface of the Active Directory Sites and Services snap-in (which can be run directly from the Administrative Tools menu or added to a custom Microsoft Management Console).

Before you start creating Active Directory sites, you need to get familiar with the meaning and characteristics of the following types of objects:

- Sites
- Subnets
- Site links
- Connections
- Site link bridges

We already discussed the concept of sites and subnets. To review, a site is a collection of one or more IP subnets, sharing fast network connections. Typically, sites correspond to physical locations (simply because computers sharing physical proximity are more likely to be connected with fast network connections).

Site links represent physical connections between sites used for replication. Without them, sites could not communicate. Active Directory contains the default site link, called `DEFAULTIPSITELINK`, which is created automatically when the first domain in the forest is installed. This link is assigned to the `Default-First-Site-Name` site. Whenever you create a new site, you can associate it with an existing site link or a newly created one. Your choice will depend on the underlying physical connections. For example, a single WAN backbone shared by multiple offices is best represented by a single site link. However, if each of the connections to these offices has different bandwidth or availability, you should create a separate site link for each. Each site link you create will link at least two sites, and each site you create will be associated with at least one link.

Each site link is assigned the IP or SMTP transport protocol, a cost, a replication frequency, and an availability schedule. All these parameters should reflect the characteristics of the physical network connection—we will cover this in detail soon.

Site links and their parameters are used when inter-site connection objects are created. The *inter-site connection object* represents a one-way replication path between two domain controllers, created on top of an existing site link (connections can use multiple, adjacent site links if site link bridging is enabled—more about this next). You can create connections manually, but typically it is better and more convenient to rely on the built-in Windows mechanism for their creation. This is done by the process called the Knowledge Consistency Checker (KCC), which runs by default on all Windows 2000/Windows Server 2003 domain controllers. The KCC analyzes all existing site links and creates inter-site connection objects. The resulting replication path forms a spanning tree (which prevents replication loops) with the lowest possible cost (calculated by adding costs of individual site links).

NOTE *Connection objects are also created between domain controllers within each site, but this is not relevant to our discussion.*

You should be able to see by now that in a multisite environment, site links form their own topology, which mirror (or at least *should* mirror) the network topology. The site link topology, in turn, is used by the KCC to create the topology of inter-site connections, used by Active Directory inter-site replication traffic.

Now, let's consider a situation in which we have three sites—A, B, and C—with one domain controller from the same domain in each (DC1, DC2, and DC3). We've created two site links—AB and BC—between the sites A and B, and B and C, respectively. We know that connection objects can be created between DC1 and DC2, and between DC2 and DC3, but can they also be created between DC1 and DC3? The answer to this question depends on whether site link bridging is enabled.

Site link bridging allows the creation of connections objects between two domain controllers residing in two sites without a direct site link between them (simply by traversing intermediate site links). Without site link bridging, replication could never take place directly between DC1 and DC3. This would create a replication problem if DC2 became unavailable.

There are two ways of enabling site link bridging:

◆ For all site links using specific transport (IP or SMTP)

◆ For two or more adjacent site links

I will describe both methods later in this chapter.

Site link bridging is sometimes compared to routing, since it resembles the process of passing traffic from one subnet (equivalent in this comparison to a site link) to another. Microsoft also refers to this functionality as *site link transitivity*.

Creating Sites

To create a site, use the Active Directory Sites and Services tool, found in the Administrative Tools group of your Start menu. You can see this tool in Figure 13.6.

FIGURE 13.6

Active Directory Sites and Services tool

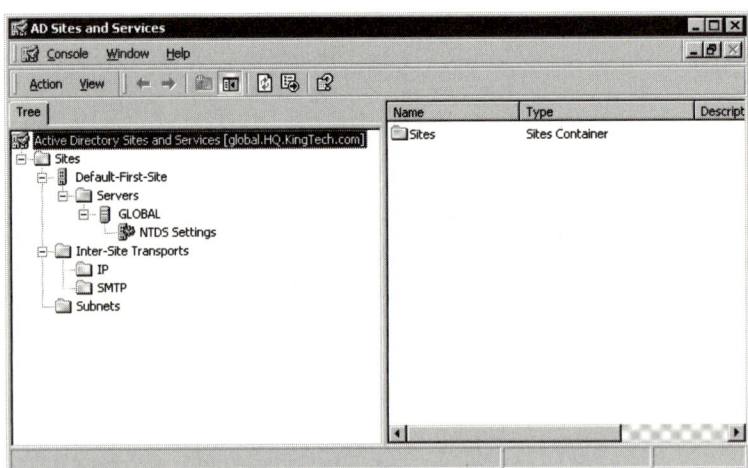

Highlight the Sites folder, right-click, and choose New Site. The New Object – Site dialog box appears, as shown in Figure 13.7.

In the Name box, enter a name that describes this site. The name should adequately describe the purpose of the site, such as the name of the physical location or the department whose servers will be a member. You also need to select a site link object that will be used by this site.

Once you have created a site, you can move servers into it by right-clicking the server and choosing Move. Just select the appropriate site from the list in the Move Server dialog box, as shown in Figure 13.8.

FIGURE 13.7

New Object – Site

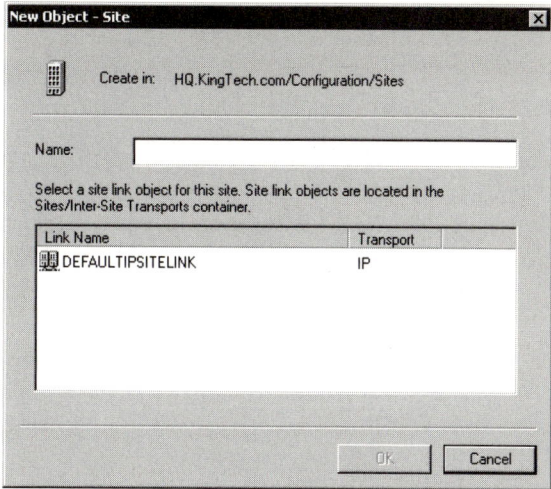

FIGURE 13.8

Moving a server
to a new site

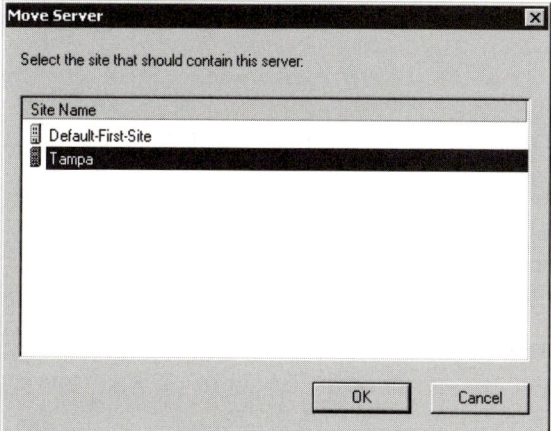

Creating Subnets

The next step in configuring a site environment is to define subnets. An AD subnet is equivalent to a TCP/IP subnet. AD subnets are created using the Active Directory Sites and Services tool. To create a subnet, right-click the subnet's container and choose New ➢ Subnet. The New Object – Subnet dialog box appears, as shown in Figure 13.9.

FIGURE 13.9

New Object –
Subnet

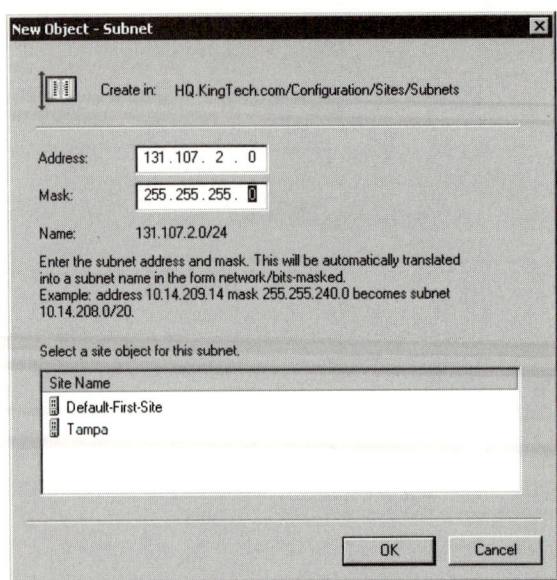

The name is made up of the IP address subnet and subnet mask for the physical network that the AD subnet will represent. If, for instance, your IP subnet were 131.107.2.0 with a subnet mask of 255.255.255.0, the name of the AD subnet would be 131.107.2.0/24. The 24 represents the number of bits being masked by the subnet mask.

NOTE *Subnet masking is a complex concept that is well beyond the scope of this book. For more information, read* TCP/IP JumpStart: Internet Protocol Basics *(2nd Edition) by Andrew Blank (Sybex, 2002) and* Windows® XP Power Tools *by Jim Boyce (Sybex, 2002).*

A computer with multiple network interface cards (also known as a *multihomed* computer) and multiple IP addresses can belong to only one site. It is recommended that all subnets attached to a multihomed computer be in the same AD site.

Associating Subnets with Sites

The next step is to associate your subnets with sites. Associating a subnet with a site tells AD which physical networks are represented by the site. If you don't select a site for the subnet, you will not be able to complete creation of the subnet. Select the appropriate site from the same New Object – Subnet dialog box shown in Figure 13.9.

If you want to change the site assignment after the subnet object has been created, access the subnet's properties. You will see the dialog box shown in Figure 13.10.

FIGURE 13.10

Properties of
a subnet

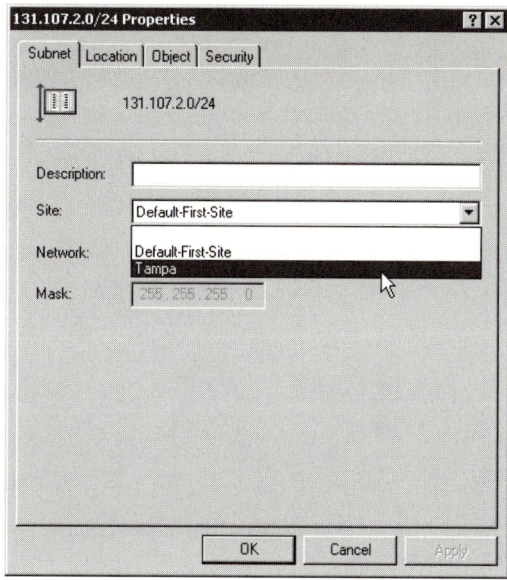

In the Description box, enter a description of the subnet, such as the physical location. In the Site list box, select the site with which you wish to associate this subnet. Click OK when finished.

Creating Site Links

So far we have created the sites and defined the scope of each site, listing which IP subnets make up our sites. The next step in the site configuration process is to configure the connections between our sites. The physical connections between sites are represented within the AD database by site link objects. There are four components to each site link:

Transport   The networking technology used to transfer the replication traffic.

Sites   The sites that the site link connects.

Cost   A value used to determine how this site link compares to others, in terms of speed, reliability, monetary charges, etc. This value is used when redundant links are available.

Schedule   The times and frequency at which the replication will occur.

Site links and their components are used when determining the path and method to transfer replication traffic. As such, a well-thought-out plan can greatly reduce congestion on wide area connections. The first step is to plan your site boundaries to minimize network traffic; the next step is to create your site links to control that traffic.

You can connect a site to other sites using any number of site links. These site links can be established over many different networking technologies, such as T1 lines, dial-up links, or ATM. Some technologies provide a "cloud" in which a single hop connects any two physical locations. This concept is shown in Figure 13.11. In this type of environment, a single site link to the cloud provides replication connections to multiple locations.

FIGURE 13.11

Multiple sites connected through a single site link

ATM Network

Tampa

Minneapolis

Reno

HOW WILL DATA BE TRANSFERRED?

When you create a site link, you will have to determine the method of data transfer. There are two options available:

IP Uses Remote Procedure Calls (RPCs) over TCP/IP to transfer data.

Simple Mail Transfer Protocol (SMTP) All replication traffic is converted to e-mail messages to send between sites.

For both types of transports, compression is applied as a means of reducing the volume of data sent over the network link.

Site links can connect multiple AD sites. This is depicted in Figure 13.12. If a company has three sites—X, Y, and Z—a single site link object can be configured to allow replication between all of them. This makes sense if the physical connection joining these three sites is the same in terms of speed, cost, and availability. If this is not the case, you should create separate site links for each and configure, for each, appropriate cost and schedule values.

FIGURE 13.12

Multiple connections with a single site link object

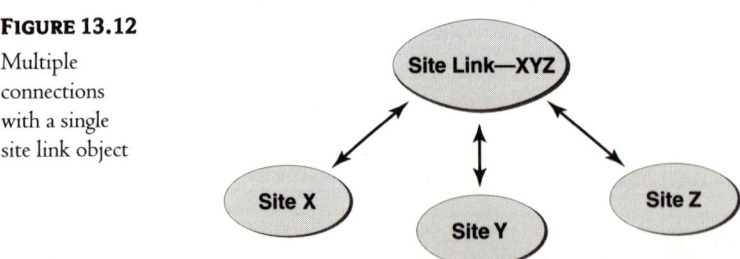

Site Link—XYZ

Site X

Site Y

Site Z

SITE LINK COSTS

A site link's *cost* represents how expensive an organization considers the network connection between two sites that the site link is connecting. Consider the environment presented in Figure 13.12. We have three sites—X, Y, and Z—connected by a single site link object; let's name it XYZ. If that site link is given a cost of 5, it means that the cost of sending traffic between any of the sites (X–Y, X–Z, Y–Z, Y–X, Z–X, Z–Y) is 5. Higher costs represent more expensive connections. If there are two site links available between two sites, the lowest cost site link will be chosen.

Now, consider the environment depicted in Figure 13.13. Sites A and B are connected through a site link named AB with a cost of 5. Sites B and C are connected through a site link named BC with a cost of 3. However, this does not mean that traffic can be routed from Site A to Site C with a cost of 8 (or at any cost). Another way to say this is that site link connections are *nontransitive* in nature. We will revisit this example shortly and discuss the ways to provide link transitivity.

FIGURE 13.13

Site link costs

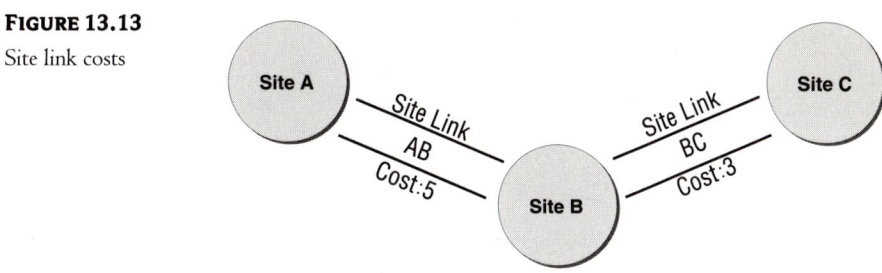

SITE LINK SCHEDULES

The site link schedule specifies the replication interval and the times during which the site link is available. Two sites, for instance, connected by a dial-up connection, might be configured to use a site link with a schedule set so that it is only available during evenings and weekends. This configuration could reduce communication costs.

SETTING UP A SITE LINK

Using the Active Directory Sites and Services tool, double-click the site's container, then double-click Inter-Site Transports. The available transports will appear within the Inter-Site Transports container, as shown in Figure 13.14.

FIGURE 13.14

Inter-Site Transports

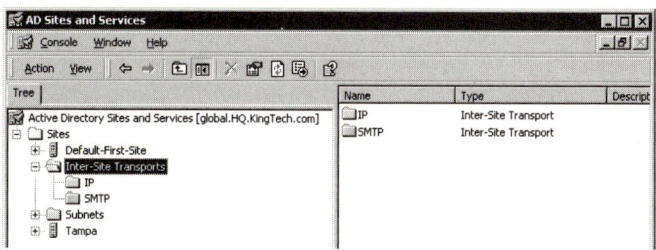

Right-click the transport to be used, and then click New Site Link. You will be presented with the New Object – Site Link dialog box, as shown in Figure 13.15.

FIGURE 13.15

New Object – Site Link

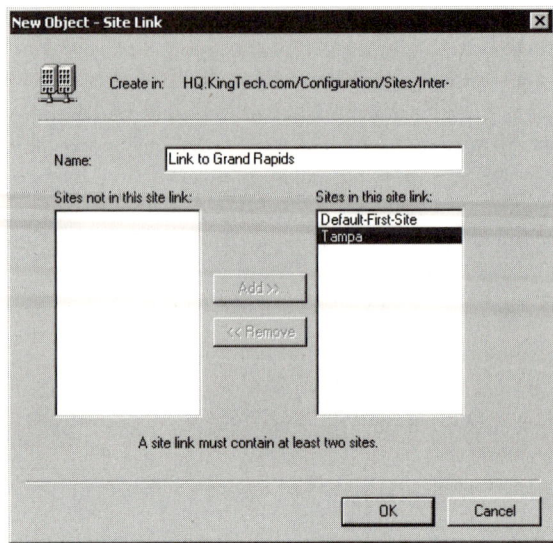

You must provide a name for the site link and a list of all sites that it should connect (at least two). The default settings for a site link object are a cost of 100 and a replication schedule set to replicate every three hours. To change either setting, right-click the site link object and select Properties.

Site Link Bridges

As we discussed earlier, a *site link bridge* is a transitive set of adjacent site links, all of which can communicate using a common transport. Since site links are inherently nontransitive, the only way to allow transitivity between them is to use site link bridging. This, in turn, allows the creation of connection objects between nonadjacent sites. One of the benefits is the increased level of fault tolerance (in case domain controllers in the intermediate site become unavailable). Another benefit is easier administration of inter-site connections, since creating and managing connections is handled automatically by the KCC. By enabling bridging for some site links and disabling it for others, you can selectively pick sites that will be able to communicate directly. Note that site link bridging is enabled by default for all site links for both transport protocols (IP and SMTP).

The main disadvantage of enabling site link bridging is the additional load placed on the KCC, since the number of possible inter-site connections that must taken into consideration increases.

To recall, there are two methods of enabling site link bridging:

◆ For all site links using specific transport (IP or SMTP)

◆ For two or more adjacent site links

To enable site link bridging for all site links using a specific transport, select the check box labeled Bridge All Site Links on the General tab of the protocol's Properties dialog box. This is, by default, enabled for both transports.

To enable site link bridging for specific site links only, disable the Bridge All Site Links setting and create a Site Link Bridge object instead. While this might create some administrative overhead, it will allow you to customize your replication topology and will have a reduced impact on the KCC.

Earlier we looked at an environment made up of three sites—A, B, and C—connected by two site links:

◆ AB (cost 5)

◆ BC (cost 3)

In a nontransitive environment, replication traffic is not routed between sites A and C. To remedy this, the site link bridge containing the site links AB and BC can be used. Once the bridge is in place, direct replication can occur between sites A and C with a cost of 8 (the cost of each site link involved in the transfer), as shown in Figure 13.16.

FIGURE 13.16

Site link bridge

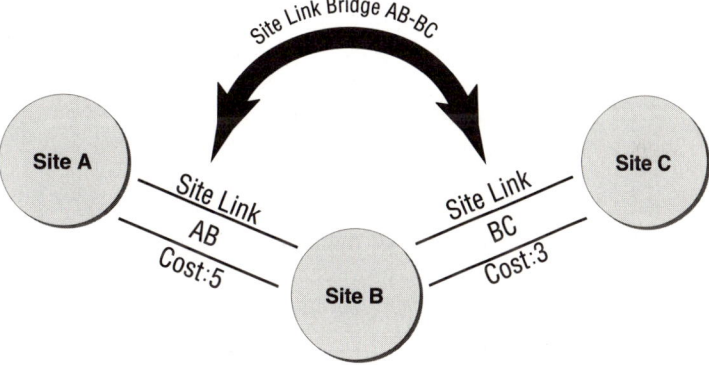

To create a site link bridge, follow these steps:

1. In the Active Directory Sites and Services tool, click the Sites container to expand it.

2. Double-click the Inter-Site Transports object.

3. Right-click the transport to be used and choose New Site Link Bridge. The New Object – (Site Link Bridge) dialog box appears, as shown in Figure 13.17.

FIGURE 13.17

New Object – (Site Link Bridge)

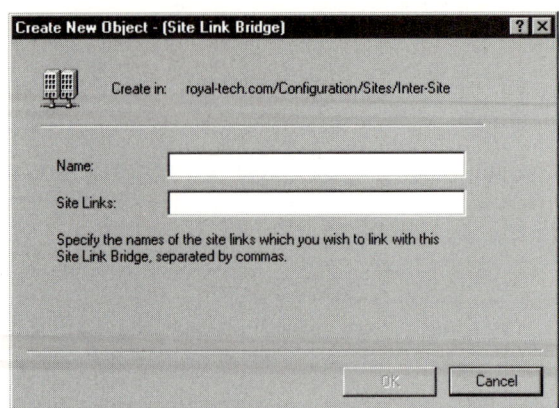

4. Give the bridge a descriptive name, and choose which site links are to be included in the bridge.

Site link bridges can reduce some of the management overhead involved in linking sites. We *could* have created another site link between sites A and C, thus negating a need for a site link bridge. Bridges reduce the effort necessary when connecting sites in a large environment.

Connection Objects

We also discussed connection objects, which represent a one-way replication path from one domain controller to another domain controller. In other words, connection objects define the two end points for replication traffic.

As you know by now, the KCC automatically creates connection objects. Although connection objects can also be created manually, this has a few drawbacks:

- Creating and maintaining connection objects manually introduces administrative overhead.

- The KCC continuously monitors existing connections and creates new ones in case a domain controller fails. This functionality, however, is available only for automatically created connections. By replacing automatic connections with manual ones, you eliminate the fault tolerance provided by the KCC.

In most cases, the criteria used by the KCC to create connection objects will suffice. In other words, in most cases, network admins will not need to manually create or configure connection objects; this work will be done automatically by the KCC. (More on the KCC later.)

Sometimes, however, creating manual connections is preferred or even required. For example, if sites are separated by a firewall, then connections often need to be restricted to specific domain controllers only. Another reason, although less likely with Windows Server 2003 domain controllers, is performance. In Windows 2000 deployments with a large number of sites, it is typical for the KCC process to consume a significant amount of CPU and memory. Fortunately, KCC implementation has been greatly improved in Windows Server 2003, which makes it possible to rely on automatically created connection objects in environments with up to 5,000 sites.

To create a connection object manually, perform the following steps:

1. In the Active Directory Sites and Services tool, click the Sites container to expand it.

2. Double-click the site where the domain controller *to* which the connection should be created resides.

3. Expand the Servers container, double-click the node representing the domain controller, and right-click the node labeled NTDS Settings.

4. Select New Active Directory Connection from the menu. This displays the Find Domain Controller dialog box.

5. Select the domain controller *from* which the replication traffic will be flowing. This will open the New Object – Connection dialog box.

6. Type in the name that appropriately describes the connection (by default, it is the name of the domain controller you selected).

NOTE *When creating a connection object manually, it is critical to remember that this object represents a one-direction, inbound replication path. For example, to configure manual replication between two domain controllers DC1 and DC2, you need to create two connection objects: the first one from DC2 to DC1 on DC1 and the other one from DC1 to DC2 on DC2.*

After the connection object is created, you can modify its properties using the connection's Properties dialog box, shown in the Figure 13.18.

FIGURE 13.18

The Properties dialog box for the Global connection

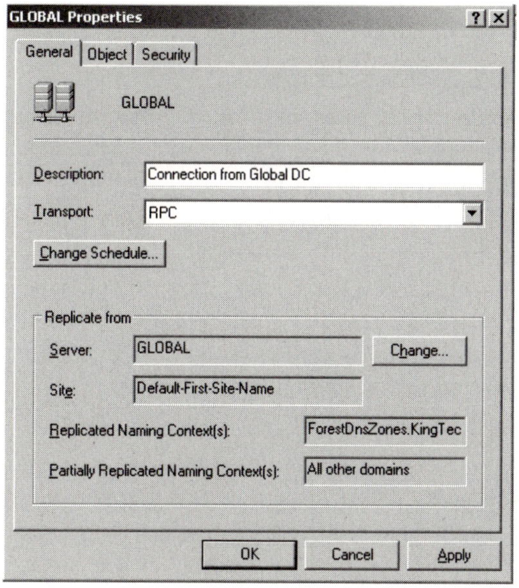

Understanding Replication

Now that we have looked at the various configuration issues involved in controlling replication traffic, we should engage in a detailed discussion of that traffic. Each Windows domain typically has multiple servers that act as domain controllers. In Windows 2000/Windows Server 2003, each domain controller is capable of making changes to the database containing accounts of domain users and computers. Earlier versions of NT were configured in a *single-master environment*. The primary domain controller (PDC) maintained and managed the master copy of the domain database and was in charge of replicating changes to the backup domain controllers (BDCs) of its domain. In a single-master environment, the master (in our case, the PDC) is a single point of failure. If for some reason the PDC is unavailable, no changes can be made to the database.

In Windows 2000/Windows Server 2003 domains, each domain controller holds a complete copy of the AD directory for its own domain. In this respect, it is much like earlier versions. The difference, however, is that each Windows 2000/Windows Server 2003 domain controller can accept and make changes to the database and then replicate those changes to other domain controllers. An environment like this, where multiple computers are responsible for managing changes, is known as a *multiple-master environment*. A multiple-master environment offers numerous advantages over the old single-master configuration. Here are some of those advantages:

◆ There is no single point of failure. Since every domain controller can accept changes to the database, no domain controller is *critical* to the process.

◆ Domain controllers that can accept changes to the database can be distributed throughout the physical network. This allows administrators to make changes on a local computer and let a background process (replication) ensure that those changes are updated on all other domain controllers in a timely and efficient manner.

Replication vs. Synchronization

The first important concept to understand when looking at AD updates is the difference between replication and synchronization. These two terms are often used interchangeably in the industry. Microsoft has a specific definition for each.

REPLICATION

Directory *replication* is the process that takes place when one Windows 2000/Windows Server 2003 domain controller updates another with changes to the AD database. Replication relies on a homogeneous environment: all domain controllers involved must be Windows 2000/Windows Server 2003 servers and have identical schemas, and there must be a high level of trust between the servers involved.

SYNCHRONIZATION

Directory *synchronization* occurs between dissimilar implementations of directory services. Through synchronization, a change made in any one implementation is automatically reflected in all related information stored in the others. For example, you might want to synchronize the following:

◆ Windows Active Directory and Novell Directory Services (NDS) databases. This way, you can create and manage accounts created in NDS using Microsoft Administrative Tools.

◆ Active Directory databases and Microsoft Exchange 5.5 Server directory services.

A number of directory synchronization products are available from both Microsoft and third-party vendors. You can manage our two examples with Microsoft Services for NetWare and Active Directory Connector (included with Exchange 2000).

Microsoft's recommended synchronization solution is Microsoft Metadirectory Services (MMS). MMS offers out-of-the-box support for a large number of different directory services, e-mail, application, and database systems, and it is extensible, which means that other, currently not supported types of repositories can be included in the future. MMS is offered through Microsoft Consulting Services and provides a unified interface to any type of information stored in all underlying systems. MMS uses management agents to connect to and synchronize information from all different sources.

Types of Replication

There are two basic types of replication in a Windows 2000/Windows Server 2003 environment:

◆ *Intra-site* replication occurs between domain controllers within a site.

◆ *Inter-site* replication occurs between domain controllers in different sites.

When planning your site structure and replication strategy, it is important to understand the methods used for each type of replication traffic.

INTRA-SITE REPLICATION

As we already discussed, intra-site replication involves domain controllers from the same site. These computers use high-speed, synchronous RPCs to perform the replication process.

Within a site, the KCC generates a *ring topology* for replication among the domain controllers within the site, as shown in Figure 13.19. This ring topology defines the path through which changes will flow within the site. Any changes will follow the ring until all domain controllers have received them.

NOTE   *Creating a ring topology ensures that there are two paths that changes can follow from one domain controller to another (either direction on the ring).*

FIGURE 13.19

Ring topology for replication

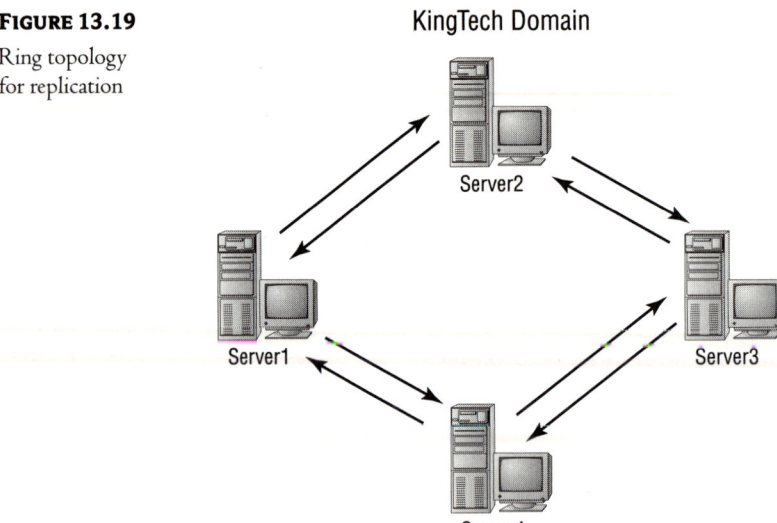

The KCC will also configure the ring so that there are no more than three hops between any two domain controllers from the same domain within the site. On occasion, this will call for the creation of multiple rings, as you can see in Figure 13.20.

FIGURE 13.20

The three-hop rule of intra-site replication

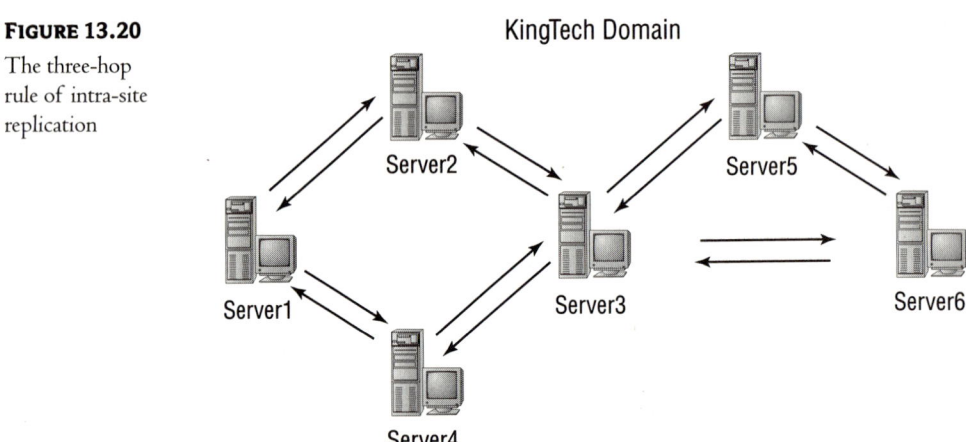

The KCC periodically analyzes the replication topology within a site to ensure efficiency. If a domain controller has been added or removed, the KCC will reconfigure the ring for optimum efficiency.

INTER-SITE REPLICATION

Inter-site replication occurs between domain controllers in different sites. If an environment has only one site, all replication will be intra-site. The biggest drawback to inter-site communication is that it is not automatic. It must be configured manually, as you saw earlier in this chapter.

TIP *Inter-site replication is the best choice if the traffic must cross a slower Internet link.*

Inter-site replication can be configured to use either low-speed, synchronous RPCs over TCP/IP or asynchronous SMTP transport.

NOTE *RPCs over TCP/IP for inter-site replication is referred to as IP in the Active Directory Sites and Services interface. Microsoft chose this rather misleading naming convention to distinguish it from the RPC over IP transport used for intra-site replication (which is referred to as RPC in Active Directory Sites and Services). RPC over TCP/IP (used for inter-site replication) permits synchronous communication over lower-speed links. Keep in mind this distinction if you decide to create manual connection objects, where you will need to specify which transport (RPC, IP, or SMTP) each connection will be using.*

The choice of the transport method depends on several factors:

Line Availability and Reliability   RPC is a synchronous protocol and requires simultaneous availability of both replication partners at the time the connection is established (according to the site link and connection schedules). SMTP, on the other hand, is asynchronous and ignores site link and connection schedules. Because of this, it is much better suited for communication over unreliable links (including the Internet).

Type of Replication Partners   SMTP replication cannot be used for replication of the domain naming context between domain controllers from the same domain. This means that if your domain spans multiple sites, you will be forced to use RPC over IP for replication. However, even if you use dial-up links, you can use properties of site links or connection objects to adjust the replication schedule with the times when dial-up connections are established. In extreme cases, you might need to modify your domain design and create a separate domain in the remote site.

Availability of Certificate Services   SMTP messages are digitally signed and encrypted (in order to increase security). This requires that you have installed Certificate Services in your domain.

Security   Due to the fact that SMTP replication is digitally signed and encrypted, it is inherently more secure. In addition, if the SMTP replication traffic needs to pass through a firewall, it is sufficient to open a single port only. RPC over IP does not offer the same level of security and requires multiple firewall ports to be opened. You can, however, use IPSec to encrypt RPC-based communication and carry it through a single firewall port.

Larger amounts of traffic are automatically compressed to reduce bandwidth utilization.

Behind the Scenes of Replication

We've discussed the objects, optimization techniques, and tools used for managing replication, but we have not yet looked at the actual process used by Windows 2000 and Windows Server 2003 domain controllers to update multiple copies of the Active Directory database. There is a very good reason for this: there really isn't much that we, as administrators, can do to influence the process, other than having a properly designed site structure.

With that said, though, most of us will have an academic interest in the replication process. Knowing how it works can also help you to design an efficient and stable site structure.

Update Sequence Numbers

When a change is made to the database stored on a domain controller, either through a user action or through replication from another domain controller, the domain controller assigns the change an *Update Sequence Number (USN)*. Each domain controller keeps its own USNs and increments the value for each change that occurs.

NOTE *With respect to a single domain controller, you can think of the USN as a change counter. Each domain controller will have different values for changes that occur on its copy of the directory database. These values are not synchronized between domain controllers within a domain.*

When the domain controller writes the change to the database, it also assigns the USN to the property that has changed. This is seen as a single transaction and will succeed or fail as a whole. In other words, AD will protect against a change being applied to the database without a corresponding USN also being recorded. This is an important feature, since USNs are used to determine which changes need to be replicated to other domain controllers. This process is depicted in Figure 13.21.

FIGURE 13.21

Applying a change to the database

Object—Bob

Property	USN	Value
Telephone number	6	555-1000

If the value of the telephone number property for user Bob needs to be changed, the domain controller will check its current value for the database USN. Let's say the last USN applied to a change was 3. When the system writes Bob's new telephone number to the database, it will increment the USN and write *both* the changed data and the USN to Bob's object. The system USN will also be incremented to reflect this new value (so that the next change to the database will receive a higher USN).

MULTIPLE USNs

There are a couple of new concepts to keep in mind here. First, notice that the domain controller is keeping track of the highest USN value that it has assigned to a change. (Microsoft doesn't really have a name for this value, but I'm going to call it the DCUSN for *Domain Controller USN*.) This allows the domain controller to increment the value for each change, ensuring that no duplicate USNs exist and that each USN is larger than the one before it. Second, each property of every object really stores two values: the actual data (like Bob's telephone number) and the USN assigned to the value the last time the attribute was changed.

NOTE   *Reread that last paragraph! Its two main concepts—a domain controller USN value that represents the highest USN assigned and the fact that every property stores the USN assigned at the time of change—are crucial to understanding how replication works.*

THE PROCESS OF REPLICATION

Now we can discuss the process of replicating Bob's new telephone number to all domain controllers within the domain. Each domain controller stores the DCUSN from all other domain controllers at the last time of replication, as shown in Figure 13.22.

FIGURE 13.22
DCUSN tables

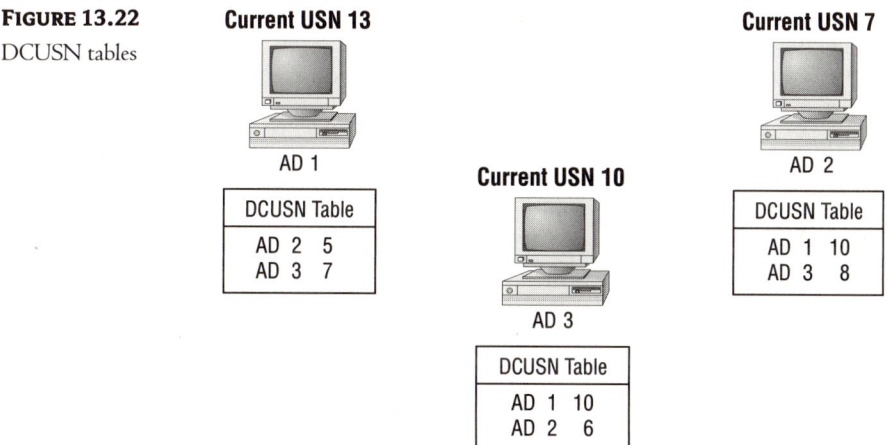

During the replication process, each domain controller sends its current DCUSN value to all of the other domain controllers in the domain. These servers compare this current value to the value that they have stored in their DCUSN table. If the current value is higher than the stored value, changes need to be replicated.

Look back at Figure 13.22. During replication, domain controller AD 2 will send its current DCUSN, which is 7, to both domain controllers AD 1 and AD 3. The last time that replication occurred with AD 1, the USN for AD 2 was 5. Since the current value is 7, AD 1 will request changes 6 and 7 from AD 2. AD 2 will search its database for the properties with these USN values and replicate them to AD 1, as shown in Figure 13.23.

FIGURE 13.23

Replication of specific changes

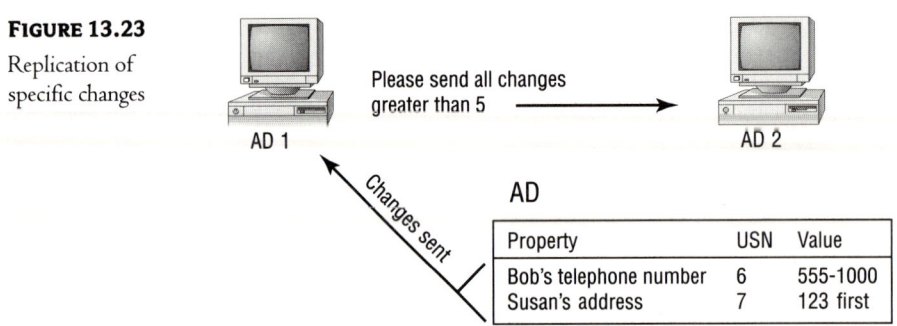

BENEFITS OF USING USNS

Using USN values to determine which changes to replicate eliminates the need for precise time stamps for changes (and for time to be synchronized among the domain controllers). Time stamps are also assigned to each change, however, for tie-breaking purposes. These time stamps decide which change should be implemented if a specific attribute was changed on two or more domain controllers during the replication interval. In that event, the change with the latest time stamp is placed in the database; any other changes are discarded.

Using USNs also simplifies the recovery process after a failure. When a domain controller comes back online after a recovery, it just needs to ask all of the other domain controllers for all changes with higher USN values than the last value stored in its DCUSN table. This is true even if the replication process is temporarily interrupted (a wide area link goes down, for instance). When communication is reestablished, the domain controller will request all changes with USNs greater than the last change applied to the database.

Propagation Dampening

As you saw earlier in this chapter, the KCC creates the replication topology for intra-site replication. The KCC creates a loop topology so that domain controllers have multiple paths for sending and receiving updates, as shown in Figure 13.24.

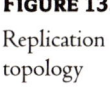

FIGURE 13.24

Replication
topology

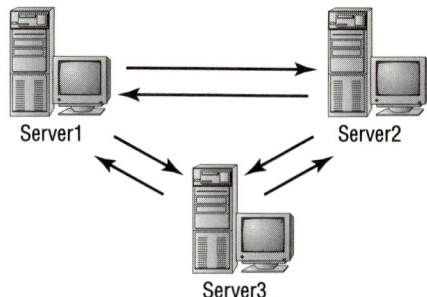

Server1   Server2

Server3

While a loop topology increases fault tolerance and can increase performance, it can also result in a domain controller receiving the same update from two different domain controllers. To prevent this, Active Directory uses a *propagation dampening* scheme. Propagation dampening is the process of preventing unnecessary replication of directory changes.

UP-TO-DATE VECTORS

While USNs can be used to determine which changes have been replicated from another domain controller, they do nothing to prevent changes from being replicated from multiple sources. This is why in addition to USNs, Windows 2000/Windows Server 2003 domain controllers also store *up-to-date vectors*. An up-to-date vector identifies the source of the *originating write* to a property. The originating write to any property identifies the source domain controller for the change. If a user changes his password, for instance, and that change is made to the copy of the directory stored on Server1, on Server1 the change would be considered an originating write; the change made there is directly related to some action performed by a user. In contrast, a *nonoriginating write* would be a change that was received through the replication process.

NOTE   *Another way to look at this is to consider the server where the change originates as the source of the originating writes.*

As an example, let's look at the process of updating a change in an environment with three domain controllers: Server1, Server2, and Server3. If a user changes her password at Server1, the server updates the value in the database and assigns that change the next incremental value for its USN. What is actually stored in the directory will contain this:

```
Password, Server1, USN-7
```

The USN value will follow the rules outlined earlier.

When this change is replicated to Server2, Server2 writes the change and increments its own USN. The actual record in the directory database remains the same as it was at Server1:

```
Password, Server1, USN-7
```

Server1 has also replicated this change to Server3. Server3 stores the same information, including the up-to-date vector information. When Server2 begins the replication process with Server3, Server3 will send its current USN value *and* all of its up-to-date vectors. Server2 compares the up-to-date vectors received from Server3 to its own. Server3 will not send any changes that have already been replicated to Server2.

In Short

Domain database replication between domain controllers in a Windows 2000/Windows Server 2003 environment is a complex process that generates traffic on the network. This traffic can be controlled (but not eliminated) through proper implementation of AD sites. The bottom line is that we can control the replication traffic generated between sites, but we cannot control the traffic generated to replicate the directory database within a site. Site boundaries define physical groupings of TCP/IP subnets and allow us to control how updates should be performed.

In the next chapter, you'll learn how to construct an infrastructure to best manage AD network traffic. You'll see how bandwidth, Active Directory site topology, replication, domain controllers, and the tools for managing network traffic figure into the mix for optimizing network transactions.

Part 3

Advanced Active Directory Administration

In this section you will learn how to:

- ◆ Manage Active Directory network traffic
- ◆ Design an Active Directory network
- ◆ Backup and Recover Active Directory
- ◆ Migrate to Active Directory
- ◆ Integrate Active Directory with Novell eDirectory

Chapter 14

Active Directory Network Traffic

ONE OF YOUR MAJOR concerns as the administrator of your organization's network is network traffic. Besides all the client activity traveling on the wire, your infrastructure must be capable of carrying server-to-server communications.

From an end-user perspective, Active Directory is a part of every transaction that requires access to a network resource. AD also coordinates communications between and among domain controllers. *Single-master operations* or *flexible single-master operations* (*FSMOs*) make designated domain controllers available to supervise server operations, and the Active Directory database must be distributed among domain controllers on a regular basis.

Domains, containers, and objects are logical structures. AD manages access to resources, wherever they are located. Your domain could span one or two or more physical locations, since AD has no awareness of physical space.

Modern Ethernet networks commonly transmit data at 10 or 100 megabits per second (Mbps), but WAN speeds can vary from 56 kilobits per second to 1Mbps. Users who log on to a local domain controller have a different experience than those who are working at a remote site. We need to factor bandwidth into our AD network design.

Featured in this chapter:

- ◆ Active Directory and bandwidth
- ◆ Active Directory naming contexts
- ◆ Global Catalog servers
- ◆ Active Directory sites
- ◆ The File Replication Service (FRS)
- ◆ Operations masters
- ◆ Database size
- ◆ Microsoft tools

Active Directory and Bandwidth

When domain controllers replicate AD information, they prefer to send updates rather than the entire file. The following circumstances require that AD transmit the entire database file. Be prepared for lots of network traffic when these events occur.

- Installation of a new domain controller in a site

- Installation of additional domain controllers in a site

- Resurrection of a domain controller that has been out of action for more than 60 days

- Installation of the first Global Catalog server in a site

- Installation of additional Global Catalog servers in a site

- Attribute changes for Global Catalogs

The three most significant factors affecting AD replication are:

- Database file size

- Frequency

- Bandwidth

How can you control these events to minimize the impact on your network? Actually, the purpose of adding a domain controller or Global Catalog is to speed up authentication and resource lookups, i.e., to improve the experience of your network users. Attribute changes on a Global Catalog server (more on Global Catalogs in a bit) are most likely the result of an application upgrade, such as Exchange. So, sometimes traffic jams are an unavoidable consequence of growth. This shouldn't deter you from upgrading your network if you are convinced you need it and your budget supports it. The best plan is to schedule these events for an evening or weekend. Pardon our dust...

Active Directory Naming Contexts

The Active Directory data warehouse is actually divided into partitions called *naming contexts* to improve administration, replication, performance, and fault tolerance. Although these portions may be distributed to different servers, the database appears to administrators and users as a single, seamless file. The AD naming contexts are:

- Domain naming context

- Configuration container

- Schema container

The *domain naming context* manages Active Directory information within a domain, including users, groups, computers, and organizational units. Domain administrators have full control but delegate authority to local managers. The *configuration container* contains forestwide information regarding domains, domain controllers, Global Catalog servers, sites, and replication topology. Enterprise administrators have full control, but domain administrators manage objects particular to each of their domains. *Schema* refers to rules for objects and attributes implemented across a forest. The schema container is controlled by the Schema administrators group.

The mechanism that distributes all this information to the domain controllers is called the *Knowledge Consistency Checker* (*KCC*), which monitors the network in 15-minute intervals. The KCC generates topologies for the domain and for the forest, based upon the number of domain controllers and physical site information.

Global Catalog Servers

Since a network can span more than one domain, Active Directory is responsible for distributing resource information for both domains and forests. The AD database contains data specific to a local domain. The *Global Catalog* is a resource of indexes for a forest. Global Catalogs are read-only, partial replicas of the AD databases of external domains, containing complete lists of objects, but not all their attributes. Global Catalogs replicate about 40 percent of the domain-naming context data of a domain.

When a user logs on to a network, the local domain controller provides her with access to resources in her domain according to her account's ACL. But, what if she needs to access a printer that's located on a different domain? Her request is sent to the nearest Global Catalog server, which allows her to search for that printer object and then checks her privileges to use it.

A Global Catalog is created automatically by DCPROMO for the first domain controller in a forest. One Global Catalog must exist in each forest, but there's no limit to how many additional catalogs can be created. Global Catalogs help to preserve bandwidth and provide security by localizing external domain information. The schema and configuration naming contexts are stored on Global Catalog servers.

The Global Catalog is required for logon to a multidomain network running in native or Windows Server 2003 mode, since it contains universal group membership information. If a Global Catalog server is not available, users other than domain administrators would not be able to log on. In a mixed-mode environment, however, logon would be successful even if a Global Catalog server were down.

WARNING *It's likely in the real world, however, that a domain controller housing a Global Catalog also functions as an operations master (see later in this chapter for details on this). Major difficulties would arise if such a server fails, since users would be blocked from accessing resources on an external domain, as well as (in the case of a PDC Emulator) authenticating passwords in their local domain.*

Creating a Global Catalog Server

Global Catalogs can be created on any domain controller with Active Directory Sites and Services. Locate a domain controller in the Server folder in its site. Right-click NTDS settings, select Properties, and then mark the Global Catalog check box as shown in Figure 14.1. Some time and several replication cycles may elapse before a new Global Catalog server is fully recognized in a forest.

FIGURE 14.1

Selecting the Global Catalog option

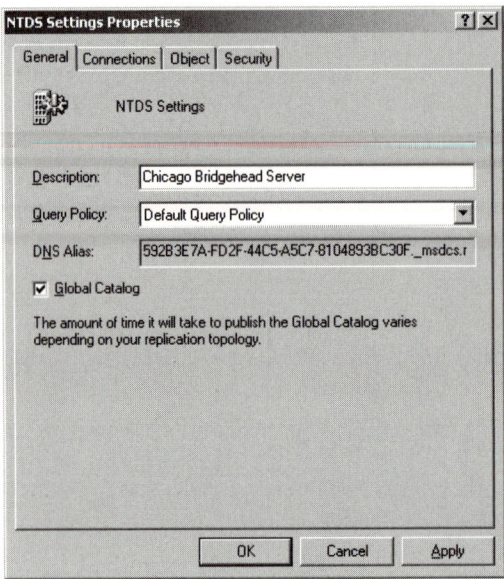

You can select which attributes will be replicated by the Global Catalog with the Schema Master console. You'll need to configure an MMC, since it's not automatically created by Windows. Here's the procedure:

1. Go to a command prompt.

2. Register `schmmgmt.dll` by typing **REGSVR32 schmmgmt.dll**.

3. Select Run at the Start menu and type MMC in the pop-up box.

4. Select Add/Remove Snap-in from the File menu, and then choose Add.

5. Select Active Directory Schema.

6. Select Save from the File menu, and name the MMC console.

Use the Schema Administrative Console to select attributes to replicate to the Global Catalog Server, as shown in Figure 14.2. Open up AD Schema in the left pane, then click Attributes to list and select an object in the details pane. As you can see in Figure 14.2, the homePhone attribute property is replicated in the Global Catalog by default. You can change any condition by clicking the appropriate check box.

FIGURE 14.2

Viewing Global Catalog attributes with the Schema Master MMC

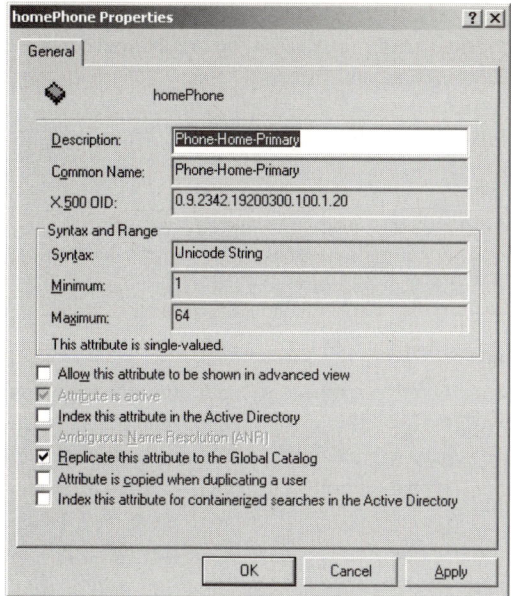

Active Directory Sites

Sites represent a geographical view of a network, as opposed to Active Directory's logical perspective. Sites provide a means to manage replication traffic for all three naming contexts. Microsoft defines a site as a group of computers that are "well-connected," using high-speed, reliable connections. This includes LANs, MANs, and WANs where bandwidth is at least 512Kbps. Segments between sites are usually WAN links. Sites are associated with one or more subnets, but a subnet can be contained in only one site. We create sites in order to:

- Manage replication routes
- Control replication traffic
- Direct clients to local domain controllers for logon
- Identify local network resources

Let's look at these four broad accountabilities in more detail in the following sections.

Sites and Replication

The replication process works differently in transmitting data within a site as opposed to between sites. The physical network topology is stored in the configuration partition of each domain controller in a forest. When a domain controller is added to a network, the Knowledge Consistency Checker automatically creates connection objects and builds a communications framework to facilitate the replication process.

Site creation directs clients to send their logon requests to a local domain controller, rather than attempt to authenticate across a relatively slow WAN link. Sites also help workstations to locate local DFS replicas, member servers, and printers.

NOTE *The* Distributed File System (DFS), *discussed later in this chapter, localizes access to files and folders stored on a server.*

Microsoft recommends that each site have at least one Global Catalog server to localize requests for network resources. For large networks, sites with more than 500 users should have more than one Global Catalog. Global Catalogs also make use of site connection objects to replicate their data.

Intra-Site Replication

Within a site, a domain controller waits five minutes after a change to its directory before notifying other domain controllers. Since bandwidth is not an issue, domain controllers can exchange data frequently. If no changes have occurred after six hours, it checks for updates anyway. These default time periods can be changed. Data is not compressed. Information is transmitted via Remote Procedure Calls (RPCs).

For up to seven domain controllers, the KCC automatically configures a bidirectional ring, as shown in Figure 14.3. Beyond that size, it will create a mesh to connect the servers to each other. Each domain controller contacts at least two other domain controllers, or replication partners. As conditions change, the KCC makes adjustments, assuming that all network paths are of equal bandwidth. Data is not compressed. We'll discuss taking control of this process in larger environments later in this chapter.

FIGURE 14.3

Ring topology for intra-site replication

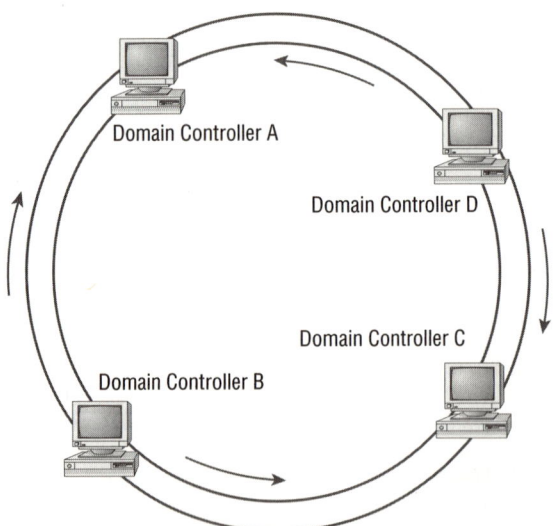

NOTE *Although you can make changes to connection objects within a site, it's not recommended. The KCC will not evaluate or change a manually created connection, and it will ignore any changes you make to KCC-generated objects when it updates its topology.*

Inter-Site Replication

Since connections between sites have limited bandwidth, we prefer to schedule replication to occur at specific times when network activity is low. Domain controllers will be updated across our WAN links, but latency becomes a factor. Transmissions between sites can use RPC over IP for synchronous connections, or SMTP for asynchronous, unreliable links. SMTP can send schema, configuration, and Global Catalog updates, but it cannot send data for the directory partition, since the File Replication Service (FRS), which is responsible for global policy data, is limited to synchronous updates. To facilitate the process, data is compressed.

Wide area networks are not ordinarily configured point to point. A router is usually connected to a telecom vendor's central office for a particular service, such as frame relay. The layout pictured in Figure 14.4 indicates all sites connected with 512Kbps links. Using this diagram, you can see that each office can contact the others. This is referred to as a fully transitive system.

FIGURE 14.4

Inter-Site
Replication

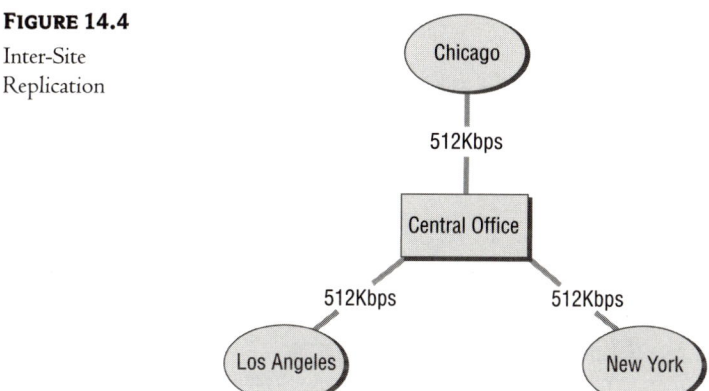

Site links represent the replication routes between two or more sites. Each link can be assigned a relative cost and a schedule. By default, the update frequency is three hours. Figure 14.4 illustrates the physical connections for three sites. For this example, you would configure one instance for the replication process, as you would schedule a conference call.

The KCC generates a spanning tree to supervise inter-site replication. The first server created at a site is assigned the role of *Inter-Site Topology Generator (ISTG)*. Its function is to create a site topology to coordinate internal and external replication traffic. If that server becomes unavailable, the next oldest domain controller at that site is promoted to ISTG status.

Bridgehead servers are gateways used to connect adjacent sites. If you have more than one domain controller at a particular site, you might want to assign one to be a bridgehead server to act as a conduit, communicating with domain controllers on other sites and exchanging updates with partners within its site. This takes the load off the other servers.

Transitive site links are created automatically, so that all site links are bridged, as in Figure 14.4. But, if you need to control part of your network because one of your links is slower than the others, or it can only connect with one site, you can turn off automatic bridging and create a site link bridge. This is a common situation with branch offices and satellite locations where fast links must be balanced with slower ones.

Creating Site Connection Objects

Figure 14.5 depicts the site layout for the Royal Tech organization. Headquarters is located in Chicago with 600 users. Branch offices, each with a staff of 200, are located in Los Angeles and New York. These locations are connected by 512Kbps frame relay. The Anaheim office, with a staff of 20, has a 128Kbps ISDN connection. Chicago manages three domain controllers and three subnets; the branch offices each have one domain controller and one subnet. The satellite office in Anaheim uses one subnet address and does not have a domain controller.

FIGURE 14.5

Site layout for
royal-tech.com

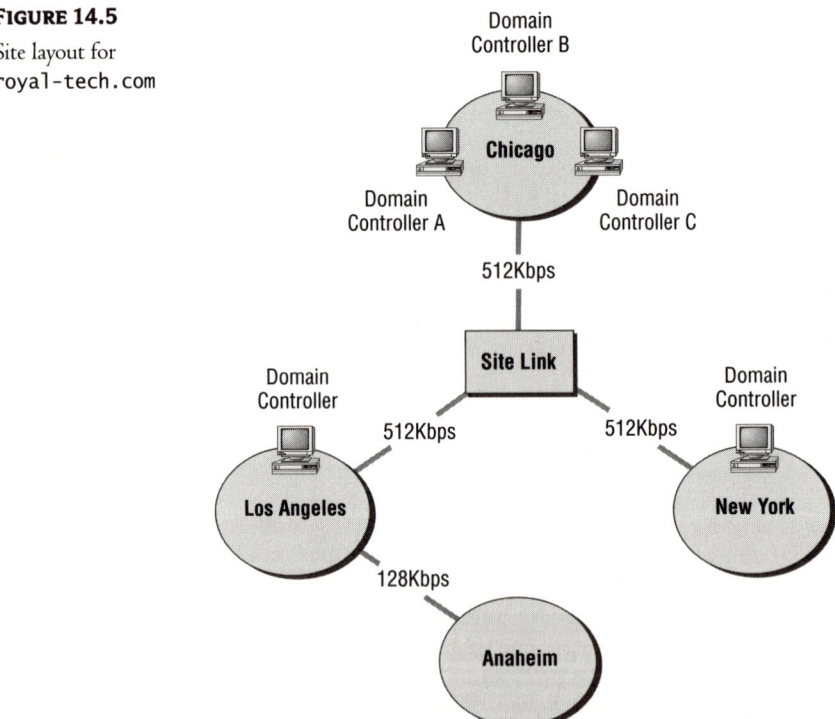

Use the following procedure to create site connection objects:

1. Create sites.

2. Create subnets.

3. Assign subnets to sites.

4. Move servers to sites.

5. Create and configure site links.

Let's look at the details in the following sections.

CREATING SITES

Open the Active Directory Sites and Services MMC. You'll notice that a default local site named *Default-First-Site* was automatically created by AD. It contains all the domain controllers on your network, as shown in Figure 14.6.

FIGURE 14.6

The AD Sites and Services MMC

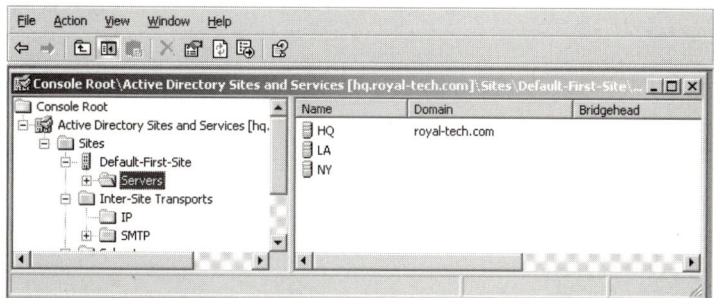

To create a new site, right-click the Site folder to display its context menu and choose New Site. As you'll see in Figure 14.7, I've named the new site LA and selected DeafultIPSiteLink for now, which is what it says, a default site link. Incidentally, you cannot use spaces in site names, so I would have typed Los_Angeles if I preferred the complete city name.

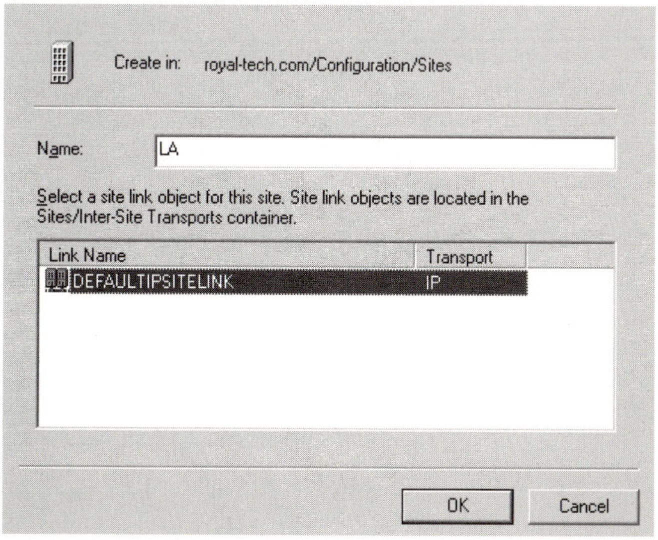

FIGURE 14.7

New site creation

Create in: royal-tech.com/Configuration/Sites

Name: LA

Select a site link object for this site. Site link objects are located in the Sites/Inter-Site Transports container.

Link Name	Transport
DEFAULTIPSITELINK	IP

OK   Cancel

The first time you create a site during a session with the MMC, Active Directory activates an information box to enumerate the tasks required to complete the process. This is illustrated in Figure 14.8.

FIGURE 14.8

An Active Directory information box

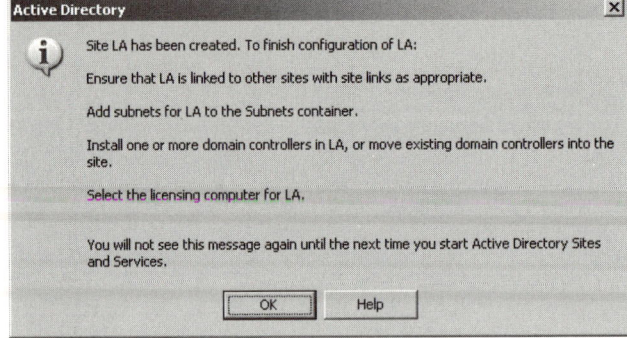

ADDING SUBNETS

After completing the site list, the next step is to create subnet objects for the local area networks and associate them with each site. Select New Subnet from the context menu available at the Subnets folder. Figure 14.9 shows you that the subnet has been recorded as 172.16.10.0/24 for the Default-First-Site, which has been renamed CHI. I'll proceed to create the other subnets on my network.

FIGURE 14.9

Adding and assigning a subnet

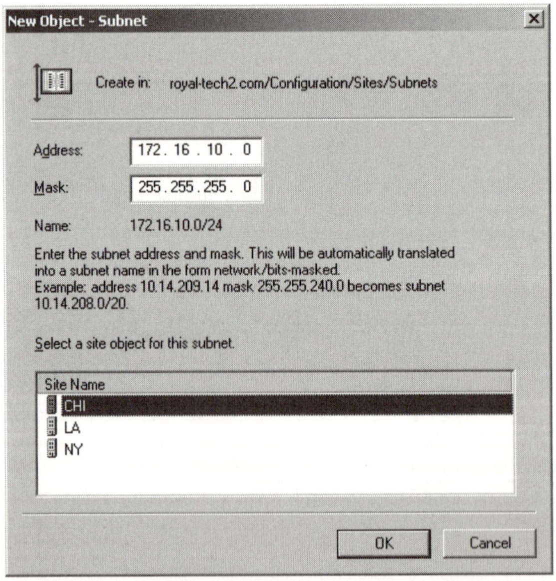

To add descriptive details for each subnet, select Properties from the context menu of the subnet and fill in the appropriate boxes on the General and Location tabs, as shown in figure 14.10. The Object tab lists the Update Sequence Numbers for this subnet object. The Security tab allows you to assign groups and users the capability of modifying the subnet.

FIGURE 14.10

General properties for a subnet object

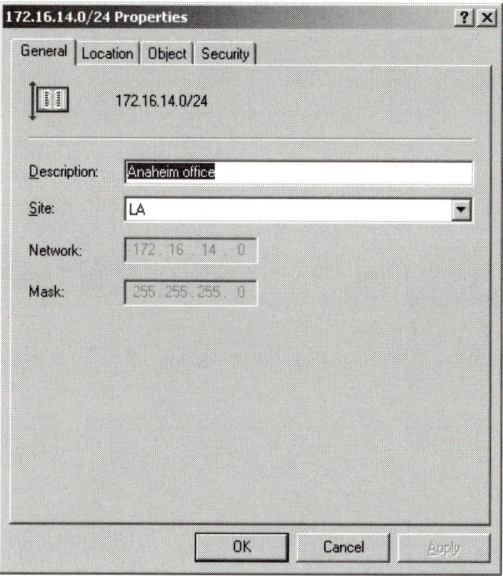

Next, move your domain controllers into the appropriate sites. Right-click a domain controller listed under the Default-First-Site Server folder, then select Move from the menu. Figure 14.11 shows the result after I first selected the NY server, then NY as the preferred target site.

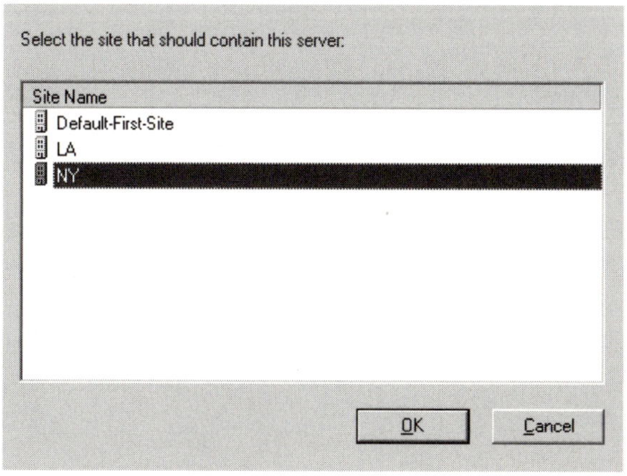

FIGURE 14.11

Moving the NY domain controller

CREATING SITE LINKS

Now that we have created sites, associated subnets for each site, and moved our servers, we need to connect our sites. To create a site link, open Inter-Site Transports, right-click IP, and select New Site Link on the menu. Supply a descriptive name, then select the sites in the left column and click the Add button to include them in this system. This procedure is illustrated in Figure 14.12.

FIGURE 14.12

Creating a site link

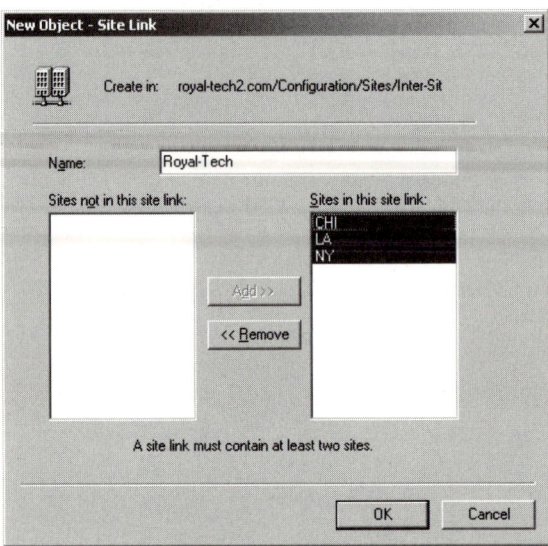

To complete the site link configuration, we need to supply a cost and a schedule. Costs are relative numbers associated with site links to reflect bandwidth and priority. Lower numbers represent higher values (speeds), which are preferred by the spanning tree topology created by the KCC. Table 14.1 below shows suggested cost values:

TABLE 14.1: SUGGESTED COST VALUES FOR SITE LINKS

NETWORK TYPE	CONNECTION SPEED	COST VALUE
ISDN	64 or 128Kbps	400–500
Frame relay	56Kbps to 1.5Mbps	201–500
T1	1.5Mbps	200
ATM	155 to 622Mbps	1–100
T3 backbone	45Mbps	1

To view and modify a site link, right-click it and select Properties, as in Figure 14.13. The General tab lists a default Cost of 100 and a 180-minute frequency between replication updates. You'll notice that I've changed the Cost to 300.

FIGURE 14.13

Modifying a site link

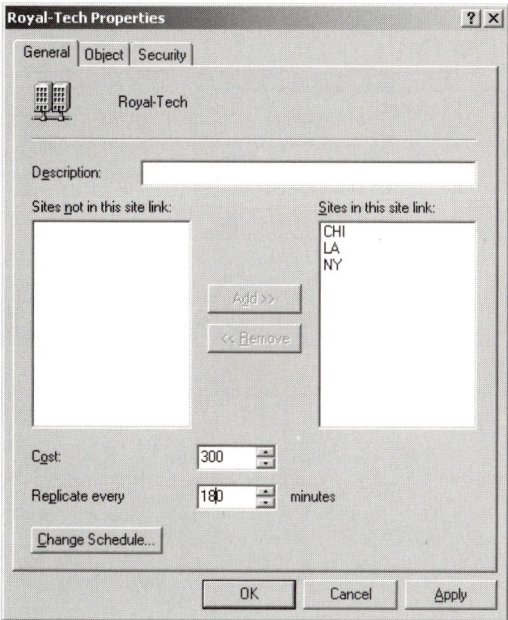

Next, click the Schedule button to access the screen in Figure 14.14. As you can see, I've removed the weekday hours 8 AM to 6 PM to prevent replication during business hours. I've also removed the hours 11 PM to 1 AM because server backups are scheduled during that time.

FIGURE 14.14

Scheduling replication

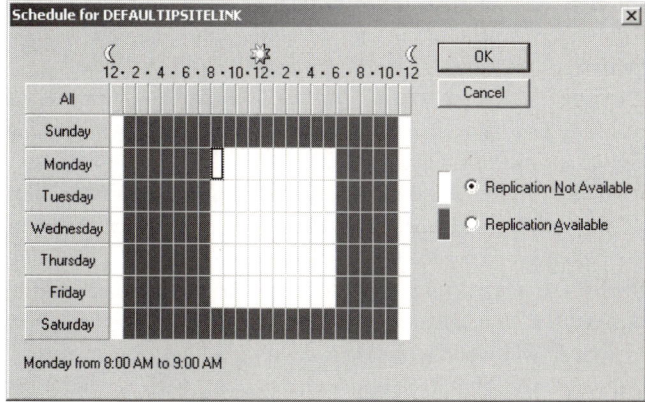

Since there are three domain controllers in our Chicago site, I've designated the HQ2 server to be a bridgehead server. This server will collect updates from HQ1 and HQ2 to replicate with servers at the NY and LA sites and relay data from those sites to the Chicago domain controllers. Select the context menu for that server to access the options box and choose the appropriate protocol, as shown in Figure 14.15.

FIGURE 14.15

Designating a
bridgehead server

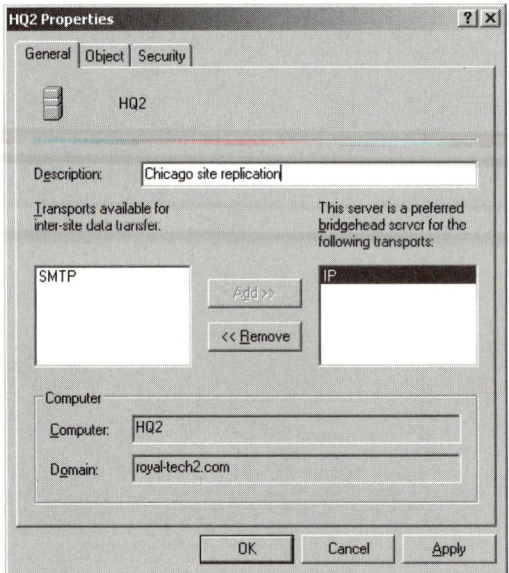

One or Multiple Sites?

Now, you may have noticed in Figure 14.10 that I placed Anaheim's subnet in the LA site. Anaheim doesn't merit its own site at this time because it does not host a domain controller that would replicate with the others. Users in that office would connect to LA's domain controller to log on and obtain access to local resources.

If that office expands in the future to a size where it becomes cost-effective to host its own domain controller and add a technical staff person, we'll have to revisit our site configuration. We would create a site for Anaheim and transfer its subnet from the LA site. We would like to add Anaheim to the Royal Tech site link, so that it would share in the replication process that has been scheduled between 6 PM and 8 AM weekdays. The problem is that it can only directly communicate with the LA router, which has been configured for ISDN as well as frame relay.

One solution is to create a new site link for the LA-to-Anaheim connection and add the LA and ANA sites to it, which is what I've done in Figure 14.16. I've also modified the cost, frequency, and schedule so it will work better for the Pacific Time zone. In this scenario, LA shares information with Chicago and New York and exchanges data with Anaheim in a separate operation.

FIGURE 14.16

The new Anaheim
office site link

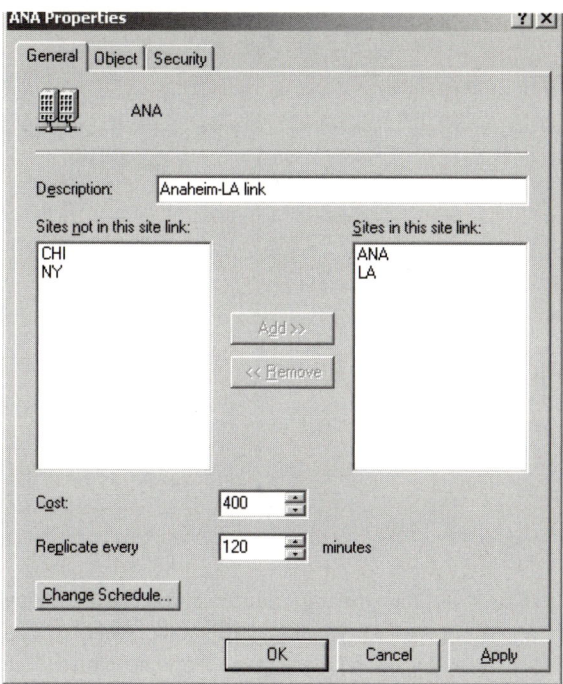

The best-case scenario is to upgrade Anaheim's connection so that it is equivalent to the other sites. We would simply incorporate the Anaheim site into our Royal Tech site link after moving its subnet and server.

Forcing Replication

One possible scenario for forcing replication is to synchronize your servers before taking one down for maintenance.

Active Directory Sites and Services can force replication between partners. When you click the destination server and open its NTDS settings, its partner(s) are listed in the details pane. Right-click to select one, then choose Replicate Now on the menu. As shown in Figure 14.17, HQ2 is the destination, while DC3, the source, is the server about to be taken offline. The fact that forced replication is a one-way street should not be a limitation, because in this scenario you would be more concerned with sending data from DC3 rather than receiving it. Later, when DC3 is reactivated, HQ2 will bring it up-to-date.

While the menu option says Replicate Now, you should be aware that this really only queues up a request to replicate. Depending upon how busy the servers in question are, and how busy the connection between them is, the actual replication process might not start for quite some time. Like Exchange Server administration, managing Active Directory is often a "hurry up and wait" process.

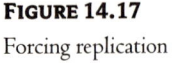

FIGURE 14.17

Forcing replication

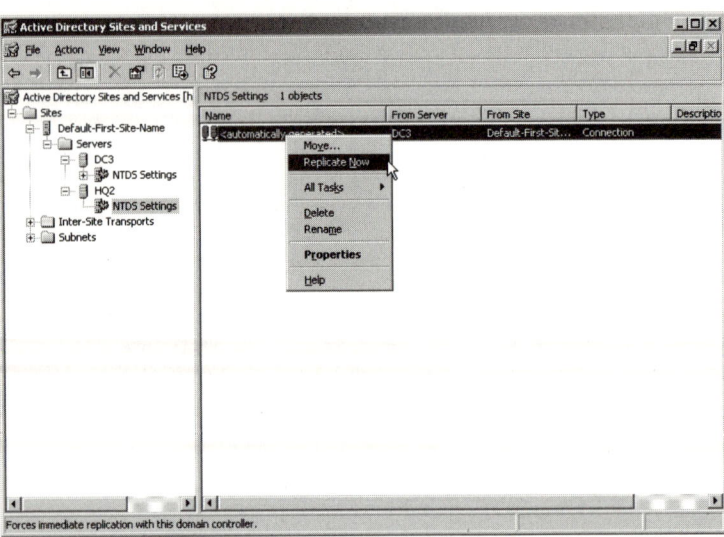

I should also mention that forcing replication has caused me more problems than it has cured in the field. In my current project, we've actually added a day to each upgrade. I come in a day early, run DCPROMO to elevate the new server to domain controller status, and then let replication occur overnight (rather than forcing the issue immediately). While I have no hard-copy proof, this seems to be more stable than trying to force immediate updates to the server's AD database. When we first started, we were coming in on Friday, running DCPROMO, and then forcing replication. We ended up have numerous replication issues—often weeks later. Now that I go in on Thursday and give the system a night to replicate, we are experiencing very few replication issues—both in the short term (the weekend of the upgrade) and in the long term.

REPLICATION ADMINISTRATION (REPADMIN)

Replication Administration (REPADMIN) is a command-line tool that monitors replication links for a specific domain controller. It's located in the Support\Tools folder on the Windows 2000/Windows Server 2003 CD. As we've done previously, double-click support.cab and copy repadmin.exe to your hard drive. Better yet, copy all those utilities, since repetition is not fascinating. REPADMIN provides information about replication partners for a particular domain controller and can also force replication.

Figure 14.18 shows the result of information gathered by using REPADMIN. Type the command as shown below, using the DNS name of the destination server. I've omitted the naming context, which is optional. The result is that REPADMIN tells us that the replication partner for DC3 is HQ2, and then it goes on to list the domain naming, configuration, and schema partitions stored on HQ2 and when they were last updated. The invocation ID is the GUID for the database.

```
Repadmin /showreps <naming-context> <destination_server>
```

FIGURE 14.18

REPADMIN displays replication information

If you plan to do some maintenance on a server and want to synchronize its AD database before taking it down, you could force it to pull replication updates from its partners with the REPADMIN command as listed below.

```
Repadmin /syncall <destination DC> <naming_context> /force
```

You'll notice in Figure 14.19 that I used the naming context this time by breaking up the DNS name and prefacing each portion of the name with dc=. If you omit the naming context, this command will automatically update the schema and configuration as well as the domain-naming context.

FIGURE 14.19

REPADMIN replicates all objects

DISABLING THE KNOWLEDGE CONSISTENCY CHECKER

At times, you may need to disable the Knowledge Consistency Checker to configure site replication manually. ldp.exe is a graphical utility that can accomplish this. It's available in the \Support\Tools folder on the Windows 2000/Windows Server 2003 installation CD. Double-click support.cab and copy ldp.exe to your hard drive. Follow these steps:

1. Run the ldp.exe program, select Connection, and click Connect on the menu, as shown in Figure 14.20.

FIGURE 14.20

Forcing replication

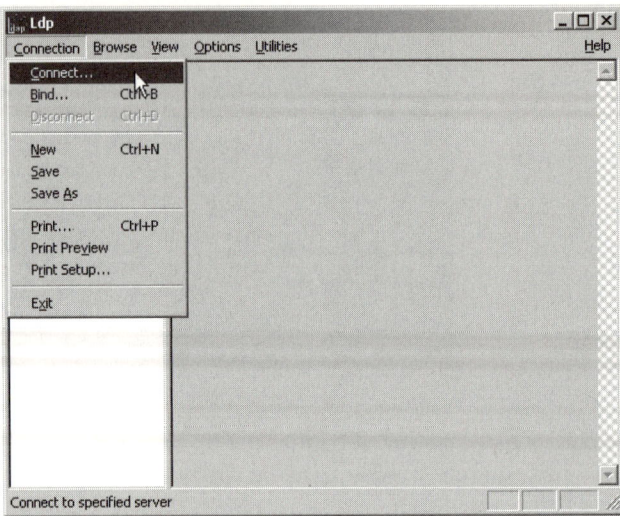

2. Insert the name of the server in the dialog box that appears and click OK. Data is displayed in the right pane, as shown in Figure 14.21.

FIGURE 14.21

Server information in LDP

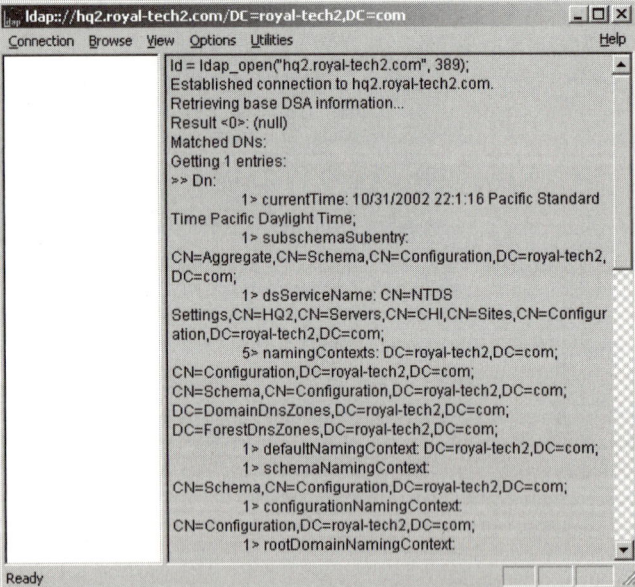

3. Click Bind on the Connection menu, then supply an administrative account and the DNS name for the domain. A comment should appear in the details pane that states you've been authenticated.

4. Select Tree on the View menu. Type the distinguished name of the container for the site object in the BaseDN box. If the object is located, it will be listed in the left pane. In our example, we would type the following:

`CN=Royal-Tech,CN=Sites,CN=Configuration,DC=hq2,DC=royal-tech2,DC=com`

5. Click the plus sign to expand the listing. Double-click the object that reads `CN=NTDS Site Settings` to display its attributes in the details pane.

6. Copy the string of data that begins with `>>Dn`, click Modify on the Browse menu, and paste the data into the Dn box.

7. Type **Options** in the Attribute box, then type a number in the Values box according to the choices listed in Table 14.2.

TABLE 14.2: OPTIONS TO DISABLE KCC WITH THE LDP UTILITY

VALUE	DESCRIPTION
1	Disables intra-site topology generation
16	Disables inter-site topology generation
17	Disables both intra- and inter-site topology generation

8. Select Replace in the Operation box, click Enter, and then click Run.

This can also be accomplished through a manual Registry edit, but that is much more dangerous than using the LDP utility.

I've had to use this process a few times in the field. If your environment includes numerous defined AD sites, the KCC will often come up with a replication topology that makes no sense whatsoever. My current project is a perfect example.

The company's network consists of 20 physical locations connected through a 56Kbps frame-relay network. Given the costs associated with each "path" established through a frame-relay environment, we configured the network as a star—the company headquarters in Minneapolis is the hub, and all of the other sites have a connection to that hub. In other words, all traffic must come through the corporate office before going to any other location (another way to look at this is that no location is more than two hops from any other).

When the KCC finished "analyzing" the AD structure, it decided that the replication topology "hub" should be one of the satellite sites. In other words, all AD replication traffic would first go to the California server, before being passed along to all of the other domain controllers throughout the network. At first glance, this doesn't seem too bad; all replication traffic passes through two hops before reaching its destination.

If you add in the physical layout of the network, though, this is a really stupid design. All of the traffic has to physically pass through the corporate hub before going anywhere. This meant that all of the AD replication traffic would first go to Minneapolis, then to California, before being directed (back through Minneapolis) to its destination. I turned off the KCC, created my own site connectors, and used the corporate domain controllers as the replication hub.

The File Replication Service (FRS)

The File Replication Service supports logon and file sharing across a network by replicating SYSVOL data and DFS root and child replicas.

SYSVOL Replication

SYSVOL is an administrative share that replaced NT's Netlogon folder. It contains Group Policy settings for Windows 2000/Windows Server 2003, Windows NT and 9x System Policies, and user login scripts. This data must be distributed to all domain controllers in a forest.

FRS replicates SYSVOL data by using the same topology and connection objects built by the KCC for intra-site and inter-site AD replication. The transmission protocol used is RPC over IP. Unlike Active Directory, FRS does not compress SYSVOL data across site boundaries. Although FRS does not have its own MMC snap-in, you can change its update schedule with Active Directory Users and Computers by following these steps. Figure 14.22 shows you the details.

1. Click View and choose Advanced Features.

2. Select System in the left pane, then click the plus sign beside File Replication Service.

3. Right-click Domain System Volume / SYSVOL to display a context menu.

4. Select Properties on the menu, then click the Change Schedule button.

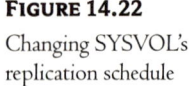

FIGURE 14.22

Changing SYSVOL's replication schedule

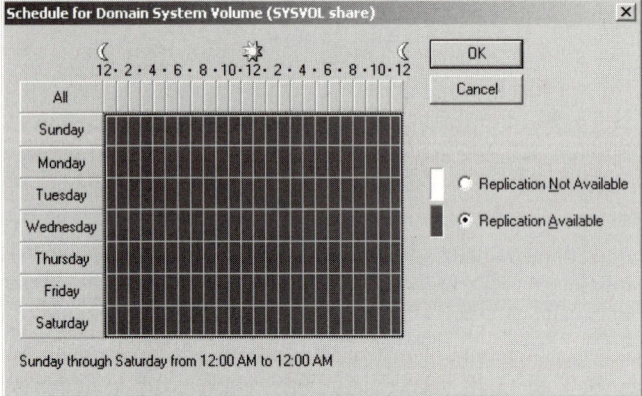

Distributed File System Replication (DFS)

Traditionally, an organization would share a folder named \\ny.tpl.org\projects by mapping drives on client desktops to the particular server on their wide area network that stores that data. Performance and availability will vary according to location, bandwidth, and traffic. DFS provides a way to create a centralized logical subdirectory to easily link to that folder without referring to the actual server. In addition, DFS can create replicas of that data to make it available on local servers, and it provides fault tolerance. How would you bind that distributed data into a unified whole? The answer, of course, is replication.

The Distributed File System centralizes access to network folders and maintains fault-tolerant data replicas in different locations. Once a DFS root folder has been designated, links are created to point to that folder. Replicas are copies of that root folder or links that are distributed to other servers. FRS synchronizes data among all the DFS replicas.

Domain-based DFS roots are integrated into Active Directory, so that details concerning the roots, links, and replica members of a DFS share are distributed by AD and replicated automatically. They must be hosted on a domain controller. Stand-alone roots can be stored on member servers, so they can make use of DFS links, but they cannot have fault-tolerant replicas.

If you've created multiple child nodes, you need to enable replication. Select the root in the left pane and select Configure Replication on the drop-down menu to enable a wizard. One target is designated as the initial master replica, as shown in Figure 14.23.

FIGURE 14.23

Selecting the master DFS replica

Next, you can select a topology, displayed in Figure 14.24.

FIGURE 14.24

Selecting a topology to replicate DFS replicas

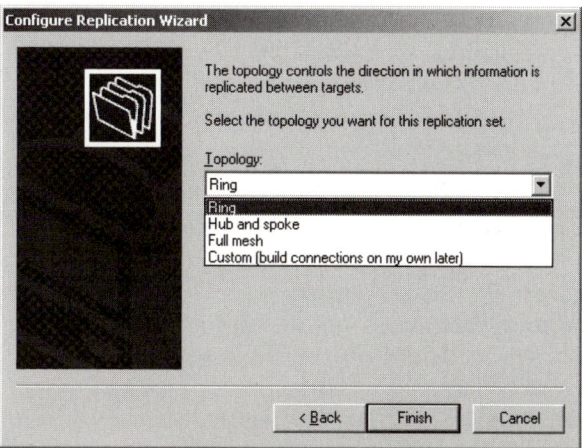

If you right-click the DFS root in the console and select Properties, you'll notice a Replication tab with a Schedule button that allows you to control the time of day when replication occurs. You can also modify the topology that you selected earlier. That Replication tab is displayed in Figure 14.25. You can also access this data in Active Directory Users and Computers by following the procedure listed earlier for SYSVOL.

FIGURE 14.25

Replication schedule and topology properties

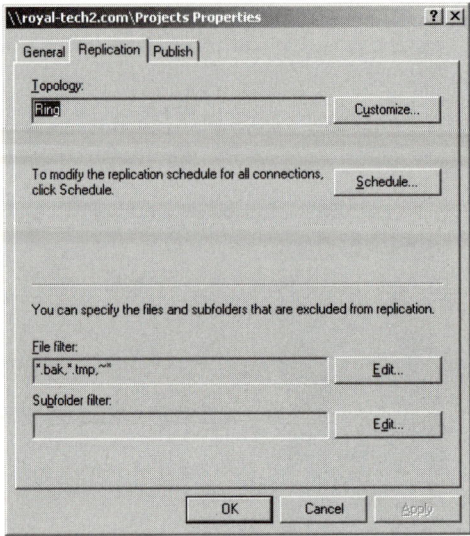

Operations Masters

In making the transition from NT's single-master model to the Active Directory multiple-master model, Microsoft was faced with the problem that certain operations require authoritative control and should not be shared on a peer basis. For example, in a distributed peer environment, two domain controllers within a domain could assign duplicate SIDs to new accounts. The solution to this problem is the adoption of flexible single-master operations in Windows 2000. Microsoft didn't like the acronym that was adopted, FSMOs, so they've been renamed *operations masters*. The word *flexible* refers to the ability to transfer a master role to different domain controllers. Any domain controller can be assigned one or more operations master roles.

There are five Operations Master roles:

♦ Schema master

♦ Domain naming master

♦ Infrastructure master

♦ PDC emulator

♦ RID master

Two of these apply to forests and three to domains, as I'll explain in the following sections.

Forest Operations Masters

As you may recall from our earlier investigation into naming contexts, two partitions contain forest-wide data: the schema and domain naming contexts. The *schema master* and *domain naming master* are responsible for those partitions. Only one domain controller can be assigned each of those roles within the enterprise. The first domain controller in a forest takes on all of them by default. Forest operations masters are usually located on the same domain controller.

The schema master oversees changes to schema classes and objects. It is managed by members of the Schema Administrators group. Exchange 2000 must be installed on the schema master domain controller, because this application doubles the number of schema objects.

Use the Schema Master MMC we created earlier in this chapter to locate the schema master. A command-line utility is available to help you find out where the schema master currently resides in your forest. Use the DSQUERY command, as listed below and illustrated in Figure 14.26.

```
Dsquery server -hasfsmo schema
```

FIGURE 14.26

Discovering the schema master with DSQUERY

There is one instance of the *domain naming master* in each forest. A domain controller assigned this role is responsible for adding and removing domains and cross-referencing to directory services on external domains. When you run DCPROMO on a server to promote it to be a domain controller, the program contacts the domain naming master for configuration information. Active Directory Domains and Trusts displays and transfers domain naming masters (see Figure 14.27).

FIGURE 14.27

Displaying the domain naming master

Change Operations Master   ? X

The domain naming operations master ensures that domain names are unique. Only one domain controller in the enterprise performs this role.

Domain naming operations master:

hq2.royal-tech2.com

To transfer the domain naming master role to the following computer, click Change.   Change...

hq2.royal-tech2.com

Close

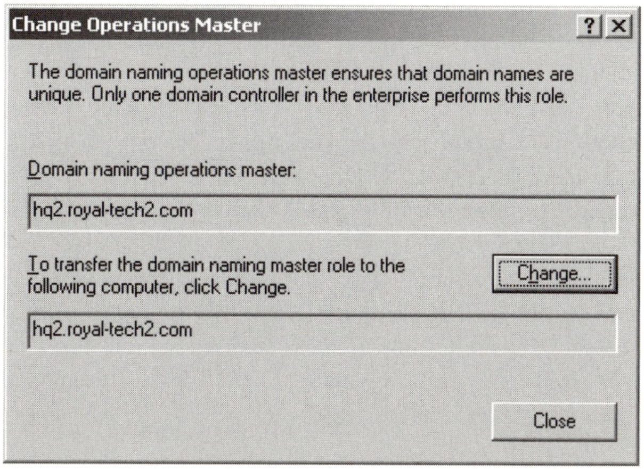

To locate the domain naming master, try the DSQUERY command below:

```
Dsquery server -hasfsmo name
```

Domain Operations Masters

The *PDC emulator master, RID master*, and *infrastructure master* are authoritative for a domain. Domain master roles are automatically assigned to the first domain controller in a new domain.

The PDC emulator takes on the role of primary domain controller for down-level clients on a network. It serves as a domain master browser, replicates data to backup domain controllers, and supervises Group Policy object changes. In native mode, the PDC emulator serves as the last word for user account passwords, since it receives all new and changed passwords. If a logon fails, the authenticating domain controller forwards the request to this server for a final decision. If you want to locate the PDC emulator in your domain, you can use the DSQUERY command below:

```
Dsquery server -hasfsmo pdc
```

The RID master parcels out *relative identifiers* to each domain controller. SIDs are actually made up of a combination of a unique security ID and the domain's relative ID. Each new security principal object (users, groups, and computers) is assigned a unique SID. This server also supervises object moves between domains. The relevant DSQUERY command would look like this:

```
Dsquery server -hasfsmo rid
```

The infrastructure master manages changes to usernames, group names, and group membership, and it exchanges that information with other domains. Use DSQUERY as listed below:

```
Dsquery server -hasfsmo infr
```

Placing Operations Masters

Microsoft warns us that a Global Catalog server should not also be an infrastructure master. Although it must have good connectivity with a Global Catalog to update references to objects that have moved or been renamed, it will not make changes to objects that exist locally.

The schema master and domain naming master should be placed on one domain controller, which should also store the Global Catalog. Administrators responsible for schema updates and domain management should have direct access. All domain controllers on the network should have good connectivity to this server. The domain masters could be assigned to other servers to help balance the load.

The locations of these operations masters will affect network traffic, because certain operations require their approval. If you add a domain controller at the LA site at our sample company, Royal Tech, you need to communicate with the domain naming master to complete the procedure. And then the new domain controller must contact the RID master to have the capability of assigning SIDs to new accounts. If an HQ server in Chicago has been assigned those roles, your new server must communicate via a WAN link. Operations master roles should be assigned to domain controllers according to the volume of work at that location. The busiest sites should have the fastest access to the domain operations masters. Forest FSMOs are not called upon every day, so their location is not so critical for branch offices.

Transferring Operations Masters

You might want to transfer operations master roles when you have to do maintenance on a domain controller, or when you want to balance the demands of your network. The procedure to transfer each role is described below.

To transfer the schema master role, open the Schema Master MMC we created earlier and right-click Active Directory Schema in the left pane. Select Change Domain Controller and add the name of the target server, as shown in Figure 14.28.

FIGURE 14.28

Changing the target domain controller

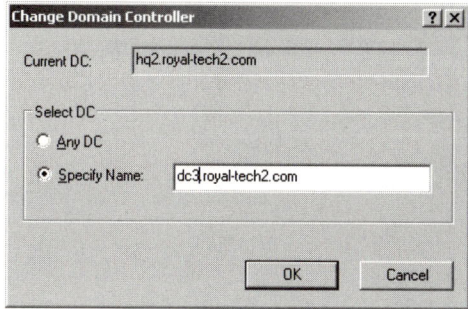

Then repeat the procedure to select Operations Master at the same menu. Click the Change button as shown in Figure 14.29.

FIGURE 14.29

Transferring the schema master

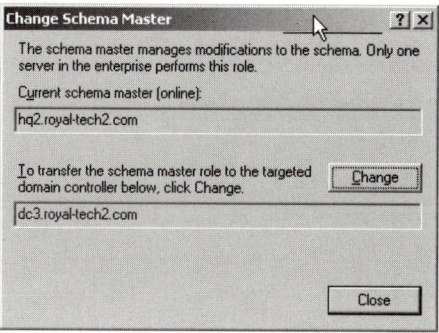

To transfer a domain naming master, use AD Domains and Trusts. Right-click Domains and Trusts and select Connect to Domain Controller. Type the name or choose the domain controller from the list. Right-click again, but choose Operations Master this time, and click the Change button. This operation is identical to the one illustrated in Figure 14.29.

To transfer the current RID, PDC, and infrastructure masters on a domain, activate Active Directory Users and Computers. The procedure should be familiar by now. Right-click your domain and select Connect to Domain Controller at the menu, as shown in Figure 14.30.

FIGURE 14.30

Selecting a domain
controller for
transfer

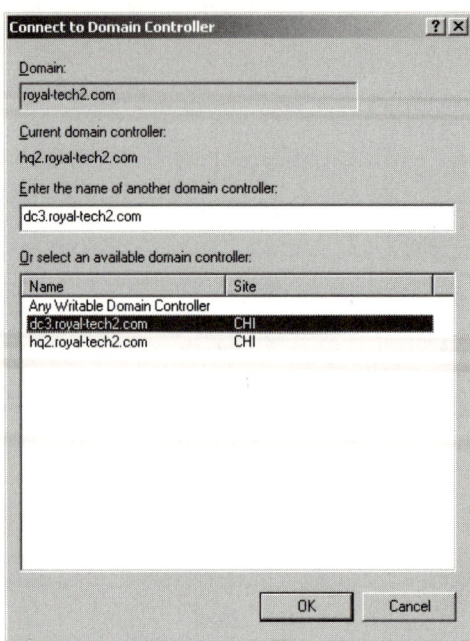

To complete the transfer procedure, right-click the domain again and select Operations Masters
at the menu. Each of these roles is accessible on a tab. Figure 14.31 displays the process of transferring the PDC master for a domain.

FIGURE 14.31

Transferring a PDC
Master

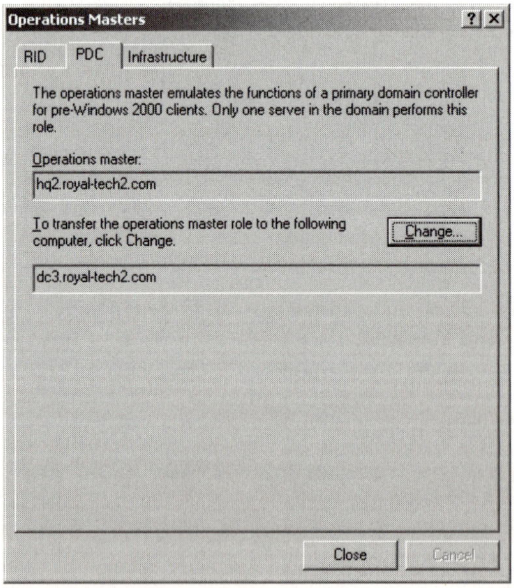

USING NTDSUTIL TO TRANSFER OPERATIONS MASTERS

The NTDSUTIL program is a powerful command-line utility that can be used to monitor or manage various aspects of a Windows 2000/Windows Server 2003 network. You must be logged on as an Administrator-equivalent user to transfer operations master roles. The command displays the prompt for you, so you type the words after the colon in the listing below. Repeat the first four lines for each role transfer. You'll need to supply the DNS name of the server, which will be designated the new operations master for the role you specify.

```
NTDSUTIL
Ntdsutil: roles
Fsmo maintenance: connections
Server connections: connect to server <server name>
Server connections: quit
```

Choose the appropriate fifth line to specify the role you wish to transfer from the commands listed below. As you might expect, Microsoft will warn you about the upcoming change before it proceeds. The activity at the command line is displayed in Figure 14.32.

```
Fsmo maintenance: transfer schema master
Fsmo maintenance: transfer rid master
Fsmo maintenance: transfer pdc
Fsmo maintenance: transfer infrastructure master
Fsmo maintenance: transfer domain naming master
```

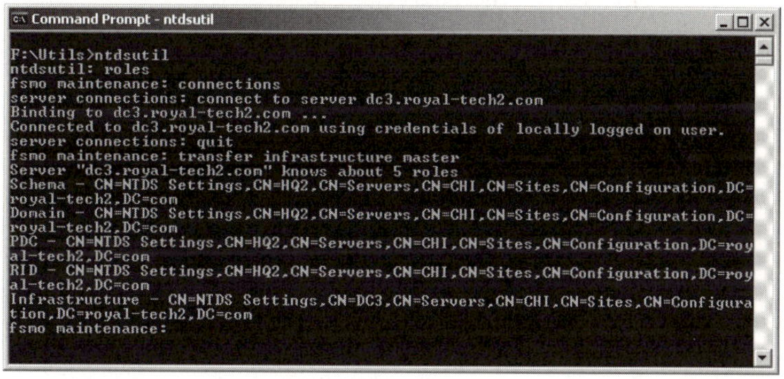

FIGURE 14.32

Transferring an infrastructure master with NTDSUTIL

SEIZING AN OPERATIONS MASTER WITH NTDSUTIL

When an operations master server fails, it's too late to transfer its role. You'll have to seize its function and assign it to another domain controller. This is a drastic measure, as the schema master, domain naming master, and RID master servers cannot be resurrected if their role is seized. If you've repaired them, you need to format their hard drives and reinstall them as new servers. Use NTDSUTIL to perform this procedure. The domain controller you connect to will take over the role you are seizing.

```
NTDSUTIL
Ntdsutil: roles
Fsmo maintenance: connections
```

```
Server connections: connect to server <server name>
Server connections: quit
Fsmo maintenance: seize <role>
```

The seize command should be followed by the role you are reassigning:

```
Schema master
Domain naming master
RID master
PDC
Infrastructure master
```

Database Size

It stands to reason that the size of the Active Directory database impacts delivery time and bandwidth. When DCPROMO installs AD on a domain controller, it creates the `ntds.dit` file in the \winnt\ntds folder. Initially this file uses approximately 12MB to store default users and groups.

Microsoft classifies network objects into two types: *security principals*, meaning those objects that have security attributes, such as users and groups, and *nonsecurity principals*, for example, organizational units. Each new object affects file size according to the data in Table 14.3. User attributes include first name, last name, e-mail address, phone number, etc. Each string attribute of 10 characters or less requires 100 bytes.

TABLE 14.3: OBJECT TYPES AND SIZES

ATTRIBUTES	OBJECT TYPE	OBJECT SIZE
Security principals	Users, groups	3,600 bytes
Nonsecurity principals	Organizational units	1,100 bytes

Table 14.4 estimates database file size by the size of the organization. I used the object size assumptions in Table 14.3 and added 14 additional attributes for each user account and four each for groups, computers, servers, and printers. The initial size of the AD database is assumed to be 12MB. According to these figures, a small organization with 500 users and 835 total network objects requires only 15.1MB for its AD database. A company with 1,000 users needs 18.2MB, while a 10,000-user firm uses 74MB.

TABLE 14.4: AD DATABASE SIZE BY ORGANIZATION SIZE

Users	500	1,000	5,000	10,000	50,000
Groups	50	100	500	1,000	5,000
OUs	10	20	100	200	1,000
Computers	250	500	2,500	5,000	25,000

Continued on next page

TABLE 14.4: AD DATABASE SIZE BY ORGANIZATION SIZE *(continued)*

Servers	5	10	25	50	200
Printers	10	20	50	100	500
Volumes	10	20	50	100	500
Total Objects	835	1,670	8,225	16,450	82,200
Total Size	15.1MB	18.2MB	43MB	74MB	322MB

Database Fragmentation

Contrary to what you might expect, deleting objects *does not* reduce the size of the AD database. Actually, deleted objects remain in AD for 60 days as tombstones, so their status can be replicated to other domain controllers. *Garbage collection* runs on each domain controller every 12 hours and removes deleted objects after 60 days (or whatever period you've set), cleans up log files, and defragments the database. Rather than reducing its size, online defrag makes space available for new objects, and reorders the database so it will run more efficiently.

WARNING   There is a way to reduce the size of ndts.dit, *but this procedure is not approved by Microsoft as a matter of routine maintenance. You take your domain controller offline and use NTDSUTIL to restore a defragmented database. This procedure is covered in Chapter 15. If you want to remove the Global Catalog from a domain controller, you can use this method to shrink the database by removing Global Catalog records and restore only local domain data.*

Linear Growth

The size of the database scales linearly with an increase in the number of users on the network. Microsoft's scalability test measured the creation of 16 million user accounts. Table 14.5 shows the results of an Active Directory scalability test, measured by the population of user accounts.

TABLE 14.5: USER POPULATION AND EFFECTS ON DATABASE SIZE

NUMBER OF USERS	FILE SIZE
10,000	62.2MB
100,000	454MB
1,000,000	4.1GB
10,000,000	41.9GB
16,000,000	68.6GB

Intra-Site Replication Traffic

As we learned earlier in this chapter, intra-site replication is not compressed. Table 14.6 depicts object sizes measured in bytes as they are replicated within a site. Notice a size efficiency at work. One user object requires 13KB to replicate; 10 users require 47KB, or four times that amount; 100 users require only about 30 times; and 1,000 users require approximately 300 times the space needed for one user object. For the purposes of this illustration, empty groups were used. This scenario assumes that the domain is in native or Windows Server 2003 mode, since universal groups are included.

NOTE *The information in Tables 14.6 - 14.13 is taken from the presentation "Active Directory Database Sizing and Traffic Analysis" found at* www.microsoft.com/seminar/includes/seminar.asp?url=/Seminar/en/ Servers/19990916TEADD/Portal.xml#aTop.

TABLE 14.6: INTRA-SITE OBJECT REPLICATION

NUMBER OF OBJECTS	USERS	GLOBAL GROUPS	UNIVERSAL GROUPS	VOLUMES
1	13,019	11,309	11,145	10,277
10	47,037	26,902	26,823	22,848
100	386,148	187,754	185,606	149,736
500	1,914,087	905,015	906,079	715,577
1,000	3,818,256	1,815,170	1,803,090	1,436,085
5,000	19,123,820	8,985,915		

Object sizes are shown in bytes.

NOTE *Traffic statistics in this section apply to full object replication, when they are first created. Modifications replicate only changed attributes.*

Microsoft compared group replication by number of members. Table 14.7 indicates that a group with 10 members increases from 13KB to 29KB, or three times when its membership grows to 100.

TABLE 14.7: GROUP MEMBERSHIP AND INTRA-SITE REPLICATION

NUMBER OF GROUPS	NO MEMBERS	10 MEMBERS	20 MEMBERS	100 MEMBERS
1	11,309	13,023	15,028	29,212
10	26,902	45,180	36,199	206,192
100	187,754	370,333	549,351	2,007,563
500	905,015	1,822,257	2,745,787	9,956,677
1,000	1,815,170	3,633,795	5,458,848	19,920,866

Member sizes are shown in bytes.

One routine network task is changing user account passwords. Since a network administrator may schedule this procedure to occur for many accounts at the same time, you should consider how it affects network traffic as those changes are replicated to other domain controllers. In Table 14.8, traffic statistics are shown according to numbers of users.

TABLE 14.8: REPLICATING PASSWORD CHANGES

NUMBER OF USERS	BYTES	BYTES / USER
1	10,805	1,842
10	12,811	385
100	59,856	509
500	275,422	533
1,000	444,085	435
5,000	3,014,610	601

Inter-Site Replication Traffic

Replication between domain controllers located on different sites is compressed to 10 to 15 percent of its original size. Compare Table 14.9 with Table 14.6 earlier to clarify the effect of compression. For example, 100 users require 39KB as opposed to 386KB for inter-site replication, and 1,000 users require 290KB, which is about 15 percent of the bandwidth required within a domain. There is a tradeoff in CPU cycles on the domain controllers, however, to compress and decompress data.

TABLE 14.9: INTER-SITE OBJECT REPLICATION

NUMBER OF OBJECTS	USERS	GLOBAL GROUPS	UNIVERSAL GROUPS	VOLUMES
1	14,108	10,437	11,227	9,667
10	45,563	25,683	26,741	21,691
100	39,583	28,743	29,675	22,602
500	173,105	102,404	119,180	81,691
1,000	291,041	194,926	199,054	151,989

Object sizes are shown in bytes.

For the purposes of this illustration, empty groups were used. This scenario assumes that the domain is in native or Windows Server 2003 mode, since universal groups are included.

Global Catalog Replication Traffic

When a domain controller becomes a Global Catalog server, it places an additional burden on that server, since it must replicate data within its domain as well as receive data for other domains. But, since Global Catalog data is a partial replica, it requires less bandwidth than the full AD database. Remember the 40 percent figure I mentioned earlier? Well, the Global Catalog adds 40 percent of each external domain's AD database to the replication burden of your catalog, in addition to its responsibility for replicating its local domain data. For example, the 10,000-user network in Table 14.4 that uses 74MB to store its Active Directory would require 40 percent, or about 30MB, for its Global Catalog. The Global Catalog for the 50,000-user company would need 129MB.

Storage requirements reported for intra-site replication in Table 14.10 represent a reduction of approximately 10 percent for the Global Catalog as compared to the figures for full AD distribution in Table 14.6. Intra-site AD replication for 100 users requires 386KB as opposed to 272KB for Global Catalog data, while the figure for 1,000 users is 3.8MB compared to 2.6MB.

TABLE 14.10: INTRA-SITE OBJECT REPLICATION FOR GLOBAL CATALOGS

NUMBER OF OBJECTS	USERS	GLOBAL GROUPS	UNIVERSAL GROUPS	VOLUMES
1	12,401	11,601	11,437	11,101
10	35,595	26,783	26,862	23,011
100	272,877	183,123	183,205	149,199
500	1,323,177	879,823	879,990	690,042
1,000	2,640,974	1,750,665	1,751,239	1,370,457
5,000	13,189,354	8,735,103	8,745,150	6,860,815

Object sizes are shown in bytes.

As expected, inter-site Global Catalog replication also requires less bandwidth than inter-site AD replication. The statistics shown in Table 14.11 compare favorably to those in Table 14.9. The transport protocol used was RPC over IP.

TABLE 14.11: INTER-SITE OBJECT REPLICATION FOR GLOBAL CATALOGS

NUMBER OF OBJECTS	USERS	GLOBAL GROUPS	UNIVERSAL GROUPS	VOLUMES
1	12,565	11,471	11,309	11,183
10	36,018	26,895	26,813	23,171
100	32,391	28,600	28,379	24,598
500	121,481	101,858	102,200	83,099
1,000	233,503	194,047	194,357	170,918

Object sizes are shown in bytes.

Universal groups publish their member lists in the Global Catalog. Global and local domain groups, however, are included by name only. This factor underlines the advantage of using nested groups to incorporate members in a group. The statistics shown in Table 14.12 measure the effect of global groups on inter-site Global Catalog replication. Table 14.13 indicates the increased burden universal groups place on Global Catalog replication between sites. That's why Microsoft urges us network admins to make use of nested groups to add members to our universal groups whenever possible. Again, the transmission protocol used was RPC over IP.

TABLE 14.12: REPLICATING GLOBAL DOMAIN GROUP MEMBERS FOR INTER-SITE GLOBAL CATALOGS

NUMBER OF GROUPS	NO MEMBERS	10 MEMBERS	20 MEMBERS	100 MEMBERS
1	10,437	11,951	11,389	11,553
10	26,683	26,141	26,223	26,223
100	28,743	28,227	28,319	28,781

Object sizes are shown in bytes.

TABLE 14.13: REPLICATING UNIVERSAL GROUP MEMBERSHIP FOR INTER-SITE GLOBAL CATALOGS

NUMBER OF GROUPS	NO MEMBERS	10 MEMBERS	20 MEMBERS	100 MEMBERS
1	11,227	17,010	15,786	32,370
10	26,741	46,898	12,999	17,902
100	29,675	39,120	46,912	107,551

Object sizes are shown in bytes.

Microsoft Tools

Microsoft has several other tools that will help you monitor and control replication on your Active Directory network. Some are graphical and menu-driven, while others are legacy command-line utilities. We'll discuss a few of those programs that didn't fit elsewhere in this chapter.

Monitoring AD with Replication Administration (REPADMIN)

We've looked at REPADMIN earlier. It can also be used to check that everything is up-to-date. After bringing a domain controller back online, you can run a KCC check immediately rather than waiting 15 minutes for the procedure to run automatically. The command listed below is illustrated in Figure 14.33.

```
Repadmin /kcc <DC_name>
```

FIGURE 14.33

KCC consistency
check with
REPADMIN

You can also persuade REPADMIN to list your domain controller's replicating partners, as well. Thus:

```
Repadmin /showvector <DC_name>
```

Performance Monitor

Performance Monitor is available in Administrative Tools. A number of counters are now available that can help you measure your database replication processes. Open up Counter Logs, then click on a log file in the details pane. On the General tab in the options box, click the Add Counters button. Change the Performance Object to NTDS, then select Counters from the list, as displayed in Figure 14.34.

FIGURE 14.34

Adding NTDS
counters to
Performance
Monitor

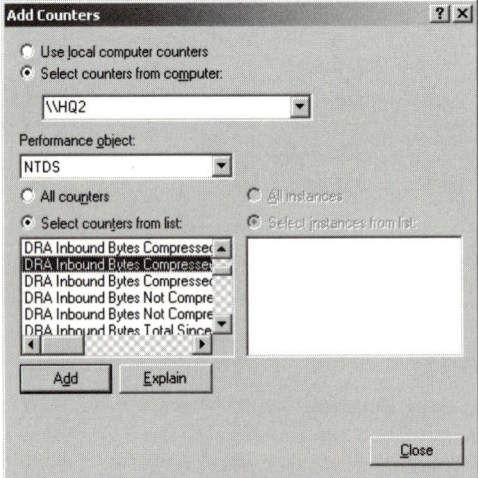

The "DRA" objects refer to Directory Replication Agents, "DS" stands for Directory Service. There are also counters for Kerberos and NTLM authentications, and LDAP and SAM activities.

Event Viewer

Event Viewer adds a Directory Services log for domain controllers, which you should monitor regularly. It can be a great source of AD-related information. Event 701 reports each time your AD database file has been defragmented online. You can also view logs recorded on other domain controllers, one at a time. Figure 14.35 displays a Warning event that should be heeded.

FIGURE 14.35

Event Viewer
Directory
Services log

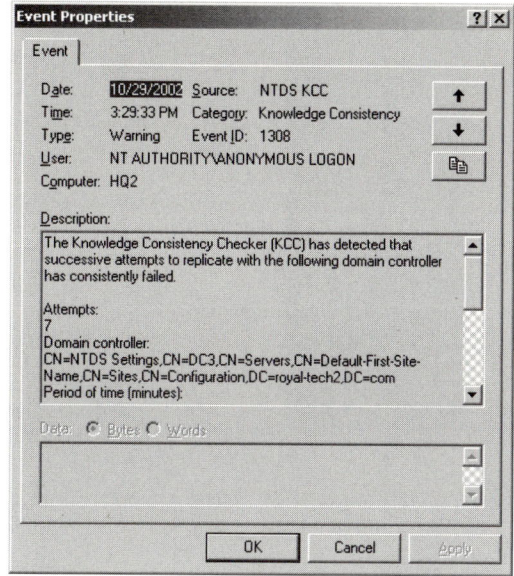

You can configure Event Viewer to monitor the KCC's activities by editing the Registry and viewing the Event Log in Event Viewer. Use REGEDT32 to locate the Registry key listed below and change the value to 3 or greater. This will record events 1009 and 1013, which signal the beginning and end of the KCC's regular network scan. Events concerning Global Catalogs and the Intersite Topology Generator may also be listed.

```
HKEY_LOCAL_MACHINE\System\CurrentControlSet\Services\NTDS\Diagnostics
1 Knowledge Consistency Checker
```

Active Directory Sizer

Active Directory Sizer, or ADSizer, helps you survey your organization to estimate the size of your Active Directory database. It's available for download at no cost on Microsoft's website. Activate the compressed **setup.exe** file that you've downloaded, and it will install the program on your computer. It does not require Windows Server 2003 or 2000; it will run on any Windows workstation.

The program looks like an MMC. Right-click Site Configuration in the left pane and provide site information about your network. Select Domain Configuration to activate a series of forms that collect information about your network in six parts, as shown in the next screens. After soliciting your network name, ADSizer asks for user data, including count and logon frequency. The count screen is shown in Figure 14.36.

FIGURE 14.36

ADSizer surveys
user details

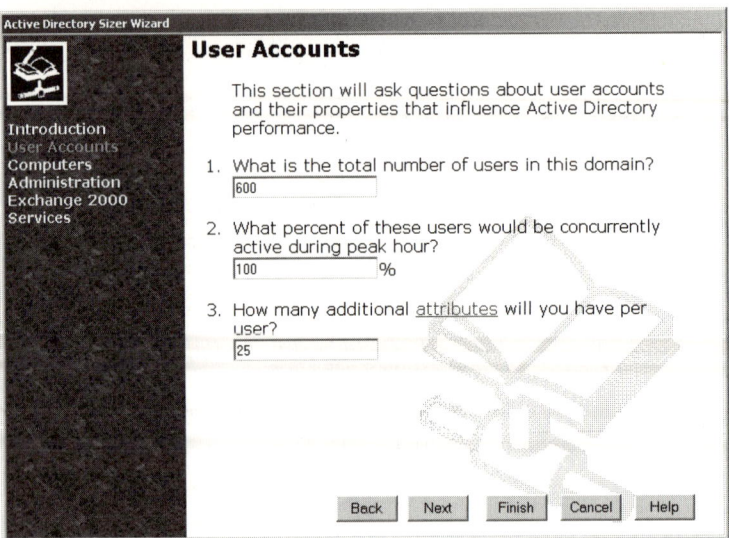

The next screen, shown in Figure 14.37, surveys workstations and printers (other objects) on your network.

FIGURE 14.37

Computer stats

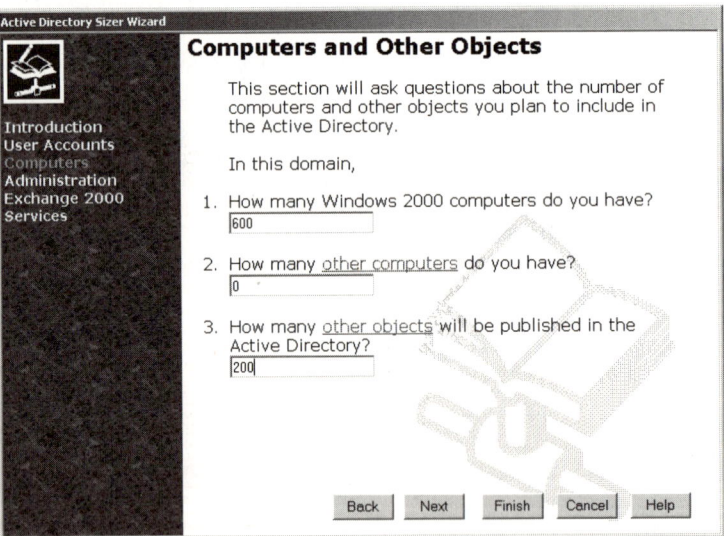

Then, the program collects information about domain controllers, including CPU type, as shown in Figure 14.38. You can supply the details, or let the program suggest a CPU and number of processors according to your needs.

FIGURE 14.38

Domain controller
information

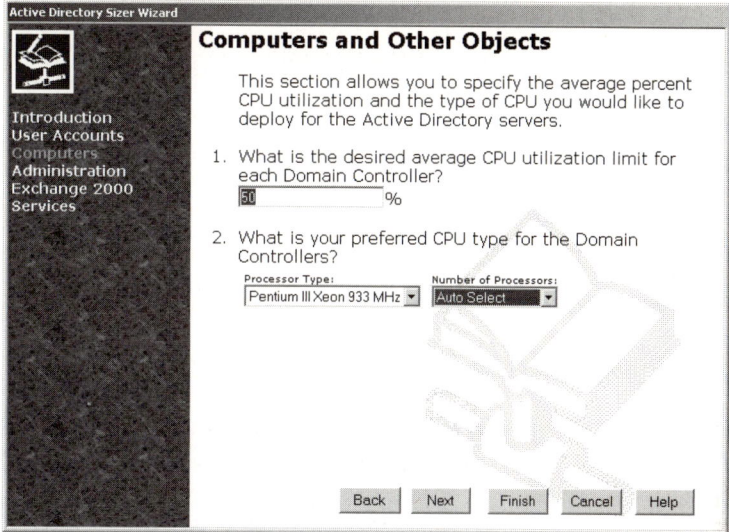

The Administration section comes up next, collecting details about the average number of objects added, deleted, and modified on a regular basis. The questionnaire goes on to survey usage of Exchange 2000. The last section surveys data about services, including DNS and DHCP.

The final screen presents a page of statistics, which summarizes the data it has collected, as shown in Figure 14.39.

FIGURE 14.39

ADSizer's final
summary page

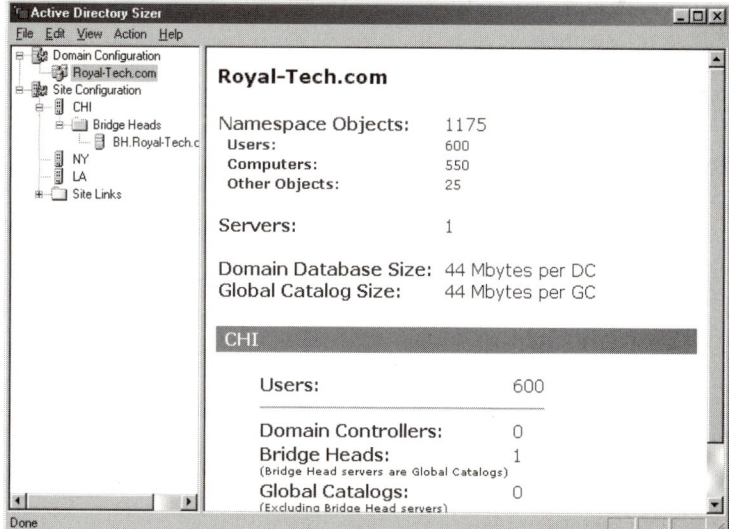

DCDIAG

DCDIAG is another command-line tool located in the CD's \Support\Tools folder that can provide a wealth of information. It checks the status of connections, replication, topology, FRS, and many other services. The best way to run it is to direct its output to a file that you can search. That command is listed below, and Figure 14.40 shows an excerpt as it inspects naming context partitions at the command line.

```
Dcdiag > <filename.txt>
```

FIGURE 14.40

Partial report from DCDIAG

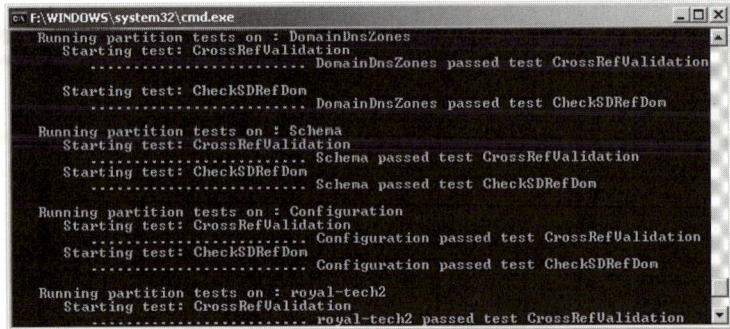

In Short

Replication is the circulatory system for your network. It distributes and collects information on every domain controller and maintains consistency. There are actually several replicating systems working simultaneously on an Active Directory network. In this chapter, we've looked at a number of ways to monitor the impact that traffic can have on a network, site creation, and measures you can take to manage it and recover from hardware failures.

In the next chapter, we'll look into implementing backups to fortify your network.

Chapter 15

Backup and Recovery of Active Directory

A DOMAIN CONTROLLER REPRESENTS a major investment in labor, so build a security net for it. Hardware can be replaced, repaired, or upgraded. Software applications can be reinstalled. But network configurations, which are created over time and probably by more than one person, are not easily recovered or reproduced. So backing up is not a question of whether, but of how and when. Your domain controller contains the Registry, Active Directory, the Windows Server 2003 operating system, and possibly data and applications. Everyone in the business knows that getting these items onto tape on a regular basis is the best way to ensure job security. I've often heard backups called the ultimate CYA (Cover Your Assets)—even if everything goes to hell in a hand-basket, with a good set of backup tapes you can recover gracefully. (Without those tapes, you are likely to find yourself looking for a new position.)

Many people seem to think that backups are basically protection against hardware failures: a hard drive dies in your server, you purchase a replacement, and you can recover the data that was lost by pulling it off your tapes. This might have been the original intent of backups, but as our world became more complex, so did our IT needs. Today, protection from hardware failure is actually not the most important consideration when deciding upon a backup strategy. Most of us purchase servers that have high levels of fault tolerance. The servers I've been buying for Cardinal Glass, for instance, have redundant system BIOSs, redundant power supplies, dual processors, and RAID 5 disk controllers, and they are (usually) even plugged into redundant UPSs (a dedicated one plugged into a buildingwide circuit—hey, we are a 24/7 shop!). Heck, one of our high-end servers even has RAID 10—two mirrored RAID 5 subsystems. On that server we would have to lose four drives (two on each RAID 5 subsystem) before we lost data.

So, if backups aren't solely for system recovery, then why are they so important? The answer to that revolves around our changing industry. First, our users are gaining more and more sophistication with the tools they use, but because those tools are designed to be transparent, they are gaining fewer skills in the actual underlying technologies. It is not uncommon to find a user who has mastered a sophisticated application, something like advanced page layout in PageMaker, but who has no real understanding of the mechanism used to store their documents. I hear "My file disappeared!" or

"The system ate my report!" from end users. This is where a consistent, well-organized, backup strategy can be a life saver. The user deletes (oops—the network eats) a file; you pull it back from last night's tape. The user is happy, you're a hero, and the expensive backup solution has once again proved its worth.

Another, and possibly more important, reason for backups is virus protection. Almost every network—no matter the size—has Internet access. As soon as you open a network to the outside world, you expose it to threats that are inherent in that environment. The smallest companies, even companies as small as my own, are hacked or infected on a regular basis. No matter how diligent you are, the people who create viruses always seem to be one step ahead of you. At best, an infestation leaves you with programs that need to be restored. At worst, virus attacks can mean a complete rebuild of your servers—from the ground up. Once again, your well-organized backup strategy will save the day!

If you have been doing your backups rigorously, you'll be rewarded one day when your server's hard drive fails, an important file is deleted, or a virus wipes your disks, because you'll be able to restore it to working condition from a recent backup. In this chapter, we'll start with an overview of backup procedures and then focus on issues specific to Active Directory.

In this chapter:

◆ Backup 101: backup methods and hardware

◆ Active Directory files

◆ Using Windows Backup

◆ Restoring Active Directory

Backup 101

Plan for disaster. Frequency should be determined by the value of your data. In most cases, your strategy should include a daily backup, regular inspection of log files, and periodic test restores. Backups should occur whenever there is low or no activity on the system, which explains why they are most commonly scheduled at night. There are five common backup methods:

Normal   Backup applications manipulate file attributes called *archive bits* to keep track of files. When a file has not been backed up, its archive bit is "on"; after a backup the bit is turned "off." A normal backup copies selected files and directories on your hard disk and turns off the archive bit for each file.

Incremental   Incremental backups use archive bits to identify and copy only those files that have been modified or created since the last backup. Then those bits are reset for each file.

Differential   Differential backups copy files changed or created since the last normal backup but do not clear archive bits.

Copy   A copy backup duplicates selected files but does not remove archive bits.

Daily   A daily backup picks up selected files that have been modified or created that day and does not clear markers.

NOTE *The term* normal *has replaced* full *when referring to a backup in which the entire system is placed on tape. Microsoft Press started this trend (to the best of my knowledge), probably to ensure that the name used was indicative of their viewpoint. Whenever possible, Microsoft likes to see daily normal/full backups! So do the tape manufacturers.*

The advantage of a normal backup is that it is a complete record of the folders you select on your hard drive; the downside is that it is slower and requires more storage space than other options. Incremental and differential settings are faster because they are partial backups, but you may have to search through several media to locate a deleted or corrupted file.

If you do a normal nightly backup, and a user reports that she is missing a file on Thursday, you would look for the file on the most recent tape, the one for Wednesday night. If it were a normal tape backup, your search would be over. If this file had been added or modified Tuesday morning, a differential backup would have copied it on Tuesday's and Wednesday's, so you would find it on Wednesday's tape. If you had used the incremental method, you would waste your time looking on Wednesday's and find it on Tuesday's tape. In other words, differential backups make for faster restores than incrementals.

NOTE *Files are not actually copied the way we copy data from a hard drive to a floppy disk, since they are packed sequentially into one large file. That's why you need a restore program—to decipher the backup file and extract the file(s) you need. See "Using Windows Backup" and "Restoring Active Directory" later in this chapter.*

The daily and copy methods are used to identify files and duplicate them to different media. For example, you could designate folders to copy to a laptop or a zip disk so that a user could transport and access the files outside of the office. The difference is that a copy backup is not limited to data that was accessed during that day.

Backup Hardware

Backup simply means file duplication. Depending upon the preferences of your software application, you may be able to use any storage media: tape, CD-R, zip drive, floppy disk, or hard disk. Tape drives are preferred because they have the capacity to store huge amounts of data. It's not likely that you'll be available to pop in a second zip disk when prompted, since you'll most likely be scheduling this operation at periods of minimal network activity, usually at night.

Your tape drive should be SCSI, for the same reason you chose it for hard drive storage: it's fast. Some applications allow you to back up data from your workstations through the network remotely to the server's tape drive, but the Registry and Active Directory files on your domain controller need to be backed up locally.

Active Directory Files

Active Directory's files are stored in the Windows\NTDS folder on your system root. When an administrator creates or modifies a network resource, data is written to the active *log file*, `edb.log`. Then that data is transferred to a database buffer. Finally, it is written to the database file, `ntds.dit`. If you do a search for `ntds.dit`, you'll find two copies on your hard drive. The second one, located in Windows\System32, is the template file that was transferred to your hard drive when you installed Active Directory.

By default, AD interacts with its log files in *sequential* mode, which means that it creates and stores historical log files. The edb.log file fills up at 10MB, creates a new log file, which is numbered sequentially (edb00001.log, edb00002.log, and so on), and moves its data to the new numbered file, purges itself, and then continues in its role as the active database log.

Circular logging is the alternative to sequential logging. This method saves disk space by overwriting edb.log when it fills up, rather than transferring data to new files. This is not recommended by Microsoft, but it can be enabled by editing the Registry.

The file edb.chk is a checkpoint log file that coordinates the data transfer between the log files and the database. You'll notice two additional log files in the NTDS folder, res1.log and res2.log. They are spaceholders that guarantee that edb.log will be able to dump its contents when the time arrives. If the hard drive fills up, these reserved log files will store any outstanding transactions and shut down the server due to low disk space.

NOTE *The reserve log files are exactly 10 megabytes in size; if their size is not exactly 10,485,760 bytes, you are probably looking at a corrupted AD database. (Time to utilize those backups you've been doing!)*

Patch files are temporary files that have a .pat filename extension. They are used to track changes made to the AD database when a backup is active. Take a look at Figure 15.1 for a listing of the Active Directory database and log files.

FIGURE 15.1

Active Directory files

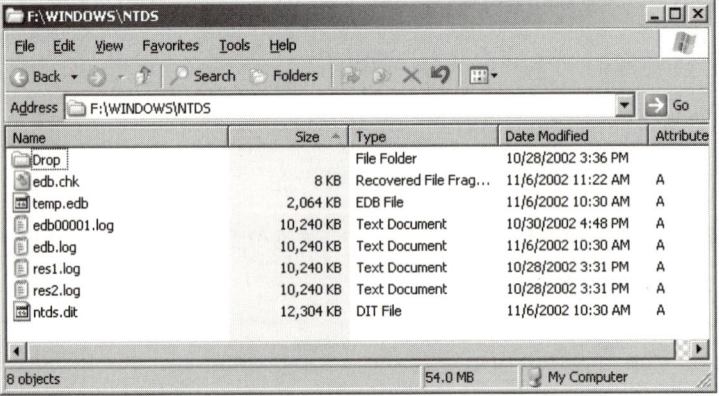

System State Data

System State Data refers to a computer's essential system files. The specific files differ according to a computer's role. *Be sure to back up these files regularly.* They are necessary to restore Active Directory Services to a domain controller. System State Data can only be backed up using normal or copy methods. Actually, I would dedicate a separate backup to System State. In the case of a domain controller, System State files include these:

◆ Active Directory

◆ Registry

- System files under Windows File Protection

- Boot files

- SYSVOL folder

- COM+ objects

- Certificate Services (if server is running Certificate Services)

- Cluster Service (if server is running Cluster Service)

Microsoft Backup lists System State Data as a separate item (as do most third-party backup applications), as you can see in Figure 15.2.

FIGURE 15.2

System State Data

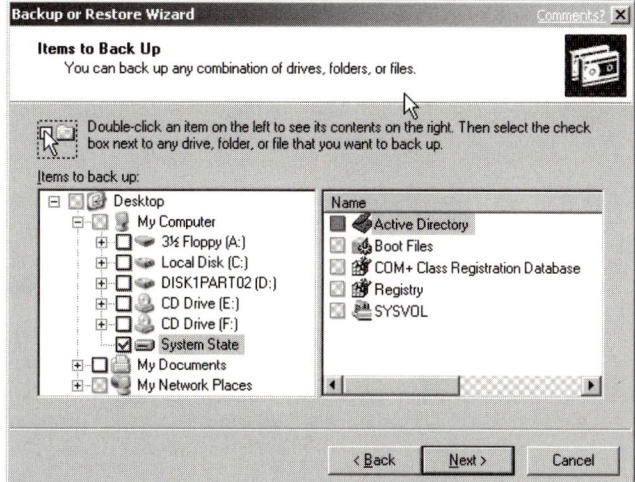

User Permissions

Of course, not every user has the right to back up and restore Active Directory files. That privilege is reserved for members of the local Administrators, Backup Operators, and Server Operators groups. This is yet another good reason to limit membership in these critical security groups. Having the ability to restore Active Directory implies the ability to really mess up your environment. Because the AD database is replicated to every domain controller, one wrong move could mess up AD across your entire environment!

The following relevant rights are granted to members of these groups:

- Log on locally

- Back up files and directories

- Restore files and directories

If, for some reason, you need to grant these rights to an individual or a group without adding them to a built-in group such as Backup Operators, access the Administrative Tools on the domain controller. Open the Domain Controller Security Policy and drill down to Computer Configuration ➤ Windows Settings ➤ Security Settings. Under Local Policies, access User Rights. To modify one of the rights listed above, double-click it and select the Add User or Group button, and browse for a name or type it in the box provided.

Using Windows Backup

Microsoft's Backup utility is new and improved in Windows Server 2003. You can back up to or restore from any media that is recognized by the *Removable Storage Manager (RSM)*, including tape, floppy disk, and zip drives. It's also possible to back up to a separate drive or partition on the server or to a network share, but be sure that these are NTFS 5–formatted so that your files do not lose certain properties, such as encryption.

Activate Backup by clicking through Programs ➤ Accessories ➤ System Tools. You'll see Windows' cascading menus in Figure 15.3. After you've run the program once, it will appear on the Start menu, which you'll notice in the left pane in Figure 15.3.

FIGURE 15.3

Running the Windows Backup utility

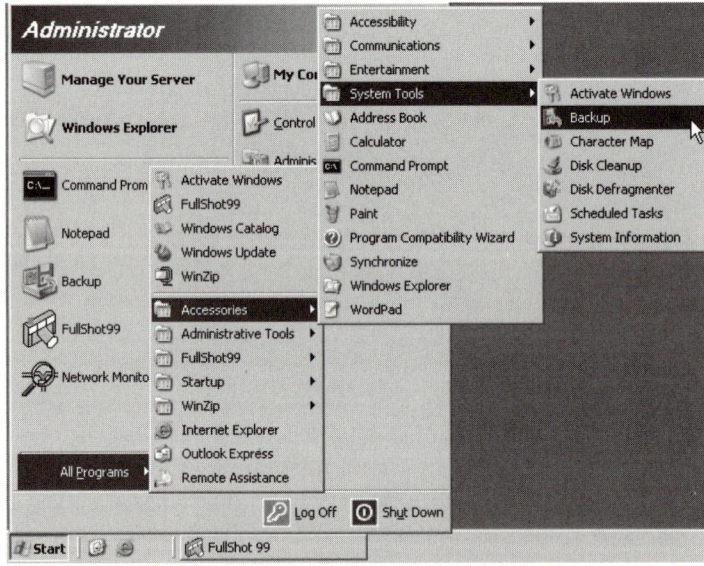

As you can see in Figure 15.4, you can use a wizard or select the Advanced Mode hyperlink for manual operation. We'll use the wizard in this example. Perform the following steps:

FIGURE 15.4

Welcome to
Windows Backup

1. Click Next for Backup or Restore operations, as shown in Figure 15.5.

FIGURE 15.5

Choosing to back
up or restore

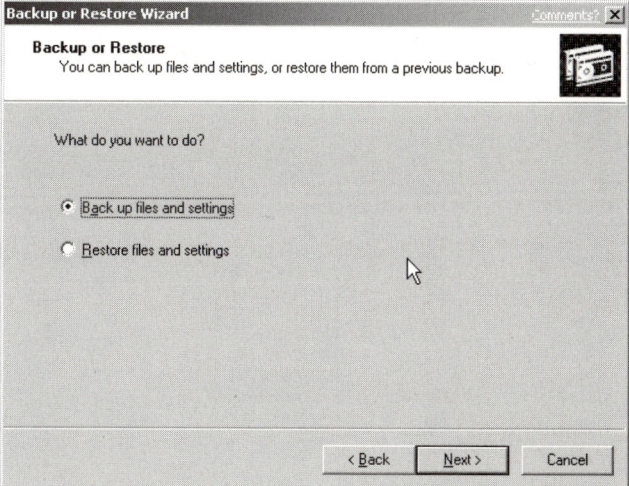

2. Select Back Up Files and Settings and click Next. The wizard asks you to select files to back up, as in Figure 15.6.

FIGURE 15.6

Having it your way

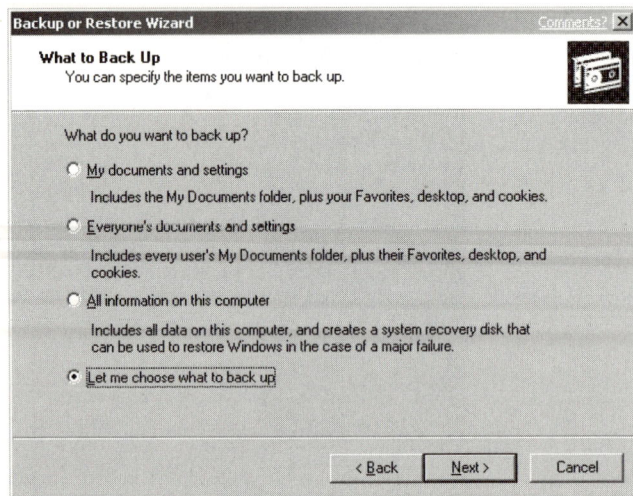

3. Choose the last option and click Next; you will see a list of the available source drives. I've checked the System State Data for our backup, as shown in Figure 15.7. Click Next.

FIGURE 15.7

Choosing source data

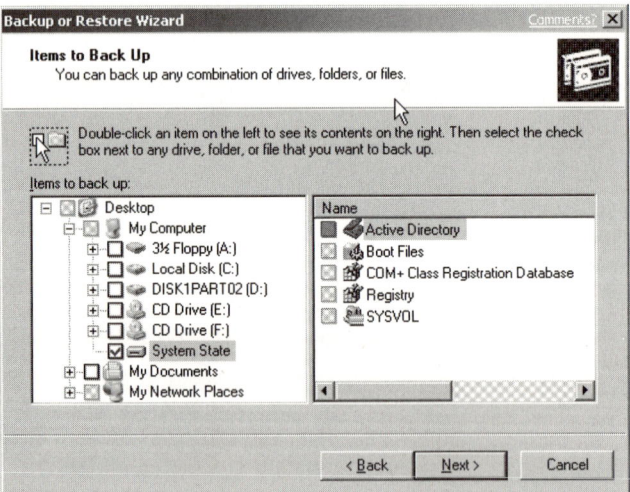

4. Windows Backup needs to know the destination drive and filename for your backup. Click the Browse button to locate your target device, most likely a tape drive. In Figure 15.8, Windows will create one huge file called `Backup.bkf` on the D drive. Click Next.

FIGURE 15.8

Choosing a target drive and filename

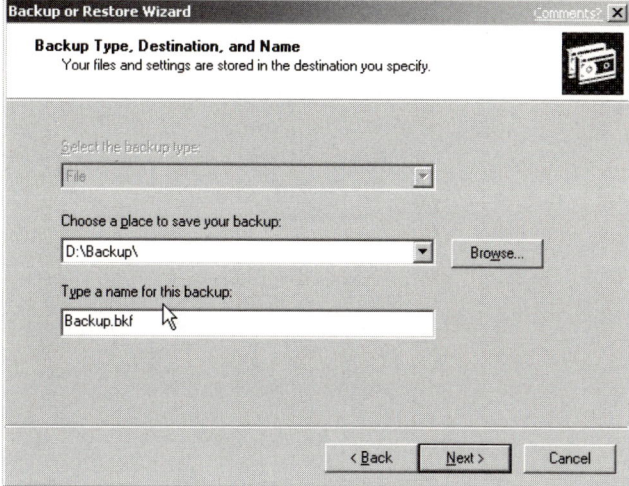

5. If you need to run the backup at this moment, you're finished. Click the Finish button on the next screen, and sit back to watch your tape drive leap into action. It would be more practical, however, to click the Advanced button, since this will allow you to name and save the backup and to schedule it to run automatically. Other options are accessible there, as well. I chose the Normal backup method at the next screen, since I am saving System State Data in this exercise, as displayed in Figure 15.9. Click Next.

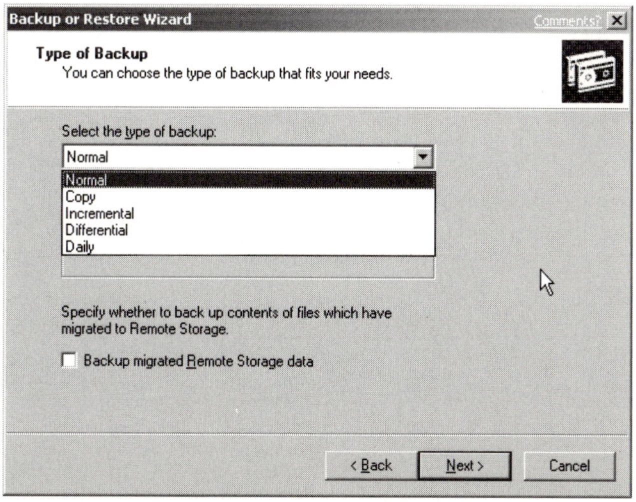

FIGURE 15.9

Choosing a backup method

6. It's a good idea to verify the backup. After copying files to your backup media, the program will verify that each file's size matches what is stored on the source drive, as in Figure 15.10. Depending upon your device, hardware compression may be available; just check the box.

FIGURE 15.10

Verifying the backup operation

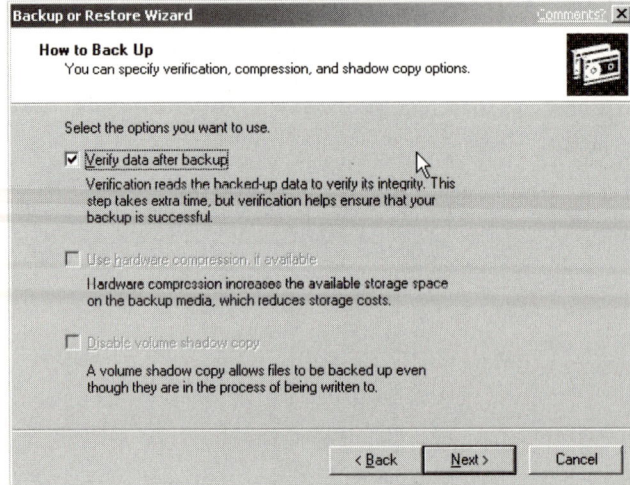

7. Do you want to overwrite your tape or add to it? Figure 15.11 illustrates the screen where you choose that setting. I would most likely use the Append option for incremental or differential backups. Click Next.

FIGURE 15.11

Append or replace

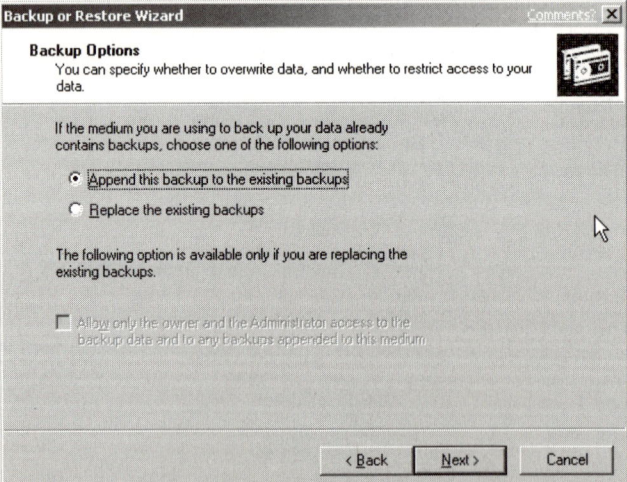

8. If you select Now, you're done, but you'll have to go through this procedure next time you want to back up. A better choice would be to name the operation by selecting the Later button, as shown in Figure 15.12, which will activate the Scheduling service. In Figure 15.13, you'll notice that I've scheduled this operation to occur weekly for Mondays at 11 PM, so I named it "Monday System backup" in Figure 15.12.

FIGURE 15.12

Naming the backup; choosing Later

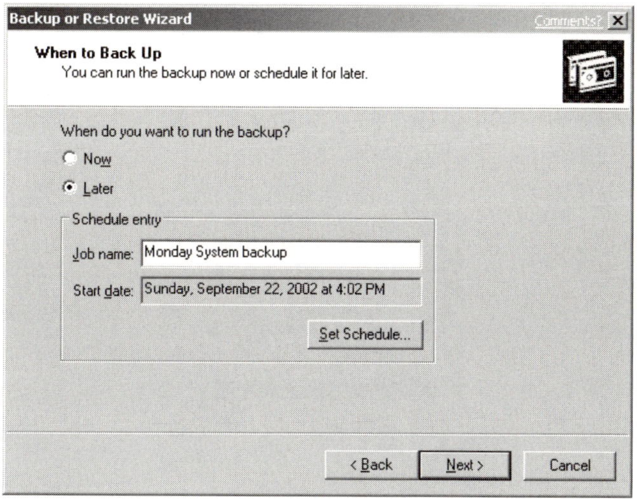

FIGURE 15.13

Scheduling the backup

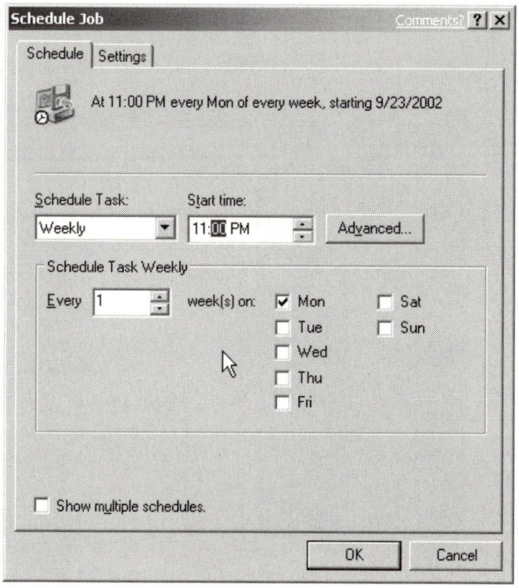

9. What to do if a problem occurs? The Settings tab displays alternative actions that the backup operation can follow if it is interrupted by a power event or some other problem. They are displayed in Figure 15.14. Click OK to return to the previous screen. Then click Next.

FIGURE 15.14

Options for incomplete backups

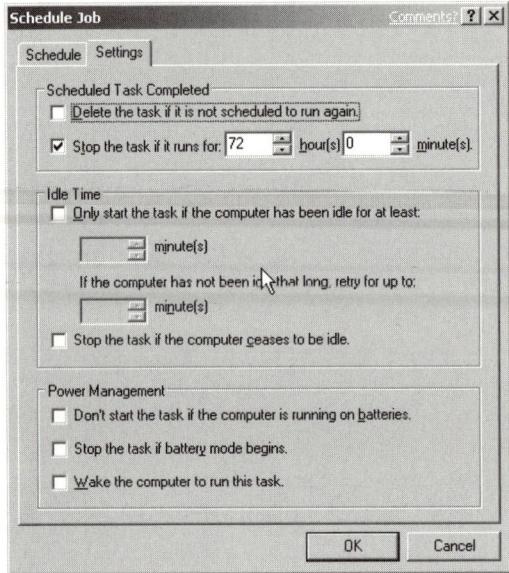

10. Voila! Figure 15.15 displays the summary screen, where you can check your settings and click Finish.

FIGURE 15.15

Completing the Backup Wizard

The preceding example of backing up the System State Data to a file is actually a real-world solution to a vexing problem. Many backup utilities are unable to back up the System State Data on remote computers. In other words, if you back up your servers across the wire to a centrally located tape device, you are unable to back up the System State Data. Our example demonstrates how to work around this issue—just back up the System State Data to a local file on each server, and then back up that file using your backup application. Depending upon the number of changes you make to your server's configurations, you could perform this type of backup weekly or even monthly.

NTBACKUP

For those of you who prefer the command prompt to a GUI, NTBACKUP is still available. You can type NTBACKUP /? to view a list of options for the command. NTBACKUP backs up but does not restore files. Using the various switches, you can accomplish any of the tasks you can do with the Backup utility. To perform a System State backup similar to the one we did using the Microsoft Backup utility, use this command:

```
NTBACKUP backup systemstate /f "D:\backup\backup.bkf" /j "Monday System backup" /l:s
/v:yes
```

To translate the switches:

/f is the backup destination folder and filename.

/j saves the job with the name you supply in quotation marks.

/l:s creates a summary log file.

/v:yes turns on verify.

Restoring Active Directory

Domain controllers do not exist in a vacuum. They have peers, or replication partners, with whom they share information on a regular basis. For example, if one domain controller goes down (let's call it FS2), the others will march on, steadfastly fulfilling their responsibilities. We then repair or replace FS2, restore it from a current backup, and put it online. When it returns to active duty, its AD database will not match those of its partners, since its information is not up-to-date. Active Directory has three restore methods, which we'll discuss in detail: Non-authoritative, Authoritative, and Primary.

Non-authoritative Restore

At this point, a replication partner would update the newly restored FS2. This scenario describes a *Non-authoritative restore*, which is the default mode for a restore operation. The assumption for a Non-authoritative restore is that new data (stored on the other domain controllers) should replace old data (restored to FS2) in case of a discrepancy. There's nothing more for the network administrator to do, since the replication process will automatically distribute its current AD database across a domain. A key is created in the Registry that notifies Active Directory that this domain controller requires updates, a consistency check, and reindexing. This key is deleted when these procedures have been completed.

For our example, we'll restore the System State Data to FS2 from the backup we created previously with the Microsoft Backup utility:

1. Restart the computer and press F8 before the Windows splash screen appears.

2. Select Directory Services Restore Mode (DSRM) at the text mode listing, which, you'll notice, includes other alternative boot options, such as Safe mode and Last Known Good Configuration.

3. Next, log on using the special username and password you created for restore mode when you promoted the server to a domain controller with DCPROMO. Windows warns you that you are running in Safe mode.

4. Run Microsoft Backup as you did earlier, choosing the Restore option.

5. On the next screen, select the files or folders you wish to restore. Notice in Figure 15.16 that I've selected the System State (you have to choose the entire item) on `Backup.bkf`.

FIGURE 15.16

Restoring System State

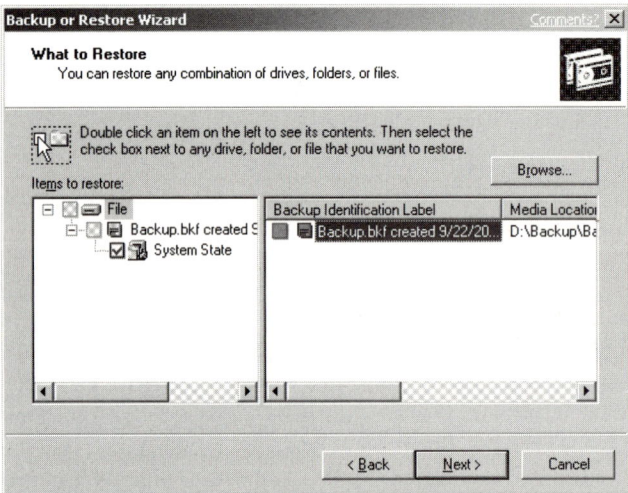

6. Click Finish on the next screen, shown in Figure 15.17, and the operation will begin.

7. After all the files have been copied to their original locations, restart the computer per the instructions, and your server will be running a healthy Active Directory, up-to-date as of the day you backed it up. The replicating partners will visit shortly, to update FS2 with current information.

FIGURE 15.17

Completing the Restore Wizard

Authoritative Restore

But what if FS2 crashed before it had a chance to share modifications to its directory with its replication partners? Or what if you had deleted an organizational unit by mistake that contained several hundred objects, and the changes (deletions) had been replicated to other domain controllers? All is not lost. If you do an *Authoritative restore*, you can select the entire AD database, or specific objects to be preserved when the server returns to service, so that it will replicate that information to its partners. Authoritative restores are limited to domain and configuration information only; they cannot restore schema. When you make your selections, the Update Sequence Numbers (USNs) for those objects will be incremented by 100,000 to make your server the authoritative source for their attributes when it communicates with its replication partners. For the next step in our Authoritative restore, we need to use NTDSUTIL (a database management utility for Active Directory) at the command line:

1. Start the procedure as you would for a Non-authoritative restore: take the domain controller offline, press F8, and select Directory Services Restore Mode.

2. Run Backup and restore the System State Data.

3. While still in DSR mode, go to the command prompt and type **NTDSUTIL /?** to display the program's various options. The screen will look like Figure 15.18.

FIGURE 15.18

NTDSUTIL
command options

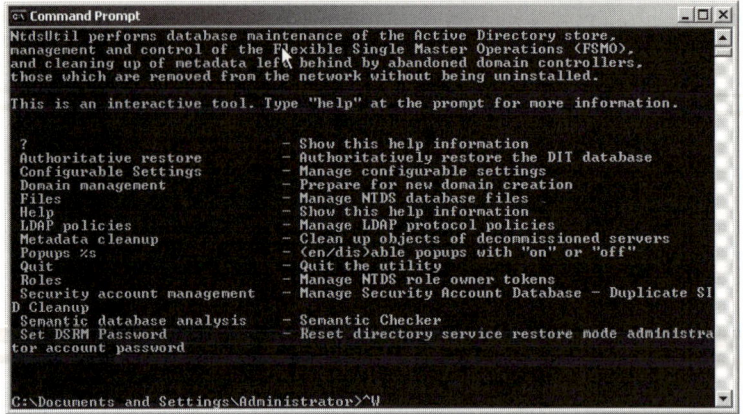

4. To restore the entire AD database, type **Restore Data** at the prompt. Figure 15.19 shows what the command looked like when I ran NTDSUTIL to authorize the restored Tech organizational unit on my domain controller.

FIGURE 15.19

Choosing
Authoritative
restore

```
E:\>ntdsutil
ntdsutil: authoritative restore
authoritative restore: restore subtree OU=Tech,DC=Royal-Tech,DC=COM
```

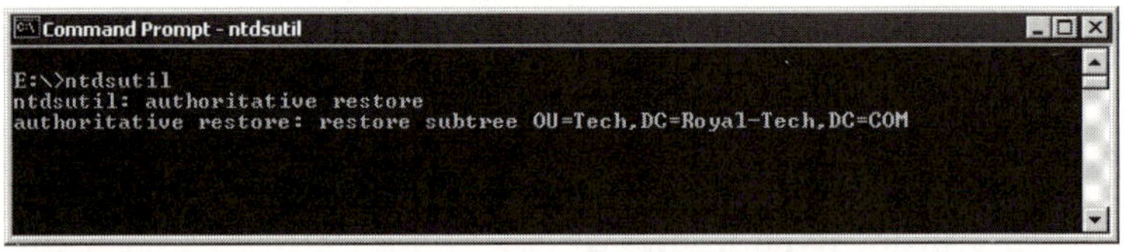

When the domain controller is restarted, it will once again display the Tech OU in Active Directory Users and Computers. Since the USNs have been incremented, this data will update replication partners and restore these objects throughout the domain.

Tombstones

Now, how could it be possible to resuscitate all those objects from the dead on your server? After all, you did remove them from Active Directory, and this information was passed along to other domain controllers. Actually, when you delete an object, it is not immediately removed from Active Directory's database. Its status changes to *deleted*, but the object remains intact for a specified period of time called a *tombstone lifetime*. For a default period of 60 days, deleted objects are in limbo, available to be restored. After that time has elapsed, however, they are removed during the process of *garbage collection*, which is a maintenance procedure that occurs every 12 hours on domain controllers.

So, this information was still stored in your domain controller's directory and on every other domain controller in the domain. When the replication partners received your instruction to delete those objects, they changed the objects' statuses. And when you Authoritatively restored those objects on your domain controller, the other servers followed suit.

The tombstone lifetime determines the lifetime of your backup media. If you resuscitate a server with a backup that is older than that period of time, it will contain objects that have already been removed from other domain controllers by the process of garbage collection. For that reason, this server's AD will never agree with those of its partners. Therefore, backups older than the tombstone lifetime are not safe to use.

Although Microsoft recommends against it, you can change the Tombstone Lifetime on your domain controller with an MMC snap-in called Active Directory Services Interface Editor, or ADSI Edit. You'll need to install the program from the \Support\Tools folder on the installation CD. Right-click `suptools.msc`, choose Install on the menu, and select a destination folder. It will create a new item called Windows Support Tools on your program menu, which doesn't seem to do much but provide a command prompt, release notes, and help. Actually, the best way to run ADSI Edit is to double-click `adsiedit.msc` in the folder you copied it to, using Explorer or My Computer. A new MMC will appear, but unfortunately you can't save it since it's in User mode. To modify the tombstone lifetime, follow these steps:

1. Click the plus sign to expand the Configuration Container in the left pane.

2. Click CN=Configuration, CN=Services, and CN=Windows NT. See Figure 15.20 for details.

3. Right-click CN=Directory Service and choose Properties.

4. In the Select a Property to View list, select Tombstone Lifetime.

5. If the number in the Value box is <not set>, it is using the default setting of 60 days. Change it at your peril.

FIGURE 15.20

ADSI Edit in action

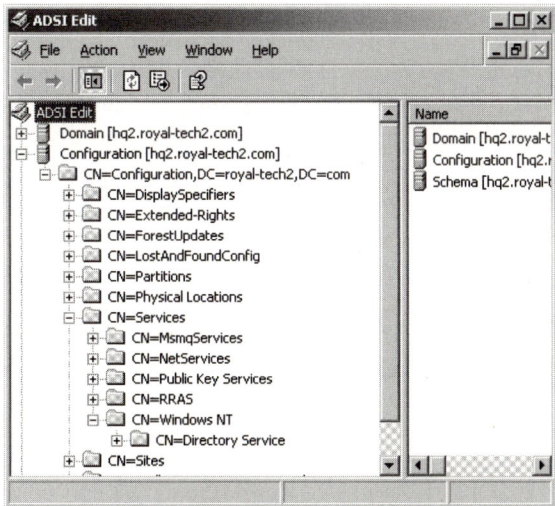

Primary Restore

What if you have a disaster and there are no replication partners? A *Primary restore* rebuilds a domain controller from backup after all domain controllers are lost. This server will become the Authority for replication in the domain. Primary restore creates a new File Replication Service (FRS) in the SYSVOL folder. All other domain controllers should use a Non-authoritative restore and replicate to the first one. Select Advanced Restore Options in Microsoft Backup as displayed in Figure 15.21 when you do a Primary restore on the first domain controller.

FIGURE 15.21

Primary restore options in Backup

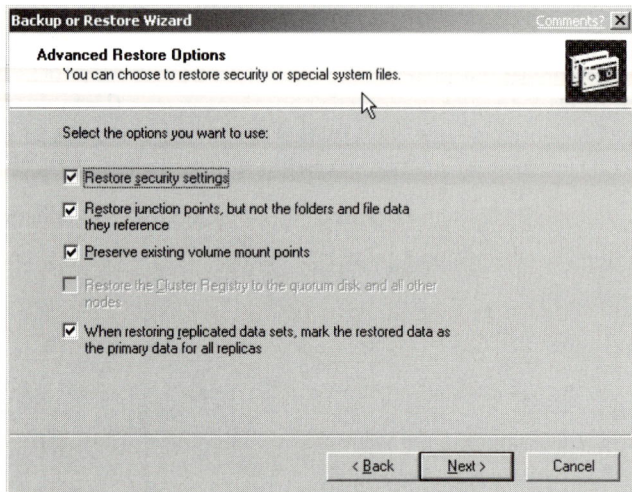

Since the domain controller has crashed, we have to reinstall Windows Server 2003/2000 Server first.

1. Reinstall Windows Server 2003/2000 Server to the repaired domain controller. Create a partition at least equal in size to the one that failed and use the same drive letter.

2. Press F8 when the server boots and select Directory Services Restore Mode.

3. Run Windows Backup and select Restore. Choose System State and System Disk, plus any data that you want to restore.

4. Click the Advanced button and select Original Location in the Restore Files To box.

5. In Advanced Restore Options, select the following, as in Figure 15.21:

   ◆ Restore security settings.

   ◆ Restore junction points and restore files and folders to their original locations.

   ◆ Preserve existing volume mount points.

   ◆ When restoring data sets, mark the restored data as the primary data for all replicas.

6. When the files have been restored, restart.

In Short

Backup and Restore operations are bulwarks against data loss. In this chapter, we identified the data files that make up Active Directory. We used Microsoft's Backup utility to demonstrate various backup operations and strategies, as well as a Non-authoritative restore. Then, we completed an Authoritative restore using NTDSUTIL.

In the next chapter, we'll discuss how to implement an effective Active Directory design that will support your business strategy, and we'll look at a few network scenarios.

Chapter 16

Active Directory Design

MANY OF THE TOPICS presented in this chapter are addressed in other contexts in this book. For example, *trees* and *forests* are discussed in Chapter 8, "Designing the Active Directory Environment," as components of Active Directory; and *namespace* is defined in Chapter 6, "Active Directory Benefits," and Chapter 7, "Network Support Services." The purpose of this chapter, therefore, is to place the design elements and principles in a broader context, one directed at the large-scale needs of your organization.

NOTE *To get the most out of this chapter, you need to understand the various components and technical issues of Active Directory—such as domains, organizational units, and schema—as described in earlier parts of this book.*

Function follows design; this is a maxim used in industry, architecture, art, and engineering. Since Active Directory represents a hierarchical database of network resources, it creates an infrastructure that directs the flow of information on a network. The design you choose should complement business processes operating within your organization.

There has been some confusion generated by that last statement, "…should complement business processes…" Before AD was a reality—back in the vaporware days—Microsoft frequently stated that Active Directory would require a whole new way of looking at your network; that the proper utilization of Active Directory would require a design that matched the environment in which it was installed. The first sets of design documents and classes all implied that the engineer/consultant responsible for the AD design would have to understand all aspects of the business into which it was placed, and would have to design an AD structure that matched the structure of the company using it. I don't necessarily agree. Although it is true that you will have to do some research into the environment, and it is also true that an understanding of the business processes in use will help design an efficient AD structure, I tend to disagree with the concept of designing to match the overall business philosophy.

Before we get into my guidelines for design, we must first have an understanding of the overall network/business structures of which you must be aware and the various AD components used to build the AD hierarchical structure. With that in mind, the first part of this chapter will concentrate on defining those components. Once we've laid our foundation, then I'll discuss various design guidelines that will help you put together a workable, efficient, and stable Active Directory structure.

In this chapter:

◆ Elements of planning and design: the business environment, technical requirements, and AD structure

◆ Designing the DNS namespace

◆ Sites: the physical composition of a network

◆ Putting it all together

Elements of Planning and Design

When you trace the path of data as it moves through your organization, you'll notice that it follows a structured pattern. Planning a network design requires that you analyze business processes and build a framework with Active Directory to conduct this flow of information. (The key word in the preceding sentence is *flow*—keep that word in mind as we continue our discussion.)

How can you improve specific operations with a better design? The decision to implement Active Directory should be based upon specific goals. Active Directory's advantages may be obvious to you as a technical person, but they may not be evident to others. Infrastructure changes have cultural consequences. During the planning phase, you will be communicating with colleagues on every level of the company. Keep in mind that change requires a team effort; the best way to successfully plan and implement major changes is by consensus and participation. Your design should transform business interactions into data transactions. Below is a list of the major topics we will cover as we investigate the design process.

◆ Business environment

◆ Technical requirements

◆ Active Directory structure

Analyzing the Business Environment

Before you implement your Windows 2000/Windows Server 2003 network with Active Directory, you need to collect information about your organization's operational, administrative, and physical requirements through a series of interviews. Your role in the organization will determine how you approach the interview task: an outside consultant needs explicit responses, while an employee may be familiar with most of this information. In any case, it's a good idea to take a step back, look at the big picture, and record data objectively to guide your design. There is no standard data bank, but here are some important queries to pose to the appropriate individuals:

◆ What is your vision of the organization?

◆ Where do you see the company in three to five years?

◆ What changes do you expect to occur in your organization in the next three to five years?

◆ List any challenges your business is currently facing and how you are responding to them.

- Do you plan to merge with or acquire another company in the near future?

- What are your plans regarding opening new locations, offices, or business divisions?

- How is your company organized geographically? Do different locations operate autonomously?

- Are your various locations affected by time zone or language problems? How do you currently handle those issues?

- What is the scope of this project?

- What are your expectations for Active Directory?

- How do you share information between different locations? Do you have teams that cross geographical barriers to work together?

- Do any of your vendors or partners access your network?

- Does your website play a role in extending relationships with customers, vendors, or partners?

- Do you use intranet or extranet technologies?

- Identify target dates, decision makers, team members, and their roles and responsibilities.

- List requirements and goals for each business unit.

- Describe the decision-making process at your company.

- How do you communicate decisions to staff members?

- Are there any laws with which you must comply?

TIP   *Microsoft's website has a wealth of resources available pertaining to Active Directory design. One publication includes a number of templates—actually a series of interviews—that walk you through the process of documenting the business model, the current operating environment, and plans for the future. As of this writing, it's at* `www.microsoft.com/technet/prodtechnol/ad/windows2000/deploy/adguide/DEFAULT.asp`.

Draw a map of the geographical divisions of the company, including their functions and the number of employees at each office. If many changes are planned, create a second diagram that illustrates plans for the future. You should also note the direction and types of data that flow through the organization.

The end result of all this reportage should be a map of the rivers of data, their sources, tributaries, and destinations. You will also have identified the prominent decision makers and the members of your team.

For example, positive responses to one or more of the following issues may lead you to consider a multiple-domain design:

- Large geographical area

- Autonomous units

- Multiple time zones

◆ Cultural differences

◆ Currency differences

◆ Legal differences

A multiple-domain framework allows technical decisions to be made locally, although resources can be shared across the domains.

Intranet and extranet issues requiring that vendors and partners access information remotely will influence DNS design. One solution is split-brained DNS, where local and remote users log on over different DNS zones. It also raises security concerns, which might call for a firewall between your LAN and WAN.

The answer to the question about impending changes may raise a red flag. Since it's difficult to modify infrastructure once it's in place, in this situation, you should probably stick to the simplest structure you can, i.e., single domain. You can always add domains later, but it's more difficult to remove or restructure them.

Mergers and acquisitions between companies with different DNS structures point in the direction of multiple trees merged into one forest to share resources. If your organization is decentralized, sites with distributed domain controllers and/or multiple domains make sense.

Remember: *separate sites do not necessarily translate into separate domains.* The domain boundary is administrative, not geographical. A company with teams that work together over a WAN can implement sites with multiple domain controllers, but a single domain may be their best path because it simplifies network administration.

Technical Requirements

Next, survey the technical issues. Collect factual information about network topologies, hardware devices, and software applications currently in place. As you interview technical staff, you should also record anecdotal information relating to their perceptions of current problems and solutions or concerns.

Do not forget to record the skill sets of each IT staffer you interview. Remember, these are the people who will first help you implement your AD design and, second, maintain it in the long term. Knowing their skills can help you when it comes time to delegate authority.

EXISTING SYSTEMS AND INFRASTRUCTURE

Document the logical topology of the wide area network for the entire organization. Note the speed of each link and the number of users at each location and add plans for new locations to your map. Then, diagram the physical WANs and LANs, including the following details:

◆ Service type (i.e., Ethernet, ISDN)

◆ Speed

◆ Subnets

◆ Cabling: vertical, horizontal

◆ Routers: interface addresses

- Firewalls

- Switches: VLANs

- Servers

Next, you'll need a detailed inventory of hardware and software at each location. Provide vendor information, RAM, hard drive, and operating systems for the computers. Licensing, version, and vendor data should be included with applications as appropriate. Take note, also, of backup and disaster recovery procedures currently in place.

- Servers: mainframes, file, print, web, fax

- Networking operating systems

- Desktops

- Network devices

- Desktop applications

- Network applications

Survey the network protocols and services that are currently in use. Examples are TCP/IP, DHCP, NetBIOS, DNS, etc. Do they use static IP addressing?

Next, measure network utilization at critical points in the company. You can run network monitor tools at servers, test Internet connection rates at various times, and so forth.

SECURITY ISSUES

Document security policies that are currently in place. This applies to local users and groups as well as to those who access the systems remotely. Use the following questions as guides:

- Who sets password policy, and what is it?

- Who defines users and provides access to resources?

- Will the organization need local groups? Global groups? Universal groups?

- How do they create access for temporary workers?

- Have duplicate and inactive users and groups been removed recently?

- Have there been any security problems recently?

- Do they use Virtual Private Networks (VPNs)?

- Is telecommuting in use?

Security is cultural behavior. Answers to these questions will help you to identify current practices, risks, and weaknesses. This information will also help you to organize resources into organizational units and identify users to whom you can delegate administrative tasks. Group Policy objects integrate password policies into your network. Policies can be assigned to OUs, sites, and/or domains to enforce security rules for accounts, such as password age and account lockout duration.

For example, we could apply Group Policies to OUs where the administrative department has different requirements than accounting. Or, we could standardize rules for the entire organization with a domainwide security policy. Universal groups are more difficult to manage than global domain groups, since only enterprise administrators can oversee them, and user accounts are on different domains. A multidomain network that requires groups to cross domain boundaries will need to be upgraded to 2000 native or Windows Server 2003 mode.

Managing temporary workers can be difficult, since hiring decisions and account changes are usually made on the departmental level. Knowledge of current practices might provide a solution. Perhaps you could create an OU reserved for temps, apply a security policy to enforce password changes, and create a group to manage that class of users, drawing members from various departments.

Duplicate and inactive user accounts should be removed regularly. Security logs must be monitored for inappropriate activity. If no procedure exists to audit and clean up accounts, you'll need to institute one and raise the awareness of the technical staff.

Remote access raises a number of technical and security issues. You'll need to unearth the details of the system currently in use, since insecure connections can compromise your company's network.

Active Directory Structure

Active Directory is composed of a hierarchy of objects, as listed below:

- Domains
- Organizational units
- Forests
- Trees

The design affects your decisions to create single or multiple objects and where to place boundaries.

DOMAINS

At what point do you create new domains? Domains are built to reflect administrative and security organizational structures that are already in place, which you discovered during the investigative phase. Since there are no hard-and-fast rules, you should compare alternative solutions.

The prototypical national-style company employs a classic hub-and-spoke arrangement, where a central headquarters functions as the decision-making body. This model uses domain policies to enforce uniform security across a single domain.

Don't assume that you need multiple domains because you have remote offices, since AD site connections will assist you in controlling replication traffic. On the negative side, network admins in the main office may not have first-hand knowledge of new users, printers, or access groups at remote sites. That's where delegation comes in (see "Organizational Units" later in this chapter for more details). You can elicit the assistance of individuals at the branch offices to help administer specific attributes of their workspace and still participate in one happy domain.

Single domains are simpler than multiple domains, but if you need to control directory services at more than one site, multiple domains are the solution. Table 16.1 lists domain creation issues.

TABLE 16.1: FEATURES OF SINGLE AND MULTIPLE DOMAIN DESIGNS

CHARACTERISTICS	SINGLE DOMAIN	MULTIPLE DOMAINS
Centralized administration	X	
Decentralized administration		X
Simplicity	X	
Single point of control	X	
Isolate or balance domain replication traffic		X
Multiple domain policies		X

Decentralized organizations use multiple domains, which creates administrative overhead, but network management controls are local. This is an administrative decision, since the organization can logistically resemble one that uses a centralized approach—the difference is that control is distributed throughout the company. Each location can manage its own resources and share with others when appropriate. Companies dispersed over large geographical distances ordinarily require autonomous units.

Two-tier designs are appropriate for branch office companies. A parent domain can be created in the center with separate child subdomains in the branches. An alternative is to use a single domain with OU containers to represent each branch office. Subsidiary and regional companies might use a parent-child arrangement, as well.

Another innovation is the empty root domain. Two merged companies that want to operate within a tree can set up separate child domains off a single domain. This design provides them the freedom to create very different organizational unit structures while maintaining a two-way trust relationship. A smaller company can accomplish this with one parent domain and two child OUs.

For large organizations, isolating and balancing replication traffic can be an important issue. Domain controllers communicating across domains share Global Catalogs, which are limited versions of the AD databases, so separating domains can help to conserve bandwidth. Installing multiple domains allows each domain to have distinct sets of controls on user and computer behavior. Other factors that encourage the use of multiple domains include geographical factors like language, currency, and time zone differences. "Political" considerations can also influence the decision to create separate domains, which exert control within their boundaries.

NOTE *The domain design must work for the designer, too. Stick to* single domains *whenever possible to save yourself from administrative headaches.*

Networks are designed to fit organizations. Let's consider three companies, each representing a different business model, to illustrate how Active Directory domains and sites might be tailored to fit their needs. In all three cases, we want to implement a framework that fits their current operation and can be modified as the company changes in the future.

Centralized Administrative Model

Small organizations that are managed at a central location are good candidates for a *centralized* domain design. Technical staff can be located at one site. As shown in Figure 16.1, `bobuniversity.net` is an example of an organization that is appropriate for this model. The company is an online training school with three locations. The first domain controller was installed in the main office in Los Angeles, where a crew of 30 handles IT, corporate planning, course development, and class scheduling. The Anaheim office has 20 employees who are responsible for accounting, personnel, and payroll tasks. The third office, located in San Diego, takes care of marketing, advertising, and website maintenance with a staff of 10.

We created site link connections between the offices to represent the WAN links for purposes of replication between the domain controllers at each site. Users have 100Mbit Ethernet access to their local LANs.

Since Active Directory is supervised by the tech group at headquarters, all network modifications are made there. Application or member servers function at each location for specific tasks. Domain controllers replicate after 6 PM every day. Domain naming is simplified with a single domain, since all resources are part of the `bobuniversity.net` domain.

FIGURE 16.1
`bobuniversity`
`.net`

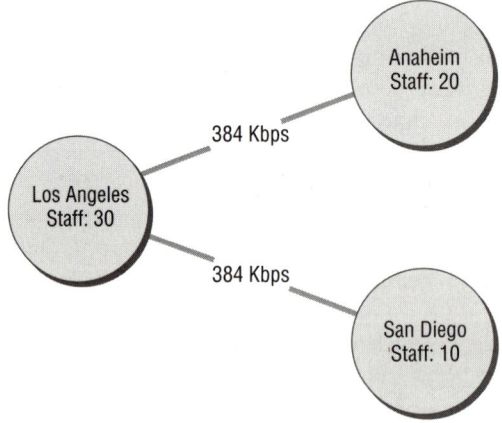

Decentralized Administrative Model

Our second example illustrates the *decentralized* model. Networks Now is a company that was formed as the result of a merger of two firms. Networks by Design, in Irvine, supports mid-sized LANs and WANs in Southern California. The second firm is Netrain, a tech training school located in Van Nuys. Each organization has 100 employees. They each wanted to retain their independence and corporate identities, but they did consolidate financial functions at the Irvine location. By employing separate domains, Netrain can enforce stricter domain security policies due to their concern about copyrighted material on their network. As a consequence of this decision, each unit will need to maintain an IT staff at its location.

Each office will continue to maintain its separate Internet domain name. The domains share a tree, `networksnow.com`, and use subdomains to identify their separate domains, `irv.networkworld.com` and `vn.networkworld.com`, for their private DNS zones. They use separate public DNS zones for Internet traffic in order to preserve their corporate identities. Their slow WAN link should not significantly impact replication traffic, since Global Catalogs are smaller than the source AD databases. They have scheduled nightly replication updates.

FIGURE 16.2

NetworksNow.com

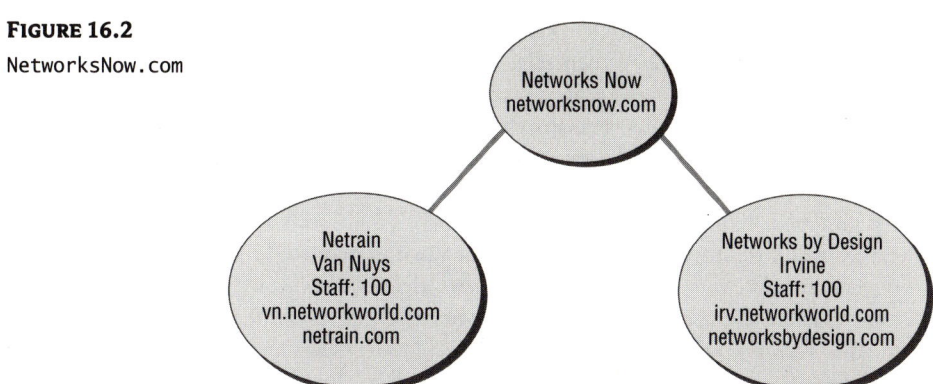

Hybrid Administrative Model

The *hybrid* model mixes ideas from the centralized and decentralized approaches. Again, the AD design follows the administrative approach of the company—management is centralized in some cases and distributed in others.

Drive Safe Motels uses a hybrid domain model for their membership-only motel chain. Locations in Tucson, Phoenix, and Las Vegas each employ a staff of 20, sharing data with the main office in Santa Fe, which employs 100. Payroll and financial functions take place in Sacramento, with 50 employees. The root domain is located in the main office in Santa Fe. Domain controllers at remote sites are members of the `drive-safe.com` domain, which they share with the main office, and their domain controllers replicate nightly. The Sacramento office houses a separate domain, due to time zone and domainwide security policy differences.

FIGURE 16.3

Drive Safe Motels

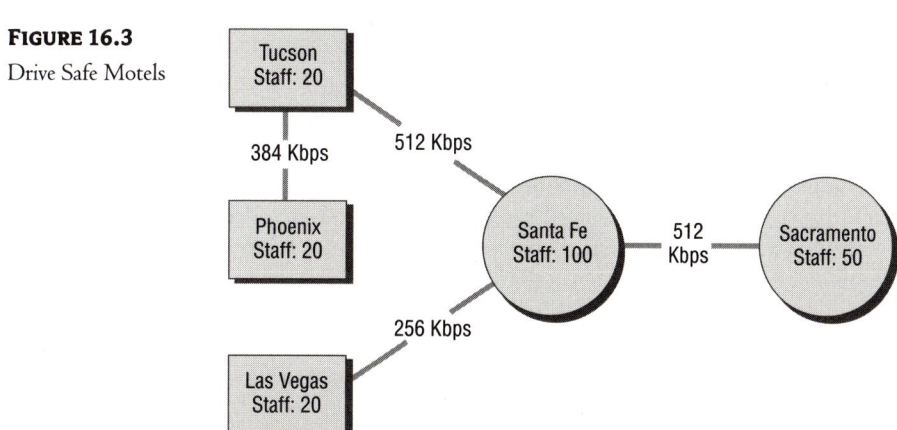

ORGANIZATIONAL UNITS

Organizational units are management containers for the network resources available in a domain. You can organize network resource objects—such as users, computers and printers—by some common element. The OU hierarchy you create should reflect an organization's culture. The structure should be static, and names should be meaningful. Some companies adhere to functional containers, such as Accounting, Personnel, Administration. Others refer to a geographical structure, for example, US, Canada, Mexico. Under the US organizational unit, you could add a second level that refers to regions, such as North, South, East, and West. This framework works well for a centralized domain model.

When should you create organizational units? You can take advantage of the delegation features that Microsoft has thoughtfully added for us with the advent of Windows 2000 Active Directory. Assign one or more individuals the task of managing objects in their OU. So, when the accounting department hires three new employees, they can add new accounts so those users can log in and use the network. When someone forgets a password, they'll speak with a supervisor in their department (who presumably has delegation powers in their OU) to reset it. You can assign certain tasks or objects to your deputy in the OU, such as Modify and Create Users and Printers, but not Delete, or you can give them free reign (do you really want to do that?).

Organizational units also enforce attached Group Policies. Since Group Policies are enforced in order—system, domain, organizational unit—OU security overrides all other policies. One example is to restrict login access for members of the sales department, who are strictly 9-to-5ers. Set a policy for all users in the Sales OU to have login privileges for those hours only. This restriction will not affect those folks in the IT container, who tend to keep late hours sometimes.

TREES AND FORESTS

Microsoft recommends single-forest designs. Domains within a forest share schema and maintain two-way transitive trust relationships. Forests and trees both share configurations, Global Catalogs, and schema. As a consequence of the DNS naming differences, forests are autonomous.

Subsidiary companies that function under the umbrella of a parent company can be assigned to separate trees under one forest. Or, to achieve a consistent namespace, an alternative design is to group several child subdomains under a parent domain in a single tree structure.

Even though Windows Server 2003 now makes it possible to move accounts between forests, the process is complex, involving the MOVETREE command-line utility. Presumably, one of our goals in designing an Active Directory network is to reduce administrative overhead and manage resource sharing. Forests maintain separate containers for their resources. Multiple-tree forests are easier to manage than separate forests. A user who needs access to data in two forests needs to log on separately. Domains in different forests that need to share resources must have explicit trusts established between them. Actually, the compelling reason to create multiple forests is to establish complete separation or limited relationships. In some organizations, unfortunately, internal politics may determine this to be a business objective. Table 16.2 compares characteristics of trees and forests, where their use is appropriate, and their effects on a network.

TABLE 16.2: FEATURES OF TREES AND FORESTS

TREES	FORESTS
Single contiguous namespace	Separate namespaces
Single business entity	Joint ventures, merges, partnerships
Simpler to navigate	Complex to navigate
LDAP searches always resolved	LDAP searches not always resolved, due to limitations of Global Catalog data

NOTE *Be advised again: keep it simple. Restrict your designs to single trees and single forests if you can.*

Since domains within a tree share DNS names, this structure is appropriate for an organization that uses a single name. Combined companies that retain their separate namespaces may opt to create separate trees within a forest, since they can combine resources and also retain their established independent identities. This independence comes at a price, however, since multiple trees are more complex than a single one. Forests do not share the entire AD database between domain controllers, but rather a more limited Global Catalog. Trust relationships are in place and resources are available, but searching across trees is more difficult than searching within a tree.

Designing the DNS Namespace

Active Directory requires that DNS be running on your network. It's a good idea to have AD integrate the DNS database as domain objects, which would be replicated among your domain controllers. But, for the sake of security, you need to separate private and public traffic.

If your organization has already registered a domain name on the Internet, you must decide whether to use that name for your network. If you haven't yet registered a name with an ICANN registrar, you should select one that represents the entire firm. Microsoft suggests that you match up DNS zones with Active Directory domains. The first DNS domain name will be the root domain for your network. It's difficult to change the DNS name, since you must uninstall Active Directory, so the name should be static.

There are three ways a company can use their established Internet domain name on their AD network, each with unique trade-offs:

◆ Use the registered Internet DNS domain name for the AD root domain

◆ Use a delegated DNS subdomain for the AD root domain

◆ Use separate DNS domains for public (external) and private (internal) use

Table 16.3 lists the features for each DNS implementation.

TABLE 16.3: SINGLE AND MULTIPLE DNS NAMES

CHARACTERISTICS	ROOT DOMAIN	SUBDOMAIN	SEPARATE DOMAINS
Single namespace	X		
Single logon for network and e-mail	X		
Multiple DNS servers	X	X	X
Two registered domain names			X
Security for internal resources		X	X
Simplicity	X		

Your company can use a single domain namespace for the Internet and for the internal AD structure, as well, but security issues complicate matters. Two DNS servers (internal and external) would refer to the same domain name, and IP addresses for internal resources would have to be applied manually to the internal DNS server. A firewall would protect your private networks from the Internet.

Or, you could use a delegated subdomain as the Active Directory root domain and leave the established Internet domain name as the authoritative root DNS server. This solution separates internal from external traffic by utilizing a second DNS server for the new delegated zone. For example, `bobuniversity.net` would be the Internet domain, and `la.bobuniversity.net` would be the delegated subdomain that exists as a separate DNS zone. The authoritative DNS server for `bobuniversity.net` would need a delegation record referring to the subdomain zone, `la.bobuniversity.net`.

Another way to secure private network traffic is to use the `.local` private domain root on the internal network. Since there are no `.local` root servers, `bobuniversity.local` would not be resolvable over the Internet, but would function quite well for LAN clients. This solution is used by companies with no Internet presence, or those that want separate namespaces. The legal DNS domain name, `bobuniversity.net`, would be used for public access. A second DNS zone would have to be maintained for local addressing.

Sites

Active Directory's domains, trees, forests, and organizational units are *logical structures*, but *sites* refer to the *physical composition of your network*. Computers are connected by high-speed (LAN) links within sites and slower, less reliable (WAN) links between them. Active Directory sites are created to manage replication and logon traffic. For purposes of "user satisfaction" (a Microsoft term), you should try to place at least one domain controller at each site to allow users to log on locally and to access a local AD resource database.

Since bandwidth is presumably not an issue, *intrasite* replication can take place at any time. *Intersite* replication links domain controllers on separate sites, where bandwidth is limited. AD databases are compressed for WAN transmission, and we can schedule updates for periods of low network activity. You create site links with Active Directory Sites and Services.

In some cases where local bandwidth is saturated, it may be appropriate to create more than one site at one physical location. In the same way that we create network segments with routers to separate broadcast domains and thereby reduce network traffic, sites are defined by their subnet addresses. So, one way to control logon and replication traffic at a busy office is to create multiple sites with different subnet addresses and to create site links with scheduled times for replication, as you would for physically distant networks.

Getting back to design issues, domain controllers at a particular site direct their attention to those domain controllers that share their domain, creating a demand for services across WAN connections. Which servers are sending updates, authority delegation, and schedules are issues for the network administrator at the main office.

Putting It Together

Now that we know the parts and pieces that make up an Active Directory structure, let's talk about how you go about designing a hierarchy that will both work and be manageable. It's important to understand that even though the concepts described earlier in this chapter are helpful, the real world has proven that a more grounded approach for those "in the trenches" has a better chance of success.

Most of us think our network should be designed for the convenience of the end user. While this is true in most respects, it is certainly not true in the design of the AD structure. (Let's face it, a properly designed AD structure will never be seen by the average end user.) This concept is especially difficult if you are coming from an environment in which the directory structure is much more visible to users, such as Novell's NDS. Here, in Active Directory, we design our structure for ease of management; in other words, we can be selfish (making our jobs as easy as possible) and still be doing the right thing.

Since our society frowns on selfishness, I've got a few guidelines that can help you overcome your giving nature. Over the years of working with AD, I've learned a few basic truths that can make designing your structure a straightforward process.

Business Analysis

Many of the ideas about analyzing the business environment so that the domain/OU structure can match the business flow are a bit too abstract and don't meet the needs of real-world organizations. In truth, you analyze the business processes with two goals in mind:

- ◆ To help you design a site strategy that controls network traffic
- ◆ To help you place servers in appropriate locations (once again, to control network traffic)

SITE STRATEGY

We have discussed the replication of AD traffic in many of the preceding chapters. By this time, you must realize that when a change is made to an AD object, that change must be replicated to all domain controllers within the domain—no matter where they are located (like across that slow, overutilized

WAN link that is always causing you headaches!). We mentioned AD sites earlier in this chapter. Now let's talk about how to use them.

First, a *site* is a collection of IP subnets. Every engineer I know has a "map" (sometimes just in his head) of the links that make up his WAN and the IP subnet addresses used in each location. In my current position, for instance, our internal network uses 192.168.*x*.0 subnets—each *x* matching the plant ID of the physical location. As an example, our corporate office has an ID number of 99. This means that the subnet address used in our LAN is 192.168.99.0. We also have a test network that uses 192.168.199.0. When we defined our AD site for the corporate office, it was defined as those networks—192.168.99.0 and 192.168.199.0.

Our current topology has a 56KB frame link to each of our 20 or so physical plants. Since our regular business traffic uses most (if not all) of that bandwidth, we could not really afford to add the burden of continuous AD replication traffic to the mix. For this reason, we defined an AD site for each location—defining the site to include any IP subnets used at the plant.

At this point you may be asking yourself, "Why?" and, "So what?" Here's the important thing to remember about sites: you can control when the AD replication traffic will be sent between sites. This means that I can configure my system so that replication traffic only crosses my WAN links late at night, when I am more likely to available bandwidth. It also allows me to control the path that the traffic will follow. Within a site all domain controllers update all other domain controllers. Between sites, however, I can define bridgehead servers that send change notifications out and accept change notifications from other sites.

SERVER PLACEMENT

There's an old networking maxim that still rings true: Place servers near those users who will use them. Basically this means that if a certain group is going to use the services offered by a server, try to locate the server physically close to that group. This accomplishes two things. First, it speeds up service. Since a user's request doesn't have to travel far to reach the server, we can assume it is less likely to encounter problems. Second, it reduces traffic on network segments that are not involved in the process. In other words, the traffic destined for a server does not clog other wires or overwhelm routers or other network hardware.

OU Structures

Microsoft has released numerous documents revolving around the design options available when it comes to organizational units. According to this information, OU design should match the business philosophy of your company: If your company follows a strict departmental management policy, then each department should have an OU. Conversely, if your company revolves around projects (sometimes known as *workgroups*), then each project should have an OU. (This seems like a reasonable idea, but you can imagine how difficult it would be to manage this one as projects come and go!) All in all, this sounds better on paper than it works in the real world. In reality, there are three basic reasons for OUs in an AD world:

◆ To act as boundaries for your AD sites

◆ To ease delegation of administrative privileges

◆ To facilitate your Group Policy implementation

Let's discuss each of these rationales.

The first, and probably most important, reason to create OUs (at least in any wide area environment) is to have structure that matches the physical layout of your network. It is much easier to manage a structure in which each AD site is defined by a matching AD OU. While it is possible to place servers from different AD sites within the same OU, keeping track of replication traffic, the location of resources, and who works where will be such a hassle you won't have time for anything else. While there might be a case where this should be done, I certainly can't think of one!

So the first reason for the creation of OUs is to organize resources by physical location (in most cases). Once you've done that, the next two reasons for OUs kind of go hand in hand. They both revolve around management.

The second use of OUs is to facilitate administrative delegation. As we've seen, it is fairly easy to delegate administrative privileges in AD. Creating an OU for each administrator (or group of administrators) can make keeping track of who has what power and where a lot easier.

In Chapter 1 we discussed Group Policies. Remember that Group Policies are implemented at the domain level, the site level, and the OU level. If you intend to implement GPOs at the OU level, then you need to create OUs for each of your GPOs. Personally, I would rather have fewer OUs and filter GPO execution through group membership—but to each his own.

Multiple Domains

Bottom line: multiple domains are a hassle to manage! Notice I didn't say impossible—just a hassle. This becomes even more of an issue when you start adding AD-integrated applications (such as Exchange 2000 Server) to your environment. Despite such concepts as automatic transitive trusts, domain versus enterprise administrators, and pass-through authentication, I've had problems with every multiple domain environment in which I've worked.

With Microsoft NT, we created multiple domains to reduce the size of the accounts database and to control replication traffic between domain controllers. With Windows 2000 and Active Directory, the database can easily handle millions of objects, and we can control replication traffic through a good site strategy. In other words, there are not many reasons to implement a multiple-domain AD structure—mostly domain-level policy needs or internal politics.

Forests

If multidomain environments are a hassle to manage, then multitree (forests) environments are a hassle-and-a-half! There are only two reasons to create more than one tree, and only one of those is technically valid:

- The need to preserve distinct namespaces—say, for instance, the merger of two companies with well-known Internet domain names. If both names need to be preserved, then two trees is your only option.

- Politics—what I call the eighth OSI layer. Sometimes, no matter how much you argue and no matter how correct your technical opinion, politics will mandate a less-than-optimum design.

While we're on the topic, I've had arguments with other consultants about this issue. They often insist that a partnership between two companies might—even if a third namespace (not the namespace of any of the members) is agreed upon—indicate the need for separate trees. While this might be true, ask yourself one question: in the event of a partnership (in which both companies remain independent), how often do the IT staffs work together? Remember, when you join your tree to a forest, then you must share (and accept) any schema changes that the other guys put in place, as well as all of the overhead of supporting a common Global Catalog. Personally, if partners need to share resources, I can find more convenient and secure ways to accommodate them, usually utilizing Internet technologies.

In Short

We have considered the design process from the perspective of Active Directory and its various components. This task requires that you collect detailed business and technical information. Then, you would consider your conclusions in the face of Active Directory's capabilities. With careful analysis, you'll be able to create an Active Directory framework that supports your business as it grows in the future.

Next, we will look at migrating to Active Directory from other network operating systems.

Chapter 17

Migrating to Active Directory

NOW THAT YOU'VE PLANNED your Active Directory architecture and documented your systems, as discussed in Chapter 16, you're ready to deal with your existing non-AD systems. In this chapter, our focus is on migrating your current network resources to AD.

First of all, why migrate? All the various benefits of Active Directory add up to one advantage: It is a superior management tool for your network resources. In the long run, it requires less effort and is more efficient to administer a system where all objects are shared on one platform. Considering its advantages, why not raise your network's standards to AD?

Migration to AD is more than a product upgrade. It's an effort to improve controls on your network. It also represents an opportunity to redesign your resource architecture. Your new Active Directory domain structure will likely differ from your NT network, since organizational units introduce new flexibility for object security and management. In order to accomplish this level of control with NT, LAN administrators routinely created several resource domains surrounding a master user domain, and set up a complex system of trust relationships between them. Active Directory doesn't need all those separate domains and extensive trust relationships, and Microsoft actually encourages the use of a single or few domains. Since the domain structure is different, you may prefer to consolidate resources currently managed on multiple NT domains into one.

There's another valid reason to upgrade that might not be as palatable as "easier management" or "more features," but it is just as valid in the workplace. Microsoft has recently defined a long-term support path for all of their product lines. For their business and development software (including operating systems), they have announced that the product support timeline will consist of five years of mainstream support, followed by two years of purchasable support, followed by a minimum of one year of self-help support (using Technet or their website). The bottom line is that Windows NT is no longer a supported platform—end of story. I know that this was a driving force in the push to upgrade our company network from NT to Windows 2000.

In this chapter:

◆ Options for migration

◆ Migrating from NT to AD

◆ Migrating from NetWare to AD

Options for Migration

There are two basic approaches to system migration: direct and gradual. The *direct* method is an all-at-once operation, so it's suitable for small networks. If your servers have sufficient resources to run Windows 2000/Windows Server 2003, you can upgrade them, as we'll see later on in this chapter. This can, of course, reduce your hardware bills. User accounts can be transferred to upgraded systems or re-created on new servers.

Since it duplicates login accounts, the *gradual* migration path represents less risk. If migration causes a major problem, you can roll back your network to its previous state. On the negative side, users will be logging on to separate networks. Gradual migration also gives you a chance to test and upgrade applications that were designed for older network systems. Restructuring complex domain and trust relationships may also require some time. Table 17.1 compares the two paths.

TABLE 17.1: COMPARISON OF DIRECT AND GRADUAL MIGRATION

FEATURE	DIRECT	GRADUAL
In-place server upgrades	X	
Lower hardware costs	X	
Higher support costs		X
Rollback available		X
Single login	X	
Maintain applications designed for NT, NetWare		X
Decentralized network administration		X
Must coexist with heterogeneous systems		X
Multiple domains with complex trust relationships		X
Restructuring domains		X

Microsoft's AD migration software for Windows 2000/Windows Server 2003 includes freely downloadable programs and products for purchase. Solutions are also available from independent software vendors, including NetIQ, Aelita, Quest Software, and Bindview.

NT to AD Migration

You have two options for migrating from NT to AD. The *in-place upgrade* calls for you to upgrade domain controllers currently running NT version 4 with Microsoft's Setup program on the Windows Server 2003 CD-ROM, assuming they have sufficient hardware to run Windows 2000/Windows Server 2003. *Over-the-wire migration* requires that you install new domain controllers and migrate resources to them *over the network* from your old servers. The following section describes these options in detail.

In-Place Upgrade

Before I begin this discussion, let me say that this is not my preferred method of migration. At the time of this writing, I was just finishing the migration from NT to Windows 2000 for my employer, Cardinal Glass Industries. We have 20 locations, each of which had at least one Windows NT 4.0/Exchange 5.5 server. Our first step was to implement a Windows 2000 domain controller at the corporate headquarters in Minneapolis, Minnesota. After that we were faced with upgrading 19 additional locations. For the first plant, we decided to perform an in-place upgrade. While everything seemed to go smoothly, that location has caused more problems in the long run than the rest of our locations combined. While I cannot say for a fact that the in-place process was part of the cause, my gut feeling is that it contributed. The problems range from AD replication storms to mysterious password issues. Given the choice, I'd go back and redo the process, moving the plant onto a new Windows 2000 server that was installed from scratch. (Unfortunately, two things prevent this: budgets and time. It's tough to tell a 24/7 plant that you want to redo a server and then tell them that you are going to charge them for the process!)

Set up your security net first. Synchronize an NT backup domain controller with the primary domain controller and take it offline to serve as a backup. If something goes awry during the upgrade, you can bring it back online and promote it to run as a PDC.

To perform an in-place upgrade at the PDC, run the Setup program on the Windows 2000/Windows Server 2003 CD-ROM. When the computer reboots, it will automatically install a new domain on Active Directory with DCPROMO and present you with questions about creating a new tree or joining an existing one.

When the domain SAM is converted to the AD database, all accounts, formerly NT, are converted to Active Directory objects. Users retain their old logon names and passwords. Trust relationships with other servers are maintained. One gotcha with this process is that the "old" trust relationships are maintained in their current state—nontransitive. In other words, you'll need to re-create the trusts to build a hierarchy that truly takes advantage of the features of Windows 2000/Windows Server 2003. The new domain will continue to use the NetBIOS name that it used on NT, so it can continue to support client systems running NT and Windows.

The in-place upgrade is straightforward, and it also preserves object properties. The first downside of this method is its insistence on creating new domains. For this reason, you cannot consolidate resources with in-place server upgrades. The second, and probably biggest, downside of this method is the fact that you are overwriting your existing server. In the event that something does go wrong (I'm a firm believer in Murphy's Law), you have to recover your server from tape (a process that often takes longer than you would like) or bring in the offline BDC and promote it to a PDC until the problem is solved.

Over-the-Wire Migration

The over-the-wire method calls for a new installation of 2000/2003 on a file server, and then the transfer of accounts from the NT 4 domain(s) to the newly created AD domain. This is the preferred upgrade method of most professional consultants. As you can see, since there is a new server involved, the old server remains untouched after the process. You can pull the old server from the wire—intact—and if something goes awry in the migration process, your old environment is still immediately available.

Depending on the tool you use, accounts can be re-created, moved, or copied. For small networks, you can do this manually or use the ADDUSERS tool available in the Windows resource kit to partially automate the process. This is called re-ACLing, in reference to Access Control Lists, or user permissions.

Another alternative is to use a migration utility to transfer your accounts. Migration offers the opportunity to consolidate resources from multiple domains into one. Copying accounts is a gradual process, since your users can continue to use their NT 4 network. You can even roll back to the old network system if you prefer it to Active Directory. But then you are faced with the complexity of managing two network accounts for each resource.

Some migration products use a new AD attribute named SidHistory. Basically, the schema has been expanded to include an attribute that can hold an old SID. Accounts created in the new AD domain are assigned new SIDs, or unique security identifiers, but some AD migration tools can attach old SIDs to the new accounts using the SidHistory attribute. This preserves your entire security environment—the new accounts will have access to anything that the old account had access to.

Although the process is more complex, the over-the-wire technique has certain advantages. In most cases, users will have to create new passwords in the new domain (this can be viewed as a plus or a minus). In contrast to the in-place upgrade, you can assign a new NetBIOS name for your domain. The most significant advantage, however, is that any number of existing NT domains can be consolidated into one AD domain.

REQUIREMENTS FOR MIGRATION

The next task is to prepare your domain controllers for migration. You'll have to adjust for the fact that NT relies on NetBIOS, and 2000/2003 servers use DNS to connect to resources, so you may have to add and configure network protocols for each server. Migration tools require that the target and server domains coexist in a two-way trust relationship. The SID history feature mentioned above will only work if the AD domain is running in native mode.

If your ultimate goal is to have AD manage all your network resources, you will eventually want to upgrade your network to enhanced, or native, mode, which requires that all domain controllers be running AD. But in order to reap the advantages of native mode, your Active Directory domain controllers will no longer share information with Windows NT PDCs and BDCs. This is, of course, no big deal since the definition of native mode is that you have no more legacy domain controllers in the domain. On the other hand, member servers and workstations can continue to run the Windows NT operating system.

Here's a server migration task list:

◆ Upgrade the NT 4 PDC to Service Pack 4 or better.

◆ Create administrative user accounts on both domains. It is best to use the same name and password for both accounts; mostly this just makes it more convenient, as you won't have to physically authenticate when moving from one to the other (your workstation will submit your current name/password to the other domain and since they match, authentication will be seamless).

◆ Point the NT 4 PDC to the DNS server on the AD domain.

◆ Activate NetBEUI on the AD domain controller.

◆ Establish two-way trust relationships between the servers.

◆ Promote the Active Directory domain to Windows 2000 native mode.

INSTALLING NETBEUI

The NetBEUI network protocol is not installed by default when you set up a domain controller with Windows Server 2003 and select network protocols, but it is available on the installation CD-ROM. (Given that NetBEUI is such a chatty protocol, your goal should be to reduce or eliminate its use anyway.) Follow the procedure below to copy files manually to the "systemroot," which is the drive and folder that stores the active Windows directory (e.g., C:\Windows), and then to activate NetBEUI in the networking Properties dialog box, as shown in Figure 17.1.

1. Navigate to the CD's folder: \Valueadd\MSFT\Net\NetBEUI.

2. Copy `Nbf.sys` to %systemroot%\System32\Drivers.

3. Copy `Netnbf.ini` to %systemroot%\Inf.

4. Open Control Panel ➢ Network Connections.

5. Right-click Local Area Connection.

6. In the Properties dialog box, click the Install button.

7. Select Protocol and click the Add button.

8. Choose NetBEUI and click OK.

FIGURE 17.1

Activating the NetBIOS protocol

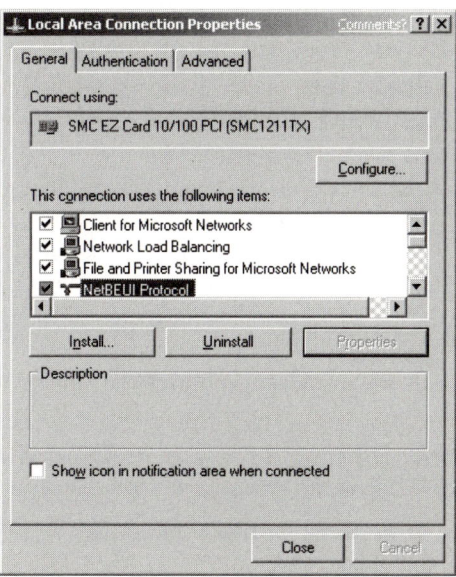

DNS CONFIGURATIONS

The PDC must point to the authoritative DNS server for the Active Directory upgrade domain. (This process will work if you have some other brand of BIND DNS in place, but I've found that I have fewer problems if I have a Windows 2000 DNS server in place during the migration/upgrade process.) Follow this procedure on the PDC:

1. Open the Control Panel and click Network Properties.

2. Access the Protocols tab, select the TCP/IP Protocol, and click the Properties button.

3. Select the DNS tab.

4. Enter the name of the computer in the Host name box.

5. Enter the Active Directory domain in the Domain box.

6. Click the Add button and enter the IP address of the network's primary DNS server.

CREATING TRUST RELATIONSHIPS

Next, you need to set up mutual trust relationships between the 2000/2003 and NT domains. The NT 4–style trust is a one-way relationship between a *trusting* and a *trusted* domain. The trusting domain accepts login from the trusted domain to share its resources. The NT master/resource model was based on this concept, storing user accounts in a centralized master domain and accounts for servers in one or more resource domains. Therefore, servers in the resource domain are trusting, allowing access to users who authenticate to the trusted master domain.

Microsoft supplies GUI tools to manage trusts: User Manager for Domains in NT and Active Directory Domains and Trusts in 2000/2003. Unfortunately, you cannot use these tools for migration, since they create down-level trusts between the network operating system products, which do not generate SID histories. We will refer to the GUI programs later, to check the status of our domain trust relationships.

USING NETDOM FOR TRUST RELATIONSHIPS

NETDOM is a Swiss army knife command-line tool that creates, validates, and manages domain relationships. As you'll see later, you can also use it to perform domain migration. Actually, NETDOM is the reason we installed NetBEUI on the target domain. The program is hidden on the Windows Server 2003 installation CD-ROM in the \Support\Tools folder. Double-click SUPPORT.cab, and you'll see a file listing that includes a number of support utilities that were not automatically installed by Setup. Copy the NETDOM.exe program to some folder on your hard drive. To create the trust relationships, you'll need to have an administrative account in both domains. Type NETDOM/? to view the many options available. The command syntax to create a mutual trust looks like this, typed on a single line at the AD domain:

```
Netdom trust ntdomain /D:ADdomain /UserO:ntaccount /PasswordO:ntpassword
➥/UserD:ADaccount /PasswordD:ADpassword /Add /Twoway
```

The D: argument refers to the Active Directory domain, admin account, and admin password. The O: pertains to the external NT domain, admin account, and admin password.

For our illustration, we will create a two-way trust between the NT domain called NT4_domain, where AaronA is the administrator using the password def, and the Active Directory Royal-tech.com domain, where BobA is the administrator using the password abc. The one-line command below uses abbreviated syntax to perform this task:

```
Netdom trust nt4_domain /D:royal-tech.com /UO:aarona /PO:def
➡/UD:boba /PD:abc /Add /Twoway
```

There should be a pause and then a response that awards your patience with a success message. To check that everything did indeed go smoothly, you can ask NETDOM to verify the operation by typing:

```
Netdom trust nt4_domain /D:royal-tech.com /UO:aarona /PO:def
➡ /UD:boba /PD:abc /Verify
```

Or, if you'd like to validate the trusts with the GUI program that you've been itching to use in Windows Server 2003, activate the MMC Active Directory Domains and Trusts on the Administrative Tools menu. Right-click the AD domain listed in the pane on the left, and then select Properties from the drop-down menu. In the dialog box that appears, click the Trusts tab, as shown in Figure 17.2.

FIGURE 17.2

The Trusts tab in AD Domains and Trusts

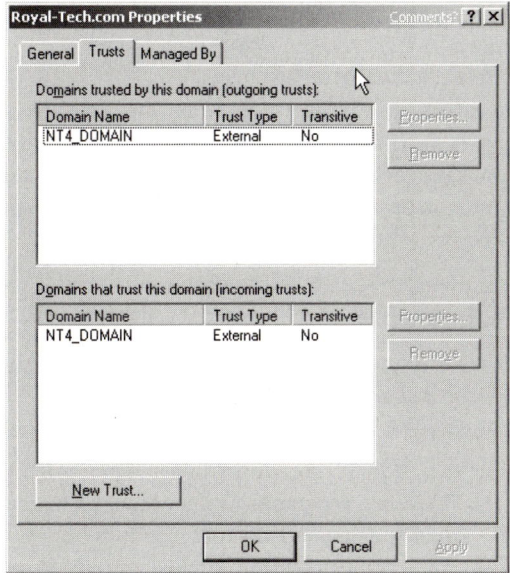

If you select either the outgoing or incoming trust, a Properties button becomes active. Click it to view details about this relationship, as indicated in Figure 17.3. Then you can click the Validate button to confirm the relationship, if you didn't trust the command-line response.

FIGURE 17.3

Trusted Domain properties

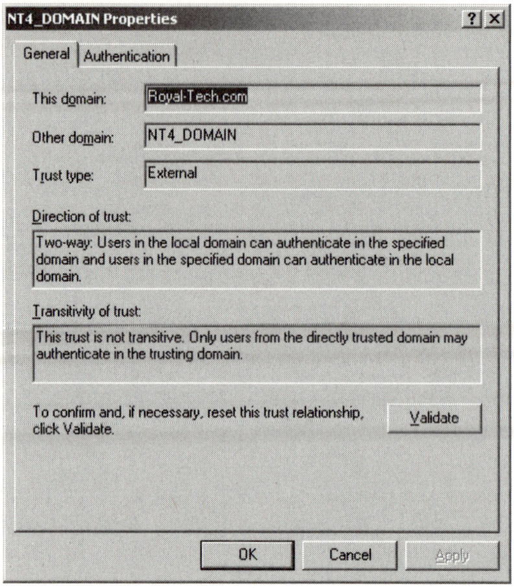

USING NETDOM TO MIGRATE DOMAINS

NETDOM can also be used to transfer accounts from one domain to another. You need to create or use an existing organizational unit on the AD domain for transferred accounts. The command will also call for the name of the PDC computer. After you've established trust between domains, use your administrative accounts to enter the following at the command line at a domain controller on the AD domain:

```
Netdom move machine /D:ADdomain /UO:NTadmin /PO:NTpassword
➥/UD:ADadmin /PD:ADpassword /OU:orgunit /reboot
```

The machine name refers to the NT PDC. The D: option, for destination, refers to the Active Directory domain, admin account, and admin password. The O: switch points to the external NT domain, admin account, and admin password. Reusing the domain names and admin users in our earlier example—an OU called ntusers and a PDC named NT4—the command would be:

```
Netdom move NT4 /D:royal-tech.com /UO:aarona /PO:def
➥/UD:boba /PD:abc /OU:ntusers /reboot
```

The reboot option will reboot the PDC after all accounts have been transferred. This is a one-way, one-time operation. After that server reboots, it will no longer supervise a domain, and all the accounts should appear in the ntusers organizational unit in the Active Directory domain.

USING ADMT TO MIGRATE DOMAINS

The Active Directory Migration Tool, or ADMT, is available on Microsoft's website at no charge. Download ADMT.exe, then double-click to install a GUI program to a domain controller on your AD domain that will be listed in the Administrative Tools folder. ADMT's wizards can copy users, groups, and trusts between domains, providing you with more control than with NETDOM. We'll examine the steps to prepare each domain for the migration process. Some requirements were already completed during the NETDOM trust operation. Here's the first set in the interest of completeness:

♦ Two-way trust relationships must exist between the source (NT) and target (AD) domains.

♦ The AD domain must be promoted to Windows 2000 native mode.

♦ Service Pack 4 or above must be installed on the NT PDC.

♦ Administrative shares must exist on both computers.

♦ You must have an account with Administrator rights to each computer and be a member of Domain Administrators in the AD domain and Administrators in the NT domain.

Next, we'll set up administrative groups on each domain. Here are ADMT's requirements:

♦ The Domain Admins global group in the source must be a member of the Administrators local group in the target.

♦ The Domain Admins global group in the target must be added to the Administrators local group in the source.

♦ A new local group called *Source Domain$$$* must be created on the source domain and remain empty.

♦ A target organizational unit for the copied accounts must be created or specified.

On the 2000/2003 domain controller, open up Active Directory Users and Computers. Open up the Builtin container, since that's where the local groups are stored. Then follow these steps:

1. Double-click Administrators.

2. Select the Member tab.

3. Click Add, select Location, and enter NT4_Domain, which is the name of our source domain.

4. Click the Advanced button, then select Find Now.

5. Double-click Domain Admins in the source domain. You should see a screen like Figure 17.4.

FIGURE 17.4

Choosing Domain
Admins from the
NT4 Domain

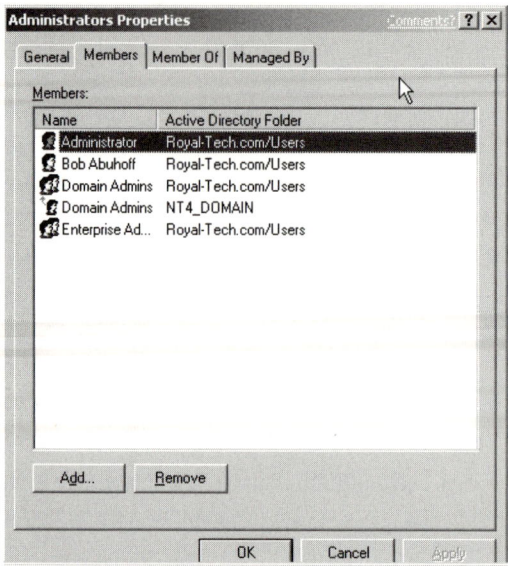

6. Move over to the PDC, activate User Manager for Domains and double-click to open up the box for the Administrators local group, as shown in Figure 17.5. Click the Add button to set up steps 6 and 7, where we will grant the Domain Administrators group on the Active Directory domain administrative rights on the NT domain.

FIGURE 17.5

Properties of the
Administrators
local group

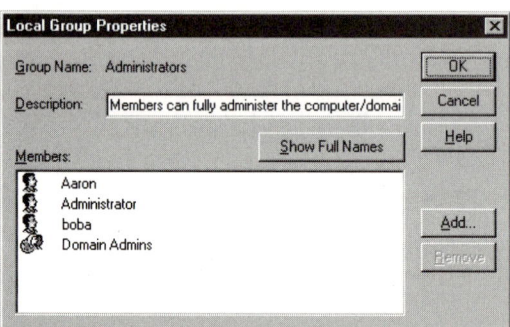

7. Select the target AD domain in the List Names From drop-down list, which in our scenario is Royal-Tech. This operation will populate the Names box below with the various groups and users contained in the Royal-Tech domain.

8. Select the Domain Admins group in the Names box, shown in Figure 17.6, and click Add.

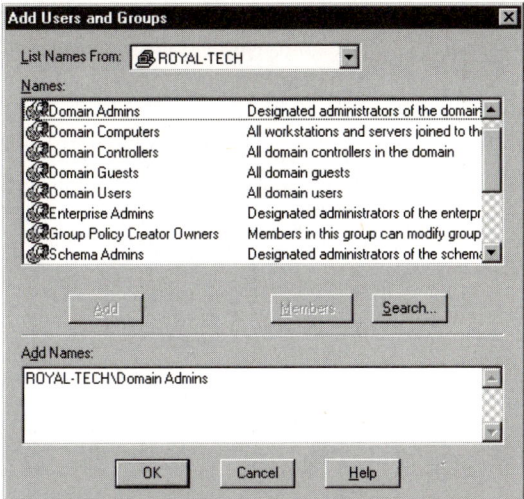

FIGURE 17.6

Adding the Domain Admins group

9. At the PDC again, create `Source Domain$$$`, a local group, and leave it empty. Then, create a new OU on the AD domain controller or make note of an existing one that will receive the NT domain's accounts.

Next, Microsoft suggests that you set up auditing on each domain controller so you have a record of what occurs when you perform the migration. In the next two steps, you will:

◆ Enable Success/Failure auditing on the source (NT) for User and Group management

◆ Enable Success/Failure auditing on the target (AD) for account management in the Default Domain Controllers policy

10. In User Manager at the PDC, select Audit on the Policies menu and choose the check boxes for Success and Failure for User and Group Management, displayed in Figure 17.7.

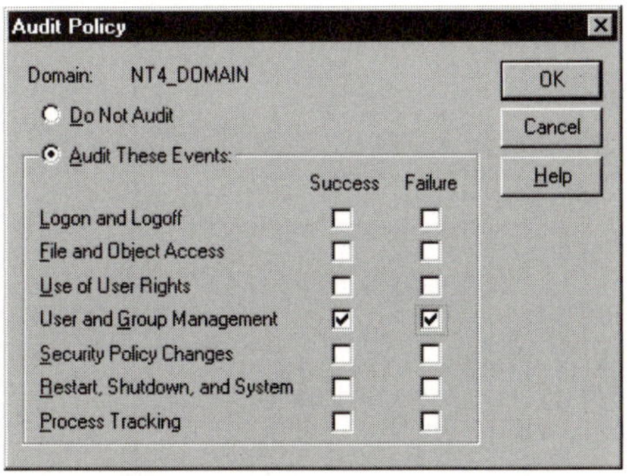

FIGURE 17.7

Setting Success/ Failure auditing in NT

11. Back at the AD domain controller, run Domain Controller Security Policy from the Administrative Tools menu. Drill down to Audit Policy by clicking Default Domain Policy ➤ Computer Configuration ➤ Windows Settings. Double-click Audit Account Management and choose Success and Failure, as shown in Figure 17.8.

FIGURE 17.8

Setting Success/
Failure auditing
in AD

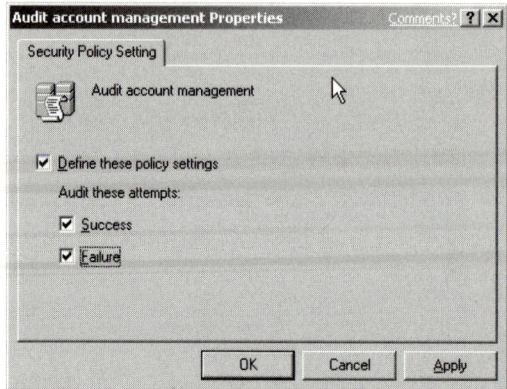

12. Now we need to add TCP/IP support for this operation at the NT server in the source domain. Since this requires editing the Registry, all the usual precautions apply. First, back up the Registry or at least the key, be careful of typos, don't use allergy medications while doing this, etc. Run Regedt32.exe, then drill down and add a new value:

A. Open the HKEY_LOCAL_MACHINE\System\CurrentControlSet\Control\LSA key, as shown in Figure 17.9.

FIGURE 17.9

Navigating
the Registry

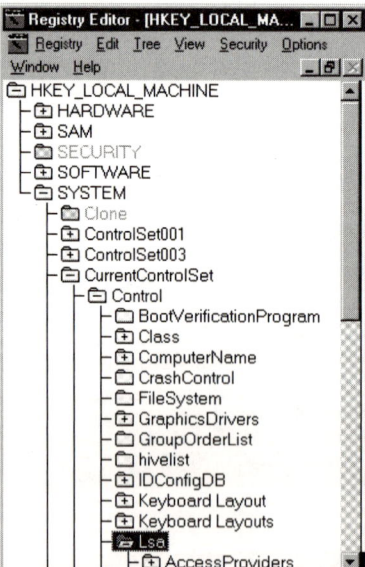

B. Select Add Value from the Edit menu to open the Add Value dialog box.

C. In the Value Name box, type **TcpipClientSupport**, and in the Data Type box, select REG_DWORD, as shown in Figure 17.10. Click OK.

D. The DWORD Editor box will open. Type the number 1 in the data entry area and select Hex from the options below. Click OK to lock in the value of the new key when you're done. Figure 17.11 illustrates the result of this procedure.

FIGURE 17.10

Adding the Value Name and Data Type to the Registry

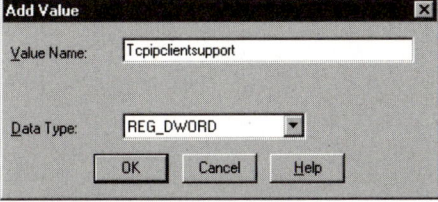

FIGURE 17.11

The completed Registry key

13. We're ready to migrate. Log on to both domain controllers with your Administrative account. At the AD domain controller, go to Administrative Tools and activate the Active Directory Migration tool, known as the Migrator. The program doesn't look like much when you first open it. Right-click Active Directory Migration Tool in the left pane to reveal the powerful wizards listed on the menu, as shown in Figure 17.12:

FIGURE 17.12

The many migration wizards

14. In our example, we'll migrate users. Select the User Migration Wizard. When you click one of the migration wizards, the program offers to test first or to migrate immediately, as shown in Figure 17.13.

FIGURE 17.13

Choosing to test or migrate immediately

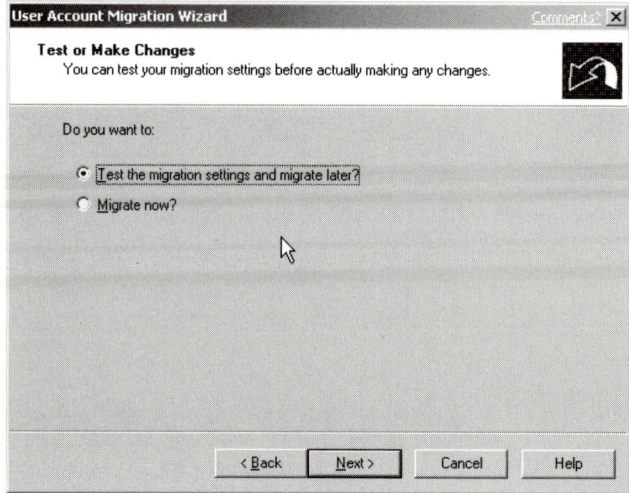

15. In the next step, you need to supply the names of the source (NT4) and target (AD) domains, or select from the lists, as in Figure 17.14.

FIGURE 17.14

Selecting the source and target domains

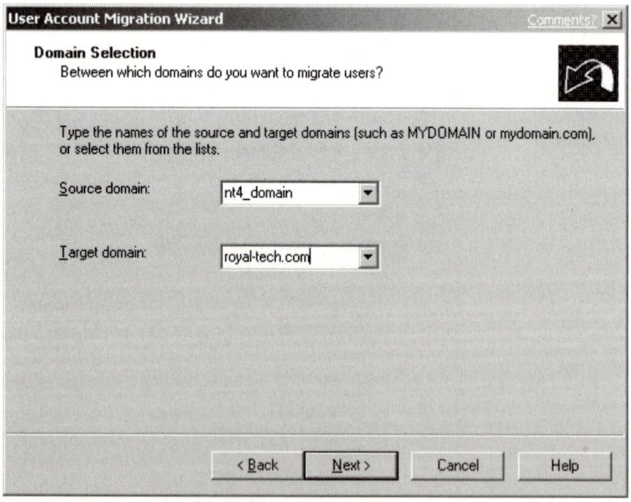

16. Since we chose to migrate users in step 14, that container shows up in the next window, where you select the source domain. The box is empty, however, so click the Advanced button and use Ctrl+click or Shift+click to select multiple users to be copied. Figure 17.15 shows the result of choosing users.

FIGURE 17.15

Selecting multiple users to migrate

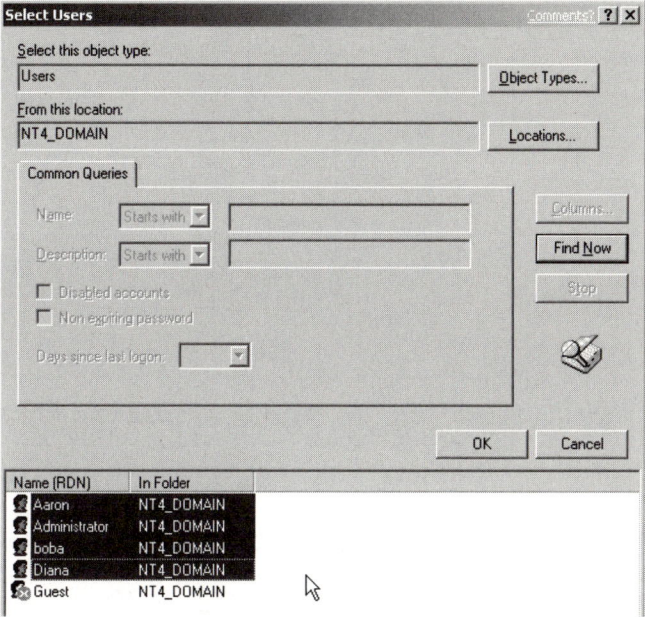

17. Click the Add button, then select the target container in the target AD domain, as shown in Figure 17.16. ADMT will interpret your selection as a fully qualified domain name (FQDN), as shown in Figure 17.17.

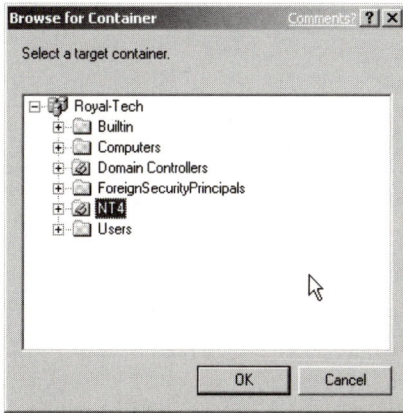

FIGURE 17.16

Locating the target domain

FIGURE 17.17

The target OU

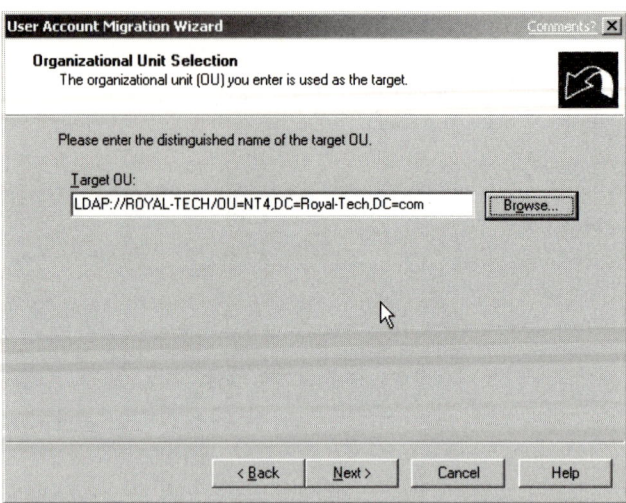

18. ADMT offers several options regarding migrated accounts. Since it cannot import passwords from the NT domain accounts, it offers to create new ones, using a complex formula or temporary passwords matching the user names, as shown in Figure 17.18.

FIGURE 17.18

Choosing
password
options

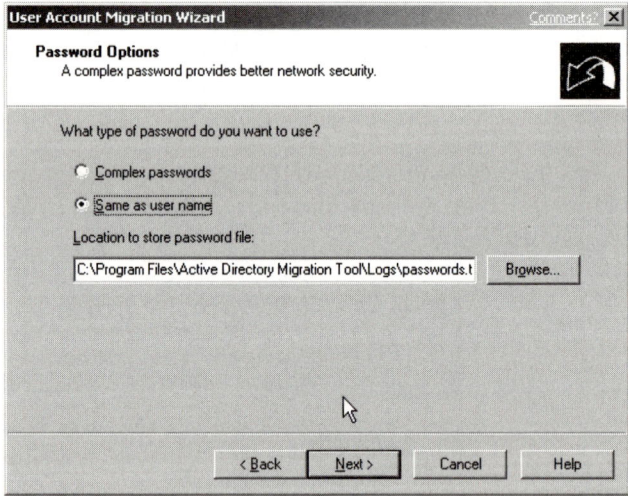

19. Once the source domain accounts have been migrated, should users retain access to the old domain? Some users may have accounts on both domains. The Account Transitions Options window lets you close source accounts immediately or to leave them open for some period of time. Notice in Figure 17.19 that I've marked the check box to migrate users' SID histories, one of the principal features of this tool.

FIGURE 17.19

Allowing access to
the old domain

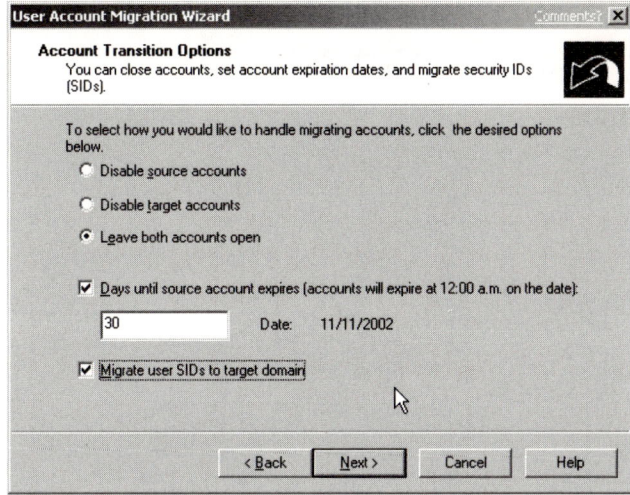

20. The next window asks you to log on to the source domain as a user with administrative rights. Click the Next button to open User Options, shown in Figure 17.20. Choices include user rights, profiles, and groups. I've directed the program to copy all accounts. You can also add a prefix or suffix to set the migrated accounts apart from those existing on the target domain.

FIGURE 17.20

Selecting user
migration options

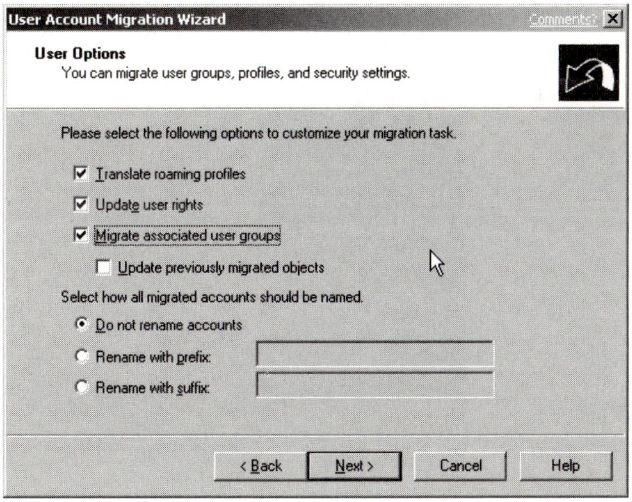

21. What to do if a migrated user account matches an existing account on the target domain? Naming conflicts are addressed in the next step, displayed in Figure 17.21. You can ignore matching accounts, replace them, or rename them with a prefix or suffix, which is the action I've chosen.

FIGURE 17.21

Adding prefixes to matching accounts

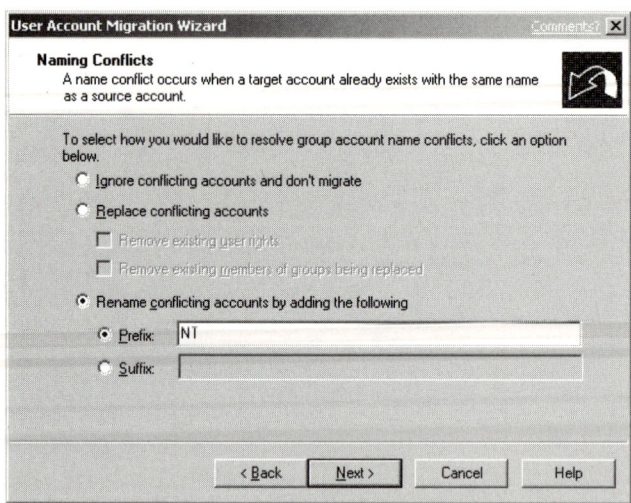

22. Next a summary box appears, like the one in Figure 17.22, where you can review your selections and go back to change them if necessary. If you're satisfied with your choices, click Finish to perform the migration.

FIGURE 17.22

Last chance to adjust your migration choices

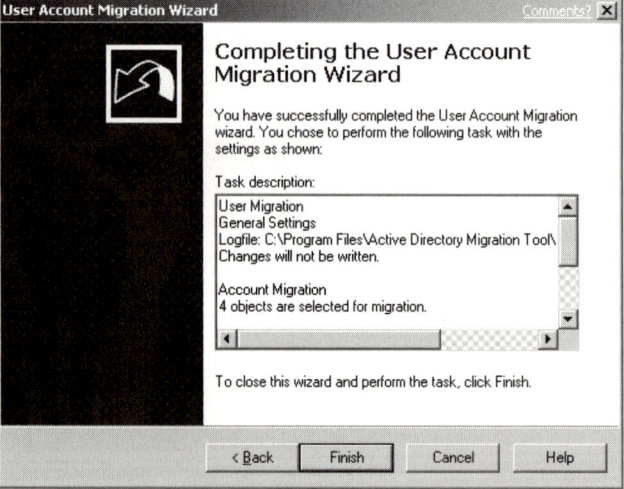

23. Finally, ADMT goes to work, displaying a status box as it migrates user accounts. Click the button to view the log, which will resemble the `Migration.log` file shown in Figure 17.23.

FIGURE 17.23

The
`Migration.log`
file

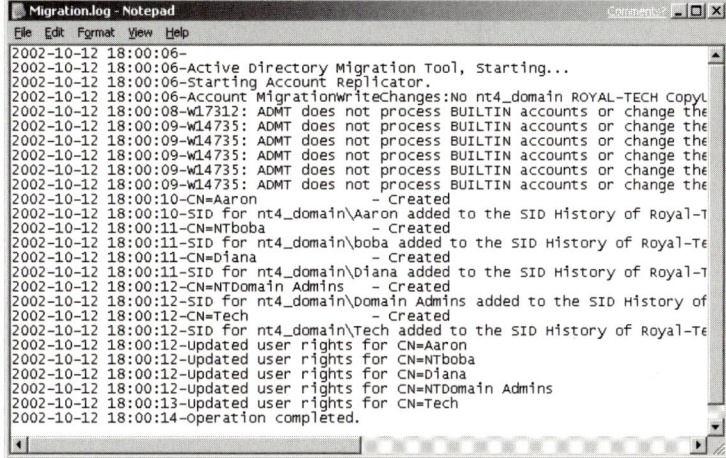

Once your user accounts have been migrated, you repeat the process to copy groups, computers, and trusts. Then, move on to migrate other PDCs. To consolidate accounts from several NT domains, continue to use the original AD domain controller as your target.

Migrating from NetWare to AD

Novell NetWare's two network operating system platforms are as different as Windows NT and 2000/2003. Version 3.*x* used Bindery Services to manage network resources. Although ancient by IT standards, some of these legacy systems are still in service. They are analogous to the NT local area network systems that can efficiently support small organizations. NetWare bindery servers do not replicate information across the network and are limited to using Novell's IPX/SPX network protocol. Novell introduced *Novell Directory Services*, or *NDS*, in NetWare 4.1. NetWare versions 4.*x*, 5.*x*, and 6.*x* use NDS to centralize network administration. Like Active Directory, NDS is a hierarchical directory service. The challenge you face in migrating NetWare to AD is that you must bridge systems with significant differences. Even where they share common features, implementations differ widely. Table 17.2 compares major features of the three products.

TABLE 17.2: COMPARING AD, NDS, AND BINDERY SERVICES

FEATURE	AD	NDS	BINDERY
File and print services	X	X	X
Replication of resources	X	X	
LDAP-compliant	X	X	
DNS support	X	X	
TCP/IP protocol support	X	X	
IPX/SPX protocol support	X	X	X
Resource catalogs available	X	X	
Kerberos authentication	X		
NetWare Core Protocol authentication		X	

NOTE *Microsoft addresses the differences between AD and NDS in several publications on its website at* `http://www.Microsoft.com/server/evaluation/compare/default.asp`.

Bindery Services

NetWare 3.x centralized management on individual servers. Binderies stored network resource data, including user accounts. Earlier network systems were usually limited to file and print services. The concept of the network in those days was limited to single-server local area networks.

Novell Directory Service (NDS)

Current versions of NetWare—4.x, 5.x, and 6—use NDS, a hierarchical namespace, to manage network resources. In reshaping their network model for multiserver wide area networks, Novell's NDS servers replicate directory service databases with each other (for more details on NDS, see Chapter 18). DNS, DHCP and LDAP version 3 are supported as generic services. Organizational units manage other objects as they do in Active Directory, but they also play a role in security. Authentication differs considerably from Microsoft's Kerberos over IP, as NDS uses Novell's proprietary implementation of RSA standards.

Microsoft's Migration Path for NetWare

Microsoft produces two solutions for bridging resources on NetWare networks to Active Directory networks:

Services for NetWare This is a separate, for-purchase product that includes several migration tools that copy or transfer accounts to AD. Services for NetWare includes Microsoft's Directory

Synchronization Services (MSDSS), which consolidates directory services on AD. MSDSS can also transfer NDS, bindery objects, and ACLs into AD containers. It can also be configured to gradually migrate accounts. Another component of the package, the File Migration Utility, copies files residing on NetWare servers with their permissions to AD domain controllers. File and Print Services for NetWare allows users on an AD domain to share NetWare bindery resources.

NetWare Connectivity Services   This comprises client-based tools that are included at no extra cost with Windows 2000/Windows Server 2003. Its principal utility is *Client Services for NetWare (CSNW)*, which serves as a redirector for Windows clients so that NetWare networks and AD networks can coexist. Since it is actually an integration tool, we will discuss CSNW in detail in Chapter 18.

In Short

In coping with a heterogeneous world, we have two options: we can strive to create a new order, or we can find a way to coexist. In this chapter, we've followed the former direction by investigating the process of migrating resources to Active Directory, using software that is freely available from Microsoft. In the next chapter, we'll examine ways to make cohabitation possible with mixed systems.

Chapter 18

Integrating Active Directory with Novell Directory Services

NETWORKS TEND TO BE multicultural or heterogeneous organisms. So you may be looking for a way to link your dissimilar systems to share resources, at least for a while. This chapter deals with coexistence and gradual migration between NetWare and Microsoft networks.

Once upon a time, Microsoft distributed a network service called *Gateway Services for NetWare* (*GSNW*). Running on a Windows NT or 2000 domain controller, GSNW acted as a proxy to link users on a Microsoft network to a NetWare file server that would make its resources available. Unfortunately, this service is no longer available for Windows Server 2003. However, a workstation-based solution does exist for accessing NetWare networks, called *Client Services for NetWare*. This product functions on the 128-bit Windows Server 2003 platform only; it is not available in the 64-bit version. Microsoft's other integration solution is *Services for NetWare*, which we discussed in Chapter 17, available as a separate product.

Truth be told, neither of the Microsoft solutions was really a viable long-term option for coexistence. For a better client-based solution, you were better served by utilizing Novell's client software (which could coexist with other Microsoft clients very well). It was faster, more stable, and specifically designed to access Novell servers in the most efficient manner. Microsoft's server-based solution was also insufficient: they were the first to admit that it was not a true *gateway* and should not be used as a long-term solution.

Choosing a directory service for your organization's network systems is a strategic decision that will have long-term consequences. Hopefully, that product will serve as a framework that can adapt to business changes without requiring major reparations. In this chapter, we'll look at Active Directory and Novell's eDirectory side by side, and consider the future possibilities for directory services.

In this chapter:

◆ Setting up Client Services for NetWare (CSNW)

◆ Comparing directory services

◆ The future of directory services

Setting Up Client Services for NetWare (CSNW)

Client Services for NetWare acts as a redirector for NetWare NDS and bindery resources for Windows Server 2003 and 2000 computers. CSNW creates NetWare Core Protocol (NCP) packets and directs them to the NetWare server you specify.

Each workstation that requires access to a NetWare network will need CSNW to be installed locally, since Windows Server 2003 no longer has a server-based gateway. To install the service, follow the steps below to activate LAN properties and add a client, as shown in Figure 18.1:

1. Open Control Panel and select Network Connections.

2. Right-click Local Area Connection.

3. Choose Properties on the context menu, then click the Install button.

4. Select Client and then click the Add button.

5. Choose Client Services for NetWare.

FIGURE 18.1

Installing a network client

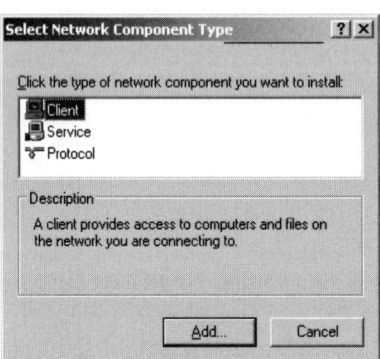

Next, Windows suggests that you restart. If all goes well after reboot, the options box shown in Figure 18.2 will solicit a name for the server or network context you prefer to set up each time you log on. Assuming that your NetWare account matches the login name and password for your Windows domain login, you'll be automatically connected to this preferred context on the NetWare network when you log in to the Windows domain. As you can see, I've used my personal account on the Windows Server 2003 domain to access the NetWare5 server, so I can sign on with a single logon.

FIGURE 18.2

Selecting a preferred server in CSNW

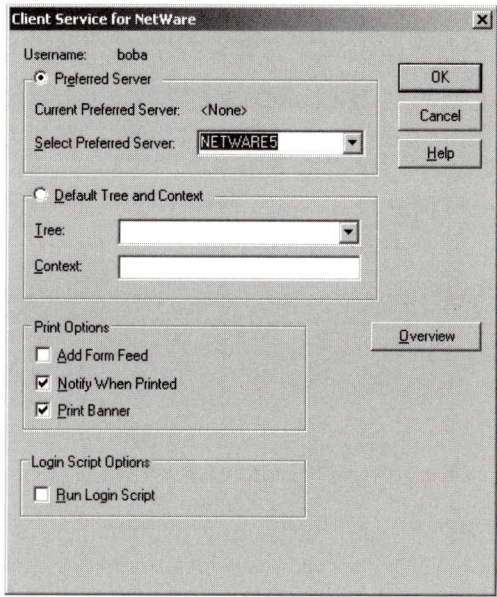

Installing NWLink

Client Services for NetWare requires the IPX/SPX protocol. The reason CSNW does not run in the 64-bit version of Windows Server 2003 is that NWLink is not available on that platform. Microsoft documentation informs us that NWLink, their implementation of IPX, is installed automatically when you enable CSNW. Check your Network Properties. For those times when the automatic feature disappoints, here's the procedure to install NWLink manually and adjust its frame type. Figure 18.3 illustrates a successful installation.

1. Open Control Panel and select Network Connections.

2. Right-click Local Area Connection.

3. Select Properties on the context menu and choose Install.

4. Select Protocol, then click the Add button.

5. Choose NWLink IPX/SPX/NetBIOS Compatible Transport.

FIGURE 18.3

NWLink successfully installed

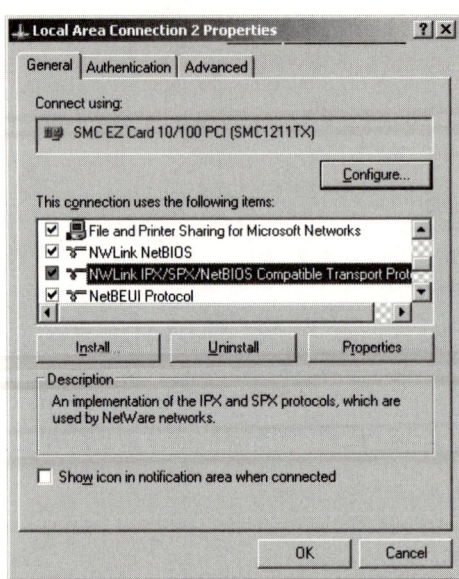

NWLink uses multiple frame types in OSI's second layer. The setting on each workstation must match the frame type in use on the NetWare server. In some cases, you can leave it at the automatic setting, but if you have difficulty, you'll need to find out which frame type is used on the NetWare network and choose the appropriate one for your network adapter. The most commonly used Ethernet frame types are 802.3, used in versions 3.x, and 802.2, for NetWare 4.x, 5.x, and 6. Windows will try to match an operating network on the wire, otherwise it defaults to 802.2. Figure 18.4 displays the details.

FIGURE 18.4

Configuring frame type properties

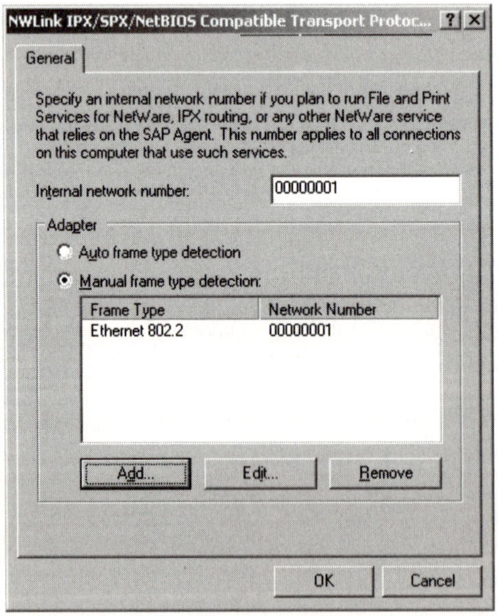

Now, you should be able to view the NetWare network in Windows Explorer under My Network Places, as shown in Figure 18.5.

FIGURE 18.5

NetWare
Network in
Windows Explorer

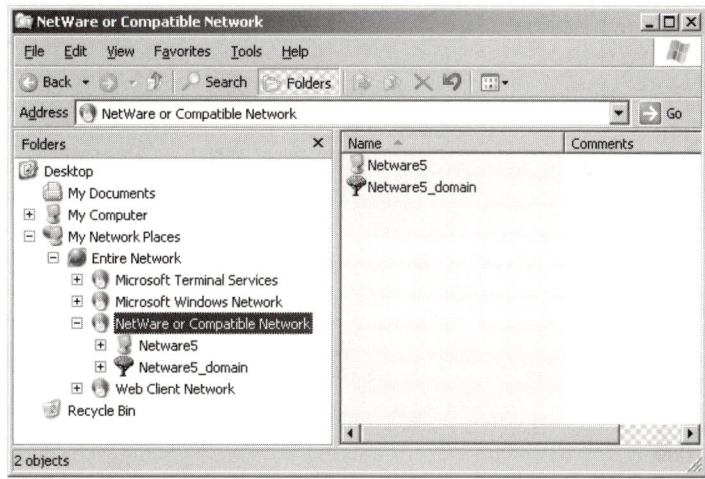

CHECK YOUR CONNECTIVITY AT THE COMMAND LINE

Alternatively, you can check your connectivity at the command line. Go to the Run box and type **CMD** to activate a 32-bit DOS box. The NET. command is a legacy utility that can provide network information, connect drives, log users on to a network, etc. Type **NET.** for more information. The following illustration displays the result of the NET USE command.

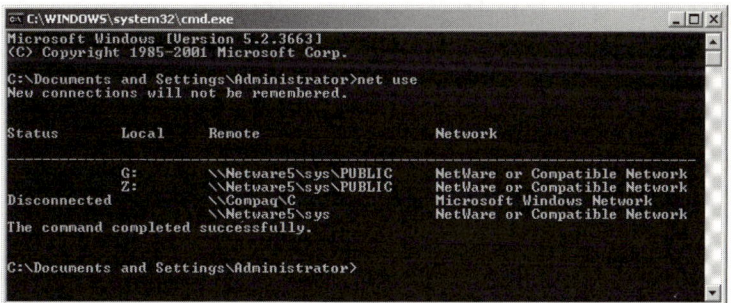

Of course, you can map network drives to NetWare folders, just as you do on your Windows network. Access should be transparent to your users. Figure 18.6 illustrates the Public folder on the NetWare5 server mapped to drive G: on a Windows workstation.

FIGURE 18.6

The Public folder on NetWare mapped to the G: drive

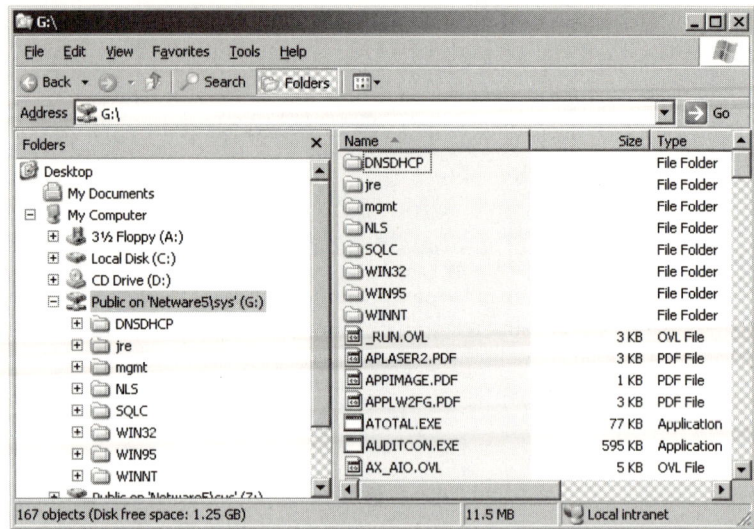

> **NOTE** *Let me stress one more time that this is probably not the best client-based solution. First, Novell's latest iterations of NetWare utilize native IP as their protocol of choice (not IPX/SPX). Adding a second protocol to your network also adds a whole new set of issues, such as traffic control, communication compatibility, routing issues, and network addressing. Second, the latest revision of NetWare does not even require that any client software be installed at all. You can attach to the NetWare server using only TCP/IP-based communication. In other words, Novell offers more flexibility and a more efficient solution than Microsoft's Client Services for NetWare.*

Comparing Directory Services

Network directory services are not applications by themselves; rather, their function is to enable other services. Until recently, we've used single-purpose applications—for example, White Pages, Yellow Pages, staff telephone extensions, e-mail address books, and network user accounts. With the growth of distributed computing and Internet technologies, there arose a need for centralized, multipurpose directory services that would facilitate network management and encourage the growth of e-commerce and distributed applications.

By making the network the focal point, directory services allow us to access resources across geographical and, in some cases, administrative boundaries. We can install and update software and enforce security on workstations. We can control mobile computers and configure roaming profiles for users. Administrative tasks can be delegated to local staff. We can inventory hardware and software for an entire organization. Users reap major benefits, too, including single sign-on, quick and convenient authentication, consistent Desktop configurations, and resource lookup from any location.

Directory service products are available from several vendors, including Microsoft, Novell, iPlanet (Sun, Netscape, AOL), IBM, and Oracle. Each vendor adheres to the industry standard definition of a directory service: a centralized, hierarchical repository of information, containing network resource information. And each product has certain features not matched by the others. In this chapter, we'll examine Novell's eDirectory and Microsoft's Active Directory.

The Development of Novell's and Microsoft's Directory Services

Early network operating systems were server-based. Novell NetWare used the bindery system, while Microsoft's LAN Manager and Windows NT supported a single-master domain model.

In 1994, Novell's first release of NDS, or NetWare Directory Services (later changed to Novell Directory Services), as part of NetWare 4 signified a shift in perspective from server-based to network-centric management. Microsoft did not develop Active Directory in a vacuum. Many features, concepts, and terminology are based on Novell's NDS product and industry standards such as X.500 and the Lightweight Directory Access Protocol (LDAP). Along the way, other standards have become important, particularly XML, which provides new opportunities for directory services.

In its most recent iteration of NDS, which has been renamed eDirectory, Novell has produced an independent product that does not require a NetWare server. Novell's goal is to provide cross-platform directory services. Microsoft's Windows Server 2003 operating system represents the second version of Active Directory.

Microsoft vs. Novell

Microsoft, Novell, and their technology partners have joined the debate claiming the superiority of their directory service product. Some of their arguments are based upon technical differences, and some are just marketing hype that attempts to produce a clear winner by drowning out competitors. The principals in the debate have, in some cases, even been guilty of comparing a current version of their product with an older version from the other vendor. The truth is that there *are* fundamental technical and philosophical differences, each product has its strengths and weaknesses, each product has been improved over time, and in some cases comparison is difficult because, in some areas, the products are very different.

Novell heralded Microsoft's first release of AD with Windows 2000 as a validation of the importance of directory services in the marketplace. Marketing executives expressed their eagerness to finally hold up NDS against a real product for comparison.

The following sections describe the crucial similarities and differences of the two platforms.

TOPOLOGY

Novell and Microsoft use similar terminology in referring to network structure. Both vendors use a logical tree topology to represent an organization's corporate framework. Trust relationships link trees to form a forest. Organizational units and leaf objects describe containers and network resources, respectively. Users, groups, and printers are managed graphically from a central point of view. This logical framework of trees and forests allows you to view objects that stand for network resources, their attributes, and the relationships among them.

As we have discussed in earlier chapters, these structural elements are neither Novell nor Microsoft solutions. They exist in each product because both products adhere to the X.500 recommendations. In other words, both products are based upon the exact same principles; most of the differences revolve around implementation, not philosophy.

DATABASE STRUCTURE

We discussed Active Directory's database structure in detail in Chapter 15. Novell's eDirectory is very similar. It is composed of several files, including a control log, transaction log, and sequential logs of record and attribute indexes. Partitions are separate indexed database files that work together to form the eDirectory.

SECURITY

Security principals are objects that apply access rights to other objects, such as users. There are two approaches to assigning access:

Dynamic Inheritance   Rights flow down the tree.

Static Inheritance   Rights are assigned to each individual object.

As an example of dynamic inheritance, let's consider Aaron, who works in the projects department. His user account has been assigned to the Projects organizational unit. This gives him access to the Projects directory and the Projects printer, since they have also been assigned to that container. In order to transfer him to the operations department, we would move his account to the Operations OU, where he would relinquish access to projects department resources and gain access to the Operations folder and printer. He would be *inheriting* trustee rights, which would change according to the location of his user account.

On a network that uses static inheritance, Aaron would be given rights to use projects resources either by assigning them to his individual account or by making him a member of the Projects group, which has been assigned access. When he is transferred to the operations department, an administrator would make the change by changing his group membership or by reassigning him individual access privileges.

NDS uses a combination of static and dynamic inheritance. NDS security principals include users, groups, workstations, organizations, organizational units, roles, and printers. Any NDS object may be granted rights to any other NDS object. Access to shared resource objects follows the NDS tree structure. So, making one change at the root of an NDS tree would affect every object. NDS actually writes properties to parent objects, so that resource lookups are not performed at the root of a tree, which is inefficient on a WAN.

Active Directory uses static inheritance to enforce security. AD objects are limited to users, groups, and workstations. All rights must be explicitly granted or denied. In order to affect all network users with a particular right, each object has to be updated. Organizational units are administrative units that can be managed by individuals or groups with specific access. But the right to access an object must be assigned to a user or group. In our example above, we would shift Aaron's folder access by modifying his group membership or his user rights. AD's static inheritance is limited to the domain and does not cross trust relationships between domains.

Since rights are explicitly recorded for each account, the static inheritance model works better for large, decentralized networks. The benefit is that access control is completed in a single step, but the directory can grow very large because each object stores all access information. Dynamic inheritance is intended for centrally administered networks. The result is that less information is written into the directory, but rights are assigned at a centralized point, which can impede the process on a WAN.

Group Policy Objects supply security for groups of objects on an Active Directory network. Novell's Inherited Rights Filter (IRF) is used to block rights that would be inherited on lower levels of a tree.

AUTHENTICATION

Microsoft adapted MIT's Kerberos model for authentication in Windows 2000/Windows Server 2003. A key feature is single sign-on to Microsoft servers. Linux programmers have warned that Microsoft's implementation of Kerberos is not a cross-platform solution.

Novell uses RSA encryption standards for user login. Additional authentication features are available by implementing the Novell Modular Authentication Service (NMAS2). Both authentication methods support smart cards, RADIUS, and LDAP.

INTERNET SECURITY

Internet-based transactions require additional security, since data is transmitted over public pathways. Both Novell and Microsoft have provided support for security APIs and services, including Virtual Private Networks (VPNs) and e-commerce transactions, by integrating authentication and encryption technologies with their directory services.

The Public Key Infrastructure (PKI) employs public and private keys to identify users. It's available on both Active Directory and eDirectory. PKI requires that a knowledgeable system administrator configure and maintain the system for tight security.

AD uses Group Policies to distribute root keys. Keys are stored on a single server. Windows 2000/Windows Server 2003 PKI is integrated with Internet Information Services (IIS) so that users can request and receive certificates using a web browser. Management features are available, including certificate revocation, through the use of an MMC.

NDS stores certificate data and keys on a central server as properties of an object that has been issued a certificate. This facilitates backup and availability, since certificates are distributed by NDS. Certificates are created and managed by the ConsoleOne administrative utility.

VPNs must encrypt data to provide secure communications over insecure transmission lines. Microsoft has integrated cryptographic services, including IPSec, originally made available in Certificate Server, into the Windows 2000/Windows Server 2003 operating system. Control is provided by Group Policies. Novell uses the Novell International Cryptographic Infrastructure (NICI) for encryption, including 40-bit and 128-bit keys. The NDS Secure Authentication Service (SAS) API supports the Secure Sockets Layer (SSL).

REPLICATION

Novell's servers replicate directory information over IP (the default protocol) or IPX, transmitting only changed or new attributes. An eDirectory tree is made up of organizational units called *partitions*, which are stored on designated servers. A replica ring distributes copies of partitions to designated servers. There is one master replica in a replica ring, which supervises all operations in a partition, including additions, edits, and deletions. The read-write replica also performs these tasks, but the master synchronizes information between the other replica servers.

The master replica is stored on a local server, while subordinate read-write and read-only replicas are copied to other servers. A read-write replica can be converted to a master replica for load balancing or in case of server failure. Filtered Replication compresses partitions for transfer over slow WAN links, using filtered read-write and filtered read-only replicas.

Each object change in eDirectory is time-stamped to keep track of updates. A NetWare Loadable Module, `Timesync.nlm`, synchronizes servers on the network. This program uses the Network Time Protocol (NTP) either over the Internet or from a trusted time source on the local network.

Using the multimaster domain model, domain controllers function as peers on an Active Directory network. Each domain controller contains a complete read-write copy of the AD database, with no divisions analogous to NDS partitions. One attribute change requires that an object be replicated to all servers. Active Directory replication is available in two flavors. A mixed-mode domain (the default setting) must contend with the NT legacy Security Accounts Manager (SAM) running on PDCs and BDCs. Native and Windows Server 2003 modes are reserved for homogeneous networks with Windows 2000 and Windows Server 2003. Improved security is available through inter-domain universal groups; global groups can be nested within other global groups, and domain local groups can be nested within other domain local groups. Nesting also reduces replication loads over a WAN.

Data integrity on Active Directory is assured by Update Sequence Numbers (USNs) assigned to each object. A time-based algorithm compares domain controller information to determine the most current updates.

A *multivalued attribute* is a directory attribute that has multiple independent values—for instance, each member of a group representing a multivalued attribute or a user who has several phone numbers listed in his account. Multivalued attributes can be replicated as a single update or through multiple updates. AD uses the first method, NDS the second.

As a network admin, you can select which partitions to replicate and where. Active Directory, on the other hand, is required to replicate all domain data. This issue and the difference in updating multivalued attributes make NDS more efficient in terms of bandwidth. But Microsoft's extensive system of site links, its scheduling capabilities, and the Knowledge Consistency Checker make its replication model more versatile.

Some administrators have discovered a shortcoming in Active Directory replication due to a timing problem. For instance, a network admin in Los Angeles adds a new user, Lance, to the IT group, currently composed of 30 members. This addition changes the group members' multivalued attribute. At the same time, an admin at the Chicago site adds Samantha to the IT group. On an NDS network, the LA server would replicate the new IT group member, Lance, to other servers, and the Chicago server would update other servers with its new IT member, Samantha. All servers would eventually include the complete 32-member IT group. Active Directory, on the other hand, shares the entire multivalued attribute, including the names of all 31 group members, during the replication process. If the domain controller at Chicago's site replicates to the New York server at the same time as LA's, it would usurp LA's changes. Consequently, the network would record an IT group with 31 members, which would be missing LA's new addition, Lance. This problem is illustrated in Figure 18.7.

This problem is exacerbated as the number of domain controllers on a network increases. Actually, it can affect other AD updates, account properties, permissions, and organizational units, as well.

FIGURE 18.7

Active Directory
Replication Problem

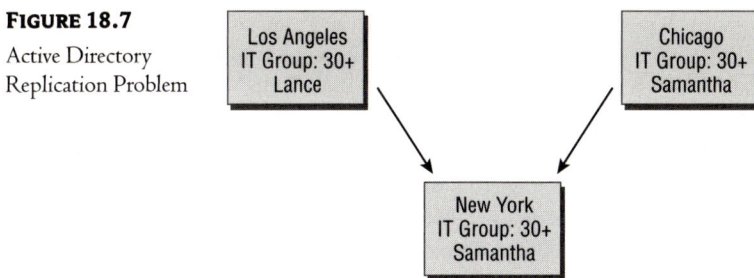

CATALOGS

Both directory products use catalogs to provide users with local access to resources available across a network. Active Directory uses Global Catalogs that are updated regularly, while NDS catalogs use a process called the *Dredger*, which runs every 24 hours and queries each partition. If a user is granted access to a catalog, she can access all objects. To add some level of security, you must customize multiple catalogs to be used by specific groups.

DESKTOP CONTROL

Active Directory's Group Policy Objects apply security rules to many users, groups, and computers. GPOs use the Windows 2000/Windows Server 2003 infrastructure to distribute software applications and upgrades and to control driver installations and desktop configurations.

Novell's ZENWorks product, which stands for Zero Effort Networks, is a separate product for desktop management. It includes the NetWare Application Launcher (NAL), a scripting tool that can be used to create roaming profiles and automated scenarios, which is equivalent to Microsoft's use of VBScript and JScript.

DNS

By integrating DNS and DHCP into Active Directory, Microsoft has moved IP and MAC addresses to the directory. AD prefers to use Microsoft's extensions or a third-party DNS server that supports RFC 2052 and RFC 2136. NDS eDirectory treats DNS and DHCP as separate services.

DNS resolves user-friendly names into IP addresses with NS records to make resources available. It also advertises network services such as mail services with MX records. DNS does not include status information, so a mail server that is listed could be offline. Microsoft resolved this limitation by adopting a proprietary extension to DNS: the Dynamic Domain Naming System (DDNS). This presents a problem for servers that do not run Windows 2000/Windows Server 2003. Another weakness of this extension is the default age-out period of seven days. This means that a resource's state change is not recognized until one week has elapsed. If you reduce this interval, you increase DNS traffic.

Novell, on the other hand, uses the IP Service Location Protocol (SLP) to record state information, which uses a 30-minute age-out period. IPX environments use the Service Advertising Protocol (SAP) which provides updates every five minutes. Like Microsoft, NDS also supports static resource lookup with NDS and the HOSTS file.

Since AD domains have a one-to-one relationship to Internet domains, clients can perform a DNS lookup, LDAP bind, and an LDAP query in one step. Also, the AD fully qualified domain name is guaranteed to be unique from all other AD objects in the world. A corporate mail server on a Windows 2000/Windows Server 2003 no longer has to do a separate lookup for internal (as opposed to Internet) e-mail accounts.

NDS objects do not incorporate DNS names. So users need to locate the appropriate NDS server first. Since NDS and LDAP use different naming syntaxes, intranet applications must access NDS using the NetWare Core Protocol (NCP), which uses different object names than LDAP.

LDAP

Both Active Directory and Novell's eDirectory support LDAP version 3 for schema management, recording attribute changes, and querying. Microsoft claims that AD was built from the ground up for LDAP compatibility, while NDS uses a separate *responder* service to process LDAP requests, translating attribute and class data between LDAP and native NDS forms to process queries. According to Microsoft, the result is that NDS servers cannot take advantage of multi-CPU configurations, and they have limited functionality for schema management.

DIRECTORY MANAGEMENT TOOLS

The Microsoft Management Console (MMC) provides a common interface for Active Directory's network management activities. Console One is the NDS administration tool that, in similar fashion, employs snap-ins for added functionality. Written in Java to run on multiple platforms, Console One can be more versatile.

NOS INDEPENDENCE

When Novell separated NDS from its networking operating system, NetWare, they were seeking to present the product as a standalone management tool. The result is NDS eDirectory, a multiplatform directory service. While Microsoft's Active Directory is available for 2000/Windows Server 2003 and requires a homogeneous network for systems to reap all its benefits, eDirectory strives to work with many open standards and various vendors' products. Novell states that their goal is to integrate intranet, extranet, and Internet directories to benefit cross-platformed e-business.

The Future of Directory Services

In a world where boundaries between internal and external networks are blurring and distributed computing is growing, the need to consolidate directory services is becoming increasingly apparent. There's a great deal of information locked up in our directories: user accounts, networking configurations, computers, network devices, and security policies. If we could somehow integrate our directory services that are currently dedicated to specific applications and network infrastructures, we could transcend vendor barriers, eliminate redundancy, simplify administration, control access, and provide network users with secure single sign-on and universal resource availability. Microsoft and Novell share this vision, and they are working to bring the future to our networks with Microsoft Metadirectory Services and DirXML, respectively.

The X.500 specification first appeared in 1988; it was revamped in 1993 to address the need to merge information contained in name directories and resource directories, open source and proprietary. Based upon X.400, which was intended to manage e-mail applications, X.500 protocols collect data from servers and use the Directory Access Protocol (DAP) as a communications protocol for clients. LDAP replaced DAP in the mid-1990s due to improvements in performance.

A *metadirectory* is a directory of directories, a set of information that is built as a result of synchronizing information from various directory sources. As a search and retrieval system, LDAP is limited, since LDAP clients are limited to retrieving information from designated servers. The metadirectory application adds a layer of security and reliability, since it refers to its own network of sources to collect data for a client, regardless of where it is located.

For instance, let's look at a real-world scenario in which a company utilizes multiple separate directories, including an Enterprise Resource Planning (ERP) database, a product database, e-mail, a telephone system, a Windows 2000/Windows Server 2003 network, and a NetWare network. Maintaining these directories requires duplication of effort, and in some cases information may not be updated at all. Distributed operations and e-business requires that this business integrate this data to ensure accuracy for vendors, partners, and clients. Figure 18.8 illustrates the role that centralized, multipurpose directory services can play in this situation.

FIGURE 18.8

Multipurpose
Directory Services

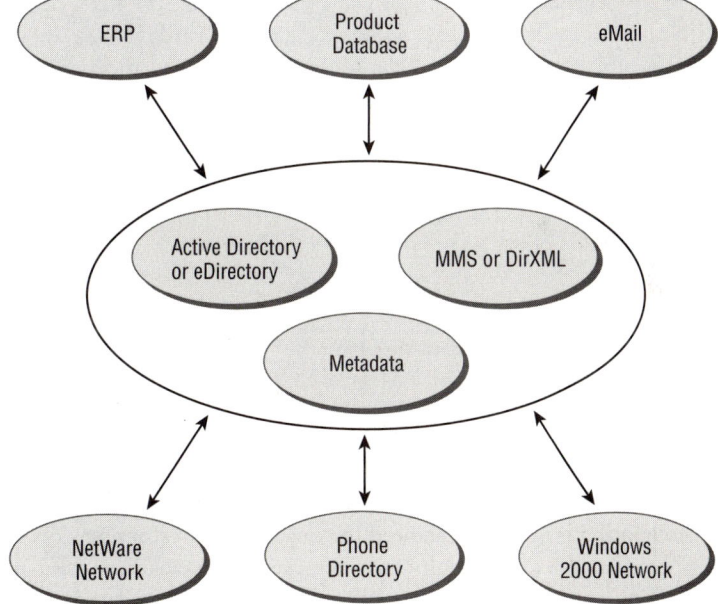

Directory Enabled Networking

Directory Enabled Networking (DEN) is an industry-standards initiative led by Microsoft and Cisco to develop next-generation networking standards. It is defined as a system that stores data in a central location, shares that data to be used by multiple applications, and is device- and platform-independent. A new DEN schema and information model will integrate network elements and services, users, and applications and make that data available, regardless of platform or location. The schema would provide security policies and profiles. The information model would be composed of relationships between objects. Directory-enabled network elements and applications would be able to discover and apply policy at any point where resources are requested. A DEN system would establish relationships between network systems, users, services, and applications.

For example, a DEN provided by Cisco will link an HP/Open View software agent with a Cisco router agent. When a new router is installed somewhere on a network, a DEN system will provide HP/Open View with the capability to discover it and produce a router configuration report based upon XML data transmitted via HTTP read directly from that router.

Microsoft Metadirectory Services

The Microsoft Metadirectory Services (MMS) product consolidates directory services information to produce the benefits underlined by the DEN initiative. Microsoft acquired the company Zoomit with the goal of incorporating the metadirectory technology built into their flagship product, VIA, into MMS.

To illustrate an MMS application, we'll link up bobuniversity with its employee benefits provider, Bitsky Benefits, a company that manages health care and 401K plans for various companies. Employee changes made by the human resources department in a database at bobuniversity are collected by MMS and published to Bitsky, while information about medical benefits and investments is available at bobuniversity over a wide area network, so that each employee can look up detailed information concerning their personal accounts. The conduit for that information transfer is MMS (see Figure 18.9).

FIGURE 18.9

A metadirectory-enabled network

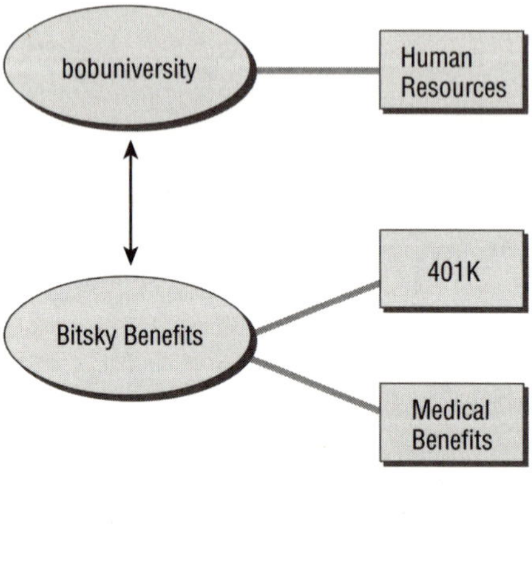

DirXML

Novell's One Net vision also recognizes the significance of consolidating directory services information with metadata. By separating NDS from the NetWare Operating System and selling it as a separate product, Novell has made directory services consolidation their *raison d'etre*.

Novell's DEN product is DirXML, which is described as a bidirectional metadata sharing service. DirXML functions as an NLM on any server that runs NDS eDirectory. Each directory product links to NDS with a specific driver to publish or subscribe to data, or both. A snap-in module is available for Console One. Filters can be created to select specific object attributes that are exchanged. Information is distributed across directories, platforms, firewalls, applications, and databases. The metadirectory publishes schema, relationships, and queries. External data and schema are integrated with NDS data.

XML is a standard metadata format for describing intranet/extranet services and resources. XML is fast becoming the standard language that facilitates communication between objects and applications. DirXML will even transfer information to non-XML legacy applications. To see how DirXML can work in a real-world situation, imagine using DirXML in place of MMS in Figure 18.9.

In Short

Microsoft has a solution for coexistence between Active Directory and other directory service products. Microsoft's CSNW synchronizes directory information between separate network systems to share their resources.

We've also taken an in-depth look at Active Directory and eDirectory, and considered the future of directory services. Metadirectory integration uses *join* technologies to create a super directory of resources. The dream of directory data integration seems to have arrived!

Index

Note to the reader: Throughout this index **boldfaced** page numbers indicate primary discussions of a topic. *Italicized* page numbers indicate illustrations.

R

U

TELL US WHAT YOU THINK!

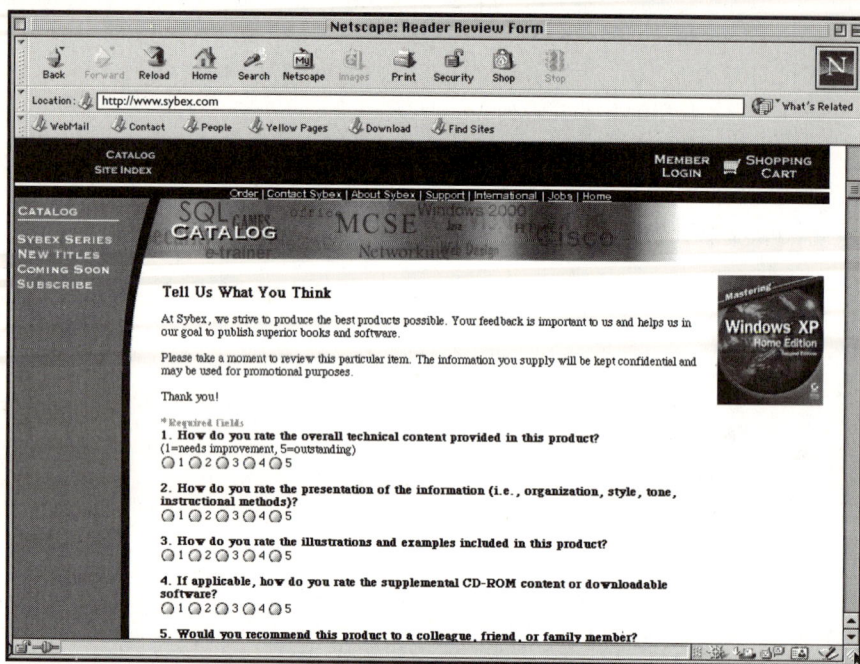

Your feedback is critical to our efforts to provide you with the best books and software on the market. Tell us what you think about the products you've purchased. It's simple:

1. Go to the Sybex website.
2. Find your book by typing the ISBN or title into the Search field.
3. Click on the book title when it appears.
4. Click **Submit a Review.**
5. Fill out the questionnaire and comments.
6. Click **Submit.**

With your feedback, we can continue to publish the highest quality computer books and software products that today's busy IT professionals deserve.

www.sybex.com

SYBEX Inc. • 1151 Marina Village Parkway, Alameda, CA 94501 • 510-523-8233